Wiltshire Record Society

(formerly the Records Branch of the Wiltshire
Archaeological and Natural History Society)

VOLUME 55

FOR THE YEAR 1999

Impression of 500 copies

*Cornbury Mill, West Lavington, c. 1855. George Butcher was the miller here until 1854/55, when his tax assessment was £100 (**315**, p. 66). His successor, Joseph Webb, appealed against his £100 assessment in 1856/57, and it was reduced to £90. It was further reduced, to £70, the following year (**343**, p. 73)*

DEVIZES DIVISION INCOME TAX ASSESSMENTS, 1842 – 1860

EDITED BY

ROBERT COLLEY
University of Wales, Aberystwyth

TROWBRIDGE

2002

ISBN 0 901333 32 8

Typeset by John Chandler
Produced for the Society by
Salisbury Printing Company Ltd, Salisbury
Printed in Great Britain

CONTENTS

PREFACE

The idea for this study by Dr. Colley was born out of research for a doctoral thesis on the mid-Victorian income tax at the Department of Law, University of Wales, Aberystwyth in the mid-1990s. During research undertaken in over twenty-five County Record Offices in England and Wales, he came upon what appeared to be a unique collection of assessments of the self-employed in mid-Victorian England, in a deposit at the Wiltshire and Swindon Record Office (WSRO 1090/81). What he found threw into sharp contrast the theoretical and actual workings of the income tax and significantly changed his preconceptions of its administration. Although essentially a legal historian, he began to see the possibility that the material offered a hitherto uncharted source of research material for other historians. His interest lies essentially in the relationship between the state and civil society, and he therefore approached the local history of Devizes with some apprehension because there are others who have devoted many years to this particular study. He decided, therefore, to concentrate purely on the material which he found without moving into this specialization, and to edit it in a way which those well versed in the story of the Devizes area can use for their own purposes.

Dr. Colley warmly acknowledges the many people who have assisted his research, through conversation and correspondence, and by providing facilities: Steven Hobbs and the staff of the Wiltshire & Swindon Record Office; Dr Lorna Haycock, Sandell Librarian, Wiltshire Archaeological & Natural History Society; the staff of the Computer Department of the University of Wales, Aberystwyth; the staff of the National Library of Wales for providing a microfilm reader and a room in which to work in peace and tranquillity for over two years; the Library of Pembroke College, Oxford, for generously supplying material from *Country Banks*; Richard Ireland of the University of Wales, Aberystwyth, and Basil Sabine, OBE, for reading the introduction to this volume. He wishes to thank Professor Jeremy Black, editor of *Archives*, for permission to use in the introduction to this volume material relating to the disposal of tax papers previously published in that journal (vol. 25, 2000, no. 102, pp. 74-87). He also wishes to pay tribute to the imagination and enthusiasm shown to him by the Committee of the Wiltshire Record Society, and to the regular advice and support, especially in the final typesetting and layout of the work, given him by me in my capacity as the Society's General Editor. Finally, Dr. Colley and the Wiltshire Record Society express our gratitude to Mr G.A. Awdry of the firm of solicitors, Messrs Awdry, Bailey and Douglas, Devizes, for permission to publish this material.

JOHN CHANDLER

INTRODUCTION

The income tax was initially a temporary phenomenon. First enacted between 1799 and 1816 as the tax that beat Napoleon, it was perceived essentially as a war tax or meant to be re-enacted only for some unique national purpose. Resuscitated by Peel in 1842,[1] the emergency was a financial one and the tax was a postulate for the extensive tariff reform that was part of his Free Trade programme. Gladstone extended its life in 1853 but with a terminable existence expressly defined, the rates of tax gradually reducing until its proposed (but unrealized) extinction in 1860.

It was expedient, both politically and methodologically, to repose the day to day administration of what was meant to be a temporary visitant in the existing centuries' old framework of tax assessment and collection which relied almost entirely on the amateur service of members of the traditional local hegemony. These personalities already had jurisdiction over the land tax and the assessed taxes (the taxes on windows, servants, carriages, sporting dogs and armorial bearings). They were, *mutatis mutandis*, Justices of the Peace, Members of Parliament, Poor Law Guardians, Street or Improvement Commissioners and Land Tax Commissioners – the wealthy, and invariably landed, representatives of politics, law, banking and church.

Peel dignified the continuance of a system of such great antiquity in his appeal to the constitutional principle that the assessment of the income tax should not depend upon the will of Government but should be undertaken by local personalities.[2] It is arguable, however, that the acceptance of the tax by Parliament was largely dependent on the continuing supremacy of these local oligarchs in its execution and their capacity to exercise patronage and influence in the control of assessment. On the one hand, it must be acknowledged that one of the distinguishing marks of landed society in the mid-nineteenth century was the acceptance and discharge of authority and responsibility which the absence of any cohesive apparatus of centralized administration left to it.[3] But on the other hand, it must equally be recognized that these local élites were strongly opposed to the extending tendrils of state intervention in the life of the individual as well as fearful of the accompanying growing erosion of their powers, any encroachment on which would have generated sufficient opposition to defeat the re-introduction of the income tax.

---

1   5 & 6 Vict., c.35
2   Hansard, *HCDebs.*, 3rd. ser., 61, col. 911, 18 Mar. 1842
3   F.M.L. Thompson, *English Landed Society in the Nineteenth Century*, 1963, p.8

THE DIVISION OF DEVIZES AND THE GENERAL COMMISSIONERS

Peel's constitutional ideal of the separation of central and local powers was translated into an intensely localized administration. The geographic jurisdiction of this local administration was the division, an area which had first been defined in 1688 when the Commissioners appointed to execute the first land tax were empowered to divide themselves into administrative units 'in such Manner and Forme as to them shall seeme expedient'.[4] They resembled more or less closely the hundred divisions of each county which were either consolidated or sub-divided into larger or smaller units respectively. These same limitations were adopted for the purposes of the income tax in 1842 resulting in 693 divisions in England and Wales.[5] These units were sometimes termed 'districts', though the correct statutory term 'division' has been preferred in this study. The division of Devizes was formed by the amalgamation of the two hundreds of Potterne & Cannings and Swanborough. The former included the town of Devizes (recorded in separate units as the parishes of St.John and St.Mary the Virgin, and the tithings of Bedborough and Week) and its environs, Bromham, Rowde, West Lavington and several smaller parishes; the latter comprised Market Lavington, Urchfont, Upavon and the several parishes along the Vale of Pewsey. These are shown in more detail on the map opposite.

At the pinnacle of the local administration were the 'commissioners for the general purposes of the (Income Tax) Act' – called almost immediately by their shortened title General Commissioners.[6] They had both an executive and appellate jurisdiction. They comprised seven men of substance and station who were to be appointed by the Land Tax Commissioners from amongst their own numbers in each division.[7] They were invariably magistrates. The first of these office holders were Thomas Henry Sutton Sotheron Estcourt, Member of Parliament for Devizes, great nephew of the former Prime Minister Henry Addington, and later President of the Poor Law Board and

---

4   1 W & M, c.20, s.5; 1 W & M, Sess. 2, c.1, s.5, (1688). The divisions were to be fixed at meetings held on or before 5 Feb. 1689. The Act 4 W & M, c.1 (1692) is generally regarded as introducing the first Land Tax proper but for the purposes of identifying the date of creation of the divisions it is necessary to refer to look to the earlier Act. W.Phillips in his article 'A New Light on Addington's Income Tax', *British Tax Review*, 1967, 271-81, at pp.275-6 firmly expounds the 'end of the 1692 myth'.

5   5 & 6 Vict., c.35, s.4. Although by 4 & 5 Will.IV, c.60, s.1, (1834), the Land Tax Commissioners were given power to transfer parishes from one jurisdiction to another or to create new divisions, there does not appear to have been any major alteration in the divisions which have been encountered by the writer during his research. The number of divisions is confirmed in House of Commons, (hereafter HC) Parliamentary Papers (hereafter PP), (1871) xxxvii 242

6   The first use of the shortened title is noted by Dr.A.Farnsworth in a side-note to an amending Act, 39 Geo.III, c.22, s.14, (1799) in his article 'The Income Tax Commissioners', *Law Quarterly Review* 64 (1948) 372-88 at p.373

7   5 & 6 Vict., c.35, s.4

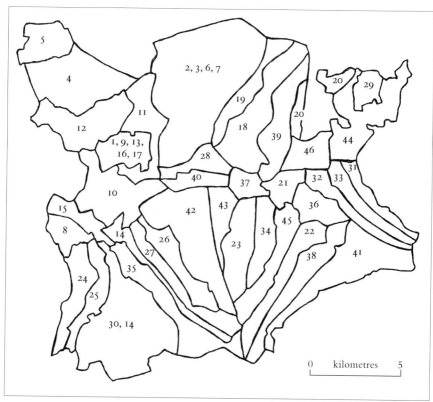

1	BEDBOROUGH	18	ALL CANNINGS	35	MARKET
2	BISHOP'S CANNINGS	19	ALLINGTON		LAVINGTON
3	BOURTON & EASTON	20	ALTON BARNES	36	NORTH NEWNTON
4	BROMHAM	21	BEECHING STOKE		& HILLCOTT
5	CHITTOE	22	CHARLTON	37	PATNEY
6	COATE	23	CHIRTON	38	RUSHALL
7	HORTON	24	CHEVERELL MAGNA	39	STANTON ST.
8	MARSTON	25	CHEVERELL PARVA		BERNARD
9	NURSTEED	26	EASTCOTT	40	STERT
10	POTTERNE	27	EASTERTON	41	UPAVON
11	ROUNDWAY	28	ETCHILHAMPTON	42	URCHFONT
12	ROWDE	29	HUISH	43	WEDHAMPTON
13	WEEK	30	LITTLETON PANNELL	44	WILCOT, OARE &
14	WEST LAVINGTON	31	MANNINGFORD ABBOTTS		DRAYCOTT
15	WORTON	32	MANNINGFORD BOHUNE	45	WILSFORD
16	DEVIZES ST. JOHN	33	MANNINGFORD BRUCE	46	WOODBOROUGH
17	DEVIZES ST. MARY	34	MARDEN		

[NOTE: WEST LAVINGTON (14) INCLUDES FIDDINGTON (DETACHED); ALTON BARNES (20) INCLUDES SHAW (DETACHED). PATNEY (37) IS INCLUDED IN THE INCOME TAX DIVISION THOUGH NOT IN SWANBOROUGH HUNDRED.]

Map of parishes and townships in the Division of Devizes

Secretary of State for the Home Office; his kinsman, Wadham Locke, son of the banker Wadham Locke who was a former Member of Parliament for Devizes; William Hughes, banker of St. John Street; Col. Henry Stephen Olivier of Potterne Manor; Thomas Hunt Grubbe of Potterne and Eastwell; Ven. Archdeacon William MacDonald, Vicar of Bishop's Cannings and Archdeacon of Wiltshire; and John Edward Andrew Starkey of Spye Park.[8] The last named died within a year of appointment and was replaced by Revd. Alfred Smith of Old Park, Perpetual Curate of Southbroom.

Clergy representation in the administration of the income tax was common, some divisions having as many as four out of the seven General Commissioners drawn from the Anglican clergy.[9] Usually every division also had among its Commissioners the incumbent Member of Parliament, in this instance Sotheron Estcourt, and one of its leading bankers. William Hughes and Wadham Locke's brother F.A.S. Locke were partners in the banking firm of Hughes, Locke & Co. This later became Locke, Olivier & Tugwell when Colonel Olivier became a partner and William Edmund Tugwell of the law firm of Tugwell & Meek, also a later Commissioner, joined the bank.[10] Alexander Meek, his partner in the firm of solicitors and a later partner in the banking firm of Locke, Tugwell & Meek, was Clerk to the General Commissioners, the officer appointed by them to deal with the day to day executive process. This was a closely-knit group with a finger on the pulse of the life of the community and a typical selection from the world of politics, law, banking and church.

THE SCHEDULAR NATURE OF THE INCOME TAX

The income tax was a duty imposed on the subject in the form of an assessment at a pound rate, of so many pence, on his income. For administrative purposes income assessable to the income tax was divided into five discrete categories, termed Schedules. These were broadly described in the taxing statute as follows: income from property was assessable under Schedule A, income from farming and market gardening under Schedule B, profits from trades, professions and vocations and wages from private sector entities under Schedule D, and income from public offices and employments under Schedule E. The receipt of interest on certain investments was also assessable under Schedule D. These were the main categories of income which were subject to many sub-divisions and as many rules but they are sufficient to give a broad outline.[11]

---

8 *Devizes Gazette*, 15 July 1842, supplemented by reference to contemporary genealogical and biographical directories

9 These were largely, but not exclusively, in rural districts. Caernarfon, in North Wales, for example, comprised 4 out of 7. In the Chester division of Wirral there were 3 out of 7.

10 M. Dawes & C.N. Ward-Perkins, *Country Banks in England & Wales, 1688-1953*, CIB, 2000, at p.198

11 5 & 6 Vict., c.35, ss. 60, 63, 100, and 146; Schedule C (s.88) related to annuities and dividends paid out of the public revenue, limited companies and other bodies corporate, and lies outside the scope of this study

Title page of Schedule D Certificate (WSRO 1090/81)

The deciding factor as to which employees should be assessed under Schedule D and which under Schedule E, was the status of the employer. Those working for a private firm or partnership would be assessable under Schedule D while those working for a limited company or public concern, under Schedule E. So, for example, Richard Falkner (**454**), most likely manager at the unincorporated bank of Locke, Olivier & Tugwell (**537**), was assessable on his salary under Schedule D, while Richard Maysmore (**556**, **797**), manager of the incorporated Wilts & Dorset Bank and Edward King (**517**), manager of the incorporated North Wilts Bank, were assessable under Schedule E.

These strict rules were not always observed (or perhaps sometimes not fully understood) and so, at times, the assessment lists include bank managers (irrespective of which bank they worked for); some curates were assessed on their stipends, like Revd. Joseph MacCormick (**543**) or Revd. William Dewdney Walke (**641**); the Relieving Officers, John Butcher (**226**) and J.P. Akerman (**1091**) were assessed; and employees such as Revd. Alexander Manning, chaplain of the New Prison (**192**) or John Thurnham [*sic*, but generally spelled Thurnam], superintendent of the County Asylum (**289**), were brought into the lists before being transferred to the Schedule E certificates. Income under each Schedule was assessed in a slightly different way and since it is with income arising from trades, professions and vocations and certain wages assessable under Schedule D with which this volume is principally concerned, a brief description of this procedure will be given.

Under Schedule D each party was required to make a return of his profits from any trade, manufacture, adventure or concern upon a fair and just average of three years ending either on the fifth day of April or on a date to which accounts had been usually made up immediately preceding the year of assessment.[12] Profits from professions, employments and vocations were computed on the basis of the income for the one year ended on the previous 5 April.[13] The term 'profits' was nowhere defined in the taxing Acts, its concept being largely parallel to that understood by the trading and professional community as being the gross income less the expenses incurred in realizing that income. The main differences were that the statute prohibited the deduction from profits of certain items which were recognized by the commercial community as proper, (the most important of which were loan interest and depreciation of plant and equipment)[14] and the profits from the trade of a married woman living with her husband were deemed to be those of the husband and charged in his name.[15] Thus, Samuel Adlam, painter and glazier of Devizes St.Mary (**667**) was also assessed in respect of his wife's profits as a straw bonnet maker.

THE ASSESSMENT

Each year the General Commissioners appointed an assessor for each parish within the division to undertake certain preliminary duties: to post a general notice on the church door or in the market place requiring returns of income to be made, to serve notices on each individual to make a return of income, to draw up the lists of those on whom assessments should be made, to insert in the list the amounts returned by the parties and to make an estimate of income where a person failed to make a return.[16] The assessor was named in vestry. He was usually a small tradesman and his office was compulsory, failure to act resulting in a fine of £20.[17] He received remuneration by way of poundage of one and a half pence for every pound of tax collected.

It was an unpopular task. His own business interests often clashed with those of the Crown, favoured customers being omitted from the assessment lists. Assessors were, at times, criticized for making assessments carelessly and inaccurately, in rural areas for being illiterate, and in towns for using their official papers for the purpose of advertising their own trades, especially those connected with debt collection.[18]

12 Ibid., s.100, r.1 of Case I
13 Ibid., r.2 of Case II confirmed by evidence given before the Hume Committee, (1852) ix qq. 949, 959-61
14 Ibid., s.100, r.3 of Case I
15 Ibid., s.45
16 Ibid., ss.46-8, 57-8
17 43 Geo.III, c.99, s.16, (1803) Examples of prosecution are given at HC, PP, (1856) l 25
18 *6th Report of the Commissioners of Inland Revenue* (hereafter CIR), PP (1862) xxvii 327, 345; *Report of the Select Committee on Inland Revenue and Customs Establishments,* (hereafter IR & CE) PP (1863) vi 303 at p.32; W.Astle, *The History of Stockport,* 1822, repr. 1971 at p.55

In order not to leave the delicate matter of the assessment of the trading community to such officers, the General Commissioners were required to appoint Additional Commissioners for the purpose of making assessments under Schedule D.[19] The assessors still dealt with the preliminary detail but the Additional Commissioners reviewed the returns, made any necessary estimates and signed the assessments. Invariably the General Commissioners selected two of their own number to act in this capacity, or two of the supply Commissioners appointed to fill vacancies in their divisional complement. Since each Commissioner had to satisfy a property qualification, this practice was encouraged because it gave a greater degree of security.[20] In Devizes the Commissioners who acted most frequently in this capacity were Revd. Alfred Smith, John Locke, a brother of Wadham Locke, Colonel H.S. Olivier and later, W.E. Tugwell, both partners in the banking firm of Locke, Olivier & Tugwell. Later in the period, W.B. Seagram, physician and John Hayward, most likely the land agent, occasionally acted in this capacity. The returns of the trading and professional community, therefore, came under scrutiny by the Commissioners themselves.

Of course, the interests of the state needed to be protected against omission and delay and to ensure the timely assessment and collection of the tax. There were some 140 centrally remunerated officials in England and Wales termed Surveyors of Taxes who represented Government at a local level for this purpose.[21] In the early years of the re-introduced income tax, their role was essentially managerial: ensuring that the assessors made assessments within the time limits stipulated by law, that tax collected was paid over to the Board of Inland Revenue and that all those who ought to be assessed were assessed. They also played a pivotal role in examining taxpayers' claims for exemption. They were each responsible for a large area of the county. Wiltshire was divided into three tax districts, of which Chippenham included the division of Devizes. Here the Surveyors were William Tennant, from Sheffield, who moved on to Chester in about 1852 and was succeeded by James Cottell, a Swindon man.

Although the Surveyor also possessed certain statutory powers in the assessment process, these were very much subordinate to the functions of the General Commissioners. Peel was careful to inculcate forbearance in trespassing on the Commissioners' jurisdiction in order to sustain deference to the parameters of local assessment and so maintain the constitutional separation of powers on which the income tax relied for its survival. But as both the assessor and Surveyor were present at the meeting at which the Additional Commissioners made the assessments, they (and the Surveyor in particular) were able to comment on the sufficiency of the returns made and offer their observations on any estimates considered necessary.[22] This was an occasion on which the Surveyor might, and often did, influence the amounts in which assessments were made.

---

19 5 & 6 Vict., c.35, s.16

20 Ibid., ss. 16, 21, 59, 111; 45 *Justice of the Peace* (1842) 706

21 Number compiled from a return by each Surveyor of Taxes to the Select Committee on the Income & Property Tax of 1851/52 (hereafter Hume Committee), HC, PP, (1852) ix pp.905-9

22 Minutes of evidence taken before the Hume Committee (hereafter Hume Committee evidence), (1852) ix qq.1517-19

Not every person made a return of income every year. Large businesses such as Paul & Edward Anstie (**375**), tobacco and snuff manufacturers, the bankers Locke, Olivier & Tugwell (**537**), Hitchcock and Ives (**1014**), the surgeons of Market Lavington, and clergymen-tutors such as Revd. George Parker Cleather, curate of Chirton (**917**), returned an exact sum each year. Many smaller businesses, too, returned exact amounts annually, *inter alia*, R & W Edmonds, French teachers (**446**), and William Blackwell Jones, law stationer (**514**), of Devizes St.John.

But more often, the taxpayer would make a return in a round sum perhaps only every three years. Although provisions existed for the imposition of penalties for default in making an annual return, alongside these sanctions was the provision to deal with the matter in another way: the propulsive force behind the income tax legislation and the machinery of its enforcement was not that those who failed to make a return of income should be punished, but that an estimated assessment should be made so that the collection of the tax should move forward as smoothly and as quickly as possible.[23] The thrust of the income tax was to get at the money in the pockets of the people, not to make criminals. The penalty provisions were meant to be experienced as a threat *in terrorem* to encourage production of a return of income.

As an, albeit primitive, check against possible omission and procrastination, the Additional Commissioners were granted the power to make an estimated assessment where the taxpayer had failed to make any return. They were also empowered to disregard the amount of income declared by the taxpayer in cases where they doubted the sufficiency of the sum returned and to make an estimate according to the best of their judgement.[24] The power of arbitrary assessment was 'necessarily entrusted to the (C)ommissioners as the last defence against the taxpayer's power of concealment'.[25] Unless an appeal were made to the General Commissioners, estimated assessments were final and conclusive.[26] These were the elementary ways in which under- or non-assessment might be minimized.

Making a best judgement assessment was a function central to checking evasion, since neither the Additional Commissioners nor the Surveyor had any powers to compel the production of information, such as trading accounts or other corroborative evidence, to support a return of income. Only the General Commissioners had the power to enquire beyond the return, but this was originated only on the taxpayer's appeal against an estimated assessment.[27] The rationale on which this was based saw the estimate as final unless the appellant could satisfy the General Commissioners that it ought properly to be reduced. This entailed producing whatever information the General Commissioners required before they altered the estimate, which often meant production of the books of account of the taxpayer.

23 5 & 6 Vict., c.35, ss.52, 55
24 Ibid., s.113
25 H.H.Monroe, *Intolerable Inquisition? Reflections on the Law of Income Tax*, 1981, p.71
26 *Allen v Sharp*, (1848), 2 Ex. 352, 361, and see Baron Parke at 363
27 5 & 6 Vict., c.35, s.120

The reluctance to reveal the true state of a man's business to Commissioners who might be his own bankers, competitors, creditors or creditors' bankers, tended to deflect the taxpayer from appeal.[28] Because of the social and commercial constraints which thus worked against making an appeal, or simply because of the desire to escape a sufficient assessment, appeals were few. The exercise of the powers of estimation using local knowledge was, therefore, an essential feature of the assessment process. The figures compiled for the purposes of the Select Committee on the Income and Property Tax of 1851/52, (hereafter called the Hume Committee), show that at least 40 per cent of Schedule D assessments in England and Wales made for 1848/49 were estimated. On average, 27 per cent of these were appealed against.[29] For Devizes itself for the same year, 38 per cent of assessments on which tax was ultimately payable were estimated either in the absence of a return or in sums increased over and above the sum returned. 25 per cent of estimated assessments either greater than £150 or increased on the return were appealed against. This compares with 21 per cent for the entire tax district of Chippenham and 21 per cent for the county of Wiltshire.

In order to overcome the apparent problem of appealing to the local Commissioners, an alternative route was permitted whereby the appellant under Schedule D could make an application to be assessed by the Special Commissioners.[30] These were three Government officials, based at Somerset House, who travelled on circuit to hear appeals. This was a provision of which few availed themselves because of the perception that remunerated officers of the Crown might be more likely to make increased assessments. In Devizes, only the solicitor John Raikes Bayley (**384**) and the law firm of MacDonald & Olivier (**544**) elected to be assessed by the Special Commissioners.

As a further measure to maintain confidentiality, (which extended only to assessments made under Schedule D), the taxpayer could elect to be assessed under letter instead of name,[31] though the degree to which strict confidentiality was thus attained is questionable. In any event, few opted for this treatment – notably George Washington Anstie, solicitor of St. Mary (**669**); Thomas Blackwell, civil engineer of Rowde (**165**); John Hayward, land agent of Rowde (**182**); Thomas Chandler, maltster of Week (**230**); John Raikes Bayley, solicitor of St. John (**384**); and innkeepers James Chandler of the Old Crown (**693**), William Grace of the Castle (**746**), James Macklin of the White Bear (**787**) and William Joyce of the Pelican (**515**).

EXEMPTION

Between 1842 and 1852 the tax threshold was £150. Those with a total annual income of £150 and above paid tax on the whole of their income, while those below were

28 Hansard, *HCDebs.*, 3rd. ser., 161, col.642, 8 Apr.1856; *The Times*, 21 Jan.1856
29 Hume Committee evidence, p.909 and PP (1851) xxxi 397 re Schedule D
30 5 & 6 Vict., c.35, s.130 (appeal), s.131 (assessment)
31 Ibid., ss.137-9

excepted, provided that they made a formal claim for exemption.[32] This entailed making a declaration of total income under all Schedules. Without such a claim, tax remained payable even though the taxpayer might be eligible for exemption. Few people with incomes well below the threshold (generally those earning between £50 and £100 annually in country parishes and in the parish of Devizes St.Mary) made returns. The Additional Commissioners exercised their powers of estimation widely in these areas. In 1848/49 (to continue the comparison with figures from the Hume Committee Report) 93 per cent of assessments made in sums below £150 in Devizes were estimated. Of the total assessments made in whatever sum, 67 per cent were discharged on a claim for exemption. Of course, proof of income is implicit in the fact that a formal claim was a precondition of relief.

Initially, an assessment had to be made on every taxpayer irrespective of the potential for exemption and the claimant had to prove the level of his income either before the Surveyor or the General Commissioners. It was a kind of means test on what might cautiously and loosely be termed the lower or lower middle classes before the assessment might be discharged. Claimants either produced calculations of their total income and were tested by oral enquiry, or acquiesced in the estimate made by the Additional Commissioners.

The formal ritual of assessment and claim for exemption was observed in the division of Devizes until 1850 when, probably in order to reduce the workload of the administrative personnel, parties who were continually being relieved from tax were eliminated altogether from the assessment process. However, after 1853 when the exemption limit was lowered to £100, a closer scrutiny of lower income taxpayers was again introduced. In the text, therefore, an assessment for the years 1850/51 to 1852/53 will sometimes be absent in respect of those whose incomes were obviously well below the exemption limit. This fact is recorded in the footnotes by stating '1850/51-1852/53 no assessments made'.

It is at the margins of tax liability that an early form of legal tax avoidance is witnessed. The exclusivity of the exemption limit where an annual income of £150 was wholly taxable while an annual income of £149 19s.11d. was wholly exempt created a fiscal precipice which tested the ingenuity of the taxpayer.[33] Employees were in a better position than most to prove the level of their incomes because they could produce corroborative evidence from their employers. Thomas Glossop Thorp, surveyor's clerk (**29**), of Bedborough, returned and was assessed on a salary of £150 up to 1847/48. For 1848/49 and 1849/50 he was assessed at £150 but proved that he had arranged with his employer a salary of £149, so making an overall saving (with a tax rate of seven pence in the pound) of £3 7s. 6d. Similar arrangements can be seen in the records of Thomas Watson Anderson, solicitor's clerk (**373**), and William Palmer Coxhead, schoolmaster (**427**), both of Devizes St.John.

---

32 Ibid., s.163
33 Hume Committee evidence, qq. 3019,3020,3235

APPEALS

Once the Additional Commissioners had made the assessment at or above £150 (or £100 after 1853) it could be displaced only by appeal to the General Commissioners. Even where made at a figure below the exemption limit, without an appeal, the figure remained the sum which had to be included in the proof of income. On appeal, the taxpayer was required to adduce such evidence as the General Commissioners considered necessary before the assessment would be reduced. This often entailed a *viva voce* examination.

The General Commissioners had wide powers of enquiry on appeal and could issue a precept for particulars in writing, for example, for a statement of debtors and creditors, or computation of profits, which might also be sworn on oath. In the main, appeals were successful but this was not universal. Often the result was a compromise after ascertaining the facts. In 1856/57 John & Thomas Chandler, corn dealers and maltsters of Week (**229**), having returned £160 were increased by the Additional Commissioners to £720; on appeal the assessment was confirmed at £550. In 1849/50 Robert Coates, innkeeper of the Odd Fellows' Arms in Sidmouth Street, Devizes (**703**), returned £100, was increased to £150 to incite an appeal and the assessment settled at £117 on which exemption was successfully claimed. Occasionally the evidence was not enough to displace the estimate: in 1842/43 John & James Sainsbury, timber dealers and wheelwrights of West Lavington (**339**), were assessed at £50 each by the Additional Commissioners and on appeal the assessments were sustained at this sum.

Statutorily no estimated assessment could be displaced except on appeal, although where exemption was clearly due and a formal claim was made, in practice, the assessment often seems to have been discharged without a formal appeal. Thus, in 1850/51, Richard Berry, miller & corndealer of Horton (**109**), who returned £100, was assessed at £150 and his assessment was reduced to £134 19s. 6d. on his proof of income alone. It may be that the figure included in the 'Amount of Income Proved' column is the total income rather then the specific Schedule D income. It is impossible to ascertain this with certainty, though isolated examples suggest this as a possibility. For example, in 1848/49 Benjamin Webb, lime burner of Bromham (**99**), was assessed at £100 but proved his income at £120. The following year he was assessed in the absence of a return at £50 which seems incongruous until it is proposed that his total income may have comprised £50 Schedule D profits and £70 other (unspecified) income. Similar examples, among many others, can be seen at entries **105, 115, 193, 214** and **311**.

In the main, up to the late 1850s, the returns of certain taxpayers were accepted as a matter of course while others were doubted. The criteria which activated the preferences and prejudices of the Additional Commissioners were inevitably many and varied and often subjective. But there is a prevailing and imperceptible undercurrent, certainly in the work of the Hume Committee, which suggests that although there would have been exceptions, returns of income above a certain figure were generally accepted by the Commissioners without question. What this figure was is difficult to ascertain. The terms 'small trader' or 'small manufacturer' were used as phrases of convenience to describe those who were scrutinized more closely. But these terms, too, present a difficulty in terminology in defining such a group for the purposes of the income tax and leave ambiguities and inconsistencies, chiefly about where to draw the high cut-off lines, although the low cut-off point was somewhere just below the exemption limit.

Throughout the evidence given before the Hume Committee, the examples of evasion put forward by the witnesses relate almost exclusively to small traders and manufacturers and instances relating to the larger industrialists and merchants are conspicuous by their absence. The presumption which pervaded the work of the Committee and was explicit in the evidence it received was that while the small trader would go to any lengths to reduce the amount returned as his profits, the larger taxpayers returned more than they needed. Contemporaries who discussed evasion in the 1840s and 1850s perceived it largely as the province of those whose incomes lay at the margins of the exemption limit. In 1848/49, nationally, 43 per cent of assessments increased over and above the return related to persons who had returned incomes below £150 but had been assessed at £150 or upwards to make them appeal or pay the tax.[34] Perhaps this mentality, which identified small traders as those who were most tempted to evade the tax, and so should be scrutinized more closely, is one of the most striking features of the mid-Victorian income tax. It can be seen particularly in the case of Isaiah Dangerfield, fishmonger of St. John (**433**).

This notion was to be shattered in the mid-1850s[35] but it can be seen in cases such as George Simpson, newspaper proprietor (**612**), Revd. Richard Elliott, dissenting minister and schoolmaster (**447**), Thomas Browne Anstie, surgeon (**670**), or William Cunnington & Sons, wine merchants of the Bottle and the Old Town Hall (**234**), among many others whose returns were largely accepted and whose assessments remained relatively constant. But instances such as the brewers James Oram of Northgate Street, Devizes (**810**) and James Banks of Bromham (**61**), the rising fortunes of George Taylor Sainsbury, brickmaker of Rowde (**201**) or of John & Thomas Chandler, retail maltsters of Week (**229**), and, to a lesser extent, of the ironfounders of Bedborough, Messrs Brown & May (**4**), reveal a policy of aggressive increases by the Additional Commissioners, perhaps stimulated, too, by attempts by the Surveyor of Taxes to raise assessment levels. It signals a move away from the general attitude that the word of a gentleman was accepted without question and perhaps indicates either a more discerning approach by the Commissioners of this division or a readiness to accede to the suggestions of the Surveyor of Taxes for an increase in the estimate.

Their reaction to local conditions and events, which reflected falling profits as well as expanding businesses, is clearly seen in the assessments of the lunatic asylums of

---

34 Hume Committee evidence, qq. 360-3 and p. 909

35 This arose primarily from the compensation claims following the Cannon Street Improvements (*Report of the Select Committee on Income Tax*, PP (1861) vi q.2174), and from the abolition of offices under the Court of Probate Act and the Matrimonial Causes Act of 1857 (Hansard, *HCDebs.*, 3rd. ser., 157, col.1203). See also 8th CIR PP (1864) xxx 423 re compensation claims upon public companies

Thomas Phillips at Bellevue, Week (**276**) and of Charles Hitchcock (successor to Robert Willett) at Fiddington House, West Lavington (**327**). These show a downturn after 1852 with the beginning of the transfer of pauper patients to the newly opened County Asylum, as recorded in a manuscript note against the name of Phillips. The assessments at Bellevue, which housed a larger proportion of paupers than Fiddington House, fell from £850 in 1852/53 to £75 by 1856/57 reflecting the fact that between 1851 and 1855 the number of pauper patients fell from 144 to 4. The assessment on Fiddington House fell from £1,000 to £380 over the same period as the number of pauper patients fell from 146 to 3, though the Commissioners in this instance were more resistant to a greater reduction, even on appeal by Hitchcock, perhaps aware of his accommodation of private patients, which continued at much the same level as before.[36]

THE CERTIFICATE OF ASSESSMENTS

The process of the assessment to income tax began when a notice of return was delivered to each inhabitant in the division by the assessors. These officers and the Schedular nature of the income tax have been described earlier, but the following will help to reinforce the essential effect of this scheme.

There was no composite return of income as there is today. Each person was required to complete a declaration of his income separately under each Schedule, so that where he owned or occupied property or used it for the purposes of farming or market gardening, he would make a return under Schedules A & B; where his income was derived from a trade, profession or vocation, from certain wages or salaries, or certain interest on investments, under Schedule D; and where he received income from a public office or employment, under Schedule E. When the declarations of income were returned, the Clerk to the Commissioners, with assistance from the assessors, drew up a list of all persons on whom a notice of return had been served, termed a Certificate of Assessments, under each separate Schedule for each township or parish within the division. These were central to the record of returns and assessments for each fiscal year and of the final charge to duty.

The Certificate of Assessments is the key administrative record. It comprised an alphabetical list of the 'Christian and Surnames of persons charged' and a 'Description of the Trade, Profession, Vocation or other Profits chargeable under Schedule D'. Against each name is written a columnar history of the stages of assessment which shows the amounts of income returned by the parties and indicates those who made no return. The next column shows the 'Amount assessed by the Additional Commissioners', from which can be deduced the estimates made both in the absence of a return and where the Commissioners were dissatisfied with the sufficiency of the sum returned. An example

---

36 *6th Report of the Commissioners in Lunacy*, PP (1851) xxiii 353 and *9th Report of the Commissioners in Lunacy*, PP (1854/55) xvii 533

of the Certificate of Assessments showing part of the entries relating to the township of Bedborough is reproduced below.

There was also a column which recorded any assessment which the Surveyor of Taxes considered insufficient so that the General Commissioners could take this into account in deciding the quantum to be assessed; but this was used infrequently and usually reserved for instances where the Surveyor laid a formal Information before the Commissioners in cases of evasion or under-assessment. In the division of Devizes this power does not seem to have been invoked. Instead, the Surveyor's observations were put forward when he attended the meeting at which the Additional Commissioners made the assessments. The forms accommodate a manuscript note for the result of appeals made to the General Commissioners against estimated assessments, from which it is possible to ascertain the proportion of taxpayers who appealed against estimated assessments and the number of appeals that were successful. Later in the period a system of abatement was introduced whereby those having an assessable income between the exemption limit and £150 were charged at a lower rate of tax. A separate column, headed 'Amount of Income Proved' records those persons relieved from the payment of duty on a claim for exemption where their total incomes lay below the tax threshold. The final columns show the amount of duty discharged, (in appropriate years) abated, and finally payable by each person.

Traders who had businesses both in Devizes and elsewhere were assessed in the division in which they resided but their presence in the division where they carried on

Sample page of a Certificate of Assessments, relating to Bedborough (WSRO 1090/81)

a trade was nevertheless noted: William Lawes & Co., carriers, who traded at the Wagon Office in Devizes St.Mary (**779**), made returns and were assessed at Chippenham, their principal place of business and residence until 1849/50 when part of the business was taken over by Horatio Nelson Perry (**24**), who resided in and was assessed at Bedborough; Jonah Reeve, upholsterer of Devizes St.John (**596**) from 1842 to 1860 also carried on the business of auctioneer, appraiser and cabinet maker at Marlborough where he made his returns; John North, coach builder at Week (**268**), made returns at Melksham between 1846 and 1855 but was assessed at Devizes St.John from 1856/57-1859/60. Thus, every businessman who traded in the division at any time between 1842 and 1860, was noted, whether or not an assessment was made.

The Certificates are signed by the Additional Commissioners at the time they made the assessments and by the General Commissioners after all appeals had been heard. By signing and, in statutory terms, 'allowing the assessments', the General Commissioners created the legal charge to tax. The Certificates for each township or parish in the division were bound together with ribbon under each Schedule, for the convenience of the Commissioners. Thus, there is a set of documents which records the number of manufacturers, tradesmen, professional men and certain classes of employees respectively and the amounts on which they paid duty. The record includes both men and women.

But however useful the statistics compiled from this source might be to the historian generally, some reorganization of the basic components included in each Certificate has been considered desirable – and indeed, necessary – if the information was to be made accessible to a wider group, for example, to the social or local historian, to the population or family historian, as well as to the casual genealogist, all of whom have a legitimate claim to be interested in this historical record. In order to achieve this, the information comprised in each Certificate has been dissected and the details for each taxpayer analysed and reallocated to form a personal history of each individual or business within the division, covering the period from 1842 to 1860. The mechanism of this process is described in more detail in the section on Editorial Method.

The question must of course be posed – how accurate a reflection of the incomes of the trading and professional people of Devizes are the assessments incorporated in the Certificates? Perhaps we shall never know for certain. The cynic may argue that their accuracy is commensurate with the honesty and integrity of each taxpayer and, in the main, he would probably be right. But the exercise by the Additional Commissioners of their judgement on the sufficiency of the sum returned and on the estimates made, under Schedule D, and the resolve of the Surveyor to ensure as high an assessment as possible, helps to lessen this concern, at least in respect of the smaller tradesmen.

Their preferences and prejudices, however, (to which reference has already been made) are still factors which must be borne in mind when considering a number of assessments made. It may well be that the incomes of the more well-to-do are understated rather than overstated. Certainly, the assessments on Tugwell & Meek, solicitors (**638**) display a remarkable uniformity, and those of Alexander Meek, solicitor (**557**) and Clerk to the Commissioners, are evidently largely repetitive amounts. On the other hand, as already noted, firms like Locke, Olivier & Tugwell, bankers (**537**) and Paul &

Edward Anstie, tobacco and snuff manufacturers (**375**) returned precise amounts. And instances such as the brewers James Oram (**810**) and James Banks (**61**) among many others, where high estimated assessments displaced the sums returned, also help to dispel fears of complacency in the assessing process.

But one answer to all such self-inflicted criticism is that this is probably the closest we will come to a construct of the incomes and profits of such a wide cross-section of people in this stratified mid-Victorian commercial community for so long a period. And in spite of nagging doubts, it is possible to discern a marked sensitivity in estimating the assessments of the various types of business. Indeed, not all tradesmen in the same category were treated the same. Each entry seems to have been considered subjectively, so that, for example, in the parish of St.Mary, the range of figures for assessments on innkeepers is significantly varied from business to business – the assessments on Henry Blencowe of the Castle (**683**) range from £118–£200; on Richard Trueman of the White Lion (**862**), £65–£100; on Isaiah Dangerfield of the White Hart (**712**), £40–£60; on James Chandler of the Three Crowns (**694**), £75–£130. And although Decimus Wild of the White Bear (**883**) made seemingly precise returns every year, these were disregarded and estimates made, rising sharply from £150 to £300 in one year. This suggests that taxpayers came under some scrutiny and that the assessments represent the exercise of local knowledge and were based on local conditions.

INCOME TAX RECORDS – THE STATUTORY REQUIREMENTS

The temporary characteristic of the income tax is reflected nowhere more clearly than in the legislative attitude to the records that were created by the system, the documents which formed the day to day administration of the income tax. This is witnessed in the legislation which envisaged a local administration, under which the custody of records was entrusted to the General Commissioners. Although the tax was a temporary measure, in order to make the system workable, custody of the records had to be subject, to an extent at least, to some continuity and the reason behind this can be seen in a consolidating Act of 1803, which related to the management of direct taxes, when it was stated (in a rather more unwieldy form than the abridged version which follows):

> ... many Difficulties and Inconveniencies have arisen to the Commissioners ... upon the Death or Removal of their respective Clerks, into whose Custody all the ... Books and Papers ... have been delivered; such Clerks so removed, or the Executors Administrators or Legal Representatives of such Clerk so dying, frequently refusing to deliver up the ... Books and Papers ... under a Pretence that the said Commissioners have no property in the same, and are without remedy for the Recovery thereof.[37]

37   43 Geo.III, c.99, s.67 (1803)

This Act, as a consequence, declared the books of assessment and all other books and papers to be the property of the local Commissioners 'for the Time being, and in succession'. The Certificates of First Assessments for the division of Devizes were prepared under the supervision of, and kept by, the Clerk to the Commissioners, Alexander Meek (**557**). He was a solicitor of 33, St.John Street, Devizes and was a partner with William Edmund Tugwell in the firm of Tugwell & Meek (**638**). The firm traced its history at least back to William Salmon in the late 18th century. After 1852, Meek practiced alone. He was also County Treasurer, Town Clerk, Clerk to the Magistrates, and a Justice of the Peace. Later he became a partner in the banking firm of Locke, Tugwell & Meek (see Locke, Olivier & Tugwell, bankers, **537**).[38]

The statutory control of local papers which was introduced by the Act of 1803 was focused on current material as opposed to past papers and concentrated on facilitating the transfer of the impedimenta of assessment and collection to newly appointed clerks on the death or retirement of their predecessors, so that the process could continue uninterrupted. The documentation created by the process was directed at a specific managerial function, that of collection of the tax for a definite period, after which such records became obsolete and, as a result, disposable. The legislation was not directed at a long-term retention of material and the Act of 1842, by which the Victorian income tax was re-introduced, still regulated by the Act of 1803, provided for the returns to be

> filed in the Office of the said Commissioners and carefully kept so long as the Accounts of the said Duties for such District, or any Part thereof, shall remain unpaid to Her Majesty.[39]

So, once the tax for the year had been paid, the purpose of the returns and assessments, or any documentation which emanated from them, became superfluous. Even papers or abstracts which the Surveyor of Taxes was permitted to take, do not appear to have been retained. For example, having been requested by the Secretary of the Board of Inland Revenue to furnish a return of assessments and appeals for the information of the Hume Committee, one Surveyor replied that he could not 'give 1842-47 because the whole of the assessments, etc., have been destroyed, agreeable to the directions given by the Board to the Clerk to the Commissioners for this district'.[40] By 1853 a general instruction to all Surveyors urged that old papers should be burned,

---

38 He remained a partner until 1883 when the bank was merged with Capital & Counties Bank. He lived at Hillworth House and at his death in 1888 left a remarkable fortune of £83,843. By his marriage to the daughter of John Grant of Manningford, he had a son Alexander Grant Meek who continued the law practice and is recorded in Trade Directories of 1875 and 1885. He married the niece of Revd. Benjamin Charles Dowding, Perpetual Curate of Southbroom (**7**) and his descendants were still living in the area in the 1950s, after which the estate passed to a kinsman and member of the Dowding family.

39 5 & 6 Vict., c.35, s.59

40 Hume Committee evidence, correspondence 29 Mar.1852 John Nicholson to Thomas Keogh

usually on a bonfire, though some seem to have been consigned to furnaces to ensure complete combustion.[41]

Although a central involvement suggests central records, these did not extend systematically, at least in relation to any other than the current or preceding two years, beyond a summary compiled from the aggregate numbers of assessments made and total incomes assessable for each division. The Surveyor of Taxes was permitted to abstract details from the Commissioners' lists of assessments but in practice appears to have used the original documents for whatever purposes he needed them. There would inevitably have been a flow of instructions and correspondence between the Surveyor and Somerset House but for perhaps the whole of the period with which this volume is concerned, the records of the Board at the Public Record Office are piecemeal, comprising, essentially, no more than random examples of correspondence and instructions, covering, in the main, only the years 1843 and 1860.[42] The record of the day to day assessment of the income tax was firmly rooted in the division. Indeed, the source of the figures from which the official income tax statistics that were compiled on a national basis for each year from 1842 onward of the total numbers of assessments made and the total amounts of income assessed under each Schedule was the divisional record of assessment.

That the documentation created by the procedure of taxation were records in the sense that they were contemporary officially authenticated statements of acts and proceedings in public affairs, is self-evident. But tax papers were not yet records in the sense that they had a secondary purpose over and above their limited function as the means of arriving at a public contribution for some specific purpose. Perhaps the word 'data', albeit the right word in the wrong century, is a better way to describe the facts which were collated as a consequence of the procedure. It might be said that such data were not processed in any way other than that for which they were brought into existence. The usefulness of the returns and assessments was essentially finite: they possessed no connotative quality beyond the immediate purpose for which they were created. For example, their application in providing a personal history of assessment for a taxpayer and hence their subsidiary utility as a means of creating an information base that could be used to detect instances of under or non-assessment over a period of time, does not seem to have been considered. There was not yet the desire, nor the manpower, to collect and organize local information for the purpose of better control; that is, there was no use of data as records of assessment which might have another dimension within a wider philosophy of taxation. This may now seem naive, but this was not yet the system of permanent taxation in which the Government Department most interested in its assessment could influence the process, nor yet the system in which the Commissioners intervened beyond the making of an assessment for one year and beyond acting as its stamp of authority. This was still the world of the autocrat not the bureaucrat. The survival of the Certificates of Assessments for Devizes, in this light, is fortuitous.

41 Chester Record Office D6148/80, The Henzell Collection, 14 June 1853. I am grateful to Mr Stephen Matthews for drawing my attention to this collection, which until recently was in private hands.
42 IR40 class file

DISPOSAL OF INCOME TAX PAPERS AND THEIR RARITY VALUE

Used paper, printed or written on, was a marketable commodity, much in demand for a great variety of uses in the wrapping of fish and groceries or many other commercial or domestic uses. Once the primary function of the income tax papers had ceased, if they no longer possessed value as a record of assessment, they did possess value as waste paper. Anecdotal evidence about the disposal of income tax papers, at first blush, seems apocryphal or at least replicated, since it normally comprises accounts of grocers delivering butter or cheese wrapped up in the customer's own return form. But the disposal of income tax returns and papers to tradesmen is recorded in several parts of the country over a substantial period, among which, the butcher at King's Cross who purchased nearly the whole of the income tax returns for the parishes of St. Mary, Islington and St. Luke in 1848;[43] the grocer near Brixton in 1851/2 who obtained for waste paper several large bales of returns, schedules and claims for exemption;[44] the shopkeeper who purchased 3cwt of returns of the inhabitants of Westbury, Devizes and Trowbridge in 1856;[45] as well as in Leeds, where the shopkeeper acquired not only returns and schedules but also 'the pieces of paper attached, with the remarks and calculations of the Commissioners'. They included the papers of two clergymen (one of whom was a distinguished leader in the Oxford movement and a chaplain to Queen Victoria) five surgeons and doctors, seven solicitors and barristers, five booksellers, six druggists, six corn-factors, eleven merchants, two curriers, five wine merchants and four tea dealers (including an alderman of the City of London).[46]

The position reached crisis point in 1858 when several hundredweight of income tax papers relating to the City of London, comprising 1000 to 1200 returns, found their way into Billingsgate fish market and the Surveyor, Edward Welsh, visited shops in several different wards and bought back as many papers as possible in order to get possession of them. A charwoman at the Commissioners' offices had sold them as waste paper and although she selected only a few at a time from various batches, the quantity discovered by Welsh was considerable: Walter Blanchard, a waste paper dealer of Bell Alley, Moorgate Street had purchased half a hundredweight from her over a three month period; Henry Barber, a fish salesman of Lower Thames Street had purchased one hundredweight and another half hundredweight was sold to Dearsley the fishmonger of Billingsgate.[47]

While revelations of laxity led to investigations by both the local personnel and the Board of Inland Revenue, the importance is, perhaps, not only that after being

---

43 *Liverpool Mercury*, 12 May 1848
44 *The Times*, 26 Jan.1852; *Chester Chronicle*, 7 Feb.1852
45 Article in *Wiltshire County Mirror* reproduced in *The Times*, 4 Dec.1856
46 *The Times*, 24, 28 & 29 Aug.1857
47 IR & CE evidence, PP (1862) xii q.2414; PP (1857/58) xxxiv 97 *et seq.*, correspondence Edward Welsh to Thomas Keogh, 11 Feb.1858; *The Times*, 12 Feb.1858; B.E.V.Sabine, 'Victorian Paper Chase', *British Tax Review*, 1969, 10-15

retained for a number of years, such records were ordered to be disposed of, but because such material found its way, whether accidentally or otherwise, into the public gaze, a more stringent policy of supervised destruction was adopted. In the City of London, for example, in the mid-fifties, it was the practice to take records 'by rail some distance from the town, and having had a good dinner, to make a good bonfire of them somewhere down the river'.[48] Gradually, probably as a result of adverse publicity, it became the practice for income tax returns and papers, once they were done with, to be sold to the highest bidder of about five persons who were in the habit of purchasing mill waste, generally Messrs Waterlow and Sons,[49] and it is apparent that, for most of the mid-Victorian period, income tax records were themselves temporary and when finished with were consigned to disposal. Sensational newspaper reports relating to such breaches of confidentiality only resulted in a stricter policy of the disposal of income tax records and even inevitably accelerated their destruction. Though it has to be said that instances existed where this, too, became lax: in Warrington in Lancashire in 1880, an inspection of the attic of the office of the Surveyor revealed the floor strewn with old letters, papers and assessments in a state of great disarray, and orders were given for their destruction.[50]

That the papers were brought into existence for only a limited purpose reflects the temporary nature of the mid-Victorian income tax: that they were sometimes disposed of in a seemingly incredible manner may account for their present-day scarcity. The survival of the Certificates of Assessments for the division of Devizes for so long a period, therefore, is remarkable, and signals the unique quality of this source of material. But it also introduces the historian to a different mentality, far removed from even the kind of bureaucracy that would later become more recognizable to the modern world. Custody of the records, while they still retained their primary utility, was entrusted to the General Commissioners and kept in the offices of a local solicitor or attorney who acted as their Clerk. The paperwork and organization of the assessments was carried out by an administrative framework which was statutorily distanced from the Government Department. This was still the world of personalities in which the executive function in relation to the income tax was carried out by members of the local oligarchy, not yet the world of officialdom. Any social disciplines which controlled the safe-keeping of the Certificates of Assessments and other books and papers were as yet largely unorchestrated by a uniform bureaucracy.

THE CERTIFICATES IN THEIR HISTORIOGRAPHICAL CONTEXT

Each of the episodes to which reference has been made suggests that the disposal of tax papers was more the rule than the exception. More than anything they stress the unique

48 *Chester Chronicle*, 12 Aug.1854
49 *Report from the Select Committee on Public Departments (Purchases and Sale of Materials and Stores)*, PP (1873) xvii 1, 364, q.8120
50 PRO IR40/1507, Report by George Phillips on George Hemment, Surveyor at Warrington, 30 Oct.1880. Similar report by William Smiles, 9 Oct.1880

quality of any surviving material. Their existence today is largely the result of the care taken by the firm(s) of solicitors which succeeded to Meek's practice and deposited the Certificates with the Wiltshire & Swindon Record Office (WSRO 1090/81). This firm is now represented by Messrs Awdry, Bailey & Douglas. The preservation of this record is important for the interpretation of official income tax statistics, as well as of the more general data obtained from these sources that might be used in population and socio-economic studies. The usefulness of income tax statistics has ever been marred to some extent by the uncertainties which surrounded them. The possibility of placing them in the context of the actual practice of taxation opens up a new awareness of these figures and may perhaps lead to a re-evaluation of accepted thinking about mid-Victorian incomes. The Certificate of Assessments provides the golden key which unlocks what was really being done at a local level, and allows us to approach more intimately the workings of the income tax which neither the statute, the Reports of the Board of Inland Revenue, central statistics or other more formalized reports, alone, permit.

Economic histories, particularly those which concern the size and distribution of middle or lower-middle class wealth have relied to some extent on official income tax statistics. These works have invariably acknowledged the limitations of these figures and that far more work needed to be done on the practices of the local administrative personnel before they could be accepted as a reasonable reflection of the social and geographic distribution of income. Social histories which have addressed the income tax have also been concerned almost exclusively with its political progress as opposed to its social impact and have been based largely on central records.

Although there have been some invaluable tax histories written during the last century or more by only a handful of writers, an understanding of the income tax in legal, social and economic terms has, in the main, been understandably doctrinal in the absence of substantive local records and the relation between the statute law and actual practice has lacked substantial empirical analysis. With some few exceptions they have had little to say about local administrative practices, which is understandable given the scarcity of surviving local material.

Almost every Record Office will boast some ephemera relating to the income tax: a batch of returns for a particular parish, the tax Commissioners' minute books recording the swearing in of the assessors and collectors, a few random notices of assessment, some minutes of appeal meetings or discrete correspondence between the taxpayer and the Clerk to the Commissioners. The density of preservation is an issue which has to be considered. The ephemera such as individual returns or assessments discovered sporadically in archival deposits may often act as tiny lanterns in a dark world in the absence of anything more substantial. But these are no more than isolated fragments which, although useful, contribute in only a minor way to a scientific understanding of the wider scheme of taxation. The value of income tax records in historical research often remains unrealized. The Certificates of Assessments for Devizes open up a new awareness of income tax records as source material for the historian.

Income statistics compiled and publicised by the Board of Inland Revenue during the third quarter of the nineteenth century were drawn directly from summaries of the Certificates of Assessments prepared by the Clerks to the Commissioners for each division. Perhaps one of the most widely held assumptions about these statistics is that they are based on information of a similar quality to the data which are created by the present day system – that is, that there is a close relation between the actual income of, the return made by, and the assessment made on the taxpayer. That the accuracy of such statistics is questionable because of the unknown quantity of evasion is generally the main concern of the historian, but the possibility that the figures may, in certain instances, be little more than estimates in the first place, is not usually considered. The usefulness of such statistics has ever been marred to some extent by the uncertainties which surrounded them. The possibility of placing them in the context of the actual practices of taxation may invite a re-evaluation of accepted thinking about how they were compiled. This is still relatively uncharted territory and more work still needs to be done to ascertain whether more examples of this primary source survive in other parts of the country. It is hoped that this study will generate a greater interest in income tax records as source material and help those who come to such material to understand its context and meaning.

EDITORIAL METHOD
EXPLANATIONS TO THE TEXT

THE MATERIAL

This volume comprises a complete analysis of the Certificates of Assessments for the year 1842/43 and the period 1846/47 to 1859/60. The first year coincides with the re-introduction of the income tax in 1842. There is a gap between 1843 and 1846 after which there is a continuous record. This record extends beyond 1860 but after this date there were subtle changes in, and outward influences on, the making of assessments which would make year on year comparisons unreliable. And as a consequence, a variety of methodological constraints make the recorded data after this date difficult to handle in a format consistent with earlier years. For this reason, this particular study ends at 1860. In order to make the material useful to historians generally, as opposed to the tax historian specifically, the data are presented in the form of a personal history of assessment for each individual or business within the division for this period.

ORGANIZATION OF MATERIAL

The division of Devizes was formed by the amalgamation of the two hundreds of Potterne & Cannings, and Swanborough. Each hundred comprised many parishes and tithings, which became the administration units within the division. A separate Certificate of Assessments was prepared for each one. The Certificates for each unit were bound together in a largely alphabetical order with two exceptions: firstly, the separation of the hundreds was observed in the ordering of the units, so that those comprised in Potterne

& Cannings are listed together, followed by those in Swanborough; and secondly, the parishes of St. John and St.Mary the Virgin, Devizes, invariably follow Worton within the hundred of Potterne and Cannings. The text, therefore, begins with Bedborough, continues to Worton, followed by St.John and St.Mary. These are followed immediately by Allcannings and continue to Woodborough. This reflects the original ordering of the Certificates of Assessments which was observed almost throughout the period.

ENTRY HEADINGS

Each entry is ordered by surname. The forename(s) are recorded where they appear at some time in the Certificates of Assessments. The heading includes the occupation(s), business name and other familial names by which the business was carried on. These are explained in more detail below:

Surnames

The first entry in each heading is the surname. Spelling variants are more frequent at the earlier dates, perhaps as a result of the lists being compiled from largely oral or hearsay evidence. Towards the middle of the period spellings were refined, perhaps when written evidence, such as returns of income and claims for exemption bearing the signatures of the taxpayers, had been obtained. On the basis that later entries reflect the accepted spelling, this form is recorded in the entry heading. Variants and the years for which they existed are recorded by way of footnote. For example, for five out of fifteen years George Randell, baker of St.Mary (**829**) is entered as George Randle; the entry heading is under Randell and the spelling variant noted by footnote.

Forename(s)

Full names are given in the entry heading where they are recorded at some time in the series. For example, J.R.Bayley, solicitor of St.John (**384**) and St.Mary (**676**) is often entered in the Certificates by initials but at other times by his full name of John Raikes Bayley. The entry heading records the full name. Where forenames (other than initials) have been ascertainable only from contemporary directories (for example the Clergy List) these are shown as follows: Cleather, Revd G(eorge) P(arker) (**917**). Variants other than initials are recorded by footnote. Original abbreviations, such as Jno. for John, Jas. for James, are replaced by the full form where this has been recorded at some time in the Certificates. Omissions have been rectified on a few occasions where this was plainly possible, for example Revd. Peter Almerick Leh(eup) Wood (**659**), or the T(urn) P(ike) Trust (**291**).

Occupations

In the entry heading all occupations recorded at any time in the period are included. For example, the heading for William Harding who was described as a farrier from 1842/43 to 1849/50 and as a veterinary surgeon between 1853/54 and 1859/60, is HARDING, William, farrier, veterinary surgeon (**15**); where dual or multiple occupations subsisted throughout the whole period for which a record exists, these are shown conjoined – PERRETT, William, baker & shopkeeper (**93**). The years for which different occupations are recorded are shown by way of footnote.

Business names

Where noted at some time in the period, the business name is given in the heading and the years noted recorded by footnote. The business name has also been included in the entry heading. This applies mostly to inns, taverns and public houses, but brewers and maltsters are also included. For example, SLOPER, Edwin, innkeeper, Elm Tree (**617**); HUMBY, Frederick Peter, Southbroom Brewery (**254**). Where the business name has been recorded for a successor only or obtained from Pigot & Co's Directory of 1842, the name is shown as follows: CROOK, William, innkeeper [by comparison Hare & Hounds] (**430**). Here, the note was recorded in the assessment record for his successor Nathaniel Millwaters.

Familial successions

Two types of succession are included in the entry heading – succession by a family member and succession by a wife or husband. An example of the first is Robert Blake, grocer, builder and assistant overseer of West Lavington between 1852/53 and 1854/55 succeeded by Christopher Blake, grocer & carpenter from 1855/56 to 1859/60. The heading reads BLAKE, Christopher, grocer, builder, carpenter, assistant overseer [also BLAKE, Robert] (**311**) on the basis that Christopher Blake was recorded in five out of eight years. An example of the second is Edward Davies, innkeeper of the Bear from 1842/43 to 1850/51 followed by Elizabeth Davies between 1851/52 and 1859/60. Here, the entry heading is DAVIES, Elizabeth, innkeeper, Bear [also DAVIES, Edward] (**434**). The entry is made under Elizabeth Davies because this is the name in which the trade was carried on for the greatest number of years recorded. The exception is where the successor has a separate entry, for example, Charles Hook, confectioner (**496**) was succeeded by Eliza & Emma Hook(**497**), who were already recorded separately as schoolmistresses but changed their occupation to confectioners after the date of succession. All successions are noted by way of footnote, recording the exact wording of the entry.

Partnerships

Partnerships are entered in headings under the name of the first named partner. For example, the partnership of tailors Spencer & Plummer is entered under SPENCER, Thomas C. and Plummer, John Alderson (**624**). Exceptionally, the changing partnership of surgeons in Market Lavington, where Charles Hitchcock appears to have been the principal partner throughout the period, is recorded under HITCHCOCK, Charles in order to maintain the integrity of this particular business entity and the heading extended to the other partners as they changed by square brackets: HITCHCOCK, Charles, surgeon [also IVES, John; HAYWARD, John; WHITE, Frederick George; PEPLER, William Brown] (**1014**) and separate headings recording individual partners occur in appropriate alphabetical places in the text and cross-referenced to HITCHCOCK.

FOOTNOTE COMMENTARY

Footnotes to each entry record all original textual commentary. This is dealt with under the following categories.

Spelling
Variants and surnames have been explained above. In all footnote entries the original spelling has been retained – for example, Cottle for Cottell; Poulshot for Poulshott.

Original comments
Comments inserted in the Certificates of Assessments have been reproduced *verbatim* and included by way of footnote with a note of the appropriate year. These are mainly comments such as 'dead', 'gone to -', 'left', 'now -', 'removed to -', 'late -', 'insolvent', 'business ceased', 'return at -', 'at Devizes', 'charged in -'.

Occupation variations
As stated above, entry headings include all occupations recorded at any given time in the period. The years for which they were recorded are given by footnote. For example, the entry heading GILLMAN, Charles, reporter, bookseller, profits on printing, dissenting preacher (**469**), would show in the footnotes 1854/55 reporter & profits on printing, dissenting preacher, 1855/56 reporter, 1856/57 reporter & bookseller, 1857/58–1859/60 bookseller.

Successions
Successions to businesses are recorded by footnote commentary showing the year in which noted. For example, JONES, William Blackwell (**514**) for 1857/58 marked 'dead, innkeeper Crown, now Charles Rhodes Plank' or LYNE, Thomas William (**542**) marked in 1850/51 'Lyne late Lavington, Samuel, grocer' and in 1856/57 'Long, John late Lyne, grocer'. This practice is extended in many instances to bank employees, as in KING, Edward, bank manager, North Wilts Bank (**517**), 1848/49 marked 'King late Copeman' in a reference to his predecessor W. W. Copeman. In 1857/58 his agency commission is marked 'transferred to Mr. Calf and Mr. Humby' in a reference to James Humby's succession as manager and Henry Calf's position as bank clerk (**57**). Occasionally the succession is implicit, for example, Eliza Allen, innkeeper of Bromham was entered and assessed in 1846/47 but in 1847/48 the entry is struck out and replaced by Richard Stone, innkeeper, in the same alphabetical position as Allen in the assessment list.

Life assurance relief
In later years relief was granted in respect of premiums paid under life assurance contracts. The relief was given in the form of a discharge of tax rather than a reduction in assessment. The amount of the premium is recorded in a footnote together with the year of note.

Schedule E
Certain employees deriving income from public offices or limited companies – for example, certain bank managers, the chaplain to the New Prison, Relieving Officers,

Prison Governors – are recorded but not assessed, since they were more correctly assessable under Schedule E. However, in the early years, the statutory requirements were at times honoured more in the breach than the observance. For example, James Humby, bank clerk at the North Wilts Bank (**256, 507**) was assessed under Schedule D between 1852/53 and 1854/55 and having been appointed manager, his name and salary were entered under Schedule D between 1856/57 and 1858/59 but marked 'Schedule E' to denote the fact that an assessment was made under another Schedule. Similarly, John Thurnham, Superintendent of the new County Asylum (**289**) was entered in 1852/43 and marked Schedule E.

CROSS REFERENCES AND NOTES

Textual cross references relate in the main to successions, where all proprietors who carried on the business at any time during the period are included. For example, under the entry JONES, William Blackwell, law stationer, innkeeper, Crown (**514**), cross references are extended not only to the immediate predecessor Benjamin Palmer and the immediate successor Charles Rhodes Plank, but to George King (including Elizabeth Gale King) who had earlier carried on the same business. Similarly the entry JOHNSTONE, Bayntun, chemist (**511**), is cross referenced to Fitzherbert Bridges, Henry Cripps and Robert Hayward. In this way a consecutive history of each business can be seen at a glance.

All appropriate entries are cross referenced to Pigot & Co's Trade Directory of 1842 which is included in Volume 47 of the Wiltshire Record Society series. For example, the footnote to the entry BIGGS, Richard William, schoolmaster, interest on securities, possessions in Ireland (**388**), records Richard W. Biggs, (boarding) school, Long Street.

Certain explanations arising from textual material accompany the entry in note form. For example, a commentary on early forms of lawful tax avoidance is included in the entry THORP, Thomas Glossop, surveyor's clerk (**29**); a comment on bank manager's salaries is included in the entry KING, Edward, bank manager (**517**); or a note concerning the brief history of the wine merchant's business in the entry relating to Edwin Giddings and George Ellis (**464, 465**).

Extra-textual cross references have been kept to a minimum and have been made only where corroboration was necessary to verify facts.

Assessment by letter
As a measure to ensure confidentiality, (which extended only to assessments made under Schedule D), the taxpayer could elect to be assessed under letter instead of name, though the degree to which strict confidentiality was thus attained is questionable. The fact that such an election was made is recorded by a capital letter placed against the sum assessed in each year. Few opted for this treatment – notably George Washington Anstie, solicitor (**669**); Thomas Blackwell, civil engineer (**165**); John Hayward, land agent (**182**); Thomas Chandler, maltster (**230**); and innkeepers such as James Chandler of the Old

Crown (**693**), William Grace of the Castle (**746**), James Macklin of the White Bear (**787**) and William Joyce of the Pelican (**515**).

Assessment by Special Commissioners

The Schedule D taxpayer could make an application to be assessed by the Special Commissioners, three Government officials based at Somerset House, who travelled on circuit to hear appeals. This was a provision of which few availed themselves because of the perception that remunerated officers of the Crown might be more likely to make increased assessments. In Devizes, only the solicitors John Raikes Bayley (**384**) and the firm of MacDonald & Olivier (**544**) elected to be assessed by the Special Commissioners. The years for which such an election was made is included in the notes to each entry.

ABBREVIATIONS

The most frequently used abbreviations in the text are 'a' against an assessment to denote that an appeal was made against an estimate; and 'i' against a sum to denote that it was interest on a loan or investment. Abbreviations specific to a particular entry are recorded separately. For example, under the entry KNEE, Nathaniel, schoolmaster, clerk, commercial traveller, baby linen warehouse (**525**), the abbreviations 's', 'c'. 'ct' and 'b' respectively are noted in the assessment record.

TERMINOLOGY USED IN THE TEXT

Much of the terminology used must be gleaned from the introduction in order to appreciate fully the meaning, but the following broadly represent a brief outline of the most common terms.

Returned – the word signifies that the taxpayer made a return of income of the amount shown.

Assessed – the word records the fact that an assessment was made by the Additional Commissioners either in the sum returned by the taxpayer or estimated by them (which one is evident from each entry).

Appeal – a formal appeal was made to the General Commissioners against an estimated assessment made by the Additional Commissioners.

Income proved – the term shows that a claim for exemption was made by the taxpayer, the exact results of which were entered in the income proved column, proving that his total income lay below the tax threshold.

Exempt – this term is used where the sum assessed is extended to the income proved column so signifying a formal claim for exemption. In later years, particularly 1856/57 to 1859/60 the names of persons continually and obviously below the tax threshold were entered but no assessments were made. In such circumstances the textual entry reads 'recorded; no assessment made; exempt.' In other cases, where the claimant was evidently below the exemption limit, the assessment was wholly discharged although no sum was recorded. The entry for the year is marked 'exempt' in the text and the fact recorded by footnote. It is important to appreciate that where any assessment is not marked 'exempt', even where the amount lay below the tax threshold, tax was payable.

First – the word "First" in the title "Certificates of First Assessments" implies that there was another, and later, assessment. The bulk of assessments were meant to be, and were, included in the Certificates of First Assessments. Any taxpayers who were omitted from the main assessment were, statutorily, included in a supplementary assessment. In the division of Devizes, these additional or supplementary assessments were very few, and were recorded by way of addition to the Certificates of First Assessments, rather than a separate list. All such entries have been included in this volume.

Assessed in absence of return – in almost every case this means that, in the absence of a return, an estimated assessment was made by the Additional Commissioners. In one or two instances the figures assessed appear to be actual rather than estimated figures, and it is possible that a late return was delivered to the Additional Commissioners before the meeting at which they made the assessments. These instances are few but needed clarification.

THE COMMISSIONERS' CERTIFICATES OF FIRST ASSESSMENTS UNDER SCHEDULE D FOR THE DIVISION OF DEVIZES 1842-1860

BEDBOROUGH

1 ABRAHAMS, Joseph, grocer, coal merchant.

Year	Amount returned £	Commissioners' estimate £	Final assessment £
1842/43	150	–	150
1846/47	110	160	160
1847/48	–	200	200
1848/49	160	200	200
1849/50	–	200	200
1850/51	200	–	200
1851/52	175	200	200
1852/53	170	200	200
1853/54	–	200	200
1854/55	–	200	200
1855/56	170	200	200
1856/57	200	–	200
1857/58	200	–	200
1858/59	170	200	200
1859/60	–	200	200

1842/43, 1846/47-1851/52 Abraham; 1852/53-1859/60 Abrahams.
1842/43, 1846/47 coal merchant & grocer; 1847/48-1859/60 grocer, etc.
Pigot & Co"s Directory, 1842: Joseph Abraham, coal merchant & dealer, grocer & tea dealer, Back Lane.

2 ASHLEY, James, mealman.

1846/47-1849/50 assessed in absence of return £50; exempt.
1853/54 assessed in absence of return £50 and £26 pension; exempt.
1854/55 assessed in absence of return £100, income proved at £70; exempt.
1855/56 assessed in absence of return £70; exempt.
1856/57-1859/60 recorded; no assessment made; exempt.

1846/47-1849/50 no occupation noted; 1853/54-1859/60 mealman.
1853/54 pension assessed.
1850/51-1852/53 no assessments made.

3 BOWERING, Benjamin, beerhouse keeper.

1842/43 returned and assessed £50; exempt.
1846/47-1849/50 assessed in absence of return £40; exempt.

Pigot & Co"s Directory, 1842: Benjamin Bowering, retailer of beer, baker, Green.

4 BROWN, William & MAY, Charles, ironfounders.

Year	Amount returned	Commissioners' estimate	Final assessment
	£	£	£
1854/55	–	–	–
1855/56	200	300	300
1856/57	300	400	400
1857/58	400	500	500
1858/59	–	500	500
1859/60	500	600	600

1854/55-1855/56 Brown & May; 1856/57-1859/60 forenames inserted.
1858/59 marked "see return".

5 CHANDLER, John, maltster & gate keeper.

1842/43 entry deleted; no assessment made.

Cross reference: Chandler, John, toll keeper & mealman, St.Mary.

6 COLE, Robert, innkeeper, brewer, Bell.

Year	Amount returned	Commissioners' estimate	Final assessment
	£	£	£
1842/43	150	200	200
1846/47	176	220a	179.16.3
1847/48	161.12.4	–	161.12.4
1848/49	203.10.8	–	203.10.8
1849/50	240	–	240
1850/51	250	–	250
1851/52	250	–	250
1852/53	250	–	250
1853/54	250	300	300
1854/55	166.13.4	300	200
1855/56	–	200	200
1856/57	150	200	200

| 1857/58 | 150 | 200 | 200 |
| 1858/59 | 150 | 200 | 200 |

1842/43, 1846/47-1853/54, 1855/56-1859/60 innkeeper; 1854/55 innkeeper & brewer.
1854/55 assessment reduced but no appeal noted.
1858/59 Bell noted.
1859/60 marked "now Decimus Wild".
Pigot & Co"s Directory, 1842: Robert Cole, innkeeper, Bell, Green.
Cross reference: Wild, Decimus, innkeeper, Bedborough; innkeeper, St.Mary.

7 DOWDING, Revd.Benjamin Charles, pew rents.

1847/48 returned and assessed £74.12.2.
1848/49-1849/50 assessed in absence of return £74.12.2.
1850/51-1851/52 returned and assessed £74.12.2.
1852/53 assessed in absence of return £74.12.2.
1853/54 returned and assessed £74.5.8.
1854/55 assessed in absence of return £74.5.8.
1855/56 returned and assessed £101.
1856/57 returned and assessed £104.2.9.
1857/58 returned £42.6.0; assessed £57.10.0.
1858/59 returned £22.10.0; assessed £55.
1859/60 returned £20; assessed £51.10.0.

1842/43 marked "clerk see Schedule A & B".
1847/48 recorded as clergyman.
1856/57 pew rents recorded.
1857/58 noted "£57.10.0 Mr.Gundry's for Mr.Dowding".
Pigot & Co"s Directory, 1842: Revd.Benjamin Dowding, Potterne Road, clergyman.

8 DURNFORD, Thomas, blacksmith.

1842/43 returned and assessed at £40; exempt.
1846/47 returned £50; increased £80 on appeal; exempt.
1847/48-1849/50 assessed in absence of return £80; exempt.

1848/49 recorded at £30 which seems a mis-numbering.
Pigot & Co"s Directory, 1842: Thomas Durnford, blacksmith, Green.

9 DYKE, Richard, plasterer & tiler.

1842/43 returned and assessed £20; exempt.
1846/47-1849/50 assessed in absence of return £20; exempt.

10 EDMONDS, Richard, teacher of French.

1848/49-1849/50 assessed in absence of return £50; exempt.

1848/49 teacher of French; 1849/50 French teacher.
Pigot & Co"s Directory, 1842: E.Edmonds, schoolmistress, Infants' School, Sheep Street.
Cross references: Edmonds, R, French teacher, St.Mary & St.John; Edmonds, R & W, school-
    masters, St.John.

11 ELLEN, Henry, lime burner. [also ELLEN, William]

1842/43 returned £60, assessed £100; exempt.
1846/47-1849/50 assessed in absence of return £50; exempt.
1853/54 assessed in absence of return £75; exempt.
1854/55 assessed in absence of return £80.
1855/56 assessed in absence of return £80; exempt.
1856/57-1859/60 recorded; no assessments made; exempt.

1842/43 William Ellen; 1846/47-1859/60 Henry Ellen.
1850/51-1852/53 no assessments made.
Pigot & Co"s Directory, 1842: William Ellen, lime burner, Green.

12 FILLIS, John, whitesmith.

1846/47-1849/50 assessed in absence of return £100; exempt.

Pigot & Co"s Directory, 1842: John Fillis, brightsmith, Green.

13 GEORGE, Frank, clerk.

1853/54-1854/55 entries made in absence of return £105 but deleted.

Cross reference: George, Francis(sic), law clerk, Week.

14 GUNDRY, George, tea dealer, grocer. [also GUNDRY, Samuel; GUNDRY & SMITH]

Year	Amount returned	Commissioners' estimate	Final assessment
	£	£	£
1842/43	208	–	208
1846/47	190	–	190
1847/48	–	190	190
1848/49	–	190	190

1849/50	–	190	190
1850/51	190	–	190
1851/52	200	–	200
1852/53	–	200	200
1853/54	150	200	200
1854/55	–	200	200
1855/56	–	200	200
1856/57	170	200	200
1857/58	150	200	200
1858/59	170	200	200
1859/60	150	200	200

1842/43, 1846/47-1850/51 Samuel Gundry; 1851/52-1853/54, 1857/58-1859/60 George Gundry; 1854/55-1856/57 Gundry & Smith.
1842/43, 1846/47 tea dealer & grocer; 1847/48-1859/60 tea dealer(s), etc.
Pigot & Co"s Directory, 1842: Peter Gundry & Son, grocer & tea dealer, agent to Imperial Fire Office, Green.

15 HARDING, William, farrier, veterinary surgeon.

1842/43 returned and assessed £40; exempt.
1846/47-1849/50 assessed in absence of return £60; exempt.
1853/54-1855/56 assessed in absence of return £70; exempt.
1856/57-1859/60 recorded; no assessments made; exempt.

1842/43, 1846/47-1849/50 farrier, 1853/54-1859/60 veterinary surgeon.
1850/51-1852/53 no assessments made.
Pigot & Co"s Directory, 1842: William Harding, blacksmith & farrier, Monday Market Street.

16 HARRISON, John, stonemason.

1842/43 assessed in absence of return £150.
1846/47 returned and assessed £76; exempt.
1847/48-1849/50 assessed in absence of return £76; exempt.
1853/54-1855/56 assessed in absence of return £75; exempt.
1856/57-1859/60 recorded; no assessments made; exempt.

1850/51-1852/53 no assessments made.
Pigot & Co"s Directory, 1842: Harrison, stone & marble mason, Green.

17 LONG, James, innkeeper, British Lion.

1858/59 entry only but deleted.
Cross references: Long, James, innkeeper, Week; West, Henry, innkeeper, Bedborough.

18 MASLEN, John, pig killer.

1842/43 returned and assessed £10.5.0; exempt.
1846-47-1849-50 assessed in absence of return £20; exempt.

19 MATTHEWS, Richard D, clerk.

1853/54-1855/56 assessed in absence of return £115.

1856/57 marked "removed to St.John's".
1858/59 marked "dead".
Cross reference: Matthews, R.D, St.John.

20 MULLINGS, Benoni, builder, etc.

Year	Amount returned	Commissioners' estimate	Income proved	Final assessment
	£	£	£	£
1852/53	100	120	100	
1853/54	–	200	116	
1854/55	100	150	–	150
1855/56	120	150	–	150
1856/57	130	150	–	150
1857/58	–	200	–	200
1858/59	160	200	–	200
1859/60	150	200	–	200

1852/53 marked "late White".
Cross references: White, Benoni Thomas, builder, Bedborough; White, T.B, St.John; Young &
    White, St.John.

21 NEATE, Charles & John, blacksmiths. [also NEATE, Mrs.]

1846/47-1849/50 assessed in absence of return £50; exempt.
1853/54 returned and assessed £80; exempt.
1854/55-1855/56 assessed in absence of return £80; exempt.
1856/57-1859/60 recorded; no assessments made; exempt.

1846/47-1849/50 Mrs Neate, blacksmith; 1853/54-1859/60 Charles & John Neate, black-
    smiths.
1850/51-1852/53 no assessments made.
Pigot & Co"s Directory, 1842: Sophia Neate, blacksmith, Green.

22 NEATE, John, carpenter, timber dealer.

1846/47-1849/50 assessed in absence of return £50; exempt.
1853/54 assessed in absence of return £50; exempt.
1854/55 assessed in absence of return £60; income proved at £25; exempt.
1855/56 assessed in absence of return £25; exempt.
1856/57-1859/60 recorded; no assessments made; exempt.

1842/43, 1846/47-1853/54 carpenter; 1854/55-1859/60 timber dealer.
1850/51-1852/53 no assessments made.

23 ORIEL, William, shopkeeper.

1842/43 returned and assessed £50; exempt.

Pigot & Co"s Directory, 1842: William Oriel, grocer & tea dealer, Green.

24 PERRY, Horatio Nelson, agent to Lawes & Co. Van, carrier.

1842/43, 1846/47-1847/48 returned and assessed £40.
1848/49 assessed in absence of return £40.
1849/50 returned and assessed £40.
1850/51 assessed in absence of return £70.
1851/52-1852/53 returned £50; assessed £70.

1842/43, 1846/47-1848/49 agent to Lawes & Co.; 1849/50-1852/53 carrier.
1849/50 [St Mary] marked "William Lawes & Co now Perry".
1852/53 marked "deceased".
Cross reference: Lawes, William & Co., carriers, wagon office, St Mary.

25 PLANK, Charles Rhodes, builder.

1842/43 returned £200; assessed £250.
1846/47-1847/48 assessed in absence of return £250.
1848/49-1849/50 returned £150; assessed £200.
1850/51 assessed in absence of return £200.
1851/52 returned and assessed £200.
1852/53 assessed in absence of return £200.
1853/54 returned and assessed £200.
1854/55-1856/57 returned £150; assessed £200.
1857/58 returned £150; assessed £225.
1858/59-1859/60 returned £150; assessed £200.

1842/43, 1846/47-1854/55, 1859/60 Charles Rhodes Plank; 1855/56-1858/59 Charles Plank.

Pigot & Co"s Directory, 1842: Charles Plank, carpenter, builder & wheelwright, Green.
Cross references: Plank, Charles Rhodes, innkeeper, St.John; Plank, Charles, builder, Week.

26 RANSOM, William, woolstapler.

1853/54 returned £32 and £30 interest; assessed £82.
1854/55 assessed in absence of return £50; increased by General Commissioners to
    £25 and £30 interest.
1855/56 assessed in absence of return £55.
1856/57 assessed in absence of return £25.
1857/58 returned £25; assessed £30.
1858/59 returned and assessed £30.
1859/60 assessed in absence of return £30.

1854/55 assessment increased by General Commissioners; no appeal noted.
1856/57 confirmed on appeal.
Cross reference: Ransom, William, woolstapler & publican, St. John.

27 SALMON, Charles, stonemason.

1858/59–1859/60 recorded; no assessments made; exempt.

28 TARRANT, Nathaniel, schoolmaster.

1858/59–1859/60 recorded; no assessments made; exempt.

29 THORP, Thomas Glossop, surveyor's clerk.

1842/43, 1846/47–1847/48 returned and assessed £150.
1848/49 assessed in absence of return £150; reduced to £149 on appeal; exempt.
1849/50 assessed in absence of return £150; income proved at £149; exempt.
1850/51 returned and assessed £149; exempt.
1851/52–1852/53 assessed in absence of return £149; exempt.

1848/49 is an example of an early form of tax avoidance. On incomes of £150, tax was payable
    on the whole amount. Incomes below this sum were eligible to be wholly relieved on a
    claim for exemption. By agreeing with the employer to fix the salary at £149, the taxpayer
    would be better off by £3.7.6. (Evidence taken before the Select Committee on the In-
    come and Property Tax, House of Commons. Parliamentary Papers. (1852) ix qq.3019,
    3235).
1849/50 no appeal noted.
1852/53 marked "removed to Southampton".
Cross references: (similar instance of early legal tax avoidance) Anderson, T.W., solicitor's clerk,
    St.John; Coxhead, W.P., schoolmaster, St. John.

30 WALKER, Frederick, silk throwster, silk manufacturer. [also WALKER, Peter]

Year	Amount returned £	Commissioners' estimate £	Income proved £	Final assessment £
1842/43	-	200	100	-
1846/47	125	169	-	169
1847/48	152	200	-	200
1848/49	-	200a	-	157
1849/50	97	-	97	-
1850/51	-	200	-	200
1851/52	135	200	-	200
1852/53	156	200	-	200
1853/54	200	-	-	200
1854/55	187	250	-	250
1855/56	163	400	-	400
1856/57	200	400	-	400
1857/58	130	300	-	300
1858/59	-	200	-	200
1859/60	100	300	-	300

1842/43 Walker, Peter, silk manufacturer, entered and deleted.
1842/43 silk manufacturer; 1846/47-1859/60 silk throwster.
1842/43 no appeal noted.
Pigot & Co"s Directory, 1842: Frederick Walker, silk throwster, Belvedere Mill.

31 WATSON, Charles, tea dealer.

1842/43 No assessment made.

Pigot & Co"s Directory, 1842: Charles Watson, tea dealer & linen & woollen draper, Green.
Cross reference: Watson, John, (Charles deleted), draper & tea dealer, St.John.

32 WEST, Henry, beerhouse keeper, British Lion.

1857/58 no assessment made.
1858/59 recorded; no assessment made; exempt.
1859/60 assessed in absence of return £80; reduced £65.

1858/59 British Lion noted.
1859/60 no appeal noted.
Cross references: Long, James, innkeeper, Bedborough; West, Henry, innkeeper, Week.

33 WHEELER, Robert, beerhouse keeper.

1842/43 assessed in absence of return £20; exempt.
1846/47-1849/50 assessed in absence of return £50; exempt.

1842/43 pig killer deleted.
Pigot & Co"s Directory, 1842: R. Wheeler, retailer of beer, Green.

34 WHITE, Benoni Thomas, builder.

1842/43 marked "return made in St. John's".
1852/53 marked "Mullings, Benoni, builder late White".
1852/53 [St.John] marked "White now Mullings, Benoni, builder".
Cross references: Mullings, Benoni, builder, Bedborough; White, T.B, St.John; Young & White, St.John.

35 WILD, Decimus, innkeeper, Bell.

1859/60 returned and assessed £200.

1859/60 marked "late Cole, innkeeper, Bell".
Cross references: Cole, Robert, innkeeper, Bedborough; Wild, Decimus, innkeeper, St.Mary.

36 WILSON, Sandar, master of workhouse.

1842/43 entered but deleted; marked "See Schedule E".

Note: Incomes from public offices and employments were assessable under Schedule E.
Pigot & Co"s Directory, 1842: Union Workhouse, Back Lane, Sandar Wilson, governor.

BISHOP'S CANNINGS

37 BERRY, Isaac, beerhouse keeper.

1846/47-1847/48 assessed in absence of return £50; exempt.
1848/49-1849/50 assessed in absence of return £90; exempt.

38 COCKLE, William, innkeeper.

1847/48 assessed in absence of return £50; exempt.

1848/49 marked "Cockle, William, late now Rumming".
Cross references: Cockle, William, innkeeper, Bourton & Easton; Rumming, Thomas, innkeeper, Bishop's Cannings.

39 DAVIS, William, provision & cheese dealer.

1858/59 returned and assessed £100.

1858/59 marked "to be charged next year in Bourton where he resides".
1859/60 marked "in Bourton".
Cross reference: Davis, William, provision & cheese dealer, Bourton & Easton.

40 KERTON, James, grocer & baker.

1853/54-1855/56 assessed in absence of return £75; exempt.

1856/57 marked "dead".

41 MACDONALD, Archdeacon [William].

1854/55 returned £393 but no assessment made.
1855/56 estimated in absence of return £268 but no assessment made.

1854/55 marked [partly illegible] "Tithe Charge".

42 RUMMING, Thomas, innkeeper.

1848/49 assessed in absence of return £50; exempt.
1849/50 assessed in absence of return £20; exempt.

1848/49 marked "Cockle, William, late now Rumming".
1849/50 marked "Rumming, Thomas late Cockle, innkeeper".
Cross reference: Cockle, William, innkeeper, Bishop's Cannings.

43 SAVAGE, William, curate.

1855/56 estimated in absence of return £268 but no assessment made. [blurred]

44 SCOTT, Revd. Thomas, curate.

1842/43 returned £70 but no assessment made.

45 SLOPER, James, miller, baker, shopkeeper, farmer.

Year	Amount returned £	Commissioners' estimate £	Final assessment £		
1842/43	50m	100	100	(70bs	30s)
1846/47	–	100	100		
1847/48	43	100	100		
1848/49	–	100	100		
1849/50	120	–	120		
1850/51	–	120a	80		
1851/52	20	80	80		
1852/53	70	80	80		
1853/54	60	80	80		
1854/55	–	110	110		
1855/56	–	110	110		
1856/57	–	110	110		
1857/58	–	125	125		
1858/59	–	130	130		
1859/60	–	130	130		

Abbreviations: m, miller at Rowde; bs, baker & shopkeeper at Bishop's Cannings; s, shopkeeper at Avebury.
1842/43 miller, baker & shopkeeper; 1847/48-1853/54, 1856/57-1859/60 baker;
1854/55-1855/56 baker & farmer; 1857/58 baker & miller.

46 SLOPER, Simon, harness maker, blacksmith.

1853/54 returned £20; assessed £75; exempt.
1854/55-1857/58 assessed in absence of return £75.
1858/59 assessed in absence of return £80.
1859/60 returned £60; assessed £80.

47 SLOPER, William, innkeeper, maltster. [by comparison, Crown]

1842/43 returned £60i, £15m; assessed £100.
1846/47 assessed in absence of return £100.
1847/48 returned £70; assessed £100.
1848/49 assessed in absence of return £100.
1849/50 returned and £115; exempt.
1850/51 assessed in absence of return £115; reduced to £103.10.0 on appeal.
1851/52 returned £50; assessed £100.
1852/53 assessed in absence of return £100.

Abbreviations: i, innkeeper; m, maltster.
1842/43, 1846/47 innkeeper & maltster; 1847/48-1852/53 innkeeper.

1842/43 possibly confirmed on appeal.
1852/53 marked "Spreadbury now".
Cross reference: Spreadbury, Charles, innkeeper, Bishops's Cannings.

48 SMITH, George, beerseller, grocer, baker.

1849/50 assessed in absence of return £20; exempt.
1853/54 returned £20; assessed £50; exempt.
1854/55-1855/56 assessed in absence of return £50; exempt.
1856/57 assessed in absence of return £100.
1857/58 assessed in absence of return £120; reduced to £100 but no appeal noted.
1858/59 assessed in absence of return £120.
1859/60 returned £100; assessed £120.

1849/50 beerseller; 1853/54-1855/56 grocer & beerseller; 1856/57-1859/60 grocer, baker & beerseller.
1850/51-1852/53 no assessments made.

49 SMITH, John, baker & beerhouse keeper.

1842/43 assessed in absence of return £75; exempt.

50 SPREADBURY, Charles, innkeeper, Crown.

1853/54 returned £60; assessed £100; income proved at £75; exempt.
1854/55-1855/56 assessed in absence of return £75; exempt.
1856/57 assessed in absence of return £100; reduced to £97 on appeal; exempt.
1857/58 returned £70; assessed £105; income proved at £70; exempt.
1858/59-1859/60 recorded; no assessments made; exempt.

1852/53 marked "Sloper, William, Spreadbury now".
Cross reference: Sloper, William, innkeeper, Bishop's Cannings.

BOURTON & EASTON

Note: Bourton & Easton was subsumed into Bishop's Cannings 1847/48; resumed separate identity 1859/60.

51 COCKLE, William, innkeeper.

1846/47 assessed in absence of return £50; exempt.

Cross references: Cockle, William, innkeeper, Bishop's Cannings; Lucas, John, innkeeper, Bourton & Easton (probable); Rumming, Thomas, innkeeper, Bishop's Cannings.

52 DAVIS, William, provision & cheese dealer.

1859/60 returned £100; assessed £120.

1858/59 [Bishop's Cannings] marked "to be charged next year in Bourton & Easton where he resides".
Cross reference: Davis, William, provision & cheese dealer, Bishop's Cannings.

53 LUCAS, John, innkeeper.

1842/43 returned and assessed £15; exempt.

Cross references: Cockle, William, innkeeper, Bourton & Easton, (probable).

BROMHAM

54 AKERMAN, James, beerseller, beerhouse keeper, innkeeper, grocer.

1842/43, 1846/47-1849/50 assessed in absence of return £20; exempt.
1853/54 returned £20; assessed £60; exempt.
1854/55 returned and assessed £20; exempt.
1855/56 assessed in absence of return £20; exempt.
1856/57-1859/60 recorded; no assessments made; exempt.

1842/43, 1846/47-1849/50 beerseller; 1853/54 innkeeper & grocer; 1854/55 beerhouse keeper & grocer; 1855/56-1859/60 beerhouse keeper.
1850/51-1852/53 no assessments made.
1857/58-1858/59 noted £80 in margin.

55 AKERMAN, John, beerhouse keeper, innkeeper, New Inn.
[also AKERMAN, Elizabeth]

1842/43, 1846/47-1847/48 assessed in absence of return £40; exempt.
1848/49 returned £25; assessed £40; exempt.
1849/50 assessed in absence of return £40; exempt.
1854/55-1855/56 assessed in absence of return £40; exempt.
1856/57-1859/60 recorded; no assessments made; exempt.

1842/43, 1846/47-1857/58 John Akerman; 1858/59-1859/60 Elizabeth Akerman.
1850/51-1853/54 no assessments made.
1854/55 New Inn noted.

56 AKERMAN, Robert, baker & shopkeeper.

1852/53 returned and assessed £70; exempt.
1853/54 returned £60; assessed £70; exempt.
1854/55-1855/56 assessed in absence of return £70; exempt.
1856/57-1859/60 recorded; no assessments made; exempt.

57 ALLEN, Eliza, innkeeper.

1846/47 assessed in absence of return £40; exempt.

1847/48 Allen is replaced by Richard Stone, innkeeper. The position of Stone in the alphabetical list suggests that he succeeded to Allen's business.
Cross reference: Stone, Richard, innkeeper, Bromham.

58 ATTWOOD, James, blacksmith.

1842/43, 1846/47-1847/48 assessed in absence of return £50; exempt.
1848/49 returned £20; assessed £50; income proved at £67.4.6; exempt.
1849/50 assessed in absence of return £50; income proved at £67.4.6; exempt.

1848/49 Atwood.

59 ATTWOOD, Thomas, smith.

1842/43, 1846/47-1849/50 assessed in absence of return £20; exempt.

1848/49 Atwood.

60 BAILEY, Thomas, innkeeper.

1842/43 assessed in absence of return £40; exempt.

61 BANKS, James, brewer, maltster.

Year	Amount returned £	Commissioners' estimate £	Final assessment £
1842/43	415	–	415
1846/47	355	415	415
1847/48	290	415	415
1848/49	240	415	415

1849/50	250	450	450
1850/51	395	450	450
1851/52	278	450	450
1852/53	310	450	450
1853/54	350	450	450
1854/55	250	450	450
1855/56	210	400	400
1856/57	320	500	500
1857/58	300	420	420
1858/59	250	500	500
1859/60	250	600	600

1842/43, 1846/47-1852/53 brewer & maltster; 1853/54-1859/60 brewer.

62 BARTON, Benjamin, miller.

1857/58 returned £150; assessed at £62; exempt.
1858/59 returned £40; assessed £100; income proved at £56; exempt.
1859/60 recorded; no assessment made; exempt.

1857/58 marked "Hitchens, John, miller, see Benjamin Barton".
1858/59 marked "no exemption claimed" but assessment discharged.
Cross reference: Hitchens, John, miller, Bromham.

63 BENGER, John, turner.

1842/43, 1846/47-1849/50 assessed in absence of return £70; exempt.
1853/54 returned and assessed £40; exempt.
1854/55-1855/56 assessed in absence of return £20; exempt.
1856/57-1859/60 recorded; no assessments made; exempt.

1850/51-1852/53 no assessments made.

64 BLACKMAN, James, baker & shopkeeper.

1842/43 returned £110; assessed £150.
1846/47 returned £68; assessed £150.
1847/48-1851/52 assessed in absence of return £150.
1852/53 returned and assessed £150.
1853/54 assessed in absence of return £150.

1854/55 marked "out of business 2 years".

65 BROWN, John, turner.

1853/54 returned and assessed £30; exempt.
1854/55 assessed in absence of return £20; exempt.
1855/56 assessed in absence of return £30; exempt.
1856/57-1859/60 recorded; no assessments made; exempt.

66 BROWN, Revd. M[eredith], clergyman.

1848/49 entry only.

67 BUTLER, Edward, miller.

1842/43 assessed in absence of return £50; exempt.

68 CHARLES, James, bailiff.

1853/54 returned and assessed £100; income proved at £90; exempt.
1854/55 returned and assessed £80; exempt.
1855/56 assessed in absence of return £90; exempt.
1856/57-1858/59 recorded; no assessments made; exempt.

1859/60 marked "now – bailiff", (no name inserted).

69 COUZENS, Jane, beerhouse keeper.

1846/47-1849/50 assessed in absence of return £50; exempt.

1842/43 recorded but no assessment made.

70 DANGERFIELD, Henry, innkeeper, Greyhound.

1855/56 assessed in absence of return £60; exempt.
1856/57-1859/60 recorded; no assessments made; exempt.

1855/56 marked "Hunt, Jacob (deleted) Henry Dangerfield".
1857/58 returned £60 but no assessment made.
1858/59 Greyhound noted.
Cross reference: Hunt, Jacob, innkeeper, Bromham.

71 DAVIS, William, grocer.

1842/43 returned and assessed £10; exempt.
1846/47-1849/50 assessed in absence of return £20; exempt.

72 DRURY, Revd. Henry, fees from private tuition.

1842/43 returned and assessed £150.

1842/43 "fees as curate" deleted; returned £9.8.0 curate deleted, marked Schedule A.

73 DUCK, Hannah, smith.

1842/43 recorded but no assessment made.
1846/47-1848/49 assessed in absence of return £10; exempt.

74 EDGELL, Revd. –, clergyman, surplice fees.

1847/48 returned £150 (deleted); assessed £10.
1848/49 returned £150 curate, £10 surplice fees; no assessment made.

75 FENNELL, William, butcher.

1853/54-1854/55 returned £25; assessed £40; exempt.
1855/56 assessed in absence of return £40; exempt.
1856/57-1859/60 recorded; no assessments made; exempt.

76 GEE, James, butcher.

1842/43 assessed in absence of return £25; exempt.
1846/47 assessed in absence of return £40; exempt.
1847/48 returned £60; exempt.
1848/49 assessed in absence of return £60; income proved at £45.2.4; exempt.
1849/50 assessed in absence of return £60; income proved at £45.2.11; exempt.

77 GEE, John, shopkeeper, baker, farmer.

1842/43 returned £50; assessed £75; exempt.
1846/47 assessed in absence of return £75; exempt.
1847/48 returned and assessed £75; exempt.
1848/49-1849/50 assessed in absence of return £75; exempt.

1851/52-1852/53 returned £50; assessed £75; exempt 1851/52.
1853/54-1854/55 returned £70; assessed £75.
1855/56-1856/57 assessed in absence of return £75.
1857/58 returned and assessed £75.
1858/59-1859/60 assessed in absence of return £85.

1842/43, 1846/47-1849/50 shopkeeper; 1851/52-1853/54, baker, etc.; 1854/55-1855/56 baker & farmer; 1856/57-1859/60 baker.
1850/51 no assessment made.

78 GIBBONS, Thomas, grocer.

1853/54 returned £20; assessed £40; exempt.
1854/55-1855/56 assessed in absence of return £40; exempt.
1856/57-1859/60 recorded; no assessments made; exempt.

79 HAND, John, innkeeper, Bell, St. Ediths Marsh.

1849/50 assessed in absence of return £70; exempt.
1853/54 assessed in absence of return £80; exempt.
1854/55-1855/56 assessed in absence of return £100.
1856/57 estimated in absence of return £60; no assessment made; exempt.
1857/58 recorded; no assessment made; exempt.
1858/59 returned and assessed £78.19.4; exempt.
1859/60 recorded; no assessment made; exempt.

1849/50 marked "Hand, John (late Smith) innkeeper".
1850/51-1852/53 no assessments made.
1858/59 Bell, St. Ediths Marsh noted.
Cross reference: Smith, John, innkeeper, Bromham.

80 HEALE, Ralph, bailiff.

1853/54-1856/57 assessed in absence of return £90.
1857/58 assessed in absence of return £90; exempt.
1858/59 returned and assessed £90; exempt.
1859/60 recorded; no assessment made; exempt.

1858/59 Hale.

81 HITCHENS, John, miller.

1842/43, 1846/47-1849/50 assessed in absence of return £50; exempt.
1853/54 assessed in absence of return £100; income proved at £95; exempt.

1854/55 assessed in absence of return £100; income proved at £80; exempt.
1855/56 assessed in absence of return £80; exempt.

1847/48-1849/50 Hitchins.
1850/51-1852/53 no assessments made.
1856/57 marked "now removed to Potterne".
1857/58 marked "see Benjamin Barton".
Cross references: Barton, Benjamin, miller, Bromham; Hitchens, John, miller, Potterne.

82 HORN, John, miller.

1853/54 returned and assessed £70; exempt.
1854/55 returned £70; assessed £75; income proved at £70; exempt.
1855/56 assessed in absence of return £70; exempt.
1856/57-1859/60 recorded; no assessments made; exempt.

1853/54 miller, etc.

83 HUGHES, -, miller.

1846/47 assessed in absence of return £75; exempt.
1847/48-1849/50 assessed in absence of return £80; exempt.

84 HUNT, Jacob, innkeeper. [by comparison, Greyhound]

1853/54 returned £30; assessed £60; exempt.
1854/55 returned £40; assessed £60; exempt.

1853/54 James entered but deleted.
1855/56 name deleted, Henry Dangerfield substituted.
Cross reference: Dangerfield, Henry, innkeeper, Bromham.

85 LEWIS, James, surgeon.

1851/52 returned and assessed £70; exempt.
1852/53 assessed in absence of return £70; income proved at £24; exempt.

1853/54-1854/55 marked "Schedule E".

86 LOTT, Thomas, innkeeper.

1842/43 returned and assessed £140; exempt.

87 MASON, Thomas, innkeeper, Shoulder of Mutton.

1858/59 returned and assessed £90; exempt.
1859/60 recorded; no assessment made; exempt.

1858/59 marked "Thomas Westaway now Thomas Mason, Shoulder of Mutton".
Cross references: Westaway, Thomas, innkeeper, Bromham; Wootten David, innkeeper, Bromham.

88 MEREDITH, Samuel, Chief Constable.

1846/47 entry only.

89 MILSOM, James, mop spinner.

1842/43 returned £10; exempt.
1846/47-1847/48 assessed in absence of return £15; exempt.

90 MOORE, Thomas, gentleman. [poet]

1842/43, 1846/47 recorded; no assessment made.
1847/48 assessed in absence of return £100.
1848/49 recorded; no assessment made.

1842/43 marked "Schedule B".
1846/47 marked "Return".

91 ORCHARD, Edward, beerhouse keeper, shopkeeper.

1842/43 returned and assessed £60; exempt.
1846/47-1847/48 assessed in absence of return £35; exempt.
1848/49 returned and assessed £64; exempt.
1849/50 assessed in absence of return £64; exempt.
1851/52 returned and assessed £70; exempt.
1852/53 assessed in absence of return £70; exempt.
1859/60 recorded but no assessment made.

1842/43, 1846/47-1849/50 beerhouse keeper; 1851/52-1852/53 shopkeeper; 1859/60 no
    occupation noted.
1850/51 no assessment made.

92 PERRETT, James, baker & retail dealer.

1842/43 assessed in absence of return £30; exempt.
1846/47-1849/50 assessed in absence of return £32; exempt.

93 PERRETT, William, baker & shopkeeper.

1842/43 returned £35; assessed £100; exempt.
1846/47–1850/51 assessed in absence of return £100.

1851/52 marked "now William Webb, carpenter".
Cross reference: Webb, William, carpenter, Bromham.

94 POWNEY, Charles.

1842/43 returned and assessed £91; exempt.
1846/47–1849/50 assessed in absence of return £91; exempt.

No occupation noted.

95 RUDDLE, James, harness maker.

1842/43, 1846/47–1849/50 assessed in absence of return £40; exempt.

96 SANSOM, James, bricklayer.

1842/43 assessed in absence of return £75; exempt.
1846/47–1848/49 assessed in absence of return £61.10.0; exempt.
1849/50 assessed in absence of return £60; exempt.

97 SMITH, John, innkeeper. [by comparison, Bell, St. Ediths Marsh]

1846/47–1848/49 assessed in absence of return £70; exempt.

1849/50 marked "see Hand".
Cross reference: Hand, John, innkeeper, Bromham".

98 STONE, Richard, innkeeper, wheelwright.

1847/48 assessed in absence of return £40; exempt.
1848/49 returned and assessed £50 innkeeper, £40 wheelwright; exempt.
1849/50 assessed in absence of return £50; exempt.

1847/48 innkeeper; 1848/49–1849/50 innkeeper & wheelwright.
Cross reference: Allen, Elizabeth, innkeeper, Bromham.

99 WEBB, Benjamin, lime burner.

1842/43 assessed in absence of return £50; exempt.
1846/47 assessed in absence of return £75; exempt.
1847/48 assessed in absence of return £100; exempt.
1848/49 assessed in absence of return £100; income proved at £120; exempt.
1849/50 assessed in absence of return £50; exempt.

100 WEBB, William, baker, shopkeeper, carpenter.

1852/53 returned £70; assessed £100; assessment discharged on appeal.
1853/54 assessed in absence of return £100; income proved at £90; exempt.
1854/55 assessed in absence of return £100; reduced to £80.
1855/56-1856/57 assessed in absence of return £80; exempt.
1857/58 returned £60; no assessment made; exempt.
1858/59-1859/60 recorded; no assessments made; exempt.

1852/53 no sum recorded.
1856/57 assessment appealed against and assessment discharged but no sum recorded.
1852/53 baker & shopkeeper; 1853/54-1855/56 baker etc.; 1856/57 shopkeeper;
1857/58-1859/60 shopkeeper & carpenter.
1851/52 marked "Perrett, William now William Webb, carpenter".
Cross reference: Perrett, William, baker & shopkeeper, Bromham.

101 WESTAWAY, Thomas, innkeeper, Shoulder of Mutton.

1856/57-1857/58 recorded; no assessments made; exempt.

1855/56 marked "Wootten, David now Thomas Westaway, innkeeper".
1858/59 marked "Westaway, Thomas now Thomas Mason, Shoulder of Mutton".
Cross references: Mason, Thomas, innkeeper, Bromham; Wootten, David, innkeeper, Bromham.

102 WOOTTEN, David, farrier, innkeeper. [by comparison, Shoulder of Mutton]

1842/43, 1846/47 assessed in absence of return £50; exempt.
1847/48 assessed in absence of return £70; exempt.
1848/49 returned £54; assessed £70; exempt.
1849/50 returned £50; assessed £70; exempt.
1852/53 assessed in absence of return £75; exempt.
1853/54 returned £20; assessed £100; reduced to £52.
1854/55 returned £60; assessed £52.
1855/56 assessed in absence of return £50; exempt.

1842/43 Wootton, Junior.
1850/51-1851/52 no assessments made.

1852/53 innkeeper & farrier.
1853/54 income proved column entered but duty marked as payable.
1855/56 marked "now Thomas Westaway, innkeeper".
Cross references: Mason, Thomas, innkeeper, Bromham; Westaway, Thomas, innkeeper, Bromham.

103 WOOTTEN, David, carpenter.

1842/43 assessed in absence of return £80; exempt.
1846/47–1849/50 assessed in absence of return £50; exempt.

1842/43 Senior.

104 WOOTTEN, Joseph, grocer, etc.

1842/43, 1846/47–1849/50 assessed in absence of return £30; exempt.

105 WOOTTEN, Stephen, carpenter.

1851/52 returned £26; assessed £50; income proved at £112.3.4; exempt.
1852/53 assessed in absence of return £50; exempt.
1853/54 returned £20; assessed £50; exempt.
1854/55–1855/56 assessed in absence of return £50; exempt.
1856/57–1859/60 recorded; no assessments made; exempt.

CHITTOE

106 EARLE, John, wheelwright.

1842/43, 1846/47–1849/50 assessed in absence of return £40; exempt.

COATE

107 NEATE, William, carpenter, timber dealer.

Year	Amount returned £	Commissioners' estimate £	Income proved £	Final assessment £
1842/43	–	75	75	–
1846/47	–	120a	80	–

1847/48	–	120	80	–
1848/49	–	80	80	–
1849/50	–	80	80	–
1851/52	80	–	80	–
1852/53	–	80	80	–
1853/54	25	80	–	50
1854/55	50	–	–	50
1855/56	–	50	–	50
1856/57	–	50	–	50
1857/58	50	–	–	50
1858/59	–	50	–	50
1859/60	–	60	–	60

1842/43 no occupation noted; 1846/47-1849/50 timber dealer; 1851/52-1858/59 carpenter; 1859/60 carpenter & timber dealer.
1850/51 no assessment made.

HORTON

108 BERRY, Isaac, baker & miller.

1848/49 returned £90 but deleted.

109 BERRY, Richard, miller & corndealer.

1850/51 returned £100; assessed £150; reduced to £134.19.6; exempt.

No appeal noted.

110 DREW, John, miller, dealer, baker, innkeeper.

1842/43 returned £150; assessed £175.
1846/47-1847/48 assessed in absence of return £125.
1848/49 returned £60; assessed £125.
1849/50 returned £60; assessed £150.
1850/51 returned £50; assessed £150.
1851/52 returned £60; assessed £175.
1852/53 assessed in absence of return £175.
1853/54-1854/55 returned £60; assessed £175.
1855/56 returned £80; assessed £175.
1856/57 returned £80; assessed £120.
1857/58 returned £100; assessed £150.
1858/59 returned £150; assessed £180.
1859/60 returned £80; assessed £180.

1842/43, 1846/47-1848/49, 1856/57-1857/58 miller; 1849/50-1852/53 miller & innkeeper;
1853/54-1855/56 innkeeper & baker; 1858/59-1859/60 miller & dealer.
1856/57 marked "baking business ceased" "Sloper, Michael late Drew, innkeeper & baker".
Cross reference: Sloper, Michael, innkeeper & baker, Horton.

111 SLOPER, Michael, innkeeper, baker, beerhouse keeper.

1856/57 assessed in absence of return £75; confirmed on appeal; exempt.
1857/58 recorded; no assessment made; exempt.
1858/59-1859/60 assessed in absence of return £100.

1856/57-1858/59 innkeeper & baker; 1859/60 beerhouse keeper & baker.
1856/57 marked "late Drew, innkeeper & baker".
Cross reference: Drew, John, innkeeper & baker, Horton".

MARSTON

112 PERRETT, James, beerhouse keeper, innkeeper, baker.

1842/43, 1846/47 assessed in absence of return £40; exempt.
1847/48 assessed in absence of return £70; exempt.
1848/49 returned £20; assessed £70; exempt.
1849/50 assessed in absence of return £40; exempt.
1850/51 assessed in absence of return £50; exempt.
1851/52 returned £10; assessed £50; exempt.
1852/53-1854/55 assessed in absence of return £50; exempt.

1842/43, 1847/48-1850/51 beerhouse keeper; 1846/47 innkeeper; 1851/52-1854/55
    beerhouse keeper & baker.

113 ROSE, Job, beerhouse keeper & maltster.

1855/56 assessed in absence of return £80; assessment deleted.

1855/56-1856/57 marked "transferred to Worton". (no entry traced in Worton)

NURSTEED

114 CALF, Henry, bank clerk.

1855/56 assessed in absence of return £100.

1855/56 marked "return in St.John" (deleted).
1856/57 marked "removed to St.John and assessed there".
1857/58 marked "charged in St.John".
Cross reference: Calf, Henry, bank clerk, St.John.

115 FARR, James, beerhouse keeper, etc.

1846/47 assessed in absence of return £50; exempt.
1847/48 assessed in absence of return £70; income proved at £108; exempt.
1848/49 assessed in absence of return £70; exempt.
1849/50 assessed in absence of return £60; exempt.
1850/51 assessed in absence of return £50; exempt.
1851/52-1852/53 assessed in absence of return £75; exempt.
1853/54 assessed in absence of return £75; reduced to £50.
1854/55-1856/57 assessed in absence of return £50.
1857/58 returned £15; assessed £50.
1858/59-1859/60 assessed in absence of return £50.

1846/47-1852/53 beerhouse keeper; 1853/54-1859/60 beerhouse keeper etc.

116 GIDDINGS, William, beerhouse keeper.

1846/47 assessed in absence of return £50; exempt.

POTTERNE

117 ADAMS, Thomas, miller.

1846/47-1849/50 assessed in absence of return £50; exempt.

118 ARMSTRONG, John.

1846/47 marked "? E Return".

Name only entered 1846/47.

119 BAKER, William, miller.

1851/52-1852/53 assessed in absence of return £100; exempt.
1853/54 returned £100 but no assessment made.

1853/54-1854/55 marked "charged in Worton".
Cross reference: Baker, William, miller, mealman, Worton.

120 BIGGS, E., miller.

1847/48-1848/49 assessed in absence of return £60; exempt.

1849/50 marked "Chandler late Biggs, miller".
Cross references: Butcher, William, miller, Potterne; Chandler, Thomas, miller, Potterne; Weeks, James, miller, Potterne.

121 BUTCHER, Mary, shopkeeper.

1842/43 returned and assessed £10; exempt.
1846/47-1848/49 assessed in absence of return £10; exempt.

122 BUTCHER, William, miller.

1857/58-1858/59 assessed in absence of return £100; income proved at £50; exempt.
1859/60 assessed in absence of return £75; exempt.

1857/58 [Weeks, James] marked "now William Butcher, miller".
Cross references: Biggs, E., miller, Potterne; Chandler, Thomas, miller, Potterne; Weeks, James, miller, Potterne.

123 CHANDLER, Thomas, miller.

1849/50-1850/51 assessed in absence of return £100; exempt.
1852/53 assessed in absence of return £100; exempt.
1853/54-1854/55 assessed in absence of return £100.

1849/50 George Chandler entered but deleted; Thomas Chandler substituted; marked "Chandler late Biggs".
1851/52 Name and occupation entered but deleted.
1853/54-1854/55 marked "now Weekes,(sic) miller"; assessment on Weeks not made until 1855/56.
Cross references: Biggs, E., miller, Potterne; Butcher, William, miller, Potterne; Weeks, James, miller, Potterne.

124 CLARKE, J. or P.C., foreign securities.

1849/50 returned and assessed £50.

125 COLEMAN, Samuel, innkeeper, Crown.

1849/50 recorded but no assessment made.
1850/51-1855/56 assessed in absence of return £60; exempt.
1856/57-1858/59 recorded; no assessments made; exempt.

1858/59 Crown noted.

126 COX, Daniel, baker.

1858/59-1859/60 recorded; no assessments made; exempt.

127 DYER, Andrew, surgeon.

1842/43 assessed in absence of return £150.

128 FAY, William, maltster & innkeeper.

1842/43 returned £70; assessed £120; exempt.

129 FRANKLIN, John, bricklayer.

1842/43 returned £30; assessed £60; exempt.
1846/47-1847/48 assessed in absence of return £75; exempt.
1848/49 assessed in absence of return £30; exempt.
1849/50 returned and assessed £25; exempt.

130 GLASS, Robert, miller.

1853/54 assessed in absence of return £75.
1854/55 assessed in absence of return £100.

1855/56 Glass, Robert deleted, Hitchens, John, miller, substituted.
Cross reference: Hitchens, John, miller, Potterne.

131 GODDEN, John, baker.

1852/53-1853/54 assessed in absence of return £50; exempt.

132 HIBBERD, John, miller, innkeeper. [by comparison, George] [also HIBBERD, Ann]

Year	Amount returned £	Commissioners' estimate £	Income proved £	Final assessment £
1846/47	–	60	60	–
1847/48	–	100	100	–
1848/49	60	100	100	–
1849/50	100	–	100	–
1850/51	–	100	100	–
1851/52	50	100	100	–
1852/53	–	100	100	–
1853/54	50	100	75	13.10.0
1854/55	–	75	–	75
1855/56	60	75	–	75
1856/57	60	75	–	–

1846/47-1855/56 John Hibberd; 1856/57 Ann Hibberd.
1846/47 miller; 1847/48-1856/57 innkeeper.
1847/48 miller deleted; tax on £13 (interest) left in charge.
1853/54 marked "pays interest"; no appeal noted.
1856/57 assessment deleted.
1857/58 marked "now Lenard, Benjamin".
Cross reference: Lenard, Benjamin Cooksey, plumber, innkeeper, Potterne.

133 HITCHENS, John, miller.

1855/56 returned and assessed £75; exempt.
1856/57-1859/60 recorded; no assessments made; exempt.

1855/56 Glass, Robert deleted, Hitchens, John, miller, substituted.
1856/57 [Bromham] marked "now removed to Potterne".
Cross references: Glass, Robert, miller, Potterne; Hitchens, John, miller, Bromham.

134 HOLLOWAY, Nathaniel, innkeeper, Kings Arms.

1859/60 assessed in absence of return £100.

1859/60 marked "Rose, John, innkeeper, Crown now Holloway" but Kings Arms noted on assessment.
Cross references: Rose, John, innkeeper, Potterne; Watts, Mary, innkeeper, Potterne.

135 HOWELL, Benjamin, tailor.

1842/43 returned and assessed £20; exempt.
1846/47 assessed in absence of return £20; exempt.

1847/48-1848/49 assessed in absence of return £40; exempt.
1849/50 returned and assessed £40; exempt.

136 LENARD, Benjamin Cooksey, plumber, innkeeper, George.

1853/54 returned and assessed £50; exempt.
1854/55-1855/56 assessed in absence of return £50; exempt.
1856/57 assessed in absence of return £50 but no assessment made.
1857/58-1859/60 recorded; no assessments made; exempt.

1853/54-1857/58 Benjamin Lenard; 1858/59-1859/60 Benjamin Cooksey Lenard.
1853/54-1856/57 plumber; 1857/58-1859/60 innkeeper.
1857/58 marked "late Hibberd, innkeeper"; "Hibberd, Ann now Lenard, Benjamin".
1858/59 George noted.
Cross reference: Hibberd, John, innkeeper, Potterne.

137 LENARD, Richard, miller.

1842/43 returned £40; assessed £60; exempt.

138 LORD, Edward, property in Australia.

1849/50 returned and assessed £1000.

139 MARSHMAN, Samuel, baker & shopkeeper.

Year	Amount returned	Commissioners' estimate	Income proved	Final assessment
	£	£	£	£
1848/49	60	100	100	–
1849/50	–	100	100	–
1851/52	84	–	84	–
1852/53	–	84	84	–
1853/54	105	–	–	105
1854/55	120	–	–	120
1855/56	100	120	–	120
1856/57	60	120	–	120

1850/51 no assessment made.
1851/52 separate figures of £74 and £14 returned but not described.
1857/58 marked "now Sedgfield, John, baker & grocer".
1858/59 marked "see Sedgfield, St.Mary".
Cross reference: Sedgfield, John, baker & grocer, Potterne and St.Mary.

140 MATTHEWS, William, brickmaker.

1846/47 assessed in absence of return £40; exempt.
1847/48-1848/49 assessed in absence of return £80; exempt.
1849/50 assessed in absence of return £100; exempt.

141 MEDLECOTT, Revd. Joseph.

1846/47 name entered but deleted.

142 MERRETT, Lucy.

1842/43 name entered but deleted.

143 MERRETT, Robert, cordwainer.

1842/43 returned £10; assessed £40; exempt.
1846/47-1849/50 assessed in absence of return £40; exempt.

144 MERRETT, Thomas, innkeeper, Bell. [also MERRETT, John]

1849/50 assessed in absence of return £50; exempt.
1853/54 assessed in absence of return £50; exempt.
1854/55 returned and assessed £50; exempt.
1855/56 assessed in absence of return £50; exempt.
1856/57-1859/60 recorded; no assessments made; exempt.

1849/50, 1853/54-1858/59 Thomas Merrett; 1859/60 John Merrett.
1850/51-1852/53 no assessments made.
1858/59 Bell noted.

145 MUNDAY, W.E., machine maker & innkeeper.

1848/49 returned £40; assessed £60; exempt.
1849/50 assessed in absence of return £60; exempt.

146 NORTH, John Bunce, miller.

1846/47-1848/49 assessed in absence of return £100; exempt.
1849/50 assessed in absence of return £80; exempt.
1850/51-1852/53 assessed in absence of return £60; exempt.

1853/54 returned £50; assessed £60; exempt.
1854/55 returned and assessed £60; exempt.
1855/56 assessed in absence of return £60; exempt.
1856/57-1857/58 recorded; no assessments made; exempt.

147 OLIVIER, Henry A., clergyman.

1850/51-1851/52 returned £80 but no assessments made.

148 OLIVIER, Henry Stephen, director of railway, interest.

1848/49 assessed in absence of return £133.0.9.
1849/50 returned and assessed £130.
1851/52-1853/54 returned and assessed £7.10.0.
1854/55 assessed in absence of return £7.10.0.
1855/56 assessed in absence of return £10.10.0.
1856/57-1857/58 returned and assessed £10.10.0.
1858/59-1859/60 assessed in absence of return £10.10.0.

1848/49-1849/50 director of railway; 1851/52-1859/60 interest.
1850/51 no assessment made.
Note: H.S. Olivier acted as an Additional and a General Commissioner.

149 PARRY, G. F or H., Esquire, foreign securities.

1850/51-1853/54 returned and assessed £100.
1854/55 assessed in absence of return £100.
1855/56 assessed in absence of return £170 and £140 as trustee.
1858/59 assessed in absence of return £80 but assessment increased to £100.

1850/51, 1852/53 Esquire; 1851/52, 1853/54-1854/55 Esquire, foreign securities; 1855/56-
   1858/59 foreign securities.
1849/50 name entered but no assessment made.
1854/55 marked "ask for return".
1856/57 marked "removed to Cheltenham".
1857/58 marked "gone to Cheltenham".
1858/59 entry deleted but assessment apparently made.

150 ROSE, John, innkeeper, Crown.

1856/57assessed in absence of return £100; reduced to £60 on appeal; exempt.
1857/58-1858/59 recorded; no assessments made; exempt.

1856/57 marked "Watts, Mary now John Rose".

1859/60 marked "now Holloway"; Crown noted.
Cross references: Holloway, Nathaniel, innkeeper, Potterne; Watts, Mary, innkeeper, Potterne.

151 SEDGFIELD, John, baker & grocer.

1857/58 assessed in absence of return £120; assessment reduced to £80.
1858/59 assessed in absence of return £100; income proved; exempt.
1859/60 returned nil; no assessment made.

1857/58 marked "Marshman, Samuel now Sedgfield, John, baker & grocer".
1858/59 income proved but no figure inserted; assessment discharged; marked "no profits"; marked [Marshman] "see Sedgfield, St.Mary".
Cross references: Marshman, Samuel, baker & grocer, Potterne; Sedgefield, (sic) Edward (for Sedgfield, John), grocer & agent, St.Mary.

152 SMITH, J.H., innkeeper.

1846/47 assessed in absence of return £120; exempt.

153 SPRULES, Ann, carpenter.

1842/43 returned £40; assessed £70; exempt.
1846/47–1849/50 assessed in absence of return £60; exempt.

154 STEVENS, Stephen, miller, carpenter.

1846/47–1849/50 assessed in absence of return £50; exempt.
1853/54–1854/55 returned and assessed £60; exempt.
1855/56 assessed in absence of return £60; exempt.
1856/57–1859/60 recorded; no assessments made; exempt.

1846/47–1849/50 Stephens; 1853/54–1859/60 Stevens.
1846/47–1849/50, 1853/54–1858/59 miller; 1859/60 miller & carpenter.
1850/51–1852/53 no assessments made.
1859/60 marked "carpenter at Worton".

155 WATTS, Mary, publican, innkeeper. [by comparison, Crown] [also WATTS, Charlotte]

1842/43 returned and assessed £20; exempt.
1846/47 assessed in absence of return £50; exempt.
1847/48–1848/49 assessed in absence of return £60; exempt.
1849/50 assessed in absence of return £40; exempt.

1853/54 assessed in absence of return £40; exempt.
1854/55 returned and assessed £40; exempt.
1855/56 assessed in absence of return £40; exempt.

1842/43, 1846/47-1848/49 Charlotte Watts; 1849/50-1855/56 Mary Watts.
1842/43 publican; 1846/47-1855/56 innkeeper.
1850/51-1852/53 no assessments made.
1856/57 marked "now John Rose".
Cross references: Holloway, Nathaniel, innkeeper, Potterne; Rose, John, innkeeper,
    Potterne.

156 WEEKS, James, miller.

1855/56 returned £40; assessed £50.
1856/57 returned £50; assessed £100.

1853/54-1854/55 marked "Chandler, Thomas now Weekes (*sic*), miller".
1857/58 marked "now William Butcher".
Cross references: Biggs, E., miller, Potterne; Butcher, William, miller, Potterne; Chandler, Tho-
    mas, miller, Potterne.

157 WILKINS, John, baker & shopkeeper.

1842/43 returned £10; assessed £40; reduced to £10.

1842/43 no appeal noted.

ROUNDWAY

158 HAYWARD, Robert, maltster.

1842/43 returned and assessed £50.
1846/47-1847/48 assessed in absence of return £70.

1848/49 marked "late"; entry deleted.
Pigot & Co"s Directory, 1842: Robert Hayward, maltster, Roundway.

159 SLOPER, Samuel, miller.

1853/54 entry only - Sloper Samuel see Cannings, miller.
Note: no reference at either Bishop's Cannings or Allcannings, but James Sloper, miller at
    Bishop's Cannings.

ROWDE

160 ALLEN, Charles, cattle dealer.

1847/48 returned and assessed £130; exempt.
1848/49 returned and assessed £50; exempt.
1849/50 assessed in absence of return £50; exempt.

1847/48 [St.Mary] "in Rowde".
Cross reference: Allen, Charles, cattle dealer, St.Mary.

161 BARKER, W.D., surgeon.

1842/43 returned and assessed £120.

Pigot & Co"s Directory, 1842: William Barker, physician, Prospect House.

162 BARNARD, Benjamin, brickmaker.

1851/52 returned and assessed £170.
1852/53 returned and assessed £180.
1853/54 returned £170; assessed £180.
1854/55–1855/56 assessed in absence of return £200.
1856/57 returned £175; assessed £200.
1857/58 returned £170; assessed £220.
1858/59 returned £140; assessed £220.
1859/60 returned £170; assessed £220.

163 BEEK, John, tailor.

1846/47–1849/50 assessed in absence of return £40; exempt.

164 BELLIS, John, gentleman.

1847/48 entered but deleted.

165 BLACKWELL, Thomas E., engineer, civil engineer.

1842/43 returned and assessed £300.
1846/47 assessed in absence of return £350.
1847/48 assessed in absence of return £500.
1848/49 returned and assessed £600.

1849/50–1850/51 assessed in absence of return £600.

1842/43 civil engineer; 1846/47–1850/51 engineer.
1842/43, 1848/49 assessed under letter.

166 BLANCHARD, Ann, innkeeper.

1842/43 returned and assessed £50; exempt.

167 BOND, James, innkeeper. [by comparison, Fox & Hounds, Picadilly]

1855/56 assessed in absence of return £75; exempt.

1855/56 Carpenter, John deleted, Bond, James substituted.
1856/57 marked "now Solomon Long".
Cross references: Carpenter, John, innkeeper, Rowde; Long, Solomon, innkeeper, Rowde; Wild,
    Henry, innkeeper, Rowde.

168 BURROWS, William, newspaper proprietor, proprietor independent newspaper.

1842/43 returned and assessed £185.
1846/47 returned and assessed £180.
1847/48 assessed in absence of return £180.
1848/49 returned and assessed £185.
1849/50–1850/51 returned and assessed £180.
1851/52 returned and assessed £182.

1842/43 proprietor independent newspaper; 1846/47–1851/52 newspaper proprietor.
1852/53–1859/60 marked "charged in St.John" or "returned in St.John".
Pigot & Co"s Directory, 1842: Mr. William Burrows, gentry, Dunkirk, publisher, Wiltshire Inde-
    pendent, Market Place.
Cross reference: Burrows, William, newspaper proprietor, St.John.

169 BUTLER, [Edward], [by reference to Bromham, miller]

1842/43 entry only marked "assessed in Bromham".
Cross reference: Butler, Edward, miller, Bromham.

170 CARPENTER, John, innkeeper. [by comparison, Fox & Hounds, Picadilly] [also CARPENTER, William]

1842/43 returned and assessed £45; exempt.
1846/47 assessed in absence of return £60; exempt.

1847/48 returned £50; assessed £60; exempt.
1848/49 returned £30; assessed £60; income proved at £30; exempt.
1849/50 assessed in absence of return £60; exempt.
1851/52 returned and assessed £50; exempt.
1852/53-1853/54 assessed in absence of return £75; exempt.
1854/55 assessed in absence of return £75; income proved at £50; exempt.

1842/43, 1846/47 William Carpenter; 1847/48-1854/55 John Carpenter.
1850/51 no assessment made.
1855/56 Carpenter, John deleted, Bond, James, innkeeper substituted.
Pigot & Co"s Directory, 1842: William Carpenter, Fox & Hounds, Picadilly.
Cross references: Bond, James, innkeeper, Rowde; Long, Solomon, innkeeper, Rowde; Wild,
    Henry, innkeeper, Rowde.

171 COONEY, William, innkeeper.

1846/47 assessed in absence of return £50; exempt.
1847/48 returned £44; assessed £50; exempt.
1848/49 returned £40; assessed £50; exempt.
1849/50 assessed in absence of return £40; exempt.

172 CROCKETT, Joseph, senior, land agent.

1842/43, 1846/47-1850/51 marked "entered in St.John", "returns in St.John" or "see St.John".
Pigot & Co"s Directory, 1842: Joseph Crockett, land agent, Bellevue.
Cross reference: Crockett, Joseph & Son, auctioneers, St.John.

173 DEVERALL, Richard, carpenter, journeyman carpenter.

1842/43 assessed in absence of return £40; exempt.
1846/47-1849/50 assessed in absence of return £50; exempt.

1842/43, 1848/49-1849/50 carpenter; 1846/47-1847/48 journeyman carpenter.

174 DEVERELL, John, blacksmith. [also DEVERELL, William]

1842/43 returned and assessed £149; exempt.
1846/47-1849/50 assessed in absence of return £135.10.0; exempt.
1853/54 returned and assessed £70; exempt.
1854/55-1855/56 assessed in absence of return £70; exempt.
1856/57-1859/60 recorded; no assessments made; exempt.

1842/43, 1846/47 Deverall.
1842/43, 1846/47-1849/50 John & William Deverell, blacksmiths; 1853/54-1859/60 John

Deverell, blacksmith.
1850/51-1852/53 no assessments made.

175 DYKE, Isaac, innkeeper, George.

1859/60 recorded; no assessment made; exempt.

176 DYKE, John, innkeeper, Cross Keys.

1853/54 returned and assessed £50; exempt.
1854/55 assessed in absence of return £50; exempt.
1855/56 assessed in absence of return £75; exempt.
1856/57-1859/60 recorded; no assessments made; exempt.

1857/58 returned £60 but no assessment made.
1859/60 Cross Keys noted.

177 FERRIS, John, shopkeeper.

1846/47 entered but deleted; illegible, perhaps butcher or hatter.

178 GABRIEL, Elizabeth, interest.

1846/47 returned and assessed £56.
1849/50 returned and assessed £20; exempt.
1851/52 returned and assessed £20.

1846/47, 1849/50 Elizabeth Gabriel; 1851/52 Miss Gabriel.

179 GIBBS, Louisa.

1849/50 returned and assessed £50.

1846/47 name entered as Louise Gibbs but deleted.
No occupation recorded.

180 GOLDING, Charles, innkeeper, Queens Head, Dunkirk.

1859/60 recorded; no assessment made; exempt.

Cross references: Harding, David, innkeeper, Rowde; Liddiard, Eaben, innkeeper, Rowde; Smith, John, innkeeper, Rowde.

181 HARDING, David, innkeeper. [by comparison, Queens Head, Dunkirk]

1842/43 assessed in absence of return £60; exempt.
1846/47 assessed in absence of return £100; exempt.
1847/48 returned £50; assessed £80; income proved at £50; exempt.
1848/49 assessed in absence of return £50; exempt.
1849/50 assessed in absence of return £80; exempt.
1850/51 returned and assessed £50; exempt.

1850/51 marked "now E. Liddiard".
Pigot & Co"s Directory, 1842: David Harding, Queens Head, Dunkirk.
Cross references: Golding, Charles, innkeeper, Rowde; Liddiard, Eaben, innkeeper, Rowde; Smith, John, innkeeper, Rowde.

182 HAYWARD, John, land agent.

1842/43 returned and assessed £1155.
1846/47 assessed in absence of return £1155.
1847/48-1848/49 returned and assessed £830.
1849/50 assessed in absence of return £1000.
1850/51 assessed in absence of return £880.
1851/52 returned and assessed £878.
1852/53-1856/57 assessed in absence of return £878.
1857/58-1858/59 returned and assessed £878.
1859/60 assessed in absence of return £878.

1842/43, 1847/48-1854/55 assessed under letter.
Pigot & Co"s Directory, 1842: John Hayward, Browfort; possibly surveyor, New Park Street, Devizes.
Note: John Hayward acted as an Additional Commissioner.

183 HIBBARD or HUBBARD, William.

1842/43 name only entered but deleted.

184 HOOKINS, John, solicitor.

1842/43 returned and assessed £196.0.5.
1846/47-1850/51 returned and assessed £200.
1851/52 returned and assessed £100.

Pigot & Co"s Directory, 1842: John Hookins, attorney, Brow Cottage.

185 KEEPENCE, Charles, bricklayer.

1846/47-1848/49 assessed in absence of return £75; exempt.
1849/50 returned and assessed £75; exempt.
1850/51 assessed in absence of return £50; exempt.
1851/52-1853/54 assessed in absence of return £65; exempt.
1854/55 assessed in absence of return £65; income proved at £50; exempt.
1855/56 assessed in absence of return £50; exempt.
1856/57-1859/60 recorded; no assessments made; exempt.

186 KINGSLAND, Revd. William, independent minister.

1853/54 returned and assessed £175 and £25 interest.
1854/55 returned £200; assessed £175.
1855/56 returned and assessed £170.
1856/57-1859/60 returned and assessed £150 and £20 interest.

1854/55 marked "£25 income on which duty is deducted".

187 KNIGHT, Henry, collector, etc.

1853/54 returned and assessed £78; exempt.
1854/55 assessed in absence of return £78; exempt.

1855/56 marked "St.Mary's". (No entry in St.Mary)

188 LEWIS, N.H., Wesleyan Minister.

1855/56 returned £98.18.0; assessed £100.

1856/57-1857/58 marked "now John Poulton, Wesleyan Minister".
Cross reference: Poulton, Revd. John, Wesleyan Minister, Rowde.

189 LIDDIARD, Eaben, innkeeper. [by comparison, Queens Head, Dunkirk]

1851/52 returned and assessed £55; exempt.
1852/53 assessed in absence of return £55; exempt.
1853/54-1854/55 assessed in absence of return £75; exempt.

1850/51 marked "Harding, David now E.Liddiard".
1855/56 marked "Smith, John late Liddiard, innkeeper".
Cross references: Golding, Charles, innkeeper, Rowde; Harding, David, innkeeper, Rowde; Smith, John, innkeeper, Rowde.

190 LONG, Solomon, innkeeper, beerhouse keeper, Fox & Hounds, Picadilly and Olive Branch.

1856/57-1859/60 recorded; no assessments made; exempt.

1856/57 beerhouse keeper; 1857/58-1859/60 innkeeper.
1856/57 marked "Bond, James now Solomon Long, Fox & Hounds".
1859/60 marked "Wild Henry now Solomon Long, Olive Branch".
Cross references: Bond, James, innkeeper, Rowde; Carpenter, John, innkeeper, Rowde; Wild, Henry, innkeeper, Rowde.

191 MACK, Robert A., Town Missionary.

1848/49 assessed in absence of return £70; exempt.
1849/50 returned and assessed £70; exempt.
1850/51 assessed in absence of return £80; exempt.

192 MANNING, Revd. Alexander, chaplain of new prison, private pupils.

1842/43 returned £150 as chaplain but deleted; marked "Schedule E".
1842/43 returned and assessed £80 private pupils.

1846/47 marked "Schedule E".
Cross reference: Manning, Revd. Alexander, private tutor, St.John.

193 MAYELL, Robert, baker.

1842/43, 1846/47-1847/48 assessed in absence of return £60; exempt.
1848/49 assessed in absence of return £75; income proved at £99.9.6; exempt.
1849/50 returned and assessed £75; exempt.
1850/51 returned £102.18.3 but deleted; assessed £80; exempt.
1851/52-1852/53 assessed in absence of return £80; exempt.
1853/54 returned and assessed £80; exempt.
1854/55-1855/56 assessed in absence of return £100; income proved at £80; exempt.
1856/57 assessed in absence of return £100; reduced to £97 on appeal.
1857/58 assessed in absence of return £97; income proved at £30; exempt.
1858/59-1859/60 recorded; no assessments made; exempt.

1856/57 marked "has house property".

194 NEALE, Henry, contractor, engineer.

1851/52 returned and assessed £160.
1852/53 assessed in absence of return £160.

1853/54 returned £100; assessed £160.
1854/55-1855/56 assessed in absence of return £160.
1856/57 assessed in absence of return £175.
1857/58-1858/59 returned £160; assessed £175.
1859/60 returned £170; assessed £175.

1851/52-1858/59 contractor; 1859/60 engineer.

195 PICTON, John Owen, clergyman.

1854/55 returned £100 but deleted.
1855/56-1859/60 recorded; no assessments made; exempt.

1853/54 marked "Query licensed?"
1854/55 marked "licensed curate".

196 POULTON, Revd, John, Wesleyan Minister.

1856/57 returned £80; assessed £100; reduced to £80 on appeal; exempt.
1857/58-1858/59 recorded; no assessments made; exempt.

1856/57 marked "late Lewis Wesleyan Minister".
1858/59 marked "Query liable?"
1859/60 marked "late Wesleyan Minister".
Cross reference: Lewis, N.H., Wesleyan Minister, Rowde.

197 PRICTOR, Job, Junior, shoemaker, innkeeper.

1842/43 returned £20; assessed £50; exempt.
1846/47 assessed in absence of return £75; exempt.
1847/48 returned £80; assessed £120; exempt.
1848/49 assessed in absence of return £120; income proved at £70; exempt.
1849/50 assessed in absence of return £75; exempt.

1842/43, 1846/47 shoemaker; 1847/48 innkeeper & shoemaker; 1848/49-1849/50
    innkeeper, etc.

198 PRICTOR, William, carpenter.

1842/43 assessed in absence of return £20; exempt.
1846/47-1849/50 assessed in absence of return £40; exempt.

199 PURNELL, Thomas, carpenter. [also PURNELL, James]

1842/43 returned £70; assessed £90; exempt.
1846/47-1849/50 assessed in absence of return £70; exempt.
1851/52 returned £60; assessed 90; income proved at £91.3.0; exempt.
1852/53 assessed in absence of return £90; exempt.
1853/54 returned £60; assessed 90 and £15 interest; exempt but £15 left in charge.
1854/55 assessed in absence of return £100.
1855/56 assessed in absence of return £100; income proved at £60; exempt.
1856/57-1859/60 recorded; no assessments made; exempt.

1842/43, 1846/47-1847/48 James Purnell; 1848/49-1859/60 Thomas Purnell.
1842/43, 1846/47-1852/53, 1857/58-1859/60 carpenter; 1853/54-1856/57 carpenter, etc.
1850/51 no assessment made.

200 PYKE, John, carpenter.

1842/43 returned £70; assessed £150; income proved at £128.14.0; exempt but £22
    interest left in charge.
1846/47-1847/48 assessed in absence of return £100; exempt.
1848/49 returned £80; assessed £100; income proved at £115.15.0; exempt.
1849/50 returned £60; assessed £100; exempt.
1850/51 returned £50; assessed £70; income proved at £50; exempt.

1842/43 marked "pays £22 interest".

201 SAINSBURY, George Taylor, brickmaker, brick, tile, manure & slate merchant.

1849/50 returned and assessed £120.
1850/51 returned £100; assessed £150.
1852/53 assessed in absence of return £200.
1856/57 returned £500; assessed £600.
1857/58 returned £600; assessed £650.
1858/59 returned and assessed £800.
1859/60 returned £700; assessed £900.

1849/50-1855/56 brickmaker; 1856/57-1859/60 brick, tile, manure & slate merchant, Devizes,
    Rowde & Seend.
1849/50 marked "St.Mary's brickmaker"; assessment in St.Mary deleted.
1851/52 marked "return in St.Mary's".
1852/53 marked "see St.Mary" but assessed in Rowde.
1853/54-1854/55 marked "see St.Mary" and "returned in St.Mary".
1855/56 marked "St.Mary's".
Note: 1842/43, 1846/47-1848/49, 1851/52, 1853/54-1855/56 assessed in St.Mary.
Cross reference: Sainsbury, George Taylor, brickmaker, St.Mary.

202 SELLIFONT, J.P., minister.

1851/52 returned and assessed £70; exempt.

203 SIMPSON, George, Junior, printer, salary, annual allowance.

1852/53 returned and assessed £178.5.0.
1853/54 returned £150 and £18 interest; assessed £170.
1854/55 returned £132; assessed £197.
1855/56 returned £65; assessed £197.
1856/57 returned £65p, £100a; assessed £200.
1857/58 returned £170; assessed £220.
1858/59 returned £65, £100; assessed £220.
1859/60 returned £160; assessed £250.

Abbreviations: p, printer; a, annual allowance.
1852/53-1854/55 George Simpson; 1855/56-1859/60 George Simpson, Junior.
1852/53, 1855/56, 1856/57 printer; 1857/58 salary; 1856/57, 1858/59-1859/60 annual allowance.
1858/59 the amounts returned of £65 and £100 are not described but following 1856/57 are likely to be printer and annual allowance respectively.

204 SIMS, Thomas, innkeeper.

1842/43, 1846/47 assessed in absence of return £40; exempt.

205 SINCLAIR, David, schoolmaster.

1846/47-1849/50 assessed in absence of return £70; exempt.
1851/52 returned and assessed £70; exempt.
1852/53-1853/54 assessed in absence of return £70; exempt.
1854/55 returned and assessed £75; exempt.
1855/56 assessed in absence of return £75; exempt.
1856/57-1858/59 recorded; no assessments made; exempt.
1859/60 assessed in absence of return £100; income proved at £82; exempt.

1850/51 no assessment made.
Pigot & Co"s Directory, 1842: David Sinclair, master, British School, Northgate Street.

206 SLOPER, James, miller.

1842/43, 1846/47-1847/48 marked "returned at Bishop's Cannings".
Cross reference: Sloper, James, miller, Bishop's Cannings.

207 SMITH, John, innkeeper, Queens Head, Dunkirk.

1855/56 assessed in absence of return £75; exempt.
1856/57 assessed in absence of return £80; exempt.
1857/58–1858/59 recorded; no assessments made; exempt.

1855/56 marked "Smith, John late Liddiard".
1856/57 Queens Head noted.
Cross references: Golding, Charles, innkeeper, Rowde; Harding, David, innkeeper, Rowde;
  Liddiard, Eaben, innkeeper, Rowde.

208 SMITH, Knightley, beerseller, innkeeper.

1846/47 assessed in absence of return £60; exempt.
1847/48 returned £40; assessed £60; exempt.
1848/49 assessed in absence of return £70; income proved at £50; exempt.
1849/50 assessed in absence of return £70; exempt.

1846/47–1847/48 beerseller; 1848/49–1849/50 innkeeper.

209 STRONG, Thomas, butcher.

1842/43 returned £60; assessed £150; income proved at £60; exempt.
1846/47 assessed in absence of return £70; exempt.
1847/48 returned £50; assessed £70; exempt.
1848/49–1849/50 assessed in absence of return £70; exempt.

210 VINCENT, Revd. Edward, foreign securities, debenture Drury Lane Company, fee admission ticket.

1842/43 returned and assessed £9.6.8f, £1.13.4d, 17.6a.
1846/47 returned and assessed £9.6.8f.
1847/48–1848/49 assessed in absence of return £9.6.8.

Abbreviations: f, foreign securities; d, debenture Drury Lane Company; a, fee admission ticket.
1842/43 marked "1/3 share debenture Drury Lane Company produce last year £5.1.3 of fee
  admission ticket, Do.".
1854/55, 1857/58 entered but deleted.
1855/56 returned nil; no assessment made.
Pigot & Co"s Directory, 1842: Revd. Edward Vincent, clergy, Rowde.

211 WESTON, Stephen, tailor.

1846/47–1847/48 assessed in absence of return £40; exempt.

212 WICKHAM, Stephen, maltster.

1842/43 assessed in absence of return £30; exempt.
1846/47 returned and assessed £30; exempt.

213 WILD, Henry, innkeeper, Olive Branch.

1854/55 assessed in absence of return £75; income proved at £70; exempt.
1855/56 assessed in absence of return £70; exempt.
1856/57-1859/60 recorded; no assessments made; exempt.

1856/57 Olive Branch noted.
1859/60 marked "now Solomon Long".
Cross reference: Bond, James, innkeeper, Rowde; Carpenter, John, innkeeper, Rowde; Long, Solomon, innkeeper, Rowde.

214 WILTSHIRE, John & William, bakers, pig butchers.

1842/43 returned and assessed £80; exempt.
1846/47 returned £52; assessed £80; exempt.
1847/48 assessed in absence of return £80; exempt.
1848/49 assessed in absence of return £80; income proved at £121; exempt.
1849/50 assessed in absence of return £20; exempt.

1842/43, 1846/47 bakers & pig butchers; 1847/48 bakers; 1848/49-1849/50 bakers, etc.

215 WITTEY, Samuel, solicitor's clerk.

1846/47 assessed in absence of return £130; income proved at £146.14.0; exempt.

Cross reference: Wittey, Samuel, solicitor, St.John.

216 WOODCOCK, Mary.

1846/47 name only entered and deleted.

WEEK

217 ABRAHAMS, Moses, jeweller.

1842/43 returned and assessed £100; exempt.
1846/47-1849/50 assessed in absence of return £80; exempt.

218 BARNARD, George, toll clerk to Kennet & Avon Canal Company, canal agent, agent GWR.

1842/43 returned £100; no assessment made and marked "Schedule E".
1846/47-1847/48 assessed in absence of return £100.
1848/49-1852/53 returned and assessed £100.
1853/54 returned £75; assessed £120; reduced to £75.

1842/43 toll clerk to Kennet & Avon Canal Company; 1846/47-1852/53 canal agent;
1853/54 agent GWR.
1847/48 estimate of £130 amended to £100.
1853/54 no appeal noted.
1854/55 marked "dead".
Pigot & Co"s Directory, 1842: George Barnard, collector for Kennet and Avon Canal Company,
    Bath Road.

219 BARNARD, William, agent, agent GWR, canal clerk.

1853/54 returned and assessed £65; exempt.
1854/55 returned and assessed £100.
1855/56 assessed in absence of return £100.
1856/57 returned £100 but deleted; marked "Schedule E".

1853/54 agent GWR; 1854/55-1855/56 agent; 1856/57 canal clerk.

220 BIGGS, Charles, innkeeper & corn dealer.

1848/49 returned and assessed £50; exempt.

221 BIRCH, Mr., innkeeper.

1846/47 entry only marked "late innkeeper".

222 BLATCHLEY, Gabriel, manure merchant.

1842/43 assessed in absence of return £40; income proved at £30; exempt.

Pigot & Co"s Directory, 1842: G. Blatchley, artificial manure manufacturer, Gunes Lane.

223 BOLLAND, James, gardener.

1842/43 entry only deleted.
Pigot & Co"s Directory, 1842: James Bolland, market gardener, Pan's Lane.

224 BOX, William, engineer, ironfounder.

1842/43 assessed in absence of return £100; exempt.
1846/47 assessed in absence of return £150.
1847/48 returned £100; assessed £200; income proved at £90.5.10; exempt.
1848/49 returned and assessed 100; exempt.
1849/50 assessed in absence of return £150; reduced to £60 on appeal.
1850/51 assessed in absence of return £100; exempt.

1842/43 engineer; 1846/47-1850/51 ironfounder.
Pigot & Co"s Directory, 1842: William Box, engineer etc., Bath Road.

225 BUNCE, John S., dissenting minister, private tuition.

1842/43 returned and assessed £130.
1846/47 returned £130m, £16t, £23.15.0i but no assessment made.

Abbreviations: m, dissenting minister; t, tuition; i, interest.
1842/43 dissenting minister; 1846/47 dissenting minister & private tuition.
Pigot & Co"s Directory, 1842: Revd. John Stacy Bunce, clergy, Hilworth (sic).

226 BUTCHER, John, Relieving Officer.

1856/57 returned £89; no assessment made; marked "Schedule E"

227 CANAL COMPANY

1842/43, 1846/47-1859/60 recorded but no assessments made; marked "return made at Bath",
    "carriers, Bath" or "carrier, return at Bath".

228 CHANDLER, James, innkeeper, farrier.

1850/51 assessed in absence of return £100; exempt.

1850/51 "& farrier" entered but deleted.

229 CHANDLER, John, corndealer, maltster. [also CHANDLER, Thomas]

1848/49 returned and assessed £30 and £13 interest.
1849/50 returned and assessed £100 and £13 interest.
1850/51-1851/52 returned and assessed £150.
1852/53 assessed in absence of return £150.
1853/54 returned and assessed £150.

1854/55 returned £150; assessed £200.
1855/56 assessed in absence of return £200.
1856/57 returned £160; assessed £720; reduced to £550 on appeal.
1857/58 returned £300; assessed £750.
1858/59 returned £385; assessed £900.
1859/60 assessed £200 and £310; assessed £1050.

1848/49-1853/54 John Chandler; 1854/55-1859/60 John & Thomas Chandler.
1848/49-1849/50 corndealer; 1850/51-1852/53 corndealer & maltster;
1853/54-1858/59 maltster(s); 1859/60 retail maltsters on commission.
1852/53 [Thomas Chandler] marked "now John".
1854/55 marked "partner" with Thomas Chandler.
1856/57 £550 confirmed on appeal.
1859/60 [Marden] John & Thomas Chandler, "charged in Week".
Pigot & Co"s Directory, 1842: Thomas Chandler & Son, maltsters, Melbourne Place.
Cross references: Chandler, Charles, maltster, Marden; Chandler, John & Thomas, maltsters,
    Marden; Chandler, Thomas, maltster, Week.

230 CHANDLER, Thomas, maltster.

1842/43, 1846/47-1849/50 returned and assessed £150.
1850/51 assessed in absence of return £150.

1842/43, 1846/47 maltster, etc; 1847/48-1850/51 maltster.
1842/43 assessed under letter.
1850/51 estimate of £200 amended to £150.
1851/52 estimate of £100 deleted.
1852/53 marked "now John".
1854/55 marked "partner" with John Chandler.
Cross references; Chandler, Charles, maltster, Marden; Chandler, John, maltster, Week; Chandler,
    John & Thomas, maltsters, Marden.

231 CHIVERS, William, carpenter.

1842/43 returned and assessed £70; exempt.
1846/47-1850/51 assessed in absence of return £70; exempt.
1851/52 returned and assessed £90; exempt.
1852/53 assessed in absence of return £90; exempt.
1853/54 returned £77.10.0; assessed £150; reduced to £125.
1854/55 returned £75; assessed £125.
1855/56 assessed in absence of return £125.
1856/57 returned £80; assessed £125.
1857/58 returned £100; assessed £125.
1858/59-1859/60 recorded; no assessments made; exempt.

1842/43 "Schedule A & B" entered but deleted.
1853/54 no appeal noted.

1858/59 marked "nil".
Pigot & Co"s Directory, 1842: William Chivers, carpenter & builder, Sidmouth Street.

232 COX, Caleb, conveyancer.

1842/43 returned and assessed £147; exempt.
1846/47 assessed in absence of return £150; reduced to £147 on appeal but altered to
     £150.
1847/48 assessed in absence of return £147 exempt.
1848/49 returned and assessed £147; exempt.
1849/50-1852/53 assessed in absence of return £147; exempt.

1846/47 duty on £150 is extended to the tax paid column despite a reduction being recorded
     on appeal.
1853/54 "gratuity" substituted for "conveyancer" but no assessment made.
1854/55 marked "gone away...to Bristol".

233 COX, George, butcher.

1859/60 returned £125; assessed £175.

1859/60 original estimate of £200 amended to £175.
1859/60 [St.Mary] marked "charged in Week".
Cross reference: Cox, George, butcher, St.Mary.

234 CUNNINGTON, William, woolstapler. [also CUNNINGTON, Messrs.; CUNNINGTON, William & Co]

1842/43 returned and assessed £365.
1846/47 assessed in absence of return £365.
1847/48 returned and assessed £365.
1848/49 returned and assessed £250.
1849/50 assessed in absence of return £300.
1850/51 returned and assessed £360.
1851/52-1852/53 returned and assessed £385.
1853/54 assessed in absence of return £385.
1854/55 returned and assessed £385.
1855/56 returned and assessed £400.
1856/57 assessed in absence of return £400.
1857/58 returned and assessed £420.
1858/59 returned £380; assessed £420.
1859/60 returned and assessed £420.

1842/43, 1846/47, 1848/49-1856/57 William Cunnington; 1847/48 Messrs Cunnington;
     1857/58-1859/60 William Cunnington & Co.

1855/56 marked "called for return".
Pigot & Co"s Directory, 1842: William Cunnington, woolstapler, Southgate House.
Cross reference: Cunnington, William & Sons, wine merchants, St. John.

235 DAVIS, John, plasterer.

1842/43, 1846/47-1849/50 assessed in absence of return £50; exempt.

Pigot & Co"s Directory, 1842: Davis & Son, plasterers & slaters, Nursery.

236 DOWSE, James, cattle dealer, dealer.

1853/54 returned £70; assessed £75; exempt.
1854/55-1855/56 assessed in absence of return £75; exempt.
1856/57-1858/59 recorded; no assessments made; exempt.

1853/54 dealer; 1854/55-1858/59 cattle dealer.
1859/60 marked "dead".

237 DREWE, John.

1842/43 marked "see return at Queen St. Park, Bristol".
1846/47 marked "returns at Bristol".

238 ELLEN, John, clerk in Stamp Office.

1842/43, 1846/47-1848/49 assessed in absence of return £150.
1849/50 returned and assessed £150.
1850/51-1851/52 assessed in absence of return £150.
1852/53 returned nil; assessed £150.
1853/54 returned and assessed £150.
1854/55-1856/57 assessed in absence of return £150.
1857/58 returned and assessed £150.
1858/59 assessed in absence of return £150.
1859/60 assessed in absence of return £100.

239 ERWOOD, Robert, innkeeper.

1842/43 assessed in absence of return £40; exempt.

Pigot & Co"s Directory, 1842: Robert Erwood, retailer of beer, shopkeeper & dealer in groceries & sundries, Nursery.

240 FRICKER, George, tailor.

1842/43 returned £8; assessed £50; exempt.
1846/47-1849/50 assessed in absence of return £50; exempt.

Pigot & Co"s Directory, 1842: George Fricker, tailor, Sidmouth Street.

241 GEORGE, Francis, law clerk, clerk.

1853/54 returned and assessed £98.15.0; exempt.
1854/55 returned and assessed £105.
1855/56 assessed in absence of return £105.
1856/57 returned and assessed £105.
1857/58 assessed in absence of return £105.
1858/59 returned and assessed £105.
1859/60 returned and assessed £110.

1853/54 clerk; 1854/55-1859/60 law clerk.
1853/54-1854/55 [Bedborough] entries made in absence of return £105 but deleted.
Cross reference: George, Frank (*sic*), clerk, Bedborough.

242 GILBERT, Henry, innkeeper. [by comparison, King's Arms]

1842/43, 1846/47-1848/49 assessed in absence of return £100; exempt.

1850/51 marked "now Truman".
Pigot & Co"s Directory, 1842: Henry Gilbert, King's Arms, Green.
Cross references: Truman, William, innkeeper, Week; Wild, Edwin, innkeeper, Week.

243 GILLMAN, Charles, reporter.

1852/53 assessed in absence of return £75; exempt.
1854/55 assessed in absence of return £100; income proved at £90; exempt.

1852/53 marked "reporter see St.John".
1853/54 marked "returned in St.John".
1855/56 marked "charged in St.John".
Cross reference: Gillman, Charles, reporter, St.John.

244 GLASS, Ann, interest.

1857/58 returned £8 but entry deleted.

245 GLASS, John, coal merchant.

1842/43 assessed in absence of return £150; income proved at £100; exempt.

Pigot & Co"s Directory, 1842: John Glass, coal merchant, Wharf.

246 GOODMAN, John, innkeeper, Artichoke.

1850/51 recorded but no assessment made.
1851/52-1852/53 assessed in absence of return £75; exempt.
1853/54 returned and assessed £80; exempt.
1854/55 assessed in absence of return £80; exempt.
1855/56 assessed in absence of return £100.
1856/57 returned £100; assessed £120.
1857/58 assessed in absence of return £120.
1858/59 returned £125; assessed £130.
1859/60 returned and assessed £130.

1850/51 marked "Phillips, George, innkeeper, now Goodman, John".
1851/52 marked "late Phillips, innkeeper".
1856/57 Artichoke noted.
Cross reference: Phillips, George, innkeeper, Week

247 HALE, James, cordwainer.

1842/43, 1846/47-1849/50 assessed in absence of return £50; exempt.

Pigot & Co"s Directory, 1842: James Hale, boot & shoe maker, Sidmouth Street.

248 HARRIS, Edward, curate.

1854/55 assessed in absence of return £80 but not completed.
1859/60 returned and assessed £100.

1854/55 assessment made by General Commissioners but no duty computed.

249 HARRIS, James, clerk agent.

1859/60 marked "from St.Mary" but no assessment made.
Cross reference: Harris, James, clerk agent, St.Mary.

250 HEALE, William, nurseryman. [also HEALE, William & Son]

1842/43 returned and assessed £180.

1846/47–1848/49 assessed in absence of return £100; exempt.
1849/50 returned and assessed £34; exempt.
1850/51 assessed in absence of return £50; exempt.

1842/43 William Heale & Son; 1846/47–1850/51 William Heale.
1842/43 nurserymen; 1846/47–1850/51 nurseryman.
Pigot & Co"s Directory, 1842: William Heale & Son, nursery & seedsmen, Wick.

251 HEEVER, Elizabeth, miller. [also HEEVER, Henry]

1842/43 assessed in absence of return £100; exempt.
1846/47–1852/53 assessed in absence of return £80; exempt.
1853/54 assessed in absence of return £100; reduced to £90.
1854/55–1855/56 assessed in absence of return £90.
1856/57 returned and assessed £100.
1857/58 assessed in absence of return £100.
1858/59–1859/60 returned and assessed £100.

1842/43, 1846/47–1855/56 Elizabeth Heever; 1856/57–1859/60 Henry Heever.
1853/54 no appeal noted.

252 HICKEY, James, schoolmaster.

1842/43 assessed in absence of return £85; exempt.

253 HILL, William, plasterer, slater.

1842/43 returned and assessed £60; exempt.
1846/47–1848/49 assessed in absence of return £60; exempt.
1849/50 assessed in absence of return £40; exempt.

1842/43 plasterer & slater; 1846/47–1849/50 plasterer, etc.
Pigot & Co"s Directory, 1842: William Hill, painter, plumber & glazier, Sidmouth Street; plasterer & slater, Back Lane.

254 HUMBY, Frederick Peter, Southbroom Brewery. [also HUMBY, Frederick & ROBBINS, Frederick]

1855/56 assessed in absence of return £150.
1856/57 returned £80; assessed £200.
1857/58 returned £120; assessed £250.
1858/59 returned £250; assessed £300.
1859/60 returned and assessed £300.

1854/55-1856/57 Frederick Peter Humby; 1857/58-1858/59 Frederick Humby;
1859/60 Frederick Humby & Frederick Robbins.
1854/55 recorded as brewer but no assessment made; 1855/56-1859/60 Southbroom Brewery.
Cross reference: Humby, Frederick Peter, innkeeper, Week & St.John.

255 HUMBY, Frederick Peter, innkeeper, Antelope.

1854/55 marked "Norton, James King now Humby".
1855/56 [St.John] innkeeper, Antelope, assessed in absence of return £50.
1857/58 [St.John] marked "now Thomas Brown" "Antelope".
1858/59 [St.John] marked "Brown, Thomas, late Humby, Antelope".
Cross references: Humby, Frederick Peter, Southbroom Brewery; Norton, James King, innkeeper, Week.

256 HUMBY, James, bank clerk.

1854/55 returned £130; assessed £150; reduced to £130.

1853/54 recorded and estimated at £150 but deleted.
Cross reference: Humby, James, bank manager, St.John.

257 LANGFORD, Peter, Supervisor of Excise.

1848/49 entry only, deleted.

258 LEWIS, David, wharfinger.

1853/54 returned and assessed £85; exempt.

259 LONG, James, innkeeper, Rising Sun.

1848/49-1849/50 assessed in absence of return £70; exempt.
1854/55-1855/56 assessed in absence of return £70; exempt.
1856/57-1857/58 assessed in absence of return £100.
1858/59 assessed in absence of return £110.
1859/60 returned £110; assessed £150.

1848/49 Packer, Samuel deleted, Long, James substituted.
1850/51-1853/54 no assessments made.
1854/55 estimate made but no assessment made.
1856/57 Rising Sun noted.
Cross references: Long, James, innkeeper, Bedborough; Packer, Samuel, innkeeper, Week.

260 MANNING, Ann.

1842/43 name only entered and deleted.

261 MARSTON, Charles Henry, Baptist minister.

1859/60 assessed in absence of return £100.

1859/60 marked "app."

262 MEAD, George, coal merchant.

1842/43 assessed in absence of return £100; exempt.

263 MULLINGS, John, basket maker.

1842/43, 1846/47-1849/50 assessed in absence of return £50; exempt.

Pigot & Co"s Directory, 1842: John Mullings, basket maker, Sidmouth Street.

264 MUSSELWHITE, John, clerk to Mr.Meek, accountant.

1858/59 assessed in absence of return £120.
1859/60 returned and assessed £120.

1859/60 accountant.
Cross reference: Meek, Alexander, solicitor, St.John.

265 NASH, Robert, shopkeeper.

1842/43 returned and assessed £75; exempt.

266 NEATE, John, innkeeper.

1846/47-1847/48 assessed in absence of return £100.

267 NISBET, Robert Parry, Esquire, property out of United Kingdom, property in British Plantations.

1842/43 returned and assessed £1000.
1846/47-1849/50 returned and assessed £750.

1850/51-1851/52 returned and assessed £250.
1852/53 returned and assessed £310.
1853/54 returned and assessed £444.
1854/55 returned and assessed £460.
1855/56 returned and assessed £450.
1856/57 assessed in absence of return £547.
1857/58 returned and assessed £244.
1858/59 returned and assessed £301.12.8.
1859/60 returned and assessed £620.

1842/43, 1846/47-1859/60 Esquire; 1853/54-1857/58 property out of United Kingdom; 1858/59-1859/60 property in British Plantations.
1854/55, 1855/56 marked "apply for return".
Pigot & Co"s Directory, 1842: Robert Parry Nisbet, gentry, Southbroom House.
Note: R.P. Nisbet acted as a General Commissioner.

268 NORTH, John, coach builder.

1856/57 assessed in absence of return £125.
1857/58 returned £105; assessed £125.
1858/59 returned and assessed £101.
1859/60 returned £102; assessed £120.

1846/47 returned £100 but deleted; marked "charged at Melksham".
1847/48-1855/56 marked "charged at" or "return at Melksham".

269 NORTON, James King, innkeeper. [by comparison, Antelope]

1851/52 estimated in absence of return £50; no assessment made.
1852/53 assessed in absence of return £50; assessment discharged on appeal but no sum recorded.
1853/54 assessed in absence of return £50; exempt.

1854/55 marked "now Humby".
Cross reference: Humby, Frederick Peter, innkeeper, Week.

270 OAKFORD, James, plasterer.

1842/43 returned and assessed £50; exempt.
1846/47-1852/53 assessed in absence of return £50; exempt.
1853/54-1855/56 assessed in absence of return £70; exempt.
1856/57-1859/60 recorded; no assessments made; exempt.

Pigot & Co"s Directory, 1842: James Oakford, plasterer & slater, Potterne Road.

271 PACKER, Samuel, innkeeper. [by comparison, Sun]

1842/43 assessed in absence of return £90; exempt.
1846/47-1847/48 assessed in absence of return £100; exempt.

1848/49 marked "Long, James, innkeeper".
Pigot & Co"s Directory, 1842: Samuel Packer, Sun, Green.
Cross reference: Long, James, innkeeper, Week.

272 PALMER, Benjamin, rent of tolls.

1851/52 assessed in absence of return £150; reduced to £100 on appeal; exempt.
1852/53 assessed in absence of return £100; reduced to nil on appeal; exempt.

1852/53 marked "gone now Commissioners of Trust".
1853/54 marked "Commissioners of T[urn] P[ike] Trust".
Cross reference: Turnpike Trust, Commissioners of, Week.

273 PEAD, George.

1842/43 name only entered and deleted.

274 PHILLIPS, George, innkeeper. [by comparison, Artichoke]

1846/47 assessed in absence of return £75; exempt.
1847/48-1848/49 assessed in absence of return £100; exempt.

1850/51 marked "now John Goodman".
Cross reference: Goodman, John, innkeeper, Week.

275 PHILLIPS, James.

1842/43 name only entered and deleted.

276 PHILLIPS, Thomas, lunatic asylum keeper. [Bellevue]

Year	Amount returned	Commissioners' estimate	Final assessment
	£	£	£
1842/43	300	500	500
1846/47	–	700	700
1847/48	500	700	700
1848/49	700	–	700

1849/50	650	–	650
1850/51	650	850	850
1851/52	600	850	850
1852/53	850	–	850
1853/54	450	550	550
1854/55	265	500	500
1855/56	–	400	400
1856/57	–	75	75
1857/58	75	–	75
1858/59	75	–	75
1859/60	–	200	200

1852/53 marked "pauper patients sent to County Asylum".
1856/57 marked "to stand over" struck out.
Pigot & Co"s Directory, 1842: Thomas Phillips, governor, Lunatic Asylum, Bellevue.

277 PLANK, Charles, builder.

1851/52 returned £200 but deleted.

Cross reference: Plank, Charles Rhodes, builder, Bedborough.

278 PLAYER, Jacob, interest.

1857/58-1859/60 returned and assessed £10.

1842/43 name only entered and deleted.

279 POOLMAN & BATT, carpenters, wheelwrights.

1842/43, 1846/47 assessed in absence of return £60; exempt.
1847/48-1849/50 assessed in absence of return £120; exempt.

1842/43 carpenters & wheelwrights; 1846/47-1849/50 carpenters, etc.
Pigot & Co"s Directory, 1842: Poolman & Batt, carpenters, builders & wheelwrights, Bath Road.

280 POULDEN, Charles, beerhouse keeper & carrier.

1854/55 assessed in absence of return £30; exempt.

281 PUGH, Samuel S., dissenting minister.

1859/60 assessed in absence of return £200.

1858/59 recorded but no assessment made; marked "late Stanford".
Cross reference: Stanford, Charles, dissenting minister, Week.

282 RIX, James, coach painter.

1842/43 returned and assessed £40; exempt.
1846/47-1847/48 assessed in absence of return £40; exempt.

283 SHIPTON, Charles B., tailor.

1842/43 returned and assessed £70; exempt.
1846/47-1849/50 assessed in absence of return £70; exempt.

1842/43 Shepton; 1846/47-1849/50 Shipton.
Pigot & Co"s Directory, 1842: Charles Shipton, tailor, Bath Road.

284 SLOPER, Edwin, innkeeper.

1842/43 assessed in absence of return £75; exempt.

Pigot & Co"s Directory, 1842: Edwin Sloper, Royal Oak, Green.

285 SPRAWSON, John, coachman.

1842/43, 1846/47-1847/48 assessed in absence of return £60; exempt.

Cross reference: Sprawson, John, coachman, St.John.

286 STANFORD, Charles, dissenting minister.

1854/55 returned and assessed £200.
1855/56 assessed in absence of return £200.
1856/57-1857/58 returned and assessed £200.
1858/59 assessed in absence of return £200.

1859/60 marked "Pugh, Samuel S., late Stanford, dissenting minister".
Cross reference: Pugh, Samuel S., dissenting minister, Week.

287 STEVENS, James, beerhouse keeper.

1842/43, 1846/47-1849/50 assessed in absence of return £30; exempt.

Pigot & Co"s Directory, 1842: James Stevens, retailer of beer, Nursery.

288 SYMES, I. or J.G., surgeon.

1853/54 returned and assessed £42.
1854/55 returned £49 but no assessment made.

1854/55 marked "gone away".

289 THURNHAM, John, superintendent County Asylum.

1852/53 marked "Schedule E".
Note: Munk's Roll gives John Thurnham, craniologist and superintendent County Asylum.

290 TRUMAN, William, innkeeper. [by comparison, King's Arms]

1849/50-1850/51 assessed in absence of return £75; exempt.

1850/51 marked "Gilbert, Henry now Truman".
1853/54 marked "Wild, Edwin, late Trueman (sic), innkeeper".
Cross references: Gilbert, Henry, innkeeper, Week; Wild, Edwin, innkeeper, Week,

291 TURNPIKE TRUST, COMMISSIONERS OF, rent of tolls.

1852/53 [Benjamin Palmer, rent of tolls] "gone now Commissioners of Trust".
1854/55-1857/58 recorded but no assessments made.
1855/56 marked "Return called for - returned under Schedule B" (in St.John deleted).
1857/58 marked "charged under A & B".
Cross reference: Palmer, Benjamin, rent of tolls, Week.

292 TYLEE, John & Thomas P., brewers.

1842/43 returned and assessed £1350.

Pigot & Co"s Directory, 1842: Tylee & Co., brewers, maltsters, Northgate Street; and East Lavington.

293 VINE, John, bailiff.

1853/54 returned £65 but no assessment made.

1853/54-1854/55 marked "Schedule E".

294 WADWORTH, William, cheese factor.

1849/50-1850/51 returned and assessed £50.

Cross reference: Wadworth, William John, baker, pig killer, St Mary.

295 WAYLEN, Edward, clergyman.

1847/48 assessed in absence of return £110; exempt.

296 WEBB, John, innkeeper.

1842/43 assessed in absence of return £60; exempt.

Pigot & Co"s Directory, 1842: John Webb, retailer of beer, Bath Road.

297 WELLS, Joseph.

1846/47 name only entered and deleted.

298 WEST, Henry, innkeeper, British Lion.

1859/60 no assessment, marked "charged in Bedborough".
Cross reference: West, Henry, innkeeper, Bedborough.

299 WHEELER, Thomas, gardener.

1842/43, 1846/47-1849/50 assessed in absence of return £50; exempt.

Pigot & Co"s Directory, 1842: Thomas Wheeler, market gardener, Pan's Lane.

300 WHITE, John, bacon factor.

1842/43 returned and assessed £20; exempt.
1846/47-1849/50 assessed in absence of return £20; exempt.

Pigot & Co"s Directory, 1842: John White, cheese & bacon factor, Green.

301 WHITE, Mary, innkeeper.

1849/50 assessed in absence of return £60; exempt.

302 WILD, Edwin, innkeeper, King's Arms.

1853/54 assessed in absence of return £100; income proved at £75; exempt.
1854/55 assessed in absence of return £75; income proved at £70; exempt.
1855/56 assessed in absence of return £70; exempt.

1856/57–1857/58 recorded; no assessments made; exempt.

1853/54 marked "late Trueman (*sic*), innkeeper.
1856/57 King's Arms noted.
1858/59 marked "Kings Arms House taken down".
Cross references: Gilbert, Henry, innkeeper, Week; Truman, William, innkeeper, Week.

303 WINTERSON, William, gardener.

1842/43, 1846/47–1849/50 assessed in absence of return £60; exempt.

Pigot & Co"s Directory, 1842: William Winterson, market gardener, Bath Road or Wick.

304 WINTERSON, William, Junior, gardener.

1842/43, 1846/47–1849/50 assessed in absence of return £80; exempt.

Pigot & Co"s Directory, 1842: William Winterson, market gardener, Bath Road or Wick.

305 WITHINGTON, W.B., Baptist Minister.

1842/43 returned and assessed £100; exempt.
1846/47–1847/48 assessed in absence of return £100; exempt.
1853/54–1855/56 assessed in absence of return £40; exempt.

1848/49–1852/53 no assessments made.
1857/58, 1858/59 marked "dead".

306 WOODMAN, John, bricklayer.

1842/43 returned £30; assessed £120; income proved at £80; exempt.

1842/43 no appeal noted.

WEST LAVINGTON

307 BAKER, George & Joseph, blacksmiths, shopkeepers. [also BAKER, George Joseph]

1842/43 returned and assessed £62.10.5; exempt.
1846/47–1848/49 assessed in absence of return £62; exempt.
1849/50 assessed in absence of return £60; exempt.

1842/43, 1846/47-1847/48 George & Joseph Baker; 1848/49-1849/50 George Joseph Baker. 1842/43, 1846/47 blacksmiths & shopkeepers; 1847/48 blacksmiths, etc; 1848/49-1849/50 blacksmith.

308 BAKER, James, beerhouse keeper, innkeeper, Wheatsheaf.

1842/43 returned and assessed £56; exempt.
1846/47-1848/49 assessed in absence of return £56; exempt.
1849/50 assessed in absence of return £50; exempt.
1853/54 assessed in absence of return £120.

1842/43, 1846/47-1849/50 beerhouse keeper; 1853/54 innkeeper.
1850/51-1852/53 no assessments made.
1852/53 marked "Hazell, John now Baker, James".
1854/55-1859/60 marked "return at" or "charged at Littleton (Pannell)".
1858/59 [1856/57 Littleton Pannell] Wheatsheaf noted.
Pigot & Co"s Directory, 1842: James Baker, retailer of beer, grocer & dealer in sundries, West Lavington.
Cross references: Baker, James, innkeeper, Littleton Pannell; Hazell, John, innkeeper, West Lavington.

309 BAKER, Joseph, grocer & mealman.

1853/54 returned and assessed £50; exempt.
1854/55-1855/56 assessed in absence of return £50; exempt.
1856/57-1859/60 recorded; no assessments made; exempt.

310 BAKER, William, mealman.

1842/43 returned £66; assessed £80; exempt.
1846/47-1849/50 assessed in absence of return £70; exempt.

Pigot & Co"s Directory, 1842: William Baker, mealman, Littleton.

311 BLAKE, Christopher, grocer, builder, carpenter, assistant overseer. [also BLAKE, Robert]

1852/53 returned £35gb, £16a; assessed £51; income proved at £83; exempt.
1853/54 returned and assessed £51gb; exempt.
1854/55-1855/56 assessed in absence of return £60; exempt.
1856/57-1859/60 recorded; no assessments made; exempt.

Abbreviations: a, assistant overseer; gb, grocer & builder.
1852/53-1854/55 Robert Blake; 1855/56-1859/60 Christopher Blake.
1852/53-1853/54 grocer & builder, assistant overseer; 1854/55 grocer & builder;

1855/56-1859/60 grocer & carpenter.
1855/56 Robert Blake deleted, Christopher Blake substituted.

312 BLAKE, William, carpenter.

1842/43 returned and assessed £20; exempt.
1846/47-1849/50 assessed in absence of return £50; exempt.

Pigot & Co"s Directory, 1842: William Blake, carpenter & wheelwright, West Lavington.

313 BLAKEMORE, Frederick, innkeeper, Churchill Arms.

1849/50 assessed in absence of return £60; exempt.

1849/50 marked "Blakemore, Frederick late Rumble (*sic*) innkeeper".
1850/51 marked "Staples, John late Rumbold innkeeper.
Cross references: House, Sarah, innkeeper, West Lavington; Rumbold, William, innkeeper, West Lavington; Staples, John, innkeeper, West Lavington.

314 BOX, John, maltster.

1842/43 returned and assessed £30; exempt.
1846/47-1849/50 assessed in absence of return £30; exempt.

315 BUTCHER, George, mealman [by comparison, Cornbury Mill].

1842/43 returned and assessed £80; exempt.
1846/47-1850/51 assessed in absence of return £80; exempt.
1851/52-1852/53 returned and assessed £80; exempt.
1853/54 returned £76; assessed £100.
1854/55 returned £75; assessed £100.

1855/56, 1856/57 marked "now Joseph Webb, mealman".
[1856/57 Webb, Joseph noted at Cornbury Mill]
Pigot & Co"s Directory, 1842: George Butcher, miller, Cornbury Mill, West Lavington.
Cross reference: Webb, Joseph, miller, West Lavington.

316 BUTCHER, Thomas, miller.

1852/53 assessed in absence of return £150 but deleted.

317 CAMERON, Revd. J[onathan] H. L[ovett], private tutor.

1847/48–1851/52 returned and assessed £150.

1850/51 marked "to be written to".

318 CASWELL, -, Revd.

1846/47 name only entered and deleted.
Pigot & Co"s Directory, 1842: Revd. Robert Casewell, clergy, West Lavington.

319 CHAPMAN, John & William, millers, Garretts Mill. [also CHAPMAN, John]

Partnership

1842/43 returned and assessed £52.10.0 each; exempt.
1846/47 returned and assessed £51.15.0 each; John Chapman exempt.
1847/48 returned and assessed £60 each; John Chapman exempt.
1848/49 returned and assessed £70 John Chapman; exempt; assessed in absence of return £70 William Chapman; exempt.
1849/50 returned and assessed £72 John Chapman; exempt; assessed in absence of return £70 William Chapman; exempt.
1850/51 assessed in absence of return £70 each; exempt.
1851/52 returned and assessed £70 John Chapman; exempt; assessed in absence of return £70 William Chapman; exempt.

John Chapman sole

1852/53 returned and assessed £70; exempt.
1853/54 returned and assessed £82; exempt.
1854/55 returned £40; assessed £100.
1855/56 assessed in absence of return £100.
1856/57 assessed in absence of return £150; reduced to £120 on appeal.
1857/58 assessed in absence of return £120.
1858/59 returned £100; assessed £120.
1859/60 returned £100; assessed £120.

1852/53 William Chapman deleted; John Chapman marked "who carried on business".
1853/54 marked "Garretts Mill".

320 COLEMAN, Mary, innkeeper. [by comparison, Black Dog] [also COLEMAN, Robert]

1842/43 returned and assessed £60; exempt.
1846/47–1847/48 assessed in absence of return £60; exempt.

1848/49–1849/50 assessed in absence of return £60; income proved at £80; exempt.
1851/52 assessed in absence of return £60; income proved at £110; exempt.
1852/53–1853/54 assessed in absence of return £60; exempt.

1842/43 Robert Coleman; 1846/47–1849/50 Mrs.Coleman; 1851/52–1853/54 Mary
    Coleman.
1850/51 no assessment made.
1854/55 marked "Whatley, Stephen late Coleman".
Pigot & Co"s Directory, 1842: Robert Coleman, Black Dog, West Lavington.
Cross reference: Whatley, Stephen, innkeeper, West Lavington.

321 DRAPER, Philip, grocer & baker.

1853/54 returned £50; assessed £120; reduced to £70.
1854/55 returned £55; assessed £120.
1855/56 assessed in absence of return £120.
1856/57 returned £70; assessed £120.
1857/58 returned £62; assessed £120.
1858/59 returned £60; assessed £120.
1859/60 returned £90; assessed £120.

1853/54 no appeal noted.
1859/60 marked "life insurance £36".

322 DUNFORD, William & James, brickmakers. [also DUNFORD, Thomas]

Sole

1842/43 assessed in absence of return £150.
1846/47 returned £60; assessed £130; reduced to £90 on appeal.
1847/48 returned £65; assessed £90.
1848/49 returned £50; assessed £90; exempt.
1849/50–1852/53 assessed in absence of return £90; exempt.
1853/54 assessed in absence of return £110; exempt.

Partnership

1854/55–1855/56 assessed in absence of return £75 each; James Dunford exempt.
1856/57 assessed in absence of return £75 James Dunford; exempt on appeal; returned
    £50 William Dunford; assessed £75.
1857/58–1859/60 James Dunford recorded; no assessments made; exempt.
1857/58 returned £70 William Dunford; assessed £75.
1858/59–1859/60 returned and assessed £75 William Dunford.

1842/43, 1846/47–1852/53 Thomas Dunford; 1853/54 James Dunford; 1854/55–1859/60
    William & James Dunford.

1853/54 entry reads Thomas (deleted) William (deleted) & James Dunford.
1854/55 composite assessment on partnership deleted; assessments made on individuals (1857/58 bracketed together).
1854/55-1855/56 Durnford.
Cross reference: Dunford, Thomas, brickmaker, Cheverell Magna.

323 FARMER, James, butcher.

1851/52 returned £50 but entry deleted.

324 GIDDINGS, James, shopkeeper.

1842/43, 1846/47-1849/50 assessed in absence of return £30; exempt.

Pigot & Co"s Directory, 1842: James Giddings, grocer & dealer in sundries.

325 GILES, James, harness maker.

1842/43 returned and assessed £40; exempt.
1846/47-1849/50 assessed in absence of return £40; exempt.

Pigot & Co"s Directory, 1842: James Giles, saddler, Littleton.

326 HAZELL, John, innkeeper, Wheatsheaf.

1842/43 returned and assessed £40; exempt.
1846/47-1847/48 assessed in absence of return £80; exempt.
1848/49-1850/51 assessed in absence of return £100; exempt.
1851/52 assessed in absence of return £150; reduced to £100; exempt.
1852/53 returned and assessed £120; assessment discharged on appeal but no sum recorded.

1851/52 no appeal noted (Statutorily an appeal had to be made to displace an assessment of £150).
1852/53 marked "Hazell, John now Baker, James".
Pigot & Co"s Directory, 1842: John Hazell, innkeeper, Wheat Sheaf, Littleton.
Cross reference: Baker, James, innkeeper, West Lavington.

327 HITCHCOCK, Charles, lunatic asylum. [Fiddington House]

1851/52 returned and assessed £1000.
1852/53 returned £500; assessed £1000.
1853/54 returned and assessed £750.

1854/55 returned £377.2.3; assessed £750.
1855/56 returned £500; assessed £600.
1856/57 returned £310; assessed £600; reduced to £380 on appeal.
1857/58 returned £155; assessed £250.
1858/59 returned and assessed £312.11.0.
1859/60 returned £320.12.0; assessed £400.

1851/52-1852/53 marked "late Willett, lunatic asylum".
Note: Between 1853/54 and 1857/58 Hitchcock was also assessed separately in West Lavington on profits as a surgeon. This related to a partnership in Market Lavington where the other partners were assessed. Hitchcock, however, had to be assessed at his place of residence, seemingly in West Lavington. But in order to reflect the integrity of the medical partnership his assessments as a surgeon have been recorded in Market Lavington.
Cross references: Hitchcock, Charles, surgeon, Market Lavington; Willett, Robert, lunatic asylum, West Lavington.

328 HOUSE, Sarah, innkeeper, [by comparison, Churchill Arms].

1842/43 returned and assessed £45; exempt.
1846/47 assessed in absence of return £45; exempt.

Pigot & Co"s Directory, 1842: Sarah House, Churchill Arms, West Lavington.
Cross references: Blakemore, Frederick, innkeeper, West Lavington; Rumbold, William, innkeeper, West Lavington; Staples, John, innkeeper, West Lavington.

329 HOWELL, Thomas, tailor & draper.

1853/54-1855/56 assessed in absence of return £50; exempt.
1856/57-1859/60 recorded; no assessments made; exempt.

1853/54-1854/55 Howle; 1855/56-1859/60 Howell.

330 INGRAM, James, baker.

1842/43 returned and assessed £50; exempt.
1846/47-1849/50 assessed in absence of return £50; exempt.

Pigot & Co"s Directory, 1842: James Ingram, baker, West Lavington.

331 KELSEY, Edw[ard] Edm[und] Peach, land agent.

1856/57 assessed in absence of return £240; reduced to £170 on appeal.

1856/57 F.James Kelsey entered but deleted; Edw. Edm. Peach Kelsey substituted.
1857/58 marked "pays in Salisbury".

1858/59-1859/60 marked "returns at Salisbury".
Cross reference: Kelsey, F.James, land agent, West Lavington.

332 KELSEY, F. James, land agent.

1851/52 returned and assessed £240.
1852/53 returned and assessed £220.
1853/54 returned £267.15.6 less £64.8.4 life insurance; estimated at £400 but reduced to £203.7.2.
1854/55 assessed in absence of return £400; reduced to £267.15.6.
1855/56 returned and assessed £240.

1853/54-1854/55 no appeal noted.
1856/57 entry deleted and Edw. Edm. Peach Kelsey substituted.
Pigot & Co"s Directory, 1842: F.J.Kelsey, land agent, West Lavington (H)ouse.
Cross reference: Kelsey, Edward Edmund Peach, land agent, West Lavington.

333 MEAD, Daniel, maltster & beerhouse keeper.

1842/43 returned and assessed £55; exempt.
1846/47-1847/48 assessed in absence of return £55; exempt.
1848/49-1849/50 assessed in absence of return £55; income proved at £40; exempt.

Pigot & Co"s Directory, 1842: Daniel Mead, retailer of beer, West Lavington.

334 MEAD, Edmund, maltster.

1842/43 returned and assessed £45; exempt.
1846/47-1849/50 assessed in absence of return £45; exempt.

335 NEWMAN, Thomas, mealman.

1842/43 returned £100; assessed £200.

1846/47 estimate of £150 deleted.

336 OATLEY, Daniel, builder, etc.

1854/55-1857/58 assessed in absence of return £75.
1858/59 returned £50; assessed £75.
1859/60 returned £40; assessed £75.

Pigot & Co"s Directory, 1842: Daniel Oatley, tiler & plasterer, Littleton.
Cross reference: Oatley, Daniel, builder, Worton.

337 PRICE, William, miller.

1846/47 assessed in absence of return £50; exempt.
1847/48-1849/50 assessed in absence of return £80; exempt.

338 RUMBOLD, William, innkeeper. [by comparison, Churchill Arms]

1847/48-1848/49 assessed in absence of return £20; exempt.

1847/48 Rumble; 1848/49 Rumbold.
1849/50 marked "Blakemore, Frederick late Rumble.
Cross references: Blakemore, Frederick, innkeeper, West Lavington; House, Sarah, innkeeper, West Lavington; Staples, John, innkeeper, West Lavington.

339 SAINSBURY, John, timber dealer, wheelwright. [also SAINSBURY, James]

Partnership

1842/43 James Sainsbury returned £25; assessed £50; confirmed on appeal. John Sainsbury assessed in absence of return £50; confirmed on appeal.

John Sainsbury sole

1846/47 returned £75; reduced to £70 on appeal.
1847/48 assessed in absence of return £120.
1848/49 returned £80; assessed £120; exempt.
1849/50-1850/51 assessed in absence of return £120; exempt.

1842/43 timber dealers & wheelwrights; 1847/48 timber dealer, etc.
Pigot & Co"s Directory, 1842: James Sainsbury, timber merchant, West Lavington.

340 SHORE, Thomas, carpenter.

1846/47 returned and assessed £35; exempt.
1847/48 assessed in absence of return £35; exempt.
1848/49-1849/50 assessed in absence of return £35; income proved at £50; exempt.

341 STAPLES, John, butcher, innkeeper, Churchill Arms.

1850/51 assessed in absence of return £70; exempt.
1851/52 assessed in absence of return £70; income proved at £80; exempt.
1852/53 assessed in absence of return £70; exempt.
1853/54 assessed in absence of return £60; exempt.
1854/55 returned and assessed £40; exempt.

1855/56 assessed in absence of return £40; exempt.
1856/57 assessed in absence of return £120; reduced to £100 on appeal.
1857/58 assessed in absence of return £100.
1858/59 returned £50; assessed £100.
1859/60 returned £60; assessed £100.

1850/51-1855/56 innkeeper; 1856/57-1859/60 innkeeper & butcher.
1850/51 marked "late Rumbold, innkeeper".
1856/57 Churchill Arms noted.
Cross references: Blakemore, Frederick, innkeeper, West Lavington; House, Sarah, innkeeper, West Lavington; Rumbold, William, innkeeper, West Lavington.

342 WEBB, James, miller.

1849/50 £13.10.0 interest assessed by General Commissioners.
1850/51 returned £50; £62.13.4 and £13.10.0 interest assessed by General Commissioners; income proved at £62 and £4.10.0 interest; £9 left in charge.
1851/52 assessed in absence of return £70; income proved at £70; exempt; £13.10.0 interest left in charge.
1852/53 assessed in absence of return £90; exempt.
1853/54 assessed in absence of return £100; income proved at £90; exempt.
1854/55-1855/56 assessed in absence of return £100.

1849/50 charged by additional assessment.
1854/55 assessment later discharged; double assessment, charged in Great Cheverell.
1856/57 marked "gone to Great Cheverell".
Cross reference: Webb, James, miller, Cheverell Magna.

343 WEBB, Joseph, miller, Cornbury Mill.

1856/57 returned £40; assessed £100; reduced to £90 on appeal.
1857/58 assessed in absence of return £90; reduced to £70.
1858/59 returned £30; assessed £80.
1859/60 returned £70; assessed £100.

1856/57 Cornbury Mill noted.
1858/59 marked "Jn?".
Cross reference: Butcher, George, mealman, West Lavington.

344 WHATLEY, Stephen, innkeeper, Black Dog.

1854/55 returned £25; assessed £60; exempt.
1855/56 assessed in absence of return £60.
1856/57 returned £24; assessed £60.
1857/58 returned £20; assessed £60.
1858/59-1859/60 returned £25; assessed £60.

1854/55 marked "late Coleman".
1858/59 Black Dog noted.
Cross reference: Coleman, Mary, innkeeper, West Lavington.

345 WILKINSON, Revd.Dr.John, private tutor.

1853/54 assessed in absence of return £586.
1854/55 returned and assessed £405.11.3.

1852/53 recorded and marked "not liable till 1855".
1855/56 Revd. John Wilkinson deleted, Revd. Matthew Wilkinson substituted.
Cross references: Wilkinson, Revd. John, tutor, Worton; Wilkinson, Revd. Matthew, private tutor, West Lavington.

346 WILKINSON, Revd.Matthew, private tutor.

1855/56 returned and assessed £506.
1856/57 returned and assessed £419.
1857/58 returned and assessed £578.14.0.
1858/59 returned and assessed £316.
1859/60 returned and assessed £387.15.0.

1855/56 Revd. John Wilkinson deleted, Revd. Matthew Wilkinson substituted.
Cross reference: Wilkinson, Revd.Dr.John, private tutor, West Lavington.

347 WILLETT, Robert, professional engagements, lunatic asylum. [also WILLETT & HOOD]

1846/47 returned £500; assessed £750.
1847/48 returned £500; assessed £850.
1848/49 assessed in absence of return £850.
1849/50 returned and assessed £850.
1850/51 assessed in absence of return £1000.

1846/47-1847/48 Robert Willett; 1848/49-1849/50 Executors of Robert Willett; 1850/51 Willett & Hood.
1846/47 professional engagements; 1847/48-1850/51 lunatic asylum.
1846/47 marked "Return vide Phillips return".
1851/52 marked "Hitchcock late Willett (& Hood deleted)".
Cross references: Hitchcock, Charles, lunatic asylum & surgeon, West Lavington; Willett, Robert, asylum keeper, Market Lavington.

348 WILTON, Revd.Edward, schoolmaster, officiating minister.

1848/49 returned and assessed £259.
1849/50-1851/52 returned and assessed £244.

1852/53 returned and assessed £240.
1853/54–1854/55 assessed in absence of return £240.
1855/56 returned and assessed £240.
1856/57 assessed in absence of return £240.
1857/58 returned and assessed £240.
1858/59 assessed in absence of return £240.
1859/60 returned and assessed £240.

1848/49–1850/51 schoolmaster, etc.; 1851/52–1855/56 schoolmaster;
1856/57–1859/60 schoolmaster & officiating minister.
1858/59 £261.3.7 entered but deleted; marked "as last year".
Pigot & Co"s Directory, 1842: Revd. Edward Wilton, clergy, master, Free School, West
    Lavington.
Cross reference: Wilton, Revd.E., clergyman & schoolmaster, Littleton Pannell.

WORTON

349 BAKER, William, mealman, miller. [by comparison, Hurst Mill]

1851/52 returned and assessed £69; exempt.
1852/53 returned and assessed £76.13.0; exempt.
1853/54 returned £67.10.0; assessed 70; exempt.
1853/54 assessed in absence of return £100 as miller.

1851/52–1852/53 mealman; 1853/54 assessments made separately as mealman and miller, sug-
    gesting two different people, especially as exemption was claimed as a mealman but tax paid
    as a miller. However, a note is recorded in 1854/55 that they are the "same person".
1850/51 marked "Chandler, George now Wm.Baker".
1851/52 marked "late Chandler".
1854/55 estimate of £150 deleted, marked "gone to Malmesbury, return there".
Cross reference: Chandler, George, mealman, Worton; Nutfield, John & George, millers, Worton;
    Sainsbury, William & John, millers, Worton.

350 BIGGS, Joseph, beerhouse keeper. [also BIGGS, John]

1854/55 returned £15; assessed £50; exempt.
1855/56 assessed in absence of return £50; exempt.
1856/57 returned £15; no assessment made; exempt.
1857/58 returned £12; no assessment made; exempt.
1858/59 returned £15; no assessment made; exempt.
1859/60 recorded; no assessment made; exempt.

1854/55 John Biggs; 1855/56–1859/60 Joseph Biggs.

351 BISHOP, John, publican, innkeeper.

1842/43, 1846/47-1850/51 assessed in absence of return £40; exempt.
1851/52 assessed in absence of return £40; income proved at £101.15.0.

1842/43 publican; 1846/47-1851/52 innkeeper.

352 BISHOP, Vincent, farmer, innkeeper, Royal Oak.

1852/53 returned £5; assessed £40; income proved at £95.
1853/54 returned £5; assessed £50; exempt.
1854/55 returned £5; assessed £50.
1855/56 assessed in absence of return £50.
1856/57 returned £20; assessed £50.
1857/58 returned £30; assessed £50.
1858/59 returned £40; assessed £50.
1859/60 returned £20; assessed £50.

1852/53-1857/58 Vincent Bishop; 1858/59-1859/60 Vince Bishop.
1852/53-1856/57 innkeeper & farmer; 1857/58-1859/60 innkeeper.
1858/59 Royal Oak noted.

353 BRIGGS, George, corn dealer.

1842/43 returned £100; assessed £200; income proved at £100; no appeal noted.

354 CHANDLER, George, mealman, Hurst Mill.

1842/43 returned and assessed £150.
1846/47-1848/49 returned £150; assessed £175.
1849/50 assessed in absence of return £175.
1850/51 returned and assessed £100; exempt.

1850/51 marked "now William Baker".
Pigot & Co"s Directory, 1842: George Chandler, miller, Hurst Mill.
Cross reference: Baker, William, mealman, Worton; Nutfield, John & George, millers, Worton;
    Sainsbury, William & John, millers, Worton.

355 COOPER, Isaac, innkeeper.

1851/52 assessed in absence of return £75; exempt.
1852/53 returned £20; assessed £75; exempt.

1851/52 marked "late Wise".
Cross reference: Wise, James, innkeeper, Worton.

356 DOWSE, George, mealman.

1842/43 returned and assessed £110.
1846/47 returned £130; assessed £150.
1847/48 returned £150; assessed £225.
1848/49 returned £100; assessed £225.
1849/50–1850/51 assessed in absence of return £350.
1851/52 assessed in absence of return £150; reduced to £100 on appeal; exempt.
1852/53 assessed in absence of return £100; exempt.
1853/54 returned £100; assessed £120.
1854/55 assessed in absence of return £120.

1855/56 marked "q. who now occupies".

357 DOWSE, Philip, baker, maltster.

1842/43 returned and assessed £80; exempt.

1842/43 baker; 1846/47 baker & maltster entered but deleted.

358 GOODALL, Hezekiah, brickmaker.

1857/58 returned £13; assessed £25.
1858/59 estimated £25 but deleted.
1859/60 recorded; no assessment made; exempt.

359 HOOKS, Joseph, miller.

1859/60 returned £77; assessed £120.

360 MASON, Robert Monck, tutor, allowance.

1852/53 returned and assessed £75 tutor, £25 allowance.

1852/53 marked "gone to Clapham?".
1853/54 tutor only noted; no assessment made.
1854/55 marked "gone away".

361 NUTFIELD, John & George, millers, Hurst Mill.

1858/59 John Nutfield assessed in absence of return £100.
1858/59 George Nutfield returned £40; assessed £100.
1859/60 John Nutfield returned £40; assessed £100.

1859/60 George Nutfield assessed in absence of return £100.

1858/59 marked "Sainsbury, William & John now Nutfield, John & George, millers".
1858/59 marked re George Nutfield "claims separate assessment".
1859/60 Nutland.
Note: in Pigot & Co's Trade Directory of 1842 the occupier of Hurst Mill was George Chandler.
Cross references: Baker, William, miller, Worton;   Chandler, George, miller, Worton; Sainsbury, William & John, millers, Worton.

362 OATLEY, Daniel, builder.

1853/54 assessed in absence of return £40; exempt.

1854/55 marked "charged before".
Cross reference: Oatley, Daniel, builder, West Lavington.

363 PARRY, G.H., Esquire.

1850/51 name entered and deleted.

364 ROSE, Job, maltster, innkeeper, Rose & Crown.

1853/54 returned £42.12.6; assessed £80; exempt.
1854/55 assessed in absence of return £60; exempt.
1856/57 returned £50; assessed £67.
1857/58 returned £30; assessed £67.
1858/59-1859/60 assessed in absence of return £67.

1853/54-1855/56 maltster; 1856/57-1859/60 maltster & innkeeper.
1855/56 no assessment made; marked "returned in Marston".
1858/59 Rose & Crown noted.
Cross references: Rose, Job, beerhouse keeper & maltster, Marston; Smith, Knightley, innkeeper, Marston.

365 SAINSBURY, William & John, millers, Hurst Mill.

1854/55 returned £100; assessed £200.
1855/56 returned £85; assessed £200.
1856/57 returned £100; assessed £200.
1857/58 assessed in absence of return £200.

1854/55 Hurst Mill noted.
1857/58 marked "left 24 June 1857".
1858/59 marked "now Nutfield, John & George, millers".

Note: in Pigot & Co's Trade Directory of 1842 the occupier of Hurst Mill is George Chandler. Cross references: Baker, William, miller, Worton; Chandler, George, miller, Worton; Nutfield, John & George, millers, Worton.

366 SMITH, Knightley, innkeeper. [by comparison, Rose & Crown]

1853/54 returned and assessed £43.10.0; exempt.
1854/55-1855/56 assessed in absence of return £43; exempt.

1856/57-1857/58 marked "now Rose".
Cross reference: Rose, Job, innkeeper, Worton.

367 STAPLES, William, innkeeper, butcher, beerhouse keeper, builder, carpenter. [also STAPLES, John]

1853/54 returned and assessed £60; exempt.
1854/55-1855/56 assessed in absence of return £60; exempt.
1856/57-1859/60 recorded; no assessments made; exempt.

1853/54 John Staples; 1854/55-1859/60 William Staples.
1853/54-1854/55 innkeeper & butcher; 1855/56 innkeeper & builder;
1856/57-1859/60 beerhouse keeper & carpenter.

368 WILKINSON, Revd. John. tutor.

1853/54 returned £526.1.3 but no assessment made.

Cross reference: Wilkinson, Revd. John, private tutor, West Lavington.

369 WISE, James, innkeeper.

1842/43 returned and assessed £100; exempt.
1846/47-1848/49 assessed in absence of return £90; exempt.
1849/50-1850/51 assessed in absence of return £80; exempt.

1851/52 Isaac Cooper substituted; marked "late Wise".
Cross reference: Cooper, Isaac, innkeeper, Worton.

DEVIZES ST. JOHN

370 A [illeg], W.J.B.

1848/49 name only entered.

371 ABRAHAM, George, hair dresser.

1846/47-1849/50 assessed in absence of return £50; exempt.

372 ALEXANDER, Alfred, New Prison.

1854/55-1855/56 noted as assessed under Schedule E.

Cross reference: Haywood, Thomas, Governor of New Prison, St.John.

373 ANDERSON, Thomas Watson, solicitors clerk.

1853/54-1855/56 returned and assessed at £120.
1856/57 returned £99, assessed £100, reduced to £99 on appeal; exempt.

1857/58 marked "gone".
1856/57 is an example of an early form of tax avoidance. On incomes of £100, tax was payable
on the whole amount. Incomes below this sum were eligible to be wholly relieved on a
claim for exemption. By agreeing with the employer to fix the salary at £99, the taxpayer
would be better off by £3.15.10. (following evidence taken before the Select Committee
on the Income and Property Tax, House of Commons. Parliamentary Papers. (1852) ix
qq.3019, 3235).
1852/53 marked "removed to Southampton".
Cross reference: (similar instance of early legal tax avoidance) Thorp, Thomas Glossop, surveyor's
clerk, Bedborough; Coxhead, W.P., schoolmaster, St. John.

374 ANSTIE, George Washington, farmer.

1842/43 entered and deleted.

Cross reference: Anstie, George Washington, solicitor, St. Mary.

375 ANSTIE, PAUL & EDWARD, tobacco & snuff manufacturers. [also ANSTIE, Benjamin]

Year	Amount returned	Commissioners' estimate	Final assessment
	£	£	£
1842/43	562	562	562
1846/47	1026	1026	1026
1847/48	1026	1026	1026
1848/49	1353	1353	1353
1849/50	1403	1403	1403
1850/51	1522	1522	1522
1851/52	2039	2039	2039
1852/53	2026	2026	2026
1853/54	1931	1931	1931
1854/55	1473	1473	1473
1855/56	1235	1235	1235
1856/57	1309	1309	1309
1857/58	1604	1604	1604
1858/59	2064	2064	2064
1859/60	2868	2868	2868

1842/43 Benjamin & Paul Anstie assessed.
Pigot & Co's Directory, 1842: Benjamin & Paul Anstie, tobacco & snuff manufacturers, Market Place.

376 ANSTIE, Thomas Brown, surgeon, etc., apothecary

1848/49 returned and assessed £305
1849/50 returned and assessed £355
1850/51 returned and assessed £360
1851/52 returned and assessed £320
1852/53 returned and assessed £350 + £20 interest

1848/49 surgeon & apothecary.
1853/54-1855/56 marked "returned in St. Mary".
Cross reference: Anstie, Thomas Browne (sic), surgeon, St. Mary.

377 BALL, James, tea dealer, etc. [also BALL, Thomas]

1842/43 returned and assessed £240.
1846/47-1848/49 returned £200 but assessed at £240.
1849/50 assessed in absence of return £240.

1849/50 Thomas Ball assessed.
1850/51 marked "Simpson late Ball, grocer".

Pigot & Co's Directory, 1842: James Ball, grocer & tea dealer, Brittox.
Cross reference: Simpson, Edward, grocer, St.John.

378 BARLOW, George, corndealer.

1853/54 returned and assessed £80.
1854/55-1855/56 returned £80 but assessed at £100.
1856/57-1859/60 returned and assessed £100.

379 BARRY, Henry George, innkeeper, spirit merchant, Dolphin. [also BARRY, William H]

Year	Amount returned	Commissioners' estimate	Income proved	Final assessment
	£	£	£	£
1850/51	–	50	50	–
1851/52	–	75	96.6.11	–
1852/53	91.12.8	–	105	–
1853/54	82.13.0	91.12.8	91.12.8	–
1854/55	–	100	–	100
1855/56	–	100	–	100
1856/57	100	–	–	100
1857/58	100	120	–	120
1858/59	100	120	–	120
1859/60	100	120	–	120

1850/51 William H Barry assessed.
1850/51-1855/56 innkeeper.
1856/57 Dolphin noted.
1856/57-1859/60 spirit merchant.

380 BARTON, Henry, shopkeeper & baker.

1842/43 returned and assessed £140; exempt.
1846/47-1848/49 assessed in absence of return £140; exempt.
1849/50 assessed in absence of return £40; exempt.

Pigot & Co's Directory, 1842: Henry Barton, baker, Bridewell Street.

381 BASTER, William, Sack Office keeper, saddler, etc. [also BASTER, Elizabeth]

1842/43 assessed in absence of return £150; reduced on appeal to £94; exempt.
1846/47-1853/54 assessed in absence of return £60; exempt.

1854/55 assessed in absence of return £50; exempt.
1855/56-1859/60 recorded; no assessments made; exempt.

1842/43 Sack Office keeper & saddler.
1855/56-1859/60 Elizabeth Baster.
Pigot & Co's Directory, 1842: William Baster, saddler & harness maker, officer Sack Office, St.John Street.

382 BATT, Moses, horse dealer.

1846/47-1848/49 assessed in absence of return £50; exempt.

383 BAYES, Frederick William, surgeon, officer.

1856/57 returned £110, assessed at £50.
1857/58 returned and assessed £120.

1856/57 marked "Schedule E", assessment reduced to £50.
1857/58 marked "Schedule E".
1858/59 marked "now Thornley, Robert".
Cross reference: Thornley, Robert, surgeon, St.John.

384 BAYLEY, John Raikes, solicitor.

Year	Amount returned	Commissioners' estimate	Final assessment
	£	£	£
1848/49	720	720	720
1849/50	730	730	730
1850/51	450	450	450
1851/52	Special Commissioners		
1852/53	Special Commissioners		
1853/54	No assessment made		
1854/55	–	400	370
1855/56	400	400	400
1856/57	–	200deleted	–

1848/49-1850/51, 1852/53, Bayley; 1851/52, 1853/54-1856/57 Bailey, but Bayley in St. Mary.
1848/49, 1850/51 assessed under letter.
1854/55 marked "qq Special Commissioners (last year ?)"
1856/57 marked "now MacDonald & Olivier".
Pigot & Co's Directory, 1842: Bayly & Bayly (sic), attorneys, John Raikes Bayly (sic), agent to Scottish Union Fire Office, High Street.
Cross references: MacDonald, Alexander & Olivier, Alfred, solicitors, St.John; Bayley, J R, solicitor, St.Mary, 1842/43, 1846/47-1849/50 name entry.

385 BENNETT, William, broker, dealer.

1847/48 returned and assessed £50; exempt.
1848/49-1849/50 assessed in absence of return £50; exempt.
1850/51-1852/53 no entries made.
1853/54 returned £52; estimate made at £62 deleted.
1854/55-1855/56 assessed in absence of return £50; exempt.
1856/57 recorded; no assessments made; exempt.
1857/58 returned £40; estimate made at £50; exempt.
1858/59-1859/60 recorded; no assessments made; exempt.

1847/48-1849/50 broker; 1853/54-1859/60 dealer.

386 BIGGS, James, grocer. [also BIGGS, Thomas]

Year	Amount returned	Commissioners' estimate	Final assessment
	£	£	£
1842/43	140	–	140
1846/47	130	150	150
1847/48	150	–	150
1848/49	150	–	150
1849/50	150	175a	150
1850/51	156	–	156
1851/52	175	–	175
1852/53	180	–	180
1853/54	200	250	201.17.3
1854/55	192	–	192
1855/56	200	–	200
1856/57	–	200	200
1857/58	210	–	210
1858/59	225	–	225
1859/60	225	–	204.12.6

1842/43 Thomas Biggs assessed.
1853/54 no appeal noted.
1859/60 assessment reduced by life assurance relief of £20.7.6
Pigot & Co's Directory, 1842: Thomas Biggs, grocer, agent to Phoenix Fire Office, Long Street.

387 BIGGS, John, tea dealer.

1842/43 assessed in absence of return £40; exempt.
1846/47-1847/48 assessed in absence of return £100; exempt.

Pigot & Co's Directory, 1842: John Biggs, tea dealer, Brittox.

388 BIGGS, Richard William, schoolmaster, interest on securities, possessions in Ireland. [also BIGGS, Richard, Senior]

Year	Amount returned £	Commissioners' estimate £	Final assessment £
Partnership			
1842/43			
Biggs, R	150	150	150
Biggs, R W	150	150	150

1842/43 marked re Richard Biggs Senior "a quarter year only".

R.W.Biggs sole

Year	Amount returned £	Commissioners' estimate £	Final assessment £
1846/47	200s 30i	–	230
1847/48	102s 10i 24bp	–	136
1848/49	70s 8i 25pI	120	153
1849/50	140s 25pI	–	165
1850/51	166s,pI	–	166
1851/52	178s 22i	–	200
1852/53	216s 42i	–	258
1853/54	223s,i	258	258
1854/55	177s,i	258	258
1855/56	130s	200	200
1856/57		200	200
1857/58	113s 16i	–	129
1858/59	75s 16i	100 –	100 16
1859/60	56s 14i	100 16	116

Abbreviations: s, schoolmaster; i, interest on securities; pI, possessions in Ireland; bp British possessions.

Richard Biggs, occasionally Richard William or Williams, Junior.

Pigot & Co's Directory, 1842: Richard W Biggs, (boarding) school, Long Street

389 BIRCH, William, horse breaker.

1842/34 returned and assessed £118; exempt.
1847/48 returned and assessed £60; exempt.
1848/49 assessed in absence of return £60; exempt.
1849/50 assessed in absence of return £60; exempt.

Pigot & Co's Directory, 1842: William Birch, livery-stable keeper, Long Street.

390 BISHOP, Thomas, plumber, glazier.

1842/43 assessed in absence of return £100; exempt.
1846/47-1848/49 assessed in absence of return £89; exempt.
1849/50 assessed in absence of return £90; exempt.
1850/51-1851/52 assessed in absence of return £120; exempt.
1852/53 returned £70; estimated at £120; assessed at £70; income proved at
    £116.6.0; exempt.
1853/54-1855/56 assessed in absence of return £80; exemption not claimed.
1856/57-1859/60 recorded; no assessments made; exempt.

1842/43, 1846/47-1847/48 plumber & glazier; 1848/49-1850/51 plumber, etc.;
1851/52-1859/60 plumber.
Pigot & Co's Directory, 1842: Thomas Bishop, painter, plumber & glazier, High Street.

391 BOURNE, Richard, innkeeper.

1842/43 returned and assessed £182.

Pigot & Co's Directory, 1842: Richard Bourne, White Swan, Market Place.
Cross references: Frayling, Edward, innkeeper, St.John; Jenkins, David, innkeeper, St.John; Wells,
    Joseph, innkeeper, St.John.

392 BOWDEN, James, butcher.

1842/43 entry only.
Pigot & Co's Directory, 1842: J. Bowden, butcher, Long Street.

393 BOWSHER, Alfred, ironmonger.

1858/59-1859/60 returned £60; estimated at £100.

1858/59 marked "in business 5 months in July".

394 BRAMBLE, J.R., surveyor.

Year	Amount returned £	Commissioners' estimate £	Final assessment £
1848/49	150	–	150
1849/50	–	200	200
1850/51	50	100	100
1851/52	120	–	120
1852/53	120	–	120
1853/54	90	–	90
1854/55	50	–	50
1855/56	10	–	10

1856/57-1858/59 marked "dead".

Pigot & Co's Directory, 1842: James Roger Bramble, agent-land, &.; Roger Bramble, surveyor, Northgate Street.

Cross reference: Bramble, J.R., land surveyor, St.Mary, 1842/43, 1846/47-1847/48.

395 BRAND, Thomas, coachman, coachmaker, coachmaster.

1849/50 recorded but no assessment made.
1852/53 returned and assessed £125; exempt.
1853/54 estimated in absence of return £125; assessed at £100.
1854/55 returned and assessed £100.
1855/56 estimated in absence of return £150, amended to £100.
1856/57 assessed in absence of return £100.
1857/58 returned and assessed £100.

1849/50 coachman; 1852/53 coachman and lodger; 1853/54-1855/56 coachman, etc.; 1856/57-1857/58 coachmaster.
1857/58 marked "gone away".

396 BRIDGES, Fitzherbert, chemist.

No assessment made. Mentioned only in notes as successor to Bayntun Johnstone, and predecessor of Henry Cripps, 1852/53.

Cross references: Cripps, Henry, chemist, St.John; Hayward, Robert, chemist, St.John; Johnstone, Bayntun, chemist, St.John.

397 BROWN, Thomas, innkeeper, Antelope.

1857/58 by note "McEwen late see Thomas Brown".
1857/58 by note "Humby, Frederick Peter, Antelope, now Thomas Brown".
1858/59 marked "late Humby, Antelope".
No assessments made.

Cross references: Humby, Frederick Peter, innkeeper, St.John; McEwin, Edwin, innkeeper, St.John; Ransom, William, innkeeper, St.John.

398 BUCKLAND, Maria Grace, schoolmistress.

1853/54-1855/56 assessed in absence of return £50; exempt.
1856/57-1859/60 recorded but no assessment made; exempt.

399 BULL, Edwin, victualler, Duke of Wellington. [also BULL, Margaret]

1847/48 returned and assessed £40; exempt.
1848/49 returned and assessed £60; exempt.
1849/50-1852/53 assessed in absence of return £60; exempt.
1853/54 returned £50; estimated at £60 but no assessment made.
1854/55-1855/56 assessed in absence of return £60; exempt.
1856/57-1859/60 recorded; no assessments made; exempt.

1856/57 noted "Duke of Wellington".
1847/48-1858/59 Edwin Bull; 1859/60 Margaret Bull.

400 BULL, Henry, bookseller, printer.

1842/43 returned and assessed £150.
1846/47-1847/48 returned £150; assessed at £200.
1848/49 assessed in absence of return £200.
1849/50 returned £150; assessed at £200.
1850/51 assessed in absence of return £200; on appeal assessment discharged but no figure recorded; exempt.
1851/52 assessed in absence of return £150.
1852/53-1859/60 returned and assessed £150.

1849/50-1850/51 bookseller, etc.; 1851/52-1855/56 bookseller; 1842/43, 1846/47-1848/49, 1856/57-1859/60 bookseller & printer.
Pigot & Co's Directory, 1842: Henry Bull, bookseller, stationer & printer, library, St.John Street.

401 BULL, Mary & Fanny, milliners & dressmakers.

Year	Amount returned £	Commissioners' estimate £	Income proved £	Final assessment £
1842/43	200	–	–	200
1846/47	150	–	–	150
1847/48	150	–	–	150
1848/49	–	150	–	150

1849/50	150	–	–	150
1850/51	–	150a	150	–
1851/52	–	150	75	75
1852/53	150	–	75	75
1853/54	100	150	75	75
1854/55	75	150	75	75
1855/56	100	–	–	100
1856/57	50	100	–	100
1857/58	100	–	50	50
1858/59	70	100	50	50
1859/60	50	100	–	50

1842/43, 1846/47-1849/50 Fanny & Mary Bull; 1850/51-1859/60 Mary &Fanny Bull.
1842/43, 1846/47-1849/50 milliners & dressmakers; 1850/51-1855/56 milliners etc.;
1856/57-1859/60 milliners.
1851/52 marked "Miss Bull relieved on appeal".
1852/53 marked against claim for exemption "Miss Bull".
Pigot & Co's Directory, 1842: M & F Bull, milliners & dressmakers, Wine Street.

402 BURGE, James, hatter.

1842/43 entry only.
Pigot & Co's Directory, 1842: James Burdge, hatter (manufacturer), Market Place.

403 BURROWS, William, newspaper proprietor.

Year	Amount returned	Commissioners' estimate	Final assessment
	£	£	£
1852/53	180	–	180
1853/54	180	250	250
1854/55	200	–	200
1855/56	–	200	200
1856/57	–	250	250
1857/58	–	250	250
1858/59	180	250	250
1859/60	180	250	250

Pigot & Co's Directory, 1842: William Burrows, Wiltshire Independent, Market Place.
Cross reference: Burrows, William, newspaper proprietor, Rowde 1842/43, 1846/47-1851/52.

404 BURT, Joseph, ironmonger.

1842/43, 1846/47-1849/50 returned and assessed £230.
1850/51-1852/53 returned and assessed £200.

1853/54 returned £230; estimated at £350; assessed at £300.
1854/55-1856/57 returned and assessed £300.
1857/58 returned and assessed £321.
1858/59 returned £320; assessed £300.
1859/60 returned £320; assessed £299.17.0.

1853/54 no appeal noted.
1859/60 assessment reduced by life assurance relief of £20.3.0.
Pigot & Co's Directory, 1842: Joseph Burt, ironmonger, brazier & tinman, St.John Street.

405 BUSH, William Robert, toyman, toy warehouse, stationer. [also BUSH, Jane]

1842/43, 1846/47 assessed in absence of return £100; exempt.
1847/48-1848/49 assessed in absence of return £60; exempt.
1849/50 returned and assessed £80; exempt.
1850/51-1851/52 assessed in absence of return £60; exempt.
1852/53 returned and assessed £135; exempt.
1853/54 returned £65; assessed £135.
1854/55-1855/56 returned and assessed £135.
1856/57-1859/60 assessed in absence of return £135.

1842/43, 1846/47-1849/50 toyman; 1850/51-1851/52 toy warehouse; 1853/54-1855/56 stationer & toy warehouse, etc; 1852/53, 1856/57-1859/60 stationer & toy warehouse.
1842/43, 1846/47-1847/48 William Robert Bush; 1848/49-1856/57 Mrs Bush; 1857/58-1859/60 Mrs Jane Bush.
Pigot & Co's Directory, 1842: William R. Bush, agent to Atlas Fire Office, Brittox.

406 BUSHELL, Ann, innkeeper [by comparison, Pelican]

1846/47-1850/51 assessed in absence of return £100; exempt.
1851/52 returned and assessed £70; exempt.
1852/53 returned £70; assessed £84; exempt.

1852/53 marked "now House (sic)".
Cross references: Howse, John, innkeeper, St.John; Joyce, William, innkeeper, St.John.

407 BUTCHER, Henry, agent to Sun Fire Office.

1842/43 returned and assessed £55.
1846/47-1847/48 returned and assessed £59.10.0.
1848/49 returned £56.9.11 marked "See Schedule E".
1849/50-1850/51 marked "under Schedule E".
1851/52 returned and assessed £62.
1852/53-1855/56 marked "Schedule E".

Note: income from public offices and employments was assessable under Schedule E.
Pigot & Co's Directory, 1842: Mr.Henry Butcher, gentry, agent to Sun Fire Office, St.John Street.

408 BUTCHER, Henry, Junior, assistant secretary to North Wilts Friendly Society.

1848/49 returned and assessed £50.
1849/50-1851/52 marked "Schedule E".

1851/52 Junior added.

409 CADBY, Robert, toyman.

1842/43 returned £26; assessed £50; exempt.
1846/47 assessed in absence of return £50; exempt.

Pigot & Co's Directory, 1842: Robert Cadby, toy dealer, Brittox.

410 CALF, Henry, bank clerk.

1852/53 returned and assessed £100; exempt.
1853/54 returned £97.14.6; assessed at £100; income proved at £98; exempt.
1854/55 assessed in absence of return £100; income proved at £90; exempt.
1855/56 no assessment made. [see Nursteed]
1856/57 assessed in absence of return £110.
1857/58 returned and assessed £126.13.4.
1858/59 returned £143.6.8; assessed £160.9.8.
1859/60 returned and assessed £150 and £15.

1852/53 marked "Knight, Henry now Calf, bankers clerk".
1858/59 marked "Query Schedule E agent".
Cross references: Calf, Henry, bank clerk, Nursteed; Knight, Henry, bank clerk, St.John.

411 CANNING, George Barnes, attorney, solicitor.

1842/43 recorded but entry deleted.
1846/47 returned and assessed £250.
1847/48-1848/49 assessed in absence of return £250.
1849/50 estimated at £150 but no assessment made.
1850/51 assessed in absence of return £120; exempt.

1842/43 attorney; 1846/47-1850/51 solicitor.
1842/43 assessed as partner with William Tanner.

1850/51 Cannings.
Cross reference: Tanner, William & Canning, George Barnes, solicitors, St.John.

412 CHANDLER, Henry, grocer.

1842/43 returned and assessed £170.
1846/47 returned and assessed £160.

1847/48 marked "late".
Pigot & Co's Directory, 1842: Henry Chandler, grocer & tea dealer, Market Place.

413 CHANDLER, John, innkeeper. [by comparison, White Hart]

1842/43 returned and assessed £140.
1846/47 assessed in absence of return £140.
1847/48 assessed in absence of return £75.

1847/48 marked "newly King".
1848/49 marked "now George King".
Pigot & Co's Directory, 1842: John Chandler, White Hart, Market Place.
Cross reference: King, George, innkeeper, St.John.

414 CLARK, John, veterinary surgeon.

1856/57–1857/58 recorded; no assessments made; exempt.

1855/56 marked "Hart, Thornton gone now Clarke (sic)".
1858/59 marked "left".
Cross references: Hart, Thornton, veterinary surgeon, St.John; Vincent, J.P., veterinary surgeon,
    St.John.

415 CLARK, William & Isaac, butchers. [also CLARK, Jacob]

Year	Amount returned	Commissioners' estimate	Final assessment
	£	£	£
1846/47	300	–	300
1847/48	–	300	300
1848/49	200	300	250
1849/50	250	300a	250
1850/51	250	–	250
1851/52	250	300	300
1852/53	250	300	200
1853/54	250	300	300

1854/55	250	300	300
1855/56	200	300	300
1856/57	300	–	300
1857/58	300	–	300
1858/59	300	–	300
1859/60	–	300	300

1842/43 Clarke
1842/43 Jacob Clarke recorded marked "return in St.Mary".
1848/49, 1852/53 no appeal noted.
1855/56-1859/60 Isaac Clark assessed sole.
Pigot & Co's Directory, 1842: Jacob Clark, butcher, Maryport Street and Brittox.
Cross reference: Clark, Jacob, butcher, St.Mary.

416 CLARKE, Charles, Professor of Music.

Year	Amount returned £	Commissioners' estimate £	Income proved £	Final assessment £
1849/50	–	150a	124.12.0	–
1850/51	125	–	125	–
1851/52	–	125	125	–
1852/53	120.2.0	–	120.2.0	–
1853/54	105	120	–	120
1854/55	108	120	–	120
1855/56	112	–	–	112
1856/57	120	–	–	120
1857/58	132	–	–	132
1858/59	130	–	–	130
1859/60	132	150	–	150

1852/53 includes assessment on lodger.

417 CLARKE, Henry Matthew, Esquire, foreign securities, furnished house, interest, New Jersey Bank.

Year	Amount returned £	Commissioners' estimate £	Final assessment £
1850/51	75	–	75
1851/52	75	–	75
1852/53	75NJ 40i	115	115
1853/54	75f	85	85
1854/55	9.19.4f	–	9.19.4
1855/56	9.18.0f	–	9.18.0
1856/57	14.10.4f	–	14.10.4

1857/58	12f	–	16.10.0
	4.10.0f		
1858/59	–	16.10.0f	56.16.0
		40h	
1859/60	16.16.0	56.16.0fh	56.16.0

Abbreviations: NJ, New Jersey Bank; i, interest; f, foreign securities; h, furnished house.
1848/49 marked "returns made in St.James, London".
1849/50-1851/52 marked "returns made in London".
Note: Henry Matthew Clarke served as Additional Commissioner.

418 CLARKE, Robert, chemist.

1842/43 returned and assessed £290.
1846/47-1847/48 returned and assessed £280.
1848/49 returned and assessed £270.
1849/50 returned and assessed £260.
1850/51 assessed in absence of return £260.
1851/52 returned and assessed £262.
1852/53-1855/56 returned and assessed £265.
1856/57 returned and assessed £260.
1857/58 returned and assessed £270.
1858/59 returned and assessed £265.
1859/60 assessed in absence of return £300.

1842/43, 1846/47-1849/50 Clark; 1850/51-1859/60 Clarke.
Pigot & Co's Directory, 1842: Robert Clark (*sic*), chemist & druggist, agent to Family Endowment Society, Market Place.

419 COOK, Charles, solicitor.

1846/47 entry only; marked "left town".

420 COOK, Mary, milliner.

1842/43 returned and assessed £100; exempt.
1846/47 assessed in absence of return £100; exempt.

Pigot & Co's Directory, 1842: Mary Cook, milliner & dressmaker, Market Place.

421 COOMBES, John, auctioneer. [also COOMBES & BRACHER; COOMBES & ELLEN]

1851/52-1852/53 assessed in absence of return £400.
1853/54-1855/56 returned and assessed £300.

1856/57–1859/60 assessed in absence of return £350.

1850/51 marked "Crockett, Joseph & Son, auctioneers, etc., now Coombes".
1851/52–1852/53 Coombes & Ellen; 1853/54–1855/56 John Coombes.
1856/57–1859/60 John Coombes & Bracher.
1854/55 "& Bracher" entered but deleted.
Cross reference: Crockett, Joseph & Son, auctioneers, St. John.

422 COOPER, Revd. James, clerk.

1858/59–1859/60 returned and assessed £100.

423 COPEMAN, W.W., bank manager.

1842/43 returned and assessed £150.
1846/47 returned £200; assessed £250.
1847/48 assessed in absence of return £250.

1847/48 marked "King late Copeman".
Pigot & Co's Directory, 1842: W.W. Copeman, manager, North Wilts Bank.
Cross reference: King, Edward, bank manager, St. John.

424 COUZENS, George, rope maker, manure merchant, brush warehouse.

Year	Amount returned £	Commissioners' estimate £	Income proved £	Final assessment £
1849/50	100	–	100	–
1850/51	100	–	100	–
1851/52	–	100	90	–
1852/53	100	–	100	–
1853/54	90	100	90	–
1854/55	90	–	90	–
1855/56	100m	–	–	100
1856/57	100	–	–	100
1857/58	120	150	–	150
1858/59	–	100	80	–
1859/60	–	100	71	–

1849/50–1854/55, 1856/57 rope maker; 1855/56 manure merchant; 1857/58–1859/60 rope maker & brush warehouse.
1855/56 initially returned £70 as rope maker and estimated at £90 but this assessment discharged and replaced by an assessment as manure merchant(m).
1856/57 [Notton, R.J., hatter] marked "now Couzens, brush warehouse"; 1857/58 marked "now Couzens, G.".
Cross reference: Notton, R.J., hatter, St. John.

425 COWARD, Thomas & Richard, grocers. [also COWARD, Charles]

1842/43 returned £160; assessed £200.
1846/47 assessed in absence of return £200; exemption claimed as partnership.

1842/43 Charles Coward assessed.
1847/48 marked "now Perry".
Pigot & Co's Directory, 1842: Charles Coward, grocer & tea dealer, High Street.
Cross reference: Perry, John & Co., grocers, St.John.
Note: Both Thomas and Richard Coward were eligible to claim exemption for 1846/47 since
their share of the assessment was £100 each and thus below the tax threshold.

426 COX, Jasper, ironmonger.

1842/43 assessed in absence of return £80; exempt.

Pigot & Co's Directory, 1842: Jasper Cox, ironmonger & cutler, Little Brittox.

427 COXHEAD, William Palmer, schoolmaster.

1856/57 assessed in absence of return £100; income proved at £99.6.8; exempt.
1857/58-1859/60 recorded; no assessments made; exempt.

This is an example of an early form of tax avoidance. On incomes of £100, tax was payable on
the whole amount. Incomes below this sum were eligible to be wholly relieved on a claim
for exemption. By agreeing with the employer to fix the salary at £99.6.8, no tax would be
payable. (Following evidence taken before the Select Committee on the Income and Property Tax, House of Commons. Parliamentary Papers. (1852) ix qq.3019, 3235).
Cross references: (similar instance of early legal tax avoidance) Anderson, T.W., solicitor's clerk,
St.John; Thorp, T.G., surveyor's clerk, Bedborough.

428 CRIPPS, Henry, chemist.

Year	Amount returned £	Commissioners' estimate £	Income proved £	Final assessment £
1853/54	72	–	–	–
1854/55	–	100	72	–
1855/56	–	72	72	–
1856/57	–	–	–	–
1857/58	–	110	–	–
1858/59	120	–	–	120
1859/60	130	–	–	130

1853/54 marked "late Bridges, chemist".
1858/59 marked "under letter Query".

1853/54, 1857/58 no assessment made; 1856/57 marked "exempt".
Cross references: Bridges, Fitzherbert, chemist, St.John; Hayward, Robert, chemist, St.John; Johnstone, Bayntun, chemist, St.John.

429 CROCKETT, Joseph & Son, auctioneers, appraisers.

1842/43 returned and assessed £500.
1846/47-1849/50 assessed in absence of return £400.
1850/51 returned £200; assessed £400; reduced to £200 on appeal.

1850/51-1851/52 marked "now Coombes".
Pigot & Co's Directory, 1842: Joseph Crockett, agent-land, &c., Bellevue; auctioneers, agent to Argus Life Office, Norwich Union Fire Office, Market Place.
Cross reference: Coombes, John, auctioneer, St.John.

430 CROOK, William, innkeeper. [by comparison Hare & Hounds]

1846/47 assessed in absence of return £100; exempt.
1847/48-1848/49 assessed in absence of return £150.
1849/50-1850/51 returned and assessed £151.

1850/51 marked "now Millwaters" by 11 October or 30 November 1850.
Cross references: Kite, Thomas, innkeeper, St.John; Millwaters, Nathaniel, innkeeper, St.John.

431 CRUDGE, William, painter & glazier.

1858/59 returned nil; no assessment made.
1859/60 returned £82.14.2; assessed £100; income proved at £82; exempt.

Cross reference: Crudge, William, painter & glazier, St.Mary.

432 CUNNINGTON, William & Sons, wine merchants.

Year	Amount returned £	Commissioners' estimate £	Final assessment £
1842/43	270	–	270
1846/47	250	–	250
1847/48	–	250	250
1848/49	290	–	290
1849/50	–	250	250
1850/51	250	–	250
1851/52	275	–	275
1852/53	320	–	320

1853/54	–	400	400
1854/55	–	400	400
1855/56	385	–	385
1856/57	520	–	520
1857/58	540	–	540
1858/59	540	–	540
1859/60	540	–	540

1842/43, 1846/47 William Cunnington & Sons; 1847/48-1850/51 William Cunnington; 1851/52-1855/56 Messrs Cunnington; 1856/57-1857/58 Messrs William Cunnington & Sons; 1858/59-1859/60 Messrs William Cunnington & Co.
1859/60 "Bottle" noted but substituted by "Old Town Hall".
Pigot & Co's Directory, 1842: William Cunnington & Sons, wine & spirit merchants, Wine Street.
Cross reference: Cunnington, William, woolstapler, Week.

433 DANGERFIELD, Isaiah, fishmonger.

Year	Amount returned £	Commissioners' estimate £	Income proved £	Final assessment £
1842/43	90	150	100	–
1846/47	65	90	–	90
1847/48	65	100	–	100
1848/49	70	100	–	100
1849/50	70	100	–	100
1850/51	50	120a	–	100
1851/52	40	100	–	100
1852/53	50	80	–	80
1853/54	50	100	–	100
1854/55	40	100	–	100
1855/56	40	100	–	100
1856/57	40	100	–	100
1857/58	50	100	–	100
1858/59	50	100	–	100
1859/60	40	100	–	100

1842/43 no appeal noted.
1856/57 marked "& innkeeper" but deleted.
Pigot & Co's Directory, 1842: Isaiah Dangerfield, fishmonger, Brittox.

434 DAVIES, Elizabeth, innkeeper, Bear. [also DAVIES, Edward]

1842/43, 1846/47-1849/50 returned and assessed £150.
1850/51 assessed in absence of return £150.
1851/52 returned and assessed £150.

1852/53 returned £150; assessed £200.
1853/54–1855/56 returned and assessed £200.
1856/57 returned £200; assessed £260.
1857/58–1858/59 returned and assessed £260.
1859/60 returned £260; assessed £400.

1842/43, 1846/47–1850/51 Edward Davies; 1851/52–1859/60 Elizabeth Davies.
1842/43 Davis.
Bear recorded 1856/57.
Pigot & Co's Directory, 1842: Edward Davies, Bear (posting house), Market Place.

435 DAVIS, Arthur, printer. [later DAVIS GILLMAN]

1852/53 estimated £80 but no assessment made.
1853/54 returned £50; assessed £70.
1854/55 returned and assessed £100.
1855/56 recorded but no assessment made.

1851/52 marked "C.E.Sartain now Davis, A., printer".
1852/53 marked "late Sartain".
1855/56 Davis Gillman.
Cross reference: Sartain, C.E., printer, St.John.

436 DERHAM, James, shoemaker.

1842/43 entry only.
Pigot & Co's Directory, 1842: James Derham, boot & shoe maker, Little Brittox.

437 DEVIZES IMPROVEMENT COMMISSIONERS

1847/48 recorded but no assessment made.

438 DEVIZES TURNPIKE

1847/48 recorded but no assessment made.

439 DODMAN, John, shopman.

1842/43, 1846/47–1848/49 assessed in absence of return £85; exempt.
1849/50 assessed in absence of return £80; exempt.
1850/51–1852/53 assessed in absence of return £50; exempt.

Pigot & Co's Directory, 1842: possibly Martha Dodman, toy dealer, Little Brittox.
1853/54 marked "gone".

440 DOWSE, Thomas, miller.

1849/50 assessed in absence of return £75; exempt.
1850/51 returned £50; assessed £60; exempt.

1849/50 Douse (*sic*) Thomas, miller, written above Haines, Daniel, miller.
1850/51 marked "Dowse, Thomas late Haines, miller".
Cross reference: Haines, Daniel, miller, St.John.

441 DREDGE, Joseph R & S., brewers, maltsters. [also DREDGE, R & S]

1842/43 returned £382; assessed £360.
1846/47-1847/48 returned and assessed £382.

1846/47-1847/48 R & S Dredge assessed.
1846/47-1847/48 brewers.
Pigot & Co's Directory, 1842: Joseph Dredge & Co., brewers, maltsters, Bridewell Street.

442 DRING, George, clerk.

1842/43 assessed in absence of return £120; exempt.
1846/47 returned and assessed £139; exempt.
1847/48 returned and assessed £148; exempt.
1848/49 assessed in absence of return £140; exempt.
1849/50-1852/53 returned and assessed £140.
1853/54 returned and assessed £135.18.3.
1854/55 returned and assessed £136.
1855/56-1859/60 returned and assessed £140.

1853/54 marked "£140 less £4.1.9 insurance".
1854/55-1855/56 assessments include interest.
Pigot & Co's Directory, 1842: George Dring, agent to Reliance Fire Office, Registrar of Marriages, St.John Street.

443 DROVER, John, shopman.

1842/43 assessed in absence of return £100; income proved £135; exempt.
1846/47-1850/51 assessed in absence of return £100; exempt.

444 DYMOND, Thomas, tailor.

Year	Amount returned	Commissioners' estimate	Final assessment
	£	£	£
1842/43	200	275	275
1846/47	205	275	275

1847/48	195	275	275
1848/49	160	275	170
1849/50	160	180	200
1850/51	175	200	200
1851/52	170	200	200
1852/53	170	200	200
1853/54	160	200	200
1854/55	165	200	200
1855/56	170	200	200

1848/49 no appeal noted.
1849/50 £180 estimated by Additional Commissioners; increased to £200 by General Commissioners; no appeal noted.
1856/57-1857/58 marked "now Gibbs" or "see Gibbs".
Pigot & Co's Directory, 1842: Thomas Dymond, tailor & draper, High Street.
Cross reference: Gibbs, Decimus, tailor, St.John.

445 EDMOND, Thomas, pork butcher.

1852/53 returned and assessed £100; exempt.
1853/54 returned £77.8.0; assessed £100; income proved £78; exempt.
1854/55 returned £100; income proved £90; exempt.
1855/56-1856/57 returned and assessed £100.
1857/58 assessed in absence of return £100; income proved £60; exempt.
1858/59-1859/60 recorded; no assessments made; exempt.

446 EDMONDS, R & W, French teachers, schoolmasters.

1846/47-1847/48 assessed in absence of return £106.11.9; exempt.
1850/51 assessed in absence of return £100; exempt.
1851/52 assessed in absence of return £95 each; income proved £194.13.4; exempt.
1852/53 returned and assessed £201.15.2; exempt.
1853/54 recorded but no assessment made.

1846/47-1847/48 R.Edmonds; 1850/51-1853/54 R & W Edmonds.
1848/49 marked "See St.James".
1854/55 marked "gone".
Pigot & Co's Directory, 1842: E.Edmonds, mistress, Infants' School, Sheep Street.
Cross references: Edmonds, R, French teacher, St.Mary, 1842/43;
Edmonds, Richard, teacher of French, Bedborough, 1848/49-1849/50.

447 ELLIOTT, Revd. Richard, schoolmaster, dissenting minister. [also ELLIOTT, Frances]

1842/43, 1846/47 returned and assessed £500.
1847/48-1848/49 returned and assessed £400.

1849/50-1850/51 assessed in absence of return £400.
1851/52 returned and assessed £400.
1852/53 returned and assessed £300.
1853/54 returned and assessed £50 school and £40 interest; assessment deleted.

1842/43, 1846/47-1850/51 schoolmaster & dissenting minister; 1851/52-1852/53 school-master.
1852/53 marked "dead".
1853/54 Frances Elliott, schoolmistress, assessed.
Pigot & Co's Directory, 1842: Revd. Richard Elliott, Long Street.
Pigot & Co's Directory, 1842: Fanny Elliott, boarding school, Long Street.

448 ELLIS, Edward, wine merchant's clerk.

1855/56-1856/57 entry only; 1857/58 marked "gone".

449 ELLIS, George Hackett, wine merchant's clerk.

1853/54 estimate £70 entered but no assessment made.
1854/55 returned and assessed £70; exempt.
1855/56 assessed in absence of return £70; exempt.
1856/57 recorded; no assessment made; exempt.

1857/58 marked "see Giddings & Ellis".
Cross reference: Giddings, Edwin & Ellis, George, wine merchants, St.John.

450 ERLE, Rebecca, haberdasher. [also EARLE, Henry]

1842/43, 1846/47-1848/49 assessed in absence of return £130; exempt.
1849/50 returned and assessed £100' exempt.
1850/51-1851/52 assessed in absence of return £100; 1851/52 income proved £120; exempt.
1852/53 returned and assessed £140; exempt.
1853/54 returned £120; assessed £150.
1854/55 returned and assessed £150.
1855/56 returned £95; assessed £150.
1856/57-1859/60 assessed in absence of return £150.

1842/43 Henry Earle; 1846/47-1859/60 Rebecca Erle.
1842/43 shopkeeper; 1846/47-1859/60 haberdasher.
Pigot & Co's Directory, 1842: Rebecca Earle, haberdasher & baby linen, Wine Street.

451 EVANS, George, schoolmaster.

Year	Amount returned £	Commissioners' estimate £	Income proved £	Final assessment £
1842/43	149	150	77.6.6	–
1846/47	130	–	130	–
1847/48	–	200	130	–
1848/49	–	120	120	–
1849/50	130	–	130	–
1850/51	–	130	130	–
1851/52	–	130	135	–
1852/53	130	–	130	–
1853/54	125	–	–	125
1854/55	125	–	–	125
1855/56	68	100	–	100
1856/57	–	100	–	100
1857/58	100	–	–	100
1858/59	96	–	–	96
1859/60	96	–	–	96

Pigot & Co's Directory, 1842: George Evans, Bridewell Street.

452 EVERETT, Dr William Giffard, physician.

1853/54-1859/60 returned and assessed £500.

Pigot & Co's Directory, 1842: William G. Everett, physician, Albion Place.
Cross reference: Everett, William Giffard, physician, St. Mary, prior to 1853/54.

453 EVERINGHAM, Henry, clerk.

1842/43 assessed in absence of return £100; exempt.
1846/47-1847/48 assessed in absence of return £125; exempt.

454 FALKNER, Richard, bank manager.

1842/43, 1846/47-1859/60 returned and assessed £400.

455 FERRIS, John, clothes cleaner.

1842/43, 1846/47-1848/49 assessed in absence of return £80; exempt.
1849/50 assessed in absence of return £50; exempt.

456 FOSTER, Misses, schoolmistresses.

1842/43, 1846/47-1849/50 assessed in absence of return £40; exempt.

1846/47-1849/50 Miss Foster assessed sole.
Pigot & Co's Directory, 1842: S.Foster, day school, Long Street.
Pigot & Co's Directory, 1842: Eliza Foster, milliner & dressmaker, Long Street.

457 FOX, John James & Co., drapers.

Year	Amount returned £	Commissioners' estimate £	Final assessment £
1842/43	410	–	420
1846/47	350	–	350
1847/48	–	350	350
1848/49	–	350	350
1849/50	350	–	350
1850/51	300	–	300
1851/52	300	–	300
1852/53	300	–	300
1853/54	350	–	350
1854/55	300	350	300
1855/56	–	300	150
1856/57	–	300a	150
1857/58	200	–	200
1858/59	200	300	300
1859/60	200	300	300

1842/43 returned £507 including rent £55; profits computed at £465 less rent £55; apparent arithmetical error in assessment.
1854/55, 1855/56 no appeal noted.
Pigot & Co's Directory, 1842: John James Fox & Co., linen & wool drapers, manufacturers of striped linseys and blankets, agent to Alliance Fire Office, St.John Street.

458 FRANCIS, Thomas, cordwainer.

1842/43, 1846/47-1849/50 assessed in absence of return £40; exempt.

Pigot & Co's Directory, 1842: Thomas Francis, cordwainer, Chequer.

459 FRANCIS, William, tailor.

1842/43, 1846/47-1849/50 assessed in absence of return £100; exempt.

Pigot & Co's Directory, 1842: William Francis, tailor, St.John Street.

460 FRASER, William, tailor.

1855/56–1856/57 returned and assessed £100.
1857/58 assessed in absence of return £150.
1858/59–1859/60 returned £100; assessed £150.

461 FRAYLING, Edward, innkeeper, White Swan.

1846/47–1849/50 assessed in absence of return £100; exempt.

1849/50 marked "now Wells, innkeeper, White Swan".
Cross references: Bourne, Richard, innkeeper, St.John; Jenkins, David, innkeeper, St.John; Wells, Joseph, innkeeper, St.John.

462 GIBBS, Decimus, tailor.

1856/57 returned £172; assessed £200.
1857/58–1858/59 returned £175; assessed £200.
1859/60 returned £170; assessed £250.

1856/57–1857/58 marked "late Dymond, tailor.
Cross reference: Dymond, Thomas, tailor, St.John.

463 GIBBS, John.

1842/43 name only entered.

464 GIDDINGS, George, grocer, chemist, bookseller. [also GIDDINGS, Edwin]

Year	Amount returned £	Commissioners' estimate £	Income proved £	Final assessment £
1842/43	81.16.6	–	–	81.16.6
1846/47	100	–	–	100
1847/48	95	–	–	95
1848/49	95	–	–	95
1849/50	100	–	–	100
1850/51	95	–	–	95
1851/52	100	–	–	100
	–	50c	50	–
1852/53	100	–	–	100
	–	50c	50	–
1853/54	35.17.2	100	–	100
1854/55	150	200	–	125

| 1855/56 | – | 150 | – | 150 |
| 1856/57 | 147 | 150 | – | 150 |

Abbreviations: c, chemist.

1842/43, 1846/47-1852/53 George Giddings; 1853/54-1856/57 Edwin Giddings.

1851/52-1852/53 Giddings, chemist, assessed and exemption claimed; seemingly Edwin Giddings by comparison with 1853/54 entry.

1842/43, 1846/47-1852/53 grocer; 1853/54-1854/55 grocer & chemist; 1855/56 grocer, chemist & bookseller; 1856/57 grocer & chemist.

1857/58-1858/59 marked "business given up".

Note: Edwin Giddings set up business with George Ellis, a wine merchant's clerk to form the wine merchants business of Giddings & Ellis.

Pigot & Co's Directory, 1842: George Giddings, wine & spirit merchant, grocer & tea dealer, Brittox.

Cross reference: Giddings & Ellis, wine merchants, St.John.

465 GIDDINGS, Edwin, & ELLIS, George, wine merchants.

1857/58-1858/59 returned £250; assessed £300.
1859/60 returned £300; assessed £350.

[Mackrell, Henry] 1856/57 marked "now Giddings & Ellis".

Note: Edwin Giddings set up business with George Ellis, a wine merchant's clerk to form the wine merchants business of Giddings & Ellis.

Cross references: Giddings, George [for Edwin], grocer & chemist, St.John; Ellis, George Hackett, wine merchant's clerk, St.John; Mackrell, Henry, wine merchant, St.John.

466 GILBERT, Henry, horse breaker.

1852/53 returned and assessed £64; exempt.
1853/54 returned £60; assessed £80 but no assessment made; exempt.
1854/55-1855/56 assessed in absence of return £80; exempt.
1856/57-1859/60 recorded; no assessments made; exempt.

467 GILBERT, Henry, solicitor.

1842/43 returned and assessed £100.

Pigot & Co's Directory, 1842: Henry Gilbert, attorney, St.John Street.

468 GILBERT, William, ironmonger.

1842/43 returned £100; assessed £200.
1846/47 returned £52; assessed £100; exempt.

1847/48 assessed in absence of return £100; exempt.
1848/49 returned and assessed £86; exempt.

1848/49 marked "Gilbert, William late now W.Hayward, ironmonger".
Pigot & Co's Directory, 1842: William Gilbert, ironmonger, Market Place.
Cross reference: Hayward, William, ironmonger, St.John.

469 GILLMAN, Charles, reporter, bookseller, printer, dissenting preacher.

1854/55 returned £95; assessed £100; income proved £95; exempt.
1855/56-1858/59 assessed in absence of return £100.
1859/60 assessed in absence of return £120.

1854/55 reporter & dissenting preacher; 1855/56 reporter; 1856/57 reporter & bookseller; 1857/58-1859/60 bookseller.
1854/55 marked "charged in Week".
1854/55 Gillman was also assessed in Week on £100 proving income at £90.
Cross reference: Gillman, Charles, reporter, Week.

470 GRANTHAM, Henry, schoolmaster. [also GRANTHAM, Mary, schoolmistress]

1842/43 returned and assessed £50 (Henry Grantham).
1842/43 assessed in absence of return £100; exempt (Mary Grantham).
1846/47-1849/50 assessed in absence of return £100; exempt (Henry Grantham).

Pigot & Co's Directory, 1842: Henry David Grantham, boarding school, Long Street.
Pigot & Co's Directory, 1842: Mary Grantham, ladies' boarding school, Long Street.

471 GREEN, William, auctioneer.

1842/43 assessed in absence of return £50; exempt.
1846/47 assessed in absence of return £130; exempt.
1847/48 estimated in absence of return £150 but entry deleted.

1847/48 marked "see St.Mary".
Cross reference: Green, William, auctioneer, St.Mary.

472 GREENLAND, Robert, bricklayer.

1842/43 returned £25; assessed £50; exempt.
1846/47-1849/50 assessed in absence of return £50; exempt.

Pigot & Co's Directory, 1842: Robert Greenland, bricklayer, Bridewell Street.

473 GRIFFIN, John, printer.

1842/43 assessed in absence of return £150; income proved at £141.14.0; exempt.

Pigot & Co's Directory, 1842: John Griffin, bookseller, stationer & printer, music seller, library, agent to Equitable Life Office, Brittox.

474 GUY, Edward Evans, watchmaker.

Year	Amount returned £	Commissioners' estimate £	Income proved £	Final assessment £
1842/43	–	100	100	–
1846/47	–	100	100	–
1847/48	–	100	100	–
1848/49	–	100	100	–
1849/50	–	80	80	–
1850/51	–	80	80	–
1851/52	–	80	102	–
1852/53	100	–	102.10.0	–
1853/54	85.6.8	100	85.6.8	–
1854/55	–	85	85	–
1855/56	–	85	85	–
1856/57	–	–	–	–
1857/58	–	100	–	100
1858/59	–	100	–	100
1859/60	80	100	–	100

1842/43, 1846/47-1859/60 watchmaker (tinman entered but deleted 1842/43).
1856/57 no assessment made; exempt.
Pigot & Co's Directory, 1842: Bush & Guy, watch & clock makers, Brittox.

475 GUY, John, ironmonger, etc.

1853/54 returned £77.7.0 but no assessment made; exempt.
1854/55-1855/56 assessed in absence of return £70; exempt.
1856/57-1859/60 recorded; no assessments made; exempt.

Pigot & Co's Directory, 1842: John Guy, brazier & tinman, St.John Street.

476 HADOW, James Remington, property out of Great Britain, interest.

1858/59 returned and assessed £1500p, £150i.
1859/60 returned and assessed £850p, £185i.

Abbreviations: p, property out of Great Britain; i, interest.

477 HAINES, Daniel, miller, carpenter, builder.

1842/43 returned and assessed £140.
1846/47 returned and assessed £150.
1847/48 assessed in absence of return £150.
1848/49 assessed in absence of return £50.

1842/43 builder; 1846/47-1847/48 carpenter & miller; 1848/49 miller & farmer.
1850/51 marked "Dowse, Thomas late Haines, miller".
Pigot & Co's Directory, 1842: Daniel Haines, carpenter & builder, timber merchant, Long Street.
Cross reference: Dowse, Thomas, miller, St. John.

478 HANCOCK, Samuel, dyer.

1842/43 returned £25; assessed £50; exempt.

479 HANN, Thomas B., commission agent, hop merchant.

1853/54 returned and assessed £80.15.0; exempt.
1854/55-1855/56 assessed in absence of return £100.
1856/57 returned and assessed £100.
1857/58-1858/59 assessed in absence of return £100.
1859/60 returned and assessed £100.

1853/54-1855/56 commission agent; 1856/57-1859/60 commission agent & hop merchant.

480 HARRISON, John.

1842/43 name only entered.

481 HART, Samuel, watchmaker.

1842/43 returned and assessed £230.
1846/47-1849/50 returned £150; assessed £210.
1850/51-1855/56 returned £150; assessed £200.
1856/57 returned £150; assessed £260.
1857/58-1859/60 returned £200; assessed £275.

Pigot & Co's Directory, 1842: Samuel Hart, watch & clock maker, Brittox.

482 HART, Thornton, veterinary surgeon.

1852/53-1854/55 returned and assessed £150.

1852/53 marked "late Vincent".
1855/56 marked "gone now Clarke (*sic*)".
Cross references: Clark, John, veterinary surgeon, St.John; Vincent, J.P., veterinary surgeon, St.John.

483 HAYWARD, John Edward, solicitor.

1848/49-1849/50 returned and assessed £200.
1850/51 returned and assessed £170.
1851/52-1854/55 returned and assessed £100.
1855/56 returned £100; assessed £200.
1856/57 returned and assessed £150.
1857/58 returned and assessed £160.
1858/59-1859/60 returned and assessed £200.

484 HAYWARD, Robert, chemist.

1842/43 returned and assessed £110.
1846/47 returned £50; assessed £100.
1847/48 assessed in absence of return £100.
1848/49 returned and assessed £100; exempt.

1848/49 marked "now Johnstone, Baynton (*sic*), chemist".
Pigot & Co's Directory, 1842: Robert Hayward, chemist & druggist, St.John Street.
Cross references: Bridges, Fitzherbert, chemist, St.John; Cripps, Henry, chemist, St.John; Johnstone, Bayntun, chemist, St.John.

485 HAYWARD, William, ironmonger.

1849/50 recorded but no assessment made.
1850/51 assessed in absence of return £120.
1851/52 assessed in absence of return £120; income proved at £100; exempt.
1852/53 returned and assessed £100.
1853/54 returned £96 and £40 interest (latter deleted); assessed £100; income proved at £136 but assessment made £136.
1854/55 returned £100; assessed £150; reduced by General Commissioners to £125.
1855/56 -1856/57 returned £100; assessed £125.
1857/58-1859/60 returned and assessed £125.

1848/49 marked "Gilbert, William late now W.Hayward, ironmonger".
Cross reference: Gilbert, William, ironmonger, St.John.

486 HAYWOOD, Thomas, governor of new prison.

1854/55 entry only marked "dead".

Pigot & Co's Directory, 1842: Thomas Haywood, Governor, House of Correction, Bath Road. Cross reference: Alexander, Alfred, Governor of New Prison, St.John.

487 HAZELAND, Abraham, coal merchant, trustee.

1842/43 returned and assessed £500.

1842/43 assessed as coal merchant and trustee for Jemima, Adam, Matthew and John surviving children of the late Matthew Hazeland.
Pigot & Co's Directory, 1842: Abraham Hazeland, salt & coal merchant & dealer, New Park Street.

488 HILL, John, plasterer.

1842/43, 1846/47-1849/50 assessed in absence of return £50; exempt.

1849/50 Hills.
Pigot & Co's Directory, 1842: John Hill, plasterer & slater, Long Street.

489 HILL, Richard, painter.

1858/59 returned nil; no assessment made.
1859/60 returned £75 but entry deleted.

1858/59 marked "query trade painter".
Cross reference: Hill, Richard, plumber, painter, St. Mary.

490 HILLIER, Martha.

1842/43 name only entered.

491 HILLS, Philip George, writing clerk, attorney's clerk.

1842/43 returned and assessed £70; exempt.
1846/47-1848/49 assessed in absence of return £70; exempt.
1849/50 assessed in absence of return £80; exempt.

1842/43, 1846/47-1847/48 writing clerk; 1848/49-1849/50 attorney's clerk.

492 HITCHMAN, James, hatter.

1842/43 assessed in absence of return £75; exempt.

Pigot & Co's Directory, 1842: James Hitchman, hatter & hosier, Brittox.

493 HOARE, George, chemist.

1842/43 returned £107; assessed £150; income proved at £107; exempt.

Pigot & Co's Directory, 1842: George Hoare, chemist, apothecary & surgeon, Market Place.

494 HOBBS, William, draper.

1842/43 assessed in absence of return £122; exempt.
1846/47 returned and assessed £170.
1847/48 returned and assessed £165.
1848/49 returned £150; assessed £165.

1849/50 marked "Lenthall & Co., late Hobbs".
Cross references: Lenthall, James & Co., drapers, St.John; Pope, John, linen draper, St.John.

495 HONEYWELL, William, shopkeeper. [also HONEYWELL, Mrs.]

1842/43 assessed in absence of return £150; income proved at £129; exempt.

1846/47 Mrs.Honeywell entered but deleted.
Pigot & Co's Directory, 1842: William Honywill, clothes dealer, linen & woollen draper, hatter, Brittox.

496 HOOK, Charles, confectioner, glass dealer.

1842/43 returned £185; assessed £200.
1846/47 returned and assessed £200.
1847/48 assessed in absence of return £200.

1842/43, 1846/47 confectioner; 1847/48 confectioner & glass dealer.
1848/49 marked "now Misses".
Pigot & Co's Directory, 1842: Charles Hook, baker, confectioner, china, glass, etc., dealer, Brittox
Cross reference: Hook, Eliza and Emma, confectioners, etc., St.John.

497 HOOK, Eliza & Emma, schoolmistresses, confectioners, glass dealers, Berlin wool.

Year	Amount returned £	Commissioners' estimate £	Income proved £	Final assessment £
Partnership				
1842/43				
Eliza	113.16.9	–	113.16.9	–
Emma	113.16.9	–	113.16.9	–
1846/47				
Eliza	100	–	100	–
Emma	100	–	100	–
1847/48				
Composite	–	–	–	–
1848/49				
Composite	175	250	250	–
1849/50				
Composite	200	–	200	–
1850/51				
Composite	–	200	200	–
1851/52				
Eliza	75	–	75	–
Emma	75	–	75	–
1852/53				
Eliza	75	–	–	75
Emma	75	–	–	75

1842/43 schoolmistresses; 1846/47 no occupation recorded; 1847/48 marked "Berlin wool"; 1848/49-1850/51 confectioners & glass dealers; 1851/52 confectioners; 1852/53 confectioners, etc.; 1847/48 recorded but no assessment made. Berlin wool work was a kind of tapestry. [1848/49-1849/50 Eliza & Emma Hook were assessed as worsted warehouse in St.Mary].
1848/49 marked "Charles now Misses Hook, confectioners & glass dealers".
1853/54 "Misses" deleted, Miss (Eliza) Hook assessed sole.

Eliza Hook sole

1853/54-1859/60 returned and assessed £150.

1853/54-1855/56 Miss Hook; 1856/57-1859/60 Miss Eliza Hook.
Pigot & Co's Directory, 1842: Eliza Hook, day school, St.John Street
Cross references: Hook, Eliza & Emma, worsted warehouse, St.Mary; Hook, Charles, confectioner, glass dealer, St.John.

498 HOOK, Mary & Theodosia, china warehouse.

1842/43 entry only.
1846/47 Mary Hook, sole entry deleted.

499 HOOPER, ———, grocer, etc.

1859/60 assessed in absence of return £150.

1859/60 marked "late Lyne, grocer".
Cross references: Lavington, Samuel, grocer, St.John; Long, John, grocer, St.John; Lyne, Thomas William, grocer, St.John.

500 HOPKINS, Thomas, linen draper.

1851/52 assessed in absence of return £119.10.0; exempt.
1852/53 returned £114; assessed £150; income proved below £150 but no sum disclosed; exempt.
1853/54 returned £107; assessed £150.
1854/55-1855/56 returned and assessed £150.
1856/57 returned £120; assessed £150.
1857/58-1858/59 returned and assessed £150.
1859/60 assessed in absence of return £150.

501 HOUSE, Robert, grocer.

1848/49-1849/50 assessed in absence of return £120; 1848/49 exempt.
1851/52 assessed in absence of return £115; exempt.
1853/54 returned £109.6.0; assessed £120.
1854/55 assessed in absence of return £120.
1855/56 returned £93.5.0; assessed £120.
1856/57 assessed in absence of return £120.
1857/58 returned and assessed £170.
1858/59-1859/60 returned £135; assessed £170.

1850/51, 1852/53 not recorded
1852/53 Howse.

502 HOWITT, George Armstrong, clerk of works, etc.

1852/53 returned and assessed £136.10.0 and £5 interest; exempt.
1853/54 returned and assessed £130.

1854/55 assessed in absence of return £130; income proved £77; exempt.
1855/56 assessed in absence of return £77; exempt.
1856/57 assessed in absence of return £100; reduced to £90 on appeal; exempt.

1857/58 marked "gone".

503 HOWSE, John, innkeeper, Pelican.

1852/53 returned £70; income proved £84; exempt.
1853/54 returned £82; exempt.
1854/55 returned £150.
1855/56 returned £100; assessed £150.
1856/57-1869/60 returned £100; assessed £160.

1852/53 marked "Bushell, Ann now House (sic)".
1853/54 marked "John Howse late Bushell".
Cross references: Bushell, Ann, innkeeper, St.John; Joyce, William, innkeeper, St.John.

504 HUBAND, John, shopkeeper.

1842/43, 1846/47-1849/50 assessed in absence of return £120; exempt.

Pigot & Co's Directory, 1842: John Huband, haberdasher, Market Place.

505 HULBERT, Henry Hale, attorney. [also HULBERT, Charles]

1842/43 returned £210; assessed £300.
1846/47-1849/50 returned and assessed £250.
1850/51-1852/53 returned and assessed £260.
1853/54-1856/57 returned and assessed £270.
1857/58 returned and assessed £300.
1858/59-1859/60 returned and assessed £350.

1842/43 Charles and Henry Hale Hulbert; 1846/47-1859/60 Henry Hale Hulbert.
1842/43 attornies; 1846/47-1859/60 attorney.
Pigot & Co's Directory, 1842: Charles & Henry Hale Hulbert, attorneys, St.John Street.

506 HUMBY, Frederick Peter, innkeeper, Antelope.

1855/56 assessed in absence of return £50.

1857/58 marked "now Thomas Brown", "Antelope".
Cross references: Brown, Thomas, innkeeper, St. John; Humby, Frederick Peter, Southbroom Brewery, Week; McEwin, Edwin, innkeeper, St.John. Ransom, William, innkeeper, St.John;

507 HUMBY, James, bank clerk, bank manager. [by comparison, North Wilts Bank]

1852/53 returned £120; assessment wholly discharged on appeal.
1853/54 assessed in absence of return £130.
1856/57 returned £220; no assessment made, Schedule E.
1857/58–1858/59 Schedule E.

1852/53–1853/54 bank clerk; 1856/57–1858/59 bank manager.
1854/55 marked "returned in Week (see assessor's note)".
1857/58 by note under Edward King, manager of North Wilts Bank, insurance commission transferred to Mr.Humby on King's removal in 1856/57.
1859/60 marked "gone".
Cross reference: Humby, James, bank clerk, Week; King, Edward, bank manager, St.John.

508 HUTCHINS, James, town crier.

1848/49–1849/50 assessed in absence of return £80; exempt.

509 JENKINS, David, innkeeper, White Swan.

1854/55 assessed in absence of return £100; income proved at £50; exempt.
1855/56–1858/59 assessed in absence of return £100.
1859/60 returned and assessed £100.

1854/55 marked "Wells, Joseph now Jenkins innkeeper".
Cross references: Bourne, Richard, innkeeper, St.John; Frayling, Edward, innkeeper, St.John; Wells, Joseph, innkeeper, St.John.

510 JENKINS, Mrs Jane, confectioner.

1849/50–1852/53 assessed in absence of return £60; exempt.
1853/54 returned and assessed £85; exempt.
1854/55 assessed in absence of return £85; exempt.

1849/50–1850/51 marked "late White, confectioner".
1855/56 marked "Taylor, Robert late Jenkins, confectioner".
Cross references: Taylor, Robert, confectioner, St.John; White, George, confectioner, St.John.

511 JOHNSTONE, Bayntun, chemist.

1849/50–1852/53 assessed in absence of return £100; exempt.

1849/50 marked "late Robert Hayward, chemist".
1852/53 marked "now Bridges, chemist".
Cross references: Bridges, Fitzherbert, chemist, St.John; Cripps, Henry, chemist, St.John; Hayward, Robert, chemist, St.John.

512 JONES, John, schoolmaster.

1859/60 returned £99; assessed £100.

513 JONES, S.H., draper.

1842/43 returned and assessed £164.5.8.
1846/47-1847/48 returned and assessed £170.

Pigot & Co's Directory, 1842: S.H.Jones, linen & wool draper, Brittox.

514 JONES, William Blackwell, law stationer, innkeeper, Crown.

Year	Amount returned	Commissioners' estimate	Final assessment
	£	£	£
1842/43	173	–	173
1846/47	86	–	86
1847/48	90	–	90
1848/49	80	–	80
1849/50	45	–	45
1850/51	42	–	42
1851/52	44	–	44
1852/53	72	–	72
1853/54	89	–	89
1854/55	84	–	84
1855/56	82	–	82
	200i	–	200
1856/57	68	–	68
	200i	–	200

Abbreviations: i, innkeeper.
1855/56 marked "W.B.Jones late Palmer innkeeper".
1856/57 marked "Crown".
1857/58 marked "dead" "innkeeper Crown now Charles Rhodes Plank".
Pigot & Co's Directory, 1842: William B. Jones, law stationer & accountant, agent to Clerical, Medical & General Life Office, St.John Street.
Cross references: King, George, innkeeper, St.John; Palmer, Benjamin, innkeeper, St.John; Plank, Charles Rhodes, innkeeper, St.John.

515 JOYCE, William, innkeeper, [by comparison, Pelican]

1842/43 assessed in absence of return £150.

Assessment made under letter.
Pigot & Co's Directory, 1842: William Joyce, innkeeper, Pelican, Market Place.
Cross reference: Bushell, Ann, innkeeper, St.John; Howse, John, innkeeper, St John.

516 KERSLEY, -, curate.

1855/56 entry only; marked "gone".

517 KING, Edward, bank manager, commission on insurance agency. [by comparison, North Wilts Bank]

1848/49 estimate in absence of return £250 deleted and marked "returned under Schedule E".
1850/51 returned £230 but noted Schedule E.
1851/52-1852/53 recorded and noted Schedule E.
1853/54 returned and assessed £42 commission.
1854/55 returned and assessed £30 commission.
1855/56 assessed in absence of return £30 commission.

1848/49 marked "King late Copeman, bank manager".
1849/50 no entry.
1856/57 marked "removed to Pall Mall"
1857/58 marked "transferred to Mr Calf and Mr Humby".
Note: Copeman was manager of the North Wilts Bank and was succeeded by King. The level of salary is consistent with other branch managers in Devizes. The transfer of the insurance agency to Henry Calf and James Humby denotes that both were employees of the same bank, Humby succeeding King as manager. Employees of public concerns were assessed under Schedule E.
Cross references: Calf, Henry, bank clerk, St.John; Copeman, W.W., bank manager, St.John; Humby, James, bank manager, St.John.

518 KING, George, innkeeper, corndealer, coachmaster, Crown and White Hart. [also KING, Elizabeth Gale]

1842/43 returned and assessed £350.
1846/47 assessed in absence of return £350.
1847/48-1849/50 returned and assessed £425.
1850/51 assessed in absence of return £425.
1851/52 returned and assessed £350.
1852/53-1853/54 returned and assessed £300.

1842/43, 1846/47-1851/52 George King; 1852/53-1853/54 Elizabeth Gale King.
1842/43, 1846/47-1849/50 innkeeper, corndealer, coachmaster; 1850/51 innkeeper;
1851/52-1852/53 innkeeper & coach proprietor; 1853/54 innkeeper, etc.

1847/48-1851/52 Crown and White Hart.
1847/48 marked "Chandler, John, newly King".
1848/49 marked "Chandler, John, now George King".
1854/55 marked "Palmer, Benjamin, late Mrs King, innkeeper".
Pigot & Co's Directory, 1842: George King, Crown, St.John Street; corn & seed dealer, maltster, Market Place.
Cross references: Chandler, John, innkeeper, St.John; Jones, William Blackwell, innkeeper, St.John; Palmer, Benjamin, innkeeper, St.John; Plank, Charles Rhodes, innkeeper, St.John.

519 KING, Robert, baker, provision dealer.

1842/43, 1846/47-1848/49 assessed in absence of return £80; exempt.
1849/50 assessed in absence of return £70; exempt.
1852/53 returned and assessed £98; exempt.
1853/54 returned and assessed £80; exempt.
1854/55 returned and assessed £88.8.0; exempt.
1855/56 assessed in absence of return £100; income proved at £90; exempt.
1856/57 assessed in absence of return £100.
1857/58-1859/60 assessed in absence of return £100.

1842/43, 1846/47-1853/54 baker; 1854/55-1859/60 baker & provision dealer.
1850/51-1851/52 no assessments made.
Pigot & Co's Directory, 1842: Robert King, baker, Long Street.

520 KING, William, baker, confectioner.

1842/43 returned and assessed £110; exempt.
1846/47-1848/49 assessed in absence of return £100; exempt.
1849/50 assessed in absence of return £70; exempt.
1853/54 returned and assessed £80; exempt.
1854/55-1855/56 assessed in absence of return £80; exempt.
1856/57-1859/60 recorded; no assessments made; exempt.

1850/51-1852/53 no assessments made.
Pigot & Co's Directory, 1842: William King, baker, Little Brittox.

521 KINGDON, William, schoolmaster, lodgings.

1857/58 assessed in absence of return £100; income proved at £78; exempt.
1858/59 returned nil; no assessment made.
1859/60 returned and assessed £66.

522 KITE, Edward, grocer.

1842/43 assessed in absence of return £130; income proved at £120; exempt.
1846/47-1851/52 assessed in absence of return £100; exempt.

1852/53-1853/54 returned and assessed £110.
1854/55-1855/56 returned and assessed £100.
1856/57 returned £90; assessed £100.
1857/58 returned and assessed £94.
1858/59-1859/50 returned and assessed £75.

Pigot & Co's Directory, 1842: Edward Kite, grocer & tea dealer, St.John Street.

523 KITE, Thomas, innkeeper. [by comparison, Hare & Hounds]

1842/43 returned and assessed £150.

Pigot & Co's Directory, 1842: Thomas Kite, innkeeper, Hare & Hounds, Bridewell Street.
Cross references: Crook, William, innkeeper, St.John; Millwaters, Nathaniel, innkeeper, St.John.

524 KITE, Thomas, yeoman.

1847/48 entry only.

525 KNEE, Nathaniel, schoolmaster, clerk, commercial traveller, baby linen warehouse.

Year	Amount returned £	Commissioners' estimate £	Income proved £	Final assessment £
1852/53	–	100s	87	–
1853/54	–	100s	90	–
1854/55	–	100s	87	–
1855/56	–	87c	87	–
1856/57	–	100c	–	100
1857/58	70c	–	73.9.0 3.9.0b	–
1858/59	100c	–	110 10b	–
1859/60	120ct 20b	– –	120 20	120 20

Abbreviations: s, schoolmaster; c, clerk; ct, commercial traveller; b, baby linen warehouse.

526 KNIGHT, Henry, auctioneer, etc.

1842/43 assessed in absence of return £122; income proved at £122.12.2; exempt.

Pigot & Co's Directory, 1842: Henry Knight, auctioneer, Brittox.

527 KNIGHT, Henry, Junior, bankers clerk, insurance office agent.

Year	Amount returned £	Commissioners' estimate £	Final assessment £
1846/47	150b 18a 7i	–	175
1847/48	150b 17i&a	– –	150 17
1848/49	–	167	167
1849/50	–	167	167
1850/51	167	–	167
1851/52	182	–	182

Abbreviations: b, bankers clerk; a, insurance agency; i, interest.
1852/53 marked "now Calf, bankers clerk"; Junior deleted.
Pigot & Co's Directory, 1842: Henry Knight, agent to Royal Exchange, Brittox.
Cross reference: Calf, Henry, bank clerk, St.John.

528 KNIGHT, Jeremiah.

1848/49 name only entered.

529 LAMBERT, Revd. Richard U., curate.

1856/57 assessed in absence of return £100.

1857/58 marked "left Devizes".

530 LAVINGTON, Samuel, grocer, etc.

1842/43 returned and assessed £295.
1846/47 returned and assessed £175.
1847/48-1848/49 assessed in absence of return £250.
1849/50 returned £200; assessed £250.

1850/51 marked "Lyne late Lavington, Samuel, grocer".
Pigot & Co's Directory, 1842: Samuel Lavington, grocer & tea dealer, High Street.
Cross references: Hooper, -, grocer, St.John; Long, John, grocer, St.John; Lyne, Thomas William, grocer, St.John.

531 LAVINGTON & NEATE, auctioneers. [also LAVINGTON, Thomas]

1842/43 returned and assessed £100.
1846/47 returned £250; assessed £300.

1847/48 assessed in absence of return £350.
1848/49 returned £240; assessed £300.
1849/50 returned £220; assessed £300.
1850/51 returned £100 but deleted.

1842/43, 1846/47-1849/50 Lavington & Neate; 1850/51 Thomas Lavington.
1850/51 marked "return in Poulshott", "late Lavington & Neate".
Pigot & Co's Directory, 1842: Lavington & Neate, auctioneers, Lovington (*sic*) & Neate, agents
   to Farmers' & General Fire Office, High Street.

532 LEACH, Robert V[alentine], mealman.

1842/43 returned and assessed £90.14.7.

533 LEACH & BOX, corn merchants.

1842/43 returned and assessed £869.8.2¾.

Pigot & Co's Directory, 1842: Leach & Box, corn & seed dealers, manure merchants, New Park
   Street.

534 LENTHALL, James & Co., drapers.

1849/50 assessed in absence of return £80; exempt.
1850/51 assessed in absence of return £150; income proved at £97.9.0 on appeal;
   exempt.
1851/52 assessed in absence of return £120; income proved at £98; exempt.
1852/53 returned and assessed £95; exempt.
1853/54 returned and assessed £115.
1854/55 assessed in absence of return £115.
1855/56 assessed in absence of return £150.

1849/50 Lenthall & Co; 1850/51-1851/52 James Lenthall; 1852/53-1855/56 James N.
   Lenthall.
1849/50 marked "late Hobbs".
1856/57 marked "now John Pope", "Pope, John, late Lenthall, linen draper".
1857/57 marked "now Pope".
Cross references: Hobbs, William, draper, St.John; Pope, John, linen draper, St. John.

535 LEWIS, David, corn dealer.

1857/58 returned and assessed £74; exempt.

1858/59 marked "left Devizes".

536 LOCKE, Francis Alexander Sydenham, Treasurer under Devizes Improvement Act.

1850/51-1851/52 returned and assessed £208.
1852/53 returned and assessed £172.
1853/54 returned £128; no assessment made.
1854/55 returned and assessed £164.
1855/56 returned and assessed £184.
1856/57-1857/58 assessed in absence of return £184.
1858/59 returned £184; no assessment made.
1859/60 assessed in absence of return £184.

1857/58 assessment on Treasurer under Devizes Improvement Commissioners.
1850/51 marked "late Saunders, interest".
1856/57 marked "Query".
1858/59 marked "chargeable under Schedule E, an office".
Cross reference: Saunders, Henry, Treasurer under Devizes Improvement Act, St.John.

537 LOCKE, OLIVIER & TUGWELL, bankers. [also HUGHES, LOCKE & CO; LOCKE, OLIVIER & SAUNDERS]

Year	Amount returned	Commissioners' estimate	Final assessment
	£	£	£
1842/43	2090.6.8	–	2090.6.8
1846/47	775.14.1	–	775.14.1
1847/48	864.17.3	–	864.17.3
1848/49	584.6.7	–	584.6.7
1849/50	732.4.4	–	732.4.4
1850/51	993	–	993
1851/52	1666	–	1666
1852/53	1492.13.6	–	1492.13.6
1853/54	1151.15.10	–	1151.15.10
1854/55	944.3.10	–	944.3.10
1855/56	1125.17.6	–	1125.17.6
1856/57	1054.16.10	–	1054.16.10
1857/58	870.14.9	–	870.14.9
1858/59	815.9.1	–	815.9.1
1859/60	871.4.0	–	871.4.0

1842/43, 1846/47-1847/48 Hughes, Locke & Co; 1848/49-1850/51 Locke, Olivier & Saunders;
1851/52-1859/60 Locke, Olivier & Tugwell.
Pigot & Co's Directory, 1842: Hughes, Locke & Co., (draw on Lubbock & Co., London).

538 LONG, John, grocer.

1856/57 assessed in absence of return £150.
1857/58-1858/59 returned and assessed £150.

1856/57-1857/58 marked "late Lyne, grocer".
1859/60 marked "Hooper, late Long, grocer".
Cross references: Hooper, -, grocer, St.John; Lavington, Samuel, grocer, St. John; Lyne, Thomas William, grocer, St.John.

539 LONG, William, corn factor.

1851/52-1853/54 returned and assessed £150.
1854/55 assessed in absence of return £200.
1855/56 returned £204, £150 substituted; assessed £250.
1856/57-1857/58 returned £250; assessed £300.
1858/59 assessed in absence of return £300.
1859/60 returned £300; assessed £400.

1851/52 [St.Mary] marked "King, George now Long, maltster".
1851/52 marked "Long, W., late King, G., corn factor".
Cross reference: King, George, maltster, St.Mary.

540 LOTT, Thomas, gunsmith.

1853/54-1855/56 assessed in absence of return £60; exempt.
1856/57-1859/60 recorded; no assessments made; exempt.

541 LOWE & SIBREE, Misses, schoolmistresses.

1842/43, 1846/47-1849/50 assessed in absence of return £65; exempt.

Pigot & Co's Directory, 1842: Low (sic) & Sibree, preparatory school, Market Place.

542 LYNE, Thomas William, grocer, etc.

1850/51 assessed in absence of return £120.
1851/52-1855/56 returned and assessed £150.

1850/51-1851/52 grocer; 1852/53-1855/56 grocer, etc.
1850/51 marked "Lyne late Lavington, Samuel, grocer".
1856/57 marked "Long, John late Lyne, grocer".
Cross references: Hooper, -, grocer, St.John; Lavington, Samuel, grocer, St. John; Long, John, grocer, St.John.

543 MACCORMICK, Revd. Joseph, curate.

1853/54 assessed in absence of return £100; income proved at £96; exempt.

1853/54 MacCormic; 1854/55 by note, MacCormick.
1854/55 marked "gone".

544 MACDONALD, Alexander and OLIVIER, Alfred, solicitors.

1856/57 assessed in absence of return £200.
1857/58 returned and assessed £72.

[Bayley, John Raikes] 1856/57 "now MacDonald & Olivier".
1857/58 Alexander MacDonald assessed sole.
1858/59 marked "assessed by Special Commissioners".
1859/60 marked "returns at Pewsey".
Cross reference: Bayley, John Raikes, solicitor, St. John.

545 MCEWIN, Edwin, innkeeper, Antelope.

1854/55 assessed in absence of return £100.
1855/56 assessed in absence of return £50.

1854/55 McEwan; 1855/56-1856/57 McEwin; 1857/58 McEwen.
1856/57 marked "McEwin late, now Humby, F.P."
1857/58 marked "McEwen late see Thomas Brown.
Cross references: Brown, Thomas, innkeeper, St.John; Humby, Frederick Peter, innkeeper, St.John; Ransom, William, innkeeper, St.John.

546 MACKRELL, Henry, wine merchant. [also MACKRELL, James]

1846/47 returned and assessed £250.
1847/48-1849/50 assessed in absence of return £250.
1850/51-1855/56 returned and assessed £250.
1856/57 assessed in absence of return £250.

1846/47-1849/50 James Mackrell; 1850/51-1856/57 Henry Mackrell.
1856/57 marked "now Giddings & Ellis".
Cross references: Ellis, George Hackett, wine merchant's clerk, St.John; Giddings & Ellis, wine merchants, St.John.

547 MANNING, Revd. Alexander, private tutor.

Year	Amount returned	Commissioners' estimate	Final assessment
	£	£	£
1849/50	35	–	35
1850/51	25	–	25

1851/52	45	–	45
1852/53	30	–	30
1853/54	37	–	37

1855/56 marked "given up to his son".
1857/58 marked "Schedule E"
Cross reference: Manning, Revd. Alexander, chaplain of new prison and private pupils, Rowde;
    Manning, Alexander, private tutor, St.John.

548 MANNING, Alexander, private tutor.

1857/58-1859/60 assessed in absence of return £50.

1855/56 marked "Manning, Revd. Alexander, private tutor, given up to his son".
Cross reference: Manning, Revd. Alexander, private tutor, St.John.

549 MARSHMENT, Samuel, artist in photography.

1859/60 assessed in absence of return £150; reduced to £55 on appeal; exempt.

550 MARTIN, Thomas, draper.

1842/43 returned and assessed £200.
1846/47-1847/48 returned £200; assessed £300.
1848/49 returned £180; assessed £300.
1849/50 returned £100; assessed £200.
1850/51 returned and assessed £200.
1851/52-1852/53 returned £150; assessed £175.
1853/54 assessed in absence of return £175.

1853/54 marked "now Tyrell, draper".
Pigot & Co's Directory, 1842: Thomas Martin, linen & wool draper, agent to Guardian Fire
    Office, Market Place.
Cross reference: Tyrell, William, linen draper, St.John.

551 MARWIN, William, innkeeper, Lamb.

1852/53 returned and assessed £100; exempt.
1853/54 returned £31.1.10; assessed £100; income proved at £75; exempt.
1854/55 returned and assessed £100.
1855/56 assessed in absence of return £150; reduced to £125.
1856/57 returned £100; assessed £120.
1857/58-1859/60 returned and assessed £110.

1852/53 marked "late Winkworth".
1854/55 Lamb Inn noted; 1856/57 Lamb noted.

1854/55 marked "£200 for 1855".
Cross reference: Winkworth, William, innkeeper, St.John.

552 MASLEN, Louisa, dressmaker.

1842/43, 1846/47 assessed in absence of return £20; exempt.

Pigot & Co's Directory, 1842: Louisa Mazlen (sic), milliner & dressmaker, New Park Street.

553 MASLEN, Maria, shoemaker. [also MASLEN, William]

1842/43 returned and assessed £75; exempt.
1846/47-1848/49 assessed in absence of return £80; exempt.
1849/50-1850/51 assessed in absence of return £100; exempt.
1851/52 assessed in absence of return £130; exempt.
1852/53 returned and assessed £130; exempt.
1853/54 returned and assessed £125.
1854/55-1858/59 returned and assessed £130.
1859/60 returned £130; assessed £150.

1842/43 William Maslen, Maria entered but deleted; 1846/47 William Maslen;
1847/48-1859/60 Maria Maslen.
Pigot & Co's Directory, 1842: William Andrews Maslen, boot & shoe maker, Brittox.

554 MASLEN, Michael, baker & grocer.

1856/57 returned £60; no assessment made; exempt.
1857/58 recorded; no assessment made; exempt.
1858/59 returned £40; no assessment made; exempt.
1859/60 recorded; no assessment made; exempt.

555 MATTHEWS, R.D., clerk.

1856/57 returned and assessed £115.
1857/58 assessed in absence of return £115.

1856/57 marked "from Bedborough".
1858/59 [Bedborough] marked "dead".
Cross reference: Matthews, R.D., clerk, Bedborough.

556 MAYSMOR, Richard, bank manager, Wilts & Dorset Bank.

1846/47 returned and assessed £250.
1847/48 assessed in absence of return £250.

1848/49 marked "See Schedule E".
1849/50 no entry.
1850/51 returned £250; no assessment made; marked "E".
1851/52-1858/59 marked "Schedule E".
1859/60 recorded; no assessment made.

1846/47-1851/52 Maysmore.
1858/59 Wilts & Dorset Bank noted.
Cross reference: Scott, H.L., bank manager, St.John.

557 MEEK, Alexander, solicitor, agent, Treasurer for Wilts interest on borrowed money for militia store.

Year	Amount returned £	Commissioners' estimate £	Final assessment £
1846/47	–	150ag	150
1847/48	–	150ag	150
1848/49	150ag	–	150
1849/50	–	150ag	150
1850/51	–	150ag	150
1851/52	150ag	–	150
1852/53	150ag	–	150
	1500s	–	1500
1853/54	150ag	–	150
	1450s	–	1450
1854/55	1450s	–	1450
1855/56	1250s	–	1250
1856/57	1250s	–	1250
1857/58	–	1250s	1250
1858/59	325t	1250s	325
			1250
1859/60	325t	1250s	325
			1250

Note: Alexander Meek was a partner in the firm of Tugwell & Meek until 1851/52. He was also clerk to the General Commissioners of income tax.

Abbreviations: ag, agent; s, solicitor; t, treasurer for Wilts on money borrowed for militia stores.

Pigot & Co's Directory, 1842: Tugwell & Meek, attorneys, St.John Street; Alexander Meek, town clerk and clerk to the magistrates, St.John Street.

Cross reference: Tugwell & Meek, solicitors, St.John.

558 MILLWATERS, Nathaniel, innkeeper & mail contractor, Hare & Hounds.

1851/52 returned and assessed £180.16.0.
1852/53 returned £150 as innkeeper, £10 as mail contractor; assessed £200.
1853/54-1855/56 returned £150; assessed £200.

1856/57 assessed in absence of return £220.
1857/58-1859/60 returned £150; assessed £230.

1851/52 marked "late Crook".
1856/57 Hare & Hounds noted.
Cross references: Crook, William, innkeeper, St.John; Kite, Thomas, innkeeper, St.John.

559 MILSOM, Robert, shopkeeper, leather cutter.

1842/43, 1846/47-1849/50 assessed in absence of return £80; exempt.
1851/52 returned and assessed £127.3.6; exempt.
1852/53 assessed in absence of return £100; exempt.
1853/54 returned £87.2.6; assessed £100; income proved at £97; exempt.
1854/55 assessed in absence of return £100.
1855/56 returned and assessed £100.
1856/57-1857/58 assessed in absence of return £100.
1858/59-1859/60 returned and assessed £100.

1842/43, 1846/47-1849/50 shopkeeper; 1851/52-1859/60 leather cutter.
1850/51 no assessment made.
Pigot & Co's Directory, 1842: Robert Milsom, leather cutter, High Street.

560 MITCHELL, John, tea dealer & draper.

1842/43 returned and assessed £78; exempt.
1846/47 assessed in absence of return £80; exempt.

Pigot & Co's Directory, 1842: John Mitchell, tea dealer, linen & wool draper, Long Street.

561 MOORE, Peter Halked, curate.

1855/56-1856/57 returned and assessed £30.

1857/58 marked "now –", "left Devizes".

562 MORRIS, Charles, clothier.

1856/57 recorded; no assessment made; exempt.
1857/58 assessed in absence of return £100.
1858/59 returned and assessed £120.

563 MORRIS, William, bacon factor.

1842/43, 1846/47-1855/56 returned and assessed £150.

1856/57 returned £100; assessed £150.
1857/58 returned and assessed £150.
1858/59 returned £125; assessed £150.
1859/60 returned and assessed £150.

Pigot & Co's Directory, 1842: William Morris, cheese & bacon factor & dealer, Market Place.

564 MUDY, William, drawing & music master.

1842/43 returned and assessed £170.

Pigot & Co's Directory, 1842: William Mudy, music teacher, Chequer.

565 MULCOCK, Ann, widow.

1842/43 name only entered.

566 MULLINGS, Thomas, shoemaker.

1842/43, 1846/47-1848/49 assessed in absence of return £40; exempt.
1849/50 assessed in absence of return £80; exempt.

Pigot & Co's Directory, 1842: Thomas Mullings, boot & shoe maker, (& parish clerk), shop keeper & dealer in groceries and sundries, Long Street.

567 MUNDAY, James, baker.

1842/43, 1846/47-1849/50 assessed in absence of return £30; exempt.

Pigot & Co's Directory, 1842: James Munday, confectioner, High Street.

568 MUSSELWHITE, Thomas, saddler. [also MUSSELWHITE, George & Henry]

1842/43 assessed in absence of return £140; exempt.
1846/47-1851/52 assessed in absence of return £100; exempt.
1852/53 returned and assessed £125; exempt.
1853/54 returned £125; assessed £150.
1854/55 assessed in absence of return £130.
1855/56 returned and assessed £130.
1856/57 returned £125; assessed £130.
1857/58 returned and assessed £130.
1858/59 returned £0; assessed £150.
1859/60 returned £125; assessed £150; exemption claimed by each partner.

1842/43, 1846/47-1858/59 Thomas Musselwhite; 1859/60 Thomas Musselwhite & Sons (George & Henry).
Pigot & Co's Directory, 1842: Thomas Musselwhite, saddler & harness maker, St.John Street.

569 NEATE, Ann, innkeeper. [by comparison, Elm Tree]

1842/43 assessed in absence of return £150.

Pigot & Co's Directory, 1842: Ann Neate, Elm Tree, Long Street.
Cross reference: Sloper, Edwin, innkeeper, St.John.

570 NEATE, John, innkeeper, maltster. [by comparison, Black Horse]

1842/43 returned and assessed £210.
1846/47 returned and assessed £200.
1847/48 assessed in absence of return £250.
1848/49 returned and assessed £200.
1849/50 returned and assessed £160.
1850/51 returned and assessed £100.

1842/43 innkeeper & maltster; 1846/47-1847/48 innkeeper, etc.; 1848/49-1850/51 maltster.
1850/51 Executors of John Neate assessed.
Pigot & Co's Directory, 1842: John Neate, Black Horse, maltster, St.John Street.

571 NORMAN , John, hair dresser, hair cutter.

1842/43, 1846/47 assessed in absence of return £140; exempt.
1847/48-1848/49 assessed in absence of return £60; exempt.
1849/50 assessed in absence of return £50; exempt.
1853/54 returned and assessed £80; exempt.
1854/55 returned £100; assessed £80; exempt.
1855/56 assessed in absence of return £80; exempt.
1856/57 recorded; no assessment made; exempt.
1857/58 assessed in absence of return £100; income proved at £79; exempt.
1858/59 recorded; no assessment made; exempt.
1859/60 returned £89; no assessment made; exempt.

1850/51-1852/53 no assessments made.
Pigot & Co's Directory, 1842: John Norman, perfumer & hair dresser, St.John Street.

572 NORRIS, Henry Kent, solicitor.

1842/43 returned £149 (deleted); assessed £100; exempt.
1846/47-1849/50 returned and assessed £120.
1850/51 assessed in absence of return £170.

1851/52-1852/53 returned and assessed £120.
1853/54 returned £120; assessed £150.
1854/55 returned and assessed £150.
1855/56 returned £120; assessed £150.
1856/57 returned and assessed £160.
1857/58 returned £120; assessed £160.
1858/59 assessed in absence of return £160.
1859/60 assessed in absence of return £200.

Pigot & Co's Directory, 1842: Henry Kent Norris, attorney, Market Place.

573 NORTH WILTS BANKING COMPANY.

1842/43, 1846/47-1859/60 recorded but marked "return at Melksham".

Pigot & Co's Directory, 1842: North Wilts Banking Company, Market Place (draw on Drewett
& Fowler, London)

574 NOTT, William, solicitor's clerk.

1858/59 returned and assessed £70.
1859/60 returned £70; reduced by life assurance relief of £1.19.2.

1858/59 marked "See Schedule E".

575 NOTTON, R.J., hatter.

1853/54 returned and assessed £80; exempt.
1854/55-1855/56 assessed in absence of return £80; exempt.

1856/57 marked "now Couzens, brush warehouse".
1857/58 marked "now Couzens, G.".
Cross reference: Couzens, George, brush warehouse, rope maker, St.John.

576 OATLEY, Cornelius, builder.

1846/47-1849/50 assessed in absence of return £100; exempt.

Cross reference: Oatley, Cornelius, carpenter, St.Mary.

577 PAGAN, Alexander, tea dealer.

1842/43 returned and assessed £80; exempt.
1846/47-1848/49 assessed in absence of return £80; exempt.

Pigot & Co's Directory, 1842: Alexander Pagan, tea dealer, linen & woollen draper, Long Street.

578 PALMER, Benjamin, innkeeper. [by comparison, Crown]

1854/55 returned and assessed £200.
1855/56 recorded but no assessment made.

1855/56 marked "now W.B. Jones".
Cross reference: Jones, William Blackwell, innkeeper, St. John; King, George, innkeeper, St. John; Plank, Charles Rhodes, innkeeper, St. John.

579 PAULING, William, fellmonger.

1842/43 returned £50; assessed £75; exempt.
1846/47-1847/48 assessed in absence of return £75; exempt.
1848/49 returned and assessed £110; exempt.
1849/50 assessed in absence of return £110; exempt.

Pigot & Co's Directory, 1842: William Pauling, fellmonger & glover, Northgate Street.

580 PEPLER, Jane, dressmaker.

1842/43, 1846/47-1849/50 assessed in absence of return £50; exempt.

Pigot & Co's Directory, 1842: Jane & Ann Pepler, milliners & dressmakers, Brittox.

581 PERRY, John & Co., grocers.

1847/48 returned £120; assessed £150; income proved at £120; exempt.
1848/49 assessed in absence of return £120; income proved at £199; exempt.
1849/50 assessed in absence of return £120; exempt.

1847/48 marked "Coward, Thomas & Richard, now Perry, grocers".
1848/49 exemption claimed as partnership.
Cross reference: Coward, Thomas & Richard, grocers, St. John.

582 PHILLIPS, Peter Pattie, draper, linen draper, warehouseman.

1851/52 returned and assessed £100; exempt.
1852/53 assessed in absence of return £150; assessment discharged but no sum recorded.
1853/54 returned £105; assessed £150.
1857/58 assessed in absence of return £100.

1858/59 assessed in absence of return £150.
1859/60 returned £130; assessed £175.

1851/52-1853/54 draper; 1857/58-1858/59 linen draper; 1859/60 warehouseman.
1854/55-1855/56 marked "gone to Australia".
1857/58 marked "late Watson, linen draper".
Cross reference: Watson, John, tea dealer & draper, St.John.

583 PHILLIPS, Thomas, shopman.

1842/43, 1846/47–1849/50 assessed in absence of return £90; exempt.

Pigot & Co's Directory, 1842: possibly Thomas Phillips, boot & shoe maker, New Park Street.

584 PHIPPS, Revd. James E., surplice fees, subscriptions for sittings.

1842/43 returned surplice fees £185 (deleted); no assessment made.
1851/52 returned and assessed subscriptions for sittings £170.
1852/53 returned and assessed subscriptions for sittings £160.

1842/43 marked "See Schedule A".
Pigot & Co's Directory, 1842: Revd. Edward James Phipps, Long Street.

585 PLANK, Charles Rhodes, innkeeper, Crown.

1857/58 assessed in absence of return £200.
1858/59 assessed in absence of return £150.
1859/60 assessed in absence of return £200.

1857/58 marked "Jones, William Blackwell, innkeeper, Crown (dead) now Charles Rhodes Plank".
Cross references: Jones, William Blackwell, law stationer, innkeeper, St.John; Plank, Charles Rhodes, builder, Bedborough; Plank, Charles, builder, Week.

586 PLANK, Sarah, glass dealer.

1842/43, 1846/47 assessed in absence of return £50; exempt.

Pigot & Co's Directory, 1842: Sarah Plank, china, glass, etc., dealer, St.John Street.

587 PLUMMER, John Alderson - see SPENCER, Thomas C & PLUMMER, John Alderson.

588 POOK, Thomas, coachman.

1842/43, 1846/47-1848/49 assessed in absence of return £80; exempt.

589 POPE, John, linen draper.

1856/57 assessed in absence of return £140; reduced to £120 on appeal.
1857/58-1858/59 returned and assessed £120.
1859/60 assessed in absence of return £150.

1856/57-1857/58 marked "late Lenthall, linen draper".
Cross references: Hobbs, William, linen draper, St.John; Lenthall, James & Co., draper, St.John.

590 PRENTIS, Charles William, chemist [also PRENTICE, J.C.].

1854/55 returned and assessed £125.
1855/56 assessed in absence of return £125.
1856/57 returned and assessed £136.
1857/58 returned £100 (deleted).

1854/55-1855/56 J.C.Prentice; 1856/57-1857/58 Charles William Prentis.
1854/55 original entry £100 deleted marked "see below".
1854/55 marked "Read now Mr or W Prentice, chemist".
1857/58 marked "now Rowland, William S., chemist".
Cross references: Read, James, chemist, St.John; Rowland, William S., chemist, St.John; Thompson, -, chemist, St.John.

591 PRICE, Andrew, innkeeper.

1846/47 entry only.

592 RANDELL, James, builder, plasterer, land and house agent.

1842/43, 1846/47-1848/49 assessed in absence of return £50; exempt.
1849/50 assessed in absence of return £80; exempt.
1853/54 returned £90; assessed £100; income proved £90; exempt.
1854/55 returned and assessed £100.
1855/56 returned and assessed £120.
1856/57 assessed in absence of return £120.
1857/58 returned and assessed £120.
1858/59 returned nil; no assessment made.
1859/60 assessed in absence of return £100.

1846/47-1849/50 Randall.

1842/43, 1846/47-1849/50 plasterer; 1853/54-1854/55 builder, etc., (land and house agent); 1855/56-1859/60 builder, etc.
1859/60 marked "app." and assessment not extended to tax paid column.
1850/51-1852/53 no assessments made.

593 RANDLE, Nathaniel Bakewell, bookseller.

1842/43, 1846/47-1858/59 returned and assessed £200.
1859/60 returned £200; assessed £250; reduced to £233 but no appeal noted.

Pigot & Co's Directory, 1842: Nathaniel Bakewell Randle, bookseller, stationer & printer, jeweller & silversmith, Market Place.

594 RANSOM, William, publican & woolstapler. [by comparison, Antelope]

1842/43 returned and assessed £130; exempt.
1846/47-1849/50 assessed in absence of return £120; exempt.

Pigot & Co's Directory, 1842: William Ransom, innkeeper, Antelope, Market Place.
Cross references: Humby, Frederick Peter, innkeeper, St.John; McEwin, Edwin, innkeeper, St.John; Ransom, William, woolstapler, Bedborough.

595 READ, James, chemist, druggist.

1846/47-1847/48 assessed in absence of return £100; exempt.
1848/49-1849/50 returned and assessed £150.
1850/51 assessed in absence of return £150.
1851/52 returned and assessed £150.
1852/53 returned £50; assessed £100; exempt.

1846/47 chemist & druggist; 1847/48-1849/50 chemist, etc.; 1850/51-1852/53 chemist.
1852/53-1853/54 marked "now Thompson, chemist".
Cross references: Prentis, Charles William, chemist, St.John; Rowland, William S., chemist, St John; Thompson, -, chemist, St.John.

596 REEVE, Jonah, upholsterer.

1842/43, 1846/47-1859/60 recorded and marked "return at Marlborough".
1857/58 marked additionally "return for both at Marlborough, see Board's letter with Mr. Cottle".
1857/58 assessment made at £200 but deleted.
Pigot & Co's Directory, 1842: Jonah Reeve, auctioneer, appraiser & cabinet maker, High Street, Marlborough.
Pigot & Co's Directory, 1842: Jonah Reeve, cabinet maker & upholsterer, Market Place and High Marlborough.

597 RENDELL, William, smith.

1853/54 returned and assessed £85; exempt.
1854/55 returned and assessed £80; exempt.
1855/56 returned and assessed £75; exempt.
1856/57 recorded; no assessment made; exempt.
1857/58 returned and assessed £75; exempt.
1858/59 returned £75; no assessment made; exempt.
1859/60 recorded; no assessment made; exempt.

1853/54-1855/56 Randell; 1856/57-1859/60 Rendell.

598 REW, Henry, hair dresser & hatter.

1842/43 returned and assessed £85 hair dresser, £25 hatter; exempt.

Pigot & Co's Directory, 1842: Henry Rew, perfumer & hair dresser, Market Place.

599 REYNOLDS, C.B., draper & tailor.

1842/43 returned £140; assessed £175.

Pigot & Co's Directory, 1842: Charles Benjamin Reynolds, tailor, Market Place.

600 RICHARDSON, George, tea dealer, etc.

1853/54 returned £90; assessed £100.

601 ROACH, Charles, hatter.

1842/43 returned £200; assessed £250.
1846/47 returned and assessed £250.
1847/48 assessed in absence of return £300.
1848/49 returned £170; assessed £300.
1849/50 returned £200; assessed £300.
1850/51 returned £200; assessed £250.
1851/52 returned £170; assessed £250.
1852/53-1853/54 returned and assessed £250.
1854/55-1856/57 returned and assessed £260.
1857/58 returned and assessed £240.
1858/59 returned and assessed £200.
1859/60 returned £200; assessed £250.

Pigot & Co's Directory, 1842: Charles Roach, straw hat maker, hatter & furrier, Brittox.

602 ROWLAND, William S., chemist.

1857/58-1859/60 returned and assessed £100.

1857/58 marked "Prentis C.W., now Rowland, William S., chemist".
Cross references: Prentis, Charles William, chemist, St.John; Read, James, chemist, St.John; Thompson, -, chemist, St.John.

603 RUDMAN, Joel, corn dealer.

1858/59 recorded; no assessment made; exempt.
1859/60 returned £60; assessed £100; income proved at £78; exempt.

604 SALMON, W.W., steward.

1842/43 returned and assessed £150.

Pigot & Co's Directory, 1842: Wm.W.Salmon, stamp distributor and Treasurer for the County, St.John Street.

605 SARTAIN, C.E., printer.

1846/47-1848/49 assessed in absence of return £70; exempt.
1850/51-1851/52 assessed in absence of return £60; exempt.

1849/50 no assessment made.
1851/52 marked "now Davis, A., printer".
Cross reference: Davis, [Gillman] Arthur, printer, St.John.

606 SAUNDERS, Henry, Treasurer under Devizes Improvement Act.

1842/43, 1846/47 returned and assessed £200.
1847/48 assessed in absence of return £160.
1848/49 returned and assessed £188.
1849/50 assessed in absence of return £188.

Cross reference: Locke, Francis Alexander Sydenham, Treasurer under Devizes Improvement Act.

607 SCORREY, -, tailor.

1853/54 estimated in absence of return £70; no assessment made; exempt.

1852/53 marked "Plummer, J.A., now Scorrey tailor".

1854/55 marked "late Plummer gone away not recorded".
Cross reference: Plummer, J.A., tailor, St.John.

608 SCOTT, H.L., bank manager. [by comparison, Wilts & Dorset Bank]

1842/43 returned and assessed £210.

Pigot & Co's Directory, 1842: H.L.Scott, bank manager, Wilts & Dorset Bank.
Cross reference: Maysmor, Richard, bank manager, St.John.

609 SEAGRAM, William Ballard, physician, visiting private lunatic asylum.

Year	Amount returned	Commissioners' estimate	Final assessment
	£	£	£
1842/43	190	–	190
	100	–	100
1846/47	200	–	285
	85p	–	–
1847/48	–	285	235(*sic*)
1848/49	–	235	235
1849/50	200	–	200
1850/51	180	–	180
1851/52	150	–	150
1852/53	170	–	170
1853/54	180	–	180
1854/55	120	–	120
1855/56	40L	–	40
1856/57	40L	–	40

Abbreviations: p, property outside Great Britain; L, visiting private lunatic asylum.
1842/43 an apparent partnership between W.B. and W.B. Seagram, M.Ds.
1846/47-1854/55 physician.
Assessments generally included "interest on property out of Great Britain" but deleted 1850/51 reinstated 1851/52.
1857/58 marked "left Devizes".
Pigot & Co's Directory, 1842: William B. Seagram, physician, the Ark.
Note: W.B. Seagram acted as an Additional Commissioner.

610 SHEPPARD, William.

1842/43 entry only; marked "left".
Pigot & Co's Directory, 1842: William Sheppard, carpenter & builder, Sheep Street.

611 SIMPSON, Edward, grocer, tea dealer.

Year	Amount returned £	Commissioners' estimate £	Final assessment £
1850/51	–	150	150
1851/52	220	–	220
1852/53	320	–	320
1853/54	320	–	320
1854/55	350	–	350
1855/56	270	350	350
1856/57	300	360	360
1857/58	300	360	360
1858/59	360	–	360
1859/60	350	360	360

1850/51-1853/54 grocer; 1854/55-1859/60 grocer & tea dealer.
1850/51-1851/52 marked "Simpson late Ball, grocer"
Cross reference: Ball, James, tea dealer, St.John.

612 SIMPSON, George, printer, newspaper proprietor.

1842/43 returned and assessed £540.
1846/47 returned £500; assessed £540.
1847/48-1848/49 returned and assessed £540.
1849/50-1850/51 assessed in absence of return £600.
1851/52-1855/56 returned and assessed £600.
1856/57-1857/58 assessed in absence of return £600.
1858/59 returned and assessed £600.
1859/60 assessed in absence of return £600.

1842/43, 1846/47-1853/54 printer; 1853/54-1859/60 newspaper proprietor.
Pigot & Co's Directory, 1842: George Simpson, printer, Devizes & Wiltshire Gazette, Market Place; agent to Alfred Life Office, Market Place.

613 SIMS, John, shoemaker.

Year	Amount returned £	Commissioners' estimate £	Income proved £	Final assessment £
1842/43	–	150	–	100
1846/47	70	100	–	100
1847/48	–	100	–	100
1848/49	50	100	100	–
1849/50	–	65	65	–
1850/51	–	150a	–	56

1851/52	56	–	–	56
1852/53	56	–	–	56
1853/54	54	–	–	–
1854/55	–	60	–	60
1855/56	50	60	–	60
1856/57	40	60	–	60
1857/58	40	60	–	60
1858/59	35	50	–	50
1859/60	40	60	–	60

1842/43 marked "statement in writing to be made". No appeal noted.
1850/51 income proved £56; income from property in addition £103.
1853/54 no assessment made.
Pigot & Co's Directory, 1842: John Sims, boot & shoe maker, St.John Street.

614 SKINNER, Joseph, tinman.

1847/48-1852/53 assessed in absence of return £90; exempt.

1847/48 [St.Mary] marked "St.John".
1854/55 marked "gone".
Pigot & Co's Directory, 1842: Joseph Skinner, brazier & tinman, Brittox.
Cross reference: Skinner, Joseph, tinman, St.Mary.

615 SLADE, Samuel, tailor, shopkeeper.

1842/43 returned and assessed £80; exempt.
1846/47-1849/50 assessed in absence of return £80; exempt.

Pigot & Co's Directory, 1842: Samuel Slade, shopkeeper & dealer in groceries & sundries, Bridewell Street.

616 SLOPER, Ann, innkeeper, Black Swan. [also SLOPER, George]

Year	Amount returned £	Commissioners' estimate £	Income proved £	Final assessment £
1842/43	270	–	–	270
1846/47	160	200	–	200
1847/48	155	200	–	200
1848/49	150	200	–	200
1849/50	–	60	100	–
1850/51	62	120	120	–
1851/52	60 52.10.0i	120a	112.11.0	100

1852/53	70pi	112	–	112
1853/54	60	90	–	137
	47i			
1854/55	60	105	–	152
	47i			
1855/56	109	152	–	152
1856/57	60	152	–	152
	47i			
1857/58	60	150	–	197
	47i			
1858/59	70	150	–	202.10.0
	52.10.0i			
1859/60	70	203	–	203
	55i			

Abbreviations: i, interest; pi, profits and interest.
1842/43 George Sloper; 1846/47-1847/48 Anne(sic) Sloper; 1848/49-1859/60 Ann(sic)
   Sloper.
1851/52 although income proved at £112.11.0, tax paid on £100.
1854/55 Black Swan noted.
Pigot & Co's Directory, 1842: George Sloper, Black Swan, Market Place.

617 SLOPER, Edwin, innkeeper, Elm Tree.

Year	Amount returned £	Commissioners' estimate £	Final assessment £
1846/47	157	–	157
1847/48	154	–	154
1848/49	154	–	154
1849/50	154	200	200
1850/51	–	200	200
1851/52	150	175	175
1852/53	150	175	175
1853/54	150	175	150
1854/55	150	–	150
1855/56	150	175	150
1856/57	150	216	216
1857/58	170	200	200
1858/59	180	200	200
1859/60	175	200	180

1853/54, 1855/56 reduced but no appeal noted.
1859/60 assessment reduced by life assurance relief of £20.
Cross reference: Neate, Ann, innkeeper, St.John.

618 SLOPER, Joseph, linen draper, worsted dealer, shoemaker.

1842/43 returned £150; estimated £175; assessment reduced to £150.
1846/47-1848/49 returned and assessed £150.
1849/50 assessed in absence of return £150.

1842/43, 1846/47-1848/49 shoemaker & worsted dealer; 1849/50 worsted dealer; 1850/51 linen draper.
1842/43 no appeal noted.
1850/51 marked "Street late Sloper, boot & shoe warehouse"; "late Sloper shoemaker".
Pigot & Co's Directory, 1842: Joseph Sloper, boot & shoe maker, Market Place.
Cross references: Sloper, Joseph, linen draper, St.Mary; Street, -, boot & shoe warehouse, St.John.

619 SLY, William, harness maker [also SLY, William, junior]

1857/58 assessed in absence of return £160.
1858/59-1859/60 returned and assessed £160.

1857/58 William Sly senior and William Sly junior.
Pigot & Co's Directory, 1842: William Sly, saddler & harness maker, Brittox.
Cross reference: Sly, William, saddler, St.Mary.

620 SMITH, Revd. A[lfred], clergyman.

1842/43 returned and assessed £30.
1847/48-1848/49 returned and assessed £25.
1849/50 assessed in absence of return £25; assessment discharged on appeal.
1852/53-1853/54 returned and assessed £24.
1854/55 returned and assessed £40.
1855/56 returned and assessed £30.
1856/57 assessed in absence of return £30.
1857/58-1858/59 returned and assessed £26.
1859/60 returned nil; no assessment made.

1842/43 marked "brickmaker".
1850/51-1851/52 no assessment made.
1852/53 marked "church at Poulshot".
1853/54-1858/59 marked "clergyman at Poulshot".
1859/60 marked "no professional income at all".
Pigot & Co's Directory, 1842: Revd. Alfred Smith, clergy, Old Park.
Note: Revd. A. Smith acted as an Additional and a General Commissioner.

621 SMITH, Elizabeth, lodging house keeper.

1842/43, 1846/47-1849/50 assessed in absence of return £60; exempt.

622 SMITH, James, currier.

1842/43, 1846/47–1849/50 assessed in absence of return £60; exempt.
1851/52 returned and assessed £126.10.0; exempt.
1852/53 returned and assessed £122.10.0; exempt.
1853/54 returned £100; assessed £122.10.0
1854/55 returned £120; assessed £122.10.0
1855/56–1857/58 returned £100; assessed £125.
1858/59 returned £110; assessed £125.
1859/60 returned £125; assessed £150.

1850/51 no assessment made.
1859/60 marked "left Devizes".
Pigot & Co's Directory, 1842: James Smith, currier & leather cutter, Brittox.

623 SMITH, Thomas B., bookseller.

1842/43 returned and assessed £100.

Pigot & Co's Directory, 1842: Thomas Burrough Smith, bookseller, printer & stationer, agent to
    Minerva Life Office, Market Place.

624 SPENCER, Thomas C & PLUMMER, John Alderson, tailors.

1842/43 assessed in absence of return £109; exempt.
1846/47 assessed in absence of return £120; exempt.
1847/48 assessed in absence of return £300; income proved at £200; exempt.
1848/49 assessed in absence of return £200; exempt.
1849/50 returned and assessed £200; exempt.
1850/51 assessed in absence of return £120; exempt.
1851/52 assessed in absence of return £120; income proved at £140.9.6; exempt.
1852/53 assessed in absence of return £80; exempt.

1842/43 Thomas Spencer, shopman's assistant; 1846/47 Thomas C Spencer, tailor;
1847/48–1849/50 Thomas C. Spencer & John Alderson Plummer, tailors;
1850/51–1852/53 John Alderson Plummer, tailor.
1852/53 marked "now Scorrey, tailor".
Exemption claimed as partnership.
Cross reference: Scorrey, -, tailor, St.John.

625 SPRAWSON, John, stage coachman, coach proprietor, coach driver.

1852/53 returned and assessed £140.15.0; exempt.
1853/54–1859/60 returned and assessed £125.

1852/53 stage coachman; 1853/54–1854/55 coach proprietor & driver;

1855/56-1859/60 coach proprietor.
Cross reference: Sprawson, John, coachman, Week.

626 STANFORD, Charles, minister.

1848/49 returned and assessed £140; exempt.
1849/50-1850/51 assessed in absence of return £140; exempt.
1851/52 assessed in absence of return £150.
1852/53 returned and assessed £140; exempt.
1853/54 returned and assessed £150.

1854/55 marked "charged in Week".
Cross reference: Stanford, Charles, dissenting minister, Week.

627 STEPHENS, William, coach proprietor.

1856/57-1858/59 recorded; no assessments made; exempt.

1857/58 margin note illegible: "114 ex. at ...."

628 STEWART. William Matthew, tea seller, commercial traveller.

Year	Amount returned £	Commissioners' estimate £	Income proved £	Final assessment £
1842/43	–	110	110	–
1846/47	–	100	100	–
1847/48	–	100	100	–
1848/49	–	100	100	–
1849/50	150 20i	–	–	170
1850/51	170	–	–	170
1851/52	170	–	–	170
1852/53	150 20i	–	–	170
1853/54	150 20i	–	–	170
1854/55	170	–	–	170
1855/56	170	–	–	170
1856/57	150 20i	–	–	170
1857/58	170 20i	–	–	190
1858/59	170 20i	–	–	190

1859/60	170	–	–	160.19.6
	20i	–	–	20

Abbreviation: i, interest.
1842/43 tea seller; 1846/47-1859/60 commercial traveller.
1847/48 assessed under letter.
1859/60 assessment reduced by relief for life assurance of £9.0.6.

629 STOCKEN, George, law clerk, school.

1852/53 returned and assessed £134.14.6; exempt.
1853/54-1857/58 assessed in absence of return £135.
1858/59-1859/60 assessed in absence of return £175.

1852/53-1856/57 law clerk, school; 1857/58-1859/60 law clerk.

630 STOCKWELL, George, beerhouse keeper.

1842/43, 1846/47-1849/50 assessed in absence of return £50; exempt.

Pigot & Co's Directory, 1842: George Stockwell, retailer of beer, shop keeper & dealer in groceries and sundries, South End.

631 STREET, -, boot & shoe warehouse.

1850/51 assessed in absence of return £100; exempt.

1850/51 marked "late Joseph Sloper, boot & shoe warehouse"; "late Sloper, shoemaker".
Cross reference: Sloper, Joseph, shoemaker, St.John.

632 TABRAM, W.M. [by comparison, clothes dealer & hatter]

1842/43 assessed in absence of return £100; exempt.

Pigot & Co's Directory, 1842: William Tabram, clothes dealer & hatter, Market Place.

633 TANNER, William & CANNING, George Barnes, solicitors.

1842/43 returned and assessed £700.

Pigot & Co's Directory, 1842: Tanner & Canning, attorneys, St.John Street; William Tanner, agent to West of England Fire Office, St.John Street.
Cross reference: Canning, George Barnes, solicitor, St.John.

634 TAYLOR, Robert, confectioner.

1855/56 assessed in absence of return £75; exempt.
1856/57 recorded; no assessment made; exempt.

1855/56-1857/58 marked "late Jenkins, confectioner"
1857/58 marked "gone".
Cross references: Jenkins, Mrs Jane, confectioner, St.John; White, George, confectioner, St.John.

635 TENNANT, William, [surveyor of taxes] interest.

1848/49 returned and assessed £28.
1849/50 returned and assessed £19.
1850/51 returned and assessed £15.

636 THOMPSON, -, chemist.

1853/54 returned £70; assessed £100; income proved at £70; exempt.

1853/54 marked "late Read chemist".
Cross references: Prentis, Charles William, chemist, St.John; Read, James, chemist, St.John; Rowland, William S., chemist, St.John.

637 THORNLEY, Robert Samuel, surgeon, etc.

1858/59 assessed in absence of return £120 (deleted) £30.
1859/60 returned £20; assessed £45; assessment reduced by relief for life assurance £6.17.4.

1858/59 marked "late Bayes".
Cross reference: Bayes, Frederick William, surgeon, St.John.

638 TUGWELL & MEEK, solicitors.

1842/43 returned and assessed £2250.
1846/47-1850/51 returned and assessed £2000.
1851/52 returned and assessed £1500.

Note: Alexander Meek continued to be assessed sole 1852/53 et seq.
Pigot & Co's Directory, 1842: Tugwell & Meek, attorneys, St.John Street.
Cross reference: Meek, Alexander, solicitor, St.John.
Note: William Edmund Tugwell acted as an Additional Commissioner; Alexander Meek was Clerk to the Commissioners.

639 TYRELL, William, linen draper.

1854/55 returned and assessed £175.
1855/56 returned £130; assessed £175.
1856/57 returned £150; assessed £175.
1857/58-1858/59 returned and assessed £175.
1859/60 returned £175; assessed £200.

1853/54 marked "Martin, Thomas now Tyrell, draper".
Cross reference: Martin, Thomas, draper, St.John.

640 VINCENT, J.P., veterinary surgeon.

1846/47 returned and assessed £156.
1847/48 assessed in absence of return £160.
1848/49 returned and assessed £154.
1849/50 returned and assessed £150.
1850/51 assessed in absence of return £150.
1851/52 returned and assessed £150.

Note: assessed in St.Mary 1842/43.
Pigot & Co's Directory, 1842: J.P.Vincent, veterinary surgeon, Northgate Street.
Cross reference: Vincent, J.P., veterinary surgeon, St.Mary.

641 WALKE, Revd. William Dewdney, curate.

1859/60 returned and assessed £80.

642 WALLACE, Hill, gentleman, income from foreign securities.

1842/43 returned and assessed £266.
1846/47 returned and assessed £289.

Pigot & Co's Directory, 1842: Captain Hill Wallace, gentry, St.John Street.
1846/47 includes income from foreign securities.

643 WARD, Isaiah, painter etc.,

1842/43 returned and assessed £130.
1846/47 assessed in absence of return £130; exempt.
1847/48-1848/49 returned and assessed £200.
1849/50 returned and assessed £122.9.0; exempt.
1850/51 assessed in absence of return £100; exempt.
1851/52-1852/53 assessed in absence of return £75; exempt.

1853/54 assessed in absence of return £100.
1854/55-1858/59 returned and assessed £100.
1859/60 returned £100; assessed £125.

1842/43, 1846/47-1850/51, 1852/53-1855/56 painter; 1851/52, 1856/57-1859/60, painter etc.
Pigot & Co's Directory, 1842: Isaiah Ward, house & ornamental painter & gilder, fancy repository & stationery, Market Place.

644 WARNE, William & Co., drapers.

1842/43 assessed in absence of return £150; assessment reduced to £120; exempt.

1842/43 no appeal noted.
Pigot & Co's Directory, 1842: William Warne, linen & wool draper, Wine Street.

645 WASTEFIELD, Andrew, music master.

1842/43 assessed in absence of return £150; assessment reduced to £125; exempt.

1842/43 no appeal noted.
Pigot & Co's Directory, 1842: Andrew Wastefield, music teacher, High Street.

646 WATSON, John, tea dealer, draper.

1848/49-1849/50 assessed in absence of return £50; exempt.
1852/53 assessed in absence of return £150.
1853/54-1854/55 returned and assessed £150.

1842/43, 1846/47-1849/50, 1852/53 tea dealer & draper; 1853/54-1854/55 draper etc.
1852/53 Charles Watson entered but deleted.
1850/51-1851/52 no assessments made.
1854/55 marked "insolvent and dead"; 1855/56 marked "dead"; 1857/58 marked "Phillips, Peter Pattie, late Watson, linen draper".
Pigot & Co's Directory, 1842: Charles Watson, tea dealer & linen & woollen draper, Green.
Cross references: Phillips, Peter Pattie, linen draper, St.John; Watson, Charles, tea dealer, Bedborough.

647 WEAVER, Henry, auctioneer & agent.

1858/59 returned £250; assessed £222.3.4.
1859/60 assessed in absence of return £300.

648 WELLS, James, innkeeper, Swan.

1850/51-1851/52 assessed in absence of return £80; exempt.
1852/53 returned £128; assessed £80; income proved £128; exempt.
1853/54 returned £53.6.8; estimated £60 but no assessment made.

1849/50 marked "Frayling, Edward now Wells innkeeper Swan".
1854/55 marked "now Jenkins, innkeeper".
Cross references: Bourne, Richard, innkeeper, St.John; Frayling, Edward, innkeeper, St.John; Jenkins, David, innkeeper, St.John.

649 WHEELER, Thomas, tailor.

1846/47-1849/50 assessed in absence of return £50; exempt.
1858/59-1859/60 recorded; no assessment made; exempt.

1858/59 marked "Qy. chd. at 90?"

650 WHITCHURCH, Samuel, ironmonger, wine merchant.

1842/43, 1846/47 returned and assessed £250.
1847/48 assessed in absence of return £250.
1848/49 returned nil; assessed £150.
1849/50-1854/55 returned and assessed £150.

1842/43, 1846/47-1848/49 ironmonger & wine merchant; 1849/50-1851/52 ironmonger etc; 1852/53-1854/55 ironmonger.
1855/56 marked "insolvent".
1856/57 marked "now Reeve, ironmonger".
Pigot & Co's Directory, 1842: Samuel Whitchurch, ironmonger, Market Place; Whitchurch & Co., wine merchants, Northgate Street.

651 WHITE, George, confectioner.

1842/43 returned £80; assessed £100; exempt.
1846/47-1847/48 assessed in absence of return £100; exempt.
1848/49 returned £60; assessed £100; exempt.

1849/50 marked "Jenkins, late White, confectioner".
Pigot & Co's Directory, 1842: George White, baker, confectioner, St.John Street.
Cross references: Jenkins, Mrs Jane, confectioner, St.John; Taylor, Robert, confectioner, St.John.

652 WILD, George, innkeeper, Three Crowns.

1856/57 marked "late Chandler 3 Crowns". No assessment made.

Cross reference: Wild, George, innkeeper, St.Mary.

653 WILTS & DORSET BANKING COMPANY.

1842/43, 1846/47-1859/60 recorded but marked "return at Salisbury" or "return at Sarum".
Pigot & Co's Directory, 1842: Wilts & Dorset Banking Company, Brittox. (draw on Williams, Deacon & Co., and the London & Westminster Bank)

654 WILTSHIRE, William Edward, saddler, harness maker [also WILTSHIRE, Mrs].

1842/43 returned and assessed £120; exempt.
1846/47-1849/50 assessed in absence of return £120; exempt.
1853/54 returned and assessed £95; exempt.
1854/55-1855/56 assessed in absence of return £95; exempt.
1856/57-1857/58 recorded; no assessments made; exempt.

1842/43, 1846/47-1848/49 possibly William & Edward Wiltshire but indistinct;
1842/43, 1846/47-1849/50 harness maker(s); 1853/54-1857/58 saddler; 1856/57 Mrs Wiltshire.
1850/51-1852/53 no assessments made.
Pigot & Co's Directory, 1842: William Wiltshire, saddler & harness maker, Market Place.

655 WINKWORTH, William, innkeeper [by comparison Lamb Inn]

1842/43 returned £80; assessed £120; income proved at £100; exempt.
1846/47-1850/51 assessed in absence of return £100; exempt.
1851/52 returned £50; assessed £100.

1852/53 marked "Marwin, William late Winkworth, innkeeper".
Pigot & Co's Directory, 1842: William Winkworth, Lamb, St.John Street.
Cross reference: Marwin, William, innkeeper, St.John.

656 WINTERSON, Joseph, gardener.

1842/43, 1846/47-1847/48 assessed in absence of return £50; exempt.

Pigot & Co's Directory, 1842: Joseph Winterson, gardener, Pan's Lane.

657 WITHINGTON, William Bamforth, watchmaker.

1858/59 returned £78.12.4; no assessment made.
1859/60 assessed in absence of return £100.

Cross references: Withington, W., watchmaker, St.Mary; Wood, John, watchmaker, St.Mary.

658 WITTEY, Samuel, solicitor, conveyancer. [also WALL, John & WITTEY, Samuel]

1853/54 returned and assessed £650.
1854/55 returned £300; assessed £650; reduced to £550.
1855/56 returned £500; assessed £600; reduced to £550.
1856/57 assessed in absence of return £600.
1857/58 returned £550; assessed £600.
1858/59 returned and assessed £600.
1859/60 returned £600; assessed £550.7.6.

1853/54 John Wall & Samuel Wittey; 1854/55-1859/60 Samuel Wittey.
1853/54 attorneys, solicitors & conveyancers; 1854/55-1857/58 solicitor etc.;
1858/59-1859/60 solicitor.
1859/60 assessment reduced by life assurance relief of £49.12.6.
Pigot & Co's Directory, 1842: John William Wall, attorney, agent to Crown Fire Office, English
    & Scottish Fire Office, St.John Street.
Cross reference: Wittey, Samuel, solicitor's clerk, Rowde.

659 WOOD, Peter Almerick Leh[eup], sittings subscriptions.

1853/54 returned and assessed £160.
1854/55 assessed in absence of return £160.
1855/56 returned and assessed £179.13.6.
1856/57 returned and assessed £186.10.0.
1857/58 returned and assessed £275.
1858/59 returned and assessed £347.18.10.
1859/60 returned £391.15.1; assessed £392.

660 WOODROFFE, William, tailor.

1842/43 assessed in absence of return £50; exempt.

Pigot & Co's Directory, 1842: William Woodroff (sic), tailor, Long Street.

661 YOUNG, John, interest.

1853/54 returned and assessed £16.16.7; income proved at £95; exempt.
1854/55-1857/58 assessed in absence of return £16.16.7; exempt 1857/58.

1857/58 marked "sunk in purchase of property last Christmas".

662 YOUNG, Joseph, innkeeper.

1858/59 returned £100; entry deleted.

1858/59 marked "assessed in St.Mary".
Cross reference: Young, Joseph Eden, innkeeper, St.Mary.

663 YOUNG, Joseph, provision dealer, carrier.

1852/53 returned and assessed £105.
1853/54 estimated £80; no assessment made.

1852/53 provision dealer; 1853/54 carrier.
1853/54 marked "given up".
Cross reference: Young, Joseph, carrier, St.Mary.

664 YOUNG & WHITE, builders [also WHITE, T.B.]

1842/43 returned £343; assessed 400; reduced to £358.
1846/47 returned and assessed £313.
1847/48 returned £295; assessed £313.
1848/49 returned £284; assessed £313.
1849/50 returned £205; assessed £350; reduced to £250 on appeal.
1850/51 returned and assessed £216.

1842/43, 1846/47-1850/51 Young & White; 1851/52 (entry only) T.B.White.
1852/53 marked "White now Mullings, Benoni, builder"; [Bedborough] marked "Mullings, Benoni late White, builder".
Pigot & Co's Directory, 1842: Young & White, carpenters & builders, Green and Bridewell Street.
Cross references: Mullings, Benoni, builder, Bedborough; White, Benoni Thomas, builder, Bedborough.

DEVIZES ST. MARY

665 ABRAHAMS, Joseph, photographic artist.

1859/60 assessed in absence of return £100; income proved at £87; exempt.

666 ADEY, John Thomas, coal merchant, tallow chandler, tallow merchant.

1849/50 assessed in absence of return £150; income proved at £120; exempt.
1850/51-1851/52 returned and assessed £180.
1852/53 returned £70; assessed £180.
1853/54-1859/60 returned and assessed £180.

1849/50, 1853/54 coal merchant & tallow chandler; 1850/51, 1852/53 tallow & coal merchant; 1851/52, 1854/55-1859/60 coal merchant; 1854/55 ironmonger deleted.

667 ADLAM, Samuel, plumber, glazier, painter. [also ADLAM, Mrs., straw bonnet maker]

Year	Amount returned £	Commissioners' estimate £	Income proved £	Final assessment £
1842/43	–	30	132.10.0	–
1846/47	100	–	–	100
1847/48	100	–	100	–
1848/49	128.7.6	153.7.6	100	–
1849/50	–	100	100	–
1850/51	81.13.1	–	81.13.1	–
1851/52	129.4.10	–	94.3.0	–
1852/53	114.6.6 20i	150	–	150
1853/54	103	150	–	150
1854/55	139	150	–	150
1855/56	67.3.6 30s	150	–	150
1856/57	136.10.0	150	–	150
1857/58	97.8.6	100	–	100
1858/59	61.10.6	100	–	100
1859/60	100	–	–	100

Abbreviations: i, interest; s, straw business.
1842/43, 1846/47-1848/49 plumber & glazier and wife as straw bonnet maker; 1849/50
plumbers (*sic*) etc; 1850/51-1852/53 plumbers (*sic*); 1853/54 plumber and millinery business; 1854/55 plumber etc; 1855/56 plumber and straw business; 1856/57-1857/58
plumber, straw business etc; 1858/59-1859/60 plumber, painter, straw business, etc.
Assessed as Samuel Adlam and wife, or Mrs. Adlam.
1848/49 no appeal noted but income proved at £100; the estimate of £25 related to the straw
bonnet business.
Pigot & Co's Directory, 1842: Lydia Adlam, milliner, straw hat maker, Brittox.
Cross reference: Stockwell, Adlam & Gregory, plumbers & glaziers, St.Mary.

668 ALLEN, Charles, cattle dealer.

1842/43, 1846/47 assessed in absence of return £40; exempt.

Cross reference: Allen, Charles, cattle dealer, Rowde.

669 ANSTIE, George Washington, solicitor.

1842/43, 1846/47-1847/48 returned and assessed £500.
1848/49 returned and assessed £400.
1849/50-1850/51 returned and assessed £450.
1851/52-1859/60 returned and assessed £300.

Assessed under letter for all years.
Pigot & Co's Directory, 1842: George Washington Anstie, attorney, agent for Britannia Fire
Office, Northgate Street.
Cross references: Anstie, George Washington, farmer, St.John.

670 ANSTIE, Thomas Browne, surgeon, apothecary.

1853/54-1855/56 returned and assessed £350.
1856/57 assessed in absence of return £340.
1857/58-1859/60 returned and assessed £350.

1853/54-1857/58 surgeon; 1858/59-1859/60 surgeon & apothecary.
Cross reference: Anstie, Thomas Brown (*sic*), surgeon, St.John.

671 ATTWOOD, John, linen draper.

Noted only in 1859/60 entry under Joseph Flower & Co., linen drapers: "now John Attwood".
Cross references: Flower, Joseph & Co., linen drapers, St.Mary; House, -, draper, St.Mary;
Matthews, William, draper, St.Mary.

672 AYTON, Jacob, chemist, surgeon dentist.

Year	Amount returned £	Commissioners' estimate £	Income proved £	Final assessment £
1842/43	–	80	80	–
1846/47	–	100	100	–
1847/48	143.14.2	–	143.14.2	–
1848/49	–	115	115	20
1849/50	66.17.7	86.17.7	–	20
1850/51	– 20i	150a	117.18.0	20
1851/52	– 20i	100	109.2.0	20
1852/53	92.4.0 20i	–	92.4.0	20
1853/54	99.3.6	100	–	100
1854/55	–	97.8.6	97.8.6	–
1855/56	–	90	90	–
1856/57	Exempt			
1857/58	Exempt			
1858/59	Exempt			
1859/60	89.2.6	100	–	100

Abbreviations: i, interest.
1842/43, 1846/47-1847/48 chemist; 1848/49-1859/60 surgeon dentist.
1849/50 entries for profits deleted.
The sums of £20 left in charge in years where exemption otherwise claimed relates to interest.
Pigot & Co's Directory, 1842: Jacob Ayton, (operative) chemist & druggist, Northgate Street.
Cross reference: Ayton, Jacob, surgeon dentist, St.John.

673 BAKER, Thomas, watchmaker.

1842/43, 1846/47-1847/48 assessed in absence of return £120; exempt.
1848/49 assessed in absence of return £100; income proved at £90; exempt.
1849/50 assessed in absence of return £100; exempt.
1853/54 returned and assessed £95; exempt.
1854/55 returned and assessed £80; exempt.
1855/56 assessed in absence of return £80; exempt.
1856/57 recorded; no assessment made; exempt.
1857/58 returned and assessed £110.
1858/59 returned £75; assessed £110.
1859/60 returned £72; assessed £110.

1850/51-1852/53 no assessments made.
Pigot & Co's Directory, 1842: Thomas Baker, watch & clock maker, Maryport Street.

674 BARNARD, George, canal agent.

1847/48 returned £100; no assessment made; marked "charged in Week".

Cross reference: Barnard, George, canal agent, Week.

675 BARNARD, John, chemist etc.

Year	Amount returned	Commissioners' estimate	Final assessment
	£	£	£
1848/49	340	–	340
1849/50	332	–	332
1850/51	327	–	327
1851/52	315	–	315
1852/53	312	–	312
1853/54	290	–	290
1854/55	287	–	287
1855/56	275	–	275
1856/57	268	–	268
1857/58	270	–	270
1858/59	260	–	260
1859/60	250	300	300

1848/49 marked "Heard, Thomas James" deleted "Barnard, chemist etc" inserted.
1849/50 marked "Heard & Barnard now Barnard, chemist"
Cross reference: Heard, Thomas James, chemist, St.Mary.

676 BAYLEY, J[ohn] R[aikes], solicitor.

1842/43 entry only; marked "return in St.John".
1846/47-1847/48 marked "Special Commissioners".
1848/49 entry only.
Pigot & Co's Directory, 1842: Bayly & Bayly (sic) attorneys, High Street.
Cross reference: Bayley, John Raikes, solicitor, St.John.

677 BERRY, William, shopman.

1842/43 assessed in absence of return £52; income proved at £79; exempt.
1846/47-1848/49 assessed in absence of return £52; exempt.

678 BERRY & OFFER, straw bonnet makers.

1842/43, 1846/47-1849/50 assessed in absence of return £40; exempt.

Pigot & Co's Directory, 1842: Berry & Offer, straw hat makers, Maryport Street.

679 BIDWELL, Elizabeth, schoolmistress. [also BIDWELL, Anna]

1842/43 assessed in absence of return £30; income proved at £40.16.8; exempt.
1846/47-1847/48 assessed in absence of return £80; exempt.
1848/49-1849/50 assessed in absence of return £80; income proved at £70; exempt.
1851/52 assessed in absence of return £80; exempt.
1852/53 returned and assessed £100; exempt.
1853/54 returned and assessed £110.16.0.
1854/55 returned and assessed £110.4.0.
1855/56-1856/57 returned and assessed £100.
1857/58 returned and assessed £130.
1858/59 returned and assessed £180.
1859/60 returned and assessed £200.

1842/43 Anna Bidwell; 1846/47 Eliza Bidwell; 1847/48-1859/60 Elizabeth Bidwell.
1850/51 no assessment made.
Pigot & Co's Directory, 1842: Elizabeth Bidwell, boarding school, New Park Street.

680 BIGGS, George, innkeeper [by comparison, White Lion].

1846/47 returned and assessed £100; exempt.
1847/48 returned and assessed £80; exempt.
1848/49 returned £50; assessed £80; exempt.

1849/50 marked "now Truman, innkeeper".
Cross references: Thomas, George, innkeeper, St. Mary; Trueman, Richard, innkeeper, St. Mary.

681 BIGWOOD, George, shoemaker.

1846/47-1849/50 assessed in absence of return £50; exempt.
1853/54 returned and assessed £60; exempt.
1854/55-1855/56 assessed in absence of return £60; exempt.
1856/57-1858/59 recorded; no assessments made; exempt.
1859/60 returned £89; no assessment made; exempt.

1850/51-1852/53 no assessments made.
Pigot & Co's Directory, 1842: George Bigwood, boot & shoe maker, Maryport Street.

682 BLACKWELL, Elizabeth & Sarah, schoolmistresses.

Partners assessed separately 1842/43, 1846/47-1849/50

Elizabeth Blackwell

1842/43 assessed in absence of return £40; income proved at £36; exempt.

1846/47–1849/50 assessed in absence of return £40; exempt.

Sarah Blackwell

1842/43 assessed in absence of return £60; income proved at £64; exempt.
1846/47–1849/50 assessed in absence of return £60; exempt.

Misses Blackwell

1852/53 returned and assessed £126.9.0; exempt.
1853/54 returned and assessed £120; exempt.
1854/55 returned and assessed £120; income proved at £119.10.0; exempt.
1855/56 assessed in absence of return £120; exempt.
1856/57–1858/59 recorded; no assessments made; exempt.
1859/60 returned £108; no assessment made; exempt.

1850/51–1851/52 no assessments made.
1856/57 Mrs. Sarah Blackwell noted.
1857/58 assessed as school; Sarah omitted, Thomas inserted.
1858/59 Thomas deleted, Sarah inserted.
Pigot & Co's Directory, 1842: Elizabeth & Sarah Blackwell, school, Sheep Street.

683 BLENCOWE, Henry, innkeeper, Castle.

1851/52 assessed in absence of return £120; exempt.
1852/53 returned £116; assessed £130; exempt.
1853/54 returned and assessed £118.
1854/55 returned £130; assessed £150.
1855/56 returned £131; assessed £150.
1856/57 returned and assessed £150.
1857/58 returned £150; assessed £200.
1858/59 returned and assessed £150.
1859/60 returned £150; assessed £200.

1851/52 marked "late Grace".
1856/57 Castle noted.
Cross reference: Grace, William, innkeeper, St.Mary.

684 BOX, Richard, corn dealer.

1846/47–1847/48 returned and assessed £500.

Richard Box was also mentioned by name only in Market Lavington 1842/43 and Cheverell
    Parva 1846/47–1847/48.
1848/49 marked "now Glass & Ferris, corn dealers".
Cross reference: Glass, James & Ferris, Thomas, corn merchants, St. Mary.

685 BRABANT R[obert] H., gentleman.

1842/43 entry only.
Pigot & Co's Directory, 1842: Robert H. Brabant, gentry, physician, Northgate Street.

686 BRAMBLE, J.R., land surveyor.

1842/43 returned £75; assessed £150; reduced to £75.
1846/47 assessed in absence of return £200.
1847/48 returned and assessed £150.

1842/43 assessment increased on objection by surveyor but reduced; no appeal noted.
Cross reference: Bramble, J.R., surveyor, St.John.

687 BRANDFORD, James, fruit dealer, etc., journeyman, journeyman saddler.

1853/54 returned and assessed £90.10.0; exempt.
1854/55-1855/56 assessed in absence of return £60; exempt.
1856/57-1859/60 recorded; no assessments made; exempt.

1853/54-1856/57 fruit dealer, etc; 1857/58 fruit dealer & journeyman;
1858/59-1859/60 fruit dealer & journeyman saddler.
1857/58 £77 returned but no assessment made.

688 BRINKWORTH, Charles, baker, pig butcher.

1842/43 returned and assessed £130; exempt.
1846/47-1847/48 assessed in absence of return £120; exempt.
1848/49 assessed in absence of return £120; income proved at £100; exempt.
1849/50 assessed in absence of return £120; exempt.
1852/53 returned and assessed £100; income proved at £127; exempt.
1853/54 returned £61.2.9; assessed £100; income proved at £72; exempt.
1854/55 assessed in absence of return £100.
1855/56 assessed in absence of return £120.
1856/57 returned £100; assessed £120.
1857/58 returned and assessed £120.
1858/59-1859/60 returned £100; assessed £120.

1842/43, 1846/47-1849/50 baker; 1852/53-1859/60 baker & pig butcher.
1850/51-1851/52 no assessments made.
Pigot & Co's Directory, 1842: Charles Brinkworth, baker, New Park Street.

689 BRISTOW, Charles, cabinet maker.

1846/47-1848/50 assessed in absence of return £90; exempt,

690 BUNTER, G.B., chemist.

Year	Amount returned £	Commissioners' estimate £	Assessment made £	Income proved £
1847/48	–	155	150	115
1848/49	–	150	134	128.17.6
1849/50	–	150	150a	138
1850/51	133.10.0	–	133.10.0	133.10.0
1851/52	–	150	150a	130
1852/53	–	130	130	130

1847/48-1849/50 marked "Late Sainsbury".
1852/53 marked "now Madge"; assessment discharged but no sum recorded.
Cross references: Madge, James Cornelius, chemist, St.Mary; Sainsbury, G.T., chemist & brickmaker, St.Mary.

691 BURGESS, Joseph, baker, grocer.

Year	Amount returned £	Commissioners' estimate £	Income proved £	Final assessment £
1842/43	–	139.10.0	139.10.0	–
1846/47	–	140	140	–
1847/48	108.10.0	–	108.10.0	–
1848/49	80	–	80	–
1849/50	–	80	80	–
1851/52	–	80	89.5.0	–
1852/53	89.5.0	105	80	–
			15.15.0i	
1853/54	–	100	80	–
1854/55	–	80	80	–
1855/56	–	80	80	–
1856/57	Exempt			
1857/58	75	–	–	–
1858/59	Exempt			
1859/60	66	100	73	–

Abbreviation: i, interest.
1842/43, 1846/47-1849/50 baker & grocer; 1851/52-1859/60 baker.
1850/51 no assessment made.
Pigot & Co's Directory, 1842: Joseph Burges (sic), baker, Burgess, grocer & tea dealer, shop keeper & dealer in groceries and sundries, Monday Market Street.

692 CATLEY, Samuel, tailor, clothes seller, dissenting preacher.

1842/43, 1846/47-1849/50 assessed in absence of return £90; exempt.
1852/53 returned and assessed 100; exempt.
1853/54 returned £78; assessed £100.
1854/55-1856/57 assessed in absence of return £100.
1857/58-1858/59 returned £90; assessed £100.
1859/60 returned and assessed £100.

1842/43, 1846/47-1849/50 tailor; 1852/53-1853/54 clothes seller & dissenting preacher; 1854/55-1857/58 clothes seller; 1858/59-1859/60 tailor & clothes seller.
1850/51-1851/52 no assessments made.
Pigot & Co's Directory, 1842: Samuel Catley, clothes dealer & tailor, Maryport Street.

693 CHANDLER, James, innkeeper & brewer [by comparison, Old Crown].

1842/43 returned £150; assessed £200 but reduced to £150. Assessed under letter. No appeal noted.

Pigot & Co's Directory, 1842: James Chandler, Old Crown, New Park Street.
Cross references: Dyke, George, innkeeper, St.Mary; Waylen, William, innkeeper, St.Mary.

694 CHANDLER, James, innkeeper, beerhouse keeper. [by comparison Three Crowns]

1846/47-1847/48 assessed in absence of return £75; exempt.
1848/49 assessed in absence of return £75; income proved at £80; exempt.
1849/50 returned and assessed £100; exempt.
1850/51 recorded but marked "charged in Week".
1851/52 returned and assessed £120; exempt.
1852/53 returned and assessed £130; exempt.
1853/54 returned £59.10.4; assessed £130; income proved at £90; exempt.
1854/55-1855/56 assessed in absence of return £90; exempt.

1846/47-1849/50 beerhouse keeper; 1850/51-1855/56 innkeeper.
1856/57 marked "now Wild"; "Wild, George, late Chandler, Three Crowns".
Cross reference: Wild, George, innkeeper, St.Mary.

695 CHANDLER, John, innkeeper.

1846/47 assessed in absence of return £40; exempt.

696 CHANDLER, John, toll keeper & mealman.

1847/48 returned £60 and £13 interest; exempt.

697 CHAPMAN, Joseph, shopkeeper, hardware & glass warehouse.
[also CHAPMAN, Stephen]

Year	Amount returned £	Commissioners' estimate £	Income proved £	Final assessment £
1842/43	70	100	70	–
1846/47	–	100a	123	–
1847/48	–	100	–	150
1848/49	–	100	–	100
1849/50	100	–	100	–
1850/51	56	–	56	–
1851/52	–	100a	100	–
1852/53	87	–	87	–
1853/54	93.8.0	100	–	100
1854/55	138	–	–	138
1855/56	–	140	–	140
1856/57	124.16.9	200	–	200
1857/58	120	200	–	200
1858/59	160.18.8	200	–	200
1859/60	118.14.0	150	–	120

1842/43, 1846/47 Stephen Chapman; 1847/48-1859/60 Joseph Chapman.
1842/43, 1846/47-1849/50 shopkeeper; 1850/51-1859/60 hardware & glass warehouse.
1847/48 marked Chapman, Stephen now Joseph, shopkeeper; note "property St.John".
1847/48 Additional Commissioners' estimate increased to £150 by General Commissioners
1856/57 marked "Devizes and Chippenham".
1859/60 includes £5 interest; marked "Thomas Church late Chapman, hardware & glass warehouse.
Pigot & Co's Directory, 1842: Stephen Chapman, china, glass, etc., dealer, Sidmouth Street.
Cross reference: Church, Thomas, hardware & glass warehouse, St.Mary.

698 CHIVERS, William, carpenter.

1859/60 returned £52; no assessment made; exempt.

Pigot & Co's Directory, 1842: William Chivers, carpenter & builder, Sidmouth Street.

699 CHURCH, Thomas, hardware & glass warehouse.

1859/60 returned £118.14.0; assessed £150; reduced to £120 and £5 interest.

1859/60 marked "late Chapman"
Cross reference: Chapman, Joseph, hardware & glass warehouse, St.Mary.

700 CLARK, Jacob, butcher.

1842/43 returned £300; assessed £350; reduced to £300; no appeal noted.

Pigot & Co's Directory, 1842: Jacob Clark, butcher, Maryport Street & Brittox.
Cross reference: Clark, William & Isaac, butchers, St.John.

701 CLARK, William, shopkeeper, grocer.

1842/43 returned £50; assessed £70; exempt.
1846/47-1849/50 assessed in absence of return £70; exempt.
1853/54 returned and assessed £45; exempt.
1854/55-1855/56 assessed in absence of return £50; exempt.
1856/57-1859/60 recorded; no assessments made; exempt.

1842/43, 1847/48-1849/50 shopkeeper; 1846/47 no occupation noted; 1853/54-1859/60 grocer.
1850/51-1852/53 no assessments made.
Pigot & Co's Directory, 1842: William Clark, grocer & tea dealer, New Park Street.

702 CLARK, William, surgeon.

1842/43 returned £150; assessed £200.

Pigot & Co's Directory, 1842: William Clark, surgeon, Lansdown Grove.

703 COATES, Robert, innkeeper Odd Fellows' Arms, earthenwareman, hardwareman. [also COATES, Joseph]

1842/43, 1846/47-1847/48 assessed in absence of return £75; exempt.
1848/49 assessed in absence of return £75; income proved at £120.
1849/50 returned £100; assessed £150; reduced to £117 on appeal; exempt.
1850/51 returned and assessed £120; exempt.
1851/52 assessed in absence of return £120; exempt.

1842/43 Joseph Coates innkeeper & earthenwareman; 1846/47 innkeeper & hardwareman; 1847/48-1850/51 innkeeper etc; 1851/52 innkeeper.
1852/53 marked "& glass warehouse".
1853/54 marked "Robert Coates H.Higgins innkeeper".
Pigot & Co's Directory, 1842: Robert Coates, Odd Fellows' Arms, hardware ironmonger, Sidmouth Street.
Cross references: Hale, Matthew, innkeeper, St.Mary; Higgins, H., innkeeper, St.Mary.

704 COLE, Daniel, innkeeper [also COLE, Jemima; by comparsion White Horse].

1842/43 returned and assessed £150.

1842/43 marked "now Jemima".
Pigot & Co's Directory, 1842: Daniel Cole, White Horse.

705 COLLINGS, John, butcher. [also LEWIS & COLLINGS]

1842/43 returned £60; assessed £120; exempt.
1846/47-1850/51 assessed in absence of return £120; exempt.
1851/52 assessed in absence of return £150; income proved at £100; exempt.
1852/53 assessed in absence of return £100; income proved and assessment discharged but no sum recorded.
1853/54 assessed in absence of return £110; income proved at £70; exempt.
1854/55 assessed in absence of return £130.
1855/56 returned £120; assessed £150.
1856/57-1857/58 returned and assessed £150.

1842/43, 1846/47-1849/50 Lewis & Collings; 1850/51-1855/56 John Collings; 1856/57-1857/58 John Lewis Collings.
1849/50 marked "now Collings butcher".
1850/51 marked "late Lewis & Collings".
1858/59 marked "now Lewis butcher".
Pigot & Co's Directory, 1842: Lewis & Collins (sic), butchers, Northgate Street.
Cross reference: Lewis, Henry, butcher, St.Mary.

706 COLLINS, John, interest.

1852/53 returned £22.10.0; no assessment made.

1852/53 marked "charged under Schedule A".

707 COOK, Elizabeth Ann, schoolmistress.

1842/43 assessed in absence of return £46; exempt.
1846/47-1849/50 assessed in absence of return £65; exempt.

1842/43, 1846/47 Ann Elizabeth Cook.
Pigot & Co's Directory, 1842: Ann Cook, boarding school, Albion Place.

708 COX, George, butcher.

1848/49 assessed in absence of return £80; exempt.
1849/50 returned £60; assessed £80; exempt.
1850/51 returned and assessed £70; exempt.
1851/52 assessed in absence of return £70; exempt.
1852/53 returned and assessed £60; exempt.
1853/54 returned and assessed £110.
1854/55 assessed in absence of return £110.
1855/56 assessed in absence of return £125.
1856/57-1857/58 returned £110; assessed £125.
1858/59 returned £110; assessed £150.

1859/60 marked "charged in Week".
Cross reference: Cox, George, butcher, Week.

709 COXHEAD, Arthur, confectioner, baker, schoolmaster.

1846/47-1849/50 assessed in absence of return £80; exempt.
1853/54 returned and assessed £56b&c, £30; exempt.
1854/55 assessed in absence of return £86; exempt.
1855/56 assessed in absence of return £70; exempt.
1856/57 returned £4c, £40s (school income deleted marked "Schedule E"); assessed £60 confirmed on appeal.
1857/58 returned £51.12.8c, £30s (school income deleted marked "Schedule E"); assessed £70; exempt.
1858/59 returned £50; assessed £70 (marked "Schedule E"); income proved at £48; exempt.
1859/60 returned £49; no assessment made; exempt.

Abbreviations: c, confectioner; s, schoolmaster; b, baker.
1846/47-1847/48 no occupation noted; 1848/49-1849/50 baker; 1853/54 baker, confectioner & schoolmaster; 1854/55-1855/56 confectioner etc; 1856/57-1859/60 confectioner & schoolmaster.
1850/51-1852/53 no assessments made.
Cross reference: Coxhead, William Palmer, schoolmaster, St.John.

710 CRUDGE, William, painter & glazier.

1856/57-1857/58 recorded; no assessments made; exempt.

1859/60 marked "See St.John".
Cross reference: Crudge, William, painter & glazier, St.John.

711 CUMNER, Charles, baker & grocer.

1853/54 returned and assessed £78; exempt.
1854/55 assessed in absence of return £78; exempt.
1855/56 returned and assessed £70; exempt.
1856/57-1859/60 recorded; no assessments made; exempt.

1857/58-1858/59 £80 returned.

712 DANGERFIELD, Isaiah, innkeeper, White Hart.

1853/54 returned and assessed £40; exempt.
1854/55-1855/56 returned £40; assessed £60.
1856/57 returned £50; assessed £60.

1856/57 White Hart noted.
1857/58 marked "Now Joseph Young".
Cross reference: Young, Joseph Eden, innkeeper, St.Mary.

713 DANGERFIELD, Thomas, shopkeeper.

1853/54 returned and assessed £50; exempt.
1854/55-1855/56 assessed in absence of return £50; exempt.
1856/57 returned £50; no assessment made.

1856/57 marked "now -".
1857/58 marked "now Chase". (no further reference to Chase).

714 DARK, George, innkeeper, Angel.

1854/55-1855/56 assessed in absence of return £70; exempt.
1856/57-1859/60 recorded; no assessments made; exempt.

1856/57 Angel noted.

715 DAY, Ozias, bacon & cheese factor.

1842/43 assessed in absence of return £80; exempt.
1846/47-1847/48 assessed in absence of return £95; exempt.
1848/49 assessed in absence of return £80; exempt.

1848/49 marked "Day, Ozias late now -".
1849/50 marked "Day, Ozias late now Staples".
Pigot & Co's Directory, 1842: Ozias Day, cheese & bacon factor, Monday Market Street, shop
     keeper & dealer in groceries and sundries, Bridewell Street.
Cross reference: Holder, Charles, grocer, St.Mary; Humphrey, Thomas & Carter, John, grocers,
     St.Mary; Staples, William, grocer, St.Mary; Vines, Uriah, grocer, St.Mary.

716 DERHAM, Joseph, shoemaker.

1846/47-1849/50 assessed in absence of return £80; exempt.

717 DEW, John, mealman, salary.

1857/58 assessed in absence of return £100.
1858/59 returned and assessed £100.
1859/60 returned £100; assessed £120.

1857/58 Dewey.
1857/58 salary Glass & Ferris; 1858/59-1859/60 mealman.

718 DOWLAND, Joseph, linen draper.

1853/54 returned and assessed £80; exempt.
1854/55–1855/56 assessed in absence of return £80; exempt.
1856/57–1857/58 assessed in absence of return £100.
1858/59–1859/60 returned and assessed £100.

[Manley, Benjamin] 1852/53 marked "now Joseph Dowland, pawnbroker."
Pigot & Co's Directory, 1842: Martha Dowland, stay maker, Northgate Street.
Cross reference: Manley, Benjamin, pawnbroker, St. Mary.

719 DOWLING, David, stay maker.

1842/43 assessed in absence of return £70; exempt.
1846/47–1849/50 assessed in absence of return £50; exempt.

1842/43 Dowland.

720 DOWLING, Edward, agent.

1842/43, 1846/47–1849/50 assessed in absence of return £50; exempt.

721 DREDGE, Stephen.

1849/50 name only entered.

722 DYKE, George, innkeeper, Old Crown.

1847/48 assessed in absence of return £100; exempt.
1848/49 returned and assessed £105; income proved at £120; exempt.
1849/50 assessed in absence of return £105; exempt.
1850/51–1851/52 returned £100; assessed £120; exempt.
1852/53 assessed in absence of return £150.
1853/54–1854/55 returned and assessed £120.
1855/56 returned £100; assessed £120.
1856/57 returned £100; assessed £200.
1857/58 returned £100; assessed £190.
1858/59–1859/60 returned £100; assessed £150.

1847/48 marked "Waylen William, innkeeper now Dyke".
1852/53, 1853/54, 1856/57 Old Crown noted.
Cross references: Chandler, James, innkeeper, St.Mary; Waylen, William, innkeeper, St.Mary.

723 EADSON, Elizabeth, dressmaker, milliner.

1842/43, 1846/47-1849/50 assessed in absence of return £50; exempt.
1851/52 assessed in absence of return £60; exempt.

1842/43, 1846/47-1849/50 milliner; 1851/52 dressmaker.
1850/51 no assessment made.
Pigot & Co's Directory, 1842: E & C Eadson, milliners & dressmakers, Maryport Street.

724 EAGLESFIELD, John C., watchmaker, confectioner.

1842/43 assessed in absence of return £100; exempt.
1846/47 assessed in absence of return £75.10.0; exempt.
1847/48-1849/50 assessed in absence of return £75; exempt.

1842/43 watchmaker & confectioner; 1846/47-1849/50 watchmaker.
Pigot & Co's Directory, 1842: John Charles Eaglesfield, confectioner, Northgate Street.
Pigot & Co's Directory, 1842: possibly Charles Eaglesfield, working jeweller, New Park Street.

725 EAGLESFIELD, Thomas, coal merchant.

1842/43 assessed in absence of return £50; exempt.

Pigot & Co's Directory, 1842: Thomas Eaglesfield, coal merchant, Wharf.

726 EDEN, Eliza, milliner.

1846/47-1849/50 assessed in absence of return £50; exempt.

727 EDEN, John, cordwainer.

1842/43 assessed in absence of return £30; income proved at £22; exempt.
1846/47-1849/50 assessed in absence of return £30; exempt.

Pigot & Co's Directory, 1842: John Eden, boot & shoe maker, Sidmouth Street.

728 EDEN, Thomas, coach maker, coach builder. [also EDEN, Joseph]

1842/43 assessed in absence of return £100; income proved at £70; exempt.
1846/47-1849/50 assessed in absence of return £100; exempt.
1854/55 assessed in absence of return £100 but deleted.
1855/56 assessed in absence of return £50; exempt.
1859/60 assessed in absence of return £100.

1842/43, 1846/47-1849/50; 1854/55-1855/56 Thomas Eden; 1859/60 Joseph Eden.
1842/43, 1854/55-1855/56 coach maker; 1846/47-1849/50 coach builder; 1859/60 coach maker.
1850/51-1853/54, 1856/57-1858/59 no assessments made.
1854/55 marked "insolvent".
1856/57 recorded but no assessment made.
1857/58 marked "dead"
1858/59 marked "dead, business ceased".
1859/60 marked "Eden, Joseph late Thomas Eden coachmaker".
Pigot & Co's Directory, 1842: Thomas Eden, coachmaker, Bath Road.

729 EDMONDS, R., French teacher.

1842/43 returned £67t and £38i; assessed £100t and 38i; exempt.

Abbreviations: t, teacher; i, interest from foreign securities.
Cross references: Edmonds, R., French teacher, St.John; Edmonds, R. & W., schoolmasters, St.John; Edmonds, Richard, teacher of French, Bedborough.
Pigot & Co's Directory, 1842: E.Edmonds, schoolmistress.

730 ELDRIDGE, Rebecca, shopkeeper.

1842/43 assessed in absence of return £50; income proved at £10; exempt.
1846/47-1849/50 assessed in absence of return £50; exempt.

Pigot & Co's Directory, 1842: Rebecca Eldridge, shopkeeper, dealer in groceries & sundries, Monday Market Street.

731 ERWOOD, James, innkeeper.

1848/49-1849/50 assessed in absence of return £50; exempt.

732 EVERETT, William Giffard, physician.

1842/43 returned and assessed £300.
1846/47-1848/49 returned and assessed £400.
1848/50 returned £400; assessed £500.
1850/51-1852/53 returned and assessed £500.

1852/53 marked "assessed in St.John". (no assessment made in St.John 1852/53)
1853/54 marked "at St.John".
Pigot & Co's Directory, 1842: William Giffard Everett, physician, Albion Place.
Cross reference: Everett, Dr. William Giffard, physician, St.John.

733 FERRIS, John, cabinet maker, auctioneer.

1842/43 returned £180; assessed £200.
1846/47 returned and assessed £120.
1847/48 assessed in absence of return £150.
1848/49 returned £110; assessed £150.
1849/50 returned £90; assessed £150.
1850/51 returned £75; assessed £150.
1851/52 returned £130; assessed £150.
1852/53 returned and assessed £150.
1853/54 returned £120; assessed £200.
1854/55 returned £150; assessed £250.
1855/56 returned £200; assessed £250.
1856/57 assessed in absence of return £300.
1857/58 returned £150; assessed £300; increased by General Commissioners to £400.
1858/59 returned and assessed £400.
1859/60 assessed in absence of return £400.

1842/43, 1846/47-1859/60 cabinet maker; 1851/52, 1853/54 cabinet maker & auctioneer.
Pigot & Co's Directory, 1842: John Ferris, land, house & estate agent, cabinet maker, inspector of
weights & measures, Brittox.

734 FIDLER, Thomas, innkeeper.

1842/43, 1846/47 assessed in absence of return £100.
1847/48 returned £50; assessed £100; exempt.

735 FLOWER, Joseph & Co., linen drapers.

1857/58-1859/60 returned and assessed £100.

1857/58 marked "late Matthews, linen drapers".
1859/60 marked "now John Attwood".
Cross references: Attwood, John, linen draper, St.Mary; House, -, draper, St.Mary; Matthews,
William, draper, St.Mary.

736 FOWLER, William, surgeon.

1842/43 returned and assessed £400.

Pigot & Co's Directory, 1842: William Fowler, surgeon, Northgate Street.

737 FRANCIS, James, innkeeper, Royal Oak. [also FRANCIS, Mary]

1842/43, 1846/47-1847/48 returned £100; assessed £150.

1848/49-1852/53 returned £90; assessed £150.
1853/54-1854/55 returned £90; assessed £120.
1855/56 returned and assessed £120.
1856/57 returned £100; assessed £180.
1857/58 returned £120; assessed £180.
1858/59-1859/60 returned £100; assessed £150.

1842/43 marked "Mary Francis now John".
1856/57 Royal Oak noted.
Pigot & Co's Directory, 1842: Mary Francis, Royal Oak, New Park Street.

738 FRANCIS, Samuel, tailor.

1853/54 returned and assessed £50; exempt.
1854/55-1855/56 assessed in absence of return £50; exempt.
1856/57-1859/60 recorded; no assessments made; exempt.

1857/58 returned £40 but no assessment made.
Pigot & Co's Directory, 1842: Samuel Francis, tailor, Green.

739 GALE, William Dathan, marine store dealer, timber merchant.

1854/55 assessed in absence of return £100.
1855/56 returned and assessed £100.
1856/57-1857/58 assessed in absence of return £100.
1858/59 returned and assessed £100.
1859/60 assessed in absence of return £100.

1854/55 timber merchant & marine store dealer; 1855/56-1859/60 marine store dealer.

740 GANE, Edward, timber dealer.

1842/43 assessed in absence of return £150; reduced by General Commissioners to
    £100; income proved at £50; exempt.
1846/47-1847/48 assessed in absence of return £150.
1848/49 assessed in absence of return £100; exempt.

Pigot & Co's Directory, 1842: Edward Gane, timber merchant, New Park Street.

741 GERRISH, Henry, dispenser of medicine.

1858/59 returned and assessed £20.

1859/60 marked "removed to Salisbury".

742 GERRISH, John, schoolmaster, stationer, collector, general agent.

Year	Amount returned £	Commissioners' estimate £	Income proved £	Final assessment £
1842/43	–	108	122	–
1846/47	–	120	120	–
1847/48	–	120	120	–
1848/49	–	120	120	–
1849/50	139.4.0	140	139.4.0	–
1850/51	142.12.0	–	126	–
1851/52	103.17.0	–	103.17.0	–
	90	–	–	90aa
1852/53	80	–	–	80
1853/54	72.16.0	–	–	72.16.0
1854/55	70	–	–	70
1855/56	70	90	–	90
1856/57	90	–	–	90
1857/58	76.13.6	100	–	100
1858/59	80.17.9	100	–	100
1859/60	84.8.0	100	–	100

1842/43, 1846/47-1847/48 schoolmaster; 1848/49-1854/55 schoolmaster & stationer, etc;
1855/56-1856/57 schoolmaster & stationer; 1857/58 schoolmaster; 1858/59-1859/60 schoolmaster, collector & general agent.
1851/52 additional assessment (aa) made in the sum of £90 on returned figure.
Pigot & Co's Directory, 1842: John Gerrish, master at the Blue Coat School, Maryport Street.

743 GLASS, Joseph, brewer.

1842/43 assessed in absence of return £100; exempt.
1846/47-1849/50 assessed in absence of return £80; exempt.
1851/52 assessed in absence of return £80; exempt.
1852/53 returned and assessed £94; exempt.
1853/54 returned £64; assessed £80.

1848/49 income proved at £97.
1850/51 no assessment made.
1852/53 marked "Gable now". (but assessments continue)
1854/55 marked "now gone".
Pigot & Co's Directory, 1842: Joseph Glass, retailer of beer, New Park Street.

744 GLASS, James & FERRIS, Thomas, corn merchants, maltsters.

1848/49-1849/50 returned and assessed £500.
1850/51 assessed in absence of return £500.

1851/52 returned £500; assessed £600.
1852/53-1855/56 returned and assessed £600.
1856/57 returned £600; assessed £900.
1857/58 returned £800; assessed £900.
1858/59 returned and assessed £900.
1859/60 assessed in absence of return £900.

1848/49-1850/51, 1853/54-1859/60 corn merchants; 1851/52-1852/53 corn merchants & maltsters.
1848/49 marked "Richard Box now Glass & Ferris, corn dealers".
1855/56 marked "return required, see below". (entry made at end of list)
1859/60 James Glass assessed sole.
Cross reference: Box, Richard, corn dealer, St.Mary.

745 GOLDSTONE, Edward, surgeon dentist.

1842/43 assessed in absence of return £100; exempt.

Pigot & Co's Directory, 1842: Edward Goldstone, surgeon dentist, Sidmouth Street.

746 GRACE, William, innkeeper. [by comparison, Castle]

1842/43 returned £150; assessed £200 under letter.
1846/47 assessed in absence of return £200.
1847/48 returned £152.7.0; assessed £200.
1848/49 assessed in absence of return £200.
1849/50-1850/51 assessed in absence of return £150.

1851/52 marked Blencowe, Henry late Grace.
Pigot & Co's Directory, 1842: William Grace, posting & commercial, Castle, New Park Street.
Cross reference: Blencowe, Henry, innkeeper, St.Mary.

747 GREEN, William, auctioneer.

1848/49 assessed in absence of return £100; exempt.
1849/50 assessed in absence of return £150; reduced to £100 on appeal; exempt.

748 GREENLAND, Charles, Professor of Music.

1853/54 returned £75 and £22 interest; assessed £75; exempt.
1854/55-1855/56 assessed in absence of return £75; exempt.
1856/57-1857/58 recorded; no assessments made; exempt.

749 GREENLAND, James, bricklayer.

1842/43 assessed in absence of return £100; income proved at £80; exempt.
1846/47-1847/48 assessed in absence of return £100; exempt.
1848/49 assessed in absence of return £100; income proved at £65.
1849/50 assessed in absence of return £100; exempt.
1853/54 returned £20; no assessment made; exempt.
1854/55-1855/56 assessed in absence of return £20; exempt.
1856/57-1857/58 recorded; no assessments made; exempt.

1850/51-1852/53 no assessments made.
Pigot & Co's Directory, 1842: James Greenland, bricklayer, Back Street.

750 GREGORY, George, painter.

1846/47 entry only.
Cross reference: Stockwell, Adlam & Gregory, painters & glaziers, St.Mary.

751 HALE, Matthew, innkeeper, Odd Fellows' Arms, horse dealer.

1854/55 assessed in absence of return £100; income proved at £50; exempt.
1855/56 assessed in absence of return £50; exempt.
1856/57-1859/60 recorded; no assessments made; exempt.

1854/55-1855/56 innkeeper; 1856/57-1859/60 innkeeper & horse dealer.
1854/55 Odd Fellows' Arms noted.
1857/58 returned £52, 1859/60 returned £54.3.0 but no assessments made; exempt.
Cross references: Coates, Robert, innkeeper, St.Mary; Higgins, H., innkeeper, St.Mary.

752 HAMPTON, Edward, surgeon.

1846/47-1849/50 assessed in absence of return £100; exempt.

753 HARRIS, James, clerk, agent.

1846/47-1849/50 assessed in absence of return £60; exempt.
1856/57-1857/58 assessed in absence of return £100.
1858/59 returned and assessed £100.

1846/47-1849/50 no occupation recorded; 1856/57 clerk; 1857/58 clerk, etc.;
1858/59 clerk, agent, etc.
1859/69 marked "removed to Week".
Cross reference: Harris, James, clerk, agent, etc., Week.

754 HEARD, Thomas James, chemist.

1842/43 returned and assessed £400.
1846/47 returned and assessed £344.
1847/48 returned and assessed £346.

1848/49 entry deleted; Barnard chemist etc., substituted.
1849/50 marked "Heard & Barnard now Barnard chemist".
Pigot & Co's Directory, 1842: Thomas James Heard, chemist & druggist, Brittox.
Cross reference: Barnard, John, chemist, St.Mary.

755 HIGGINS, H., innkeeper. [by comparison Odd Fellows' Arms]

1853/54 assessed in absence of return £100; income proved at £70; exempt.

1853/54 marked "Robert Coates H.Higgins innkeeper".
Cross references: Coates, Robert, innkeeper, St.Mary; Hale, Matthew, innkeeper, St.Mary.

756 HIGGS, Elijah Andrew, grocer, etc.

1857/58 assessed in absence of return £125.
1858/59 returned and assessed £125.
1859/60 returned £95; assessed £125.

1856/57 marked "Weston, John now Higgs, baker, etc".
Cross reference: Weston, John, baker, St.Mary.

757 HILL, Richard, plumber, glazier, painter. [also HILL, William]

1842/43 assessed in absence of return £100; exempt.
1846/47-1849/50 assessed in absence of return £80; exempt. (income proved at £35
    1848/49).
1852/53 returned £80; assessed £120; income proved at £80; exempt.
1853/54 returned £75; assessed £120; income proved at £75; exempt.
1854/55 assessed in absence of return £76; income proved at £70; exempt.
1855/56 assessed in absence of return £70; exempt.
1856/57-1858/59 recorded; no assessments made; exempt.

1842/43, 1846/47-1849/50 William Hill; 1852/53-1858/59 Richard Hill.
1842/43, 1846/47 plumber & glazier; 1847/48-1849/50 plumber, etc; 1852/53 plumber.
1850/51-1851/52 no assessments made.
1853/54-1858/58 plumber & painter.
1858/59 marked "Query St.John".
Pigot & Co's Directory, 1842: William Hill, painter, plumber & glazier, Sidmouth Street.
Cross reference: Hill, Richard, painter, St. John.

758 HOLDER, Charles, grocer.

1856/57 assessed in absence of return £125; entry deleted.

1856/57 marked "Staples, William now Holder, grocer".
1856/57 appeals include Charles Holder assessment discharged.
Cross references: Day, Ozias, bacon & cheese factor, St. Mary; Humphrey, Thomas & Carter, John, grocers, St.Mary; Staples, William, grocer, St.Mary; Vines, Uriah, grocer, St.Mary.

759 HOLLOWAY, Joseph, whitesmith.

1842/43 returned £50; assessed £100; exempt.
1846/47-1849/50 assessed in absence of return £80; exempt.

Pigot & Co's Directory, 1842: Joseph Holloway, brightsmith, New Park Street.

760 HOOK, Eliza & Emma, worsted warehouse.

1848/49 assessed in absence of return £60; income proved at £70; exempt.
1849/50 assessed in absence of return £60; exempt.

1849/50 marked "Each" ?
Cross reference: Hook, Eliza & Emma, confectioners, etc., St.John.

761 HOUSE, -, draper.

1857/58 by way of note "Matthews, William now House, draper".
No assessment made.
Cross references: Attwood, John, linen draper, St.Mary; Flower, Joseph & Co., linen drapers, St.Mary; Matthews, William, draper, St.Mary.

762 HULL, Samuel, butcher. [also HULL, James]

1842/43 returned £120; assessed £200; reduced to £150 but no appeal noted.
1846/47 assessed in absence of return £175.
1847/48 returned £150; assessed £200.
1848/49-1849/50 returned £175; assessed £200.
1850/51 assessed in absence of return £200.
1851/52 returned £150; assessed £200.
1852/53 assessed in absence of return £200.
1853/54-1854/55 returned and assessed £200.
1855/56 returned £175; assessed £200.
1856/57-1858/59 returned and assessed £200.
1859/60 assessed in absence of return £200.

1842/43, 1846/47-1847/48 James Hull; 1848/49-1859/60 Samuel Hull.
1847/48-1848/49 marked "now Samuel".
Pigot & Co's Directory, 1842: James Hull, butcher, Brittox.

763 HUMPHREY, Thomas & CARTER, John, [by succession, grocers]

1857/58 entry only marked "Staples, William late Holder now Humphrey & Carter".
Cross references: Day, Ozias, bacon & cheese factor, St. Mary; Holder, Charles, grocer, St.Mary;
Staples, William, grocer, St.Mary; Vines, Uriah, grocer, St.Mary.

764 HUNT, George, shoemaker, cordwainer, linen draper.

1848/49 returned £85; assessed £120.
1849/50, 1852/53 assessed in absence of return £120.
1853/54 returned £90; assessed £120.
1854/55 returned and assessed £120.
1855/56 assessed in absence of return £150.
1856/57 returned and assessed £150s, £100l.
1857/58-1858/59 assessed in absence of return £150.
1859/60 returned £150s, £100l; assessed £300.

Abbreviations: s, shoemaker, l, linen draper.
1842/43 cordwainer; 1848/49-1858/59 shoemaker; 1859/60 shoemaker & linen draper.
1842/43, 1846/47-1847/48 recorded marked "return in Bath"; 1850/51 no assessment made;
1851/52 estimated in absence of return £120 but no assessment made.
1849/50-1850/51 marked in brackets "Bath".
Pigot & Co's Directory, 1842: George Hunt, boot & shoe maker, Brittox.

765 HURST, Joseph, baker.

1842/43, 1846/47-1847/48 assessed in absence of return £100; exempt.

Pigot & Co's Directory, 1842: Joseph Hurst, baker, Sidmouth Street.

766 HUTCHINS, William, innkeeper.

1846/47-1847/48 assessed in absence of return £50; exempt.

767 JACKSON, D.D., dyer & bird stuffer.

1846/47-1848/49 assessed in absence of return £20; exempt.
1849/50 assessed in absence of return £50; exempt.

768 JEFFERIES, Charles, cabinet maker.

1846/47-1854/55 assessed in absence of return £70; exempt.
1855/56 assessed in absence of return £70; income proved at £75; exempt.

769 JEFFERIES, Cornelius, carver & gilder, painter, etc.

Year	Amount returned £	Commissioners' estimate £	Income proved £	Final assessment £
1842/43	60	125	–	125
1846/47	–	150	–	150
1847/48	–	150	120	–
1848/49	–	120	70	–
1849/50	–	120	120	–
1850/51	116.7.0	–	116.7.0	–
1851/52	–	120	104.15.0	–
1852/53	80	120	115	–
1853/54	80	100	–	100
1854/55	–	100	–	100
1855/56	60	100	–	100
1856/57	60	100	–	100
1857/58	110	–	–	110
1858/59	50	100	–	100
1859/60	–	75	–	75

1842/43 carver & gilder; 1846/47-1859/60 painter, etc.
1859/60 estimated at £100 but reduced to £75; no appeal noted.
Pigot & Co's Directory, 1842: Cornelius Jefferies, painter & gilder, Sidmouth Street.

770 JEFFERIES, Joseph, bacon factor.

1842/43, 1846/47-1855/56 assessed in absence of return £75; exempt.
1856/57-1859/60 recorded; no assessments made; exempt.

Pigot & Co's Directory, 1842: Joseph Jefferies, cheese & bacon factor, butcher, Maryport Street.

771 JEFFERIES, Priscilla, dressmaker.

1842/43, 1846/47-1849/50 assessed in absence of return £40; exempt.

Pigot & Co's Directory, 1842: Priscilla Jefferies, milliner & dressmaker, Maryport Street.

772 JEFFERIES, Samuel, shoemaker.

1842/43, 1846/47-1849/50 assessed in absence of return £50; exempt.

Pigot & Co's Directory, 1842: Samuel Jefferies, boot & shoe maker, Maryport Street.

773 KER, C., shopkeeper.

1846/47 assessed in absence of return £50; exempt.
1847/48 returned and assessed £130; income proved at £53; exempt.
1848/49 assessed in absence of return £53; exempt.
1849/50 assessed in absence of return £50; exempt.

774 KING, George, maltster.

1842/43 returned and assessed £150.
1846/47-1847/48 returned £100; assessed £150.
1848/49-1849/50 returned and assessed £150.
1850/51 assessed in absence of return £150.

1851/52 marked "now Long, maltster".
Pigot & Co's Directory, 1842: George King, corn & seed dealer, Market Place.
Cross reference: Long, William, cornfactor, St.John.

775 KING, Thomas G., corn dealer.

1848/49 assessed in absence of return £100; income proved at £88.3.0; exempt.

776 KINGSTON, William, cooper.

1842/43 returned £80; assessed £100; exempt.
1846/47-1849/50 assessed in absence of return £85; exempt.

1842/43 Kingstone.
Pigot & Co's Directory, 1842: William Kingston, cooper, New Park Street.

777 KNEE, Joseph, shoemaker.

1842/43, 1846/47-1851/52 assessed in absence of return £90; exempt.
1852/53 returned and assessed £90; exempt.
1853/54 assessed in absence of return £90; exempt.
1854/55 assessed in absence of return £90; income proved at £75; exempt.
1855/56 assessed in absence of return £50; exempt.
1856/57-1859/60 recorded; no assessments made; exempt.

778 LANSDOWN, Richard, painter, gilder, picture frame maker.

1853/54 returned £85; assessed £100; income proved at £85; exempt.
1854/55 assessed in absence of return £80; exempt.
1855/56 assessed in absence of return £100; income proved and assessment discharged, sum not recorded.
1856/57 recorded; no assessment made; exempt.
1857/58 assessed in absence of return £90; exempt.
1858/59-1859/60 recorded; no assessments made; exempt.

1853/54 painter, gilder & picture frame maker, (glazier deleted); 1854/55-1856/57, 1859/60 painter & gilder, etc.; 1857/58-1858/59 painter & gilder.

779 LAWES, William & Co., carriers, wagon office.

1842/43 Carriers; 1846/47-1848/49 Wagon Office.
1842/43, 1846/47-1848/49 marked "return made at Chippenham".
1849/50 marked "now Perry".
Cross reference: Perry, Horatio Nelson, carrier, Bedborough (formerly agent to Lawes & Co.)

780 LENARD, Sarah, dressmaker.

1842/43, 1846/47-1848/49 assessed in absence of return £100; exempt.
1849/50 assessed in absence of return £60; exempt.

Pigot & Co's Directory, 1842: Sarah Lenard, straw hat maker, Maryport Street.

781 LENARD, William, glazier, painter.

1842/43, 1846/47-1849/50 assessed in absence of return £40; exempt.

1842/43 glazier & painter; 1846/47 glazier; 1847/48-1849/50 glazier, etc.
Pigot & Co's Directory, 1842: William Webb Lenard, painter, plumber & glazier, Maryport Street.

782 LENTHALL, Joseph, attorney's clerk.

1853/54 returned £90; assessed £100; income proved at £90; exempt.
1854/55 assessed in absence of return £90; exempt.
1855/56 assessed in absence of return £100; income proved and assessment discharged, sum not recorded.
1856/57-1859/60 recorded; no assessments made; exempt.

783 LEVANDER, H.C., schoolmaster.

1859/60 assessed in absence of return £110.

Assessment made by General Commissioners; recorded on a separate page inserted into certificates of assessment.

784 LEWIS, Henry, butcher.

1858/59-1859/60 assessed in absence of return £150.

1858/59 marked "Collings, John now Lewis, butcher".
Cross reference: Collings, John, butcher, St.Mary.

785 LEWIS, Jonathan, butcher, lodgings.

1842/43 assessed in absence of return £90.
1846/47 returned and assessed £60b, £40l.
1847/48 assessed in absence of return £100; income proved at £60; duty of £1.15.0 left in charge.

Abbreviations: b, butcher; l, lodgings.
Pigot & Co's Directory, 1842: Jonathan Lewis, butcher, New Park Street.

786 MABBETT, Betty, innkeeper. [by comparison Angel]

1842/43 assessed in absence of return £50; exempt.

Pigot & Co's Directory, 1842: Elizabeth Mabbett, Angel, Sheep Street.

787 MACKLIN, James, innkeeper. [by comparison White Bear]

1842/43 returned £150; assessed £180 under letter.
1846/47 returned £180; assessed £200.
1847/48-1849/50 returned £150; assessed £200.
1850/51 assessed in absence of return £200.
1851/52 returned £140; assessed £175.
1852/53 assessed in absence of return £175.

1842/43, 1846/47-1847/48 Maklin.
1852/53 marked "now Decimus Wild".
Pigot & Co's Directory, 1842: James Macklin, White Bear, Monday Market Street.
Cross reference: Wild, Decimus, innkeeper, St.Mary; Macklin, Thomas, innkeeper, St.Mary.

788 MACKLIN, Thomas, innkeeper, White Bear.

1859/60 assessed in absence of return £300.

1859/60 marked "Wild, Decimus (deleted)".
Cross reference: Macklin, James, innkeeper, St.Mary; Wild, Decimus, innkeeper, St.Mary.

789 MADGE, James Cornelius, chemist.

1853/54 assessed in absence of return £70; exempt.
1854/55 assessed in absence of return £100; income proved at £90; exempt.
1855/56 assessed in absence of return £100.
1856/57 returned and assessed £100.
1857/58 returned £118; assessed £130.
1858/59 returned and assessed £127.
1859/60 returned and assessed £132.

1853/54 marked "late Bunter, chemist".
Cross reference: Bunter, G.B., chemist, St.Mary; Sainsbury, G.T., chemist & brickmaker, St. Mary.

790 MANLEY, Benjamin, pawn broker.

1842/43 returned £120; assessed £150; income proved at £120; exempt.
1846/47 assessed in absence of return £102; income proved at £100; exempt.
1847/48 returned and assessed £134; exempt.
1848/49 assessed in absence of return £134; exempt.
1849/50 returned and assessed £125; exempt.
1850/51 returned and assessed £130.
1851/52 assessed in absence of return £100; exempt.
1852/53 assessed in absence of return £80; exempt.

1852/53 marked "now Joseph Dowland, pawnbroker". (note: Dowland assessed as linen draper)
Pigot & Co's Directory, 1842: Benjamin Manley, pawnbroker, Maryport Street.
Cross reference: Dowland, Joseph, linen draper, St.Mary.

791 MANNINGS, Mary, dressmaker.

1855/56 returned and assessed £70; exempt.
1856/57-1859/60 recorded; no assessments made; exempt.

792 MANNINGS, Michael, woolstapler.

1853/54 returned £90; exempt.
1854/55 recorded; no assessment made; exempt.

793 MARTEN, -, linen draper.

1850/51 assessed in absence of return £100; exempt.

1849/50 marked "Overy, Alfred now Marten linen draper".
1850/51 marked "Marten late now Walker linen draper".
Pigot & Co's Directory, 1842: Thomas Martin (*sic*), linen & woollen draper, Market Place.
Cross reference: Overy, Alfred, linen draper, St.Mary; Walker, John, linen draper, St.Mary.

794 MASLEN, David, grocer, etc.

1856/57 assessed in absence of return £93; reduced to £80 on appeal.
1857/58 returned £52; assessed £80.
1858/59 returned £50; assessed £80.
1859/60 returned and assessed £80.

795 MASLEN, Ellen Ann, milliner, dressmaker.

1842/43 returned and assessed £100; exempt.
1846/47-1847/48 assessed in absence of return £75; exempt.

1842/43 milliner & dressmaker; 1846/47-1847/48 milliner.
1848/49 marked "now Mrs.J.Perry" "milliner".
Pigot & Co's Directory, 1842: Ellen Ann Mazlen (*sic*), milliner & dressmaker, Brittox.

796 MATTHEWS, William, draper.

1842/43, 1846/47 assessed in absence of return £120; exempt.
1847/48 returned and assessed £100; exempt.
1848/49 assessed in absence of return £100; income proved at £116.18.9; exempt.
1849/50 assessed in absence of return £150; reduced to £112 on appeal; exempt.
1850/51 returned and assessed £120; exempt.
1851/52 returned £116; no assessment made; exempt.
1852/53 assessed in absence of return £120.
1853/54-1854/55 returned and assessed £102.
1855/56 returned and assessed £100.
1856/57 returned and assessed £102.

1857/58 marked "now House".
Pigot & Co's Directory, 1842: William Mathews (*sic*), linen & woollen draper, New Park
    Street.
Cross references: Attwood, John, linen draper, St.Mary; Flower, Joseph & Co., linen drapers,
    St.Mary; House,-, draper, St.Mary.

797 MAYSMORE, Richard, bank manager.

1856/57-1858/59 marked "Schedule E".
1859/60 name and occupation recorded but no assessment made.

Cross reference: Maysmor(sic), Richard, bank manager, St.John.

798 MEAD, James, coal merchant.

1842/43 assessed in absence of return £100; income proved at £80; exempt.
1846/47-1847/48 assessed in absence of return £53; exempt.

Pigot & Co's Directory, 1842: George Mead, coal merchant, Wharf.

799 MEDLAND, William Thomas, baker, grocer.

Year	Amount returned £	Commissioners' estimate £	Income proved £	Final assessment £
1842/43	–	150	130	–
1846/47	–	117	117	–
1847/48	–	117	117	–
1848/49	–	117	130	–
1849/50	125	150a	135.13.4	–
1850/51	–	135	135	–
1851/52	–	135a	129.16.0	–
1852/53	84.18.0	100	138	–
1853/54	54.8.0	100	–	100
1854/55	100	–	–	100
1855/56	–	100	–	100
1856/57	100	–	–	100
1857/58	–	100	–	100
1858/59	100	–	–	100
1859/60	100	–	–	100

1842/43 baker & grocer; 1846/47-1859/60 grocer, etc.
Pigot & Co's Directory, 1842: William T.Medlam (sic), grocer & tea dealer, Maryport Street.

800 MONTGOMERY, Ronald, surgeon, visitor private lunatic asylum.

Year	Amount returned £	Commissioners' estimate £	Final assessment £
1846/47	180	–	180

1847/48	206	–	206
1848/49	170	–	170
1849/50	186	–	186
1850/51	295	–	295
1851/52	233.5.9	–	233.5.9
1852/53	252	–	252
1853/54	250	–	250
1854/55	265.10.0	–	265.10.0
1855/56	256.16.6	–	256.16.6
1856/57	266.10.8	–	266.10.8
1857/58	256.18.10	–	256.18.10
1858/59	222.7.6	–	222.7.6
1859/60	202.17.11	–	202.17.11

1859/60 additional entry as visitor private lunatic asylum deleted.

801 MORGAN, Mary, dressmaker & fancy repository.

1842/43 returned £30; assessed £50; income proved at £47; exempt.
1846/47-1848/49 assessed in absence of return £50; exempt.
1849/50 recorded but no assessment made.

Pigot & Co's Directory, 1842: Mary Morgan, fancy repository, Sidmouth Street.

802 MULLINGS, Benoni, cabinet maker.

1842/43 assessed in absence of return £90; exempt.

Pigot & Co's Directory, 1842: Benoni Mullings, cabinet maker, Northgate Street.

803 MULLINGS, John, cordwainer, grocer.

1842/43, 1846/47-1849/50 assessed in absence of return £50; exempt.

Pigot & Co's Directory, 1842: John Mullings, boot & shoe maker, Maryport Street.

804 MUNDY, A.B., tailor.

1846/47-1847/48 assessed in absence of return £50; exempt.

1848/49 marked "late tailor".

805 NOYES, Edwin, cooper.

1853/54 returned and assessed £75; exempt.

1854/55-1855/56 assessed in absence of return £75; exempt.
1856/57-1857/58 recorded; no assessments made; exempt.

1857/58 marked "dead" but remains in list for 1858/59 and 1859/60 as if exempt.

806 OAKFORD, Edward, tiler & plasterer.

1846/47 assessed in absence of return £80; exempt.
1848/49-1849/50 assessed in absence of return £80; exempt.

1847/48 entry deleted.
Pigot & Co's Directory, 1842: Edward Oakford & Son, plasterers & slaters, New Park Street.

807 OAKFORD, T.D. Junior, tiler & plasterer.

1842/43 returned and assessed £35; exempt.
1846/47-1849/50 assessed in absence of return £80; exempt.

Pigot & Co's Directory, 1842: Edward Oakford & Son, plasterers & slaters, New Park Street.

808 OATLEY, Samuel, carpenter. [also OATLEY, Cornelius]

1842/43, 1846/47-1852/53 assessed in absence of return £100; exempt.
1853/54 assessed in absence of return £100; income proved at £80; exempt.
1854/55 assessed in absence of return £80; exempt.

1842/43 Cornelius Oatley; 1846/47-1854/55 Samuel Oatley.
Pigot & Co's Directory, 1842: Cornelius Oatley, carpenter & builder, Sheep Street.
Cross reference: Oatley Cornelius, builder, St.John.

809 OFFER CHARITY or OFFER, Charity.

1846/47-1849/50 assessed in absence of return £50; exempt.

810 ORAM, James, brewer.

Year	Amount returned £	Commissioners' estimate £	Income proved £	Final assessment £
1842/43	–	150	130	–
1846/47	–	200a	–	150
1847/48	150	200	–	200
1848/49	200	–	–	200

1849/50	200	–	–	200
1850/51	200	–	–	200
1851/52	200	–	–	200
1852/53	200	250	–	250
1853/54	250	300	–	300
1854/55	225	300	–	300
1855/56	250	300	–	300
1856/57	300	450	–	450
1857/58	400	600	–	600
1858/59	500	600	–	600
1859/60	500	700	–	700

Pigot & Co's Directory, 1842: James Oram, brewer, Northgate Street.

811 OVERTON, John, dissenting minister.

1846/47 entry only.

812 OVERY, Alfred, linen draper.

1842/43 returned and assessed £150.
1846/47-1847/48 assessed in absence of return £175.
1848/49 returned £150; assessed £175.
1849/50 assessed in absence of return £175; assessment discharged on appeal but no
    figure recorded.

1849/50 marked "now Marten linen draper".
Pigot & Co's Directory, 1842: Alfred Overy, linen & woollen draper, Maryport Street.
Cross references: Marten, -, linen draper, St.Mary; Walker, John, linen draper, St. Mary.

813 PARADISE, John, orange dealer.

1846/47-1848/49 assessed in absence of return £30; exempt.

814 PARKER, Sarah Jane, straw bonnet maker.

1842/43, 1846/47-1848/49 assessed in absence of return £20; exempt.
1849/50 assessed in absence of return £50; exempt.

Pigot & Co's Directory, 1842: Sarah Jane Parker & Co., straw hat maker, Maryport Street.

815 PEACOCK, Mary & Samuel, carriers.

1842/43, 1846/47 entries only marked "return at Bath".
1842/43 Mary & Samuel John Peacock; 1846/47 M & S Peacock.

816 PERRETT, Charlotte, coal dealer.

1859/60 returned and assessed £100.

817 PERRETT, George, coal merchant, shopkeeper.

Year	Amount returned £	Commissioners' estimate £	Income proved £	Final assessment £
1842/43	–	115	115	–
1846/47	120	–	–	120
1847/48	120	–	–	120
1848/49	–	120	–	120
1849/50	132	150a	132	–
1850/51	135	–	135	–
1851/52	–	135	135	–
1852/53	80	135	129.2.0	–
1853/54	118.10.0	–	–	118.10.0
1854/55	116.3.6	–	–	116.3.6
1855/56	100	–	–	100
1856/57	100	–	–	100
1857/58	120	–	–	120
1858/59	100	120	–	120
1859/60	–	120	–	120

1842/43, 1846/47-1857/58 George Perrett; 1858/59-1859/60 James Phipp as Executor of George Perrett.
1842/43, 1846/47 shopkeeper, etc; 1847/48-1850/51 coal merchant & shopkeeper; 1851/52-1857/58 coal merchant.
Pigot & Co's Directory, 1842: George Perrett, shopkeeper & dealer in groceries & sundries, New Park Street.

818 PERRETT, Reuben, boat owner, coal merchant.

Year	Amount returned £	Commissioners' estimate £	Income proved £	Final assessment £
1842/43	80	–	80	–
1846/47	–	80	80	–
1847/48	–	80	80	–
1848/49	–	80	103.10.0	–
1849/50	95	–	95	–
1850/51	30	–	30	–
1851/52	–	95	94	–
1852/53	50	95	124	–
1853/54	25	100	–	100

1854/55	–	100	–	100
1855/56	100	–	–	100
1856/57	42	100	–	100
1857/58	65	100	–	100
1858/59	100	–	–	100
1859/60	100	–	–	100

1842/43, 1846/47-1852/53 boat owner; 1853/54-1859/60 coal merchant.

819 PHILLIPS, George, boat owner, coal merchant.

1842/43, 1846/47-1847/48 assessed in absence of return £100; exempt.

Pigot & Co's Directory, 1842: George Phillips, coal merchant, Wharf.
1842/43, 1846/47 boat owner & coal merchant; 1847/48 boat owner, etc.

820 PHIPP, Daniel, coal merchant, wharfinger, carter, corn merchant.

Year	Amount returned £	Commissioners' estimate £	Income proved £	Final assessment £
1842/43	95w 43c	150	–	150
1846/47	–	100	100	–
1847/48	–	100	100	–
1848/49	100	–	100	–
1849/50	100	150	–	150
1850/51	–	150	–	150
1851/52	–	150	–	150
1852/53	150	–	–	150
1853/54	–	150	–	150
1854/55	150	–	–	150
1855/56	150	200	–	200
1856/57	200	350	–	350
1857/58	350	400	–	400
1858/59	400	500	–	500
1859/60	–	500	–	500

Abbreviations: w, wharfinger; c, carter.
1842/43, 1846/47-1852/53 Phipps; 1853/54-1859/60 Phipp.
1842/43 wharfinger, carter; 1846/47-1849/50 wharfinger, etc.; 1850/51 wharfinger;
1851/52 coal merchant, etc.; 1852/53-1854/55 corn (sic) merchant;
1855/56-1859/60 coal merchant.
1842/43 returned £15 as farmer but deleted.
1856/57 marked "Devizes and Bath"; 1858/59 marked "Devizes"; 1859/60 marked "Devizes
and Bristol".

Pigot & Co's Directory, 1842: Daniel Phipps (*sic*), wharfinger, Devizes Wharf.

821 PHIPP, James, innkeeper, Cross Keys.

1853/54 returned and assessed £65.15.0; exempt.
1855/56 assessed in absence of return £100.
1856/57 returned £100; assessed £200.
1857/58 assessed in absence of return £200.
1858/59 returned £150; assessed £200.
1859/60 assessed in absence of return £200.

1854/55 no assessment made. Marked "Ponting, George Butler, late Phipp, innkeeper; (assessments resume 1855/56) 1856/57 Cross Keys noted.
Cross reference: Phipp, John, farrier & innkeeper, St.Mary; Ponting, George Butler, innkeeper, St.Mary; Truman, Samuel, innkeeper, St.Mary.

822 PHIPP, John, farrier, innkeeper, beerhouse keeper. [by comparison, Cross Keys]

1851/52 returned and assessed £140; exempt.
1852/53 assessed in absence of return £150.
1853/54 assessed in absence of return £100.
1854/55 assessed in absence of return £50; exempt.

1851/52 farrier & beerhouse keeper; 1852/53-1853/54 farrier & innkeeper; 1854/55 farrier.
1855/56 "John" deleted, "James" substituted.
Pigot & Co's Directory, 1842: James Phipps, blacksmith, Monday Market Street.
Cross reference: Phipp, James, innkeeper, St.Mary; Ponting, George Butler, innkeeper, St.Mary; Truman, Samuel, innkeeper, St.Mary.

823 PHIPP, Samuel, corn porter.

1853/54 returned £50; exempt.
1854/55-1855/56 assessed in absence of return £50; exempt.
1856/57-1857/58 recorded; no assessments made; exempt.
1858/59 assessed in absence of return £80.
1859/60 returned £80; assessed £100.

1859/60 assessment increased possibly on objection by surveyor of taxes.

824 PHIPPS, David.

1842/43 name only entered.

825 PILE, Benjamin, tea dealer, grocer.

1842/43, 1846/47-1847/48 assessed in absence of return £80; exempt.
1848/49 assessed in absence of return £80; income proved at £81.16.0; exempt.
1849/50 assessed in absence of return £80; exempt.

1842/43 tea dealer & grocer; 1846/47-1849/50 tea dealer.
Pigot & Co's Directory, 1842: Benjamin Pile, shopkeeper & dealer in groceries & sundries.

826 PONTING, George Butler, innkeeper. [by comparison, Cross Keys]

1854/55 returned and assessed £125.

1854/55 marked "late Phipp, innkeeper".
Cross references: Phipp, James, innkeeper, St.Mary; Phipp, John, farrier & innkeeper, St.Mary;
    Truman, Samuel, innkeeper, St.Mary.

827 PRICE, Ezra, piano forte seller, music seller.

1859/60 assessed in absence of return £130.

1858/59 marked "see Market Lavington".
1859/60 marked [Market Lavington] "at Devizes, removed to St.Mary".
Cross reference: Price, Ezra, grocer & piano forte tuner, Market Lavington.

828 PRITCHARD, George, tailor.

1842/43, 1846/47-1849/50 assessed in absence of return £50; exempt.

Pigot & Co's Directory, 1842: George Pritchard, tailor, Sheep Street.

829 RANDELL, George, baker, grocer.

1842/43 returned and assessed £150.
1846/47 returned and assessed £160.
1847/48 returned £160; assessed £150 and £13 interest.
1848/49 assessed in absence of return £163; income proved at £125.6.0; exempt.
1849/50 returned £131.12.0; assessed £150.
1850/51-1854/55 returned and assessed £160.
1855/56-1857/58 returned £155; assessed 160.
1858/59-1859/60 returned and assessed £160.

1846/47-1849/50, 1853/54 Randle.
1842/43 baker & grocer; 1846/47-1849/50 baker, etc.; baker 1850/51-1859/60.

1846/47-1847/48 interest included in total figure.
1856/57 returned £160 but no assessment made.
Pigot & Co's Directory, 1842: George Randell, baker, New Park Street.

830 RANDELL, J.Ashley, cabinet maker, auctioneer.

1846/47-1852/53 assessed in absence of return £80; exempt.

1846/47-1849/50 cabinet maker; 1850/51-1852/53 auctioneer & cabinet maker.
1853/54 marked "late, now -," "gone".

831 RANDELL, James T., tallow chandler, brickmaker, coal merchant.

1842/43 returned £200; assessed £400.
1846/47-1847/48 returned £250; assessed £350.
1848/49 returned and assessed £350.

1842/43 tallow chandler & brickmaker; 1846/47-1848/49 tallow chandler, brickmaker & coal
merchant; 1849/50 brickmaker & coal merchant.
1842/43 James, otherwise J.T.
1849/59 marked "see Rowde" (no assessment made in Rowde).
Pigot & Co's Directory, 1842: James Randell, coal merchant, Maryport Wharf; tallow chandler,
Maryport Street.

832 REYNOLDS, Charles, butcher.

1842/43 assessed in absence of return £54.6.8; exempt.

Pigot & Co's Directory, 1842: Charles Reynolds, butcher, Sidmouth Street.

833 REYNOLDS, William & Stephen, curriers. [also REYNOLDS, Robert]

1842/43 returned and assessed £150.
1846/47-1847/48 assessed in absence of return £300.
1848/49 returned and assessed £190; exempt.
1849/50 returned and assessed £168; exempt.
1850/51 assessed in absence of return £168; exempt.
1851/52 returned and assessed £220; exempt.
1852/53 returned and assessed £220; income proved at £262; exempt.
1853/54 returned and assessed £225.
1854/55 returned and assessed £240.
1855/56 returned £220; assessed £240.
1856/57 assessed in absence of return £260.
1857/58-1859/60 returned and assessed £260.

1842/43 Robert Reynolds.
1848/49–1852/53 entitled to exemption as partnership income.
Pigot & Co's Directory, 1842: Robert Reynolds, currier & leather cutter, Maryport Street.

834 ROBBINS, Samuel, timber merchant.

1848/49 returned and assessed £100.
1851/52–1852/53 returned £80; assessed £100.

1849/50–1850/51 marked "return at Woodborough".
Pigot & Co's Directory, 1842: Samuel Robbins, timber merchant, Wharf.
Cross reference: Robbins, Samuel, timber merchant, Woodborough.

835 ROMAIN, William, builder. [also ROMAIN, John]

1842/43 returned £40; assessed £130.
1846/47–1849/50 returned £130; assessed £150.
1850/51 returned and assessed £150.
1851/52 returned and assessed £130.
1852/53–1855/56 returned £130; assessed £150.
1856/57–1857/58 returned £120; assessed £150.
1858/59 returned and assessed £100.
1859/60 assessed in absence of return £100; exempt.

1842/43, 1846/47–1858/59 William Romain; 1859/60 William & John Romain.
1859/60 entitled to exemption as partnership income.
Pigot & Co's Directory, 1842: William Romain, builder, carpenter & wheelwright, timber merchant, New Park Street.

836 RUTTER, John.

1842/43 name only entered.

837 SAINSBURY, George Taylor, slate merchant, brickmaker, druggist, chemist.

Year	Amount returned £	Commissioners' estimate £	Income proved £	Final assessment £
1842/43	150b 170d	320	–	320
1846/47	120b	120	–	120
1847/48	150b 50c	– –	– 50	150 –
1848/49	130b	–	–	130
1851/52	150	200	–	200
1853/54	200s	–	–	200

	200b	-	-	200
1854/55	500	-	-	500
1855/56	500	600	-	600

Abbreviations: b, brickmaker; c, chemist; d, druggist; s, slate merchant.
1842/43, 1846/47-1852/53 brickmaker; 1842/43 druggist; 1847/48 chemist; 1853/54-1855/56 slate merchant & brickmaker.
1847/48-1849/50 marked "G.B.Bunter chemist, late Sainsbury"
1849/50-1850/51, 1852/53, 1856/57-1859/60 assessed in Rowde.
1855/56 marked "at Seend & Rowde".
The exemption claimed in 1847/48 is anomalous but entry is made against George Taylor Sainsbury.
Pigot & Co's Directory, 1842: George Taylor Sainsbury, chemist & druggist, Market; agent to Economic Life Office, Market Place.
Cross references: Bunter, G.B., chemist, St.Mary; Madge, James Cornelius, chemist, St.Mary; Sainsbury, George Taylor, brickmaker, Rowde.

838 SAINSBURY & SAUNDERS, coal merchants. [also SAUNDERS, Henry]

1846/47 returned and assessed £600.
1847/48-1849/50 returned £500; assessed £600.
1850/51-1852/53 returned and assessed £500.
1853/54-1854/55 returned and assessed £250.
1855/56-1856/57 returned £250; assessed £300.
1857/58 returned and assessed £250.

1846/47-1852/53 Sainsbury & Saunders; 1853/54-1857/58 Henry Saunders.
1858/59-1859/60 marked "Nursteed". (no assessments made in Nursteed).

839 SAPP, Elias.

1846/47-1848/49 assessed in absence of return £90; exempt.

No occupation noted.

840 SAYER, John, shoemaker.

1842/43, 1846/47-1849/50 assessed in absence of return £60; exempt.

Pigot & Co's Directory, 1842: John Sayer, boot & shoe maker, New Park Street.

841 SEDGEFIELD, Edward, grocer, Fire Office agent. [also SEDGEFIELD, Mrs Sarah, SEDGFIELD, (sic) John]

1842/43, 1846/47 returned and assessed £200g, £15f.
1847/48 assessed in absence of return £215.

1848/49 returned and assessed £215.
1849/50-1851/52 returned and assessed £190.
1852/53 assessed in absence of return £190.
1853/54 returned £5; no assessment made.
1854/55 returned £30; assessed £100.
1855/56-1856/57 returned and assessed £110.
1857/58 assessed in absence of return £120.
1858/59-1859/60 returned and assessed £120.

Abbreviations: g, grocer; f, Fire Office agent.
1842/43, 1846/47-1849/50 Edward Sedgefield; 1850/51-1852/53 Mrs Sedgefield;
1853/54-1855/56 Sarah Sedgefield; 1856/57-1859/60 John Sedgfield (sic).
1842/43, 1846/47-1854/55 grocer & Fire Office agent; 1855/56-1859/60 grocer & agent.
1852/53 marked "now Jarman". (no reference elsewhere to Jarman)
1857/58 [Potterne] "Marshman, Samuel now Sedgefield, John, baker & grocer".
1858/59 [Potterne] "Marshman, Samuel - see Sedgefield, St.Mary"
Pigot & Co's Directory, 1842: Edward Sedgefield, grocer, wine merchant (British wines & spirits), agent to County (Fire) & Provident (Life) Office, Maryport Street.
Cross references: Marshman, Samuel, baker & grocer, Potterne; Sedgefield, John, baker & grocer, Potterne.

842 SELBY, Thomas, bacon factor. [also SELBY, Harriet]

1842/43, 1846/47-1850/51 assessed in absence of return £100; exempt.
1852/53 returned £88.4.0; assessed £100; income proved at £88.4.0; exempt.
1853/54-1854/55 returned and assessed £120.
1855/56-1856/57 assessed in absence of return £150.
1858/59-1859/60 returned and assessed £150.

1842/43, 1846/47-1857/58 Thomas Selby; 1858/59-1859/60 Harriet Selby.
1851/52 no assessment made.
1857/58 marked "dead"; no assessment made.
Pigot & Co's Directory, 1842: Thomas Selby, cheese & bacon factor, Northgate Street.

843 SHEPHERD, James, carpenter.

1846/47-1848/49 assessed in absence of return £20; exempt.
1849/50 assessed in absence of return £50; exempt.

844 SHEPPARD, William, coachman, coachmaster, innkeeper. [by comparison, Nags Head]

1842/43 returned and assessed £70; exempt.
1846/47-1848/49 assessed in absence of return £70; exempt.
1849/50 assessed in absence of return £150; reduced to £120 on appeal; exempt.
1850/51 returned and assessed £120; exempt.

1851/52 assessed in absence of return £120; income proved at £95; exempt.
1852/53 assessed in absence of return £120; income proved and assessment discharged but no sum recorded.
1853/54 returned and assessed £100.

1842/43 coachman, 1846/47-1849/50 coachmaster, 1850/51-1852/53 coachmaster & innkeeper, 1853/54 innkeeper.
1854/55 Sheppard deleted, Joseph Willis substituted.
Cross reference: White, William, innkeeper & cheese factor, St.Mary; Willis, Samuel & Son, coachmaker & innkeeper, St.Mary.

845 SHILSTONE, John, broker.

1853/54 returned £94; assessed £100; income proved at £94.
1854/55-1856/57 assessed in absence of return £100.
1857/58-1858/59 returned and assessed £100.
1859/60 returned £100; assessed £150.

1854/55 Shilston.

846 SIVELL, Henry, grocer.

1842/43 returned and assessed £250.
1846/47-1847/48 assessed in absence of return £250.
1848/49 returned £250; assessed £300.
1849/50 returned £127.8.0; assessed £250.
1850/51-1855/56 returned £200; assessed £250.
1856/57-1859/60 returned £250; assessed £300.

1842/43, 1846/47-1851/52 Sivill.
Pigot & Co's Directory, 1842: Henry Sivell, grocer & tea dealer, New Park Street

847 SKINNER, Joseph, tinman, agent.

1842/43 assessed in absence of return £100; income proved at £133.6.2.
1846/47 assessed in absence of return £90; exempt.

1842/43 tinman & agent; 1846/47 tinman.
1847/48 marked "St.John".
Pigot & Co's Directory, 1842: Joseph Skinner, brazier & tinman, Brittox.
Cross reference: Skinner, Joseph, tinman, St.John.

848 SLADE, John, solicitor.

1842/43 returned £250; assessed £300.
1846/47 returned and assessed £300.

Pigot & Co's Directory, 1842: John Slade, attorney, New Park Street.

849 SLOPER, Joseph, linen draper.

1850/51 assessed in absence of return £150.
1851/52 assessed in absence of return £100; income proved at £132.10.0; exempt.
1852/53 assessed in absence of return £120; assessment discharged on appeal but no
sum recorded.
1853/54 returned £70 and £24 interest; assessed £120.
1854/55 returned and assessed £100.
1855/56 assessed in absence of return £100.
1856/57–1859/60 returned £70; assessed £120.

1850/51 marked "late Wolfe linen draper".
Cross reference: Sloper, Joseph, linen draper, St.John; Wolfe, John, draper, St.Mary.

850 SLY, William, saddler, trumpeter in yeomanry.

Year	Amount returned	Commissioners' estimate	Final assessment
	£	£	£
1842/43	160	–	160
1846/47	150	–	150
1847/48	150	–	150
1848/49	140	150	150
1849/50	150	–	150
1850/51	140	150	150
1851/52	138.10.0	150	150
1852/53	139.15.0	150	150
1853/54	114.3.8 10t	150	150
1854/55	123	150	150
1855/56	124	150	150
1856/57	120	160	160

Abbreviation: t, trumpeter in yeomanry.
1842/43, 1846/47–1856/57 saddler; 1853/54–1854/55 trumpeter in yeomanry.
1857/58 marked "Charged Sly & Son see St.John".
Pigot & Co's Directory, 1842: William Sly, saddler & harness maker, Brittox.
Cross reference: Sly, William, harness maker, St.John.

851 SMALLBONES, James, linen draper.

Year	Amount returned	Commissioners' estimate	Final assessment
	£	£	£
1842/43	300	–	300

1846/47	270	350	350
1847/48	300	350	350
1848/49	250	350	350
1849/50	250	300a	250
1850/51	300	-	300
1851/52	300	-	300
1852/53	250	300	300
1853/54	300	-	300
1854/55	200	250	250
1855/56	300	-	300
1856/57	200	300	300
1857/58	250	-	250
1858/59	150	200	200
1859/60	200	250	250

Pigot & Co's Directory, 1842: James Smallbones, linen & woollen draper, Sidmouth Street.

852 SMITH, George, William & Mary, linen drapers.

1842/43 returned and assessed £300.
1846/47 assessed in absence of return £300.
1847/48 returned and assessed £300.
1848/49-1850/51 assessed in absence of return £200; exempt.
1851/52-1852/53 assessed in absence of return £315; £210 exempt.
1853/54 assessed in absence of return £115.
1854/55-1859/60 assessed in absence of return £300.

1842/43, 1846/47-1847/48 George Smith; 1848/49-1850/51 George & William Smith;
1851/52-1859/60 George, William & Mary Smith (sometimes Mrs Smith)
1851/52-1852/53 £105 left in charge, 1852/53 marked "Mrs Smith liable".
1853/54 assessment on Mrs Smith only, G & W Smith being exempt.
Pigot & Co's Directory, 1842: George Smith, linen & woollen draper, Brittox.

853 STAPLES, William, grocer.

1849/50 assessed in absence of return £80; exempt.
1850/51 assessed in absence of return £100; exempt.
1853/54 returned and assessed £84; exempt.
1854/55 assessed in absence of return £84; exempt.

1849/50 marked "Day, Ozias late now Staples, grocer";Vines, Uriah now Staples".
1851/52-1852/53 no assessments made.
1855/56 marked "gone".
1856/57 marked "now Holder".
1857/58 marked "late Holder now Humphrey & Carter".
Cross references: Day, Ozias, grocer, St.Mary; Holder, Charles, grocer, St.Mary; Humphrey,Thomas & Carter, John, grocers, St.Mary;Vines, Uriah, grocer, St. Mary.

854 STEVENS, Jonathan, fruiterer.

1846/47–1849/50 assessed in absence of return £50; exempt.

855 STOCKWELL, John, plumber, glazier. [also STOCKWELL, ADLAM & GREGORY]

1842/43 assessed in absence of return £232.10.0; exempt.
1846/47–1848/49 assessed in absence of return £100; exempt.
1849/50 assessed in absence of return £60; exempt.
1853/54 returned and assessed £120.
1854/55 assessed in absence of return £120; reduced to £100 but no appeal noted.
1855/56 returned and assessed £100.
1856/57 recorded but no assessment made.
1857/58 assessed in absence of return £100.
1858/59 returned and assessed £100.
1859/60 assessed in absence of return £130.

1842/43 Stockwell, Adlam & Gregory; 1846/47–1854/55 John Stockwell; 1855/56–1859/60 John Stockwell & Son.
1842/43 plumbers & glaziers; 1846/47 glazier; 1847/48–1849/50, 1853/54–1859/60 plumber.
1842/43 entitled to exemption as partnership income.
1850/51–1852/53 no assessments made.
Cross reference: Adlam, Samuel, plumber, glazier, painter, St.Mary; Gregory, George, painter, St.Mary.

856 STRANGE, Robert, attorney, solicitor.

1842/43 returned £80; assessed £120.
1846/47 returned £50; assessed £120; reduced to £80 on appeal.
1847/48–1849/50 returned and assessed £80; exempt 1848/49.
1850/51 assessed in absence of return £80; exempt.

1842/43 solicitor; 1846/47–1850/51 attorney.
Pigot & Co's Directory, 1842: Robert Strange, attorney, agent to Globe Fire Office, New Park Street.

857 TABOIS, F[rederick] W[illiam], cutler, etc.

1842/43, 1846/47–1847/48 assessed in absence of return £100; exempt.

Pigot & Co's Directory, 1842: Frederick William Tabois, ironmonger & cutler, Brittox.

858 THOMAS, George, innkeeper. [by comparison, White Lion]

1842/43 assessed in absence of return £100; exempt.

Pigot & Co's Directory, 1842: George Thomas, White Lion, Northgate Street.
Cross references: Biggs, George, innkeeper, St. Mary; Trueman, Richard, innkeeper, St.Mary.

859 THOMPSON, Peter, baker, pork butcher.

1842/43 returned and assessed £150.
1846/47 assessed in absence of return £120; assessment discharged on appeal but no sum recorded.
1847/48 assessed in absence of return £160; income proved at £120; exempt.
1848/49 assessed in absence of return £120; income proved at £94.7.0; exempt.
1849/50-1851/52 assessed in absence of return £120; exempt.

1842/43, 1846/47-1847/48 baker; 1848/49 baker, etc.; 1849/50-1851/52 baker & pork butcher.
Pigot & Co's Directory, 1842: Peter Thompson, baker, cheese & bacon factor, New Park Street.

860 THOMPSON, Stephen, tailor.

1842/43 assessed in absence of return £120; exempt.
1846/47 returned and assessed £150.
1847/48 assessed in absence of return £150.
1848/49-1849/50 returned and assessed £150.
1850/51 assessed in absence of return £150.
1851/52-1858/59 returned and assessed £150.
1859/60 assessed in absence of return £150.

Pigot & Co's Directory, 1842: Stephen Thompson, tailor, Northgate Street.

861 TRINDER, Charles, surgeon, medicine.

1842/43 returned and assessed £350m, £25 bond security.
1846/47 returned and assessed £321.13.4.
1847/48 returned and assessed £350s, £21.13.4 interest.
1848/49 assessed in absence of return £271.6.8.
1849/50 returned and assessed £250s, £21.13.4 interest.
1850/51 returned and assessed £200.

Abbreviations: m, medicine; s, surgeon.
1842/43 medicine; 1846/47-1850/51 surgeon.
1846/47 includes "interest on money".
Pigot & Co's Directory, 1842: Charles Trinder, surgeon, New Park Street.

862 TRUEMAN, Richard, innkeeper, White Lion.

1853/54 assessed in absence of return £100; income proved at £65.
1854/55-1856/57 assessed in absence of return £100.
1857/58 returned £80; assessed £100.
1858/59 returned and assessed £100.
1859/60 assessed in absence of return £100.

1856/57 White Lion noted.
Cross references: Biggs, George, innkeeper, St. Mary; Thomas, George, innkeeper, St.Mary.

863 TRUMAN, Samuel, innkeeper [by comparison, Cross Keys].

1842/43, 1846/47-1849/50 assessed in absence of return £80; exempt.

Pigot & Co's Directory, 1842: Samuel Truman, Cross Keys, Market Street.
Cross reference: Phipp, James, innkeeper, St.Mary; Phipp, John, farrier & innkeeper, St.Mary;
    Ponting, George Butler, innkeeper, St.Mary.

864 VINCENT, J[ohn] P[hillips], veterinary surgeon.

1842/43 returned and assessed £158.15.4.

Pigot & Co's Directory, 1842: John Phillips Vincent, veterinary surgeon, Northgate Street.
Cross reference: Vincent, J.P., veterinary surgeon, St.John.

865 VINES, Uriah, grocer.

1842/43, 1846/47-1849/50 assessed in absence of return £100; exempt.

1849/50 marked "now Staples".
Pigot & Co's Directory, 1842: Uriah Vines, baker, grocer, Northgate Street.
Cross references: Day, Ozias, bacon & cheese factor, St. Mary; Holder, Charles, grocer, St.Mary;
    Humphrey, Thomas & Carter, John, grocers, St.Mary; Staples, William, grocer, St.Mary.

866 WADWORTH, William John, baker, pig killer.

1842/43 assessed in absence of return £150; income proved at £146; exempt.
1846/47 assessed in absence of return £160.
1847/48 assessed in absence of return £160; income proved at £120; exempt.

William Wadworth Junior 1848/49.
1842/43 baker & pig killer; 1846/47-1847/48 baker, etc.
1848/49 marked "now in Week".
Pigot & Co's Directory, 1842: William Wadworth, baker, cheese & bacon factor, New Park Street.
Cross reference: Wadworth, William, cheese factor, Week.

867 WAITE, Ann, blacksmith.

1842/43, 1846/47-1849/50 assessed in absence of return £80; exempt.

Pigot & Co's Directory, 1842: Ann Waite, blacksmith, Sheep Street.

868 WALKER, John, draper.

1851/52-1854/55 returned and assessed £160.
1855/56 assessed in absence of return £160.
1856/57 returned and assessed £160.
1857/58-1859/60 returned £160; assessed £200.

1850/51 marked "Marten late now Walker, linen draper".
1855/56 figures indistinct, seemingly £100 but likely to be £160.
Cross references: Marten, -, linen draper, St.Mary; Overy, Alfred, linen draper, St.Mary.

869 WARD, Thomas Ponson, cabinet maker.

1842/43 assessed in absence of return £50; exempt.

870 WATTS, William, bricklayer.

1854/55 assessed in absence of return £100.
1855/56-1856/57 returned and assessed £100.
1857/58 returned £80; assessed £100.
1858/59-1859/60 returned and assessed £100.

871 WAYLEN, George, surgeon

Year	Amount returned £	Commissioners' estimate £	Final assessment £
1846/47	–	125	125
1847/48	125	210	210
1848/49	200	–	200
1849/50	200	–	200
1850/51	–	250	250
1851/52	190	250	250
1852/53	–	250	250
1853/54	200	250	250
1854/55	200	250	250
1855/56	–	250	250
1856/57	–	142	142

1857/58	–	150	150
1858/59	200	–	200
1859/60	250	–	250

1846/47 assessed in partnership with William Waylen.
Cross reference: Waylen, William, surgeon, St.Mary.

872 WAYLEN, Robert, schoolmaster, education, wine manufacturer.

Year	Amount returned £	Commissioners' estimate £	Final assessment £
1852/53	160s 50w	–	210
1853/54	140s 50w	–	190
1854/55	150	–	150
1855/56	128	–	128
1856/57	117	–	117
1857/58	150	–	150
1858/59	193	–	193
1859/60	241	–	241

Abbreviations: s, schoolmaster or education; w, wine manufacturer.
1852/52-1853/54 education; 1854/55-1859/60 schoolmaster; 1852/53-1855/56 wine manufacturer.

873 WAYLEN, William, innkeeper. [by comparison, Old Crown]

1846/47 assessed in absence of return £100; exempt.

1847/48 marked "William Waylen, innkeeper, now Dyke".
Cross reference: Chandler, James, innkeeper, St. Mary; Dyke, George, innkeeper, St.Mary.

874 WAYLEN, William, surgeon.

1842/43 returned and assessed £200.
1846/47 assessed in absence of return £125.
1847/48 returned and assessed £40.
1848/49 returned and assessed £90.
1849/50 Schedule E £50; exempt.

1846/47 assessed in partnership with George Waylen.
Pigot & Co's Directory, 1842: William Waylen, surgeon, Brittox.
Cross reference: Waylen, George, surgeon, St.Mary.

875 WESTON, Henry, hair dresser, grocer.

1842/43, 1846/47-1848/49 assessed in absence of return £100; exempt.
1849/50 assessed in absence of return £50; exempt.
1852/53 returned and assessed £95; income proved at £110; exempt.
1853/54 returned £72.14.0; assessed £100; income proved at £72.14.0; exempt.
1854/55 assessed in absence of return £80; exempt.
1855/56 assessed in absence of return £80.
1856/57 assessed in absence of return £80; confirmed on appeal.
1857/58 returned £62; assessed £80; exempt.
1858/59 recorded; no assessment made; exempt.
1859/60 returned £82; no assessment made; exempt.

1842/43, 1846/47 hair dresser, etc; 1847/48-1849/50 hair dresser; 1852/53-1859/60 grocer, hair dresser (etc., 1852/53-1853/54).
1850/51-1851/52 no assessments made.
Pigot & Co's Directory, 1842: Henry Weston, perfumer & hair dresser & toy dealer, shopkeeper & dealer in groceries & sundries, Chapel Corner.

876 WESTON, John, baker, grocer.

1848/49 assessed in absence of return £120; income proved at £90; exempt.
1849/50-1850/51 assessed in absence of return £120; exempt.
1851/52 returned £80; assessed £120; exempt.
1852/53-1853/54 assessed in absence of return £100; exempt.
1854/55 returned £100; assessed £150; reduced to £125 but no appeal noted.
1855/56 returned £80; assessed £125.
1856/57 returned £100; assessed £125.

1848/49-1850/51, 1856/57 baker; 1851/52-1855/56 baker & grocer.
1857/58 marked "now Higgs, baker, etc."
Cross reference: Higgs, Elijah Andrew, grocer, St.Mary.

877 WHEELER, Mary Ann Elizabeth, schoolmistress, shopkeeper.

1842/43, 1846/47-1849/50 assessed in absence of return £65; exempt.

1842/43 schoolmistress & shopkeeper; 1846/47-1849/50 schoolmistress.
Pigot & Co's Directory, 1842: Mary & Elizabeth Wheeler, grocers & tea dealers, Sidmouth Street.

878 WHEELER, Richard, pork butcher, dairyman.

1842/43, 1846/47-1850/51 assessed in absence of return £60; exempt.
1851/52 assessed in absence of return £60; income proved at £57; exempt.

1852/53-1855/56 assessed in absence of return £60; exempt.
1856/57 recorded; no assessment made; exempt.
1857/58 returned £41.12.0; no assessment made; exempt.
1858/59 recorded; no assessment made; exempt.
1859/60 returned £52; assessed £100.

1842/43, 1846/47-1856/57 pork butcher; 1857/58-1859/60 pork butcher & dairyman.
Pigot & Co's Directory, 1842: Richard Wheeler, pork butcher, Sidmouth Street.

879 WHEELER, Robert, tailor.

1842/43, 1846/47-1855/56 assessed in absence of return £60; exempt.
1856/57-1859/60 recorded; no assessments made; exempt.

Pigot & Co's Directory, 1842: R.Wheeler, tailor, New Park Street.

880 WHEELER, Thomas, gunsmith.

1842/43, 1846/47-1855/56 assessed in absence of return £75; exempt.
1856/57-1859/60 recorded; no assessments made; exempt.

Pigot & Co's Directory, 1842: William Wheeler, gun maker, Little Brittox.

881 WHITE, George, ironmonger.

1842/43, 1846/47-1847/48 assessed in absence of return £95; exempt.
1848/49 assessed in absence of return £95; income proved at £113; exempt.
1849/50 assessed in absence of return £95; exempt.
1850/51 assessed in absence of return £95 and £32 interest; income proved at £110;
    exempt.
1851/52 assessed in absence of return £120 and £32 interest; income proved at £120;
    exempt.
1852/53 returned £115; assessed £120; income proved at £117; exempt.
1853/54 returned £115; assessed £150; reduced to £125 but no appeal noted.
1854/55 returned £110; assessed £125.
1855/56 returned £112; assessed £125.
1856/57 returned £110; assessed £125.
1857/58 returned £120 and £41.12.0 interest; assessed £130.
1858/59-1859/60 returned £115; assessed £130.

1851/52 interest charged under Schedule C.
Pigot & Co's Directory, 1842: George White, ironmonger, Sidmouth Street.

882 WHITE, William, innkeeper, cheese factor. [by comparison, Nags Head]

1842/43 returned £70; assessed £125; exempt.

Pigot & Co's Directory, 1842: White, -, Nags Head, New Park Street.
Cross references: Sheppard, William, innkeeper, St.Mary; Willis, Samuel & Son, innkeeper,
St.Mary.

883 WILD, Decimus, innkeeper, White Bear.

1853/54 returned £140; assessed £150.
1854/55 returned £110; assessed £150.
1855/56 returned £120; assessed £150.
1856/57 returned £130; assessed £300.
1857/58 returned £205; assessed £300.
1858/59 returned £180; assessed £300.

1852/53 marked "Macklin now Decimus Wild innkeeper".
1853/54 marked "late Macklin innkeeper".
1859/60 marked "Macklin, Thomas, innkeeper, White Bear".
1859/60 [Bedborough] marked "late Cole, innkeeper, Bell".
Cross reference: Macklin, James, innkeeper, St.Mary; Macklin, Thomas, innkeeper, St.Mary;
Wild, Decimus, innkeeper, Bedborough.

884 WILD, George, innkeeper, Three Crowns.

1856/57 assessed in absence of return £100.
1857/58-1859/60 returned and assessed £100.

1856/57 [St.John] entered but deleted.
1857/57-1859/60 marked "late Chandler, Three Crowns".
Cross reference: Chandler, James, innkeeper, St.Mary.

885 WILLIS, Samuel.

1850/51-1851/52 assessed in absence of return £57.2.6; exempt.

No occupation noted.

886 WILLIS, Samuel & Son, coachmakers, innkeeper, Nags Head. [also WILLIS, Joseph]

1842/43 assessed in absence of return £130; exempt.
1846/47-1847/48 assessed in absence of return £120; exempt.
1848/49 assessed in absence of return £120; income proved at £110; exempt.
1849/50 returned and assessed £110; exempt.
1850/51-1851/52 assessed in absence of return £110; exempt.
1852/53 returned and assessed £110; income proved at £142; exempt.
1853/54 returned £100; assessed £130.

1854/55 returned £100; assessed £150.
1855/56 returned and assessed £150.
1856/57 returned £150; assessed 80c, 160i.
1857/58 returned £200; assessed £240.
1858/59 returned £200; assessed £250.
1859/60 returned £210; assessed £300.

Abbreviations: c, coachmaker; i, innkeeper.
1842/43 Samuel Willis & Son; 1846/47-1849/50 Samuel & Joseph Willis;
1850/51-1859/60 Joseph Willis.
1842/43, 1846/47-1855/56 coachmaker(s); 1855/56-1859/60 coachmaker & innkeeper.
1854/55 marked "Return to make for innkeeper".
1857/58 Nags Head noted.
Pigot & Co's Directory, 1842: Samuel Willis & Son, brightsmiths, coachmakers, Maryport Street.
Cross references: Sheppard, William, innkeeper, St.Mary; White, William, innkeeper, St.Mary.

887 WISE, Joseph, coachmaker.

1842/43 assessed in absence of return £60; exempt.

Pigot & Co's Directory, 1842: Joseph Wise, coachmaker, Maryport Street.

888 WITHINGTON, W., watchmaker.

1856/57-1857/58 recorded but no assessments made.

1855/56 marked "Wood, John now Waddington (sic) watchmaker".
1858/59 marked "removed into St.John".
Cross references: Withington, William Bamforth, watchmaker, St.John; Wood, John, watchmaker, St.Mary.

889 WOLFE, John, draper.

1842/43, 1846/47-1848/49 assessed in absence of return £100; exempt.
1849/50 returned and assessed £100; exempt.

1850/51 marked "Sloper, Joseph late Wolfe, linen draper".
Pigot & Co's Directory, 1842: John Wolfe, linen & woollen draper, Brittox.
Cross reference: Sloper, Joseph, linen draper, St.Mary.

890 WOOD, John, watchmaker.

1842/43, 1846/47-1853/54 assessed in absence of return £80; exempt.
1854/55 assessed in absence of return £60; exempt.

1855/56 marked "now Waddington (*sic*), watchmaker".
Pigot & Co's Directory, 1842: John Wood, watch & clock maker, Northgate Street.
Cross reference: Withington, W., watchmaker, St.Mary; Withington, William Bamforth, watchmaker, St.John.

891 WOODMAN, John, bricklayer.

1846/47-1847/48 assessed in absence of return £97; exempt.
1848/49 assessed in absence of return £97; income proved at £65.11.7; exempt.
1849/50-1850/51 assessed in absence of return £97; exempt.
1851/52 assessed in absence of return £100; exempt.
1852/53 assessed in absence of return £50; exempt.
1853/54 returned £33; assessed £60; exempt.
1854/55-1855/56 assessed in absence of return £60; exempt.
1856/57-1859/60 recorded; no assessments made; exempt.

Pigot & Co's Directory, 1842: John Woodman, bricklayer, Green.

892 YOUNG, Joseph, carrier.

1853/54 returned £75.8.0; assessed £80; exempt.
1854/55 assessed in absence of return £80; exempt.
1855/56-1856/57 assessed in absence of return £100.

Cross reference: Young, Joseph, carrier, St.John.

893 YOUNG, Joseph Eden, innkeeper, White Hart.

1857/58 returned £60; assessed £100.
1858/59-1859/60 returned and assessed £100.

1857/58 marked "Dangerfield, Isaiah now Joseph Young". White Hart noted.
Cross reference: Dangerfield, Isaiah, innkeeper, St.Mary.

ALLCANNINGS

894 AKERMAN, Stephen, baker, brewer.

1851/52 returned and assessed £100; exempt.
1852/53-1854/55 returned £50; assessed £100; exempt 1852/53.
1855/56 assessed in absence of return £100.

1856/57 marked "now Bailey".
Cross reference: Bailey, John, grocer, baker & brewer, Allcannings.

895 BAILEY, John, baker, grocer, brewer. [also BAILEY, Joseph]

1848/49 returned £50; assessed £75; exempt.
1849/50-1850/51 assessed in absence of return £70; exempt.
1851/52 returned £50; assessed £70; income proved at £50; exempt.
1852/53 assessed in absence of return £70; exempt.
1853/54 returned and assessed £60; exempt.
1854/55 returned £50; assessed £100.
1855/56-1856/57 assessed in absence of return £100.
1857/58 returned £50; assessed £100.
1858/59 returned £20b&g, £30br; assessed £100.
1859/60 assessed in absence of return £100.

Abbreviations: b&g, baker & grocer; br, brewer.
1848/49-1853/54 Joseph Bailey; 1854/55-1859/60 John Bailey.
1848/49-1855/56 baker & grocer; 1856/57-1859/60 baker, grocer & brewer.
1856/57 marked "Akerman, Stephen now Bailey".
Cross reference: Akerman, Stephen, baker, brewer, Allcannings.

896 CANNING, Jane, interest on money.

1853/54 returned and assessed £90; exempt.

897 CHANDLER, Thomas, baker, brewer, maltster.

1842/43 returned £200; assessed £150.

1842/43 baker, brewer & maltster; 1846/47 baker & brewer.
1846/47 marked "q.left".

898 HISCOCK, John.

1842/43 name only entered.

899 M [illeg] Revd. A.

1850/51 returned £451.3.0 or £1151.3.0 but no assessment made.
By comparison with *Clergy List*, this entry relates to Revd. T.A. Methuen.

Figures illegible.

900 MASLEN, Daniel, maltster, baker, butcher.

1842/43 returned and assessed £100.
1846/47 returned £20; assessed £85; income proved at £70 but assessment stood.
1847/48 returned £20; assessed £85; income proved at £70; exempt.
1848/49 returned £40; assessed £70.
1849/50-1850/51 assessed in absence of return £70.
1851/52 returned £20; assessed £40.
1852/53 returned £30; assessed £70; income proved at £109; exempt.
1853/54 returned £20; assessed £100; reduced to £65 but no appeal noted.
1854/55 returned £20; assessed £65.
1855/56-1856/57 assessed in absence of return £65.
1857/58-1858/59 returned £20; assessed £65.
1859/60 assessed in absence of return £65.

1842/43 maltster; 1846/47-1852/53 baker & butcher; 1853/54-1855/56 baker & farmer; 1856/57-1859/60 baker.

901 MASLEN, James, butcher, innkeeper, miller, grocer, baker. [possibly Kings Arms]

Year	Amount returned £	Commissioners' estimate £	Income proved £	Final assessment £
1842/43	–	30	30	–
1846/47	30	100	100	–
1847/48	20	100	100	–
1848/49	80	100	100	–
1849/50	–	100	100	–
1850/51	–	100	100	–
1851/52	60	100	80	–
1852/53	40	–	–	40
1853/54	20	50	–	50

1854/55	10	50	50	–
1855/56	–	150	–	150
1856/57	–	150	–	150
1857/58	65	150	–	150
1858/59	5b	150	–	150
	10g			
	5ba			
1859/60	–	150	–	150

Abbreviations; b, butcher, ba, baker, g, grocer.
1842/43 innkeeper; 1846/47-1848/49 innkeeper & butcher; 1849/50-1854/55 butcher; 1855/56-1857/58 butcher & miller at Stanton; 1858/59 butcher, grocer, & baker at Stanton; 1859/60 butcher, grocer & baker.
1855/56 marked "Mill at Stanton".
Cross reference: Maslen, James, miller, Stanton St. Bernard.

902 MASLEN, Joseph, shoemaker.

1846/47-1849/50 assessed in absence of return £40; exempt.

903 MASLEN, Michael, baker, shopkeeper, property out of Great Britain, interest. [also MASLEN, Richard]

1842/43 returned and assessed £40; exempt.
1846/47-1847/48 assessed in absence of return £40; exempt.
1848/49 returned £50; assessed £40; exempt.
1849/50-1850/51 assessed in absence of return £40; exempt.
1851/52 returned and assessed £45; income proved at £49; exempt.
1852/53 returned £14 and £37 interest; assessed £51; exempt.
1853/54-1855/56 assessed in absence of return £50; exempt.
1856/57 recorded; no assessment made; exempt.

1842/43, 1846/47 Richard Maslen; 1847/48-1856/57 Michael Maslen.
1842/43 baker; 1846/47-1856/57 baker & shopkeeper; 1846/47 property out of Great Britain; 1853/54-1856/57 interest.

904 MASLEN, Thomas, butcher, maltster.

1851/52 returned £45; assessed £90; income proved at £45; exempt.
1852/53 returned and assessed £60; exempt.
1853/54 returned £45; assessed £60; exempt.
1854/55-1855/56 assessed in absence of return £60; exempt.
1856/57-1859/60 recorded; no assessments made; exempt.

905 TASKER, Robert, blacksmith, innkeeper, Kings Arms.

1850/51 assessed in absence of return £100; exempt.
1851/52 returned £45; assessed £100; income proved at £50; exempt.
1852/53 returned and assessed £60; exempt.
1853/54 returned £40; assessed £50; exempt.
1854/55 returned and assessed £40; exempt.
1855/56 assessed in absence of return £20; exempt.
1856/57 recorded; no assessment made; exempt.
1857/58 returned £20i, 20b; assessed £90.
1858/59 returned £20o, 20b; assessed £90.
1859/60 assessed in absence of return £90.

1850/51-1852/53 innkeeper; 1853/54-1859/60 innkeeper & blacksmith.
1856/57 Kings Arms noted.

906 WALTER, Thomas, coal merchant.

1842/43 returned and assessed £20; exempt.
1846/47-1850/51 assessed in absence of return £20; exempt.

907 WHITE, Jane, shopkeeper & baker.

1846/47 returned £40; assessed £100; income proved at £126; exempt.
1847/48-1848/49 returned £40; assessed £100; exempt.
1849/50-1850/51 assessed in absence of return £100; exempt.

ALLINGTON

908 GODWIN, James, maltster, profits arising from a horse called Hotspur.

1842/43 returned and assessed £25.
1855/56 returned and assessed £84.5.0.
1856/57 assessed in absence of return £100.
1857/58 returned £47; assessed £100; reduced to £62 but no appeal noted.
1858/59 assessed in absence of return £80; reduced to £60 but no appeal noted.
1859/60 returned £35; assessed £50.

1842/43 maltster; 1855/56 profits arising from a horse called Hotspur;
1856/57-1859/60 profits from stallion Hotspur.
1856/57 marked "property in A & B...to be charged".

ALTON BARNES

909 SMITH, W. Anderton, clerk in holy orders.

1848/49 returned and assessed £70.

CHARLTON

910 BAYNHAM, Arthur, private tutor.

1853/54-1854/55 assessed in absence of return £80.
1855/56-1856/57 assessed in absence of return £50.
1857/58-1858/59 assessed in absence of return £25.

1859/60 marked "ceased for 18 months".

911 COBDEN, Revd. H.E., private tuition.

1846/47 recorded but no assessment made.
1847/48 marked "Returns in London".

912 HEAD, William, innkeeper. [by comparison, Poores Arms]

1842/43 returned and assessed £120.

1846/47 marked "Witchell, John late Head, innkeeper".
Cross reference: Witchell, John, innkeeper, Charlton.

913 SKRINE, Revd. Wadham Huntley.

1848/49 entry only, deleted.

914 WITCHELL, John, innkeeper, Poores Arms.

1846/47 assessed in absence of return £120; reduced to £74 on appeal; exempt.
1847/48-1850/51 assessed in absence of return £100; exempt.
1851/52 returned £85; assessed £100; exempt.
1852/53 returned £60; assessed £100; reduced to £75; exempt.
1853/54-1854/55 returned and assessed £120.
1855/56-1856/57 returned £100; assessed £120.
1857/58-1859/60 returned and assessed £120.

1846/47 marked "Witchell, John late Head, innkeeper".
1852/53 no appeal noted.
1856/57 Poores Arms noted.
Cross reference: Head, William, innkeeper, Charlton.

CHIRTON

915 CHANDLER, Charles, miller, maltster. [by comparison, Church Mill]

Year	Amount returned	Commissioners' estimate	Final assessment
	£	£	£
1842/43	60	100	80
1846/47	–	80	80
1847/48	–	80	80
1848/49	80	–	80
1849/50	80	–	80
1850/51	80	120	120
1851/52	60	100	100
1852/53	80	100	100
1853/54	120m	140	140
	80mr	–	80
1854/55	–	300	300
1855/56	237	300	300
1856/57	300	500	500
1857/58	250	600	600
1858/59	–	200	200

Abbreviations: m, miller; mr, maltster.
1842/43, 1846/47-1852/53 miller; 1853/54-1858/59 miller & maltster.
1851/52 £70 maltster returned but deleted.
1857/58 marked "see explanation in return".
1858/59 marked "Chandler, Charles now Thomas Tanner, maltster. No malthouse in Chirton
   but both malthouses are in Marden".
Cross references: Chandler, Charles, maltster, Marden; Charlton, Thomas & John, maltsters,
   Marden & Week; Tanner, Thomas, miller, Chirton.

916 CLEATHER, Revd. G[eorge] E[llis], private tuition.

1855/56 returned and assessed £180.
1856/57-1857/58 returned and assessed £100.
1858/59 returned and assessed £96.
1859/60 returned and assessed £95.

Cross reference: Cleather, Revd. G.P., tutor, Chirton.

917 CLEATHER, Revd. G[eorge] P[arker], tutor, pupils, private tuition, curate.

1842/43 returned and assessed £321.
1846/47 returned and assessed £350.
1847/48 returned and assessed £280.
1848/49 returned and assessed £370.
1849/50 returned and assessed £360.
1850/51 returned and assessed £370.
1851/52 returned and assessed £345.
1852/53 returned and assessed £300.
1853/54 returned and assessed £100t, £100c.
1854/55 returned and assessed £200.

Abbreviations: t, tuition, c, curate.
1842/43 (curate entered but deleted) tutor; 1846/47-1847/48 pupils;
1848/49-1853/54 private tuition; 1853/54-1854/55 curate.
1842/43 £80 curate entered but deleted.
1846/47 figures entered on 1847/48 certificate of assessment.
1853/54 marked "gone".
Cross reference: Cleather, Revd. G.E., private tuition, Chirton.

918 HOWELL, John, shopkeeper.

1842/43, 1846/47-1849/50 assessed in absence of return £50; exempt.

919 SHEPPARD, William, harness maker.

1842/43, 1846/47-1849/50 assessed in absence of return £50; exempt.

920 TANNER, Thomas, miller, Church Mill.

1858/59 returned £310; assessed £500.
1859/60 returned and assessed £500.

1858/59 marked "Chandler, Charles now Thomas Tanner".
1859/60 "maltster" entered but deleted, marked "Query this".
Cross reference: Chandler, Charles, miller, maltster, Chirton.

921 WITCHELL, John, blacksmith, beerseller. [also WITCHELL, George]

1846/47-1849/50 assessed in absence of return £50; exempt.
1857/58-1859/60 recorded; no assessments made; exempt.

1846/47-1849/50 John Witchell, blacksmith; 1857/58-1859/60 George Witchell, blacksmith
    & beerseller.
1857/58 £40 returned but no assessment made.

CHEVERELL MAGNA

922 BUTCHER, James, mealman.

1848/49 returned and assessed £40; exempt.
1849/50 assessed in absence of return £30; exempt.

923 BUTCHER, John, Junior.

1848/49 returned and assessed £30; exempt.
1849/50 assessed in absence of return £30; exempt.

No occupation noted.

924 CHAPMAN, Thomas, cordwainer.

1842/43 returned and assessed £50; exempt.
1846/47 assessed in absence of return £50; exempt.
1847/48 assessed in absence of return £60; exempt.
1848/49 returned and assessed £58; exempt.
1849/50 assessed in absence of return £40; exempt.

925 COOK, Revd. Thomas, annuity.

1846/47-1848/49 recorded; no assessments made.
1846/47 marked "Return".

926 COOMBE, W.W., shopkeeper.

1857/58 returned £65; no assessment made; exempt.
1858/59-1859/60 recorded; no assessments made; exempt.

927 DEANE, Robert, innkeeper, Bell, engine master.

1848/49-1850/51 assessed in absence of return £70; exempt.
1851/52 returned and assessed £90; exempt.
1852/53 returned and assessed £90; income proved at £94; exempt.
1853/54 returned £80; assessed £90; exempt.
1854/55 returned £70; assessed £100.
1855/56 returned £80; assessed £100.
1856/57 returned £40i, £30e; assessed £100.
1857/58 returned £60; assessed £100; income proved at £80; exempt.
1858/59-1859/60 recorded; no assessments made; exempt.

Abbreviations: i, innkeeper; e, engine master.
1848/49-1851/52 innkeeper; 1852/53 innkeeper, etc; 1853/54-1859/60 innkeeper & engine master.
1848/49 Hannah Edwards deleted, Robert Deane substituted.
1856/57 Bell noted.
Cross reference: Edwards, Hannah, innkeeper, Cheverell Magna.

928 DUNFORD, Giffard, millwright.

1857/58 returned £60; no assessment made; exempt.
1858/59-1859/60 recorded; no assessments made; exempt.

929 DUNFORD, William, brickmaker.

1848/49 returned and assessed £50; exempt.
1849/50 assessed in absence of return £50; exempt.

1847/48 Durnford, Thomas entered but deleted; 1848/49 William Dunford.
1842/43 marked "See West Lavington".
Cross reference: Dunford, Thomas, brickmaker, West Lavington.

930 DUTCH, James, carpenter, joiner.

Year	Amount returned	Commissioners' estimate	Income proved	Final assessment
	£	£	£	£
1842/43	80	–	80	–
1846/47	95	–	95	–
1847/48	–	95	90	–
1848/49	84	100	100	–
1849/50	–	50	50	–
1850/51	No assessment made			
1851/52	70	70	90	–
1852/53	76	–	98	–
1853/54	76	90	–	90
1854/55	30	100	–	100
1855/56	–	100	–	100
1856/57	No assessment made			
1857/58	40	No assessment made		

1842/43 carpenter; 1846/47-1849/50 carpenter & joiner; 1851/52-1856/57 carpenter.
1856/57-1857/58 marked "dead".

931 DUTCH, Joseph, shopkeeper, carpenter, grocer.

1848/49 returned and assessed £24; exempt.
1849/50 assessed in absence of return £24; exempt.

1857/58-1859/60 recorded; no assessments made; exempt.

932 EDWARDS, Hannah, innkeeper. [by comparison, Bell]

1842/43 returned and assessed £70; exempt.
1846/47-1847/48 assessed in absence of return £70; exempt.

1848/49 Hannah Edwards deleted, Robert Deane substituted.
Pigot & Co's Directory, 1842: Hannah Edwards, Bell, Great Cheverell.
Cross reference: Deane, Robert, innkeeper, Cheverell Magna.

933 GALE, Thomas, blacksmith.

1846/47-1847/48 assessed in absence of return £40; exempt.
1848/49 returned £50; exempt.
1849/50 assessed in absence of return £50; exempt.

934 HAYDEN, Thomas, mason.

1846/47-1847/48 assessed in absence of return £50; exempt.
1848/49 returned £40; exempt.
1849/50 assessed in absence of return £40; exempt.

935 LIGHT, William, baker, grocer.

1842/43 returned and assessed £90; exempt.
1846/47-1849/50 assessed in absence of return £90; exempt.
1851/52 returned and assessed £60; exempt.
1852/53 assessed in absence of return £60; exempt.
1853/54 returned £20; assessed £60; income proved at £40; exempt.
1854/55-1855/56 assessed in absence of return £40; exempt.
1856/57-1859/60 recorded; no assessments made; exempt.

1842/43, 1846/47-1849/50 baker; 1851/52-1859/60 baker & grocer.
1850/51 no assessment made.

936 MATTHEWS, William.

1846/47-1849/50 marked "Return in Potterne". (No occupation noted).
Cross reference: Matthews, William, brickmaker, Potterne.

937 POTTER, James, bellman, bellmaker, baker.

1842/43 returned and assessed £40; exempt.
1846/47 assessed in absence of return £30; exempt.

1847/48 assessed in absence of return £50; exempt.
1848/49-1849/50 assessed in absence of return £30; exempt.
1851/52 returned £12; assessed £50; income proved at £44; exempt.
1852/53-1855/56 assessed in absence of return £60; exempt.
1856/57-1859/60 recorded; no assessments made; exempt.

1842/43, 1848/49 bellmaker; 1846/47, 1847/48, 1849/50 bellman; 1851/52-1859/60 baker.
1850/51 no assessment made.
1857/58 returned £20 but no assessment made.

938 PRICE, William, pork butcher.

1846/47-1849/50 assessed in absence of return £20; exempt.

939 PRICE, William, Junior, miller.

1842/43 returned £40; assessed £50; exempt.
1846/47-1849/50 assessed in absence of return £50; exempt.

940 PURNELL, Ann, baker. [also PURNELL, Samuel]

1842/43 returned and assessed £20; exempt.
1846/47-1847/48 assessed in absence of return £20; exempt.
1848/49 returned and assessed £10; exempt.
1849/50 assessed in absence of return £10; exempt.

1842/43 Samuel Purnell; 1846/47-1849/50 Ann Purnell.
1846/47-1849/50 baker, etc.

941 SAWYER, Mark & Son, millwrights. [also SAWYER, Joseph & Nathaniel]

Year	Amount returned	Commissioners' estimate	Income proved	Final assessment
	£	£	£	£
1842/43	100	–	100	–
1846/47	–	120	120	–
1847/48	–	120	120	–
1848/49	–	150	110	–
1849/50	–	110	110	–
1850/51	–	110	110	–
1851/52	60	110	104.10.0	20
	20interest			
1852/53	130	150a	119.6.8	–

	20interest			
1853/54	100	120	-	130
1854/55	50	150	-	150
1855/56	-	150	-	150
1856/57	-	150a	-	112.10.0
1857/58	70	112	52	-
1858/59	75	-	-	75
1859/60	-	75	-	75

1842/43, 1848/49-1852/53 Mark Sawyer; 1846/47-1847/48 Mark Sawyer & Son; 1853/54-1854/55 Joseph Sawyer; 1855/56 Joseph & Nathaniel Sawyer; 1856/57-1857/58 Nathaniel Sawyer; 1858/59-1859/60 Joseph Sawyer.
1853/54 assessment increased by General Commissioners to £130.

942 WEBB, John, miller, Cheverell Mill. [also WEBB, James & Joseph]

Year	Amount returned	Commissioners' estimate	Income proved	Final assessment
	£	£	£	£
1846/47	-	30	30	-
1847/48	-	30	30	-
1848/49	180	-	180	-
1849/50	-	180	180	-
1850/51	-	180	180	-
1851/52	80	120	80	-
1852/53	100	-	107.3.4	-
1853/54	50	100	-	100
1854/55	80	100	-	100
1855/56	80	100	-	100
1856/57	-	100	-	100
1857/58	80	100	-	100
1858/59	-	100	-	100
1859/60	-	100	-	100

1846/47-1847/48, 1851/52-1859/60 John Webb; 1848/49-1850/51 John James & Joseph Webb.
1848/49-1850/51 exemption claimed as partnership.
1856/57 Cheverell Mill noted.

943 WILLIAMS, Thomas, cutler.

1842/43 returned and assessed £40; exempt.

1842/43 marked "charged in . . ." (illegible).
1846/47 marked "q. Return in London".
1847/48 marked "gone. q. in London" or "given up" (illegible).

CHEVERELL PARVA

944 BOLTER, Isaac, brickmaker.

Year	Amount returned £	Commissioners' estimate £	Income proved £	Final assessment £
1842/43	30	–	30	–
1846/47	–	50	50	–
1847/48	–	70	70	–
1848/49	–	70	70	–
1849/50	–	70	70	–
1852/53	50	–	70.10.0	–
1853/54	50	–	50	–
1854/55	–	50	50	–
1855/56	30	50	50	–
1856/57	40	–	–	–
1857/58	–	50	50	–
1858/59	15	50	–	–
1859/60	40	60	–	60

1850/51-1851/52 no assessments made.
1856/57, 1858/59 no assessments made.
1858/59 marked "Has 2 brickyards".

945 BOLTER, Samuel, grocer.

1858/59 returned £15; no assessment made; exempt.
1859/60 returned £10 but deleted.

946 BOX, Richard.

1846/47-1847/48 marked "returned at Devizes".
No occupation noted.
Cross reference: Box, Richard, corn dealer, St. Mary.

947 INGRAM, James, shopkeeper, etc.

1853/54-1855/56 assessed in absence of return £50; exempt.
1856/57-1859/60 recorded; no assessments made; exempt.

1853/54 shopkeeper, etc; 1854/55-1859/60 shopkeeper.
1858/59 returned £15.
Pigot & Co's Directory, 1842: James Ingram, grocer & dealer in sundries, West Lavington.

948 JAMES, Alfred, maltster.

1842/43 returned and assessed £30; exempt.

949 SELF, Harry, mealman.

1842/43 assessed in absence of return £50; exempt.
1846/47-1849/50 assessed in absence of return £70; exempt.

Pigot & Co's Directory, 1842: Henry Self, miller, Great Cheverell.

950 WARD, Benjamin, baker.

1842/43 returned and assessed £20; exempt.
1846/47-1847/48 assessed in absence of return £20; exempt.
1848/49-1849/50 assessed in absence of return £50; exempt.

EASTERTON

951 COLLINGBORN, John M., baker & shopkeeper.

1842/43 assessed in absence of return £20; exempt.

1846/47 marked "given up business".

952 DAVIS, Thomas, innkeeper. [by comparison, Royal Oak]

1842/43 returned £5; assessed £75; exempt.
1846/47-1848/49 assessed in absence of return £75; exempt.
1849/50-1852/53 assessed in absence of return £100; exempt.
1853/54 assessed in absence of return £80; income proved £85; exempt.

1854/55 entry deleted Philpott, John, innkeeper, Royal Oak substituted.
Pigot & Co's Directory, 1842: Thomas Davies (sic), Royal Oak, Easterton.
Cross reference: Philpott, John, innkeeper, Easterton.

953 DRAPER, James, dealer & baker.

1854/55-1855/56 assessed in absence of return £40; exempt.
1856/57-1859/60 recorded; no assessments made; exempt.

1855/56 marked "Draper, Philip given up to James Draper".
Cross reference: Draper, Philip, dealer, baker, Easterton.

954 DRAPER, Philip, dealer, baker.

Year	Amount returned £	Commissioners' estimate £	Income proved £	Final assessment £
1846/47	–	50	50	–
1847/48	–	120	96.14.0	–
1848/49	70	96.14.0	96.14.0	–
1849/50	–	50	50	–
1850/51	–	50	50	–
1851/52	–	50	104	–
1852/53	–	104	–	152
1853/54	30	–	–	30
1854/55	–	30	–	30

1846/47-1852/53 dealer; 1853/54-1854/55 dealer & baker.
1854/55 marked "£120 in Market Lavington"; (no assessment in Market Lavington).
1855/56 marked "given up to James Draper".
Pigot & Co's Directory, 1842: Philip Draper, baker, grocer & dealer in sundries, Easterton.
Cross reference: Draper, James, dealer, baker, Easterton.

955 GRANT, John, maltster. [also GRANT, William]

1842/43 returned £20; assessed £40 but reduced to £20.
1846/47 assessed in absence of return £20; exempt.
1847/48 assessed in absence of return £20; income proved at £50; exempt.
1848/49-1850/51 assessed in absence of return £50; exempt.
1851/52 assessed in absence of return £20; income proved at £35; exempt.
1852/53 assessed in absence of return £50; exempt.
1853/54 returned £3; assessed £40; exempt.
1854/55 assessed in absence of return £40.

1842/43 John Grant; 1846/47-1847/48 John Grant & Brother; 1848/49-1854/55 John & William Grant.
1842/43 assessment reduced but no appeal noted.
1855/56 marked "left Easterton business ceased".
1856/57 marked "removed from Easterton".
1857/58 marked "removed from Easterton to Wilcot".
Pigot & Co's Directory, 1842: John Grant, maltster, Easterton.
Cross reference: Grant, John & James, maltsters, Wilcot.

956 HOBBS, Charles P., minister.

1842/43 returned and assessed £100; exempt.
1846/47-1847/48 assessed in absence of return £100; exempt.
1848/49-1849/50 assessed in absence of return £110; exempt.

957 MAYNARD, William, blacksmith.

1842/43, 1846/47-1849/50 assessed in absence of return £30; exempt.

Pigot & Co's Directory, 1842: William Maynard, blacksmith, Easterton.

958 MEREDITH, Samuel, Chief Constable.

1842/43 entry only, marked "Schedule E".

959 NEVILLE, John.

1846/47-1848/48 name only entered, no assessments made.
1846/47 marked "q. who or what".
Pigot & Co's Directory, 1842: John Neville, draper, grocer & dealer in sundries, Littleton.

960 PHILPOTT, John, innkeeper, Royal Oak. [also PHILPOTT, Caroline]

1853/54 assessed in absence of return £70; reduced to £60.
1854/55 assessed in absence of return £100.
1855/56 returned £60; assessed £100.
1856/57 assessed in absence of return £100; reduced to £90 on appeal; exempt.
1857/58-1859/60 recorded; no assessments made; exempt.

1853/54-1855/56 John Philpott; 1856/57-1859/60 Caroline Philpott.
1854/55 Davis, Thomas deleted, Philpott, John substituted.
1854/55 marked Royal Oak.
1856/57 marked "now Caroline".
Cross reference: Davis, Thomas, innkeeper, Easterton.

961 STILL, James.

1854/55-1855/56 assessed in absence of return £50; exempt.
1856/57-1859/60 recorded; no assessments made; exempt.

No occupation noted.

962 WILSON, David, yeoman.

1851/52 entry only, no assessment made.

ETCHILHAMPTON

963 BLEE[C]K, Revd. William.

1848/49 returned £30.19.4 but deleted.

964 COCKELL, Revd. H., stipend.

1842/43 returned £105 but deleted.

965 PLANK, George, pig dealer.

1858/59 assessed in absence of return £110; income proved at £75; exempt.
1859/60 returned £39 and £6.5.0 interest; assessed £75 and £6.5.0.

966 RUDMAN, Noah, carpenter.

1857/58 returned £45; no assessment made; exempt.
1858/59-1859/60 recorded; no assessments made; exempt.

967 WESTON, John, auctioneer.

1858/59-1859/60 recorded; no assessments made; exempt.

968 WAYLEN, James, artist.

1851/52 returned and assessed £50.
1852/53 returned and assessed £50; exempt.
1853/54-1854/55 assessed in absence of return £50.
1855/56 returned and assessed £50.
1856/57 returned and assessed £57 and £25 interest.
1857/58 returned and assessed £42.6.0 and £25 interest.
1858/59 returned and assessed £37.14.11 and £24.11.8 interest.
1859/60 returned and assessed £33.12.0 and £24.6.0 interest.

Pigot & Co's Directory, 1842: James Waylen, teacher of painting, Bellevue, Devizes.

LITTLETON PANNELL

969 BAKER, James, innkeeper, Wheat Sheaf.

1854/55 assessed in absence of return £100; reduced to £95.
1855/56 assessed in absence of return £100.
1856/57 assessed in absence of return £130.
1857/58 assessed in absence of return £175.
1858/59 returned £125; assessed £175.
1859/60 assessed in absence of return £175.

1856/57 Wheat Sheaf noted.

970 BAKER, William, baker, mealman.

1848/49-1849/50 assessed in absence of return £90; exempt.
1850/51 assessed in absence of return £250; reduced to £100 on appeal; exempt.
1851/52 assessed in absence of return £100; income proved at £80.

1848/49-1849/50 baker; 1850/51-1851/52 baker & mealman.
Pigot & Co's Directory, 1842: William Baker, miller, Littleton.

971 BUTCHER, Thomas, miller.

1852/53 returned £90; assessed £150; reduced to £115 on appeal; exempt.
1853/54-1856/57 assessed in absence of return £150.
1857/58 assessed in absence of return £160.
1858/59 returned £105; assessed £160.
1859/60 assessed in absence of return £160.

972 FARMER, John Seymour, miller.

1852/53 returned and assessed £65; exempt.
1854/55-1855/56 assessed in absence of return £100.
1856/57 assessed in absence of return £125.
1857/58-1859/60 assessed in absence of return £130.

1853/54 recorded but no assessment made.

973 MEAD, Henry, grocer, maltster.

1852/53 returned £20; assessed £50; income proved at £20; exempt.

1853/54-1855/56 assessed in absence of return £50; exempt.
1856/57-1859/60 recorded; no assessments made; exempt.

1852/53 grocer; 1853/54-1859/60 grocer & maltster.
1852/53 bears illegible note.

974 NEWMAN, Thomas, mealman.

1846/47-1847/48 assessed in absence of return £200.
1848/49 returned £200.
1849/50 returned £150; assessed £200.

Pigot & Co's Directory, 1842: Thomas Newman, grocer & dealer in sundries, chymist (sic), East Lavington; miller, Littleton.

975 PEPLER, -.

Surname only entered 1858/59.

976 WILKINS, John, carpenter. [also WILKINS, Christopher]

1857/58 assessed in absence of return £30.
1858/59 returned and assessed £30.
1859/60 assessed in absence of return £30.

1857/58 Christopher Wilkins; 1858/59-1859/60 John Wilkins.
1857/58 "agency" entered but deleted.

977 WILTON, Revd. E[dward], clergyman & schoolmaster.

1853/54 returned £250 but entry deleted.

Pigot & Co's Directory, 1842: Revd. Edward Wilton, clergy, West Lavington.
Cross reference: Wilton, Revd. Edward, officiating minister & schoolmaster, West Lavington.

MANNINGFORD ABBOTTS

978 HAINES, John, miller, mealman.

1854/55-1856/57 assessed in absence of return £100.
1857/58 returned and assessed £100.
1858/59-1859/60 assessed in absence of return £100.

1854/55-1855/56 miller; 1856/57-1859/60 mealman.
1854/55 marked "late Sherry, miller".
Cross reference: Sherry, James, miller, Manningford Abbotts.

979 SHERRY, James, miller.

1842/43 returned and assessed £50.
1846/47-1847/48 assessed in absence of return £150.
1848/49 returned and assessed £150.
1849/50 returned £100; assessed £150.
1850/51 assessed in absence of return £150; reduced to £59.12.0 on appeal; exempt.
1851/52 assessed in absence of return £60; exempt.
1852/53 assessed in absence of return £100.
1853/54 returned and assessed £100.

1853/54 marked "now Haines miller".
Cross reference: Haines, John, miller, Manningford Abbotts.

MANNINGFORD BOHUN

980 COX, William, victualler.

1842/43 returned and assessed £25; exempt.
1846/47-1849/50 assessed in absence of return £15; exempt.

981 GALE, Henry, victualler, brewer Bottlesford.

1848/49 returned and assessed £30; exempt.
1849/50 assessed in absence of return £30; exempt.
1859/60 returned £60; assessed £100.

1848/49-1849/50 victualler; 1859/60 brewer Bottlesford.

982 WRIGHT, Joseph, carpenter.

1848/49 returned and assessed £50; exempt.
1849/50 assessed in absence of return £50; exempt.

MANNINGFORD BRUCE

983 GRANT, Alexander, parish priest.

1848/49 returned £318.5.0 but deleted.

984 ROBERTS, William, shopkeeper, grocer.

1842/43 returned and assessed £5; exempt.
1846/47-1850/51 assessed in absence of return £50; exempt.
1851/52-1855/56 assessed in absence of return £60; exempt.
1856/57-1859/60 recorded; no assessments made; exempt.

1842/43 shopkeeper; 1846/47-1859/60 grocer.

985 WAITE, Nathaniel, carpenter.

1857/58 returned and assessed £100.
1858/59-1859/60 assessed in absence of return £100.

MARDEN

986 CHANDLER, Charles, maltster. [also CHANDLER, John and Thomas]

1842/43 returned and assessed £50.
1846/47 returned and assessed £70.
1847/48 returned £70; assessed £100.
1848/49-1849/50 returned and assessed £70.
1850/51 assessed in absence of return £80.
1851/52 assessed in absence of return £100.
1852/53 returned £70; assessed £120.
1858/59 assessed in absence of return £150.

1842/43, 1850/51-1852/53 Charles Chandler; 1846/47-1849/50 Thomas Chandler;
1858/59 John & Thomas Chandler.
1853/54-1857/58 marked "charged in Chirton".
1858/59 marked "see Chirton".
1859/60 marked "maltsters, charged in Week".
Pigot & Co's Directory, 1842: Charles Chandler, maltster, Nursery, Devizes.
Cross references: Chandler, Charles, miller & maltster, Chirton; Chandler, Thomas & John, retail
    maltsters, Week.
Note: [Chirton] "both malthouses are in Marden".

987 GERRISH, James, miller.

1848/49 returned and assessed £70; exempt.
1849/50-1851/52 assessed in absence of return £70; exempt.

1852/53 marked "see Wells below".
Cross reference: Wells, Jasper, miller & shopkeeper, Marden.

988 MASTERS, Beatrice, schoolmistress.

1846/47-1849/50 assessed in absence of return £50; exempt.

989 NEATE, Stephen R., maltster.

1842/43 returned and assessed £20;
1846/47 returned £5; assessed £20.
1847/48 returned £12; assessed £20.
1848/49 assessed in absence of return £20; exempt.
1849/50 returned and assessed £10.
1850/51 assessed in absence of return £10.
1851/52-1854/55 returned and assessed £10.
1855/56 assessed in absence of return £10.

1856/57 marked "discontinued malting last year".

990 SKIPPER, Revd. J.B.

1848/49 name only entered.

991 STRATTON, Jacob, miller. [also STRATTON, Frederick]

1842/43 returned and assessed £160.
1846/47 returned and assessed £80.
1847/48 returned £50; assessed £80.
1848/49 returned and assessed £90; exempt.

1848/49 Stratton, Jacob Exors deleted, Frederick Stratton inserted.
Cross reference: Stratton, Jacob, maltster, Wilsford.

992 WELLS, Jasper, miller & shopkeeper.

1851/52 returned and assessed £70; exempt.
1852/53 assessed in absence of return £70; exempt.
1853/54 returned £55; assessed £60; exempt.
1854/55-1855/56 assessed in absence of return £60; exempt.
1856/57 recorded but no assessment made.
1857/58-1859/60 assessed in absence of return £60.

1852/53 Gerrish, James, miller, deleted marked "see Wells below".
1858/59 marked "has £48.15.0 real property".
Cross reference: Gerrish, James, miller, Marden.

MARKET LAVINGTON

993 ASHLEY, George.

1859/60 name only entered.

994 BOWLES, John Thomas, seedsman, corndealer.

1842/43, 1846/47-1849/50 assessed in absence of return £50; exempt.
1853/54 returned and assessed £60; exempt.
1854/55-1855/56 assessed in absence of return £100.
1856/57 returned £40; assessed £100.
1857/58 returned £50; assessed £105.
1858/59 returned £40; assessed £105.
1859/60 assessed in absence of return £105.

1842/43, 1846/47-1849/50 Bowle; 1853/54-1859/60 Bowles.
1842/43, 1846/47-1849/50 seedsman; 1853/54-1859/60 corndealer.
1846/47, 1847/48 [Newman] marked "now John Bowle druggist".
1850/51-1852/53 no assessments made.
Pigot & Co's Directory, 1842: John Thomas Bowle, corn dealer, East Lavington.
Cross reference: Newman, Thomas, druggist.

995 BOX, John, maltster.

1851/52-1852/53 assessed in absence of return £50; exempt.
1853/54 returned and assessed £53.10.0; exempt.
1854/55 returned £25; assessed £70; income proved at £50; exempt.
1855/56 assessed in absence of return £50; exempt.
1856/57-1859/60 recorded; no assessments made; exempt.

1854/55 [Box, Thomas] marked "not in business, his son Jno has business".
Cross reference: Box, Thomas, maltster, Market Lavington.

996 BOX, Richard, cornfactor.

1842/43 marked "returned at St.John".
Note: Assessed in St.Mary.
Cross reference: Box, Richard, corndealer, St.Mary.

997 BOX, Thomas, maltster.

1842/43, 1846/47-1852/53 assessed in absence of return £80; exempt.

1853/54 assessed in absence of return £50; exempt.

1854/55 marked "not in business, his son Jno has the business".
Pigot & Co's Directory, 1842: Thomas Box, maltster, East Lavington.
Cross reference: Box, John, maltster, Market Lavington.

998 BOX, William, contractor.

1855/56 assessed in absence of return £100.
1856/57 returned and assessed £100.
1857/58 returned £50; assessed £105.
1858/59 returned £100; assessed £105.
1859/60 returned £100; assessed £150.

1856/57 marked "q. brick yard".

999 CAMBRIDGE, William, machine maker.

1842/43, 1846/47 returned and assessed £210.
1847/48 returned £200; assessed £210.
1848/49 returned and assessed £210.

Pigot & Co's Directory, 1842: William Cambridge, engineer, ironfounder & manufacturer of agricultural implements, East Lavington.

1000 CANNINGS, Henry, plumber, glazier.

1842/43, 1846/47-1848/49 returned and assessed £160.
1849/50 assessed in absence of return £160.
1850/51 returned and assessed £90; exempt.
1851/52-1852/53 assessed in absence of return £90; exempt.
1853/54-1855/56 assessed in absence of return £40; exempt.
1856/57-1859/60 recorded; no assessments made; exempt.

1842/43 plumber & glazier; 1846/47-1851/52 plumber, etc; 1852/53-1859/60 plumber.
Pigot & Co's Directory, 1842: Henry Cannings, painter, etc., East Lavington.

1001 CLEAVER, Henry, draper & grocer.

1842/43 returned and assessed £100; exempt.
1846/47-1848/49 assessed in absence of return £100; exempt.
1849/50 assessed in absence of return £100; income proved at £120; exempt.
1850/51-1852/53 assessed in absence of return £100; exempt.
1853/54-1855/56 assessed in absence of return £40; exempt.

1856/57-1859/60 recorded; no assessments made; exempt.

Pigot & Co's Directory, 1842: Henry Cleaver, grocer & dealer in sundries, draper, East Lavington.

1002 DRAPER, Samuel, carpenter. [also DRAPER, Thomas]

1842/43 assessed in absence of return £100; exempt.
1846/47-1849/50 assessed in absence of return £88; exempt.
1850/51 assessed in absence of return £88; income proved at £80; exempt.
1851/52 assessed in absence of return £88; income proved at £135.5.0; exempt.
1852/53 assessed in absence of return £130; exempt.
1853/54 returned £46; assessed £100; income proved at £50; exempt.
1854/55 returned £40; assessed £50; exempt.
1855/56 returned £30; assessed £50; exempt.
1856/57 returned and assessed £100.
1857/58 returned £50; assessed £100.
1858/59-1859/60 returned and assessed £100.

1842/43, 1846/47-1855/56, 1857/58 Samuel Draper; 1856/57, 1858/59-1859/60 Samuel & Thomas Draper.
Pigot & Co's Directory, 1842: Samuel Draper, carpenter & wheelwright, East Lavington.

1003 DRAPER, Stephen, innkeeper. [by comparison, Kings Arms]

1850/51-1852/53 assessed in absence of return £80; exempt.
1853/54 assessed in absence of return £100; income proved at £75; exempt.

1850/51 marked "late Lawes, innkeeper".
Cross reference: Lawes, Joseph, innkeeper, Market Lavington; Reed, John, innkeeper, Market Lavington.

1004 ELLIS, John, tailor. See SMITH, Frederick & ELLIS, John, tailors.

1005 FARMER, James, butcher.

1851/52 returned and assessed £50; income proved at £62; exempt.
1853/54 returned £50; estimated at £60 but no assessment made.
1854/55 returned £50; assessed £150; reduced to £135.
1855/56 returned £100; assessed £135.
1856/57-1859/60 returned £100; assessed £150.

1852/53 no assessment made.
1854/55 Assessment reduced but no appeal noted.

1006 GAUNTLETT, Caroline, butcher. [also GAUNTLETT, George]

1842/43 assessed in absence of return £100; exempt.
1846/47 assessed in absence of return £67; exempt.
1847/48-1849/50 assessed in absence of return £90; exempt.

1842/43 George Gauntlett; 1846/47-1849/50 Caroline Gauntlett.
Pigot & Co's Directory, 1842: George Gauntlett, butcher, East Lavington.

1007 GAUNTLETT, Henry, baker, confectioner.

1842/43 assessed in absence of return £100; exempt.
1846/47 assessed in absence of return £90; exempt.
1847/48-1852/53 assessed in absence of return £100; exempt.
1853/54 returned £91.6.0; assessed £100; income proved at £91.6.0; exempt.
1854/55 assessed in absence of return £100.
1855/56-1856/57 returned £75; assessed £100.
1857/58-1858/59 assessed in absence of return £100.
1859/60 returned £80; assessed £100.

1842/43, 1846/47-1849/50 baker; 1850/51-1859/60 baker & confectioner.
Pigot & Co's Directory, 1842: Henry Gauntlett, baker & confectioner, East Lavington.

1008 GRAY, John, gardener.

1842/43, 1846/47-1849/50 assessed in absence of return £40; exempt.

1842/43, 1846/47-1847/48 Gray; 1848/49 Grey.

1009 HAWKINS, Bryant Tinkes, baker, innkeeper, Bell.

1853/54-1855/56 assessed in absence of return £70; exempt.
1856/57-1859/60 recorded; no assessments made; exempt.

1856/57 Bell noted; "now J. Reed" deleted.
Cross reference: Reed, John, innkeeper [Kings Arms], Market Lavington.

1010 HAYWARD, John, surgeon

See composite entry for partnership under HITCHCOCK, Charles et alii.

1011 HAZELL, John, brewer, maltster.

1853/54 returned £80; assessed £120.

1854/55-1855/56 returned and assessed £120.
1856/57 returned and assessed £125.
1857/58-1858/59 returned £120; assessed £200.
1859/60 returned £80.10.0; assessed £100; income proved at £73; exempt.

1853/54-1855/56 brewer; 1856/57-1858/59 brewer & maltster; 1859/60 maltster.

1012 HERRIOTT, James, surgeon.

1848/49 returned £200; assessed £250.
1849/50 returned and assessed £250.
1850/51 assessed in absence of return £250.
1851/52-1854/55 returned and assessed £200.

1013 HINTON, James, bailiff.

1858/59-1859/60 returned and assessed £120.

1014 HITCHCOCK, Charles, surgeon. [also IVES, John; HAYWARD, John; WHITE, Frederick George; PEPLER, William Brown]

	Year	Amount returned £	Commissioners' estimate £	Income proved £	Final assessment £
CH	1842/43	239.17.6	–	–	239.17.6
JI		119.18.8	–	119.18.8	–
CH	1846/47	230.2.8	–	–	230.2.8
JI		115.1.4	–	115.1.4	–
CH	1847/48	204.13.0	–	–	204.13.0
JI		102.6.6	–	102.6.6	–
CH	1848/49	282.3.0	–	–	282.3.0
JI		94.1.0	–	–	94.1.0
CH	1849/50	–	371.5.0	–	371.5.0
JI		123.15.0	–	123.15.0	–
CH	1850/51	350.8.0	–	–	350.8.0
JI		116.15.0	–	116.15.0	–
CH	1851/52	251.10.0	–	–	251.10.0
JH		251.10.0	–	–	251.10.0
CH	1852/53	244.16.0	–	–	244.16.0
JH		244.16.0	–	–	244.16.0
CH	1853/54	217.4.0	–	–	217.4.0
JH		217.4.3	–	–	217.4.3
CH	1854/55	254.19.0	–	–	254.19.0
JH		254.19.0	–	–	254.19.0

CH	1855/56	263.18.6	–	–	263.18.6
JH		263.18.6	–	–	263.18.6
CH	1856/57	277.1.9	350a	–	202
JH		277.1.9	304a	–	231
CH	1857/58	293.13.0	–	–	293.13.0
JH		293.13.0	–	–	293.13.0
CH	1858/59	222.5.7	250c	–	250
JH		147.5.7	250c	–	250
FGW		159.5.7	250c	–	250
WBP		–	120	–	120
CH	1859/60	214	–	–	214
JH		214	–	–	214
FGW		214	–	–	214
WBP		214	–	–	214

Abbreviations: CH, Charles Hitchcock; JI, John Ives; JH, John Hayward; FGW, Frederick George White; WBP, William Brown Pepler; a, appeal; c, composite assessment.

1842/43, 1846/47-1847/48 2/3 share of profits Hitchcock, 1/3 share of profits Ives; 1848/49-1850/51 3/4 share of profits Hitchcock, 1/4 share of profits Ives; 1851/52-1857/58 equal share of profits Hitchcock & Hayward; 1858/59 equal share of profits Hitchcock, Hayward & White, reduced share to Pepler; 1859/60 equal share of profits Hitchcock, Hayward, White & Pepler.

1858/59 surgeons & apothecaries, otherwise surgeons throughout.

1849/50 return for Hitchcock appears to have been submitted to the Additional Commissioners rather than the assessor.

Note: 1851/52-1859/60 Hitchcock also ran the lunatic asylum at Fiddington House, West Lavington where he seemingly resided; for 1853/54-1857/58 the assessments on his profits as a surgeon in Market Lavington were made in West Lavington, (statutorily the assessment had to be made in the place of residence) separate assessments being made in respect of the lunatic asylum and the surgery; during this period the partners continued to be assessed in Market Lavington. In order to retain the integrity of the partnership business entity Hitchcock's assessments as a surgeon have been recorded in Market Lavington.

For 1857/58 White was assessed as a surgeon in Urchfont. His 1858/59 assessment was made originally in Urchfont but deleted and restated in Market Lavington.

Cross references: Hitchcock, Charles, lunatic asylum, West Lavington; Hayward, John, surgeon, Rushall; White, Frederick George, surgeon, Urchfont.

Pigot & Co's Directory, 1842: Hitchcock & Ives, surgeons, East Lavington.

1015 HOUSE, James, foundry.

1853/54 returned £60 but no assessment made.
1854/55 returned £30; assessed £60; exempt.
1855/56 assessed in absence of return £60; exempt.
1856/57-1859/60 recorded; no assessments made; exempt.

1016 HOUSE, William P., post master, innkeeper, Green Dragon.

1853/54 returned £72.15.0; assessed £100.
1854/55 assessed in absence of return £100.

1855/56 returned £85; assessed £100.
1856/57 returned £73; assessed £90.
1857/58 returned £100; assessed £160.
1858/59 returned £125; assessed £160.
1859/60 returned £75; assessed £160.

1853/54-1856/57 innkeeper; 1857/58-1859/60 innkeeper & post master.
1853/54 marked "Henry Philpott now House (Miss deleted) Mr".
1854/55 Green Dragon noted; marked "late Philpott".
Cross reference: Philpott, Henry, innkeeper, Market Lavington.

1017 HULBERT, Robert.

1842/43 name only entered.

1018 HUSBAND, John, interest.

1853/54 returned £900 but deleted.

1019 HUSSEY, William Slade, grocer.

1853/54 returned £62 but no assessment made.
1854/55 returned £40; assessed £62; exempt.
1855/56 assessed in absence of return £62; exempt.
1856/57-1859/60 recorded; no assessments made; exempt.

1020 IVES, John, surgeon.

See composite entry for partnership under HITCHCOCK, Charles et alii.

1021 LAWES, Joseph, innkeeper, [by comparison Kings Arms]

1842/43, 1846/47-1849/50 assessed in absence of return £80; exempt.

1850/51 marked "Draper, Stephen late Lawes".
Pigot & Co's Directory, 1842: Joseph Lawes, Kings Arms, East Lavington.
Cross reference: Draper, Stephen, innkeeper, Market Lavington; Reed, John, innkeeper, Market Lavington.

1022 MAYOW, Revd. Wynell Mayow, foreign securities, interest, pupil, other profits.

1853/54 returned and assessed £13.10.0F, £115o.

1854/55 returned and assessed £16ii, £15i, £115o.
1855/56 returned and assessed £48, £30, £10.
1856/57 returned and assessed £78f, £40p.
1857/58 returned and assessed £48f, £30i.
1858/59 returned and assessed £48fb, £135f, £90s.
1859/60 returned and assessed £189fb, £54s, £36s.

Abbreviations: f, foreign securities; F, French — illegible; fb, securities in British Plantations; i, interest on money; ii, interest on money in land (illegible); o, other profits; p, pupil; s, foreign securities as agent to Revd. Alfred Smith and Miss Smith.
1853/54 marked "query to be assessed under number or letter".
1853/54 returned in addition to amounts assessed but deleted, £500i; £805f.
1854/55 marked "interest on which duty is not deducted" and "profits from a resident in family".
1855/56 income not described.
Pigot & Co's Directory, 1842: Revd. M.W.Mayow, vicar, Vicarage, East Lavington.

1023 MEAD, Henry, corndealer, grocer, cordwainer.

1842/43 returned £60; assessed £100; exempt.
1846/47-1850/51 assessed in absence of return £100; exempt.
1851/52 returned £30; assessed £100; income proved at £60; exempt.
1852/53 returned £20; assessed £70; exempt.
1853/54 returned £45; estimated £70; no assessment made.
1854/55 assessed in absence of return £150.
1855/56 returned £100; assessed 150; reduced to £125.
1856/57-1859/60 returned £100; assessed £125.

1842/43 corndealer & cordwainer; 1846/47-1850/51 corndealer; 1851/52-1859/60 grocer, etc.
1855/56 Mary Mead entered and deleted.
Pigot & Co's Directory, 1842: Henry Mead, corn & seed dealer, boot & shoe maker, East Lavington.

1024 NEATE, James, brewer.

1859/60 returned and assessed £100.

1025 NEWMAN, Thomas, druggist.

1842/43 assessed in absence of return £50; exempt.
1846/47 assessed in absence of return £70; exempt.

1846/47, 1847/48 marked "now John Bowle druggist.
Cross reference: Bowles, John, seedsman, corndealer, Market Lavington.

1026 ORAM, John.

Name only entered 1855/56.

1027 PEERLESS, Thomas, mealman.

1855/56 returned £100; assessed £150.
1856/57 returned and assessed £150.

1855/56 marked "late Saunders, mealman.
1856/57-1859/60 marked "late Saunders".
Cross reference: Saunders, A.E., mealman & baker, Market Lavington.

1028 PERRETT, Richard, innkeeper, New Inn.

1853/54 returned £20; estimated £40; no assessment made.
1854/55-1855/56 assessed in absence of return £40; exempt.
1856/57-1859/60 recorded; no assessments made; exempt.

1856/57 New Inn noted.
Cross reference: Philpott, William, innkeeper, Market Lavington.

1029 PHILPOTT, Henry, innkeeper, maltster, brickmaker [by comparison, Green Dragon]

1842/43, 1846/47-1848/49 returned and assessed £200.
1849/50 assessed in absence of return £200.
1850/51 returned £160; assessed £200.
1851/52-1852/53 returned and assessed £200.

1849/50 Estimate of £300 deleted, £200 substituted.
1852/53 marked "dead".
1853/54 marked "now House (Miss deleted) Mr".
Pigot & Co's Directory, 1842: Henry Philpott, Green Dragon Inn & Excise Office, maltster, agent to Norwich Union Fire Office, East Lavington.
Cross reference: House, William, P., innkeeper, Market Lavington.

1030 PHILPOTT, John, maltster.

1842/43 returned £20; assessed £100; exempt.
1846/47-1852/53 assessed in absence of return £100; exempt.
1853/54 assessed in absence of return £100.

1854/55 marked "does not carry on malting".
Pigot & Co's Directory, 1842: John Philpott, maltster, West Lavington (sic).

1031 PHILPOTT, William, innkeeper & butcher. [by comparison New Inn]

1842/43, 1846/47–1849/50 assessed in absence of return £80; exempt.

Pigot & Co's Directory, 1842: William Philpott, butcher, innkeeper, New Inn, East Lavington.
Cross reference: Perrett, Richard, innkeeper, Market Lavington.

1032 PIPER, Joseph, grocer, maltster. [also PIPER, John]

1842/43, 1846/47–1852/53 assessed in absence of return £100; exempt.
1853/54 assessed in absence of return £100; income proved at £90; exempt.

1842/43, 1846/47–1849/50 Joseph Piper; 1850/51–1853/54 John Piper.
1842/43, 1846/47–1850/51 grocer; 1851/52–1853/54 maltster.
1854/55 marked "does not carry on any business".
Pigot & Co's Directory, 1842: Joseph Piper, grocer & dealer in sundries, East Lavington.

1033 POMROY, Daniel, shopkeeper, draper.

1842/43, 1846/47–1852/53 assessed in absence of return £80; exempt.
1853/54–1854/55 returned and assessed £80; exempt.
1855/56 assessed in absence of return £80; income proved at £75; exempt.
1856/57 returned £75; assessed £100.
1857/58 recorded; no assessment made; exempt.
1858/59–1859/60 returned £70; assessed £100.

1842/43, 1846/47–1855/56 shopkeeper; 1856/57–1859/60 draper.
Pigot & Co's Directory, 1842: Daniel Pomroy, boot & shoe maker, draper, East Lavington.

1034 POTTER, Thomas, innkeeper, dealer, brewer, beerseller, butcher, Angel.
[also POTTER, Jane]

1842/43, 1846/47–1849/50 assessed in absence of return £100; exempt.
1851/52 returned £50; assessed £100; exempt.
1852/53 assessed in absence of return £100; exempt.
1853/54 returned £44.10.0; assessed £160; income proved at £80; exempt.
1854/55 returned £30; assessed £100; income proved at £50; exempt.
1855/56 assessed in absence of return £50; exempt.
1856/57–1859/60 recorded; no assessments made; exempt.

1842/43, 1846/47–1853/54 Thomas Potter; 1854/55–1859/60 Jane Potter.
1842/43, 1846/47–1849/50 innkeeper & dealer; 1851/52–1852/53 brewer & dealer; 1853/54
    beerseller & innkeeper; 1854/55–1855/56 butcher (Angel); 1856/57–1859/60 butcher &
    innkeeper (Angel).
1850/51 no assessment made.
1853/54 illegible entry after "beerseller & innkeeper".

1854/55 Thomas deleted Jane substituted.
Pigot & Co's Directory, 1842: Thomas Potter, butcher, innkeeper, Angel, East Lavington.

1035 PRICE, Ezra, grocer & piano forte tuner at Devizes.

1856/57 returned £20g, £56p; assessed £100; reduced to £90 on appeal; exempt.
1857/58-1858/59 assessed in absence of return £120.

Abbreviations: g, grocer; p, piano forte tuner.
1859/60 returned £82 but deleted; marked "removed to St.Mary".
Cross reference: Price, Ezra, piano forte seller, St.Mary.

1036 REED, John, innkeeper, Kings Arms.

1858/59-1859/60 recorded; no assessments made; exempt.

1856/57 marked "Hawkins, B.T., now J. Reed, innkeeper". (Hawkins recorded at Bell and assessments continue)
Cross reference; Hawkins, Bryant Tinkes, innkeeper, Market Lavington; Draper, Stephen, innkeeper, Market Lavington; Lawes, Joseph, innkeeper, Market Lavington.

1037 SAINSBURY, Samuel, draper & grocer.

1842/43 returned and assessed £95; exempt.
1846/47-1850/51 assessed in absence of return £95; exempt.
1851/52 assessed in absence of return £20; exempt.
1852/53-1853/54 assessed in absence of return £80; exempt.
1857/58-1858/59 recorded; no assessment made; exempt.
1859/60 assessed in absence of return £100.

1854/55 estimate of £100 but no assessment made.
1855/56-1856/57 marked "insolvent".
Pigot & Co's Directory, 1842: Samuel Sainsbury, grocer & dealer in sundries, draper, East Lavington.

1038 SAUNDERS, A[braham] E[dward], mealman & baker. [also SAUNDERS, A.E. & Sons]

1842/43 returned and assessed £120. (illegible £620)
1846/47 returned and assessed £120.
1847/48 returned and assessed £150.
1848/49-1850/51 assessed in absence of return £150.
1851/52 returned and assessed £150.
1852/53-1854/55 returned £150; assessed £200.

1842/43, 1846/47-1848/49 A.E.Saunders & Sons; 1849/50-1854/55 A.E.Saunders.
1842/43, 1846/47-1848/49 mealmen & bakers; 1849/50-1854/55 mealman & baker.
1854/55 marked "now Thomas Peerless".
Pigot & Co's Directory, 1842: Abraham Edward Saunders, miller, East Lavington.
Cross reference: Peerless, Thomas, mealman, Market Lavington.

1039 SAXTY, James, draper, etc.

1848/49-1849/50 assessed in absence of return £90; exempt.

1848/49-1849/50 draper; 1855/56-1859/60 draper, etc.
1850/51-1854/55 No assessments made.
1855/56-1859/60 marked "returns made at Trowbridge".

1040 SMITH, Frederick & ELLIS, John, tailors. [also SMITH, Frederick]

1853/54 returned £40; no assessment made.
1854/55-1855/56 assessed in absence of return £40; exempt.
1856/57-1859/60 recorded; no assessments made; exempt.

1853/54 Frederick Smith; 1854/55-1859/60 Frederick Smith & John Ellis.

1041 STAGG, Thomas, wine merchant.

1853/54 returned and assessed £125.
1854/55 returned £120; assessed £125.
1855/56 returned and assessed £125.

1856/57 marked "dead", "query successor", "now Wm. Titt".
1857/58 marked "see William Wallace Titt".
Cross reference: Titt, William Wallace, spirit merchant, Market Lavington.

1042 TITT, William Wallace, spirit merchant.

1857/58-1859/60 returned and assessed £100.

1856/57 marked "Stagg, Thomas, wine merchant now Wm. Titt".
1857/58 marked "Stagg, Thomas, spirit merchant, see William Wallace Titt".
Cross reference: Stagg, Thomas, wine merchant, Market Lavington.

1043 TUCKER, William, surgeon.

1842/43 returned and assessed £205.
1846/47 returned £205; assessed £250.

Pigot & Co's Directory, 1842: William Tucker, surgeon, East Lavington.

1044 TUCKER, Walter, cabinet maker & auctioneer.

1842/43 returned £145; assessed £175.
1846/47 assessed in absence of return £175.
1847/48-1849/50 assessed in absence of return £200.
1850/51 returned £120; assessed £150.

1851/52, 1857/58, 1859/60 marked "return at Salisbury".
1858/59 recorded; no assessment made.
Pigot & Co's Directory, 1842: Walter Tucker, cabinet maker, agent to Farmers' & General Fire
Office, auctioneer, East Lavington.

1045 WARD, Benjamin, grocer.

1842/43, 1846/47-1849/50 assessed in absence of return £60; exempt.

Pigot & Co's Directory, 1842: Benjamin Ward, grocer & dealer in sundries, East Lavington.

1046 WEBB, John, bricklayer.

1842/43 assessed in absence of return £10; exempt.
1846/47-1849/50 assessed in absence of return £20; exempt.

Pigot & Co's Directory, 1842: John Webb, bricklayer, East Lavington.

1047 WILLETT, John, Doctor of Medicine.

1846/47 returned and assessed £200.
1847/48 assessed in absence of return £200.

Pigot & Co's Directory, 1842: Dr.John Willett, M.D., gentry, surgeon, physician at Lunatic Asylum, Fiddington.

1048 WILLETT, Robert, Asylum keeper.

1846/47-1847/48 marked "return in West Lavington".

Pigot & Co's Directory, 1842: Robert Willett & Son, proprietor, Lunatic Asylum, Fiddington.
Cross reference: Willett, Robert, lunatic asylum, West Lavington.

1049 WILLETT, Robert Smith, spirit merchant.

1846/47-1847/48 assessed in absence of return £100; exempt.

NORTH NEWNTON & HILLCOTT

1050 DOWSE, James, baker & grocer.

1856/57 returned and assessed £35.
1857/58-1859/60 recorded; no assessments made; exempt.

1051 DUNFORD, George, butcher.

1842/43 returned and assessed £50; exempt.
1846/47-1848/49 assessed in absence of return £50; exempt.

1052 EDWARDS, William, tailor.

1852/53-1855/56 assessed in absence of return £50; exempt.
1856/57-1859/60 recorded; no assessments made; exempt.

1053 HUNTLEY, John Simster(?), mealman.

1859/60 returned £50; assessed £100; income proved at £50; exempt.

1054 KEEPENCE, George, builder.

1856/57 assessed in absence of return £100; reduced to £83 on appeal; exempt.
1857/58-1858/59 recorded; no assessments made; exempt.
1859/60 returned £70; assessed £80; exempt.

1055 KNEE, James, miller.

1842/43 returned and assessed £20; exempt.
1846/47-1847/48 assessed in absence of return £20; exempt.
1848/49 assessed in absence of return £60; exempt.

1056 MARTIN, George, brewer, grocer. [also MARTIN, Henry Alexander]

1842/43 returned and assessed £18; exempt.
1846/47-1849/50 assessed in absence of return £30; exempt.
1854/55 returned and assessed £60; exempt.
1855/56 assessed in absence of return £60; exempt.
1856/57 returned £60 but no assessment made.

1857/58-1858/59 recorded; no assessments made; exempt.
1859/60 returned £50 but no assessment made.

1842/43, 1846/47-1849/50, 1854/55-1855/56 George Martin; 1856/57-1859/60 Henry Alexander Martin.
1842/43, 1846/47-1849/50 brewer; 1854/55-1859/60 grocer & brewer.
1850/51-1853/54 no assessments made.
1856/57 George deleted, Henry Alexander substituted.

1057 PAGE, Thomas, mealman.

1854/55 returned £105; assessed £150; reduced to £105.
1855/56 returned £65; assessed £105.

1854/55 no appeal noted; marked "q. deductions".
1856/57 marked "now Stratton & Skeate (sic), mealmen"; "Page, Thomas ceased business in September 1855".
1857/58 marked "now Stratton & Keate (sic)"; "no trade carried on".
Cross reference: Stratton & Skeate, mealmen, North Newnton & Hillcott.

1058 ROGERS, Francis James H., barrister.

1842/43 entry only.

1059 SKEATE, -, (possibly KEATE, S.) mealman.

1857/58 assessed in absence of return £105.

1857/58 marked "late Stratton & Skeate"; Page, Thomas now Stratton & Keate (sic), mealmen".
1858/59-1859/60 marked "late S".
Cross reference: Page, Thomas, mealman; North Newnton & Hillcott; Stratton & Skeate, mealmen, North Newnton & Hillcott.

1060 STRATTON, William, trustee for Strattons Estate, mealman.

1857/58-1859/60 recorded but no assessments made.

1857/58 trustee for Stratton Estate; 1858/59-1859/60 trustee for Strattons (sic) Estate, mealman.
1858/59 marked "Query".
Cross reference: Page, Thomas, mealman, North Newnton & Hillcott; Stratton & Skeate, mealmen, North Newnton & Hillcott.

1061 STRATTON & SKEATE, Mealmen - See Stratton, Frederick; Skeate, -.

1062 WELLS, Joseph, innkeeper.

1856/57-1857/58 recorded; no assessments made; exempt.
1858/59 assessed in absence of return £50.
1859/60 returned and assessed £50; exempt.

1063 WILD, Robert, land measurer.

1853/54 returned £95; assessed £100; income proved at £95; exempt.
1854/55 assessed in absence of return £95; exempt.
1855/56-1856/57 assessed in absence of return £100.
1857/58 returned and assessed £100.
1858/59 assessed in absence of return £100.
1859/60 returned and assessed £100.

PATNEY

1064 AKERMAN, Stephen

1842/43 name only entered and deleted.

1065 HAILSTONE, John, carpenter.

1842/43 returned and assessed £65; exempt.
1846/47-1849/50 assessed in absence of return £65; exempt.

1066 WELLS, John, cordwainer.

1842/43 returned and assessed £10; exempt.
1846/47-1849/50 assessed in absence of return £30; exempt.

RUSHALL

1067 BARTLETT, John, surgeon, etc.

1846/47 returned and assessed £230.
1847/48-1848/49 returned and assessed £255.
1849/50 returned and assessed £250.

1850/51 entry deleted, Cream, Robert Chevalier, surgeon substituted.

Cross references: Cream, Robert Chevalier, surgeon, Rushall; Febb, Thomas H., surgeon, Rushall; Hayward, John, surgeon, Rushall.

1068 CREAM, Robert Chevalier, surgeon.

1850/51 assessed in absence of return £250.
1851/52 returned £150; assessed £250.
1852/53 returned and assessed £200.
1853/54 assessed in absence of return £200.
1854/55 returned and assessed £200.
1855/56 returned £150; assessed £250.
1856/57 assessed in absence of return £250.

1854/55, 1858/59 Chevallier.
1857/58 faint illegible; no assessment made.
1858/59 marked "now Hayward, John".
Cross references: Bartlett, John, surgeon, etc., Rushall; Febb, Thomas H., surgeon, Rushall; Hayward, John, surgeon, Rushall.

1069 FEBB, Thomas H., surgeon.

1842/43 returned and assessed £230.

Cross references: Bartlett, John, surgeon, etc., Rushall; Cream, Robert Chevalier, surgeon, Rushall; Hayward, John, surgeon, Rushall.

1070 HAYWARD, John, surgeon.

1858/59 marked "Cream, Robert Chevallier, surgeon now Hayward, John".
1859/60 marked "charged in Market Lavington".
Cross references: Bartlett, John, surgeon, etc., Rushall; Cream, Robert Chevalier, surgeon, Rushall; Febb, Thomas H., surgeon, Rushall; Hayward, John, surgeon, Market Lavington.

1071 LEWIS, James, blacksmith.

1842/43 returned and assessed £57.6.8.
1846/47 assessed in absence of return £100.
1847/48 assessed in absence of return £100; income proved at £80; exempt.
1848/49 returned and assessed £150.
1849/50 assessed in absence of return £150; assessment discharged on appeal but no sum recorded.

1847/48 £2.6.8 left in charge.

1072 LLOYD, Revd. William.

1842/43 name only recorded.

1073 SIMPSON, Edward.

1851/52 marked "of Netteravon".

STANTON ST. BERNARD

1074 ABRAHAMS, Morris, tailor.

1846/47-1850/51 assessed in absence of return £130; exempt.
1851/52-1852/53 assessed in absence of return £100; exempt.
1853/54-1855/56 assessed in absence of return £80; exempt.
1856/57-1859/60 recorded; no assessments made; exempt.

1075 BERRY, Isaac, miller.

1850/51-1852/53 assessed in absence of return £70; exempt.
1853/54 recorded but no assessment made.

1850/51 marked "late John Stadden miller".
1854/55 marked "late now Maslen, James".
Cross references: Maslen, James, miller, Stanton St. Bernard; Stadden, John, miller, Stanton St. Bernard.

1076 CHANDLER, Thomas, innkeeper, grocer.

1851/52 returned and assessed £130; exempt.
1852/53 assessed in absence of return £130; reduced to £120 on appeal.
1853/54-1855/56 assessed in absence of return £130.
1856/57 recorded but no assessment made.
1857/58-1859/60 recorded; no assessments made; exempt.

1851/52 innkeeper, grocer, etc.; 1852/53-1855/56 innkeeper, grocer;
1856/57-1859/60 grocer.
1852/53 marked "Wiltshire, William see Chandler".
1856/57 marked "Query".
Cross reference: Wiltshire, William, brewer, cooper, Stanton St. Bernard.

1077 CLARKE, John, coal & platt merchant, coal & slate merchant. [also CLARKE, William, CLARKE, Executors of William]

1842/43 returned and assessed £200.
1846/47 returned £160; assessed £200.
1847/48 assessed in absence of return £200.
1848/49 returned £160; assessed £200.
1849/50 returned £150; assessed £200.
1850/51 assessed in absence of return £250.
1851/52 returned £160; assessed £250.
1852/53 returned £150; assessed £250.
1853/54 returned £120; assessed £250.
1854/55-1856/57 assessed in absence of return £250.
1857/58 returned £160; assessed £250.
1858/59 assessed in absence of return £150.
1859/60 recorded but no assessment made.

1842/43, 1846/47-1852/53 John Clarke; 1853/54-1858/59 William Clarke; 1859/60 Executors of William Clarke.
1842/43, 1846/47-1847/48 coal & platt merchant; 1848/49-1859/60 coal & slate merchant.
1858/59 marked "see return".
Pigot & Co's Directory, 1842: John Clarke, coal, salt & slate merchant, Wharf, Devizes.
Cross reference: Hilliard, Benjamin, agent to Clark (sic), Stanton St. Bernard.

1078 HILLIARD, Benjamin, agent to Clark, accountant.

1858/59-1859/60 assessed in absence of return £75.

1858/59 agent to Clark (sic); 1859/60 accountant.
1858/59 William inserted but deleted, Benjamin substituted.
Cross reference: Clarke, John, (for William) coal & slate merchant, Stanton St. Bernard.

1079 MASLEN, James, miller.

1854/55 assessed in absence of return £100.
1855/56 estimated at £100 but no assessment made.
1858/59-1859/60 recorded but no assessments made.

1854/55 marked "Berry, Isaac late, now Maslen, James, miller".
1855/56 marked "late Berry, charged at Allcannings".
1856/57-1857/58 marked "charged at Allcannings".
Cross references: Berry, Isaac, miller, Stanton St. Bernard; Maslen, James, butcher, Allcannings; Stadden, John, miller, Stanton St. Bernard.

1080 MASLEN, John, innkeeper, Barge.

1859/60 assessed in absence of return £120.

1859/60 marked "Sparks, William Henry now Maslen, John, innkeeper (Barge)".
Cross references: Naish, Jacob Hobbs, innkeeper, Stanton St. Bernard; Sparks, William Henry, innkeeper, Stanton St. Bernard.

1081 NAISH, Jacob Hobbs, innkeeper, Barge.

1856/57 assessed in absence of return £120.
1857/58 returned and assessed £120.
1858/59 assessed in absence of return £120.

1858/59 marked "now William Henry Sparks, innkeeper, Barge".
Cross references: Maslen, John, innkeeper, Stanton St. Bernard; Sparks, William Henry, innkeeper, Stanton St. Bernard.

1082 SPARKS, William Henry, innkeeper, Barge.

1859/60 marked "Naish, Jacob Hobbs now Sparks, William Henry, innkeeper, Barge"; entry deleted, marked "now John Maslen, innkeeper".
Cross references: Maslen, John, innkeeper, Stanton St. Bernard; Naish, Charles Hobbs, innkeeper, Stanton St. Bernard.

1083 STADDEN, John, miller.

1842/43 returned and assessed £70; exempt.
1846/47-1849/50 assessed in absence of return £70; exempt.

1850/51 marked "Berry Isaac late John Stadden, miller".
Cross references: Berry, Isaac, miller, Stanton St. Bernard; Maslen, James, miller, Stanton St. Bernard.

1084 TASKER, Michael, blacksmith, etc.

1842/43 returned and assessed £80; exempt.
1846/47 returned and assessed £20.
1847/48 assessed in absence of return £20; exempt.
1848/49 returned and assessed £60; exempt.
1849/50-1852/53 assessed in absence of return £60; exempt.
1853/54 returned £20; assessed £40.
1854/55-1855/56 assessed in absence of return £40; exempt.
1856/57-1859/60 recorded; no assessments made; exempt.

1842/43, 1846/47-1847/48, 1856/57-1859/60 blacksmith; 1848/49-1855/56 blacksmith, etc.

1085 WILTSHIRE, William, brewer, cooper, dealer.

1842/43 returned and assessed £80; exempt.

1846/47 returned and assessed £95; exempt.
1847/48 assessed in absence of return £95; exempt.
1848/49 returned and assessed £100; exempt.
1849/50-1850/51 assessed in absence of return £100; exempt.
1851/52 assessed in absence of return £60; exempt.

1842/43 brewer, cooper & dealer; 1846/47-1851/52 brewer, cooper, etc.
1852/53 marked "see Chandler".
Pigot & Co's Directory, 1842: Wiltshire, William, saddler, East Lavington.
Cross reference: Chandler, Thomas, innkeeper, grocer, Stanton St. Bernard.

STERT

1086 BEAVEN, John, miller.

1853/54 returned and assessed £40; exempt.
1854/55 assessed in absence of return £100; income proved at £50; exempt.
1855/56 returned and assessed £50; exempt.
1856/57-1857/58 recorded; no assessments made; exempt.
1858/59 returned £25; no assessment made; exempt.
1859/60 returned £30; no assessment made; exempt.

1087 COOKE, George, brickmaker.

1859/60 assessed in absence of return £25 (Stert), £65 (Etchilhampton); assessment on
profits at Stert deleted.

1859/60 marked "at Stert & Etchilhampton"; against Stert entry marked "commenced in May
1859".
1859/60 marked "Dunford, James, brickmaker now George Cooke".
Cross reference: Dunford, James, brickmaker, Stert.

1088 DUNFORD, James, brickmaker.

1853/54 returned and assessed £20; exempt.
1854/55 assessed in absence of return £100.
1855/56 returned £20; assessed £100.
1856/57-1857/58 assessed in absence of return £100.
1858/59 returned £30; assessed £100.

1853/54-1856/57 Durnford; 1857/58-1858/59 Dunford.
1854/55 [Wedhampton] Dunford, James, brickmaker Stert.
1859/60 marked "now George Cooke".
Cross references: Cooke, George, brickmaker, Stert; Dunford, James, brickmaker,
Wedhampton.

1089 HISCOCK, Abel, miller. [also HISCOCK, Mary]

1855/56 returned £15 miller, £20 interest; assessed £50; exempt.
1856/57-1857/58 recorded; no assessments made; exempt.
1858/59 returned £16 but no assessment made.
1859/60 returned £25 miller, £25 interest but no assessment made.

1855/56-1858/59 Abel Hiscock; 1859/60 Mary Hiscock.

1090 POPE, James, miller.

1853/54 returned and assessed £10; exempt.
1854/55-1855/56 assessed in absence of return £50; exempt.
1856/57-1859/60 recorded; no assessments made; exempt.

UPAVON

1091 AKERMAN, J.P., Relieving Officer.

1842/43 returned £40 interest on money on loan but deleted.
1846/47-1848/49 marked "Schedule E".
1851/52 returned and assessed £111; income proved at £134.9.8; exempt.
1852/53 assessed in absence of return £134 but deleted; marked "Schedule E".
1853/54 returned and assessed £70; exempt.
1854/55 returned £109.3.8 but deleted; assessed £70.
1855/56 returned and assessed £40.17.4.
1856/57-1859/60 marked "Schedule E"; no assessments made.

1849/50-1850/51 no assessments made.

1092 BONNER, John, beerseller, butcher.

1842/43 returned and assessed £50; exempt.
1846/47-1849/50 assessed in absence of return £50; exempt.
1851/52 returned and assessed £80; income proved at £83.10.0; exempt.
1852/53 returned £70; assessed £80; exempt.
1853/54 returned £60; assessed £80; exempt.
1854/55 returned £75; assessed £100.
1855/56 returned £90; assessed £100.
1856/57 assessed in absence of return £100.
1857/58-1858/59 returned and assessed £100.
1859/60 returned two amounts of £30; assessed £100.

1842/43 butcher & beerseller; 1846/47-1849/50, 1851/52-1857/58 butcher; 1858/59-1859/60
butcher & retailer of beer.

1850/51 no assessment made.

1093 CARTER, Henry, draper & grocer.

1842/43 returned and assessed £150.
1846/47-1847/48 assessed in absence of return £150.
1848/49-1855/56 returned and assessed £150.
1856/57 assessed in absence of return £150.
1857/58-1859/60 returned and assessed £150.

1094 COPELAND, -.

1846/47-1847/48 surname only entered; no assessments made.

1095 CROOK, Revd. Henry S.C., private tutor.

1842/43 returned and assessed £100.
1850/51-1851/52 returned and assessed £70.
1852/53 returned and assessed £80.

1846/47-1847/48 recorded but no assessments made; 1846/47 marked "Return".
1853/54 recorded but no assessment made; marked "call for return".
1854/55 marked "nil".
1855/56 marked "none in year".
1856/57-1859/60 recorded but no assessments made.

1096 CROOK, Miss Sarah.

1848/49 name only entered but deleted.

1097 FORD, Edward, mealman, miller, baker.

1842/43 returned and assessed £80; exempt.
1846/47-1849/50 assessed in absence of return £80; exempt.
1851/52 returned £25; assessed £50; income proved at £80; exempt.
1852/53 assessed in absence of return £80; exempt.
1853/54 returned £40; assessed £70; income proved at £50; exempt.
1854/55 assessed in absence of return £100; income proved at £80; exempt.
1855/56 assessed in absence of return £80; exempt.
1856/57-1859/60 recorded; no assessments made; exempt.

1842/43, 1846/47-1849/50 mealman; 1851/52-1852/53 baker; 1853/54-1859/60 miller.
1850/51 no assessment made.

1098 HEDGES, John, innkeeper.

1842/43 returned £95; assessed £120; exempt.
1846/47-1852/53 assessed in absence of return £120; exempt.

1099 HUTCHENS, John, innkeeper & baker.

1842/43, 1846/47-1849/50 assessed in absence of return £50; exempt.

1842/43, 1846/47 Hutchins; 1847/48-1849/50 Hutchens.

1100 LANCASTER, William, brewer.

1851/52 returned and assessed £50; exempt.
1852/53 returned and assessed £70; exempt.
1853/54 returned £50; assessed £70; exempt.
1854/55-1856/57 assessed in absence of return £100.
1857/58 returned and assessed £100.
1858/59 returned £70; assessed £100.
1859/60 returned £100; assessed £120.

1101 MASTERSON, John, drillman.

1842/43 returned £50; assessed £75; exempt.
1846/47-1848/49 assessed in absence of return £130; exempt.
1849/50 assessed in absence of return £130; assessment discharged on appeal but no
    amount recorded.

1102 ORAM, John, baker.

1842/43 returned and assessed £100; exempt.
1846/47-1849/50 assessed in absence of return £80; exempt.

1103 SMITH, Edward, grocer, shopkeeper.

1842/43, 1846/47-1849/50 assessed in absence of return £100; exempt.
1851/52 returned and assessed £70; exempt.
1852/53 returned £70; income proved at £107.15.0; exempt.
1853/54 assessed in absence of return £100; income proved at £60; exempt.
1854/55-1855/56 assessed in absence of return £70; exempt.
1856/57 recorded; no assessment made; exempt.
1857/58-1858/59 returned and assessed £75 and £18 interest.
1859/60 returned £70 and £18 interest; assessed £93.

1842/43, 1846/47-1849/50 shopkeeper; 1851/52-1859/60 grocer.
1850/51 no assessment made.
1857/58-1859/60 returned "interest of money".

1104 SMITH, James, carrier.

1842/43 returned and assessed £30; exempt.
1846/47-1849/50 assessed in absence of return £30; exempt.

URCHFONT

1105 BURT, John, cordwainer.

1842/43 returned £20; assessed £50; exempt.
1846/47-1849/50 assessed in absence of return £50; exempt.

1106 BUNGLEY, George, tailor.

1842/43 returned £30 but no assessment made.
1846/47-1849/50 assessed in absence of return £30; exempt.

1107 CLELFORD, William, cordwainer.

1842/43, 1846/47-1849/50 assessed in absence of return £50; exempt.

1108 DAVIS, George, tailor.

1846/47-1849/50 assessed in absence of return £50; exempt.

1109 DOWSE, John, innkeeper, farmer, Bell.

1846/47 assessed in absence of return £150; income proved at £136; exempt.
1847/48 assessed in absence of return £150; income proved at £120; exempt.
1848/49-1850/51 assessed in absence of return £120; exempt.
1851/52 returned and assessed £116; exempt.
1852/53 returned £100; assessed £120.
1853/54 returned £40; assessed £120.
1854/55 assessed in absence of return £120.
1855/56 returned £40; assessed £120.
1856/57 returned £80; assessed £120.
1857/58 returned £40; assessed £120.

1846/47-1850/51, 1855/56-1857/58 innkeeper; 1851/52-1854/55 innkeeper & farmer.
1846/47-1847/48 no appeal noted.
1856/57 Bell noted.
1858/59 marked "now Charles Hobbs Naish.
Cross reference: Naish, Charles Hobbs, innkeeper, Urchfont.

1110 EDWARDS, James, innkeeper, Nags Head. [also EDWARDS, Jane; EDWARDS, William]

1842/43 returned £50; assessed £100; exempt.
1846/47-1849/50 assessed in absence of return £100; exempt.
1851/52 returned £35; assessed £70; income proved at £55; exempt.
1852/53 returned £50; assessed £55; exempt.
1853/54 returned and assessed £35; exempt.
1854/55-1855/56 assessed in absence of return £100.
1856/57 returned £100; assessed £150.
1857/58 returned £90; assessed £160.
1858/59-1859/60 returned £100; assessed £160.

1842/43, 1851/52-1854/55 James Edwards; 1846/47-1850/51 Jane Edwards;
1855/56-1859/60 William Edwards.
1850/51 no assessment made.
1856/57 Nags Head noted.

1111 EDWARDS, John, lime burner.

1857/58 assessed in absence of return £20.
1858/59 returned and assessed £20.
1859/60 returned £10; assessed £20.

1112 EDWARDS, William & Thomas, blacksmiths, etc.

1842/43, 1846/47-1849/50 assessed in absence of return £60; exempt.

1842/43, 1846/47 blacksmiths; 1847/48-1849/50 blacksmiths, etc.

1113 GIDDINGS, Robert, baker & mealman.

1842/43 returned £30 and £7.10.0 interest; assessed £120 and £7.10.0 interest.
1846/47-1848/49 returned £30; assessed £130.
1849/50 assessed in absence of return £130.
1850/51 returned £15; assessed £150.
1851/52 returned £20; assessed £150.
1852/53-1854/55 returned £30; assessed £150.
1855/56-1859/60 assessed in absence of return £150.

Pigot & Co's Directory, 1842: Robert Giddings, miller, Urchfont.

1114 GIDDINGS, Sarah, grocer, chandler. [also GIDDINGS, Robert]

1842/43 returned and assessed £10; exempt.
1846/47-1848/49 assessed in absence of return £10; exempt.
1849/50 returned and assessed £25; exempt.

1842/43 Robert Giddings, chandler; 1846/47-1849/50 Sarah Giddings, grocer.

1115 GILLETT, James, bricklayer, grocer & tea dealer.

1842/43 returned and assessed £15g, £50b; exempt.
1846/47-1849/50 assessed in absence of return £65; exempt.
1851/52-1855/56 assessed in absence of return £50; exempt.
1856/57-1859/60 recorded; no assessments made; exempt.

Abbreviations: b, bricklayer, g, grocer & tea dealer.
1842/43, 1846/47-1849/50 bricklayer, grocer & tea dealer; 1851/52-1859/60 bricklayer.
1850/51 no assessment made.

1116 HAMLEN, John, innkeeper.

1842/43 returned £50; assessed £150; income proved at £100; exempt.

1842/43 no appeal noted.

1117 HIBBERD, Robert, carpenter.

1842/43 returned £70; assessed £100; exempt.
1846/47-1849/50 assessed in absence of return £80; exempt.
1851/52 returned and assessed £50; exempt.
1852/53 returned and assessed £50; income proved at £64.3.3; exempt.
1853/54 returned and assessed £65; exempt.
1854/55-1855/56 assessed in absence of return £65; exempt.
1856/57-1859/69 recorded; no assessments made; exempt.

1850/51 no assessment made.
Pigot & Co's Directory, 1842: Robert Hibbard (sic), carpenter & wheelwright, Littleton.

1118 HIBBERD, William, carpenter, beerseller.

1842/43 returned £20; assessed £50; exempt.
1846/47-1849/50 assessed in absence of return £50; exempt.

1852/53 returned £30; assessed £50; exempt.
1853/54-1855/56 assessed in absence of return £50; exempt.
1856/57-1859/60 recorded; no assessments made; exempt.

1842/43, 1846/47-1849/50 carpenter; 1852/53-1859/60 beerseller.
1850/51-1851/52 no assessments made.

1119 LANCASTER, John, castrator.

1842/43 returned and assessed £85; exempt.
1846/47-1848/49 returned and assessed £85 and £12.10.0 interest; exempt.
1849/50 returned and assessed £85 and £2.2.0 interest; exempt.
1851/52 returned and assessed £85.
1852/53 returned £80; assessed £85; income proved at £87.14.0; exempt.

1850/51 no assessment made.

1120 LYNE, John, butcher.

1842/43 returned £30; assessed £75; exempt.
1846/47-1849/50 assessed in absence of return £130; exempt.
1851/52 returned £20; assessed £50; exempt.
1852/53-1855/56 assessed in absence of return £50; exempt.
1856/57-1859/60 recorded; no assessments made; exempt.

1850/51 no assessment made.

1121 MATTHEWS, Roger, chandler, baker.

1842/43 returned and assessed £25; exempt.
1846/47-1849/50 assessed in absence of return £25; exempt.
1851/52 returned and assessed £20; exempt.
1852/53 assessed in absence of return £20; exempt.
1853/54 returned and assessed £20; exempt.
1854/55-1855/56 assessed in absence of return £60; exempt.
1856/57-1859/60 recorded; no assessments made; exempt.

1842/43, 1846/47-1849/50 chandler & baker; 1851/52-1859/60 baker.
1850/51 no assessment made.

1122 NAISH, Charles Hobbs, innkeeper. [by comparison, Bell]

1858/59-1859/60 returned £40; assessed £120.

1858/59 marked "late Jno. Dowse innkeeper".
Cross reference: Dowse, John, innkeeper, Urchfont.

1123 NEW, James, bailiff.

1842/43 returned and assessed £40; exempt.
1846/47-1849/50 assessed in absence of return £40; exempt.

1124 PIERCE, James, tailor.

1842/43 assessed in absence of return £45; exempt.
1846/47-1849/50 assessed in absence of return £40; exempt.

1125 PLANK, Thomas, shoemaker.

1842/43 returned and assessed £20; exempt.
1846/47-1849/50 assessed in absence of return £20; exempt.

1126 RUDMAN, Noah, carpenter.

1842/43, 1846/47-1849/50 assessed in absence of return £30; exempt.

1127 SCOTT, Richard, bailiff.

1842/43 returned and assessed £80; exempt.

1128 SMITH, Richard, cooper, maltster.

1842/43 returned £35; assessed £80; exempt.
1846/47 assessed in absence of return £80; income proved at £99.13.7; exempt.
1847/48-1848/49 assessed in absence of return £80; exempt.
1849/50 assessed in absence of return £85; exempt.
1851/52 returned £20; assessed £60; income proved at £88.5.1; exempt.
1852/53 returned £18; assessed £40; income proved at £107.9.0; exempt.
1853/54 returned £18; assessed £50; exempt.
1854/55 assessed in absence of return £75.
1855/56 assessed in absence of return £60; exempt.
1856/57 recorded; no assessment made; exempt.
1857/58 returned £18; estimated at £40 but no assessment made; exempt.
1858/59 returned £5; assessed £50.
1859/60 returned £10; assessed £50.

1842/43 cooper & maltster; 1846/47-1849/50, 1851/52-1859/60 cooper.
1850/51 no assessment made.

1129 SMITH, Thomas, shopkeeper.

1842/43 returned and assessed £20; exempt.
1846/47-1849/50 assessed in absence of return £40; exempt.

1130 SNOOK, John Swallow, threshing machine owner, maltster, thrasher.

1842/43 returned £18; assessed £25; exempt.
1846/47-1849/50 assessed in absence of return £25; exempt.
1850/51 assessed in absence of return £25; assessment discharged on appeal but no sum recorded.
1851/52 returned nil, no assessment made.
1852/53 recorded but no assessment made.
1853/54 assessed in absence of return £20; exempt.
1854/55 assessed in absence of return £50; exempt.
1855/56-1859/60 recorded; no assessment made; exempt.

1842/43, 1846/47-1850/51 maltster; 1851/52-1857/58 threshing machine (owner);
1858/59-1859/60 thrasher.
1850/51 on appeal marked "business given up. No successor".
1855/56 marked "discontinued".

1131 STAPLES, James, grocer, draper, bacon factor, shopkeeper, innkeeper.

1842/43 returned £60; assessed £100; income proved at £60.
1846/47-1849/50 assessed in absence of return £73; exempt.
1852/53 returned and assessed £42; income proved at £84.5.10; exempt.
1853/54 assessed in absence of return £84; exempt.
1854/55 assessed in absence of return £100; reduced to £75.
1855/56 assessed in absence of return £75; exempt.
1856/57-1859/60 recorded; no assessments made; exempt.

1842/43, 1846/47-1848/49 grocer, draper & bacon factor; 1849/50 draper, grocer, etc.; 1852/
53-1857/58 shopkeeper; 1858/59-1859/60 innkeeper.
1850/51-1851/52 no assessments made.

1132 WHATLEY, Evi, beerseller, brewer.

1842/43 returned £40; assessed £60; exempt.
1846/47-1850/51 assessed in absence of return £100; exempt.
1851/52 returned £30; assessed £80; exempt.
1852/53 returned £30; assessed £80; income proved at £86.11.0; exempt.
1853/54 returned £20; assessed £86; exempt.
1854/55 assessed in absence of return £100; income proved at £50; exempt.
1855/56 assessed in absence of return £50; exempt.

1856/57-1859/60 recorded; no assessments made; exempt.

1842/43 beerseller (brewer entered but deleted); 1846/47-1859/60 beerseller & brewer.

1133 WHITE, Frederick George, surgeon.

1857/58 returned and assessed £200; reduced to £137.

1858/59 returned £159.5.7 but deleted and marked "returned at Market Lavington".
1858/59-1859/60 also marked "Schedule E".
Cross reference: White, Frederick George, surgeon [under Hitchcock, Charles], Market Lavington.

1134 WISE, Thomas, brickmaker.

1842/43 recorded but no assessment made.
1846/47-1849/50 assessed in absence of return £40; exempt.

WEDHAMPTON

1135 DUNFORD, James, brickmaker. [also DUNFORD, Thomas]

1842/43 returned and assessed £50; exempt.
1846/47 assessed in absence of return £50; exempt.
1847/48-1852/53 assessed in absence of return £100; exempt.
1853/54 assessed in absence of return £100; income proved at £90; exempt.

1842/43, 1846/47-1847/48 Thomas Dunford; 1848/49-1853/54 James Dunford.
1854/55-1857/58 marked "return in Stert". [1853/54 assessed also in Stert].
1853/54-1856/57 [Stert] Durnford.
1858/59-1859/60 recorded but no assessment made.
Cross reference: Dunford, James, brickmaker, Stert.

1136 FAY, Timothy, woolstapler.

1842/43 returned and assessed £50; exempt.
1846/47 assessed in absence of return £100.
1847/48 returned and assessed £100.
1848/49 assessed in absence of return £140.
1849/50 returned £139; assessed £150.
1850/51-1852/53 returned and assessed £150.
1853/54 returned and assessed £400.
1854/55 assessed in absence of return £400.

1855/56 returned £186; assessed £400.
1856/57 returned £150; assessed £300.

1857/58 marked "dead".

1137 MANNINGS, George, woolstapler.

1842/43 returned and assessed £122.
1846/47-1847/48 returned and assessed £150.
1848/49 assessed in absence of return £140; exempt.
1849/50 returned £105.3.8; assessed £150.
1850/51 returned £117; assessed £150.
1851/52-1852/53 returned and assessed £150.
1853/54 returned and assessed £200.
1854/55 assessed in absence of return £200.
1855/56 returned £100; assessed £200.
1856/57 returned £150; assessed £200.
1857/58 returned and assessed £200.
1858/59 returned £150; assessed £200.
1859/60 returned and assessed £300.

1842/43 marked "pays £25 interest"; 8/9 duty left in charge, otherwise exemption claimed.

1138 RICKETTS, James, beerhouse keeper.

1842/43 returned and assessed £50; exempt.
1846/47-1849/50 assessed in absence of return £50; exempt.

1139 WITCHELL, James, blacksmith.

1842/43 returned and assessed £50; exempt.
1846/47-1849/50 assessed in absence of return £50; exempt.

WILCOT, OARE & DRAYCOT [FITZPAYNE]

1140 CHANDLER, Elizabeth, innkeeper.

1842/43 returned and assessed £20; exempt.
1846/47-1849/50 assessed in absence of return £20; exempt.

1141 COLLARD, G.P., shopkeeper.

1846/47-1849/50 assessed in absence of return £20; exempt.

1142 EDMONDS, John, maltster, baker.

1842/43 returned and assessed £70.
1846/47-1847/48 assessed in absence of return £80.
1848/49 returned £60; assessed £80.
1849/50 returned £50; assessed £80.
1850/51 assessed in absence of return £80.

1842/43 maltster & baker; 1846/47-1850/51 maltster.
1851/52 marked "no business done for 12 months".
1852/53 marked "left the parish".

1143 FERRIS, William, valuer.

1857/58 returned and assessed £150.
1858/59 returned and assessed £275.
1859/60 returned and assessed £320.

1144 GRANT, John & James, maltsters.

1857/58-1859/60 recorded but no assessments made.
Cross reference: Grant, John, maltster, Easterton.

1145 GRANT, Jonathan, valuer.

1850/51-1851/52 assessed in absence of return £67.
1852/53 returned and assessed £83.
1853/54 returned and assessed £46.
1854/55 assessed in absence of return £60.
1855/56 returned and assessed £60.
1856/57 assessed in absence of return £80.
1857/58 returned and assessed £80.
1858/59-1859/69 returned £60; assessed £80.

1146 MARKES, Frances B.

1842/43 name only entered; no assessment made.

1147 WILSON, David, shopkeeper.

1842/43 returned and assessed £20; exempt.

1846/47 marked "left the parish".

WILSFORD

1148 BOLTER, John, beerhouse keeper.

1857/58 returned £60; no assessment made.
1858/59-1859/60 recorded; no assessments made; exempt.

1149 DUNFORD, James, baker & shopkeeper.

1857/58 returned £30; no assessment made.
1858/59-1859/60 recorded; no assessments made; exempt.

1150 LEONARD, Jesse, maltster.

1851/52 assessed in absence of return £100.
1852/53 assessed in absence of return £100; exempt.
1853/54 returned £77; assessed £100; exempt.

1851/52 marked "late Exors. of Jacob Stratton".
1853/54 marked "see Marden". (no entry in Marden)
1854/55 marked "gone".
Cross reference: Stratton, Jacob, maltster, Wilsford.

1151 ORAM, Mary, blacksmith.

1857/58-1859/60 recorded; no assessment made; exempt.

1152 SIMONS, Revd. N., clerk.

1842/43 returned and assessed £100; exempt.

1846/47 marked "q.pupils. return".

1153 SPRINGBETT, Thomas, mealman.

1842/43 returned and assessed £50; exempt.
1846/47 assessed in absence of return £50; exempt.
1847/48 assessed in absence of return £150.
1848/49 returned £75; assessed £150; reduced to £110; exempt.
1849/50 assessed in absence of return £110; exempt.
1850/51-1852/53 assessed in absence of return £120; exempt.
1853/54-1856/57 assessed in absence of return £120.

1857/58 returned £100; assessed £120.
1858/59-1859/60 assessed in absence of return £120.

1848/49 no appeal noted.

1154 STRATTON, Jacob, maltster.

1842/43 returned and assessed £90.
1846/47-1847/48 assessed in absence of return £90.
1848/49 returned and assessed £100.
1849/50 returned £100; assessment discharged on appeal but no sum recorded.

1848/49-1849/50 Executors of Jacob Stratton.
1851/52 marked "Leonard, Jesse, maltster late Stratton, Jacob".
Cross reference: Leonard, Jesse, maltster, Wilsford.

WOODBOROUGH

1155 BROWN, Job, innkeeper, smith.

1842/43, 1846/47-1852/53 assessed in absence of return £75; exempt.
1853/54 returned £15; assessed £75; exempt.
1854/55-1856/57 assessed in absence of return £75.
1857/58 returned £70; assessed £75.
1858/59 returned £50; assessed £75.
1859/60 returned and assessed £75.

1842/43, 1846/47-1852/53, 1858/59-1859/60 innkeeper; 1853/54-1857/58 innkeeper & smith.

1156 BROWN, Philip, blacksmith.

1846/47-1849/50 assessed in absence of return £20; exempt.

1157 CALLADINE, Samuel, tailor, draper.

1842/43 assessed in absence of return £80; exempt.
1846/47-1849/50 assessed in absence of return £70; exempt.
1851/52 returned and assessed £100; income proved at £135; exempt.
1852/53 assessed in absence of return £135; exempt.
1853/54 returned £4; estimated at £135 deleted.

1842/43, 1846/47-1849/50 tailor; 1851/52-1852/53 draper; 1853/54 draper & tailor.

1850/51 no assessment made.
1851/52 entered as Mr.Culladine.
1852/53 marked "late draper".

1158 FIDLER, Hezekiah, smith.

1846/47-1849/50 assessed in absence of return £20; exempt.

1159 FIDLER, William, harness maker, grocer. [also FIDLER, Sarah]

1846/47-1849/50 assessed in absence of return £40; exempt.
1857/58 returned £65; assessed £100; reduced to £75.
1858/59-1859/60 returned and assessed £75.

1846/47-1849/50, 1857/58 William Fidler; 1858/59-1859/60 Sarah Fidler.
1846/47-1849/50, 1857/58 harness maker; 1858/59-1859/60 harness maker & grocer.
1850/51-1855/56 no assessments made.
1856/57 recorded as harness maker & grocer but no assessment made.
1857/58 no appeal noted.
1858/59 marked "Q. Fidler journeyman harness maker".

1160 HIBBERD, John, maltster, grocer, shopkeeper.

1842/43, 1846/47-1849/50 assessed in absence of return £60; exempt.

1842/43 maltster & grocer; 1846/47-1849/50 shopkeeper.

1161 NORTH, John B., miller.

1842/43 assessed in absence of return £80; exempt.

Cross reference: North, John Bunce, miller, Potterne [possible].

1162 PAVEY, James, miller.

1846/47-1849/50 assessed in absence of return £80; exempt.

1163 PINNIGER, Thomas, traveller.

1857/58-1859/60 returned and assessed £120.

1164 ROBBINS, Samuel, timber merchant, coal merchant, tonnage agent, slate merchant, Post Master.

1842/43 returned £150tc, £100a; assessed £300.
1846/47 assessed in absence of return £400.
1847/48 returned £350; assessed £400.
1848/49 returned £300; assessed £400.
1849/50-1850/51 returned £380; assessed £500.
1851/52 returned £300; assessed £400.
1852/53 assessed in absence of return £400.
1853/54 returned and assessed £400.
1854/55 assessed in absence of return £500.
1855/56 returned £500; assessed £600.
1856/57 assessed in absence of return £600.
1857/58 returned and assessed £600.
1858/59 returned £600; assessed £800.
1859/60 returned £700; assessed £800.

Abbreviations: t, timber merchant; c, coal merchant; a, tonnage agent.
1842/43, 1846/47 timber & coal merchant, tonnage agent; 1847/48-1849/50 timber merchant
    & tonnage agent; 1850/51-1858/59 timber merchant; 1859/60 timber merchant, coal &
    slate merchant, Post Master.
1849/50 marked "& at Devizes".
Cross reference: Robbins, Samuel, timber merchant, St.Mary.

1165 SHIPMAN, Thomas, baker.

1842/43, 1846/47-1849/50 assessed in absence of return £50; exempt.

1166 TURNER, William, draper & tailor.

1853/54 returned and assessed £110.
1854/55 assessed in absence of return £100.
1855/56 returned and assessed £100.
1856/57 assessed in absence of return £100.
1857/58 returned £72; assessed £100.
1858/59-1859/60 returned and assessed £100.

1167 WILTSHIRE, Mary, collar & harness maker.

1842/43, 1846/47 assessed in absence of return £30; exempt.

1168 WYLD, Revd. W.T.

1848/49 name only entered and deleted.

INDEX OF OCCUPATIONS

NOTE: References are to entry numbers, not to pages.

INDEX OF BUSINESS NAMES

Note: Businesses outside the parishes of St.John and St.Mary, Devizes, are shown with the parish or township in which they are recorded; otherwise, remaining businesses are recorded in either the parish of St.John or St.Mary. References relate to both text and footnotes

INDEX OF NAMES

WILTSHIRE RECORD SOCIETY
(As at May 2002)

President: PROF. C.R. ELRINGTON, F.S.A.
General Editor: DR JOHN CHANDLER
Honorary Treasurer: IVOR M. SLOCOMBE
Honorary Secretary: JOHN N. D'ARCY

Committee:
D. CHALMERS
DR D.A. CROWLEY
S.D. HOBBS
M.J. MARSHMAN
MRS S. THOMSON
MRS I.L. WILLIAMS
K.H. ROGERS, F.S.A., representing the Wiltshire Archaeological and Natural History Society

---

Honorary Independent Examiner: J.D. FOY
Correspondent for the U.S.A.: CHARLES P. GOULD

PRIVATE MEMBERS

ADAMS, Ms S, 23 Rockcliffe Avenue, Bathwick, Bath BA2 6QP

ANDERSON, MR D M, 20 Shakespeare Road, Stratford-sub-Castle, Salisbury SP1 3LA

APPLEGATE, MISS J M, 55 Holbrook Lane, Trowbridge BA14 0PS

ASAJI, PROF K, 5-35-14 Senriyama-nishi, Suita, Osaka, Japan 565-0851

AVERY, MRS S, 33 Cardigan Street, Oxford OX2 6GP

BADENI, COUNTESS JUNE, Norton Manor, Norton, Malmesbury SN16 0JN

BAINES, MRS B M, 32 Tybenham Road, Merton Park, London SW19 3LA

BALL, MR S T, 19 The Mall, Swindon SN1 4JA

BARNETT, MR B A, 17 Alexandra Road, Coalpit Heath, Bristol BS36 2PY

BATHE, MR G, Byeley in Densome, Woodgreen, Fordingbridge, Hants SP6 2QU

BAYLIFFE, MR B G, 3 Green Street, Brockworth, Glos GL3 4LT

BENNETT, DR N, Hawthorn House, Main Street, Norton, Lincoln LN4 2BH

BERRETT, MR A M, 10 Primrose Hill Road, London NW3 3AD

BERRY, MR C, 9 Haven Rd, Crackington Haven, Bude, Cornwall EX23 0PD

BISHOP, MRS S M, Innox Bungalow, Market Place, Colerne, Chippenham SN14 8AY

BLAKE, MR P A, 18 Rosevine Road, London SW20 8RB

BLAKE, MR T N, Glebe Farm, Tilshead, Salisbury SP3 4RZ

BOX, MR S D, 73 Silverdale Road, Earley, Reading RG6 2NF

BRAND, DR P A, 155 Kennington Road, London SE11 6SF

BRITTON, MR D J, Overbrook House, The High Road, Ashton Keynes, Swindon SN6 6NL

Brooke-Little, Mr J P, Heyford House, Lower Heyford, Bicester, Oxon OX25 5NZ

Brown, Mr D A, 36 Empire Road, Salisbury SP2 9DF

Brown, Mr G R, 6 Canbury Close, Amesbury, SalisburySP4 7QF

Bryant, Mrs D, 1 St John's Court, Devizes SN10 1BJ

Burgess, Mr I D, 29 Brackley Avenue, Fair Oak, Eastleigh, Hants SO5 7FL

Burgess, Mr J M, Tolcarne, Wartha Mill, Porkellis, Helston, Cornwall TR13 0HX

Burnett-Brown, Miss J M, Lacock Abbey, Lacock, Chippenham SN15 2LG

Carew Hunt, Miss P H, Cowleaze, Edington, Westbury BA13 4PJ

Carr, Prof D R, Dept. of History, 140 7th Ave South, St Petersburg, Florida 33701 USA

Carrier, Mr S, 9 Highfield Road, Bradford on Avon BA15 1AS

Carter, Dr B J, JP PhD BSc FSG, 15 Walton Grange, Bath Road, Swindon SN1 4AH

Cawthorne, Mrs N, 45 London Road, Camberley, Surrey GU15 3UG

Chalmers, Mr D, Bay House West, Bay House, Ilminster, Somerset TA19 0AT

Chandler, Dr J H, Jupe's School, The Street, East Knoyle, Salisbury SP3 6AJ

Chard, Mr I, 35 Thingwall Park, Fishponds, Bristol BS16 2AJ

Chave, Mr R A, 39 Church Street, Westbury BA13 3BZ

Church, Mr T S, Mannering House, Bethersden, Ashford, Kent TN26 3DJ

Clark, Mr A G, Highlands, 51a Brook Drive, Corsham SN13 9AX

Clark, Mrs V, 29 The Green, Marlborough SN8 1AW

Clegg, Ms R, 12 Brookes Road, Broseley, Salop TF12 5SB

Cobern, Miss A M, 4 Manton Close, Manton, Marlborough SN8 4HJ

Colcomb, Mr D M, 38 Roundway Park, Devizes SN10 2EO

Cole, Mrs J A, 113 Groundwell Road, Swindon SN1 2NA

Coleman, Miss J, Swn-y-Coed, Abergwili, Carmarthenshire SA32 7EP

Collins, Mr A T, 11 Lemon Grove, Whitehill, Bordon, Hants GU35 9BD

Colman, Mrs P, 28 Abbey Mill, Church Street, Bradford on Avon BA15 1HB

Congleton, Lord, West End Farm, Ebbesbourne Wake, Salisbury SP5 5JW

Coombes, Mr J, 85 Green Pastures, Heaton Mersey, Stockport SK4 3RB

Coombes-Lewis, Mr R J, 45 Oakwood Park Road, Southgate, London N14 6QP

Cooper, Mr S, 12 Victory Row, Wootton Bassett, Swindon SN4 7BE

Coram, Mrs J E, 38 The Parklands, Hullavington, Chippenham SN14 6DL

Coulstock, Miss P H, 15 Pennington Crescent, West Moors, Wimborne, Dorset BH22 0JH

Covey, Mr R V, Lower Hunts Mill, Wootton Bassett, Swindon SN4 7QL

Cowan, Col M, 24 Lower Street, Harnham, Salisbury SP3 8EY

Crighton, Mr G S, 68 Stanford Avenue, Springfield, Milton Keynes MK6 3NH

Crook, Mr P H, Bradavon, 45 The Dales, Cottingham, E Yorks HU16 5JS

Crouch, Mr J W, Kensington House, Pensford Hill, Pensford, Somerset BS39 4AA

Crowley, Dr D A, 16 Greater Lane, Edington, Westbury BA13 4QP

d'Arcy, Mr J N, The Old Vicarage, Edington, Westbury

Davies, Mrs A M, 283 Longstone Road, Iver Heath, Bucks SL0 0RN

Dibben, Mr A A, 18 Clare Road, Lewes, East Sussex BN7 1PN

Draper, Miss R, 12 Sheep Street, Devizes SN10 1DL

Ede, Dr M E, 12 Springfield Place, Lansdown, Bath BA1 5RA

Edwards, Mr P C, 33 Longcroft Road, Devizes SN10 3AT

Elrington, Prof C R, 34 Lloyd Baker Street, London WC1X 9AB

FALCINI, Ms L, Old Forge Cottage, North Lane, West Tytherley, Salisbury SP5 1JX

FAY, Mrs M, 40 North Way, Porton Down, Salisbury SP4 0JN

FICE, Mrs B, Holt View House, 9 Rosemary Lane, Rowledge, Farnham GU10 4DB

FIRMAGER, Mrs G M, 72b High Street, Semington, Trowbridge BA14 6JR

FLOWER-ELLIS, Dr J G, Swedish Univ of Agric Sciences, PO Box 7072 S-750 07, Uppsala, Sweden 1972

FORBES, Miss K G, Bury House, Codford, Warminster

FOSTER, Mr R E, The New House, St Giles Close, Gt Maplestead, Halstead, Essex CO9 2RW

FOY, Mr J D, 28 Penn Lea Road, Bath BA1 3RA

FREEMAN, Rev Dr J, 1 Cranfield Row, Gerridge Street, London SE1 7QN

FROST, Mr B C, Red Tiles, Cadley, Collingbourne Ducis, Marlborough SN8 3EA

FULLER, Mrs B, 65 New Park Street, Devizes SN10 1DR

GALBRAITH, Ms C, Box 42, 17 Gill Street, Coldwater, Ontario L0K 1EO, Canada

GALE, Mrs J, 169 Spit Road, Mosman, NSW 2088, Australia

GHEY, Mr J G, 18 Bassett Row, Bassett, Southampton SO1 7FS

GIBBS, Mrs E, Home Farm, Barrow Gurney, Bristol BS48 3RW

GINGELL, Ms B M, 32 Cambridge Lodge, Bonehurst Road, Horley, Surrey RH6 8PR

GODDARD, Mr R E H, Sinton Meadow, Stokes Lane, Leigh Sinton, Malvern, Worcs WR13 5DY

GOODBODY, Mr E A, Stockmans, Rectory Hill, Amersham, Bucks

GOODFELLOW, Mr P S, Teffont Selby, 47 High Street, Mow Cop, Cheshire ST7 3NZ

GOSLING, Rev Dr J, 1 Wiley Terrace, Wilton, Salisbury SP2 0HN

GOUGH, Miss P M, 39 Whitford Road, Bromsgrove, Worcs B61 7ED

GOULD, Mr C P, 1200 Old Mill Road, San Marino, California 91108 USA

GOULD, Mr L K, 263 Rosemount, Pasadena, California 91103 USA

GRIFFIN, Dr C J, School of Geographical Sciences, University of Bristol, University Road, Bristol BS8 1SS

GRIFFITHS, Mr T J, 29 Saxon Street, Chippenham SN15

GRUBER VON ARNI, Col E E, 11 Park Lane, Swindon SN1 5HG

HAMILTON, Captain R, 1 The Square, Cathedral Views, Crane Bridge Road, Salisbury SP2 7TW

HARE, Dr J N, 7 Owens Road, Winchester, Hants SO22 6RU

HARTCHER, Rev Dr G N, 3-5 Vincentia Street, Marsfield, NSW 2122, Australia

HATCHWELL, Mr R C, Cleeve House, Rodbourne Bottom, Malmesbury SN16 0EZ

HAYWARD, Miss J E, Pleasant Cottage, Crockerton, Warminster BA12 8AJ

HELMHOLZ, Prof R W, Law School, 1111 East 60th Street, Chicago, Illinois 60637 USA

HENLY, Mr H R, 99 Moredon Road, Swindon SN2 2JG

HERRON, Mrs Pamela M, 25 Anvil Crescent, Broadstone, Dorset BH18 9DY

HICKMAN, Mr M R, 184 Surrenden Road, Brighton BN1 6NN

HICKS, Mr I, 74 Newhurst Park, Hilperton, Trowbridge BA14 7QW

HICKS, Prof M A, King Alfred's College, Winchester SO22 4NR

HILLIKER, Mr S, Box 184, Sutherland, NSW 2232, Australia

HILLMAN, Mr R B, 18 Carnarvon Close, Chippenham SN14 0PN

HINTON, Mr A E, Glenside Cottage, Glendene Avenue, East Horsley, Surrey KT24 5AY

HOBBS, Mr S, 63 West End, Westbury BA13 3JQ

HOLLEY, Mr R J, 120 London Road, Calne SN11 0AH

HORNBY, MISS E, 70 Archers Court, Castle Street, Salisbury SP1 3WE

HORTON, MR P.R.G, OBE, Hedge End, West Grimstead, Salisbury SP5 3RF

HOWELLS, Jane, 7 St Mark's Rd, Salisbury SP1 3AY

HUGHES, PROF C J, Old House, Tisbury, Salisbury SP3 6PS

HUGHES, MR R G, 60 Hurst Park Road, Twyford, Reading RG10 0EY

HULL, MR J L F, Sandown Apartments, 1 Southerwood Drive, Sandy Bay, Tasmania 7005, Australia

HUMPHRIES, MR A G, Rustics, Blacksmith's Lane, Harmston, Lincoln LN5 9SW

INGRAM, DR M J, Brasenose College, Oxford OX1 4AJ

JACKSON, MR D, 2 Byways Close, Salisbury SP1 2QS

JAMES, MR & MRS C, 18 King Henry Drive, Grange Park, Swindon SN5 6BL

JAMES, MR J F, 3 Sylvan Close, Hordle, Lymington, Hants SO41 0HJ

JEACOCK, MR D, 16 Church Street, Wootton Bassett, Swindon

JELLICOE, RT HON EARL, Tidcombe Manor, Tidcombe, Marlborough SN8 3SL

JOHNSTON, MRS J M, Greystone House, 3 Trowbridge Road, Bradford on Avon BA15 1EE

KENT, MR T A, Rose Cottage, Isington, Alton, Hants GU34 4PN

KING, MR S F, Church Mead House, Woolverton, Bath BA3 6QT

KIRBY, MR J L, 209 Covington Way, Streatham, London SW16 3BY

KITE, MR P J, 13 Chestnut Avenue, Farnham GU9 8UL

KNEEBONE, MR W J R, 20 Blind Lane, Southwick, Trowbridge BA14 9PG

KUNIKATA, MR K, Dept of Economics, 1-4-12, Kojirakawa-machi, Yamagata-shi 990, Japan

LANSDOWNE, MARQUIS OF, Bowood House, Calne SN11 0LZ

LAURENCE, MISS A, 1a Morreys Avenue, Oxford OX1 4ST

LAURENCE, MR G F, Apt 312, The Hawthorns, 18-21 Elton Road, Clevedon BS21 7EH

LAWES, MR G, 48 Windsor Avenue, Leighton Buzzard LU7 1AP

LEGGATT, MR A, 48 High Street, Worton, Devizes SN10 5RG

LODGE, MR O R W, Southridge House, Hindon, Salisbury SP3 6ER

LONDON, MISS V C M, 55 Churchill Road, Church Stretton, Salop SY6 6EP

LUSH, DR G J, 5 Braeside Court, West Moors, Ferndown, Dorset BH22 0JS

MARSH, REV R, Maybridge Vicarage, 56 The Boulevard, Worthing, West Sussex BN 13 1LA

MARSHMAN, MR M J, 13 Regents Place, Bradford on Avon BA15 1ED

MARTIN, MR D, 21 Westbourne Close, Salisbury SP1 2RU

MARTIN, MS JEAN, 21 Ashfield Road, Chippenham SN15 1QQ

MASLEN, MR A, 8 Alder Walk, Frome, Som BA11 2SN

MATHEWS, MR R, P O Box R72, Royal Exchange, NSW 2000, Australia

MATTHEWS, CANON W A, Holy Trinity Vicarage, 18a Woolley St, Bradford on Avon BA15 1AF

MATTINGLY, MR N, Freshford Manor, Freshford, Bath BA3 6EF

MERRYWEATHER, MR A, 60 Trafalgar Road, Cirencester, Glos GL7 2EL

MILLINGTON, MRS P, Hawkstone, Church Hill, Lover, Salisbury SP5 2PL

MOLES, MRS M I, 40 Wyke Road, Trowbridge BA14 7NP

MONTAGUE, MR M D, 115 Stuarts Road, Katoomba, NSW 2780, Australia

MOODY, MR R F, Harptree House, East Harptree, Bristol BS18 6AA

MORIOKA, PROF K 3-12, 4-chome, Sanno, Ota-ku, Tokyo, Japan

MORLAND, MRS N, 33 Shaftesbury Road, Wilton, Salisbury SP2 0DU

MORRISON, MRS J, Priory Cottage, Bratton, Westbury BA13

MOULTON, DR A E, The Hall, Bradford on Avon BA15

NAPPER, MR L R, 9 The Railway Terrace, Kemble, Cirencester GL7 6AU

NEWBURY, MR C COLES, 6 Leighton Green, Westbury BA13 3PN

NEWMAN, MRS R, Tanglewood, Laverstock Park, Salisbury SP1 1QJ

NOKES, MR P M A, Wards Farm, Ditcheat, Shepton Mallet, Somerset BA4 6PR

O'DONNELL, MISS S J, 42 Wessington Park, Calne SN11 0AU

OGBOURNE, MR J M V, 14 Earnshaw Way, Beaumont Park, Whitley Bay, Tyne and Wear NE25 9UN

OGBURN, CHIEF JUDGE ROBERT W, 317 First Avenue, Monte Vista, CO 81144, USA

OSBORNE, COL R, Unwins House, 15 Waterbeach Road, Landbeach, Cambridge CB4 4EA

PARKER, DR P F, 45 Chitterne Road, Codford St Mary, Warminster BA12 0PG

PARROTT, MRS M G, 81 Church Road, Christian Malford, Chippenham SN15 4BW

PATIENCE, MR D C, 29 Priory Gardens, Stamford, Lincs PE9 2EG

PATRICK, DR S, The Thatchings, Charlton All Saints, Salisbury SP5 4HQ

PERRY, DR S H, Priory Cottage, Broad Street, Bampton, Oxon

PERRY, MR W A, Noads House, Tilshead, Salisbury SP3 4RY

POWELL, MRS N, 4 Verwood Drive, Bitton, Bristol BS15 6JP

RADNOR, EARL OF, Longford Castle, Salisbury SP5 4EF

RAYBOULD, MISS F, 20 Radnor Road, Salisbury SP1 3PL

REEVES, DR M E, 38 Norham Road, Oxford OX2 6SQ

ROGERS, MR K H, Silverthorne House, East Town, West Ashton, Trowbridge BA14 6BE

ROOKE, MISS S F, The Old Rectory, Little Langford, Salisbury SP3 4NU

SHELDRAKE, MR B, 28 Belgrave Street, Swindon SN1 3HR

SHEWRING, MR P, 73 Woodland Road, Beddau, Pontypridd, Mid-Glamorgan CF38 2SE

SIMS-NEIGHBOUR, MR A K, 2 Hesketh Crescent, Swindon SN3 1RY

SINAR, MISS J C, 1 Alton Road, Wilcot, Pewsey SN9 5NP

SLOCOMBE, MR I, 11 Belcombe Place, Bradford on Avon BA15 1NA

SMITH, DR C, 2 Wesley Villas, Church Street, Coleford, Frome BA3 5ND

SMITH, MR P J, 6 Nuthatch, Longfield, Kent DA3 7NS

SNEYD, MR R H, Court Farm House, 22 Court Lane, Bratton, Westbury BA13 4RR

SOPP, MR G A, 23952 Nomar Street, Woodland Hills, California 91367, USA

SPAETH, DR D A, School of History and Archaeology, 1 University Gardens, University of Glasgow G12 8QQ

STEELE, MRS N D, 46 The Close, Salisbury SP1 2EL

STEVENAGE, MR M R, 49 Centre Drive, Epping, Essex CM16 4JF

STEWARD, DR H J, Graduate School of Geography, 950 Main Street, Worcester, Mass 01610-1477, USA

STEWART, MISS K P, 6 Beatrice Road, Salisbury SP1 3PN

SYKES, MRS M, Conock Manor, Conock, Devizes SN10 3QQ

SYLVESTER, MR D G H, Almondsbury Field, Tockington Lane, Almondsbury, Bristol BS12 4EB

TAYLOR, DR A J, Rose Cottage, Lincolns Hill, Chiddingfold, Surrey GU8 4UN

TAYLOR, MR C C, 11 High Street, Pampisford, Cambridge CB2 4ES

TAYLOR, MRS J B, PO Box 3900, Manuka, ACT 2063, Australia

TELFORD, MRS L, 1 Dauntsey Court, Duck St, West Lavington, Devizes SN10 4LR

THOMPSON, MR & MRS J B, 1 Bedwyn Common, Great Bedwyn, Marlborough SN8 3HZ

THOMSON, MRS SALLY M, Home Close, High St, Codford, Warminster BA12 0NB

TIGHE, MR M F, Strath Colin, Pettridge Lane, Mere, Warminster BA12 6DG

TOMKOWICZ, MRS C, 2 Chirton Place, Trowbridge BA14 0XT

TSUSHIMA, MRS J, Malmaison, Church Street, Great Bedwyn, Marlborough SN8 3PE

TURNER, MR I D, Warrendene, 222 Nottingham Road, Mansfield, Notts NG18 4AB

WAITE, MR R E, 18a Lower Road, Chinnor, Oxford OX9 4DT

WALKER, MR J K, 82 Wainsford Road, Everton, Lymington, Hants SO41 0UD

WARNEFORD, MR F E, New Inn Farm, West End Lane, Henfield, West Sussex BN5 9RF

WARREN, MR P, 6 The Meadows, Milford Hill Road, Salisbury SP1 2RT

WEINSTOCK, BARON, Bowden Park, Lacock, Chippenham

WELLER, MR R B, 9a Bower Gardens, Salisbury SP1 2RL

WENDEN, MRS P, 21 Eastern Parade, Fareham, Hants PO16 0RL

WHORLEY, MR E E, 190 Stockbridge Road, Winchester, Hants SO22 6RW

WILLIAMS, MRS I L, 7 Chandler Close, Devizes SN10 3DS

WILTSHIRE, MRS P E, 23 Little Parks, Holt, Trowbridge BA14 6QR

WOODWARD, A S, 28-840 Cahill Drive West, Ottawa, Ontario K1V 9K5, Canada

WORDSWORTH, MRS G, Quince Cottage, Longbridge Deverill, Warminster BA12 7DS

WRIGHT, MR D P, Haileybury, Hertford SG13 7NU

YOUNGER, MR C, The Old Chapel, Burbage, Marlborough SN8 3AA

UNITED KINGDOM INSTITUTIONS

Aberystwyth
    National Library of Wales
    University College of Wales
Bath. Reference Library
Birmingham
    Central Library
    University Library
Brighton. University of Sussex Library
Bristol. University Library
Cambridge. University Library
Cheltenham. Bristol and Gloucestershire Archaeological Society
Chippenham. Wiltshire College
Coventry. University of Warwick Library
Devizes
    Wiltshire Archaeological & N.H. Soc.
    Wiltshire Family History Society
Dorchester. Dorset County Library
Durham. University Library
Edinburgh
    National Library of Scotland
    University Library

Exeter. University Library
Glasgow. University Library
Leeds. University Library
Leicester. University Library
Liverpool. University Library
London
    British Library
    College of Arms
    Guildhall Library
    Inner Temple Library
    Institute of Historical Research
    London Library
    Public Record Office
    Royal Historical Society
    Society of Antiquaries
    Society of Genealogists
    University of London Library
Manchester. John Rylands Library
Marlborough
    Memorial Library, Marlborough College
    Merchant's House Trust
    Savernake Estate Office

Norwich. University of East Anglia Library
Nottingham. University Library
Oxford
    Bodleian Library
    Exeter College Library
Poole. Bournemouth University
Reading
    Central Library
    University Library
St Andrews. University Library
Salisbury
    Bourne Valley Historical Society
    Cathedral Library
    Salisbury and South Wilts Museum

Sheffield. University Library
Southampton. University Library
Swansea. University College Library
Swindon
    English Heritage
    Swindon Borough Council
Taunton. Somerset Archaeological and
    Natural History Society
Trowbridge
    Wiltshire Libraries & Heritage
    Wiltshire and Swindon Record Office
Wetherby. British Library Document Supply
    Centre
York. University Library

INSTITUTIONS OVERSEAS

AUSTRALIA

Adelaide. Barr Smith Library, Adelaide
    University
Crawley. Reid Library, University of Western
    Australia
Melbourne
    Baillieu Library, University of Melbourne
    Victoria State Library
Sydney. Fisher Library, University of Sydney
    Law Library, University of New South
    Wales

CANADA

Halifax, Nova Scotia. Dalhousie University
    Library
London, Ont. D.B. Weldon Library, Univer-
    sity of Western Ontario
Montreal, Que. Sir George Williams
    University
Ottawa, Ont. Carleton University Library
Toronto, Ont
    Pontifical Inst of Medieval Studies
    University of Toronto Library
Victoria, B.C. McPherson Library, Univer-
    sity of Victoria

EIRE

Dublin. Trinity College Library

GERMANY

Gottingen. University Library

JAPAN

Osaka. Institute of Economic History, Kansai
    University
Sendai. Institute of Economic History,
    Tohoku University
Tokyo. Waseda University Library

NEW ZEALAND

Wellington. National Library of New
    Zealand

UNITED STATES OF AMERICA

Ann Arbor, Mich. Hatcher Library, Univer-
    sity of Michigan
Athens, Ga. University of Georgia Libraries
Atlanta, Ga. The Robert W Woodruff
    Library, Emory University
Baltimore, Md. Milton S. Eisenhower
    Library, Johns Hopkins University
Bloomington, Ind. Indiana University
    Library
Boston, Mass.
    Boston Public Library
    New England Historic and Genealogi-
    cal Society

Boulder, Colo. University of Colorado Library

Cambridge, Mass.

Harvard College Library

Harvard Law School Library

Charlottesville, Va. Alderman Library, University of Virginia

Chicago.

Newberry Library

University of Chicago Library

Dallas, Texas. Public Library

Davis, Calif. University Library

East Lansing, Mich. Michigan State University Library

Eugene, Ore. University of Oregon Library

Evanston, Ill. United Libraries, Garrett/Evangelical, Seabury

Fort Wayne, Ind. Allen County Public Library

Houston, Texas. M.D. Anderson Library, University of Houston

Iowa City, Iowa. University of Iowa Libraries

Ithaca, NY. Cornell University Library

Las Cruces, N.M. New Mexico State University Library

Los Angeles.

Public Library

Young Research Library, University of California

Minneapolis, Minn. Wilson Library, University of Minnesota

New Haven, Conn. Yale University Library

New York.

Columbia University of the City of New York

Public Library

Notre Dame, Ind. Memorial Library, University of Notre Dame

Piscataway, N.J. Rutgers University Libraries

Princeton, N.J. Princeton University Libraries

Salt Lake City, Utah. Family History Library

San Marino, Calif. Henry E. Huntington Library

Santa Barbara, Calif. University of California Library

South Hadley, Mass. Williston Memorial Library, Mount Holyoke College

Stanford, Calif. Green Library, Stanford University

Tucson, Ariz. University of Arizona Library

Urbana, Ill. University of Illinois Library

Washington. The Folger Shakespeare Library

Winston-Salem, N.C. Z. Smith Reynolds Library, Wake Forest University

LIST OF PUBLICATIONS

The Wiltshire Record Society was founded in 1937, as the Records Branch of the Wiltshire Archaeological and Natural History Society, to promote the publication of the documentary sources for the history of Wiltshire. The annual subscription is £15 for private and institutional members. In return, a member receives a volume each year. Prospective members should apply to the Hon. Secretary, c/o Wiltshire and Swindon Record Office, County Hall, Trowbridge, Wilts BA14 8BS. Many more members are needed.

The following volumes have been published. Price to members £15, and to non-members £20, postage extra. Available from the Wiltshire and Swindon Record Office, Bythesea Road, Trowbridge BA14 8BS.

1. *Abstracts of feet of fines relating to Wiltshire for the reigns of Edward I and Edward II*, edited by R.B. Pugh, 1939
2. *Accounts of the parliamentary garrisons of Great Chalfield and Malmesbury, 1645-1646*, edited by J.H.P. Pafford, 1940
3. *Calendar of Antrobus deeds before 1625*, edited by R.B. Pugh, 1947
4. *Wiltshire county records: minutes of proceedings in sessions, 1563 and 1574 to 1592*, edited by H.C. Johnson, 1949
5. *List of Wiltshire boroughs records earlier in date than 1836*, edited by M.G. Rathbone, 1951
6. *The Trowbridge woollen industry as illustrated by the stock books of John and Thomas Clark, 1804-1824*, edited by R.P. Beckinsale, 1951
7. *Guild stewards' book of the borough of Calne, 1561-1688*, edited by A.W. Mabbs, 1953
8. *Andrews' and Dury's map of Wiltshire, 1773: a reduced facsimile*, edited by Elizabeth Crittall, 1952
9. *Surveys of the manors of Philip, earl of Pembroke and Montgomery, 1631-2*, edited by E. Kerridge, 1953
10. *Two sixteenth century taxations lists, 1545 and 1576*, edited by G.D. Ramsay, 1954
11. *Wiltshire quarter sessions and assizes, 1736*, edited by J.P.M. Fowle, 1955
12. *Collectanea*, edited by N.J. Williams, 1956
13. *Progress notes of Warden Woodward for the Wiltshire estates of New College, Oxford, 1659-1675*, edited by R.L. Rickard, 1957
14. *Accounts and surveys of the Wiltshire lands of Adam de Stratton*, edited by M.W. Farr, 1959
15. *Tradesmen in early-Stuart Wiltshire: a miscellany*, edited by N.J. Williams, 1960
16. *Crown pleas of the Wiltshire eyre, 1249*, edited by C.A.F. Meekings, 1961
17. *Wiltshire apprentices and their masters, 1710-1760*, edited by Christabel Dale, 1961
18. *Hemingby's register*, edited by Helena M. Chew, 1963
19. *Documents illustrating the Wiltshire textile trades in the eighteenth century*, edited by Julia de L. Mann, 1964
20. *The diary of Thomas Naish*, edited by Doreen Slatter, 1965
21-2. *The rolls of Highworth hundred, 1275-1287*, 2 parts, edited by Brenda Farr, 1966, 1968
23. *The earl of Hertford's lieutenancy papers, 1603-1612*, edited by W.P.D. Murphy, 1969
24. *Court rolls of the Wiltshire manors of Adam de Stratton*, edited by R.B. Pugh, 1970
25. *Abstracts of Wiltshire inclosure awards and agreements*, edited by R.E. Sandell, 1971
26. *Civil pleas of the Wiltshire eyre, 1249*, edited by M.T. Clanchy, 1971
27. *Wiltshire returns to the bishop's visitation queries, 1783*, edited by Mary Ransome, 1972
28. *Wiltshire extents for debts, Edward I - Elizabeth I*, edited by Angela Conyers, 1973
29. *Abstracts of feet of fines relating to Wiltshire for the reign of Edward III*, edited by C.R. Elrington, 1974

30. *Abstracts of Wiltshire tithe apportionments*, edited by R.E. Sandell, 1975
31. *Poverty in early-Stuart Salisbury*, edited by Paul Slack, 1975
32. *The subscription book of Bishops Tounson and Davenant, 1620-40*, edited by B. Williams, 1977
33. *Wiltshire gaol delivery and trailbaston trials, 1275-1306*, edited by R.B. Pugh, 1978
34. *Lacock abbey charters*, edited by K.H. Rogers, 1979
35. *The cartulary of Bradenstoke priory*, edited by Vera C.M. London, 1979
36. *Wiltshire coroners' bills, 1752-1796*, edited by R.F. Hunnisett, 1981
37. *The justicing notebook of William Hunt, 1744-1749*, edited by Elizabeth Crittall, 1982
38. *Two Elizabethan women: correspondence of Joan and Maria Thynne, 1575-1611*, edited by Alison D. Wall, 1983
39. *The register of John Chandler, dean of Salisbury, 1404-17*, edited by T.C.B. Timmins, 1984
40. *Wiltshire dissenters' meeting house certificates and registrations, 1689-1852*, edited by J.H. Chandler, 1985
41. *Abstracts of feet of fines relating to Wiltshire, 1377-1509*, edited by J.L. Kirby, 1986
42. *The Edington cartulary*, edited by Janet H. Stevenson, 1987
43. *The commonplace book of Sir Edward Bayntun of Bromham*, edited by Jane Freeman, 1988
44. *The diaries of Jeffery Whitaker, schoolmaster of Bratton, 1739-1741*, edited by Marjorie Reeves and Jean Morrison, 1989
45. *The Wiltshire tax list of 1332*, edited by D.A. Crowley, 1989
46. *Calendar of Bradford-on-Avon settlement examinations and removal orders, 1725-98*, edited by Phyllis Hembry, 1990
47. *Early trade directories of Wiltshire*, edited by K.H. Rogers and indexed by J.H. Chandler, 1992
48. *Star chamber suits of John and Thomas Warneford*, edited by F.E. Warneford, 1993
49. *The Hungerford cartulary: a calendar of the earl of Radnor's cartulary of the Hungerford family*, edited by J.L. Kirby, 1994
50. *The Letters of John Peniston, Salisbury architect, Catholic, and Yeomanry Officer, 1823-1830*, edited by M. Cowan, 1996
51. *The Apprentice Registers of the Wiltshire Society, 1817-1922*, edited by H.R. Henly, 1997
52. *Printed Maps of Wiltshire 1787–1844: a selection of topographical, road and canal maps in facsimile*, edited by John Chandler, 1998
53. *Monumental Inscriptions of Wiltshire: an edition, in facsimile, of* Monumental Inscriptions in the County of Wilton, *by Sir Thomas Phillipps*, edited by Peter Sherlock, 2000
54. *The First General Entry Book of the City of Salisbury, 1387-1452*, edited by David R. Carr, 2001

VOLUMES IN PREPARATION

Wiltshire glebe terriers, edited by S.D. Hobbs and Susan Avery; *Marlborough probate inventories*, edited by Lorelei Williams; *Wiltshire papist returns and estate enrolments, 1705-87*, edited by J.A. Williams; *The Diary of William Henry Tucker*, edited by Helen Rogers; *Early vehicle registration in Wiltshire*, edited by Ian Hicks; *Wiltshire probate records index*, edited by Lucy Jefferis; *Crown pleas of the Wiltshire eyre, 1268*, edited by Brenda Farr; *The Hungerford cartulary, vol.2: the Hobhouse cartulary*, edited by J.L. Kirby; *The Parish registers of Thomas Crockford, 1613-29*, edited by C.C. Newbury; *Farming in Wiltshire during the seventeenth century*, edited by J.H. Bettey. The volumes will not necessarily appear in this order.

A leaflet giving full details may be obtained from the Hon. Secretary, c/o Wiltshire and Swindon Record Office, County Hall, Trowbridge, Wilts. BA14 8BS.

Songbirds

Brought up in London, Christy Lefteri is the child of Cypriot refugees. She is a lecturer in creative writing at Brunel University. Her previous novel, *The Beekeeper of Aleppo*, is an international bestseller, selling over half a million copies worldwide.

Songbirds

CHRISTY LEFTERI

**MANILLA
PRESS**

First published in the UK in 2021 by
MANILLA PRESS
An imprint of Bonnier Books UK
80–81 Wimpole St, London W1G 9RE
Owned by Bonnier Books
Sveavägen 56, Stockholm, Sweden

A CIP catalogue record for this book is
available from the British Library.

Hardback ISBN: 978-1-83877-376-2
Export ISBN: 978-1-78658-082-5
Special edition ISBN: 978-1-78658-125-9

Also available as an ebook and an audiobook

1 3 5 7 9 10 8 6 4 2

Typeset by Palimpsest Book Production Ltd, Falkirk, Stirlingshire
Printed and bound in Great Britain by Clays Ltd, Elcograf S.p.A.

Manilla Press is an imprint of Bonnier Books UK
www.bonnierbooks.co.uk

For Marianne

1

Yiannis

ONE DAY, NISHA VANISHED AND turned to gold. She turned to gold in the eyes of the creature that stood before me. She turned to gold in the morning sky and in the music of the birds. Later, in the shimmering melody of the maid from Vietnam who sang at Theo's restaurant. Later still, in the faces and voices of all the maids that flowed along the streets like a turbulent river of anger, demanding to be seen and heard. This is where Nisha exists. But let's go back. We need to go back.

2

Petra

THE DAY NISHA DISAPPEARED WE went to the mountains. The three of us put on our hiking boots and waited for the bus that goes up to Troodos, which comes just twice a day. Nisha would normally go out on her own on Sundays but this time, for the first time, she decided to come along with Aliki and me.

Oh, it was beautiful up there! The autumn mist mingled with the ferns and pines and twisted oaks. These mountains rose from the sea when the African and European tectonic plates collided. You can even see the Earth's oceanic crust. The rock formations, with their veins and lava pillows, look like they are wearing snake skins.

I love thinking about beginnings. Like that story my aunt used to tell in the back garden: *When the Creator finished his creation of the world – Petra, are you listening?! – he shook the remaining clumps of clay from his hands and they fell to the sea and formed this island.*

Yes, I love thinking about beginnings. I don't like endings, though I suppose I'm like most people in that. An ending can be staring you right in the face without your knowing it. Like the last cup of coffee you have with someone when you thought there would be many more.

Aliki played with leaves as Nisha and I sat beneath the heater at one of the small taverns on the trail we were taking, and drank coffee. I remember the conversation we had.

Nisha had been unusually quiet, stirring her coffee for some time without drinking it. 'Madam,' she said, suddenly, 'I have a question to ask.'

I nodded and waited while she shifted in her seat.

'I would like to take tonight off to—'

'But Nisha, you had the whole day off!'

She didn't speak again for a while. Aliki was gathering armfuls of the leaves and placing them on a bench. We both watched her.

Nisha had decided to spend her free day with us, to join Aliki and me on this trip. I shouldn't be expected to give her more time off.

'Nisha,' I said, 'you have all day off on Sunday. In the evening, you have things to do. You need to help Aliki get her bag ready for school, and then put her to bed.'

'Madam, many of the other women have Sunday night off too.' She said this slowly.

'I know for a fact that other women are not allowed to go gallivanting around at night.'

She acted like she hadn't heard this and said, 'And I don't think madam has plans tonight,' giving me a sly look before returning her gaze to the coffee. 'So maybe madam could put Aliki to bed just for tonight? I will do extra duties next Sunday to make up for it.'

I was about to ask her where she intended to go; what was so important that she was willing to disrupt our routine. Perhaps she saw the disapproving look in my eyes, but there was no time for either of us to say anything because at that moment an avalanche of leaves was released over our heads. Nisha screeched, making a pantomime of it, waving her hands in the air and chasing Aliki, who was slipping away down a path that led into the woods. I could hear them after a while in the forest, like two children, laughing and playing, while I drank my coffee.

By the time we got home that evening, Nisha hadn't mentioned again taking the night off. She made dhal curry, and the house filled with the smell of onions and green chillies, cumin, turmeric, fenugreek and curry leaves. I looked over her shoulder as she sautéed the onions and combined the spices with the split red lentils, finally adding a splash of coconut milk. My mouth was watering. Nisha knew this was my favourite dish. I lit the fire in the living room. It had rained earlier that afternoon and from the living-room window I could see that Yiakoumi opposite had his canopy open, and the cobbled streets glimmered beneath the warm lights of his antique shop.

We do not have central heating, so we sat as close as we could to the flames with the bowls of dhal curry on our laps. Nisha brought me a glass of sweet *zivania* – the aromatic type with caramel and muscat, so warming on this chilly night – and tested Aliki on the nine times table.

'Seven times nine?' Nisha said.

'Sixty-three!'

'Good. Nine times nine?'

'Eighty-one! And there's no point in doing this.'

'Why not?'

'I know them.'

'But you haven't practised.'

'I don't need to. You just have to see the pattern. If you ask me what seven times nine is, I will know that the answer begins with a six. I know that the second number is always one lower than the previous one. So, eight times nine is seventy-two.'

'You're too cheeky for your own good, you know? I'm going to test you anyway.'

'Go ahead. If it helps you.' Aliki sighed and shrugged as if she had resigned herself to this pointless fate of learning something that she already knew. She had every bit the spunk of a nine-year-old girl.

Yes, I remember it all very well, the way that Aliki was munching and yawning and shouting out the answers, the way that Nisha kept her attention on my daughter, saying hardly a word to me. The TV flickered in the background. The news was on with the volume turned low: footage of refugees rescued by coastguards off one of the Greek islands. An image of a child being carried to the shore.

5

I would have forgotten all of this, but I have been over it again and again, like retracing footsteps on the sand when you have lost something precious.

Aliki lay on her back and kicked her legs up in the air.

'Sit up,' Nisha scolded, 'or you will be sick in your mouth. You've just eaten.' Aliki made a face but she listened: she perched on the sofa and watched TV, her eyes moving over the faces of people as they trudged out of the water.

Nisha refilled my glass for the third time, and I was starting to get sleepy. I looked at my daughter then; a monster of a child, she's always been too big for me, even her curly hair is too thick for me to get my hands around. Curls so thick, like the tentacles of an octopus; they seem to defy gravity, as if she lives in an underwater world.

In the light of the fire, I noticed that Nisha's face was pale, like one of those figs blanched in syrup that have lost their true colour. She caught my eye and smiled, a small, sweet smile. I shifted my gaze over to Aliki.

'Do you have your bag ready for school?' I asked.

Aliki's attention was on the screen.

'We are doing it now, madam.' Nisha got up hastily, gathering the bowls from the coffee table.

My daughter never really spoke to me anymore. She never called me Mum, never addressed me. At some point a seed of silence had been sowed between us and it had grown up and around and between us until it became almost impossible to say anything. Most of the time, she would talk to me through Nisha. Our few conversations were functional.

I watched Nisha as she licked a handkerchief and wiped

a stain off Aliki's jeans and then took the bowls and spoons to the kitchen. Maybe it was the alcohol, or the trip up to Troodos, but I was feeling more tired than usual, a heaviness in my mind and my limbs. I announced that I was going to bed early. I fell asleep straightaway and didn't even hear Nisha putting Aliki to bed.

3

Yiannis

THE DAY THAT NISHA VANISHED, before I even realised she'd gone, I saw in the forest a mouflon ovis.
I thought it was odd. These ancient sheep, native
to the land, are wild and rare. With a yen for solitude, they
usually roam secluded parts of the mountains. I'd never seen
one on flat terrain, never this far east. In fact, if I told anyone
that I saw a mouflon on the coast, nobody would believe me;
it would make national news. I should have known at the
time that something was wrong. A long time ago, I understood that sometimes the earth speaks to you, finds a way to
pass on a message if only you look and listen with the eyes
and ears of your childhood self. This was something my
grandfather taught me. But that day in the woods, by the
time I saw the golden ovis, I'd forgotten.

It began with a crunch of leaves and earth. A late October

morning. I'd returned to collect the songbirds. I'd driven out to the coast, west of Larnaca, near the villages of Alethriko and Agios Theodoros where there are wild olive and carob groves and plantations of orange and lemon trees. There is also a forest of dense acacia and eucalyptus trees – an excellent spot for poaching. In the small hours of the morning, I'd put out the lime sticks – a hundred of them strategically placed in the trees where the birds come to feed on berries. I'd also hidden amongst the leaves devices that played recordings of calling birds, to lure my prey. Then I found a secluded spot and lit a fire.

I used olive branches as skewers and toasted haloumi and bread. I had a flask of strong coffee in my backpack and a book to pass the time. I didn't want to think about Nisha, of the things she had said the night before, the stern look on her face when she left my flat, the tightness of the muscles in her jaw.

These thoughts fluttered around me with the bats and I waved them away, one by one. I warmed myself and ate and listened to the birdsong in the dark.

So far, it was a normal hunt.

I fell asleep by the fire and dreamt that Nisha was made of sand. She dissolved before me like a castle on the shore.

The rising sun was my calling. I had a last shot of coffee to wake myself fully and threw the rest on the fire, then stamped out the remaining flames and forgot about the dream. The thick woods began to stir, to wake. I usually make more than 2,000 euros for each hanging, and this one was a good one – there were around two hundred blackcaps stuck on the lime sticks. They are worth more than their weight in gold. Tiny songbirds migrating from Europe to Africa to escape the winter. They fly in from the west, over the mountains, stopping here on our island before heading out to sea, towards Egypt. In the spring, they make the return journey, coming from the southern coast. They are so small that we can't shoot them. They're also endangered, a protected species.

I was always frightened at this point, looking over my shoulder, expecting that this time I would be caught and thrown in jail. I'd be totally screwed. This was always my weakness – the fear, the anxiety I felt before killing the birds. But the woods were quiet, no sound of footsteps. Just the birdsong and the breeze through the tree branches.

I removed one of the attached birds from the stick, gently prying its feathers from the glue. This one had tried hard to free itself, it seemed. The more they try to escape, the more stuck they get. I held it in my palms and felt its tiny heart racing. I bit into its neck to end its suffering, and dropped it, lifeless, into a large, black bin-liner. This is the most humane way to kill them – a quick, deep bite to the neck.

I'd filled up the first bag and begun to remove the feathers and berries from the lime sticks with my lips so I could reuse them, when I heard the crunch of leaves.

Shit. I froze for a moment and held my breath. I scanned the surroundings and there it was, in a clearing between the bushes. The mouflon was calmly staring at me. It stood in the long shadows of the trees and it wasn't until the light shifted that I saw the most extraordinary thing: instead of the usual red and brown, its short-haired coat was gold; its curved horns, bronze. Its eyes were the exact colour of Nisha's – the eyes of a lion.

10

I thought I must be dreaming, that I must still be asleep by the fire.

I took a step forward and the golden mouflon took a small step back, but its posture remained straight and strong, its eyes fixed on mine. Moving slowly, I removed my backpack from my shoulders and took out a slice of fruit. The mouflon shuffled its feet and lowered its head so that its eyes now looked up at me, half-wary, half-threatening. I placed the slice of peach in my palm and held out my hand. I stayed like that, as still as a tree. I wanted it to come closer.

Seeing the beauty of its face, a memory came to me, sharp and clear. Last March, Nisha and I had gone to the Troodos mountains. She loved to go for long walks on Sunday mornings when she wasn't working. She'd often come with me into the forest to pick mushrooms, wild asparagus, blue mallow or to collect snails. On this day, I had wanted to see if we could spot a mouflon ovis. I hoped that we would see one in the depths of the woods or the verge of the mountains, at the threshold to the sky. We were so high up and she slipped her hand in mine.

'So, we're looking for a sheep?' she'd said.

'Technically, yes.'

'I've seen plenty of sheep.' There was a mocking smile in her eyes.

'I told you, it doesn't look like a sheep! It's a magnificent creature.'

'So. We're looking for a sheep that doesn't look like a sheep.' She was holding her hand over her eyes, scanning the area around us, pretending to look.

11

'Yes,' I said, matter-of-factly.

This made her laugh and her laughter escaped into the open sky. I felt in that moment that she had never been a stranger.

We'd been walking around for hours and were about to turn back, as the evening was closing in, when I suddenly spotted one standing at the edge of a steep cliff. I could tell it was female as it had smaller curved horns and no ruff of coarse hair beneath its neck. I pointed so that Nisha could see.

The mouflon saw us and faced us straight on.

Nisha stared at it in amazement. 'It's so pretty,' she said. 'It looks like a deer.'

'I told you.'

'Nothing like a sheep.'

'See!'

'Its fur is smooth and brown . . . and such a gentle look on its face. It's like it's going to speak to us. Doesn't it look like it wants to say something?'

I didn't reply and instead watched Nisha watch the animal, her face bright with curiosity.

There was a flash in her eyes, as if the colours of the forest shone through them, as if some secret energy, some nimble animal hiding amongst the trees, had suddenly come to life. She let go of my hand and took a few steps towards the mouflon. Strangely, it stepped away from the edge of the cliff and came slightly closer. I had never seen one approach a human before. Nisha was so gentle in the way she stretched out her hand, in the way she waited for the animal. But there was tension in her. This was all in her eyes: they burned with an emotion that I didn't recognise.

In that moment, I felt such a distance from her and the animal, like they shared something I couldn't understand.

However, in the next moment she turned to kiss me. One soft kiss.

Now, dawn in the forest, and the memory of that day brought a sharp pain to my heart. The mouflon ovis gazed at me, transfixed, tilting its head slightly, making a sound which was like a question. A question of a single word.

'I won't hurt you,' I said, and realised suddenly how loud my voice was in the woods, how it disturbed the peace. The Ovis shook its head and took another step back.

'Sorry,' I said to it, this time softly.

For the first time, it broke its gaze. It seemed to rest its eyes on the bucket of birds beside me.

'Sure,' I said. 'I don't blame you. I'm basically a murderer offering you a peach.' I laughed a bit, at the irony of it, as if the Ovis might share the joke.

I threw the slice of fruit on the ground, and this time I walked backwards, retreating into the shadows and the trees. I continued to watch the mouflon from there for a while, this incredible animal, strong and beautiful. It was very still, then it looked at something over to the left and turned its back to me and walked away, into the forest.

I removed the rest of the birds from the lime sticks as quickly as I could, so I could return home and find Nisha. I couldn't wait to tell her what I'd seen. I was hoping that perhaps this story about the mouflon would make her shine again.

4

Petra

I WOKE UP IN THE MIDDLE of the night because something broke. I heard a crashing noise, loud and clear, like a window smashing or a glass dashed on the floor with force. The sound had come from the garden, I was sure about that. The clock on my bedside cabinet showed 12 a.m. Could it be the wind? But the night was still and apart from the sound I had heard, there was a deep silence. Maybe it had been a cat?

I put on my slippers and opened the shutters, then the long glass doors to the garden. It was a clear night with a full moon. My house is a three-storey Venetian property in the old part of the city, east of Ledra and Onasagorou, leading to the Green Line that has divided the island since 1974. Sitting in the crystal blue waters of the eastern Mediterranean, our small island has long felt the influence of both Europe and the Middle East. We have been occupied by the Ottomans. We have been colonised by the British. And then we became a battleground between the Greeks and the Turks, our population split, until peacekeeping forces stepped in and, literally, drew the line. This partition continues to hold our island in a tentative peace, although missives about reunification are constantly in the news. Our city of Nicosa, on the Greek side, brushes the Green Line right where I live. When I was a little girl, I thought the end of our street reached the end of the world. There is no violence today with our Turkish Cypriot neighbors in the north, but it is an uneasy peace, to be sure.

We live only on the ground floor, each of our bedrooms looking out onto the garden. Two years ago, I rented out the storey above me to a man called Yiannis, who made a living by collecting mushrooms and wild greens from the forests. A bit reclusive, but he was a good tenant, always paid his rent on time. The top floor is empty, or full of ghosts, as my mother used to say, which would make my father scoff at her and respond always with the same words: *Ghosts are memories. Nothing more, nothing less.*

In the garden, there is boat. There were times in the past, on long nights when I couldn't sleep, that I would see Nisha sitting out in my father's tiny fishing boat, *The Sea Above the Sky* painted in pale blue on its hull. The paint is peeling, and the wood is crumbling. It's a boat that has made so many journeys. Nisha would sit in it and stare out into the darkness. The boat has one oar – the other has been missing for as long as I can remember – but someone placed an olive tree branch in its place. Because my bed is next to the window, I would watch her for a while through the slits of the shutters, and wonder what was going through her mind, alone like that, in the middle of the night.

But on this night, she wasn't there. I looked around to try to determine the cause of the crashing noise. I was half expecting the crunch of glass beneath my feet. But there didn't seem to be anything broken or out of place.

The moon illuminated the pumpkins, the winding jasmine and vines, the cactus and fig tree to the far right, near the glass doors of Aliki's room, and, in the middle, on a slightly raised patch of earth, where the roots have cracked through the concrete, the orange tree – like a queen on her throne. I always felt, growing up, that this tree quietly commanded the garden.

Everything was so still. Still and quiet. Hardly a leaf moved. I walked around the garden. Near the steps that lead up to Yiannis's flat, I finally discovered the source of the noise: a ceramic money-box that I'd had since I was a child – it had smashed on the ground, its white shell broken and hundreds of old lira scattered about, making tiny pools of gold.

It was the kind of money-box that you have to break in order to get to the treasure inside. I remembered dropping in the coins, imagining a day when I would retrieve them. My aunt Kalomira had made it for me in the village of Lefkara, where she lived with her husband, who used to eat the balls of a goat or the brain and eyes of a lamb with lemon and salt. I had watched her spinning the clay on the wheel. Her husband offered me an eye. I refused. Later, she had painted the pot white and added a funny sketch of a dog. It was ready for me and waiting on a shelf when I returned with my mother to see her many weeks later.

I had never broken it; the time was never right. So, I had left the coins safely inside, like wishes or secret dreams collected from childhood.

But who had broken it now? How had it fallen from the garden table?

I decided to go back to bed and ask Nisha to deal with it in the morning.

I pulled the covers over me and in the dark and quiet of my room, I remembered my mother by my side.

'What will you do with all that money?' she had asked.

'I will buy wings!'

'Like the wings of a bird.'

'No, more like the wings of a firefly. They will be transparent and when I wear them, I will fly around the garden at night and glow in the dark.'

She had laughed and kissed me on the cheek. 'You will be beautiful as always.'

The memory faded and I suddenly felt a deep pang of guilt for the absence of words and dreams and laughter with my own daughter. How had I lost her?

Or had she lost me?

5

Yiannis

WHEN I GOT BACK FROM hunting it was still early afternoon. I couldn't wait to tell Nisha about the mouflon ovis I'd seen in the woods. I wanted to describe its incredible beauty, how unusual its golden fur had been and how, oddly, it had had the eyes of a lion.

The more I said these things in my head, however, the crazier they sounded. I knew that Nisha would listen to me. She would look at me like I was bat-shit crazy, humour me with that slow nod of her head, but she would also suggest we return later that afternoon so that she could see it for herself.

I knocked on the glass doors of her bedroom and waited. I usually heard her flip-flops on the marble floor, but this time there was silence. I knocked again and waited a few minutes, then again and waited a further five. Maybe she had walked down to the grocery store, or she could have gone to the church. Although she wasn't Christian, she liked to light a candle and appreciate the peace and quiet. In church there were no demands of her, no tuts, no shaking heads. Nobody disturbed her. The locals just saw a good Christian woman praying amongst other good Christians. In there, she'd said, everyone was equal as long as you were one of them.

I decided to head upstairs and start cleaning the birds. I sat on a stool in the spare room and, one by one, I plucked out their feathers and threw the birds into a large basin. This was a task that took some time, and one that I never looked forward to. It was tedious work I did automatically, and left my hands covered in feathers and sticky blood. Once this task was complete, I would soak them in water or pickle them in vinegar, place them in various sized containers depending on the order, and take them out to restaurants, hotels and venues around the island.

As I held one of the birds in my left hand, about to pluck its feathers with my right, I felt an unexpected vibration on my palm. I paused and looked down and noticed that the soft brown feathers on the bird's chest rose; its right wing twitched. It suddenly felt heavy on my palm, as if I was holding a paperweight, and the vibration seemed to travel through me – along my arteries, up my arm, until I felt a terrible sensation, a deep tremble in my chest.

I felt nauseous. I dropped the bird onto the table and shifted on the stool, taking long, deep breaths. The bird lay there, breathing, its chest rising and falling more visibly now.

I was four or five years old, walking with my dad in the wild fields of the mountains. He stopped to pick some hawthorn berries. On the ground something bright caught my eye: a yellow wagtail. Even at this age, I knew the names of some of the bird species, migratory and native, because my grandfather had taught me. I loved the birds. I watched them building their lives high up in the trees and sky. I was desperate to catch them, hold them in my hands, to look closely at their feathers and decipher their amazing colours.

Here was my opportunity! This yellow wagtail was motion-less amongst the brambles. Even as I approached, it didn't move. I picked it up and nestled it in my palms – it was so dead that it was dry. I examined it: its small, silver-grey bill, brown tail and brown primary feathers; while its chin and breast, belly and under-feathers were the brightest yellow I'd ever seen. Its crown, shoulder and back were a darker yellow, greyish in tone. I examined its eyeline and eyestripe, its open blank eyes, its wing-bars and lores, its twiglike feet.

I imagined I was holding gold. In my hands I held pure gold.

I lived simply and saved money so that I could stop the poaching. All my neighbours thought that I made a living picking and selling wild asparagus and mushrooms, wild greens, artichokes and snails – depending on the season. I mean, of course, that kind of foraging was my day job and

20

provided pocket money. But I would never have been able to build a future for myself relying on the measly income of selling vegetables and snails. Not after what had happened. It was a risk I couldn't take.

I hated lying to Nisha. I'd managed to keep the poaching a secret for so long: it wasn't difficult – when I came back with bulging bin bags, people would assume I'd collected other things from the forest. People didn't question much around here, and many of the houses were empty because so few wanted to live so close to the Green Line. It reminded them of the war, of division, of abandoned homes and lost lives. This isn't something one wants to be reminded of on a daily basis.

I had my reasons for choosing to rent a flat there. It was reasonably quiet, most of the residents were old, and I knew I could get away with more. And besides, I enjoyed sitting on the balcony in the evening, listening to the bouzouki from Theo's restaurant, and watching the old men eating, drinking and playing cards. I joined them sometimes, but mostly I kept my distance. In this part of old Nicosia there were brothel-type bars, and when the men finished eating and drinking at the restaurant, they usually made their way to them.

There was one such bar at the end of our street, called Maria's. Its windows were frosted, and through the old wooden door wafted the heavy scent of sweat mingled with cigarette smoke and old beer. The barmaid, in tight black clothing, served sliced apples and peanuts, olives and hummus. I have been there twice, on both occasions to meet Seraphim.

21

I watched the bird on the counter now, the way its beak opened and closed, the way its matted feathers twitched. I checked its neck and saw that the wound I had made wasn't that deep. It looked up at me, straight into my eyes, and seemed to be saying, 'You sick prick, I can see you.'

I put some water on my finger and brought it to its beak. At first it didn't drink but I kept my hand there for a while, and, after a few minutes, it dipped its bill into the droplet of water and tilted its head to swallow it. I decided to line a small container with a clean towel and I put the bird in there to rest. I sat there and watched it for a while. It was suspicious of me, kept giving me that look.

Some time later, I had filled a whole bin-liner with feathers. The little bird was lying still in the container, breathing steadily. The naked birds were piled up in the basin by my side.

I thought you were a different person, Nisha had said.

I put some water in the basin, using a hose, and left the birds in there for a while to soak. Then, I dipped my finger into a glass of water and brought it to the little bird's beak again. This time, it dropped its bill immediately into the water and tilted its head so that it could swallow. It seemed to be treating me less like a killer and this was reassuring. I did it a few more times until it didn't want any more.

I thought you were a different person.

After I had finished cleaning the birds, I made myself some supper and sat on the balcony, eagerly awaiting Nisha's knock at the door. Most evenings, she would wait for Petra to go to bed before sneaking out into the garden. The staircase was on the far left, behind a large fig tree, so Petra wasn't able to see it from her window. Nisha didn't want Petra to know. She wasn't allowed to have a boyfriend. Nisha would slip out at around 11 p.m., unnoticed. She would stay with me for a few hours – we would talk for a while and make love and fall asleep. Then her alarm would go off at 4 a.m., and she would unfurl herself from my arms, go out into the garden and sit in the boat while the sun rose. I was never sure why she didn't just go straight to her room, but the time she spent alone in the old fishing boat seemed to be important, and I didn't question it. I would turn off the light and go back to sleep for a few hours.

When she came last night, things felt different. We sat by the open doors of the balcony, overlooking the street below, with the sound of the bouzouki and a sky full of stars. It was chilly and she had a throw wrapped around her. She was quieter than usual, as if there was something on her mind, but then she started telling me a story about her grandfather and how he'd ended up with a glass eye.

Nisha was in the middle of saying, '... and then he chased him with a baseball bat . . .' when I placed the ring in front of her on the table.

She looked down at it, then picked it up and put it, not on her finger, but on her open palm. She was gazing down at it so I couldn't see her eyes, just the soft darkness of her lids and lashes.

'Will you marry me, Nisha?' I asked.

She said nothing.

'I've had the ring for a while. I wanted to ask you this summer . . .' I paused there, as I couldn't finish the sentence: I couldn't bring myself to remind her of what had happened just two short months earlier. '. . . and then you were so heartbroken.'

She nodded.

'But I meant everything I said.'

She looked up at me. Straight lips. Hard eyes.

She didn't believe me.

'We can still do all of the things we were going to do. We can still go together to Sri Lanka, back to your home. You can be with Kumari. We can have a family.'

'I fell in love with you as soon as I saw you.' Her voice was barely a whisper.

I tried to remember the first time she'd seen me. What had I been doing? What had she seen in me in that moment?

'But I loved my husband too.' Then the muscles of her jaw clenched, her shoulders and body stiffened. She closed her fingers around the ring, tightening her fist, possessing it.

Without a further word, without a yes or a no, she walked towards the back door that led to the stone staircase.

'What was I doing when you first saw me?' I asked.

She stopped in her tracks, but did not turn around. 'Feeding the chickens.'

'Feeding the chickens?'

She didn't reply. Instead, she turned and looked at me over her shoulder, and then said, 'You see, I thought you were a different person.'

24

She didn't sit in the boat that night; she went straight to bed.

Around 11 p.m. I expected to hear Nisha's gentle tapping on the back door, but it didn't come. Sunday was one of the nights she usually called Kumari, so I was sure she would appear. She always spoke to her very early in the morning because of the time difference, and she liked to do it at my place due to the fact that I had a tablet and she wanted to be able to see Kumari while she spoke to her. Before she met me, she had talked to Kumari on the phone. To give her some privacy, I would sit out on the balcony and wait for her to finish.

However, she told me once that it was also her way of keeping the two worlds of her life apart, separate but in harmony at the same time.

'What did you mean by that?' I'd asked her one night, when she'd finished the call with Kumari. I came back inside and she crawled into bed with me.

'Well,' she'd replied, 'downstairs at Petra's I am nanny to Aliki. But when I come up here – and everyone is asleep and there are no demands of me – I remember who I really am. I can be a real mother to my own daughter.'

Now, I made myself a coffee and sat on the balcony and listened to the sound of the bouzouki. I took the little bird from the container and sat holding it in my palms. It took a bit of convincing to get it to stay there, but then it slept, breathing slowly, steadily, its tiny body expanding and releasing. When it woke up, I gave it water, drop by drop, until it didn't want any more.

An hour passed and still there was no sign of her. At midnight, I decided to go downstairs and knock on her bedroom door.

On the last step, something got tangled in my feet – one of the stray cats, the black one, the one with the different-coloured eyes. I lost my balance and grabbed on to a small garden table to stop myself from falling. The table tipped and from it fell an old ceramic money-box that belonged to Petra. It smashed on the ground, the coins spilling out, and when I saw the light of Petra's room turn on, I rushed back up the stairs, closing the door gently.

I couldn't sleep that night. I couldn't stop thinking about Nisha.

Where had she disappeared to?

Had I scared her away?

You see, I thought you were a different person.

I sat on the balcony with the bird for the rest of the night, until the sun began to rise behind the buildings to the east. Far away, I imagined the sun's rays lighting up the sea. And the little bird filled its lungs and began to sing.

The red lake at Mitsero reflects a sunset, captures it, holds it, even when the sun has died.

Red lake, toxic lake, copper lake. Mothers and fathers tell their children stories about it. Never go near the red lake at Mitsero! Tales of deep passages underground, where men crawled like animals and died in darkness. Stay away from the red lake at Mitsero! By all means, run along the dust paths and into the fields – as long as you avoid the snakes and hornets – but whatever you do, keep well away from the water.

On this day, in late October, there is a dead hare on the rocky terrain by the lake. So fresh it is still intact. The wind blows its fur the wrong way. Its footprints are scoured into the earth beside it. There are no wounds on its body; it seems to have run out of life, for one reason or another. Soon the hare will return to the earth, but for now it lies still, in a running position, as if it had been hoping to make it further, like we all do.

What a beautiful lake it is. Copper bleeds into it from the past. The lake is a consequence of what has been left behind: when the mines were abandoned a crater was left. As winter approaches, just as it does now, the crater fills with water. After a rainstorm, rivers of yellow and orange trickle into the red water, changing its colour – this is how the sunset appears.

But why not a sunrise?

Because a sunrise is infused with the promise of a new day.

A sunset holds the expectation of something else – the hush and darkness of the night. The lake exists on the verge of darkness.

6

Petra

I T WAS 6.30 A.M. WHEN I woke up. Nisha would have just had a shower and gone out into the garden with long, damp hair, picking oranges and collecting fresh eggs. After bringing in the eggs, she would fry or boil them. When we had courgette flowers or wild greens, she would scramble the eggs over them and add lots of lemon and pepper. This was Aliki's favourite.

On this morning, Nisha was not outside. A silvery mist rested over the leaves, as if the garden had exhaled. The lira on the ground now glimmered in the sun.

In the kitchen, Aliki was sitting at the table, still in her pyjamas, swinging her legs and playing a game on her iPad. Her loose hair fell about her face and shoulders. By this time, it was usually in a neat ponytail and she should have been wearing her school uniform and finishing off her orange juice.

29

'Where is Nisha?' I said.

Aliki looked up from the screen and shrugged.

'Have you eaten?'

She tutted, no. I saw a stroke of uncertainty in her eyes. I thought she would speak but she slouched and sank further down into her seat.

I went into Nisha's room and found that she wasn't there. In fact, her bed looked like it hadn't been slept in.

Returning to Aliki, and with as much cheer as I could muster, I said, 'Why don't you go and get changed and I'll make breakfast? Then I'll take you to school.'

She got up, reluctantly, but did as I'd suggested. In the meantime, I called Nisha's mobile a few times, but it went straight to voicemail.

'Nisha,' I said. 'Where are you? Call me back.'

I began to boil the eggs and make toast, opening all the cupboards to find where Nisha kept the fig jam. I was becoming increasingly irritated – fear hadn't gripped me yet.

It was Aliki who had the deeper instincts that I lacked. After I had peeled the eggs and laid the table, Aliki still hadn't come back to the kitchen so I went to her room and found her in front of the mirror, crying. She'd put on her uniform, but she'd been unable to tie up her hair. The elastic band was stuck in a knot of curls.

I told her to sit on the bed and I perched beside her and gently untangled the band. Then, with a wide hair-brush, I tried to bring all that hair together into a high ponytail, like Nisha did. But the curls were wild and unruly and tried to escape – as I brought one side up, the other side fell out of my grip and tumbled back down to her shoulder.

I could feel her shifting, uncomfortable and impatient.

'I'll tell you what!' I said. 'Forget the ponytail. Let's do something different.'

So, I plaited her hair and she pulled the thick black braid over her right shoulder and stood to look at herself in the mirror. Her patio doors were open and the room was full of sunlight and music from the birds. Even the mist came in, like a lost spirit.

Such a crisp autumn day, and it should have been a happy morning, like every other. But what I saw in Aliki's eyes as she stared at her reflection was a broadening expanse of worry.

I took Aliki to school, something Nisha usually did. I also had to leave work for an hour to collect her in the afternoon – my shop assistant, Keti, didn't work on Mondays. I then had to bring Aliki back to work with me for a while. We made our way through heavy traffic to Onasagorou Street, just by Eleftheria Square, to the main branch of my clinic, Sun City – I am an optician – which sat in a stately row of expensive boutiques, ice-cream parlours, patisseries, restaur-ants, galleries, cafes, and also the base of the British Council – a converted townhouse on Solomou Square. Aliki amused herself by trying out the least expensive pairs of glasses and doing impressions of people in front of the large mirror at the front. In a pair of metal-rimmed, round specs she pretended to be Gandhi; in some round transparent anti-blue light glasses she was a K-pop star; in a plain brown-framed pair she was Nisha, and she grabbed the feather duster and cleaned the shelves.

That night, Nisha still hadn't returned. I made some dinner, but Aliki wasn't hungry. She sat in front of the TV.

'Your food is on the table. I've covered it to keep it warm,' I said. 'I'm just popping out to speak to Mrs Hadjikyriacou next door. Find out if she's seen Nisha. I'll be outside if you need anything.'

Aliki nodded and continued to watch the news, which I'm sure she wasn't really paying any attention to. She seemed preoccupied, and she was sucking the knuckle of her index finger as she had done when she was much younger.

I'd never paid much attention to the other maids in our neighbourhood before. The maids here did everything – they were hired and paid (lower than the minimum wage) to clean the house, but ended up being child-carers, shop assistants, waitresses. Outside, two women, probably Filipinos, walked along the street with a young Cypriot child between them – a little girl with pigtails, holding each by the hand. She ran and skipped and they lifted her by the arms. In a house down the road a maid whacked the dust out of a rug on the railing of the porch. She waved at the two who were passing. Now, turning the corner, another maid was being pulled along by a huge sand-coloured hunting dog. Outside,

Yiakoumi's shop, yet another maid was bringing in the antiques – displayed on a table during the day – in order to shut up shop for the night. To the right, Theo's restaurant was starting to get busy, as it was close to dinner time. His two Vietnamese maids dashed about in their rice hats, holding drinks or trays of dips. Each time I saw one of these women, my heart dropped, hoping that Nisha might appear beside them.

Right next door sat Mrs Hadjikyriacou, who Aliki called the Paper-Lady. She was sitting on her usual deckchair, in the front garden next door to ours. Her skin was so white and creased that she looked as though someone had scrunched her up into a ball and opened her up again. She sat there most of the day, and late into the evening, sometimes until midnight, watching the day go by, the seasons change, and she remembered everything – her mind like a journal, full of pages and pages of the past, or at least every bit of the past that has walked her way. It is a well-known fact that her hair turned white overnight, during the war, when the island was divided. That's when she started storing everything in her mind, so that nobody could take her soul from her. This is what she told me once, many years ago.

She sat there now, perched on her chair, watching TV, which had been brought outside; the wire was stretched almost to breaking point, plugged into a socket in the living room. She spat phlegm into a handkerchief, inspected it, then shouted at the TV. She was furious, it seemed, about a decision the president had made.

I hoped that she might have seen Nisha leave.

I watched as her maid came out with a tray of fruit and water, placing it on a small table by the old lady's side.

'I don't want any,' she said, flicking her wrist in dismissal, and the maid mumbled something in her own language before returning to whatever she had been doing inside. This maid was new and hadn't yet learned a word of Greek or English, so they communicated with their respective mother tongues, plus gestures and eye-rolls.

As usual the Paper-Lady was surrounded by cats, all of which Aliki had named. One of the cats was sitting to attention, staring at her, meowing.

'What is it, my dear?' she asked, with a sigh. 'What is it, my darling sesame dough? You want to drink? You want to eat? Come to me and I'll kiss you!' In response, the cat turned its back to her. Then, without even looking my way, she lowered the volume on the TV, and said, 'Petra, come over and have some fruit.'

I approached, with usual pleasantries about the weather, taking a slice of orange out of courtesy, and then I asked whether she had seen Nisha the previous night or, in fact, that morning.

Sitting back with her fingers laced together, she searched her mind, her head tilted slightly to the right, towards the light of Yiakoumi's shop. She fixed her gaze on the window display. 'According to seven of Yiakoumi's clocks, it was ten thirty when I saw her. According to one, it was midnight.'

I waited for her to say more but instead she scooped up

one of the cats and placed it on her lap. The black cat's eyes were gold, with an area of patchy blue that looked like the Earth from a great distance.

'Did she say where she was going?'

'She was in a hurry. She said something about meeting a man.'

'Who?'

'Do you think if I sniff my nails they will tell me the answer?' Her stock phrase.

She stared at me for a while, as if she was waiting for me to stop chewing. When I swallowed the last bit of orange she tapped the plate with her finger.

'Have some more.'

I could see that her attention would remain on the plate until I obliged, so I took another slice. She watched me as I bit into it, and as I wiped juice from my chin.

'Was there anything unusual . . . ?' I began.

'My daughter is coming next week from New Zealand. She's coming to see me from the other side of the world.'

'That's wonderful.' Through the crocheted curtain I could see her maid's silhouette; she looked like she was bending down to wipe the coffee table, the glow of an orange lamp behind her. She was shaking her head, talking to herself about the old lady, no doubt – unless there was something else that had peeved her so badly that she looked like she had taken a bite of a lemon straight from the tree.

Just at that moment, the bouzouki started playing in the restaurant and the cats, as if on cue, scurried off in that direction.

'Did she say anything else?' I said. 'Nisha, I mean.'

'No.'

'Which way did she go?'

She pointed to the right. 'Then she turned left at the end of the road.'

'But that way's a dead end,' I said. What would Nisha be doing going down there? It only led to the Green Line, to the military base and the buffer zone that separated the Turkish and Greek parts of the island. Nobody went that way.

Mrs Hadjikyriacou was looking up at me, examining me. From her corneas, triangular films of tissue threatened to take over her eyes.

'What's the problem?' she asked.

'I don't know where Nisha is. I'm sure it's nothing to worry about, she probably just—'

She interrupted me: 'Just what? You mean to tell me she hasn't returned?'

I nodded.

'I presume you've tried her phone?'

I nodded again and she looked up to the sky, her silvery eyes restless. She looked so worried that I suddenly had the urge to reassure her.

'Honestly, I'm sure it will be fine. There has to be a reasonable explanation.'

'No,' she said.

'Maybe she went to see a friend.'

'No,' she said again. 'Nisha would never take off like that, even for a day. You must know that. She is an extremely conscientious young woman.'

She picked up a slice of orange, brought it to her lips and, seeming to remember that she didn't want any, tore it up into sections, throwing the pieces on the ground for the cats when they returned.

Then she reached out and placed a sticky hand on my arm. 'Petra,' she said, staring at me hard, like she was trying to see me through a thick mist, 'there is something not right here.'

I returned home and checked on Aliki. I found her sitting on her bed in the dark. She was in her pyjamas and sipping a mug of warm milk, which she cradled in her palms. Her school bag was at the foot of the bed and her uniform was hanging ready, on the back of her chair by the desk. If I hadn't known better, I would have thought Nisha had been here.

'You've eaten?' I said, and Aliki glanced at me over the mug and nodded. 'You're OK?' Again, she nodded.

I went over and gave her a kiss on the forehead. That's when I noticed that the black cat with the different-coloured eyes was sleeping on the bed beside her, at first glance just a gleam in the moonlight, its shiny black fur oily in the darkness. I was about to say that she knew very well that cats weren't allowed in the house, but, anticipating my admonishment, she quickly said, 'Monkey has had a tough day. He needs some tender loving care.'

'You've named him Monkey?'

'Look at his long, bent tail. I think he swings from trees.'

I smiled. *My clever girl.* I backed out of her room and closed the door.

But I was on edge. I couldn't shake the feeling of Mrs Hadjikyriacou's hand on my arm, her insistence that something was amiss. I peered out of the window to see that she had gone inside, the street now dark and empty.

7

Yiannis

IN THE MIDDLE OF THE night, Seraphim and I drove out to a beach in Protaras. Once a week, during the autumn migration, he and I would go out to sea to catch birds. These were our most lucrative hunts. We drove to the east coast in Seraphim's van. Although it was cold in the early hours, Seraphim had his window wide open and drank in big gulps of air. He always did this as we approached the water. I hardly spoke. I couldn't stop thinking about Nisha. I tried to imagine where she might be, but my mind met only darkness. I had tried ringing her many times but her phone was switched off.

The villages around us were quiet, only one light was on in a house on a hillside. Soon I could hear the waves.

You see, I thought you were a different person.

It was Seraphim who had got me into poaching. Seraphim

was in love with money – but I'd be lying if I didn't say the same about myself. Once upon a time, I had been an executive at Laiki Bank. I lived in a luxury apartment on the other side of the city – the sparkly, fashionable district. My grandfather was a farmer in his former years, and a park ranger thereafter. My ancestors lived the rural life, farmers and shepherds who worked the land. Father was determined that I would make it in the world. He encouraged me to study hard so that I would *climb from the soil to the stars!*

And, of course, I did. The banker's life was appealing, stable. I would be financially secure, rich even, and wouldn't have to rely on the weather and the seasons, like my forefathers had. At least this was what my father told me. I hadn't realised then that the financial world had its own storms and droughts.

Before the financial crisis of 2008, Laiki Bank was booming – it was set to become the European investment vehicle of Dubai's sovereign wealth fund, and it played a pivotal role in the island's financial services industry, welcoming fresh-faced Russian entrepreneurs who arrived with cash-filled suitcases then set up companies on the island, run by local lawyers and accountants. At one point, bank transfers between Russia and Cyprus were astronomical. Laiki had even handled the affairs of Slobodan Milosevic. His administration moved billions of dollars in cash through Laiki in the 1990s in spite of UN sanctions.

I loved to tell these stories at swanky dinner parties – people were always impressed. Teresa, my wife at the time, loved that sort of life. She would never have married me if

40

I'd followed the life of my grandfather. Our story was a simple one: she worked at Laiki's rival bank, we met, we fell in love.

But Laiki got into fatal trouble because of aggressive expansion into Greece. The balance sheet was overstretched and then the global financial crisis hit and everything went wrong. Laiki was placed under administration and I lost my job, my savings, my wife – in that order. But while the humiliating turn in the bank's fortunes reflected Cyprus's deeper troubles, the turn of events in my life shone a light on the black hole that existed at its centre.

The van rattled along a dirt path. Seraphim began, as usual, to hum an old children's song. He always hummed this rhyme as we approached the water, something that harked back to the days before the war. But the memory was too buried for me to retrieve it and I never asked him.

'You need to loosen up,' he said now. 'I've told you so many times, come down to Maria's with me – I'll get you sorted. Last night I was with the Filipino girl again. She's very sweet, you know. If it wasn't for my wife I think I might fall in love.'

I remained silent, staring out of the window, watching the approaching opaque darkness of the sea and sky.

'What's wrong with you?' Seraphim asked, flicking his eyes towards me. He was about two years older than me and, in spite of all his money, dressed like an odd-job man no matter the occasion. He was a small, dark man with large hands, his hair was mostly uncombed and was receding at the front. Usually unshaven, he reminded me of the rats that live in the sewers along the banks of the Pedieos River. He was married to a Russian woman called Oksana, whom he spoke about often and fondly; but most nights he visited the bars in old Nicosia, searching for the women who had to find another way to make ends meet – as he put it. Nice Romanian, Moldavian, Ukrainian girls – not too expensive – Sri Lankan, Vietnamese, Nepalese maids. Women who came here to make money, one way or another – as he put it. As if he was doing them a favour.

I turned a blind eye to the crap Seraphim spewed. He was dodgy to the core, but there was something charming about him, a certain warmth. And he was good at keeping secrets. He held steadily to the steering wheel as the van bounced over the rough terrain. Seraphim was the only person in the world who knew about my relationship with Nisha.

'Nisha's gone,' I said.

I could hear the sea now, below us to the right, breathing heavily. The clouds parted and the sky around the moon turned silver. I realised he'd been silent for too long.

'Nisha is gone,' I said again.

'That's not possible.'

'Why not?'

He was quiet again and he made a right turn now, onto the road that would lead down to the jetty of a small private cove. There was a tiny church made of limestone on this corner, with a huge white cross that was illuminated at night.

'Why would she leave?' he asked, finally.

42

'I don't know,' I said. 'She just disappeared.' I paused. 'I proposed to her on Saturday night and she disappeared on Sunday night. Well, any time on Sunday, I guess.'

'Sunday night,' he said. Not a question, but a statement. But before I could say anything else, he'd brought the van to a swift halt, turned off the engine and opened the driver's side door.

Vyacheslav was waiting for us as usual by one of the boats, holding his silver thermal flask, smoking a cigarette and reading the news on his phone, his hair so blond it was almost white. He grinned when he saw us, throwing the butt on the ground and greeting us as usual.

Seraphim and I pulled a huge, rolled-up mist net from the back of the van, one side each, rather like we were carrying a body. I kept looking over my shoulder, sweating. These sea-hunts were the most dangerous. If we were caught, we'd be fined 20,000 euros and land ourselves in jail. Each time we went out to sea, I thought: *Surely this time we will be caught.*

Vyacheslav began to unwind the mist net in order to attach either end to the two boats. He would sail with Seraphim, as usual, and I would go out alone. I think he preferred Seraphim's company.

'It's clear now,' Vyacheslav said, looking up at the sky, his eyes narrowing, his face creasing into a big smile. 'This'll be a good hunt.'

'Let's hope so,' Seraphim said. We all spoke to each other in English, in our respectively heavy accents.

Vyacheslav lit another cigarette and recited the main

43

headlines of the day, something he always did, while Seraphim made sure that the nets were attached securely. I placed a couple of calling devices in each boat.

Thousands of migrating birds sweep down as the sun begins to rise, coming to the island to stop for a rest on their arduous journey across the Mediterranean Sea. This island, this little sea rock, is along one of the major migration routes. The birds see the lights of the town and fly towards them. Some birds even use the coast as a leading line, helping them to find their way. The mist nets are so fine that the birds fly straight into them. Every attempt to escape causes further entanglement. It's not just blackcaps we catch, but all kinds – the nets are indiscriminate. Summer is relatively quiet, but during passage times, particularly autumn and spring, more birds move through – so many in fact, that we make a killing.

As we sailed out to sea, I was suddenly hit by the feeling that I was drifting further away from Nisha: that some invisible cord that kept us together was being stolen by an invisible but powerful current. She always seemed to know what I was feeling, or rather she carried my feelings, even the ones I didn't know I had. She would rest her chin on her fist, lying on my bed, or sitting at the dining table, and look into me with her lion eyes.

'What's making you so sad?' she would say, or 'Why are you angry today?' or 'Where have you disappeared to?' She knew my moods better than I knew them myself. The only other person who had ever paid me that kind of attention was my grandfather, when I was a boy. He was always so aware, as we walked through the woods: where I was stepping,

44

whether I was too excited and would frighten the animals, whether I was tired, hungry. Once, after my dog had died, he let me talk about her all the way from Troodos to the East coast. We got off the bus, and although I was animated and told him joyful stories, he knew from the way I dragged my feet that my heart was heavy, and that when we went for our swim I would have sunk if I hadn't given him those memories to carry.

Last summer, I had shown Nisha a photo of myself when I was six, taken in front of the farmhouse in Troodos. There was a cow in the yard just behind me, and I was crouching down tying my laces and looking at the camera, smiling. It was my mother who had taken that photo; I remember her carrying my sister on her hip. She had come back from taking my father and grandfather their lunch in the fields, her face red, a scarf tied around her head. Nisha cried when she saw it. She was sitting naked on my bed by the open doors of the balcony, the air hot, sticky, full of night jasmine and the perfume of women who roamed the streets. It was nearly midnight and the music from Theo's drifted up to us. We had the fan rotating between us. Her yellow eyes had welled up and tears dropped down onto my wrist as I held the photo.

'Why are you crying?'

'You were just so beautiful and sweet,' she said, wiping her face with the back of her hands. Then she lay down in my arms and I could feel her tears on my chest. I held her tight, not knowing if I was comforting her or if in fact it was she who was comforting me. I didn't really understand what had made her cry. What had she seen in my face from all those years ago? What unfathomable dreams had she projected into the future?

As the boats went further out into the water, broadening the distance between us, the mist net stretched out, almost invisibly, just above the sea, between the two boats. The lights of the town became smaller as we drifted further, steering the boats so that the distance between them remained stable and we were running parallel to each other. It took some careful sailing not to tear the nets or let them droop, but I'd had a lot of practice and Vyacheslav had taught me well.

Once we had gone out far enough, Vyacheslav raised his hand in the air and we turned off the engines. The boats bobbed on the soft waves now, and we waited. The horizon was still black.

You were just so beautiful and sweet.

I must have fallen asleep because when I woke up I saw a thousand wings silhouetted against the sky, the sun cracking through the edge of the world. The birds that flew highest missed the net and made it to the shore; the others, the hundreds that skimmed the water or flew a few metres above it – their journeys ended there. They crashed into an invisible barrier, the fine threads of our massive net, and there they would flap, screech and cry. But there they would stay.

Before the sun rose completely, we steered our boats back to shore and the three of us pulled the net out of the water. Some birds were drowned, others were still trying to escape. We lay the net out on the sand and began to remove the birds, one by one. Amongst the blackcaps were robins and redwings, grey and purple herons, honey buzzards, red-footed falcons, goldcrests and some large wintering black gulls.

We threw the dead into the bin bags and the others – the ones that were still moving – we bit into their necks, severing the artery for a quick death, and adding their bodies to the rest. Other birds were still coming in to land on the shore, and tiny sparrows hopped beside us on the sand. A stray cat with bulging eyes came to sniff out what was happening, winding its way between us, head-butting our knees and elbows for attention. Seraphim threw it one of the birds and the cat took it in its jaw and sprinted off.

'You shouldn't do that,' Vyacheslav said, with creased brows. 'You might as well throw the vermin money.'

'It's only one!' Seraphim laughed. 'Keep your hair on, as they say in English. Cats are hunters, just like us.'

'They hunt to survive and they hunt for the sake of it, depending on their circumstances,' I said. I'd been quiet until that point, and the two men flicked their eyes towards me without much interest and continued with their task. The sky was lightening now and we had to be faster – we had to have all this sorted and cleared before people in the town began to wake up.

On the way home, I wanted to talk to Seraphim more about Nisha's disappearance, but he was distracted, giddy from our big take of the morning. He was jabbering incessantly about the plans for our next hunt: we would go to the

Akrotiri peninsula, a good place to trap – being part of the British military base there, it was largely undeveloped. We would take lime sticks and mist nets to the Akrotiri marsh reserve and to the pools behind Lady's Mile beach. We would need quite a lot of lime sticks, so he was going to prepare them in advance.

It was Seraphim who kept our small organisation running, and above him were men who gave him orders. We had the bags of birds with us in the back: Seraphim and I would take a few bags each, clean them, and then give Vyacheslav a cut of the profit. Vyacheslav was exempt from cleaning the birds because the boats belonged to him. We would each make about 3,000 euros from the morning's efforts.

As I got out of the van, I paused with the passenger door open. 'Sunday,' I said to him. 'Nisha disappeared on Sunday. Was there anything particular about that day? Do you remember anything?'

'No, why would I?' he said.

'Because earlier you said it wasn't possible. That Nisha wouldn't have run away. What did you mean by that?'

'I think you misheard me, my friend. You know what these women are like – they come and go like the rain.'

Not Nisha, I was going to say. But I didn't.

When I got home, I brought the bags of birds upstairs and placed them in the spare room. I proceeded to the kitchen to check on the little bird. It was sleeping. I stroked its feathers. I imagined that birds have no memory, that they

48

live only in the present, that the past washes away behind them and disappears like each wave on the ocean.

I thought of the bags of dead birds in the spare room. I had no energy to clean them, so I stored them in the industrial-sized fridge, and I decided to leave the job for the next day.

I had a long nap as I hadn't slept the night before. When I got up, it was already dark. I rang Nisha a few more times. Again, it went straight to voicemail. I made myself some dinner of couscous and snails and sat out on the balcony to eat, the throw that Nisha always used over my shoulders. The blanket smelled of her – wood polish and bleach, spices and milk. She felt so far away. Where had she gone? What had Seraphim meant? Did he know something? You never knew with him.

Seraphim is the son of an old family friend. When I was a kid, he would come with his parents and sister to visit a couple of times a year. Being two years older than me, he either ignored me or bossed me around. Then our families drifted apart, and I went off to university in Athens. When I returned, I moved to the heart of the city centre. Years later, after I lost my job at Laiki and started renting the flat above Petra's, I bumped into him again in the grocery store down the road. He recognised me immediately, embracing me, whacking my back with his big hands. He told me about his Jaguar (he collected antique cars), his property (a sprawling villa), and his beautiful Russian wife. It seemed that there should have been a parenthesis there too, but he left it out.

I was envious. There he was, his life pretty much sorted, while mine was falling apart.

'So, how are you, my friend?' he said. 'I heard you're flying high in the financial world?'

I had been about to nod and simply agree with him, but then he added, 'Or has this crisis been a blow?'

So, I told him, matter-of-factly, that yes, in fact, it had been a blow. I didn't mention, however, that I'd been looking for work with zero success and wasn't even sure how I was going to make next month's rent payment to Petra.

He nodded, thoughtfully. 'And I heard you got married . . . and so young!'

'Yes,' I said, 'she's wonderful. Very supportive.' I didn't tell him that I'd lost her too.

The first loss had led to the second, and those two had in fact led to a third – the loss of my naivety, which in reality I should have outgrown already. It was only when we knew each other better that I confessed to him that she had, in fact, left me.

'Do you live around here now?'

Yes, I had said, and told him the name of the street.

'Great. We're practically neighbours.' He had hesitated for a moment. 'I'll tell you what . . . I have a proposal for you. I think you'll like it. Will you meet me at eleven thirty tomorrow evening?' From his pocket he took out a crumpled-up receipt, flattened it out on the grocery story counter, and wrote down the name of a street, the name of a bar and his mobile number. He also wanted to take mine – 'Just to be sure,' he said.

50

I wanted to go and meet him. There was something about him, some energy, that said: *Follow me and I'll show you a life that's better.* He had an infectious smile and his eyes always shone with possibilities.

When I looked at the scribbled address, it turned out to be Maria's. I should have known from the time he wanted to meet – it ran until the early hours.

Maria's bar was an open ground for sex workers, pimps and drunk old men. Just off the main street with dark windows and a wooden door. On the dance floor, an older woman threw tiny pieces of paper into the air as if she was showering herself with confetti.

Seraphim was sitting at the bar talking to the barmaid, who was dressed in her habitual tight black. He spotted me straightaway and waved. He had clearly been looking out for me.

I joined him. Without asking what I wanted, he ordered a couple of beers. He was grazing on some nuts. He pushed the bowl towards me. 'Help yourself,' he said.

'No, thank you.'

'You must try them. Fresh from the trees. Lightly roasted. No added salt.'

I felt that I couldn't refuse. It was the same when we were kids. One time, when I was thirteen and he was fifteen, he convinced me to climb a tree. He told me about a beautiful bird he had seen up there, a rare species that he'd never encountered before. Of course, I was excited, and I went up quite easily, as I was agile and strong. But coming down was a problem. Trees are notoriously difficult to climb down. I was stuck up there for a good hour before my grandad came up the hill carrying two bales of hay on his shoulders, which he placed on the ground below me so that they would break my fall.

The nuts did look good and I'd been anxious about meeting him, curious about what this proposal might be, so I'd hardly eaten. Now I took a handful of them and threw them in my mouth.

The barmaid placed two bottles on the bar and Seraphim reached for his wallet to pay. I was his guest, he said, he would be treating me. I drank the beer quickly. On the stool beside us, a man with grey hair was playing with the hair of a young woman, her arms hung around his neck. She was dark skinned and looked barely eighteen. A few seats down a bald man was trying to kiss the neck of another woman – she looked familiar, but I couldn't think where I'd seen her. Seraphim ordered another couple of beers. This time the barmaid placed in front of us bowls of sliced apples, olives and crisps. This time he didn't pay. We were drinking the beers at top speed and the barmaid kept replacing the empty ones.

On a table behind us, two beautiful women sat in the laps of two very old men. 'Those are lovely Romanian girls,' Seraphim said. 'Not too expensive.'

The beer had started to go to my head. So far we'd spoken about nothing much. He had told me a bit more about his cars. A Porsche 911, in mint condition. 'There's magic in that car,' he said. 'You should come with me some time, we'll go up to the mountains. You'll see its power.' He told me about his Mercedes SL 300 Gullwing. 'One of the first sports cars of the post-war era. Silver. Doors open up like the wings of a bird. You can fly in that thing.' He preferred not to drive that one around too much, he said. He kept it in tip-top condition in his garage, took it out for a spin once a week, to keep it alive and breathing.

Even slightly pissed, I had been struck by how shabby his clothes were. His T-shirt was old and worn, as were his jeans; his hair barely brushed, it flicked out in various directions. With all that money I wondered why he wore clothes that looked twenty years old.

The beers kept coming, and I was drinking more slowly now.

Two Filipino women approached us: one younger, heavily made up; the other, slightly older woman, hardly wore a speck of makeup and her skin shone in the dim lights. Seraphim was well acquainted with them. There was a lot of small talk.

'When shall I take you two out in my car? Seraphim had said.

The older woman smiled politely but didn't answered. The younger one brushed her hair away from her forehead and placed both of her hands between her knees. These small movements told me that the women were not comfortable. I downed another beer. The two women disappeared into the crowd.

Seraphim ordered couscous from one of the barmaids.

'Couscous?' I said, and he winked.

In a short while she returned carrying a ceramic pot on a silver tray. She placed the pot and two small plates and cutlery on the bar.

'Have a look at this, my friend,' said Seraphim. 'In season. Organic. You must love them.'

He opened the pot and dug into it with a fork – pulling out a tiny poached songbird. Steam wound in ribbons out of the pot, mixing with the cigarette smoke already in the air. He delicately placed a couple on my plate and a couple on his. Then he threw one into his mouth, crunching into its bones with relish.

'Go for it,' he said. Mouth full. 'You must like them. I've never met anyone who doesn't. Didn't you have them when you were a boy?' He spat on the counter.

I told him that I did. And that I knew that it was illegal to eat these birds.

'I'm not too hungry,' I said. 'I had a huge meal before I came out. Still bloated.'

'Looks like it might be harder for me to get you on my side than I thought.' Seraphim swallowed the last bit of bird and used the nail of his pinkie finger to remove meat from his tooth. I felt like gagging.

'I don't understand.'

'These songbirds – how shall I put it? They are on your plate courtesy of me. You can say that I'm keeping the tradition alive. But I catch them in their thousands. Another pair of hands would double my income. It's just a few traps a week during the hunting seasons.' He paused, considering me. 'After all, how did you think I lived so well?'

I didn't respond.

'I see your dapper clothes and your good looks are your cover-ups. But you're struggling, my friend – don't think I can't see that. I saw it in your eyes in the grocery store. It was right there, slashed across your face like a huge scar.'

Once again, I said nothing. But Seraphim had sussed me out. It was his mighty skill.

'You don't have to give me an answer now. Think about it, and I'll call you in a week. If you say yes, we'll start straight away. I need an apprentice. Someone I can trust. You've always been trustworthy, haven't you?' He grinned broadly for a moment and then pushed the plate towards me. 'If nothing else, at least try one. It'll take you right back to your childhood.'

I realised I had hardly touched my dinner. I got up and put it in a Tupperware box to store in the fridge. I gave the little bird some more water and it drank, drop by drop. I had put out a plate of seeds in the morning and it had eaten quite a bit. Then I nestled it in my palms and took it out, once again, to the balcony to wait for 11 p.m. I watched it as its jet-bead eyes opened and closed, its feathers fluffing up as it settled in my hands. I had an image in my mind of the other birds, the dead ones, thousands of them in the black bin-liners, feathers stuck together with their own blood and the blood of the other birds. Beady eyes open forever to the darkness.

I was even more uneasy that night. Below, on the street,

the light from Petra's living room shone on the cobblestone street. There were shadows on the stones, the movement of people within. Yes, one was Petra's – long and slim, hair up. The other was Aliki's – shorter and broader – coming to the window intermittently to stand silently, no doubt, beside her mother. Then, on one occasion, there was a third, softer, rounder – standing alone. This must have been Nisha. But I could hardly go and check. I rang her, and once again it went straight to voicemail. I could think of no good reason to knock on their door at this hour. But I kept thinking – *She'll be back*. Unless she went back to Sri Lanka . . . No, I was sure that Nisha would knock on the back door at eleven, like she always did, and the memory of waiting for her would fade into the past and be forgotten.

Mrs Hadjikyriacou was outside again, talking nonsense to the cats. I couldn't hear was she was saying, though – the bouzouki wasn't playing that night; instead, a girl was singing in another language, and the foreign words flew in their hundreds over the streets and consumed them. I'd never seen her before, and she was beautiful: dark, with dark eyes. Her right hand was smaller and seemed damaged in some way, perhaps a birth defect. It remained scrunched up, close to her breast. Her left hand, however, danced as she sang, rose and fell with the mesmerising tone of her voice, her fingers tapping the air as if she was playing an invisible instrument. Her voice was extraordinary, clear as glass. On the tables around her, the men, many of whom had once been officers in the military, who probably had medals and flashbacks locked away somewhere, knocked back shots of ouzo, sucked

56

snails with their gums, laughed – and ignored her. She was merely background noise.

I saw Yiakoumi come out of his shop. He sat down on a wicker chair to drink coffee and hear the music. The clocks behind him were lit up – it was 10.30 p.m.

I sat there holding the bird, listening to the music, waiting for the next half hour. But Nisha didn't come.

At 5 a.m. I was awakened by the sound of my iPad ringing. I jumped up to answer it, thinking it was Nisha, but the name that was flashing brightly on the screen was Kumari. I stood and watched it for a while not knowing what to do. What would I say to her?

In a moment it stopped. But not even ten seconds later, it began to ring again and once more I could do nothing but stand there, imagining the little girl on the other end, waiting eagerly to speak to her mother.

8

Petra

THE NEXT MORNING, AS SOON as the cockerel started to crow, I made myself some tea and toast and went to Nisha's room. I looked around, without knowing what I was searching for. Her makeup was on the dressing table, neatly lined up. The brushes sparkled with rouge. Then I noticed a journal and, resting on top of it, a gold engagement ring. I had never seen her wearing this before – it was simple, with a decent sized diamond in a raised clasp. I placed the ring on the dresser and opened the journal. On the first page was a rough sketch of the garden – there was the boat and the orange tree. The rest of the pages were full of writing in Sinhalese.

In the drawer of her bedside cabinet, I found a gold locket. It was heart shaped and inside were two, roughly cut out photographs – one of her, and one of a young man. She never wore this locket but sometimes, in the evenings, when she sat down to rest and watch TV, she held it tightly in her palm or coiled the gold chain around her finger, like a Christian would their rosary.

In another drawer, I found a lock of hair.

'That's my Sri Lankan sister's hair.' I turned and Aliki stood in the doorway. 'Her name is Kumari. She is two years older than me – she's eleven.' She stared at me. 'Did you know that?'

'Not really,' I said. It occurred to me that I had never bothered to ask about her daughter, about what she looked like, what she was like, how she was doing without her mother by her side. When did Nisha even speak to Kumari?

The lock of hair was in a clear plastic bag, the type you might keep coins in to take to the bank.

'But my hair is curly and hers is straight.'

I nodded.

'That is a locket that Nisha's husband gave her before he died. He is inside that heart. She would never, ever leave without him.'

So, these were Nisha's most precious possessions.

None of Nisha's clothes or shoes were missing. She owned three handbags, but only two were there, lined up at the bottom of her wardrobe. Her reading glasses were resting on her pillow. Her bed was neatly made, the covers folded at the corners meticulously.

Turning around to ask Aliki a question, I realised that she had slipped out of the room. Probably gone to make herself some breakfast.

There was a small antique desk by the glass doors and when I opened the top drawer, I found her passport. At this point I sat down on the chair, I was so confused. A part of me had hoped that I wouldn't find these items, particularly the passport. I wanted to believe that Nisha had taken off somewhere – and that would mean she was safe. But, if she had, why would she leave her passport? The locket? I opened the journal again and ran my fingers over the foreign words, the beautiful lines that ran along the paper like the vines in the garden. I wished I could read it, hoping it would give me some clue to Nisha's whereabouts.

She had simply vanished.

I took the locket and held it tightly in a closed fist, like Nisha did when she watched TV. It reminded me of Aliki's tiny heart, during the last ultrasound I had had when I was pregnant, before going into labour.

Stephanos hadn't been there. He had been an army officer and worked at the British base, which was why we had decided to stay here – in my parents' house – after we got married. Stephanos was a British Cypriot, born in Islington, raised in Edmonton. His parents moved to London as refugees after the war. He'd enlisted in the army in England, but one summer he came to Cyprus to stay with relatives and we met and fell in love. After that he requested to be transferred here. The British still have a base in Cyprus, a remnant of their occupation of the island until its independence in 1960.

It was convenient for him to get to work, as he could walk

there in ten minutes, or drive in two. By that time, Mum had already passed away and Dad had moved to a small flat in the mountains, so we moved into this beautiful Venetian property in the old city – the house I had grown up in.

It belonged to my dad's aunt, and for a few years, when I was between the ages of five and seven, she lived above us, where Yiannis now lives. I remembered her as a tiny, pretty, old lady, with silver hair, which she always wore in a net. She used to sit in the garden and crochet tablecloths, curtains, wedding dresses and veils. She told me stories about the beginning of time and the end of time, her hands always busy. She told me once that she was buying time, that she would work until she was ready to leave this world and reunite with the man she loved – my father's uncle, who had died fighting for the British in the Second World War.

Stephanos was diagnosed with cancer when I was five weeks pregnant with Aliki. It travelled from his prostate, to his bones, to his liver. He went from a man leaving the house in his military gear every morning, a man who ran laps around the old city in the evenings, a man who made me laugh till I burst, into a . . . something. Something shrivelled, not human. Something not alive and not dead. A creature; a tiny, dying bird.

Aliki continued to grow. She grew and she grew like a fruit on a tree, like a plump fig, growing and expanding my insides till I was ready to burst. She writhed and wriggled and pushed, and that's when the idea of an octopus came to me.

By the time of the mid-pregnancy ultrasound, Stephanos

was bed-bound. I promised to bring him the scan to see. He hoped, he'd said, that Aliki would be as beautiful as me. He had chosen her name. When he spoke like that, looking right into my eyes, I knew that he was still there. But then I would take in the rest of him; how alien he looked – bones crumbling, spine twisted, neck bent forward like a vulture's – and I had a feeling that I wanted to melt away. I wanted to disappear into him, into his eyes, so that I could rest inside him and hold on to his soul. I began to see his eyes like tiny doors, leading to the man that I had always known. I would wait for him to wake up each morning, sitting by his side in the hospital. I would look at this shrivelled form on the bed, wired up to machines, and wait for those doors to open. When his eyes closed forever, I'd lose him completely.

The day of the scan, the nurse spread gel over the bump and ran the cold wand over my skin. But I couldn't bring myself to look at the screen. I just thought of the first scan at twelve weeks. Stephanos had come with me to the appointment – we knew his diagnosis by then, but he hadn't deteriorated yet. We had both stared rapt at the screen, not even sure what we were looking at. The foetus, the size of a raspberry, had barely looked human. The heartbeat was faint and muffled, so far away. But now if I looked at the screen there would be a real child, and I wasn't ready to imagine her. Not without Stephanos. Still, I heard her heartbeat. It was steady and strong and full of life; it knocked on the boundaries of this world demanding to be heard. I heard it. Oh, I heard it! I had no choice. Aliki was announcing herself, forging a path for her arrival.

At the same time, my heart vanished. It turned to mist and disappeared.

I hired Nisha as soon as Stephanos died. She was even there for the birth. Most of the other women in the city had domestic workers, so I saw no harm in having one too. I did my research and realised that it wouldn't be too expensive, no more than I could afford. I would offer her accommodation and food, so the monthly fee was minimal. The fact was, I couldn't manage on my own and I knew I would need to return to work sooner rather than later. It was my own business, after all. This is how I reasoned, anyway.

Aliki was an 8lb baby with a full head of hair. She looked exactly like Stephanos. I'm petite with mousy-brown, straight hair and olive skin. I saw nothing of me in her. Even my breasts were too small for her and I never produced enough milk. She pulled at my skin and sucked my nipples raw, trying in desperation to get more than I could give her. I have to admit, I was jealous of how Nisha was able to love her, hold her in her arms, so close to her skin.

Aliki would cry and cry.

'Madam,' Nisha would say, 'your baby is crying. Go to her, she needs you.'

I couldn't go. I couldn't move. 'Please, Nisha, can you go, just this once? I will go next time.'

'OK, madam, if that is what you want.'

She would pick up the wailing child and walk around, but Aliki would not stop. Then, one day, for some reason, Nisha decided to lie on the floor on her back, lift up her top, and place the baby on her naked chest. Aliki suddenly stopped crying. She whimpered for a while, then slept. Sitting back in the armchair and watching them like that – Aliki's white, curled-up body against Nisha's darker skin – reminded me of the night cradling the moon.

Aliki fell in love with Nisha: she desired her odours and the warm touch of her skin. I imagined that in the beating of Aliki's heart, Nisha could feel that of her own child. I didn't want to think about this. I dashed the thought aside, to a safe place, where the guilt couldn't reach me.

Nisha never gave up trying to bring me closer to my child. She tried to get me to hold Aliki, to be still with her. But I couldn't. In Aliki's face, in her eyes, in the soft curve of her chin, the pink freshness of her skin, even in the mole on her cheek, I saw Stephanos. I had nightmares. I would sit up and see huge white spiders the size of shoes crawling to the baby's room. I'd follow them, stamp on them, trying to keep them from reaching my baby. Then I would wake up, standing over the cot, Nisha by my side with her hand on my back, rubbing it.

'Shush now, shush, madam. Everything will be OK.'

She would take my hand and place it on Aliki's chest so that I could feel her chest expanding as she breathed,

'You see,' Nisha whispered beside me, 'your daughter is just fine. When she wakes up, you can take her outside and enjoy some sunlight. It will be warm tomorrow.'

Then she would calmly lead me back to bed, holding my hand, tucking me in, whispering, 'Sleep now.'

No, Nisha would never leave Aliki without saying goodbye. This I knew for certain.

I placed the locket back in the drawer and, taking the passport with me, headed outside to see if Mrs Hadjikyriacou was there. She was sitting on the deckchair by the front door and her maid was kneeling in front of her, rubbing *zivania* into her legs, her translucent skin creasing like tiny waves under the maid's fingers. It was warmer but windy that morning. When she saw me, she shooed her maid away and propped her legs up on a stool.

'It's a bit early for you,' she said, without even looking in my direction. She was gazing up at the sky and straining her neck to do so. It was early; Yiakoumi hadn't even opened his shop yet, and all his timepieces, apart from one, read seven o'clock.

She straightened her neck now and turned to look at me. The wind blew stronger and the alcohol evaporated from her legs and drifted towards me. She smelled like she'd spent the whole night in a bar. I brought my hand up to my nose and she noticed the passport I was holding.

'My darrrrling,' she said in English, then in Greek: 'Where are you going?'

'Nisha hasn't returned.'

'I know,' she replied, nodding.

'This is her passport.'

65

'Ah.'

'If she'd intended to leave, then wouldn't she have taken this with her? She's even left the locket her husband gave her before he died, and her daughter's lock of hair.'

I waited, expecting to hear another *ah*, but Mrs Hadjikyriacou remained silent. She seemed to be thinking.

She looked up and down the street then turned to face me, her eyes filled with anxiety, with intensity. 'She was wearing a long-sleeved black dress,' she said, 'with white trainers. She had a green scarf wrapped around her neck, which partly covered her mouth. She wore that scarf like it was the middle of winter, though I know it must have been a warm Sunday night because my woman didn't bring me a blanket.'

'Why was she dressed like that?'

'Do you think if I sniff my nails they will tell me the answer?'

I rolled my eyes without her seeing.

One of the cats jumped onto the stool and walked along her leg as if it was a tree branch, then settled in her lap. She stroked it while it purred. 'Petra,' Mrs Hadjikyriacou said, 'if she's not back by tomorrow, you must go to the police.'

I looked down at my watch. There was no time to think about this right now, as I needed to get Aliki ready for school.

Once again, I left work early to collect Aliki from school in the afternoon. I had no option but to bring her to work with me again. This time, she sat behind the counter doing her homework with Keti's help. She was learning the periodic table.

'It's amazing to see all the elements of the whole universe on one page!' I heard her saying with excitement, as I led a client into my office for an eye exam.

That evening, after work, I made some pasta with haloumi and mint for dinner. Aliki and I ate in silence. Aliki's eyes flicked towards Nisha's empty chair now. The photograph of Stephanos in his uniform sat behind her on a console table. Sometimes I would catch Aliki stop in front of it while she was playing, pausing to stare at it. Could she see how much they looked alike? Their pale skin, wide-set eyes and round faces – even the small moles on their right cheeks.

I tried to engage Aliki, ask her questions. How was school, and do you have homework tonight? She replied with a nod, a shrug or a shake of the head, but she never spoke. Not a word. Sometimes I thought she wanted to speak, but then whatever words were hovering would be swallowed, gulped down with the pasta.

When we had finished, I helped Aliki with her homework at the kitchen table, then settled her into bed. We both pretended she was going right to sleep, but no doubt she would stay up reading for a while.

When I heard no more sounds from her room, I tiptoed to the front door, quietly closing it behind me before crossing the street to Theo's restaurant. He was in the kitchen shouting at the chefs. I stood and waited for him to stop and finally he turned to me with a smile. 'Petra, my dear, table for tonight? A late supper?'

'No, Theo, I've come to speak to your maids.' He raised

his eyebrows. 'It's about an important matter regarding Nisha. She's gone missing and I want to see if they know anything.'

'Take a seat,' he said. 'I'll bring you a coffee on the house. They are busy in the back but they can take a break soon.'

I sat down beneath the vine-covered trellis, sipping my coffee. It was just after 9 p.m. and there were a few diners at the table and a couple of punters at the bar. After about fifteen minutes, the women emerged from the kitchen, both in black trousers and white shirts, their usual rice hats tied at the chin with a red ribbon. It occurred to me then how awful it was that Theo was making the women wear these hats; I couldn't imagine that it was their own choice. This wasn't a Vietnamese restaurant, after all, it was Greek. The hats were exotic, a fetish, of course. The men ogled from their seats. How had I never noticed this before?

Theo gestured in my direction, and they approached my table, clearly tired but smiling.

'Madam,' said the one on the left. 'Sir said you wanted to talk about something important.'

'We are just having a break. We've been working from six this morning,' said the other, in a tone that was both joyful and irritated.

The shorter one nudged her and gave her a look to be quiet. 'Sorry, madam,' she said, holding out her hand. 'I am Chau and this is my sister, Bian.'

I shook both of their hands. 'I live across the street,' I said. 'I am Petra.'

They both laughed. 'We know, madam,' said Chau. 'We see you every day and we are friends with Nisha.'

68

'I was hoping you might know where she is. I haven't seen her since Sunday evening.'

'No, madam,' said Chau, shaking her head. 'She comes to say hello every morning after taking Aliki to school, but we have not seen her for a few days. We were thinking maybe she went away.'

'We work here in the morning for the breakfast customers,' added Bian, 'then we go to sir's house to clean, then we come back here in the afternoon until very late. We see Nisha once in the morning and sometimes in the afternoon. Now, for few days, nothing.'

The word 'nothing' stabbed me like a knife. It reminded me of the emptiness that Nisha had left behind.

Bian eyed Theo watching us from behind the bar. Several customers had left their tables, and dirty dishes had started to pile up at the bussing stations.

Chau looked over, concerned. 'We must go,' she said. 'Sir will be angry. We have much more to clean before closing time.'

'Hold on,' I said. 'Please, if you hear anything, will you come and knock on my door straightaway?'

They both stared at it me for a moment too long and then nodded.

'Of course, madam,' said Bian. 'We will come to tell you first.'

When I got home, the house was quiet. I peeked into Aliki's room and she was asleep, a book lying across her chest.

Feeling restless, I went to the garden to collect the pieces of broken money-box and coins from the ground. I put all the lira in a glass bowl and sprayed them with water until they gleamed. The black cat sat by my feet.

Then I went out to the front porch to sit for a while. I watched the neighbourhood go about the business of shutting down. Mrs Hadjikyriacou was indoors tonight. Yiakoumi's maid was taking the antiques inside in order to shut the shop. To the right, Theo's restaurant was getting quiet, just a few customers remained, finishing drinks and paying their bills. Bian and Chau dashed about, wiping down tables and preparing them with fresh tablecloths for the next day.

I had started to see the rhythm of these women with new eyes – how the whole neighbourhood pulsed with their activity. They had been invisible to me before Nisha had gone missing: all I had seen before was a little Cypriot girl walking excitedly down a street with two adults; the shining antiques outside Yiakoumi's shop every day; the clean and well-kept front garden down the road; the happy customers at Theo's. I had not really seen the women.

When I went to bed, I heard my daughter's voice; it struck me, since I had craved the sound of it all through dinner. I had the window slightly open, the sky a deep blue, when her voice came to me with the wind. Such a soft voice, but textured, rising with excitement, falling with lilting sadness. I peered out of the shutters and was surprised to see her sitting in the boat. When had she woken up? This time she was holding the oar and the olive branch but not rowing. Then she laughed, holding her sides, as if someone had said something funny. I called her inside and lay back on my bed and closed my eyes.

I must have fallen asleep because when I woke up it was completely dark and I heard knocking coming from the garden. I got out of bed and opened the glass doors. Yiannis was standing by Nisha's room, tapping on the glass.

Startled, he turned to me. 'Petra,' he said.

'What are you doing?'

'I heard a noise.'

'But you were the one making the noise,' I said. 'Was there another noise?'

He didn't respond to this.

'Do you know where Nisha is?'

'No,' he said, bluntly. And then it seemed that he regretted this and said, 'I wanted to ask her something. Do you know where she is?'

'Unfortunately, I don't.'

Then there was anguish on his face, anguish in his eyes. The moonlight illuminated the streaks of silver in his hair and I thought to myself what a beautiful and lonely man he was.

A gallows frame looks over the red lake at Mitsero, a colossal rusty carcass that creaks in the wind. It is quiet by the lake, on this bright day in October. The hare is exposed to the sun, its body bloated as gases stretch its insides and skin, as bacteria eat soft tissue. The hare is still intact, in the running position, but its powerful hind legs have lost their purpose. It is lying on a slab of yellow stone about five metres from where the crater wall drops to the water.

A praying mantis flies down – green as another land in another time – all five eyes alert for any movement or changes of light. It scuttles a short distance across the yellow stone where the bloated hare is lying, back legs pushing its green frame forward, the front two – sharply spined – reach out and capture and hold a roaming fly.

The hare's head is slanted slightly upwards, away from its front paws. It would seem that it is looking at the mantis eating the fly, but its left eye, the colour of amber, is flat against the earth, and its right eye looks directly into the sun, golden. The hare's black-tipped ears give the impression that they are blowing backwards in the wind. As if it were running.

No vegetation grows around the lake, the soil is arid. But, further out, the soil is rich in copper and pyrite and gold, and there are barley and wheat fields and sunflowers leading to the village. There are fruit trees in the fields beyond the village, and from there come the distant sounds of life – of leaves rustling, wings flapping, animals moving amongst the cherry and pecan trees as they begin to shed their golden leaves.

The hare's carcass reeks now, and the smell is carried by a soft breeze over the red water of the lake, through the hollow gallows frame into the fields, where it meets rosemary and thyme, eucalyptus and pine.

9

Petra

I CALLED UP NISHA'S AGENCY. I asked them if they'd heard from her.

'No,' the woman said, after checking the system. 'We log everything and there's nothing here.'

I told her that Nisha had gone missing three days ago, that I couldn't get through to her on her mobile, either.

'Well,' the woman said, 'keep us posted because she still has an outstanding debt.' She had a voice like a foghorn. It was awful and too loud, and it said nothing helpful.

'How much?' I said, but the woman wouldn't tell me, it was confidential information. However, I knew that the agencies charged the workers a considerable amount of money to sign up and secure a placement abroad.

Then I rang Nicosia hospital to see if Nisha had been admitted, but they had no record of her.

When I got off the phone, I looked around and saw that the dinner plates from the night before were still in the sink unwashed, and the ones from breakfast were piled up on top of them. Dust had gathered on the furniture and the marble flagstones.

It was only 9 a.m., but I felt like I'd already had a full day.

I'd woken up early, left a message for Keti to tell her I'd be taking the whole day off, made breakfast for Aliki – finding a jar of her favourite fig jam in the cupboard felt like a small victory – and rushed Aliki off to school.

Now, I went to Nisha's room and gathered what I needed: her passport, her contract, the locket and the lock of hair. I was going to the police station.

I drove to Lykavitos station at Spyrou Kyprianou, an old white building with blue shutters. I'd passed the building many times but had never been inside. I told the officer at reception that I wanted to report a missing person. The woman took down my name and asked me to take a seat, saying someone would be with me in a minute.

A minute turned to five, ten, twenty, half an hour. Phones rang in rooms along unseen corridors; occasionally an officer would pass by and wish me good morning. Footsteps on flagstones reminded me for a moment of all those hours I had spent in hospital waiting-rooms, praying for Stephanos: the intermittent whispers, the soft footfalls; disinfectant and coffee; smiles from distracted doctors. I would nod politely, but I found that I couldn't smile, my hand resting on my stomach as the baby grew day by day, week by week, month by month.

'Mrs Loizides?'

Looking down at me, as if from a great height, was a man in his sixties, taller than the average Cypriot, stomach spilling over his trousers, sleeves rolled up.

'Yes,' I said. 'That's me.'

He held out his hand, either to shake mine, or to help me to stand – for a moment I wasn't sure, and hesitated.

'Vasilis Kyprianou,' he said.

'Nice to meet you,' I said, and shook his hand, and with a smile he led me down one of the corridors and into a small room with a cluttered desk, a filing cabinet and a fan that was blowing some paperwork to the floor. He rushed to scoop up the papers with large, clumsy hands, straightening them into a pile and plonking it back on the desk – whereupon, once again, when the fan arced back around, the paperwork flew back down to the floor. This time he left it and picked up a small cup of coffee and took a sip. He grimaced.

'Cold,' he said, noticing that I was looking at him. 'Always.'

With the shades drawn, the office was dim, streaks of sun reaching through the dusty slats. He sat down, the light cutting across his face and highlighting his white stubble. He signalled for me to take one of the vacant chairs opposite him.

'Loizides,' he said. 'Why does that name sound familiar?' He thought for a moment. 'Ah, it was an old colleague of mine. Yes. Nicos Loizides. We trained together. Do you know him?'

'No. I don't believe I do.'

He smiled and leaned forward on his elbows. His face

77

reminded me of a red helium balloon that had begun to sag, those balloons that slowly deflate after a birthday until they are wrinkled and bobbing on the ground.

'So, how can I help you today?'

I took Nisha's things out of my handbag and laid them out on the desk. 'My maid has gone missing,' I said. 'Her name is Nisha Jayakody. She is thirty-eight years old and she's been missing since Sunday night.'

'Today is Wednesday,' he said, as if I didn't know.

'Yes.' I opened the passport and placed it in front of him. I explained everything in detail: the trip to Troodos, Nisha asking me if she could take the night off, returning home, what we had eaten, what time we had eaten, how I had gone to bed leaving Nisha to take care of Aliki, and, how I had woken up in the morning to find that Nisha had gone. Finally, I explained that a reliable neighbour had seen Nisha heading out at ten thirty that same night.

'She hasn't taken her passport,' I said, pushing it still closer to him, because he had not yet even looked at it. 'If she had intended to leave, she would have taken this with her.'

'Ha,' he said simply, bringing the back of his hand to his mouth, wiping it as if he had just finished eating, and leaning back in the chair.

'Where is she from?' he asked.

'Sri Lanka. She has been working for me for nine years. She has helped to bring up my daughter. Nisha would never leave without saying goodbye to her.'

There was a moment of silence. Then Officer Kyprianou sighed deeply, and looked me straight in the eyes, as if willing

78

me to understand his thoughts, like I was missing some joke. Then he said, 'It's only been a few days. Why don't you leave it and see how it goes?'

'But she's never done this before,' I said. 'I know something is wrong. Look' – I tapped the locket and the lock of hair on the desk in front of him – 'these are her most prized possessions. She wouldn't even wear the locket for fear of losing it. It was a gift from her late husband. This is a lock of her daughter's hair. She hasn't seen her daughter for nine years, since she came here. She would never leave these items behind.'

He picked up the coffee again and took another dissatisfied sip, nodding his head as if to himself.

I wished I had a pin to burst his big, hollow head.

'I was wondering if you could take down Nisha's details, investigate—' but he interrupted me before I had even finished speaking.

'I can't concern myself with these foreign women. I have more important matters to attend to. If she doesn't return, my guess would be that she's ran away to the north. That's what they do. She's gone to the Turkish side to find better employment. These women are animals, they follow their instincts. Or the money, more likely. That's what I have to say on the matter. You would do best to go home and start cleaning out her room. If she's not back by the end of the week, call up the agency to find another maid.'

With that, he stood up to signal that our meeting was over, holding out his hand to me.

I rose from my chair and looked at his hand, but didn't

shake it. There was so much I wanted to say, but it was clear this man wasn't capable of hearing me. I gathered Nisha's things from the desk and tucked them back into my bag, purposely stepped on the paperwork that was scattered on the floor, and walked out of his shabby little office.

When I got home, I saw that Yiakoumi's maid was in the antique shop, polishing things. I went across the street to have a chat with her, to see if she knew anything.

Yiakoumi was in the back with his feet up on a messy desk. He nodded at me when I entered. 'Get Nilmini to help you,' he said. 'I'm waiting for an important call.'

'Nilmini,' I said. She was sitting on a stool amongst items of copper. She looked up. How young and self-contained she was. A beautiful Sri Lankan woman in her early twenties, with such long hair it looked as though it had never been cut.

'That's a lovely name,' I said.

'It means "ambitious woman".' She continued to polish an old urn.

I noticed behind her a pile of tattered books – *Alice's Adventures in in Wonderland*, *Huckleberry Finn*, *Peter Pan*. One of them was open on the floor in front of her, pages held back with two pebbles from the beach. She saw me looking.

'I love reading, madam. In Sri Lanka I wanted to study literature. Sir bought me these books from the market. He said I can read as long as I do my work.'

80

I nodded and glanced up at Yiakoumi, who was yawning and reading something on his phone.

'I am wondering, Nilmini, if you have seen Nisha or heard from her.'

She paused and looked up at the ceiling where a brass chandelier hung above her.

'The last time I saw Nisha, madam, was Sunday night.'

'What was she doing?'

'Usually, madam, she comes to say hello. This time she was walking very quickly.'

At that point Yiakoumi's mobile rang and he got up to speak in the storage room at the back.

'What time was that?' I asked.

'I arrived here maybe an hour earlier, so I think it was after ten. Sir wanted me to work Sunday night because customers come in the morning. I cleaned his house in the morning, had a break and then came here at nine o' clock.'

'Did Nisha say anything to you?'

'No, madam, she said nothing. Normally she waves, sometimes she comes in and makes a joke and we laugh, often she brings me fruit. No, she didn't stop to see me and I tell you, she looked worried.'

'Are you sure?'

'Yes, madam. I have been working here opposite Nisha for a year. I know her face. I know my friend's face when she's happy, sad, angry, tired. This time I tell you she was worried.'

'Do you remember anything else at all?'

'Well, madam, maybe this not an important thing, but the cat was following her.'

'The cat?'

'Yes. I looked down the road as she walked off. I was outside. The cat followed her all the way and turned the corner when she turned. So the cat might know where Nisha is.'

I stared at her. Was she being serious?

'It was this cat, madam.' She pointed out of the window, where the black cat with the different-coloured eyes was sitting on the table, washing itself amongst the pots and vases. The one my daughter now called Monkey.

That afternoon, I picked up Aliki from school. I didn't take the car because I wanted to walk with her. She was wearing her favourite K-pop idol girl T-shirt with some light blue jeans, and she'd released her hair from its ponytail so it hung in thick waves over her shoulders.

'Aliki,' I said, 'I went to the police today.'

She quickly glanced up at me, cheeks rosy.

'I went to report Nisha missing, but they wouldn't help me. They said she's probably run away to the north. But I don't believe them,' I said.

Suddenly, her eyes filled with tears.

'I'm not saying this to upset you. I want you to know what's happening. I'm looking for Nisha but I'm confused. Did she say anything to you? Do you know anything that might help me to understand what is going on?'

Aliki looked down at her feet as she walked.

'Aliki?' I said. But this just made her withdraw further –

she walked over to a shop front and stared at the shoes on display. She'd cut herself off from me completely.

At home, I made potato salad. The vegetables in the fridge had started to rot – Nisha had always done the shopping – so I chopped them all up and threw them in the salad: red peppers, tomatoes, spring onions and parsley. Aliki poked at the food with her fork, humming something under her breath.

Later, I stood by the large window at the front of the house, looking out onto the street, hoping with each second that passed that I would see Nisha turning the corner. I couldn't tamp down that hope. Maybe any moment she would appear in the lights of Yiakoumi's shop and Theo's restaurant, coming to our door and turning the key in the lock, putting down her handbag and explaining where she had been.

I must have stood like that for half an hour, maybe more. Like a cat, Aliki came in and out of the living room, standing beside me for a while and leaving again. She was anxious. I could hear it in the way she moved, in the urgency of her footsteps.

The olive tree opposite was illuminated by the shop lights. Yiakoumi came out and sat beneath it with a coffee. A woman was singing at Theo's restaurant – I couldn't see her because the men sitting beneath the grapevine at the tables around her obscured the view, but her voice was pitch-perfect, so full of pathos, so full of beauty and sadness, that something welled up inside me and I began to cry.

Who was this woman who sang in a foreign tongue? Where had she come from? What had she wished for before coming here? These questions brought me back to Nisha in a way that I had never thought about her before. I had failed to recognise that she too was a woman with pain and hopes. I had known this only as a distant thought – I had never absorbed it into my heart. For she too had lost her husband. She too had come from an island ravaged by war over the years, one besieged by colonialists. Its beauty and its people had suffered too. And these things live on: they carry themselves silently into the future. Who was Nisha? What had life taught her? Why had she travelled such a great distance? To save her daughter . . . from what?

I had never asked these questions.

I knew that she treasured the locket. I knew how she loved Aliki. I knew the taste of her food, the spices and curries and creams. I knew how she dusted and vacuumed, how she ironed the clothes, how she wrote careful shopping lists, taking her time with each letter, each word, as if she were writing a poem. I knew how she packed the groceries in perfect order so that she could unpack them more easily. I knew she had a copy of the Buddhist scriptures by her bed and a fat little statue of the Buddha beside it. I knew that when she washed fruit, she'd watch the water fall and get lost for a while.

I didn't know Nisha.

Now that I could hear this woman's song – a melody that told a story I couldn't understand – I hoped with all of my heart that it wasn't too late.

I felt Aliki standing beside me; I thought she was going to put her hand in mine. But when I turned, she was nowhere to be seen.

Aliki was sitting out in the garden in the boat again. She was rowing and humming to herself. I went outside, turned an empty plant pot over and sat on it, a little distance away from her. The trees around the garden created a shelter from the wind. Above, the moon shone brightly in the dark sky but, around it, thick clouds were gathering – an indication of a brewing storm. The black cat was in the garden now, sprawled across the patio, purring. I watched it, contemplatively. If only it could speak.

'Would you like to come in?'.

I turned and saw that Aliki was looking in my direction. 'You want me to sit in the boat?' I asked.

She nodded.

So, I climbed in opposite her and she gave me the olive branch to hold. The cat jumped in with us and snuggled up against her thigh. I glanced over at the glass doors of Nisha's room.

'She loves me,' Aliki said, and I wasn't sure if she was talking about Nisha or the cat.

'I know,' I replied, and whichever it was, this seemed to satisfy her as she started to row with the oar she was holding.

'You have to row on the other side, because if you don't we'll end up just going around in circles. This is why it's important to be balanced. Because then you'll go around in circles if you're not.'

Her words made me chuckle there was so much truth in them. I moved to sit beside her, and began to row with the olive branch, to the rhythm that Aliki had set.

'Where are we going?' I said.

'To the Sea Above the Sky. This is where I go with Nisha. It's lovely up there. Sometimes a bit scary, but not always.'

'I see,' I said, matching her movements still.

I was hoping that she would tell me more, but she had fallen silent. Her last words had floated away, high into the sky, and were mere dots up above, like helium balloons at carnivals when I was a girl: after all the sweets and colour and noise, I would release them at the end of the day and watch them float away.

Finally, Aliki spoke. 'Mum, please find her,' she said. 'I really want you to find her.'

At that moment, the sky opened, and rain began to pour down on us.

The hare is drenched. Its fur looks oily in the sunlight that shines intermittently through the clouds. The rain falls into the red lake. The rain falls onto the yellow rocks, forming streams of gold. The rain clangs against the steel of the gallows frame and the metallic structure creaks. Water begins to fill its hollow shell.

In the fields beyond, it falls through the leaves of the pecan and fruit trees. It falls down upon the wheat and barley fields. No one is out today; even in the village, doors and windows and shutters are closed, and water runs from the eaves of buildings.

Rain is always a surprise. The villagers are relieved because the earth needs to drink. Not so long ago were the scorching summer days when the water barrels were empty, the land dry as a bone. Now, the trees are cool in the drenching. When the rain stops, the locals will come out to collect the pecans before the crows do.

There is a chapel in this village which is silent and empty, but slightly further away, in Agrokipia the church bells can be heard this morning and every morning. Built by the Hellenic mining company, the church served as a protector of the miners, who risked their lives underground. Far away, across the dividing line, the birds can hear the very distant sound of morning prayer from the mosque.

Somewhere in the middle, amongst the rainfall, the two sounds meet and touch and join in union and fall down upon the hare, washing away the dirt and the hatching maggots, washing away the dried blood, the skin that has cracked open into wounds.

10

Yiannis

FOR TWO DAYS IT RAINED. It was so bad that water streamed into small rivers along the cobbled streets. At night, the customers at Theo's reluctantly went inside because nobody could sit beneath the vines in the pouring rain. We can survive the cold – with the warmth of outdoor heaters and clay ovens in the taverns – but the rain, though rare, sends everyone indoors. Even Mrs Hadjikyriacou locked herself away. Even the cats disappeared.

For those two days I stayed in. It took me almost that long to clean all the birds from the hunt with Seraphim, to pull out their feathers and soak them. I had to do it in batches. In the spare room I had three large fridges, industrial size. I checked the orders and separated the birds into containers of various sizes and labelled them, before storing them in the fridges. There were one or two establishments – a hotel and a restaurant in Larnaca – who had requested the birds be pickled, so those I soaked in vinegar.

During these dark days, I tried not to think about Nisha. But it didn't work – of course it didn't. The rain pelted down on the window from the gutters, drowning out all other sound, so that I felt my solitude keenly.

Nisha's absence was even louder than the rain.

Down in the garden, the boat filled with water and looked like it was going to sink, like it was doomed.

Nisha loved the rain. She would lie on my bed, near the long glass doors, and watch it coming down. She liked to watch water falling. It reminded her of something, she'd said, though what that thing was, I didn't know. A secret memory.

When it rained, she wanted me to make her Turkish coffee in a small cup, with some sesame biscuits in a saucer.

'It's nice to be served sometimes,' she said, laughing. How she savoured that coffee, dipping the biscuit in until it became moist and dark.

'Back home we drink tea and chew betel,' she would say. Always. A mantra. As if she couldn't quite allow herself to enjoy the pleasures of one world without being pulled into the other. Her home was always waiting for her. This was the feeling I had and it made me want to touch her, to feel the soft dark skin on her thighs and stomach, to wrap my limbs around her and hold her there. But instead,

I would simply sit beside her, sensing that at these times she needed company more than comfort.

'It's weird to think,' she said once, 'how the British occupied both of our countries. What they took and what they left behind . . .' and the sentence remained incomplete as Nisha's sentences often did, so that I had to imagine what might have come after. I guess we both finished her sentences with our own thoughts.

She told me about Nuwara Eliya, up in the hills of central Sri Lanka, far from her hometown of Galle in the south. 'That's where most of the English people settled,' she said, 'up there – because they liked the cold weather. It's about fifteen degrees! And they built *typical* English houses.' There was a note of disgust in her voice on the word *typical*, a scrunching of her eyes.

I felt close to her at these times – there was this thing we shared, the British occupation, something we could both understand: tales passed down, culture and land stolen, that insatiable fight for freedom and identity. I imagined these houses built with red brick and slanting roofs and neat front gardens, misplaced amongst the rainforest and blue magpies and jackfruit trees. But then, I had never set foot in the place where Nisha had grown up, never seen the paddy fields that she'd speak of so often.

'*Tiryak* is one of the six realms of rebirth in Buddhism,' she said once, when the rain had just stopped, and she was watching snakes and snails coming out on the street below, the birds re-emerging from the trees. 'This is when one is reborn as an animal. It makes me wonder ... imagine being reborn as a snail!' She had taken a sip of thick black coffee and been thoughtful for a while. 'When I was a child in Galle, there was a frogmouth owl that visited me at night. It was a female, so lightly spotted and white, about twenty centimetres tall, with a large head and a flattened, hooked bill. In the daytime it must have slept in the forest. Its wings were so soft that it flew silently. One night, on my sister's eleventh birthday, it came to our bedroom window. After that, it came every night for a week, so I started to leave the window open, and then it would fly in and sit on my sister's bed. But she wasn't there. She had already died.'

'You had a sister?' I asked. She had never mentioned a sister before.

'She died when she was ten. She was born with a broken heart. This is what my mother said – that some babies are born with a broken heart because they felt so much sadness in a past life, and they are not ready to live again. She had an operation when she was three, had a scar running down her chest like a beautiful tree branch. Sometimes she got me to draw flowers around it, with my mum's lip pencil. She wanted the scar to look pretty, like the places in the tropical forest. That's what she said. One day, she just didn't wake up.'

I reached out and took Nisha's hand in mine; it was warm, and she squeezed my fingers.

'The owl would come in and sit down on my sister's favourite book – *The Mahadenamutta and His Pupils*. She loved those stories. She would ask me to read them to her every night. One day, I shooed the owl off the book and started to read. The owl sat beside me and watched me turning the pages. I think it was listening! It came again and again for a whole year, and I read that book every time. On my sister's next birthday, it disappeared.'

She squeezed my fingers again and remained silent. She looked out of the window, and I did too.

'I love the way the snail trails glimmer in the light,' she had said.

'I love you, Nisha,' I had replied.

There wasn't even a pause.

'I didn't come here to love *anyone*,' she said, pulling her hand out of mine. 'I came here to send money to my daughter.' She was so deliberate with her words, as if she had rehearsed them. The way she had stressed *anyone*, with a fierceness in her eyes, made me reluctant to say anything else to her. I nodded and she put her hand on my knee, then dunked a biscuit in the coffee.

Remembering this now, I was all the more convinced that I had scared Nisha away with my proposal, that it had finally been the thing that had been too much for her. She had probably packed her belongings and gone home without telling me. But I had proposed on Saturday and she had left on Sunday. How would she have had time to reserve a flight so quickly? Something didn't quite add up. Perhaps she had already decided to leave before my proposal? And, once I had proposed, that had made it even harder to tell me, so she had just left. I decided that this was the most probable explanation. But I still couldn't be sure.

I noticed that the little bird was struggling to open its right wing. I filled up a smaller container with about an inch of water and placed it in there to bathe. I didn't think its wing was dislocated and I hoped it was bruised rather than broken. The bird moved around in the container, splashing its beak into the water, turning once or twice to glance in my direction. Each time it did this my heart fell to my stomach. When the bird finished its bath it hopped out, without opening its right wing at all, and ate some of the berries that I had put on a plate beside the container.

Eventually, it stopped raining and the sun came out. I decided to head to the river to find some snails: there'd be an abundance of them now after the rain, and I just couldn't sit still.

It seemed that the river had overflowed, carrying along with it all manner of detritus. There were plastic containers and plastic bags, barbed wire, car wheels and hubcaps, a pair of sunglasses, a yellow foam mattress clinging to the side of a tree, even a dead cow. A stench travelled along with it, most likely from the north part of the island, which was often polluted by spills from a badly maintained sewage system. The smells travelled across the water with a southern blowing wind, like today.

Suddenly, I heard a voice – a woman's cry – so quick and sharp I wasn't sure I actually had heard it. I couldn't distinguish voice from wind from rush of river.

'Hello?' I called across the water. But no reply came, even when I called again.

In the mountains, the water is clear and fresh, nothing like the water down here. Before it gets contaminated by human waste, you can drink from it and swim in it; there are waterfalls that pour down amongst the trees. It's the kind of water one might imagine in paradise, if such a place existed.

I went up with Nisha last winter, up to the hills above the valley to sit by the river. She wanted me to show her where my grandparents and parents had lived, where I had grown up – the old farmhouse with the arches was now owned by tourists, who came only in the summer. The rest of the time the building was dark and empty. Nisha wore an abundance of clothing: a scarf, a woolly hat, thick gloves, two pairs of socks, thermal tights beneath her jeans, a thermal top beneath her jumper, and her big puffy coat with the fake fur running around its hood. All this, and her teeth were still chattering! 'See,' she had said, 'isn't it nice to see the place where you grew up, because now I think I know you better.' She planted a big, cold kiss on my cheek.

You see, I thought you were a different person.

If I followed the river through time, would I find Nisha at the top dressed in all her cold weather abundance? Would I find my father and grandfather there with flocks of sheep, both with high boots so they could walk easily though the fields, sheepdogs by their side? The sheep roamed free in the pastures – back then, the borders between farms were fluid, they weren't divided by fences but instead by trails of wild herbs, like rosemary and thyme.

There had been two sheds attached to the farmhouse, one for churning the milk to make haloumi and *anari*, and the other for spinning wool into yarn. My mother and grandmother used the yarn to knit blankets. The men – including me, though I was just a boy – would load the mules with cheese, yoghurt, milk and rolled-up warm woollen throws and head out to the farmers' market. My grandfather, strong as an ox and with a head of thick white hair, loved his animals, caring for them as if they were his children; although it's true that he killed around four or five lambs a year – one especially for Easter after the long fast. The meat was clean and pure. We also had some chickens for fresh eggs, and a dozen turkeys.

I told Nisha all this when we went to the hills, and she had a similar look on her face as she did that day when she had seen the photograph. She held my hand tightly, as if the wind might blow me away.

What I didn't tell her was that sometimes my grandfather and I would go hunting for songbirds. I didn't want to tell her this. My grandfather had shown me how to make the lime sticks. We would make them together in the farmhouse and put them out in the sun to dry, then we would go to the woods and catch about ten birds. He had a singing bird mechanism which had been made in Paris by a French watchmaker who had perfected the sound. There was a bird on this automaton, meticulously crafted, adorned with real feathers. A wind-up key animated the bird and produced the sound. This device, which fit comfortably into the palm of my grandfather's hand, was made of brass and steel components and had a leather bellow. When he wound the key, the movement pumped the bellow which sent air through a tiny whistle, producing the most extraordinary song. If the key was fully wound, the bird would sing for about half an hour.

He would always ask me to wind the key, while we stood in the forest of the mountains, just above the valley. Then he would balance the device in the branch of a tree, covering the metal with leaves so that the birds would not see it glinting in the sun. He made sure not to put up too many sticks. He didn't want to kill any birds unnecessarily. He just wanted to catch enough so that the family could eat some meat in the winter months. Once the lime sticks were set, we would find ourselves a spot in another part of the woods and wait. To pass the time, he often told me stories – Greek myths and legends of Panhellenism and of fantastical beings – all things that, according to my grandfather, had spurred the Greek Cypriots to fight for independence but, at the same time, had convinced some of them of their invincibility. They had a sense of entitlement and desire to join with Greece that was fierce and unforgiving. 'The voice of myth is powerful,' he would say. These were his favourite words.

But sometimes we just waited quietly, listening to the sound of the machine, which was loud and clear, even at a distance.

'Sounds like a real bird, Grandad,' I said, on one such occasion.

'It has a voice of brass and steel,' he said. 'Never confuse the two things.'

At the time, I had no idea what he meant, but I nodded dutifully, like I always did.

He went on: 'You see, we have to eat, and we have to survive, and yet we must protect our dignity and our identity. There are things we do to achieve those things. But we can respect the land and the animals that are on it. Always be kind to the land, the people and the animals that are on it. Remember that. It's the most important rule in the world.'

This was just after the war, when the island had been divided. My father had fought, and he came back without his right hand and with a new voice. When he came trudging up the mountain, a week after we'd heard on the radio that the war had ended, his eyes were different – they had spots of blood in them, and he barely spoke. He only opened his mouth to complain, or yell about one thing or another. I remembered how his voice would suddenly break the silence. Our Turkish friends had disappeared from their houses in the hills and now we were supposed to refer to them as our enemies. The only thing my father said in his old voice – which I remembered as so earnest, so thoughtful – was that he'd killed a friend down there. Though he never told us who it was.

After the war, I learnt a lesson I would never forget: how a person can disappear inside themselves, and that, sometimes, like my father, they are never able to find their way back.

There it was again – the sound of a woman's voice. As if the wind had opened its mouth and let out a cry. I suddenly remembered where I was: the river to my right, the field to the left. Was that just the wind? A crow maybe? Was my mind playing tricks on me? I looked around.

'Is anyone there?' I called again, but there was no reply. I walked up and down the river, I trudged through the rain-soaked land, I walked far and wide, covered as much distance as I could, until I was convinced that I was alone.

I hadn't collected any snails, and the memories of Nisha and my childhood had drained me. I decided to head back home. But I couldn't spend another night wondering about Nisha, thinking I had seen her shadow, questioning whether she had gone or not.

So, before heading up the stairs to my flat, I knocked on Petra's front door.

11

Petra

ALIKI LOOKED OUT OF THE car window at the rain pelting down on the pavement as we waited at the traffic light, on the way to school. She seemed thoughtful and faraway. She'd done her own hair – two plaits hung over each shoulder – and she was wearing a bright blue raincoat over a grey tracksuit and her P.E. trainers. I knew she didn't want to get any of her Converse wet and dirty. She had about six pairs of various colours and designs, some with flower patterns, others with stars or planets or polka dots. Sometimes she purposely wore odd pairs; how she matched them was of some importance. She kept them in a neat row against the wall just outside her bedroom door, and I'd watch her from time to time as she tried out different combinations, sometimes shaking her head and trying another until she felt that her look was just right. She was very particular about her footwear; she wouldn't even let the cats sleep on them: pointing a finger, and in her most adult voice, she instructed the cats to sit *beside* the shoes, not *on* them. If they didn't cooperate, which they often didn't, she showed them the door. As a rule, I didn't allow cats in the house – they are vermin in these areas – but still they would stroll in when doors were left open in the summer months.

I stood at the gate, as Nisha would have done, and watched as Aliki walked to the entrance of the school. She was slow in her movements, avoiding the puddles as if they were landmines. Normally she would jump in them in order to make Nisha scold and laugh. Nisha would tell me about it later: 'That daughter of yours! She drenched her shoes and trousers. She jumps in those puddles like she is Indiana Jones!'

As Onasagorou is pedestrian only, I parked in one of the back streets and made my way on foot through the rain. By the time I arrived at Sun City, Keti was turning over the open sign on the shop door. She stepped aside to let me in and ran to get me a towel and a coffee. Always eager to please and to learn, she was an aspiring eye surgeon, training at the university of Nicosia, who worked part-time as my assistant. She was brilliant at her job, attentive, meticulous. Sun City attracted an elite clientele; indeed, the city's most important politicians, actors, hotel owners – and even an Indian prince – came to us so that they could see the world more clearly and with style, so I only hired the best staff. Keti had 20/20 vision, but shrewdly wore a pair of Chanel tortoiseshells without prescription: she knew how to represent our interests. We sold the latest designs from Tom Ford, Cartier, Versace, Dior, Bvlgari and Chopard. I even had embroidered eyewear by Gazusa, and in an alarmed cabinet behind the counter, I kept the most expensive pair – gold framed with pink lenses and encrusted with 2.85 carats of pink diamonds. I loved the craftsmanship of the individual glasses, each a work of art.

'Where is Nisha?' Keti said, handing me a warm mug of coffee.

'Nisha?'

'It's Thursday,' she said. 'And you are late – we were meant to go through the stock and you have a client in' – she looked at her watch – 'twenty-three minutes.'

'Thursday?' was all I could say at this point. Thursday was the day I brought Nisha in to clean the shop. She would be relieved of her household duties for the day and join me at Sun City to mop and clean the floor, wipe down the shelves and polish the glasses. She would then clean my clinic, followed by the kitchen at the back. She put her heart into it: she knew how important it was to make the shop sparkle.

'Are you OK?' Keti had lifted her glasses, as if this would make her see better, and she was examining my face closely.

'Yes, I'm fine.'

'So where is Nisha?' she asked again.

'Nisha,' I repeated.

Once again, she waited, glasses hovering above her eyes.

'I have no idea.'

She creased her brow.

'I have no idea. I don't know where she is. She's gone.'

'Gone?' She now lowered the glasses onto her nose and bombarded me with questions: Where did she go? Did she say she was leaving? Do you think she went back to Sri Lanka? Any chance she had enough of you? ('Joking – don't look at me like that!')

I answered her questions as best I could. I was exhausted. I realised in that moment that the last few days had caught up with me.

Soon, our first customer came in to collect her prescription sunglasses: Porsche Design with an 18 carat gold frame. She was a new client, with an accent I didn't recognise. Tall, severe blonde bob, sharp fringe, dressed all in black. She'd first visited the shop a couple of weeks earlier when I'd given her an eye test. She put the glasses on now, and stared at herself in the mirror for a while, then she popped the case into her handbag, paid the rest of the money – she had left a deposit of 250 euros – and went out into the rain wearing her new sunglasses.

Keti would normally have had a great deal to say about a customer like this. She would have mused about who she was, where she might have come from. She would have come up with ludicrous and yet at the same time almost plausible stories about why she needed to wear such an expensive pair of sunglasses in the middle of a storm. But today she was quiet, and she looked over at me from the back of the store, where she was checking the stock, and I could see that she was concerned.

The morning proceeded with a few more appointments, some cancellations due to the weather, and just one or two browsers, but it was a mercifully quiet day. Keti went out at lunch and came back with warm haloumi and tomato sandwiches for us both; she closed the shop and brewed coffee. We sat in the kitchen to eat, while the rain continued to fall outside.

'So, let's examine this,' she said, placing one hand on the table, opening it, palm facing up, as if she was holding an eyeball that she was about to dissect.

I nodded.

'She decided to waste her one day off to spend it with you and Aliki in the mountains?'

I nodded again, ignoring Keti's little embellishments, which I had been expecting anyway.

'And while you were there, she asked if she could take the evening off – seeing as she had spent the day practically looking after Aliki – in order to visit—?'

I nodded.

'To visit whom?' Keti prompted.

'I don't know,' I said, and added reluctantly, 'I interrupted her before she could finish her sentence.'

'So, you told her, quite clearly, that she couldn't go.'

'I didn't say no, as such. But it was clear that I disapproved.'

'And you have no idea whom she might have wanted to visit?'

'None whatsoever.'

'So, you went back home, she made dinner, you all sat together to eat, right?'

'Right.'

'Then what?'

'Then I went to bed. I was tired, I wanted an early night. I left Nisha to put Aliki to bed and ready her things for school in the morning.'

'And then in the morning . . .'

'In the morning she was gone. She left her passport and a number of other things that are very special to her. I also found a gold ring, like an engagement ring, on her dresser, that I'd never seen before.'

Keti nodded now, presumably at a loss.

'It's Thursday today,' she said. 'You've been to the police?'

'Yesterday.'

I told her about the whole sorry encounter at the station: what the officer had said, and how I had finally walked out of his office, stepping on his paperwork. But as I relayed the story, I felt a dull ache in my stomach, like something was amiss, something I didn't understand. And it was then that I realised the officer's voice had sounded somehow familiar, as if I had been hearing an echo of something that was coming from inside me.

I couldn't say this to Keti, but I felt a bloom of guilt at this acknowledgement. Blushing self-consciously, I focused on her.

'You've got to search for her yourself,' she said, slapping her hand meaningfully on the table between us.

'How? I don't even know where to begin.'

'You'll figure it out. You can't leave it like this! You can't let a woman who has lived with you and helped you for so many years just vanish, as if she was meaningless.'

I nodded. She was right.

'And your instinct tells you something is wrong?'

'Yes. Absolutely.'

'And this is out of character?'

'Yes.'

'Well, then. You have no other choice.' And that was the last thing she said, before looking at her watch and informing me that lunch was over and our next client would be arriving in about three minutes.

That evening it continued to rain. The boat was brimming over with water. Water fell through the trees in the garden; it saturated the soil and made the patio glisten like a lake. Aliki stalked around the house, holding onto the black cat as if it was her salvation. Sometimes the cat obliged, purring and rubbing its nose on her ear; other times, it pushed her face away with its paw, scrambled out of her arms with a hiss, and dashed for the window.

I couldn't eat that night, but I made a light meal for Aliki. I couldn't stop thinking about my conversation with Keti and the things Nilmini had said. I walked in and out of Nisha's room, hoping to spark a memory, a revelation. Was there something I had missed? Had she mentioned anything that I'd forgotten? It was like attempting to recall a half-forgotten dream.

I kept hearing Keti's words: *You've got to go and search for her yourself.* Heavy words; words that hit me hard with the weight of responsibility. And last night Aliki had asked me to find her.

Yes, this was something I had to do, although I hadn't the slightest idea how.

I decided that I would speak to more of Nisha's friends. It seemed like a place to start. I wondered if they knew anything – and if they did, whether they would tell me.

I knew Nisha was friends with the maids at the gated mansion at the end of the street, the one with two hunting dogs so, on Friday afternoon, I shut my practice early and headed home. The rain had finally stopped, but very few customers had come in – I had been alone in the shop, as Keti studied at university on Fridays.

I decided to make dinner early, then walk over to the gated mansion down the street. But before I'd even started cooking, while Aliki was in the garden attempting to empty the boat of water, the doorbell rang.

It was Yiannis from upstairs. The light from Yiakoumi's shop glowed around him and he stood there staring at me for a moment too long before he spoke.

'Petra,' he said, 'sorry to disturb you. I am wondering . . .' There was a pause, and a shuffle of his feet, as if he was about to change his mind and walk away. '. . . is Nisha in?' He was almost a silhouette, so I couldn't see the expression on his face, but there was something guarded, uncertain, in the tone of his voice.

'No,' I said. 'I'm sorry, Yiannis, but she's not.'

He ran his hand through his hair, streaks of silver illumi- nated in the light that poured from the display window behind him. His movements were so hesitant that I could almost hear all those clocks ticking.

'Do you know where she is?'

'Why?' I said, perhaps too quickly, and he brought his hand to his face and rubbed his stubble. Then he looked over my shoulder, into the open-plan living room, his eyes scanning.

'Well . . . because I haven't seen her,' he said. 'I haven't seen her all week, and I've been worried.'

There was a desperation in him now that I didn't understand. He was lost and vulnerable, like those stray dogs that wander the neighbourhood looking for someone to love. Why was he so concerned about Nisha? There was something niggling at me, something I think I had known for a long time but refused to believe, and it was this thought that made me invite him in.

He was dressed nicely, as if he was heading to a bar for a drink – a perfectly ironed black shirt, opened slightly at the collar, a pair of dark blue jeans – but mud covered his shoes. Mud that hadn't yet dried and crusted.

He stood awkwardly in the middle of the room: it was the first time he'd been inside, and he glanced left and right at the furniture, the photographs on the console table, the dining table. He looked over to the kitchen, where Nisha had spent so much of her time, scrubbing and cooking. It was strange, though – he looked around like he knew the place.

Now, in the light, I could see clearly the desperation that I had sensed in the darkness; it was mainly in the deep crease of his brow and the restlessness of his eyes. We stood there

108

for a moment, neither of us speaking. He was a good-looking man: very dark eyes with thick lashes, and a soft beard that was neatly trimmed, partly black, partly grey. It was strange to have him standing in my living room. We hardly ever spoke, apart from short pleasantries in the garden about the chicken pen or the weather or how the tomatoes and prickly pears were doing.

I wanted to understand his connection to Nisha. I had seen them talking many times in the garden; I had seen the looks they gave each other, of course I had – a touch of the hand, low whispers in the evening . . . but, if there had been something going on between them, I may have needed to dismiss Nisha, even though I couldn't imagine my life without her. Nobody allowed their maids to have sexual or romantic relationships – it was almost unheard of, apart from those maids who ended up marrying their employers.

I couldn't help glancing down at the mud on his shoes, wondering where he'd been. I suddenly realised I should have told him to take them off at the door – *It's not as though Nisha's here to keep the floors clean.* And that thought alone made me suddenly feel so alone, the house so empty without her.

I offered him a drink and he thanked me and asked for alcohol. 'Anything,' he said. 'Something strong.'

I went to the kitchen and poured us both some *zivania*.

When I came back, Yiannis had taken off his shoes and was standing by the console table in his socks, looking at the photographs. He must've seen me looking at his feet.

'I'm sorry that I came in with such muddy shoes,' he said. 'I was out collecting snails. I've had so much on my mind that I'm finding it hard to think.' Before I could respond, he said. 'Is that your husband?' signalling with his eyes Stephanos in his military gear.

'It is.'

He nodded. 'Your daughter looks like him.'

I noticed now that his shoes were lined up neatly by the door.

I put the drinks down on the coffee table and lit the fire. He joined me, perching, uncomfortably, on the edge of the L-shaped sofa. He took a long gulp of *zivania* and for a second it made his jaw clench and his eyes shine. This wasn't a man who was used to drinking spirits.

I wasn't sure if he was waiting for me to speak, but I didn't know what to say anyway. I could have started talking about Nisha, telling him what had been going on this week, but apart from being my tenant, this man was more or less a stranger.

He took another big gulp from his glass and this time scrunched up his eyes. Then he ran his finger over the rim of the glass, again lost in thought.

Eventually I said, 'So, you're worried about Nisha? Do you know her well?' This made him put the glass on the table and rub his eyes with his hands, as if I had just woken him up. He nodded and picked up the glass again.

He was nervous, I could see that, and he opened his mouth a few times to say something, but at first no voice came out. 'When was the last time you saw her?' he eventually asked.

'Last Sunday evening,' I said, cautiously. 'I woke up in the morning on Monday, and she was gone.'

110

This seemed to worry him even more and he stood up and paced up and down in front of the fire, his feet padding softly on the rug, so that his faint moving shadow drifted over the furniture. I thought how absurd it was that this man was in my living room all of a sudden, in his socks.

'I don't know where she is,' I said.

'Do you think she went home?'

'No.'

'How can you be so sure?'

I thought for a few moments, while he stared at me with wide eyes, waiting for an answer. Perhaps it was the fact that he seemed to share my confusion and concern, that I went into Nisha's bedroom and came back with her belongings, those I had taken to the police station. I didn't bring the gold ring. I placed them all on the coffee table without saying a word.

He sat down again and looked at the items. He opened the passport and stared at her picture for a long time. Then he picked up the locket, as if he'd seen it before, and wrapped his hand around it. As for the lock of hair in the plastic bag – he pressed it between his palms, so tight, that I could see blue veins bulging in the backs of his hands.

'So she hasn't gone home.' He said this more to himself than to me. His voice had changed: it rang out clear, filling the quiet room, hovering over us for a while, much like the sound of a gong that reverberates before vanishing into silence.

'Have you been to the police?'

'Yes, I went on Wednesday.'

'What did they say?'

I paused, considering whether to tell him the whole unpleasant story. 'They were no help. They have no interest in searching for her. They said she's probably run away to the north to find other work.'

'Nisha would never do that,' he said. And suddenly I understood clearly – it was the way her name rolled off his tongue, as if he'd said it a thousand times before – that he knew her. He loved her.

There were questions – so many – I could have asked him. But I decided to keep us on our shared concern and knowledge that anyone who knew Nisha even a little bit would know that she would never take off in that way.

'The only time she went away,' I said, 'was a few months ago. She went for the entire weekend to stay with a cousin of hers in Limassol. This woman was about to leave Cyprus and Nisha wanted to take her some things to give to Kumari. She gave me the woman's name, her employer's name, their telephone number – in case her battery went dead or something . . . she didn't just take off. It was all organised.'

Yiannis was silent for a while.

'When was this?'

'In August,' I said. 'Yes, I'm pretty sure that's when it was. I remember the heat that day. She packed an overnight bag and wore an orange linen dress that I had given her. I dropped her off at the coach station in the early morning. She was teary in the car. When I asked her what was wrong, she said she was going to miss Aliki. I remember saying, "Don't be silly! You're only going for a weekend!" But since

Aliki was born, Nisha has never spent a weekend away from us.'

Realisation hit me. Nisha had lived here for nearly ten years and in that entire time, had only spent two days away from us. She had taken care of my daughter and loved her, she had scrubbed my floors and toilets, she had made us hot dinners and kept the garden looking beautiful. She even polished the frame of Stephano's photo every day, and it broke my heart when I recalled the look on her face as she did this. She had lost a husband, too. She gave us everything. In this generosity, she had been the heart of this house. And yet, I had no idea about her life. I knew she held the heart locket some nights, and I knew there was a new gold ring on her dressing table that I had never seen before. How had her husband died? She had never told me, and I had never asked. How had she felt? What was it like to feel something for another man, after losing him? Had Yiannis given her the ring? Had she loved both these men in the way that I had loved Stephanos? Did she love this man sitting before me? Or did he have something to do with her disappearance? I could barely hold one thought before I jumped to another.

I heard a soft bump and saw the toe of a red Converse poking out from the doorway. Aliki was eavesdropping, but the intensity of Yiannis's words surrounded me and pressed down on me. I didn't want to break the spell to scold her.

'Did she say anything?' Yiannis asked now. 'Before she disappeared. Did she say or mention anything that could help us to understand where she might have gone?'

113

'We went up to the mountains on Sunday for a day out. While we were there, she asked if she could take the night off. It seemed as if she wanted to meet someone.'

'Who?'

'I have no idea. She didn't say. And I didn't approve of her going.' I didn't tell him about the whole conversation I'd had with Mrs Hadjikyriacou – that she had seen Nisha leaving that night around ten thirty. Something told me not to.

'So, on Sunday afternoon she was with you in the mountains.' He seemed to be turning this around in his mind. 'And there was someone she wanted to meet that night. You say you didn't approve of her going, but you haven't said if she went or not.'

'Nisha came home with us and I went to bed at nine o'clock. Nisha was here, putting Aliki to bed. Look,' I said, standing up, suddenly exhausted, 'I can see that you're concerned but there's nothing more I can tell you.' I saw that Aliki's shoe had vanished from the entrance to the hallway. 'And plus, it's late, and I haven't made dinner yet. Aliki hasn't eaten and I've been working all day.'

He stood up too, looking dismayed. 'Yes, of course – I'm sorry, Petra. I didn't mean to bother you.' He hesitated for a moment, as if he wasn't sure whether to go out of the front door or the back – either way, there was a stairway that would lead him to his flat. Then he seemed to remember his shoes and went to the front door, bending over to put them on. The mud had dried now and was breaking off in flakes on the rug.

'Thank you for your time, Petra. And if you hear anything . . .'

'I will tell you straightaway.'

He left. After closing the door, I went to the window and saw that he was standing again in the light of Yiakoumi's shop, staring up at his flat, reminding me again of one of those wandering dogs, the ones that people leave on the streets when, for whatever reason, they are no longer good for hunting.

At night, a bat circles the lake, almost invisible against the black water. For a brief moment, the clouds part and the moon catches its large wings, its fragmented flight.

The new moon quickly disappears behind the clouds, as if it had never been there.

The earth around the crater smells fresh from the rain, and the fur of the hare has begun to dry. Earlier, when the sun was high and the air was warmer, the blow flies returned to lay their eggs once more in the open wounds of cracked skin, while the flesh flies deposited larvae around the eyes and in the mouth.

On this night the earth and the sky join without a seam. There are white flowers in the fields, hundreds and thousands of them. Had there been a fuller moon, had there not still been thick clouds in the sky, they would glow like stars, and heaven and earth would be mere reflections of each other.

A man arrives, by foot. He lights up the path with the light of his phone. He has walked for miles along the bank of the river. The artificial light has a metallic quality. He has nothing else on him, no bag, no wallet, just the phone that he holds like a torch in his hand. The light drifts over the hare – he winces – then he directs the light over the lake and it catches the flight of the bat. He walks a few yards until he reaches the gallows frame, his heavy army boots leaving prints in the forgiving soil.

12

Yiannis

I COULDN'T GO UPSTAIRS. I WAS restless.

'Darrling,' a voice said in English to my left. I turned and saw Mrs Hadjikyriacou on her deckchair, a thick throw over her shoulders. Then she reverted back to her native tongue, a concerned look on her face: 'My love, you look heartbroken.'

I said nothing at all.

'How about some baklava?' On a small table beside her, she had an assortment of miniature cakes, as if she was expecting visitors.

'No, thank you, Mrs Hadjikyriacou. I think I'm going to go for a walk. It's a nice evening, if a bit chilly.'

'I wouldn't know. I'm numb to the cold. I have felt nothing, not heat, nor cold, since the war. It's Ruba – she insists on putting this stupid blanket on me. She says I'll catch my death. I tell her I've already caught him, many times before. And I'm stronger than him.'

I nodded. I was sure she was right.

'And I've said to you before, call me Julia. Mrs Hadjikyriacou makes me sound old.' This almost made me laugh, because she looked as though she'd fought her way out of the grave.

She reached over and selected two small portions of baklava, then gingerly folded them in a tissue and pressed them into my hand. She insisted that I looked malnourished and hungry – but then again, every person without a huge gut looked hungry to Mrs Hadjikyriacou.

Thanking her, I took her carefully wrapped parcel and walked past Theo's, where outdoor heaters had been lit and smoke rose from the ovens. Some of the men waved at me and I raised my hand and tried to smile. I continued on down the road, nearing the Green Line, where cats darted from one end of the street to the other, jumping over the dividing fence into the buffer zone. Everything seemed so surreal, like the world was ticking away without me. The only thing that seemed true was the moon.

A cat was trying to get my attention, chirping, weaving through my legs as I walked. The black cat that often hung around with Aliki and Nisha.

I thought about Nisha's passport – the fact that she hadn't taken it with her clearly meant that she had not gone back to Sri Lanka, as I had suspected. This made me feel relief and anxiety at the same time. If she hadn't gone home, then where was she? Why had she not informed anybody? I thought about the locket her late husband had given her and the lock of Kumari's hair. She would absolutely never leave without those two items. Even when she had gone away for those two days, she had taken them with her, neatly tucked into her wallet.

The cat yowled at me now and, when I paused, sprawled itself expectantly on the ground in front of me, paws up, stomach exposed.

I leaned down and stroked it, felt the vibration of its deep, contented purrs. I sat down on the ground, cross-legged, and continued to pet the cat. It seemed to have decided that this was what we both needed to do right then. The street was dark, deserted, with no lights on in any of the houses: most of them probably abandoned this far down the street, near the buffer zone. A new moon hung in the sky, still tinged with red.

I thought about Nisha's orange linen dress and the weekend she had left to stay with her cousin Chaturi in Limassol. The story wasn't as simple as Petra thought.

It began one Sunday in August. Petra had left Nicosia to spend the day with Aliki at Makronisos beach in the east. They'd left early in the morning, as it was a two-hour drive, packing deckchairs, towels and sun hats into the boot of the car. Petra had informed Nisha that they would be gone all afternoon, and would likely have supper in Ayia Napa with a friend. So Nisha and I had the whole day and evening to laze about together. It had been too hot to go anywhere except the sea, and Nisha hated the sea, so we had decided to stay in the cool darkness of the bedroom, with the balcony doors wide open. I will never forget that day. There was

121

hardly a breeze: not even a leaf stirred on the trees. The sound of the cicadas and the smell of jasmine filled the room. Whenever the wind blew, it was hot and brought no relief.

Before noon, Nisha spent some time talking to Kumari on my tablet. She sat at the desk while I lay on the bed, listening to them speaking in Sinhalese, their voices sometimes joyful, sometimes serious, a few words in English. Though I couldn't understand their conversation, I knew Nisha well enough to pick up on the fact that she was distracted. I went to the kitchen and made us both some frappe, with lots of ice cubes and extra milk and sugar for Nisha, just as she liked. I handed it to her as she finished the call; she took one small sip and left it on the side of the desk, then she sat staring out of the open doors, hardly saying a word. We made lunch together, eating hoppers – Sri Lankan pancakes. She stirred the mixture and said a few things like, 'Pass the rice flour' or 'Splash some coconut milk into it now.' I added a ladle of batter to the wok and swirled it around, then she cracked an egg into the bowl-shaped pancake and began to make the garnish of onions, chillies and lemon juice while I fried the rest. 'Don't you think that one's ready?' she said, when I'd left the pancake in the wok too long, because I too had become distracted, wondering what was wrong with her. I knew she didn't like to be asked, so I waited.

Later that night, a full moon hung in the sky. Theo's was bustling with people, the bouzouki was playing and Nisha was lying on her side looking up at the sky. She wanted all the lights off: she felt cooler that way, she'd said. The moonlight was cool. She stared at it, her eyes glazed, as if she was staring at the space between her and the moon.

After what felt like a long time, she sat up, folded her legs, and faced me. I did the same. She looked at me straight in the eyes.

'I'm pregnant.'

'Pregnant?'

She nodded.

'You're pregnant.'

She nodded again. 'We were so careful,' she said. I could make out no obvious expression on her face, it was as blank as a stone. But then she leaned into me and rested her head on my chest and we lay down together.

'What are you thinking?' she asked.

'I think it's great.'

'Do you?'

'Yes.'

She turned on her back, took my hand and placed it on her stomach, then she rested her hand on top of mine. I'd never felt as close to anyone as I did in that moment. Our bodies connected – mine, Nisha's and this little foetus that was growing inside her. Our baby. Mine and hers. A wave of happiness came over me, like someone had opened a window that overlooked the landscape of my childhood and reminded me of what it felt like to be filled with love and wonder. What would this child look like? Perhaps these were premature thoughts, but I imagined that he or she would be everything like Nisha. These images fell into my mind as fresh and cool as rain in the heat of that room.

'What are you thinking?' she said again.

'I think it's wonderful. I love you.'

'That's because you're feeling and not thinking.'

'That's not true,' I said. 'My feelings and thoughts are perfectly in sync!' Then I added, 'For once!' And I laughed at how often we'd both said the words *feelings* and *thoughts*.

But Nisha didn't laugh. She gently lifted her hand from mine, lifted my hand from her stomach and continued to gaze out of the window. Finally, she said: 'I will lose my job. Nobody wants a pregnant maid.'

'We'll find a way. I'll help you find something else to do. Or I'll take care of you. Whatever you want, we'll make it work.'

'You don't understand,' she said. 'What about Kumari? I have to send money. If I lose my job, how will she live? I have debts to pay off. I have debts with the agency, Yiannis – I'm still paying them for bringing me here. And what about my mother? She is relying on me, too. It's because of the work I do here that they have money to eat and live and go about their everyday lives. What would happen if I lost this job? It's not just you and me and this baby.'

She said all this in one breath and her voice broke, though tears didn't come: she seemed to swallow them.

'I understand,' I said. I brought her closer to me, held her. 'What if I helped you financially? What if I gave you money to pay off your debt and also to send back home?'

'With what?' she said. 'Wild asparagus and snails?' Her voice held an edge of derision.

And she was right, because if that was the whole truth

124

then I'd be nothing short of a lunatic. I wanted to tell her about the songbirds. But if I told her, it would break her heart.

'The thing is,' she said, 'if I didn't have this debt, I probably would have been able to go home by now, and we wouldn't be here . . . we wouldn't be in this situation anyway.'

She was matter-of-fact, decisive; her words a brutal blow to a fragile dream. But then she took my hand again, and this time pressed it down onto her stomach so that I could feel the weight of her love in that small push.

The following evening, I decided to tell her about the songbirds. It was the only chance I had to get her to believe that I had the means to help her financially. I wanted this baby, our baby, more than anything. It was late when she appeared at my door – we were back to our usual 11 p.m. rendezvous, since Petra and Aliki had returned from the beach. After Nisha had made them dinner and put Aliki to bed, she came up to my flat. I took her by the hand and led her to the spare room. I unlocked the door and for a few moments she stood there, confused, looking around, resting her eyes on one of the industrial fridges.

'What is all this?' she said.

'I have another way of making money,' I said. 'I want you to know that I've saved enough and I can support you, Kumari, and your mother.'

'But you told me this door was always closed because it was such a mess in here.'

In fact, it was relentlessly tidy and I could see her taking all this in, looking around at the lime sticks, the wicker shoulder-pouch I took with me on hunts, the black calling devices lined up on the small desk, the containers stacked against the wall.

'It's like Indiana Jones with fridges. What have you been doing?' she said

'After I lost my job at Laiki, I became involved in hunting. I was desperate. I could never have survived selling mushrooms and—'

'Hunting what?' she interrupted me.

'Songbirds,' I said, quietly.

'Songbirds?'

She went straight to one of the fridges, opened it and looked inside. Luckily, they were all empty on that day. Then she shut it and opened the second fridge, and the third. Leaving this last door open, she turned to face me.

'Where are they?' she asked.

'I don't have any right now. I just made a delivery.'

She nodded, and there was a look of disappointment on her face. But this feeling belonged only to her; she wasn't willing to share it with me in words.

'I don't want to do it,' I said, trying to make her understand. 'Once you get into it, it's hard to stop. It's a bit like drug dealing – there's a huge underground organisation, and they won't let you go, it's too risky for them.' I didn't tell her that the previous week a man I knew had handed in his notice, and that night his boat shed had mysteriously burnt to the ground.

'Who are *they*?' Nisha asked.

'The men at the top.'

'So, once you make a decent amount of money, you want out and you're stuck?'

'Yes.'

She closed the fridge door and brought her hand to her stomach, her eyes to the ground.

'What I'm saying to you is that I'm going to find a way out of this. I will. But I have more than enough money to be able to support us until I find a different job. The recession has passed now. I have experience in finance. I know the way I made my money isn't ideal, but we can be a family.'

'Not ideal.' She repeated faintly. She turned and walked out of the spare room, then headed for the back door. Her hand on the door knob, she turned back to me and said, 'I'll think about it,' then disappeared down the stairs.

After that, she didn't come to see me for several days. But about a week later, she turned up at my door – I remember it was a Friday morning and I was surprised to see her in the light of day. She looked so beautiful, in a vibrant orange dress that brought out the gold in her eyes. Her hair was tied up in a ponytail. Her lips glimmered with gloss. On her feet she still wore her practical, scuffed, high-impact walking sandals.

I wanted to reach out and hold her. 'Come in,' I said.

'No. I've just come to tell you that I'm going to Limassol for the weekend, to stay with my cousin Chaturi. Do you remember when she came to visit me?'

'Of course,' I replied.

'Well, she's leaving to go back to Sri Lanka next week and I'm going to give her a few things to take to Galle.'

I nodded.

'I need some time away from here so that I can think.'

I nodded again.

'Don't call me or try to contact me. It's just for a few days.'

'Don't worry,' I said, 'I understand.'

Her lips broke into a small smile, but her eyes carried a lingering sadness. Then she walked down the stairs and I watched her as she went into her bedroom through the patio doors.

After the weekend passed, Nisha returned. Late on Monday night, I heard a knock at the door. She was standing there in a bright white nightdress, a pink cardigan draped over her shoulders. Her hair was loose, her face flushed like she'd been running.

'I couldn't wait to see you,' she said.

She put her arms around me immediately and tucked her face into the crook of my neck; I felt the damp warmth of her body against mine, her breath against my skin. I was flooded with relief, joyful at her return, grateful to have her in my arms again.

'I wanted to come last night, but Aliki was running a fever. I couldn't leave her,' she said.

We lay down on the bed. There was a soft summer breeze. She lay on her back, I on my side; I kissed her shoulder and stroked her hair, just as she liked. I almost couldn't believe that she was there.

'How is Chaturi?' I asked.

'Do you like my nightdress? She gave it to me as a gift. She made it herself. It's beeralu lace.'

'It's beautiful,' I said. And it was so beautiful. I ran my hand over the fine patterns of flowers. It was like a pure white garden.

'She drew it on graph paper first, then attached it to the *kotta boley* with pins. She then took each thread around the pin. Can you imagine what a task it is?'

'I can.'

'Her employers were away this weekend, so we had the house to ourselves. I helped her with the chores, then we sat the rest of the time in the garden. We talked while she weaved. She was desperate to finish it before I left. She said she had a feeling she would not see me for a very long time.'

Over the years, Nisha had seen Chaturi every couple of months, usually when Chaturi came with her employers to Nicosia for a Sunday visit. They had family there and they would drop her off at Petra's for the day, then collect her in the evening before heading back to Limassol. It was always a special occasion for Nisha. The two women would spend time making *aluwa*, a nutty sweetmeat with cashews, or my favourite, *aasmi*, made with coconut milk and the juice of cinnamon leaves. Chaturi would leave with a couple of Tupperware boxes filled with sweets. Nisha would always set aside a few slices in foil and bring them up for me later in the evening, telling me all about their conversations, Chaturi's jokes, the news from home.

'I hope she is wrong about that,' she said. 'That it will be a long time before she sees me again.' She ran her fingers over the flowers of her nightgown.

'I'm sure it won't be too long' I said, reassuring her.

She paused a moment, and then said: 'I made an appointment at the clinic in Limassol to end the pregnancy, but I couldn't do it.' Her eyes were wide now, fearful. 'This baby is going to start growing and I'm going to be left without a job and without a home. Do you know what happens to women like me who break the rules?'

Her words were tumbling from her mouth now, and I could barely keep up.

'My friend, Mary, from the Philippines, well, her employer saw her jumping over the fence at night to see her boyfriend and fired her on the spot. It was almost impossible for her to find work after that, because this employer was very well known in the community, and respected. She had to move into a hostel with fifteen other women on the other side of the island. The conditions were so bad that she ended up selling her body to stay in an old man's villa by the sea with three other women.'

I reached for her, but she pushed me away. She distanced herself from me, so she could look me in the eyes.

'And little Diwata down the road, well, her ex-employer beat her. She had bruises on her arms and legs and was only allowed to eat such a small amount of food each day that she ended up shrinking down to nearly nothing. She looked like she was twelve! Well, she was lucky because she found another employer. He has bought her a car, he never bruises her body, and he buys her new clothes and gives her his credit card to buy whatever she likes. Why do you think that is?'

She stared at me without blinking. I said nothing.

'Petra will fire me. She will. Who knows where I will end up? And if I want to find another job, I will have to give up the baby. But what if I can't do it? Just like I couldn't terminate the pregnancy.' Tears fell from her eyes now and she briskly wiped them with the back of her hand. 'I stepped through the door. I actually went to the clinic.'

There was nothing I could say. I wanted to tell her it would be OK, that for her the outcome would be different, I would help her. But what did I know of her world? Of what she owed. I couldn't bring myself to make promises I couldn't understand.

After a silence, she finally spoke. 'Whatever happens,' she said, 'you have to promise me that you will stop what you are doing to the songbirds. It's not a good thing.'

'I promise,' I said. 'I can promise that.'

Suddenly the cat's ears flattened and it hissed. From behind I heard footsteps approaching. I turned and saw Spyros with his poodle. Spyros, the postman. A well-built guy, covered in tattoos from the neck down. His poodle, tiny, well-groomed, in a khaki military bomber jacket designed especially for dogs. In the summer it had a sun umbrella attached to its leash. The discrepancy between them always made Nisha laugh when she saw the pair from my balcony on Sundays. She would lean forward carefully, so that prying neighbours would not see her, and whistle the theme tune of Indiana Jones, and he would whistle it back. It meant: *I know you're there and your secret is safe with me.* Spyros the postman knew most things, everyone in the neighbourhood knew that Spyros the postman knew most things, but his lips were always sealed. Nisha loved this game they played – it made her feel more accepted, more human, she said. She had told me that *Indiana Jones and the Temple of Doom* had been filmed in Kandy in the eighties, and as a child she had loved to imagine all the adventures taking place just 200 km or so from her home.

The cat now hissed, circling Spyros's dog, who growled in return, making a show of pulling at his lead. The dog bared its tiny teeth and the cat hissed again. It was an amusing stand-off, and if I hadn't been so upset, I would have laughed.

'Sit, Agamemnon!' Spyros said. The dog obeyed – sort of – continuing to growl from deep in its chest.

'What are you doing here, mate?' he asked, looking down at me.

'Thinking.'

'On the ground? In the middle of the street?'

'Yes.'

He sat down beside me. 'Something's wrong.'

'Nisha is missing. I don't know where she's gone.'

'How long?'

'Nearly a week now. Last Sunday night or Monday morning.'

Spyros furrowed his brow, seemed caught up in thought. 'I saw her on Sunday,' he said, 'around ten thirty in the evening. I took Agamemnon out later than usual because my mum had come to visit. I took my usual route, I was heading down *this* street and she walked past me pretty fast. She was in a rush. I asked her where she was off to and she said she was going down the road to Maria's bar to meet Seraphim.'

'Seraphim?' A jolt like a rush of ice went down my spine. 'Why?'

'I have no idea,' he said. 'That's all I know. But I saw her and I'm certain it was Sunday night.'

The cat followed me home like a tiny shadow, then disappeared into the darkness of the back garden. I was surprised to find the little bird sitting on the rug in the hallway near the door when I arrived. It was hopping about now. I put out some fresh water and bread and went out to sit on the balcony. I opened a cold beer and drank it quickly. Why was Nisha meeting Seraphim? And why had he not told me he had seen her? And what in God's name would she be doing in a place like that? I knew the bar. It was the place I had met Seraphim back when he first recruited me.

I couldn't sleep for thinking about it all, and was awake when, once again, at 5 a.m., my iPad started to ring. I got up and saw Kumari's name flashing on the screen. It stopped and started again. Once again I could do nothing: I was frozen to the spot. But the name begged me to answer, it pounded at the darkness with desperation.

I answered.

Kumari blinked at me, shocked to see my face. 'Where is Amma?' she said in English, stretching her neck in an attempt to see behind me. The girl was wearing her school uniform and had a rucksack with purple straps on her shoulders.

'I'm Yiannis,' I said. 'Do you remember me?'

She nodded. 'Of course I remember you, Mr Yiannis. We have spoken so many times! You are Amma's friend.'

'That's right. Is your grandmother there? Can I speak to her?'

'She just go to shop.'

'Your mum is at work. She left the tablet here with me. She told me to tell you that she loves you, to be good at school and that she'll speak to you very soon.'

Kumari nodded. 'Okay, Mr Yiannis,' she said. 'Thank you. You be good at work too.' Then she smiled. There was a cheekiness to her, like her mother. It made my heart ache.

Then she was gone, and the screen was blank once more.

13

Petra

ON SATURDAY MORNING, I DECIDED to visit the gated mansion at the end of the street. I told Aliki that Mrs Hadjikyriacou would be keeping an eye on her, but she was free to play in the garden. She nodded, without seeming too bothered, picking up a favourite book and heading out the door to the boat. She got in and started reading. I brought her out a plate of orange slices and kissed her head, then thanked Mrs Hadjikyriacou and told her I wouldn't be gone long. She knew my errand and was happy to help.

My first stop was Yiakoumi's shop. I had brought Nisha's journal with me and now clutched it to my chest as I stepped into the shop. There were no customers yet this early on a Saturday, but, as I had expected, Nilmini was there cleaning, bending over wiping dust from the glass cases under the counter. Yiakoumi was nowhere to be seen.

'Good morning,' I said.

'Good morning, madam,' she said. She paused in her dusting, standing up and eyeing the journal in my hands.

'Nilmini, will you do me a favour? Or, in fact, a favour for Nisha?'

'Of course, madam,' she said.

'This is a journal that Nisha kept,' I said, placing it on the counter. 'Would you be able to read it and tell me if there is anything in it that might help me to find her?'

She took the journal from my hands and opened it, flicking through, glancing at the pages. 'I will do it, madam,' she said. 'I will read this for you.'

I was in a hurry so I thanked her and left, and she watched me from the large window and waved as I continued down the street.

I walked past the church and caught wafts of lavender from its garden. The sun was still low in the sky in this early part of the day, and it promised to be a sunny and crisp autumn afternoon. A maid swept the path in front of the church, clearing it of leaves and cockroaches. She looked up and nodded as I passed.

There was a sculptor's workshop further down the street: a terraced property with no front wall or door or window, just a large mouth of an entrance that was always open – there was not even a shutter which came down at night to secure the premises. The cavernous space was strewn with broken planks, rusty nails, boxes of tools and twisted tree branches scattered about like severed limbs. From time to time the owner, a middle-aged man called Muyia, appeared in there, working, but more often than not it looked like a ramshackle, abandoned garage. However, Muyia was there this morning and I could see that he was focused on a piece of wood, chipping away, shaping something that seemed to mean very much to him: his concentration was so intense, his brow was furrowed and his lips were pressed together tightly.

Hearing my footsteps, he looked up and then raised his hand in greeting. 'Petra! How was your trip to the mountains?' he called.

'Mountains?' I said, coming up to the entrance.

'Yes, Nisha said she was going with you to the mountains. Come in, come in! Let me show you something.'

I stepped over bits of twisted wire and scrap wood. The space was deep and should have been dark but he had two bright lamps over his work station. This was the first time I'd been inside, and I realised that it wasn't as much of a mess as I'd thought. In fact, there was a gigantic shelf that held beautiful, carved wooden sculptures. They were mostly faces of people, but also animals: a snake, an elephant, three dragonflies hovering on invisible strings. There were finely carved flowers and various birds and fish, even a globe of the Earth – all crafted intricately with minute, precious details. They were unpainted, so they retained their soft honey colour and you could see the wood's grain. I felt as though I'd stepped into some kind of magical forest.

'Do you like them?' he said.

'They are extraordinary.'

He smiled at the compliment, and said, 'Have a look at this.'

I turned to see the piece he had just been working on. It was a Madonna and child, enormous, almost life-sized. There was a quiet beauty to the woman, to the curve of her cheek bones and the soft sweep of her eyes and nose, her heart-shaped face. A strand of hair fell down over one eye, and a small owl perched on her shoulder. But what truly struck me was how life-like she was – not just in her fine appearance, but in her essence, her energy; her strength and practicality. It was in the soft but certain gaze of her eyes as she looked down at the child in her arms, the firm and tender touch of her fingers on the child's thigh.

'She is holding *her* child,' he said, deeply emphasising the word *her*.

He looked at it now, staring at his creation, as though he had forgotten that I was there. Squinting his eyes, he ran his thumb over the wing of the owl. 'Hmm,' he said, 'I need to fix that bit. Do you see how the angle there is too sharp, in the wing? It gives the character of the bird the wrong quality, wouldn't you say?'

'I wouldn't know what quality the owl is supposed to have.'

At that point he looked at me for a moment, then creased his brow and nodded slightly, as if he had understood or remembered something. Then he said, 'You know, we've never really spoken before. Imagine, all these years as neighbours and this is the first time we've said more than a few words to each other.'

I looked again at the statue and saw something I hadn't noticed before: there was a deep sadness in the woman. It emanated not just from her eyes, but from everywhere, her posture, her enduring silent touch, even her stillness; it was even in the grain of the wood. And there was something else about her – she looked remarkably like Nisha.

'Would you like a coffee?' he said. 'I can bring another stool for you to sit down.'

'No,' I replied. 'I'm afraid I'm out on an errand and I don't have much time.'

Suddenly, I felt a desperate urge to leave. My mind was rattling with questions, but I wasn't ready to ask them. Did she pose for this statue, was she his muse? How many other men in the neighbourhood did she know? I had started to become worried about what else I might discover about this stranger who had lived in my house, brought up my daughter, orchestrated our lives, made our house a home after Stephanos died. Who was this woman who I had previously seen only as a shadow of myself? A dark and beautiful shadow, who rattled around in old sandals and with fire in her eyes.

It struck me now that it was I who had been her shadow.

I quickly took leave of Muyia, stuttering my apologies and promising to come back for a coffee another time. I did want to speak to him more, but I had to sort out my questions. And anyway, I'd already been delayed and didn't want to leave Aliki with Mrs Hadjikyriacou all morning.

I hustled along the street, to the gated mansion, a colossal neoclassical building with balconies flowering at every window. I pressed the buzzer and looked into the intercom. After a moment there was a crackly voice: 'Madam, come in!' followed by a loud click. The gate creaked open.

I'd visited Mr and Mrs Kosta's mansion once before when they'd thrown a New Year's party. All the neighbours – well, the ones they deemed worthy – had been invited, and I had made the cut. I supposed it was because I mixed with the rich and famous in my work; perhaps they thought I would have some good stories. This oversized house was their retirement home: they'd repatriated from the UK, where Mr Kostas had owned a chain of insurance firms in London.

I walked along a path, through the meticulously kept orchard: on one side were shoe-fig trees, cacti and apple and pear trees; on the other, lemon, cherry and apricot trees, grape-vines and tomato plants. Winter was approaching so the trees were losing their leaves, but I knew in just a few months tiny buds would appear on the branches and in a few weeks after that this whole place would smell like a perfumerie.

Halfway down the path I hesitated, expecting someone to come out to greet me.

'Madam, come in!' a voice called, and I followed the path around the house to the back garden, where there was an open lawn and a large metallic cage that held two sand-coloured hunting dogs. They were lean and muscular, and should have looked fierce, but their eyes were docile and calm. Inside the cage, one of the maids was bent over, cleaning the dog's backside.

'Madam,' she said, standing up, holding her gloved hands

behind her back, 'Binsa . . . she opened for you. She is inside. Please go inside.' She pointed at the door beneath the terrace. 'I have to clean the dog, he has a bad stomach today.' While she spoke, the dog remained with its hind end up in the air, its front paws stretched in front, obediently waiting for her to continue.

I thanked her and walked up a couple of steps to the patio, where a glass door was open and smells of cooking wafted out.

'Madam, this way!'

Binsa was in the kitchen, deep-frying. 'I'm sorry, madam, I couldn't come to the door. I am making *keftedes* for sir and madam. You know, you can't leave these things in the oil. It is no good for them. And how is Nisha, madam? She hasn't come to the gate to talk for a long time. We miss her. I called her phone but nothing. You know that madam doesn't let us go out, so I couldn't come to see her. I hope she is OK, madam?' She flicked her eyes towards me now, but swiftly returned her attention to the oil and the fire.

'Where are sir and madam?' I said.

'They're out shopping today, madam. If you come back in one hour, they will be here.'

'Actually, Binsa, it was you I wanted to speak to.'

She looked up from her work again for a moment, furrowed her brow, then quickly said, 'OK, madam. I will take out this lot, three minutes, and talk to you before I do others. Can you wait a few minutes?'

'Of course, Binsa,' I said. 'Take your time.'

On the counter by her side there was a large platter full

of raw meatballs dusted with flour, ready for the oil. Nisha had spoken to me many times about Binsa and Soneeya from Nepal. Both in their twenties, about ten years younger than Nisha, their journey to Cyprus was the first time either of them had been away from their families. Before making the decision to migrate, Binsa had been a young radio host at her local radio station, and Soneeya had been a nursery nurse, I think. Their English wasn't as good as Nisha's, because Nisha had learnt it back in Sri Lanka when she was a little girl. But Binsa and Soneeya had been here for two years and were already speaking quite well. Apparently, Mrs Kosta gave them classes in the evenings. Nisha had told me how they were not allowed out of the grounds because the Kostas were worried that they would be led astray.

Soon Soneeya came in, taking off her blue rubber gloves, chucking them in the bin and washing her hands thoroughly with plenty of soap. Before long, I was sitting in the living room with a cup of tea in my hand, the two women looking at me intently.

'I'm worried about Nisha,' I said.

At this, Soneeya nudged Binsa hard in the thigh with her fist and scrunched up her lips, saying something in Nepali. Then Soneeya got up and left the room, returning with something shiny in her hand. She offered it to me. It was a bracelet, a silver bangle with a single evil-eye charm. I held my breath and picked it up, turning it around in my hand. And there it was. The inscription of Aliki's name, engraved on the inner side of the bracelet. We had given this bracelet

142

to Nisha for her birthday a few years earlier. She wore it every day. The clasp was broken now.

I looked up at Soneeya and Binsa. 'How do you have this?' I asked, my breath quickening, panic blooming in my chest.

'I told Binsa many times this week to ask madam to give us your phone number so we could call you, madam. We tried Nisha's mobile and there was no answer. I didn't ask madam because Binsa is her best maid. I am number two here. Binsa needed to ask her.'

'Soneeya found it, madam,' Binsa quickly broke in. 'She was walking the dogs, to the end of the street by Maria's. There is an old house there. No one lives there. Soneeya sometimes lets the dogs go do their business in that yard,' she said, shooting Soneeya a reproving look. 'And she saw something shiny by the front door. It was Nisha's bracelet. We became worried.'

'Very worried,' agreed Soneeya.

'And then Nisha didn't answer her phone,' Binsa said, 'and we thought that maybe Nisha went to see her cousin, maybe she went away again. It is none of our business. This is what I said to Soneeya.'

I put the tea-cup on the coffee table. 'The thing is,' I said, cautiously, 'I have no idea where Nisha is. She has simply disappeared. She left her passport and other important items. I can't get through to her on her phone, either. Her friend Yiannis has not seen her, but several neighbours say they saw her going out on Sunday evening.'

I waited as the women looked at each other and chatted,

143

quickly, passionately, in Nepali. Soneeya's voice rose now and then with alarm, whereas Binsa sounded calmer.

'Madam,' Binsa said suddenly, 'have you been to the police station?'

I explained to them that I had, but the police would not help; leaving out, of course, what Officer Kyprianou had said about foreign workers.

'I came to you,' I said, 'because I was hoping you might know something about where she went.'

They both shook their head.

'Did she ever mention leaving me? Maybe going over to the north to find other work?'

'Never!' said Soneeya, quickly. 'Madam, Nisha would never even think of doing this. That is not Nisha.'

I nodded. I knew of course that she was right.

'Do you know anything about Yiannis?'

The girls started speaking in Nepali again, whispering, as if there was a chance I might understand them. They were clearly in disagreement, but after some time, Soneeya turned to me.

'Madam, Binsa is unsure about speaking to you but I think you care about Nisha. I would like to say this to you because Yiannis maybe knows something that you don't know.'

I sat up straighter at this point and I think Binsa noticed, as she looked concerned. She mumbled a few words under her breath and Soneeya shushed her.

'This man, Yiannis, he loves Nisha so much. He *loves* her, madam. I don't know how to say this to you. He *loves* her from here to the moon.' She made a huge gesture with her hands at this point, opening them wide.

'I see,' I said. 'Does she love him, too?' It seemed like a reasonable question to ask.

'Yes, madam,' said Soneeya. 'If anybody knows a thing about where Nisha is, he will know. She tells him all her secrets, everything.'

I nodded, a knot forming in my stomach, like a stone. It was clear from how anxious Yiannis had been last night that he did not know a thing.

'Madam,' said Binsa now, interrupting my thoughts, 'do not tell Nisha we told you this information. She will be unhappy with us. She loves her job too, madam, she never wants to lose this job with you. She worries that you will not like her being with Yiannis.'

'I promise,' I said. 'I won't say a thing.'

At that point the sound of a buzzer rang through the room.

'Ah!' Binsa exclaimed, jumping up and heading to the large front window. From her apron pocket she retrieved a gate remote and clicked it a few times.

'Sir and madam are here!' Soneeya said, beginning to gather up our tea-cups.

I heard the creak of metal gates and the soft sound of an engine, followed by the thump of car doors. Quickly, I riffled through my purse, found an old receipt and wrote my phone number on it. 'Soneeya' – I pressed the paper into her hand – 'please call me if you think of anything else. Anything at all.'

Soneeya nodded and tucked the receipt into her pocket, spiriting the tea tray off into the kitchen.

Binsa opened the front door and Mr and Mrs Kosta came in. They were both wearing soft cashmere jumpers, with jeans and tennis shoes. Mrs Kostas lifted her gold-framed Armani glasses (I recognised them; I'd sold them to her), pushing them up into her hair.

'Petra!' she said, 'how nice to see you. What brings you here?' Before I could reply she turned to Soneeya. 'Soneeya, the shopping's in the car. Go.'

Soneeya nodded and said, 'Yes, madam, I'll go now.' She rushed out to help Binsa, who was already bringing in bags from the car and placing them in the hallway.

Mr Kostas, with a mop of thick brown hair, greeted me and excused himself to make a phone call. Binsa now returned to the kitchen, working quickly to finish the meatballs she had left during our chat, clearly trying to make up for lost time. Mrs Kostas placed her keys in a large bowl in the middle of a round marble table and hung her bag on a coat stand by the door, then turned to speak to me.

'Petra, have you been well? I haven't seen you for so long. Did my girls take care of you? I do hope so. They are improving. I've been teaching them, but I tell you, I'm thinking of separating them, sending one to work elsewhere. They distract each other too much when they're together and, realistically, do I really need two maids?' She paused in front of me now and lowered her glasses onto her nose again. It was clear that she'd had some work done on her forehead and her lips.

'Well, I don't know,' I said. 'I guess it depends how much needs to be done.'

146

'I'm *inundated* with work from the charity events I organise. And this is *such* a big house.' She laughed and sighed and shook her head, as if there was always way too much work to even mention, and then she offered me a seat in the living room with a wrinkled hand that was tipped with long, red, coffin-shaped nails.

'Oh, thank you,' I said, 'but I really must be going.'

'But I've only just come through the door!'

'Actually, I came to speak to Binsa and Soneeya.'

'Oh?' She eyed me suspiciously.

'The thing is that Nisha, my maid, my . . . girl, has . . . well, how shall I put this? She has been gone for several days and I wanted to see if Soneeya and Binsa have heard from her or if they know anything.'

'I see,' she said, glancing over to the kitchen, where her maids were working. 'I doubt they know anything, as they really don't have many friends and acquaintances. I make sure of that.'

Soneeya came out of the kitchen holding a tray with a tea-pot and two cups with saucers.

'Are you sure you won't have a drink? I could get Soneeya to bring an extra cup, there's always plenty in the pot. Soneeya! What did I tell you? We drink our tea with milk in this house! Go and bring some. Pour a little into the small jug. Goodness, I've told her so many times. These girls have the attention spans of fleas.' She sighed, then continued. 'Petra, dear, don't look so worried! Don't overly concern yourself. If Nisha has gone, she's gone. They do that some-times, you know? These women can drift around the world without a second thought. Oh, how I wish I had that luxury!' Her face creased into a grimace, but her forehead remained smooth as stone.

'Well . . .' I began.

'Well,' she said, in a pronounced whisper, 'no more distractions for Soneeya and Binsa, hmm?' With that, she stepped towards the front door, signalling that our chat was over, and waved at me as I weaved back through the orchard to the gate, which was now creaking open. 'Come again for a coffee!' she called. 'Call me soon!'

In the late afternoon light, the sunset and the lake are one. Beautiful streaks of pink and red wash through the sky, which is luminous and silky. The hare is no longer distinct. Its skin has ruptured further and is almost completely decayed. Fly eggs have hatched into maggots in its eye and in the expanding wound around its neck, while the larvae in the mouth have grown, feeding on flesh. The same kind of larvae have also filled the rotten hole in the abdomen; feeding and feeding, converting the tissue of the hare into their own. The hare is slowly disappearing. But its hind legs still look strong and its ears still look as though they are blowing in the breeze; its fur is still the warm colour of the earth.

The rusty metal of the gallows frame looks ochre, bathed in the pink light. On clear and quiet afternoons such as this, the locals believe they can hear the ghosts of the men underground working, endlessly working until they die. Their effort is lost now but it was also lost then – not to their families, no doubt, but to the rest of the world. On they worked, like ants, while copper blazed in the light of the upper world.

If you listen carefully, apparently, you can still hear them calling to one another beneath the soil.

14

Yiannis

HY WOULD NISHA HAVE GONE to the bar to meet Seraphim? I had been stuck on this since Friday night. All day Saturday, packing up the birds and preparing for deliveries, ticking off the orders against the containers, making sure all the inventory was properly distributed, I thought about it. I wanted to call him and confront him, but he had gone away for a couple of nights so I decided to wait. I'd be meeting him for a hunt in a few days and I would rather speak to him face to face, see his expression as well as hear his voice.

On Sunday, I set out on deliveries. They would take me all day, and most were usual customers, so I could drive the route practically without thinking. While part of my mind steered my truck down the narrow streets, navigating intersections and traffic, another part of my mind travelled the past.

I thought about the night Nisha came to my apartment, after her visit to Chaturi. It had been the middle of August and extremely hot. When she told me she could not terminate the pregnancy, I had gone out the next day to buy her a ring. I visited the jewellers on Ledra Street and bought a simple gold ring with a blossom-cut diamond. I was not *simply* going to propose, but suggest that we leave Cyprus together, and move to Sri Lanka. In my mind, this would solve two problems: the first, that Nisha would finally be with Kumari; the second, that I could stop the poaching without having to face the consequences. I reasoned that it wouldn't be too difficult for me to find a job in Sri Lanka, particularly with my background in finance and my experience working with foreign markets. I am fluent in both English and Greek.

While this may sound well thought out, it was impulsive. It is my nature, and it's what made me good at banking. But the truth is, I was following my heart and not my head and therefore failed to recognise the challenges to my plan. Like how Nisha would feel being completely reliant on me financially. Like whether we would have enough money to settle Nisha's debts to her hiring agency in Cyprus, or did I think we could just run out of town and leave them unsettled? Like whether Nisha would want to leave Petra and Aliki – as much as she wanted to return to her own daughter, would it be so easy for her to leave behind the Cypriot girl she had raised? All of these thoughts, these contingencies, I tucked away somewhere, refusing to derail my dream of a free life with the woman I loved.

The weekend after her return from Chaturi, I went to the supermarket to buy the ingredients for Nisha's favourite vegetable rice and curry. I had some *kakulu* rice at home, plus basics such as coconut and turmeric, and some chillies that Nisha had grown and dried in the garden. I bought pineapple, sweet potatoes, aubergines. It was a simple meal, but one that I knew reminded Nisha of home.

That Sunday, she sat on a kitchen chair while I made lunch. Aliki and Petra had gone to the beach again and wouldn't be back until very late, so Nisha had the whole day and night off. I didn't want her to lift a finger: she was constantly working, hardly ever taking a break for herself. She had her bare feet up on the chair, arms around her legs, chin resting on her knees. She was wearing a pale blue summer dress, a pass-me-down from Petra. One of the straps had fallen off her shoulder, which was smooth and golden-brown. The chalky blue contrasted with her skin so much that it almost glowed. She was beautiful. Nisha was always beautiful, in every single way.

I was dicing the pineapple when she said, 'I'd recognise you if you were a lion.'

'What?' She often came out with bizarre things, but this was odd even for her.

'If in another life you were a lion, I think I would recognise you and still love you.'

'What if I were a snake?'

'Still, I'd know it was you.'

'A jellyfish?'

'Yes.'

'Cockroach?'

'Absolutely.'

'Is this assuming we are both lions or both cockroaches?'

'Yes,' she said.

'OK, what if you were a deer and I was a lion? Would you still love me?'

She thought about this as I threw the pineapple in the wok and began to cut the aubergine.

'I think we will meet again in all our future lives.'

I added the spices to the vegetables and began to boil the rice.

'Do you mind if I lie down?' she said.

'Of course not. I'll call you when it's ready.'

She went over to the bedroom and I could hear that she had turned on the fan. I thought about what she had said: *I'd recognise you if you were a lion,* and suddenly a different meaning came to mind. Because, in fact, in this life, I *was* a predator. First with stocks and shares, and now with the songbirds. Had she been somehow referring to this? I could not be sure. But a deep feeling of guilt overtook me. I had promised Nisha that I would stop hunting and I was planning on keeping that promise. But was it enough? Would that change who I was, a hunter, a predator? Or was the poaching only part of that truth?

I had the odd feeling that she was in love with the man I should have been.

I poured myself a large glass of wine and gulped it down to wash away all the questions.

When dinner was ready, I went into the bedroom to tell

Nisha. She was lying on her back on the bed with her eyes closed.

'Are you asleep?' I whispered.

She shook her head. I sat beside her on the bed.

'In one story,' she said, 'a married couple ask the Buddha how they can remain together in this life and be together in future lives as well. The Buddha said, "If both husband and wife wish to see one another not only in this present life but also in future lives, they should have the same virtuous behaviour, the same generosity, the same wisdom." I know you're not my husband but if we want to stay together we have to try and be on the same . . .' She hesitated, wincing.

'What's wrong?' I said

'It hurts.'

'Where?'

She took my hand and placed it low on her stomach, close to her pelvis, in exactly the same location she had placed my hand two weeks before. I leaned down and kissed her just below her belly-button. When I sat up, I noticed that blood was leaking from beneath her body onto the white sheets.

Either she saw the expression on my face, or she felt the dampness on her skin, for Nisha jumped from the bed and looked down at the covers. I noticed in that moment that the back of her dress was soaked and blood was trickling down her leg.

Trying to keep my hands from shaking, I called my doctor's emergency number to request a home visit. Nisha had made her way to the bathroom and was sitting on the toilet with the door open.

Her face was red and bloated with pain, drenched knickers around her ankles, streaks of red on her thighs. She was mumbling, saying something to me that I couldn't understand.

I sat down beside her and took her hand; she held it tight, as if she were about to fall from a cliff. Her words became more audible: she was repeating something in Sinhalese, maybe a prayer.

I couldn't move or speak, I just held her hand to stop her from falling into the black abyss that had opened up before us.

Dr Pantelis arrived silently: I saw only the headlights of his car distorted through the privacy glass of the bathroom window. I tried to release my hand from Nisha's so that I could open the door for him, but she wouldn't let go.

'Can you get up?' I asked.

She nodded and stood, slowly and with great effort. She held on to me as we made our way to the front door. By this time Dr Pantelis had come up the stairs. He took charge immediately, swiftly and professionally. Only then did Nisha allow her hand to loosen from mine. He asked me to fetch a chair. I did so. My next task was to get a glass of water. I did that too. Meanwhile, he had opened his bag on the floor and checked her blood pressure and oxygen levels, her heart rate and pupils. He then gave her a small canister of oxygen to hold over her mouth.

Once she started breathing into it, I could see her shoulders relaxing. She glanced at me over the mask and I knew what her eyes were saying.

The doctor and I lifted her onto the bed and I tucked the covers around her. Then, at his request, I led him into the bathroom as he wanted to see what had come out of her body.

He looked into the toilet bowl.

'I'm afraid she has lost the baby,' he said, bluntly, but with a softness to his voice that made me want to break down and cry.

I swallowed hard. 'What can I do?'

'Make sure you keep giving her oxygen through the night. Stay with her. If you find she bleeds again and it doesn't stop, you may need to take her to the hospital. But for the time being she is fine to stay here.'

I stayed by her side all night. I peeled her out of her wet clothes, helped her into one of my T-shirts and sat by her side. We did all this without speaking. She wanted me to hold her hand so she could sleep.

'How are you doing?' I would say, whenever I saw her eyes flicker open.

'Yes, I'm doing OK.'

Beyond the glass doors of my bedroom, I could hear murmurs from the people passing in the street, the barking of a dog, the wheels of a car, footsteps, clattering plates at Theo's. It all seemed miles away. I was in between worlds: behind me was a road that reached a dead end and would never now open up; a child that would not come into existence. Yet, I could see him or her, a half-formed shadow with Nisha's bright eyes. Maybe I'd been too hasty. I'd made too many plans. I had been too sure of myself. This unliving child was so real to me. It filled the cocoon in which I sat and Nisha slept, like the light from the sun and the song of the birds that came through the window that morning.

Of course, I thought, *birdsong glows like sunlight.* A strange thought, which was snatched away from me as sleep tried to catch me. I stood, by the window, making sure to stay awake.

When Nisha woke up around five o'clock, I was seated upright on the bed beside her.

'Good morning,' she said, with such sadness that it broke my heart.

'Good morning. Did you sleep OK?'

'Yes,' she said.

'How are you feeling?'

'The pain has gone. I'm tired.'

I nodded, kissed her on the cheek and went to fetch a glass of water, which I held to her lips. She had a few sips and handed it to me.

'I'm empty,' she said. A clear and quiet truth.

The air in my apartment was heavy and humid. I had sweated through my clothes. There were a few items of clothing that Nisha had left over at my place – some under-wear, and a red beach dress with yellow flowers that she often wore in the garden. I helped her to get dressed. It was as if she was half-asleep, her arms and body malleable, like soft clay – she allowed me to move her without resistance. It was the first time I had seen such vulnerability in her. Nisha was always strong, fearless, practical. Now, she had handed her power over to me.

She said only a few things. Namely that she would tell

Petra that she was unwell with a stomach bug and that hopefully after a little more rest she would be able to return to her duties. With every word she spoke, every small decision she made, I could see her strength returning, her back straightening, the colour gradually returning to her face.

We walked through the garden to her room. The red dress kept reminding me of her blood-soaked blue dress. I tucked her up in bed in order for her to get some rest before Petra and Aliki woke up.

'Stay with me for a few minutes?' she said, quietly, and I heard the deep sadness in her voice again.

'Of course.'

I sat beside her on the bed and stroked her hair.

'You know,' she said after a long silence, 'every person comes into this life with a certain amount of breaths. You live until those breaths run out. It doesn't matter where you are or what you're doing, if you have no breaths left, your energy will pass. This baby just didn't have enough breath to come into this world.'

I took in her words but said nothing. There was a stillness in the room; the fan was off and the heat was immense.

'When you die,' she said finally, 'your energy passes into another form. Imagine having two candles. You pass the flame from one candle to the other.'

I knew she was talking about our unborn child, the child that would never be born as our daughter or our son. But I didn't respond. I found it hard to speak, to know what to say. I simply listened and stroked her hair. Soon she was asleep.

I looked around the room. On the nightstand was a religious statue and her reading glasses. On the old wood dressing table, her makeup and jewellery. In the far corner of the room was an ironing board next to a laundry basket filled with clean and fresh towels and bed linen that had already been ironed. Behind this, a feather duster and a couple of multicoloured aprons hung on a hook on the wall.

Of course, I'd seen her tending the garden, but I had never, ever imagined her life beyond her bedroom door, her life as a maid in this house.

I gave Nisha a soft kiss on her forehead as she slept and left her room through the glass doors. Back in my flat, in the bathroom, the toilet was still full of Nisha's blood and what looked like clots and grey tissue. I heaved. There was nothing else I could do but flush the toilet and leave the room.

The meal we had not eaten was still in the kitchen, the glasses empty on the counter. The ring was in my pocket. I took it out and stared at the light bouncing off the diamond. Then I put it away in the cabinet. I knew I couldn't propose now: I would have to wait until Nisha was better, wait for the right time.

The sun was setting as I made my final delivery. I was ready to return to my apartment, the spare room now empty and, well, spare. But not for long. Seraphim and I would be hunting again in just under a week. And I had a lot to ask him.

160

15

Petra

O<small>N MONDAY MORNING AT THE</small> shop, I showed Keti the bracelet. She examined it closely, turning it over in her hands, her brow furrowing at the broken clasp.

'It doesn't look like she took it off herself, on purpose,' she said.

'No.'

'Will you take it to the police?' she asked.

'What's the point?'

Keti nodded in understanding.

'Why don't we make posters,' she suggested. 'Maybe someone saw her . . . I could draft a flyer on the computer,'

'Could you?' I nodded. 'I think it's a good idea.'

'Do you have any photographs of Nisha on your phone?' she asked.

I scrolled through and found one. It was a close-up I had

taken of Nisha and Aliki on Aliki's birthday almost a year ago. They were in the garden beneath the tree, Nisha's arm around Aliki's shoulder. They were both smiling.

Keti sat down at the computer in the back office and drafted a flyer:

MISSING PERSON
IF ANYONE HAS SEEN THIS WOMAN
PLEASE CALL 9-------
THERE WILL BE A GENEROUS REWARD

She cropped the photograph I had given her to remove Aliki from the photo, and zoomed in on Nisha's face. Her eyes were arresting: anyone who saw this would recognise her immediately if they'd ever seen her. Nisha's eyes aren't something you forget.

Keti printed many copies of the flyer and we split them between us. Even though Keti lived near the university, we thought it wouldn't be a bad idea to show them beyond my neighbourhood.

Before we locked up that night, I thanked Keti heartily.

'Of course,' she said. 'Nisha was a friend. You don't have to thank me.'

Soon Nisha's face stared out of flyers on every street in the area.

I was managing to keep my business running smoothly– no small thanks to Keti, who had even begun coming in early to dust and sweep the shop, trying to make up for the cleaning that Nisha would have done. I couldn't bring myself to hire a new cleaner, not yet. It would feel like an admission that Nisha was really gone.

Life at home, however, was falling apart. My mornings were put back by having to make Aliki breakfast and take her to school, and I had to let Keti open the shop on her own. I would run out after lunch to pick up Aliki, and Mrs Hadjikyriacou would watch her in the afternoons, while I returned to work. I would come back again in the evenings often later than I had planned, due to trying to finish enough work at the shop, squeeze in as many appointments as I could. I was exhausted. I felt like I was failing on all fronts.

At home, Aliki was restless. She would wander around the house, putting on and taking off her Converse trainers. She would match different colours then regret the choice. She'd walk around with one pink shoe, one chequered. Then one green shoe, the other striped. The cat called Monkey followed her around, sniffing her feet, rubbing its face against her hands as she tied the laces. She avoided the garden and I could hardly blame her: the garden was covered in snails. On the boat, particularly, there must have been about thirty, of various sizes, with their glossy shells and nimble eyes at the tips of their tentacles, slithering over the bow and stern, climbing languidly up its hull. After rain, Nisha would have peeled the snails off the boat, one by one, gently so as not to hurt them. But in her absence, nature had taken over.

On Tuesday night I had to stay at work very late. When

I got home, it was past nine o'clock and Mrs Hadjikyriacou was asleep in the armchair by the fire. On her lap, with her hands resting on it, was the framed photograph of Stephanos in his military gear. When she heard me, she opened her eyes. The fire was dwindling.

'Ah, Petra,' she said. 'You're back.' And then she seemed to remember that she was holding the photograph, and she looked down at it and ran her white fingers over the glass.

'He was so handsome, wasn't he?' she said.

I nodded.

'And such a kind heart. He would always bring me BBQ when he made it. And do you remember that time he came to pick me up from the airport? It was a Sunday and his only day off, but he came.'

'I do remember.'

'I'm sorry, my love,' she said. 'I'm sure you don't want these things darkening your heart right now. I always feel lonelier at night, don't you?'

I nodded again.

'You're lucky you have Aliki. She's a little genius, that girl. She tells some good stories too. She told me a story from *The Mahadenamutta and his Pupils*. Fascinating and hilarious!' She handed me the photograph and slowly got up.

I thanked her for helping me out, for watching Aliki and for staying so late.

'It's my pleasure, my love,' she said, and went home, where I suspect Ruba was waiting up for her.

I found Aliki sleeping on Nisha's bed with Monkey. In her arms she held the little Buddha that Nisha kept on her bedside cabinet. I didn't wake her; I put a throw over her and kissed her on the cheek. She didn't stir. The cat gave me a dirty look for disturbing it and went straight back to sleep.

I considered Nisha's room. It was so austere, with only the barest of essentials. She had hung a few pictures on the wall, but after living here for nearly ten years, it still felt temporary. My eyes fell on Nisha's dressing table, and it occurred to me that I hadn't searched the drawers there; I had just searched the desk, the most obvious place.

Aliki was sleeping comfortably and, quietly, so as not to wake her, I pulled out the dresser drawers one by one. In one, I found Nisha's underwear – cotton, white and cream-coloured knickers – all neatly folded. How strange it was to find her undergarments, to be rummaging through another woman's most intimate things.

In the third drawer, underneath a pile of neatly folded T-shirts, I found a photo album. Its cover was soft blue leather, the colour of the sea. The first photographs were from Nisha's wedding day. She was so much younger, her face fresh; she looked like a different Nisha to the one I knew. She was a young woman with dreams for the future. Her husband had been young too, clean-shaven, quite small in build, and he seemed to sparkle. I imagined that he would have been the kind of man to tell jokes at parties. She was wearing a white dress, embroidered with red flowers. She held a small bunch of red roses. There were dates beneath each photo that I could barely make out in the half-darkness.

The album was a window into Nisha's life back in Sri Lanka. A visual story. Her husband standing on his own on the side of a street carpeted with red flowers, on the road a red bus with a lit-up sign on its front reading 22 Kandy, above it the canopy of trees adorned with red blossoms. Another of a waterfall, rushing down a cliff, falling somewhere behind a bustling market; amongst this crowd Nisha and another woman both waved at the camera. I could almost hear the sounds that these people could hear.

Towards the end of the album, her husband was suddenly missing, and I knew these photos must have been taken after his death.

The final pages of the album were pictures of Kumari, from when she was a baby until she was about two years old, the age she was when Nisha left and came to us. My eyes rested on the last photograph in the album, where Nisha was holding Kumari in her arms. It reminded me of Nisha holding Aliki in her arms at that same age, but my daughter had been a plump toddler, though both girls had thick, shiny, dark hair. Nisha held them the same way.

I thought of the wooden statue that Muyia had made. The mother and child. It was Nisha. Yes, I was sure. The woman holding the child was Nisha and the child was Kumari. I lay down beside Aliki and the now-purring cat and fell asleep.

The next morning, while Aliki was eating her breakfast, I went to see Nilmini.

166

'I know you said you'd read Nisha's journal,' I said to her as she swept the floor, 'but I also found this photo album last night and I wanted to give it you as well, in case it helps you to identify anyone from the journals.'

Leaning the broom against the wall, Nilmini took the album from my hands and held it to her chest, just as she had done with the journal.

'I suppose I just thought you might like to see it.'

'Thank you, madam,' she said. 'I have begun reading the journal. What I can tell you is that in this journal are twelve letters written for her daughter Kumari, during her first year here in Nicosia.'

'So there is nothing more recent?'

'No, madam. They are dated.'

'I see.'

I must have looked disappointed and at a loss, for she said: 'Madam, even if we do not find anything obvious, there may be other information which might give us a better understanding.'

'That's true,' I said, smiling. And, just for a moment, she grabbed my fingers and squeezed them with hands that were softer and warmer than I had expected. I looked up and saw she had tears in her eyes.

'It is beautiful, the journal. Nisha should be a writer. In the letters, she tells all about her life back home and about her life here. I can hear my friend's voice as I read. I miss her very much.'

'I know Nilmini,' I said, 'So do I.'

'I'm sorry, madam.'

'What for?'

'Because I have not found what you are looking for.'

In the evening I invited Mrs Hadjikyriacou to stay and join us for supper. She demurred at first, saying that Ruba wouldn't know what to do without her there for the evening meal, but Aliki pleaded and finally she agreed. I made dhal curry but it was nothing like Nisha's – it lacked flavour and I added way too much coconut milk so it was like mush. But Aliki ate it regardless. After dinner, we sat by the fire drinking tea.

Mrs Hadjikyriacou's cloudy, silvery eyes regarded me with certainty and warmth. Then she turned her attention to Aliki. 'Come here, child,' she said. 'I can tell you a story. What is your favourite? And why in God's name are you wearing odd shoes?'

Aliki giggled. 'I like odd things,' she said. 'I'd like to hear a story.'

It was lovely to hear Aliki's voice, I drank it in. With Nisha gone, my daughter had no one else to speak to at home. Except the cats. Her voice was lost to me, we both knew that.

'Fair enough,' Mrs Hadjikyriacou said. 'Sit here beside me. I'll tell you about Foinikas, or Palm Tree village, the place where I was born. I lived there all my life, I got married there and had five children there. It's such an old place. People lived there since the times of the crusaders. Do you know about the crusaders?'

168

Aliki nodded. 'We learnt about it at school. Is that when you were born?'

'No!' She laughed. 'How the hell old do you think I am, you little monkey? Eight hundred years old?'

Aliki laughed and laughed and then she quietened at the sight of the old woman's knitted brow.

'Well, let me begin,' she said. 'Are you ready?'

Aliki sat straight and nodded.

'The knight commander's residence was built on the highest point of the village. The village was abandoned in 1974 after the war that divided the island. Today it is often flooded by water from the dam, but back in the day – well, what can I tell you, it was a place of beauty.'

Seeing my daughter held rapt by Mrs Hadjikyriacou's tale, I felt a pang of jealousy. I had never been able to command Aliki's attention, but then what did I offer her? Nisha had told her the stories, Nisha had played the games, teasing her imagination and teaching her how to see the world. I remembered the day we had gone up to the mountains and Nisha and Aliki had sat together on the bus, while I sat opposite them across the aisle, next to an old man who had been carrying a jasmine plant on his lap. He must have been growing it indoors by a sunny window for the flowers smelled as if it were summer and I remembered how strange it was to be enveloped by the scent during that chilly October day. The old man had snored, his head bopping gently to the movement of the bus as we headed up the mountain, and Nisha and Aliki had played I Spy.

'I spy with my little eye, something beginning with N!' Aliki said.

'Hm, that's a hard one,' Nisha said. She pretended to look all around the bus, then leaned over Aliki and made a big deal of looking out of the window.

Aliki giggled.

'Hmmm, let me see. Nature?'

'Nope.'

'Erm . . . nuts!'

'Where do you see nuts?'

'There are almond trees on the hills.'

'Well, if there are, I can't see them.'

'How about' – Nisha was looking around again, this time at the other passengers – 'novel!'

'Nope.'

'Aliki, this is too difficult.'

'Keep going!' she said.

'Nylon? And before you ask, the woman who is reading the novel – to your right – is wearing nylon tights.'

'That's very good,' Aliki said. 'But no.'

'Necklace.'

'No.'

'Neck!'

'No.'

'Nun?'

I remembered Aliki looking around her at this point, then she started to laugh again. 'Nisha, where do you see a nun?'

'We passed a church and a nun was outside in the garden.'

'You see everything,' Aliki said.

'You should be more observant,' Nisha said.

'OK, do you give up?'

'Let me try one last time . . .' There was a long pause. 'Nostril!'

'The answer,' said Aliki, 'is Nisha.'

'Me?'

Aliki had nodded.

'That's cheating! I can't see me!'

'Why?' she said. 'I see you!'

'I would never have guessed that. I could have gone on all week and I would never have guessed that.'

'Isn't it funny,' Aliki said, in her most adult voice, 'that you saw everything but yourself?'

On Friday night, around 10 p.m., I received a phone call from Soneeya. She was frantic. 'Madam, please come meet me at the gate, I have some information. Will you come right away?'

I told her yes, of course. I looked in on Aliki, who was sleeping peacefully in her room. Mrs Hadjikyriacou was still out, sitting in her garden as usual, and I asked if she wouldn't mind coming in and staying with Aliki for a while.

'Of course, my love,' she said, placing her hand on mine. 'My daughter is no longer coming to see me – something to do with work – they had to cancel the trip. So I have all the time in the world. Go and do what you need to do and don't worry about me.'

I thanked her by placing a kiss on her cheek, like I would have done with my own mother or grandmother, and left

171

her sitting in the living room by the fireplace flicking through a fashion magazine.

When I arrived at the mansion, Binsa and Soneeya were both waiting for me, standing behind the bars of the huge gate, beneath the glare of the security light. The two hunting dogs were out of their cages. One had its nose pressed between the bars of the gate, sniffing the air; the other lay flat, its huge head resting on its front paws. Their sand-coloured coats were shiny, their muscles defined in the spotlight.

'Madam,' Soneeya said. 'There has been another woman who vanished.'

'What do you mean, Soneeya?'

'Soneeya is saying there is another woman who is missing. This week, we called on a few friends to see if anyone has heard from Nisha. Our friend told us that her friend's sister, who works in a house with a family on the other side of Nicosia, well, she vanished one day. She went out at night and never came back.'

I tried to sort this out in my head.

'How long ago?'

'About three week ago, madam,' said Binsa.

'And they've heard nothing from her?'

'Nothing, madam. Not one thing,' replied Soneeya.

This made my mouth dry. I was still hoping that, at any moment, Nisha would return, but here they were telling me a story of another maid going missing without explanation.

'We don't know anything about the circumstances,' I said. 'There could be very good reasons why your friend's sister is missing from her place of work.'

Soneeya shook her head but said nothing.

Binsa reached into her apron pocket and took out a small scrap of paper. 'We have a number, a person for you to call. You can go see him.'

Through the bars, I took the piece of paper from Binsa's hand and read the details that had been hastily scribbled across it: *Mr Tony The Blue Tiger, Limassol 09* ----------------

'Who is this Mr Tony? What is the Blue Tiger?'

'The Blue Tiger, madam, is a place I have never been. It is a lovely place, they say, where all the workers meet on Sunday and make food and dance and eat. It is Mr Tony's restaurant the rest of the week. But Sunday he looks after all the workers. He finds them jobs. He helps them when they're in trouble. Sometimes girls stay at his home until they find an employer who is kind. They say Mr Tony is a good man and he knows so many things. If there is a problem, every maid goes to Mr Tony.'

'I don't see how he will be able to help me,' I said. 'The Blue Tiger is in another town. What information could he possibly have about Nisha?'

However, I remembered that Nisha had recently been to Limassol. Maybe he would know her, or her cousin Chaturi?

'He knows about the other woman who vanished. We do not have any more answer, but Mr Tony, he may have more answer.' Soneeya's eyes penetrated mine with urgency, as though she were about to take flight and go and find Nisha herself – if only she had had the freedom to do so.

The dogs picked up on her restlessness, for they were both pacing about behind her. With their coats golden in the

173

lamplight, their heads bowed, muscles rippling, tails down, for a moment they looked to me like lions. Lions in captivity. Lions who had been stolen from their land.

As I turned towards home, it occurred to me to go to the late-night bar by the Green Line, Maria's, which was located at the end of the street in the direction that Mrs Hadjikyriacou had seen Nisha heading the night she had disappeared. I wondered if someone there might know something about Nisha. I knew I was on borrowed time with Aliki home in bed, but maybe I would just stop in. Even just leave a flyer with them.

Two women were standing outside beneath a lamp-post smoking. In spite of the chilly night, they wore strappy tops and mini-skirts and were deep in conversation. I entered a place full of smoke. It reeked of beer. On a nearly empty dance floor there was a belly dancer in sequins and bright pink, rolling her stomach and tinkling bells. Men lined the bar. Waitresses in tight black clothes came and went with silver trays of dips and drinks. Candles had been lit on some of the tables, but nothing could make this bar look elegant: it was seedy and dark and it smelled of lust and greed and desperation.

I felt very out of place in my jogging bottoms, trainers and woolly cardigan whose sleeves were too long, but I was inside now, and knew it would be worth asking some questions. A few men turned with leering eyes to look at me but, to my relief, turned away again. I went to the bar and ordered a sparkling mineral water: I wanted to keep my wits about me in this place. The man beside me had a girl who barely looked eighteen sitting on his lap. As she licked his ear, he played with the strap of her pink dress and kissed her upper arm. I looked away. On my other side, a woman sat alone, smoking an e-cigarette that smelled like cherries. Her black hair reached the small of her back.

Once I paid for my drink, I asked the waitress if I could speak privately to the manager.

'Why?'

'I'm looking for work.'

She looked me up and down as if to say *Really?* and pointed to a wooden door at the back of the bar.

'He's in his office,' she said. 'Knock three times and wait.'

I did as she said. I waited for more than five minutes before the door opened and a small man who looked a lot like a hamster opened the door. He had a huge grin, dead-white teeth and a pot belly that spilled over his trousers. But he carried himself like a king.

'What can I do for you, young lady?' he said.

'Well, I'm not exactly a young lady anymore,' I said.

'You'd be surprised.' He smiled widely.

I had no idea what he meant.

He invited me into his office and I sat on a low stool by a high antique desk. He sat in a pivoting office chair – soft leather with broad arms – and looked down at me.

'You knocked three times. You're looking for work.'

'No.'

He raised his eyebrows and, for the first time, irritation erupted on his face. He glanced at the clock on the wall. In spite of the music outside, this office was strangely quiet.

'I know that many foreign domestic workers *work* here,' I said, 'and because of that I wondered if you have ever seen this woman.' From my handbag I pulled out one of the flyers Keti and I had made and pointed at Nisha's picture.

From the top pocket of his shirt the man retrieved a cheap pair of gold-rimmed glasses and put them on, taking the flyer from me and studying it. He seemed deep in thought for a very long time. Finally, he looked at me and said, 'No.'

'You've never seen her?'

'No.'

'She's never been in here?'

'Well, if she has, I never saw her. But I don't sit by the front door and memorise faces.' He glanced again at the clock and stood up.

'There are so many foreign workers here, they might have seen Nisha, they might know something,' I continued, desperately.

'Nisha, huh?' he said and smiled. 'Do you know that in Sanskrit, Nisha means "night"?'

I told him that I didn't know that.

'All the women I have ever met called Nisha are beautiful and mysterious. If I had met her, I definitely would have remembered. Leave the flyer with me and I'll put it up. Don't worry.'

I decided to hand out flyers to some of the women. Many of them were foreign domestic workers; there was a chance that they may have known Nisha, or at least someone may have seen her that night. The women here were usually tucked away, wrapped up safely in our domestic routines. It

176

struck me how one person's emancipation sometimes relies on the servitude of another. These thoughts tormented me. I feared that I would never be able to tell Nisha what I had understood.

I stood there in the candlelight, clutching on to Nisha's flyers.

On the table near me, three young women sat talking. They laughed. They drank hot tea in tiny glasses.

'Hello,' I said, awkwardly, feeling that I was intruding.

All eyes looked up. 'Good evening madam,' said the woman closest to me.

'I'm wondering if you have seen this woman?' I placed one of the flyers on the table and they leaned in to take a look.

'Yes!' the one on the left said. 'I know her!' She was a slim woman with thick black curls.

'Me too!' said the one next to her. 'That is Nisha . . . I forget her family name now.'

The first, who had placed her cup of tea on the table, was leaning in, looking concerned. 'Well, that is my friend, Nisha. Sometimes we go to church on Sundays, when she is free; she meets me at the other café around corner from here, the one where all of us girls meet on Sundays, and we have a cup of tea together.'

'Nisha has gone missing,' I said.

'When?' asked the woman who hadn't spoken yet, startled.

'Two weeks ago. Do you know anything? The police said she might have gone to the north of the island.'

The first woman laughed now, but with a darkness that

177

seemed to extinguish even the dim light. 'They always think these things. They think we are thieves, too. My madam thought I stole her wedding ring. That's how I go fired. That's how I ended up here.' The woman shook her head and suddenly glanced down at Nisha's poster. She stared at it for a long time. 'I hope you find her, madam,' she said.

As I walked away, I realised that I had not asked the women their names. They had called me 'Madam'. From that point on, I held out my hand and introduced myself.

'Good evening. My name is Petra.'

I met so many women that night. Diwata Caasi, a sixty-one-year-old woman from the Philippines, who had been forced to drink water from a jam jar because she was only a maid, and the food was rationed so that she was eating less than the cat. She eventually left her employer and had nowhere to turn.

Mutya Santos, from the bay-side city of Manila, who used to be a midwife. She loved her elderly employer and had dinner with her every night, but when the old lady passed away Mutya was placed with a man who kept touching her, who walked in on her while she showered, who came to her room while she slept. She had complained to the agency who did nothing to help. When her employer found out, he fired her. Again, she was left with nowhere to go and huge debts.

Ayomi Pathirana, from Sri Lanka. Her parents were both farmers. As a child she would wake up early every morning to help her parents on the farm before going to school. Later, she left college as they were financially hard-up and

178

found a job in a bookstore for two years; but the money was not good, she could not progress and her parents were getting old. Her cousin encouraged her to apply for work as a nanny abroad. She went to Kuwait, where she was faced with difficulties. Eventually, she made plans to come to Cyprus, where she found similar problems. She was so young when she came here. Then she met a Cypriot man who promised to get her work, and though it was the wrong kind of work, she could not return to Sri Lanka because of the debts she had.

Etisha, from Nepal, who had to leave her one-year-old daughter, Feba, the source of her light, because she and her husband could not find work back home. Initially she came here as a student; she was promised work, but when she arrived there was nothing.

Every single one of them had a story. I could have sat there all night listening. But the bars on the windows, the flailing light, made me feel trapped. I just wanted to get out of there. But the women's stories . . . they moved me, they opened something inside me.

One of the girls I spoke to began to cry. She wasn't intending to. I showed her the flyer of Nisha. She didn't recognise her. Then I asked her where she was from, and instead of words, tears flowed out, down her cheeks, smudging her makeup. For a moment I slipped my hand in hers. She looked at me with black eyes that reflected the candlelight. 'I want to go home, madam,' was all she said. She did not tell me where home was.

'Can't you go? Just pack your bags and go.'

Through her tears, she laughed. 'It's not as easy as that. If only you knew.'

As I was leaving, I recognised a man at the bar. I was sure it was the guy who often visited Yiannis – Seraphim was his name. I assumed they worked together, as he sometimes dropped him off after they'd gone foraging in the forest for snails and mushrooms. He'd greet me politely whenever he saw me. Scruffy guy, uncombed hair. He sat at the bar on his own, drinking whisky. I was about to leave but I had a couple more flyers in my purse and decided to approach him.

'Good evening, Seraphim,' I said, standing beside him.

He glanced up. 'Petra!' he said, startled. 'What are you doing here?'

'I'm looking for my maid,' I said. 'Nisha. Do you remember her?'

'Of course,' he said. 'I know Nisha.'

'Have you seen Yiannis lately? Did he mention to you that she's missing?'

'I can't say that I can recall that conversation,' he said. 'But I am sorry to hear that.'

'Well, since you're here . . .' I handed him one of the flyers and he spent a long time looking at the picture of Nisha. The music seemed to go up a few notches, and the belly dancer was still twinkling and jingling in the candlelight.

'Very beautiful woman,' I heard him say, through all the noise. 'Don't you think? It's her eyes, isn't it? They seem to know a lot.'

I didn't reply. He handed the flyer back to me. 'I'm sorry,' he said. 'She must have been an asset to your household. But I suspect she will be back, and if she isn't, don't be surprised. These women come and go like the rain, you know?'

He grinned at me but I did not smile back. I didn't like this man. He was always so courteous when I saw him outside mine waiting for Yiannis to come down, but now I could see an intensity to him that I'd never noticed before. In fact, he seemed to be made of sharp edges – his nose, his cheek bones, even his elbows. There was a sharpness to his entire frame and bone structure; it was evident now in the candle-light. Or was it my mind playing tricks on me? I knew I was becoming more anxious, more unsettled with each passing day that Nisha was away.

'Hey, join me for a drink, won't you? You're lucky to catch me here tonight – I've been away for a few days, came back a bit earlier than anticipated.'

'I'm OK, thanks,' I said, 'so, when you're not away, do you come here a lot?'

He raised his eyebrows.

'I'm asking because I wonder if you ever saw Nisha here? You see, the old lady who lives next door to me told me that Nisha was heading this way the night that she vanished.'

'What night was that?' he said.

'Two weekends ago, on the Sunday.'

Again, he was silent for a while, thinking. 'I wish I could tell you that I've seen her, but I haven't.'

*   *   *

181

I inhaled the cold air out on the street. The night was fresh and I walked away briskly from the bar. I could still hear the voices of the women inside. I was eager to get home, but as I passed Muyia's workshop, I remembered the sculpture. Suddenly, I had to see it again. I felt compelled to go inside – the entrance, as usual, was gaping open. It was so dark in there I had to be careful not to trip over the debris on the floor. Slowly my eyes adjusted and I could make out the vague shape of the worktop, feeling with my hands to find the light switch on one of the lamps.

The sculpture of the mother and child had been covered in a white cloth. I lifted off the sheet and sat down on the stool opposite, struck again by the resemblance to Nisha. I could almost feel the energy emanating from her; so many emotions, she had a history, she had a whole life. And she had an enduring and powerful love for the child in her arms. A love that could not be replaced. Why had Muyia made this? It was Nisha, to be sure, her heart-shaped face, her fiery eyes. Even the tiny dimple in her right cheek. I reached out and touched her hand. I wanted her to speak. I was desperate that she would break out of her wooden case and speak to me.

'Nisha,' I said, gently. 'Tell me where you are.'

I waited as if I might hear her voice. I looked at her unmoving face, but I heard only the sound of the wind – nothing else, just the wind through leaves.

I covered up the statue and headed back home.

In the village there is a guest house: a small, rickety building with brown shutters and whitewashed walls in the back garden of a widow's home. There have been no guests, though, for many years. Once in a blue moon, someone will call from a distant land and make a booking and the old woman will take down the details in a black notebook she keeps by the phone. Then she will go to great efforts to clean, and fluff up the towels and cushions. She will place fresh tea-bags and honey and sugar on a tray, and lay sugared almonds on the pillows and bake pistachio cakes, which she'll wrap in cellophane decorated with paper daisies and display on the dressing table. She will sweep the leaves and dust from the patio and leave a tourist brochure by the bed.

It is dark when the phone rings. A young man, calling from a hotel in Beirut, with one of those transatlantic accents she has only ever heard on TV. He is travelling around Europe with his new wife, they will be arriving next week, all being well. The old lady jots down his name and number and date of arrival in the black notebook beneath a doodle of a clown riding a donkey that her granddaughter has drawn.

The nights are getting longer and colder and she goes out to collect the washing from the line. The children across the street have gone in and their maid is out picking apples from the tree in the dark. A breeze blows. Good evening, she says, but her voice is carried away. Along the path a mist settles and darkness settles too, as there are no houses there to light up the way. Further along, there are only trees and clouds and sky, until the earth becomes jagged and dry and drops down to the red water of the lake, which is as black as the night and as the empty eye socket of the hare glaring up at the sky.

16

Yiannis

O N Saturday, before dawn, Seraphim picked
me up in his van. We drove to the Akrotiri base,
an hour and a half away. Our ride was mostly
silent: we were sleepy; Seraphim looked like he'd been out
late. I was biding my time. I wanted his full attention for our
conversation.

This time he'd brought with him four calling birds in two
cages: three blackcaps and a blackbird. These caged callers
would have been caught and kept in the dark for months so
that when they were finally taken out into the light, they
would sing their hearts out, unwitting decoys to lure as many
birds as possible into the trap.

The cages were in the back of the van with black blankets
draped over them. I dozed until we reached the wetland, an
area of 150 hectares known for its bird life and protected by

various agencies because of it. If we succeeded, it would be a good hunt, but we had to be careful.

With Nisha gone, however, and the memories of her tugging at my insides, I began to feel nauseous at the thought of killing all those birds, imagining them trapped in the mist nets.

They flap and they flap and they try to fly, but the sky has caught them.

I thought of the little bird back home, how it trusted me now.

If Seraphim smelled my apprehension, there'd be trouble, so I pushed these thoughts aside. There had been another arson attack a few days ago: a man named Louis, who had never been suited to hunting. They had set his car on fire, like the man before him, but this time Louis's teenage son was in there, apparently sneaking a cigarette. The boy had managed to get out, but with a badly burnt arm. It was all over the local news. There was an ongoing investigation, but, of course, Louis wouldn't let on what he knew. He would never tell the police anything.

I knew Seraphim had been the one to snitch on him. Well, of course he had. He is a weasel, this man: stealthy, sharp-eyed, cunning, shifty, sneaky, scheming. Above all, and this was the most dangerous part, he was loyal to the men in charge. I had met Louis – he came out with us a couple of times. He had still been learning the trade, and we introduced him to some good poaching locations. But then he wanted out, and Seraphim was pissed off – this Louis had been his next prodigy. 'Best to snitch before they snitch,' was his motto

186

– he'd said this with a wide grin and narrow eyes. The arson attacks were meant as a warning.

'You're even quieter than usual,' Seraphim finally said. 'Thinking about Nisha?'

'Yes.'

I could see the moon in the stretch of water outside the window.

Seraphim parked the van and we pulled the mist nets and poles from the back of the van, carrying them across the muddy terrain. We returned for the calling birds. There's a British military base there and the English are very strict about hunting, regularly searching the area for poachers, so we had to be extra careful. It was unlikely, though not impossible, that someone would be checking so early in the morning – it was 3.30 a.m., and because the land was so flat and open, we would see anyone approaching from quite a distance. If we stayed vigilant, we would not be caught.

Seraphim wore a head-torch and led the way. We put the nets up, securing them to eight-foot poles. Then he turned off the torch and carefully lifted the blankets from the cages. The birds were quiet, as it was still dark out. The blackbird's feathers were a deep ebony, like the night. I suddenly had the urge to open the door of its cage, to let it free so it could merge with the sky.

We placed their cages on the ground of the shimmering wetlands, just beneath the mist nets that hovered like ghosts above the earth, then we found a secluded spot nearby among

187

some pine trees and rosemary bushes. Seraphim had brought a small gas canister and I took out from my rucksack bread, haloumi and olives. We toasted the food on sticks over a small fire. Shadows from the flames licked over Seraphim's face.

'That Sunday, when Nisha went missing,' I began, and he nodded, still staring at the olives on the stick that he held over the fire. 'Did she come to meet you?'

Seraphim looked at me now. 'Why would you ask me that?'

'I was chatting to someone, a friend, and they thought Nisha was on her way to meet you that evening. Around ten thirty.'

'Why would Nisha be coming to meet *me*?'

'I was hoping you would be able to answer that question.'

Seraphim was silent for a while. The darkness was thick behind him.

'Whoever told you that was not telling you the truth.'

'Why would they lie?'

'They might not be lying. They are just not telling truth. They may have had their wires crossed. If, on the other hand, they did lie deliberately, I assume they have their reasons for doing so, but I cannot possibly begin to speculate because I have no idea who this person is.'

Then Seraphim lay back with his hands behind his head, signalling that our conversation was over. He told me to stay alert and closed his eyes to nap. He fell asleep quickly, his mouth hanging open and emanating a faint snore.

The land stretched for miles all around, dark, with shivers of silver where the moon caught the water. I watched as a sliver of light emerged on the horizon, darkness becoming less opaque. At this first sign of day, the caged birds began to sing. Their voices rose in a swelling, melodic chorus – a burst of music after so much time in silence.

And that's when I heard it again: the voice of a woman, calling. Calling something which I could not understand, her voice mixed with the song of the birds

I stood up. Looked around. I shouldn't have left Seraphim alone, sleeping like that, but I instinctively followed the voice to the mist nets. When I got to the water's edge, it ceased abruptly. There didn't seem to be anyone there. In every direction, the land was open and empty.

Then the birds filled the sky – their music filled the sky. They swooped down in their thousands, their wings alight in the sunrise – gold and red and blue. They veered down sharply, diving towards the calling birds, to the song that was luring them to their death, down, down, down to the water's edge.

I stood frozen, watching them as their journeys ended, the mist net suddenly enveloping them. So many wings tangled, so many birds suspended mid-flight. Their song changed – from trills to shrieks, or so it seemed to me. But some, I thought, continued their melodic song, as if the sky might just open up again and release them.

'What are you playing at?' a voice said behind me. I turned. Seraphim was there, fire in his eyes.

'I thought I heard something,' I said.

'So you leave me sleeping on my own? What if somebody had come? I would have been done for!'

189

'I made a mistake.'

He stared at me without blinking. 'A mistake? A mistake is forgetting to bring the gas canister or the olives.' His eyes narrowed. The birds' cries filled the air around us. 'Well,' he said, 'let's not dwell on it now. We've caught enough.' He glanced at the net, sizing up the success of the hunt. 'Let's just take down what we have and head home.'

We brought the nets down and began pulling the birds from it, killing them one by one as we did so. We did this without speaking, in synchronicity with one another. I was freeing the birds from the net, passing each one to Seraphim so that he could bite its neck and put it into the black bin-liner. I could feel each one trembling in my hands, tiny heart racing, wings twitching and beating in my palms. The soft touch of feathers on my skin. There must have been twenty different species. But I was careful not to hesitate – I didn't want Seraphim to notice anything was amiss. The birds were still singing, though. That was what disturbed me the most. They sang until their last breath.

I got home around 9 a.m., fed the bird, and lay down. I was so tired. The conversation with Seraphim had been unsatisfying. Was he lying? Had Spyros been mistaken about what Nisha had said? Or was Seraphim trying to throw me off the scent of something else? I missed Nisha keenly.

I fell asleep with dreams of her in the wetlands. She stood in the water, which came to her ankles. A clear blue sky behind her. She was wearing her nightdress of beeralu lace with the garden of white flowers, the one Chaturi had made her. She was saying something to me, her lips moving, but I heard nothing.

'What is it Nisha?' I asked.

She pointed at something behind me, up in the sky. When I turned to look, the sky became black, it was suddenly night. When I looked back at Nisha, she was gone. In her place, the moon hung over the horizon, so big I thought I could reach out and touch it. I noticed its reflection in the water, painfully bright; a silver pool of light in the middle of black water. I took my shoes off and walked in: I wanted to find her, but when I got there, I saw that what I thought had been the moon's refection was in fact a deep well. A well that seemed endless. It was not a dark well. A bright white light glowed from within, illuminating its cobbled walls, spilling out onto the water. From it came immense heat.

I woke up drenched in sweat, a bright winter sun shining through the window, bathing me in its light. The little bird was sitting on my chest, chirping gently to itself. I stroked its soft feathers. Winter was coming. October had passed and Nisha was still missing. The bird sang to the sun and for the first time in many years, I began to cry.

I heard the sound again, the woman's cry, and I realised that this time it was coming from inside me, drifting around the dark corners of my mind. It was a pure and unpredictable sound: like the wind, it ebbed and flowed, it quietened down and came back with force. The sound was coming from a place that didn't belong just to me. It was such a strange

191

and terrifying sensation that I jumped off the bed, the bird fluttering to the ground. And the sound of its wings, as soft as they were, startled my mind back to reality, back to the room I was in with the winter sun beaming through the window.

I felt nauseous, acid coming up from my stomach, burning my oesophagus. I went to the bathroom and vomited in the toilet. As I flushed it, I remembered the blood and grey tissue in the toilet bowl – the child that would never be.

I lay down on the bed again. After the night of the miscarriage, Nisha changed. She would come late at night, as usual, and lay down where I was lying now, hands crossed over her stomach, protectively – like the position in which one places a corpse, except her hands were on her stomach instead of her chest.

She would look out of the window and watch summer fade, each passing day an equation: 'On this day,' she would say, 'I would have been eight weeks pregnant, but instead I have been empty for seven days.' Or, 'On this day I would have been nine weeks pregnant, but I have been empty for fourteen days.'

At 5 a.m., she would wake up and speak to Kumari on the phone. It would have been 7.30 in the morning in Sri Lanka and Nisha wanted to catch her daughter before her school day. I would be half-asleep, the feel of Nisha's warmth still beside me on the bed. She would sit at the desk and her conversation and the light from the tablet would reach me. Sometimes my eyes would flicker open and I would see her silhouette, hear her words in Sinhalese and Kumari's response.

Though I didn't understand the language, I got to know their tones and rhythms. I could understand if they were having a joke, or an argument, or a light-hearted conversation about school or Kumari's homework or her friends. I could tell when Nisha was annoyed about something, or when she was firm and insistent. Sometimes I heard love in her voice; other times concern, joy, irritation, determination. Kumari was sometimes cheeky, sometimes agreeable, often so chatty that Nisha couldn't get a word in edgeways; other times quieter and solemn, moody. There were a few occasions when I could even hear the first signs of adolescent rebellion sneaking in. All the emotions that one would expect between a mother and a burgeoning teenager, but all of this was through a screen.

Many early mornings Nisha would teach Kumari English. They each had copies of *The Secret Garden* and they would take turns reading the pages aloud. They sometimes both got stuck on a word, but Nisha kept a dictionary by my bedside – a gift from her friend, Nilmini – and she would consult it for assistance. Their chatting drifted over my dreams like the echo of a birdsong.

One time, she said, 'Yiannis, come here. Kumari wants to say hello.'

'You've told her about me?' I mimed.

'Of course,' she said, her eyes bright and encouraging.

It was roughly a year ago, so Kumari must have been about ten at the time. She was wearing her uniform, ready for school, with a massive rucksack on her shoulders.

'Hello, Mr Yiannis,' she had said, smiling. Although she

had darker skin and eyes than her mother, her smile and expressions were exactly the same.

'Hello, Kumari, it's lovely to finally meet you!'

'Finally? Have you heard stuff about me?'

'Of course.'

'Good stuff?'

'Wonderful stuff.'

'That's OK then.' She scrunched up her face. 'So you are my amma's friend?'

'I am.'

'She said you feed the chickens in the garden downstairs.'

'I guess I do.'

'What else do you do, Mr Yiannis. Or are you just a chicken feeder?'

I laughed. 'I'm not *just* a chicken feeder. I go into forests and pick wild vegetables and snails.'

'Hmmm. What do you do with them after you pick them?'

'I sell them.'

'Hmmm.' She nodded. 'I guess that sounds all right.'

After that particular call, Nisha lay down next to me, entwining her limbs with mine. 'I have an extra hour or so before I should leave. Hold me really tight.'

And of course, I did. It was all I wanted to do. She would set her alarm for just before 6 a.m. I would drift in and out of sleep, and sometimes I would hear her crying.

'What is it, Nisha?' I would whisper in the dark.

'Oh, it's nothing, I just remembered something.'

'What did you remember? Tell me.'

During this time of grief for the lost child, Nisha told me

194

three stories of loss. The first was of her sister's death. The second of her husband's. The third of making the devastating decision to leave Kumari in order to come here. Her sister's death had coincided with the Vesak Poya festival of lights, on the first full moon in the month of May, when she was twelve years old and her sister, Kiyoma, had been ten. She told me about the white lanterns at night, hanging over the door of every home in the street apart from theirs. Her sister had died that morning. The year before her death, they went together to the Koggala lagoon and took a gondola to the tiny island where a Buddhist temple was located. There were hundreds of lanterns, and a thousand lights floating on the water as they glided across the lake. Her sister had called them *tiny moons in a starry sky*. Tiny moons that filled up the world.

The temple was covered in flowers, lights and incense; there were dancers and singers and firewalkers. Her sister's face was lit up by all the lights as she held onto Nisha's hand. Kiyoma was only a couple of years younger, but because of her heart condition she was small for her age and if someone didn't know they would think she was much younger. She had been named Kiyoma, which means *good mother*, because her own mother, Lakshitha, wished that Kiyoma would grow up to be a wife and a mother herself. It was the greatest wish that Lakshitha had for her daughter. But Nisha imagined her sister's heart like a tiny bird fluttering in her chest: she knew one day, before long, that it would break free of its cage and fly away. She knew because she could hear the changed rhythm of her breathing. It was so subtle, anyone else would have missed it, but Nisha could hear it because they shared a bed.

Kiyoma always wore a *panchauda* – a gold pendant embellished with five weapons: a bow and arrow, a sword, a disc, a trident and a conch, to ward off the evil eye. Lakshitha made sure Kiyoma never took it off and Nisha saw it glimmering in the light of the lanterns and the fires while they were on the little island visiting the temple. But when they got off the gondola on their return, the necklace had disappeared. It was Nisha who noticed. 'Where is your pendant?' she'd said to her sister with fearful eyes. Kiyoma had shrugged.

Later, their mother was beside herself. 'What could this mean? Nisha, did you see her drop it? Kiyoma, did you not feel it fall? Did either of you not hear it fall?'

Lakshitha had become obsessed with Kiyoma's heart condition. Some days she would be calmer and accept that her beautiful daughter might have less breaths to take in this life and in this world, which is really an almost impossible thing for any mother to come to terms with; other times, and most of the time, she would consult astrologers, or watch out for good or bad omens, such as who Kiyoma might have met at certain times of day, what somebody had said to her, or what they might have been carrying while they spoke to her. She bombarded poor Kiyoma with questions. Other times still, she used lotions, potions and oils on the scar that ran vertically down her youngest daughter's chest to her navel.

Kiyoma was a perceptive girl for her age. One day, while

they were walking back home from the paddy fields where their parents worked, she confided to Nisha that she had thrown the pendant into the lagoon while they were on the gondola on the night of Vesak Poya.

'Why, why, why would you do such a thing?' Nisha scolded.

'Because,' her little sister had said with candid eyes, 'the pendant felt like a chain around my neck.'

Exactly a year later, on the morning of Vesak Poya, just before light filled the sky, Kiyoma drew her last breath and her heart flew away out of the window. Nisha was fast asleep, but she dreamt of a bird with golden feathers as soft as waves that hovered over her for a while, and then flew out of the open window.

She woke up immediately and turned in the half-darkness to face her sister. She noticed that her chest was not rising gently, that her eyes were not moving inside her dreams. She leaned over her, placing her ear close to her mouth and nose. And that's when she heard and felt something that was, up to that point in time, completely unknown to her. The stillness and soundlessness of death.

Kiyoma's body was kept at the house for a few days in an open casket. Monks came to chant prayers and eulogise about the impermanence of life. Her body was placed facing west, and their mother stayed in the room with her day and night, to prevent evil spirits from taking up residence in the house. Pictures had been turned around on the walls, or placed facing down on tabletops; family and friends came to the house with offerings of white and yellow flowers.

Lakshitha did everything she could to ensure that Kiyoma's

197

transition to the next life was assured. She offered the monks white cloth to be stitched into monastic robes. Then relatives and friends poured water from a vessel into an overflowing cup while reciting prayers.

Nisha listened to the prayers and watched the water over-flowing – how it momentarily caught the light like crystals and seemed like the most beautiful thing in the world. And she understood for the first time that everything – everything – must come to an end.

17

Petra

THAT SUNDAY I GOT READY to go to Limassol. I had arranged to meet Mr Tony at the Blue Tiger at 3 p.m. and I had about an hour's drive ahead of me. After lunch, I took Aliki over to Mrs Hadjikyriacou, who was sitting outside with the cats. It was a rather last-minute plan, but when I had asked her the previous afternoon, she seemed excited at the prospect of spending more time with Aliki. 'She's a funny little girl. Watch her!' she said, beaming from ear to ear, so that her paper-like skin had creased a thousand times.

Aliki took her time to decide which shoes she was going to wear. Eventually, she settled on one grey denim and one bright blue with a flower pattern. Finally, she picked up another odd pair: one with red cat paws and the other bright red.

199

'You're taking a spare pair of shoes?' I asked.

'No.'

When we got to Mrs Hadjikyriacou's, Aliki placed the shoes on the floor beside her and the old woman looked down at them.

'They're for you,' Aliki said.

'For me?'

'They're a present. And, plus, I don't like your old-lady shoes. They won't do.'

Mrs Hadjikyriacou laughed out loud.

'Last time we learnt that we're the same shoe size,' the old lady said to me. Then to Aliki: 'Well, I must say, they are a perfect odd choice!' Then she called Ruba to come and help her change into her new shoes.

Ruba came out holding a tea-towel. She greeted us warmly before kneeling down by Mrs Hadjikyriacou's feet, pulling off her old-lady shoes and putting on the Converse sneakers.

The shoes were quite remarkable beneath her calf-length black skirt and against her dead-white skin. She leaned over herself with great effort and looked down at her feet, clicking her heels. Aliki laughed. The cats ran off on some urgent business. At this, I quietly took my leave, hearing Aliki's laughter rippling behind me.

It was a bright and beautiful day. I rolled down the windows of my Range Rover as I drove southwest to Limassol. It was a bit chilly, but I welcomed the fresh breeze that came down from the mountains, which was soon replaced with a breeze from the sea, drifting in with the sound of the birds.

Everything seemed to melt as I neared the water. The salty air, the way it enveloped me, wrapped me up in a time long gone. *All the water on Earth once arrived on asteroids and comets.* Yes, that is what my father told me. He was a fisherman. He had a library of books in the cellar – where he also kept potatoes – and this was where he got all his information. During the war, the library was taken from him, but until the day he died, he could recall the title and author of every book. In the car, with the windows down and the sea opening up and glistening before me, I could almost hear my father's voice: *Since it came to Earth, the water has been cycling through air, rocks, animals and plants. Each molecule has been on an incredible journey. When you feel alone, try to remember that at some point the water inside you would have been inside dinosaurs, or the ocean, or a polar ice-cap, or maybe a storm cloud over a faraway sea at a time when that sea was still nameless. Water crosses millennia and boundaries and borders.*

For years, I'd forgotten my father's words, and they came back to me now. *Remember we all have something in common, and that is the water that runs through us.*

The Blue Tiger was not too far from the beach, just off one of the side streets that leads down to the sea. It was a dilapidated, double-fronted building, with colourful murals on its walls, mostly of sports scenarios: football players in a packed stadium, basketball players crouched on a court. Above these, on the concrete wall and continuing onto the concrete canopy, were painted vines, large and winding, with thick

201

stems and giant leaves that climbed up to a bright blue sky. On the far left – just above a barred window and two air-conditioning units – looking out through the leaves, was a blue tiger with striking yellow eyes.

I looked at the time on my phone: 14.46.

Below the tiger was a sign that read:

DWA
DOMESTIC WORKERS ASSOCIATION OF CYPRUS
LIMASSOL
REGISTERED OFFICES

Beside the double doors of the entrance was a blackboard pavement sign, with a menu: BURGERS, HOT DOGS, SUPER DOGS, CHILLI CON CARNE.

Two men stood beside it, leaning on a motorbike, smoking. 'You are lost?' one of them asked, in a heavy, unfamiliar accent.

'I'm looking for Mr Tony,' I said, my voice croaky as if I had just woken up. 'I have an appointment.'

'You are not lost,' he said, smiling, 'He is inside the office. On the right.'

I could hear music coming from the depths of the place, and smell spices. I thanked the man and stepped through the open doors. I still didn't know what I was doing there or how this Mr Tony could help me, but by that point I was grateful to speak to anyone who might be able to offer a glimmer of hope.

In an open kitchen on the left, women were cooking in

large pans and woks; other women were scattered about, sitting at tables drinking hot tea or eating steaming dumplings that they dipped into a bright orange sauce. Most of the people were domestic workers from Nepal or the Philippines, Sri Lanka or Vietnam. A local man sat on his own, noticeable due to his bald head, white stubble and gleaming eyes – leering at the girls as they passed with trays of tea. He looked like he was about to drool. He glanced at me, smiling, and I turned away, disgusted. At the back of the kitchen was a set of doors that opened up to a large hall and stage. This was where the music was coming from. People were dancing there, men and women, beneath a canopy of multi-coloured flags.

I spotted what must have been Mr Tony's office: a rectangular glass booth on the far right of the dining area. A large man with broad shoulders and white hair sat behind a desk, a fan spinning above him blowing his hair while he spoke on the phone, a conversation that was clearly making him agitated. He hung up. I waited a minute, then approached the booth and knocked on the door.

'Enter!' he called.

He was sitting on a swivel chair in front of a computer. He smiled and raised his eyebrows. I went to close the door behind me.

'Leave the door open. We need some air in here.'

'Mr Tony?'

'Tony is fine.'

'I'm Petra.' I held out my hand.

'Ah, yes, of course.' He wiped his hand on his trousers and

shook mine; his grip was warm and sweaty. 'Take a seat.' He pointed at a plastic chair in the corner of the booth.

The entire place was awash in laughter and music and spices, and it all swirled around the little booth as it seeped in through the open door.

'What you have here is amazing,' I said. 'You run this organisation yourself?'

He nodded, smiled and said, 'Don't get me wrong – these Asians are ungrateful people.' But then his smile faded, and he glanced down at the ground.

'Really? So why do you help them?'

'I was married to one. Do you mind if I smoke?'

'Not at all.'

Taking a cigarette out of a box, he lit it with a large match, shaking out the flame and chucking it into a crystal ashtray that sat on a notebook.

'And plus, I found a lot of injustice around.'

At that moment the phone rang; he looked down at the flashing screen on his desk and sighed. 'Excuse me,' he said, and picked it up. 'Good afternoon, Mrs Kaligori, can I call you back in about—'

'No.' The voice on the other end interrupted. 'She's no good for me, Tony. She doesn't even speak any English.' The woman said a lot more but I turned my attention to outside the booth, where a beautiful young woman in a green and gold sari was passing by holding a bowl of steaming noodles. Beyond her, I saw the women in the kitchen still sweating and chopping, emptying the contents of their woks into large blue dishes.

'No problem, we'll sort this out,' Tony said loudly. 'I have someone here. Let me call you back in around thirty minutes.'

The woman seemed to acquiesce, although her voice was much quieter now and it was hard to hear.

'I don't work like the agents,' he said to me, when he had hung up. 'The employers come to me directly. They can try out the women, and if they don't like them they send them back. Like Mrs Kaligori. You're not getting some person from Nepal that you are tied to blindfolded. These people' – he waved his hand around him – 'need someone to help them. To the agents they are merchandise, not people.'

'So, the women aren't indebted to you?'

'No! That is the whole point. The agents are furious.'

I nodded and watched him as he sucked deeply on his cigarette, narrowing his eyes at a streak of light from the sliding doors at the front. I noticed on his desk, propped up on some paperwork, a tiny grainy photo of a woman in a bronze frame. He followed my gaze.

'Your wife?'

'Ex-wife. Vietnamese.'

It seemed to me that he was about to say more about this as he opened his mouth, but then he pursed his lips and took a long, hard drag of the cigarette, blowing the smoke in a straight line towards the fan.

'So, you're looking for a girl?' he said.

'Not exactly,' I said.

'On the phone you said you wanted to see me about an

urgent matter. In my experience most urgent matters come from women who are looking for a new maid because they are dissatisfied with the one they have.'

'I see.'

'So how may I be of assistance?' he asked, grinning even more broadly now. He was like a gambling saint – there was a disparity, a weird dissonance about this man.

'Well,' I hesitated, and he nodded, urging me on patiently and impatiently. 'I *had* a maid, and she has disappeared. She just vanished one day. I was told that you might be able to help.' I could hear my voice crack. Saying it out loud to a stranger, and a strange stranger at that, made it so much worse.

'Vanished?'

I nodded.

'When?'

'Two Sundays ago.'

'And you've been to the police.'

There was no question mark to this question. I told him I had.

'How did that go?'

'It was a useless waste of my time. They told me she must have run away to the north. I know she hasn't.'

He hastily grabbed the notebook that the ashtray was sitting on and leafed through it. Without looking at me he said, 'What is her name?'

'Nisha Jayakody.'

'Where do you live?'

I told him and he continued to search his notebook, his

finger running along the pages. He took another deep drag of the cigarette and I watched him as the fan swirled the smoke around him, as his eyes skimmed over the words, as he turned the pages, flicking forwards and back again, as he placed the cigarette in the ashtray and ran his hand through his hair. I'm not sure what he was searching for but then he grabbed a pen and jotted something down.

'In the last month,' he said finally, 'two other maids have been reported missing to me.' He stressed the last two words and looked up with a deep frown, his eyebrows raised at the edges.

'Two?'

'Both Filipino. One worked in Akrotiri, the other in Nicosia. Where is your maid from?'

'Sri Lanka.' He jotted this down in the notebook too. I felt my body turn cold, despite the heat in the booth. Two other women had gone missing.

'What could this mean?' I managed to say. I found that I couldn't speak much, my mouth dry, my tongue stuck to the roof of my mouth. Perhaps sensing this, he called out to one of the maids who was passing the booth.

'Bilhana! Bilhana!'

A woman in an orange sari turned on her heel and arrived in the open doorway of the booth.

'Tell Devna – two coffees.' He spoke slowly, holding up two fingers. 'Sugar?' he said to me.

I shook my head. 'Do you think they are connected?' I said, once the woman had gone.

He responded by raising his eyebrows and opening both

of his palms – he was at a loss. 'I knew there was a problem when the first girl went missing,' he said. 'Rosamie. I placed her. She came here three years ago through an agency; she worked for a man who was no good to her. He beat her. God knows what else. She came to me for help. With some difficulty, I got her out of the clasp of her agent and found her a better home. She moved in with a British family in Akrotiri. They were good to her, and she was pleased with them. She would come here on Sundays, eat and talk with the other women. She was a good dancer too, loved the music here. One Sunday she didn't come.'

He paused there and stubbed out his cigarette. The phone rang again, but this time he turned it over and ignored it. 'Billie Jean' was playing in the back hall, and a couple of women were standing close to the booth chatting.

'The next Sunday,' he continued, 'she didn't turn up again, and I thought it was odd. The following one, her employer came here to tell me that she'd gone.'

'She'd gone,' I repeated. It seemed the only thing I could manage to say.

'Mrs Manning went to the police, but they convinced her that Rosamie had run away to find employment in the north of Cyprus. Poor woman didn't know what to believe. But I knew Rosamie. She came here beaming every Sunday because her bruises had faded, because she was happy with Mr and Mrs Manning. She would bring me a cake or biscuits, always thanking me. She said I had saved her life. Why would she run away? It doesn't make sense. You see, when you clump people together and don't understand their personal stories, you can make up any bullshit and convince yourself it's the truth.'

By now the ash from his cigarette was long and he threw it in the ashtray and took another out of the box, holding it between his fingers without lighting it. At this point Devna came in with a tray of coffee, two glasses of water and a plate of sesame fingers. She was a slim girl who looked like she could easily have been fifteen, but there was an assurance and confidence to her movements and posture which made me think she was older. I hoped she was, at least. She wore faded jeans with slits at the knees and a brightly coloured shirt. Large, silver, hooped earrings shone through her dark hair as she leaned over the desk, placing the tray on top of some paperwork.

'They don't know anything about life,' Tony said, looking at Devna. 'They've come from small communities, labourers in fields.' I watched Devna's fingers as she took the glasses and cups from the tray, placing them on the table – long, dark, beautiful fingers, her nails painted earth-green.

'They say they want to send money to their families, but a lot of them come to find freedom. They think they're going to be flying free in Europe. Back home they usually earn 200 euros a month; here it's around 500. But what do they do? They look at TikTok and photographs on their phones all day and think about which boys they like. Isn't that right, Devna?'

Devna laughed but said nothing.

'Don't you like boys?'

'I do,' she replied with a smile, 'but that is not why I am here.'

'So why are you here? Tell Petra why you are here.'

'Please, madam,' she said, smiling again with glistening lips, 'this is your coffee and water.'

'If they were clever,' Tony said loudly, more to Devna than to me, 'they would save!'

Devna turned her back to him and winked at me. There was a faint smile about her lips, a knowing in her pitch-black eyes. I took the wink to mean: *Don't listen to him, we know perfectly well why we are here.*

Someone called Tony from the kitchen. 'Excuse me a moment,' he said, leaving me in the booth with Devna.

'I'll tell you why I'm here,' she said; and now that Tony was gone her voice was sharper, louder. 'Tony is a good man, but he still doesn't really understand. I came because I saw no other way forward at home. There was no work, nothing I could do. I have a brother who is disabled, he can't walk or talk. My parents are old now. I have to send him money. Tell me, who will do this if I don't? I was working night and day at home and it wasn't enough. They say we have a better life here, but is that a reason to treat us like children, or worse, animals?' There was a fierceness to her words. 'Do you understand what I'm saying?' Her gaze was firm and penetrating.

'Yes,' I said, without looking away, feeling the full force of this woman's determination and strength. 'Yes,' I said, 'I do. Have you told Tony this?'

'Of course I have,' she said. 'He knows. He knows. He likes to tease me. The others don't know, though. They see me as a robot.'

I gulped down the water and placed the empty glass back on the tray.

Tony returned and Devna winked at me again, smiled and left.

'I can see that you're distressed,' he said. 'And I want to hear your story. But first, let me tell you about the other missing girl, Reyna . . . Reyna was a different matter altogether. She came here five years ago with her sister, through an agency. Her sister, Ligaya, was relatively happy with her employers but Reyna was miserable. She worked for an old woman who shouted at her and she felt pretty homesick most of the time. One night, she went out and never returned. Ligaya came here, a wreck, a week later. She was crying a lot and I had to calm her down before I could understand anything. Reyna's phone was switched off. She had left everything – her passport, other precious items, she went out with the clothes she was wearing and the shoes on her feet and never returned. The old woman wasn't bothered – she was advised to find another maid, and she did. Poor Ligaya got my details from some other girls and came to me because she was afraid to go the police.'

'Afraid? Was she an illegal immigrant?'

'No,' he said bluntly. 'She came here legally. She was afraid about how she would be treated.'

He struck a match on the box and it sizzled into a flame. He lit his cigarette and the smoke came out of his mouth in rings, which disintegrated and dispersed in grey wisps around the booth. He picked up his coffee and had a sip. 'Help yourself,' he said, signalling with his eyes to my coffee and the biscuits on the tray.

I took a sip. It was packed full of sugar, but I decided to

drink it anyway — I needed it in the heat and stuffiness of the tiny booth with the fan that circulated the same smoky air. Scenarios flashed through my mind. Had all three women got involved with something that had led to their disappearance? Could Nisha have known Reyna and Rosamie? A shadow loomed in the corner of my thoughts. Had something else occurred, something darker . . . I couldn't bear to think about it.

'So, tell me,' he said. 'What makes you think Nisha hasn't run away? Because I guess that is why you are here?'

I drank the rest of the coffee in one go, took a deep breath and told him the whole story: the trip to the mountains; her request to go out that evening which she hadn't mentioned again; the crash I heard in the garden that night; realising the following morning that Nisha had gone; that her bed had not been slept in; that she had left her passport, her locket, her daughter's lock of hair; and, most importantly, that she had not said goodbye to Aliki. I told him that she had been seen heading out at 10.30 on Sunday night, after I had gone to bed, and that she had been heading in the direction of Maria's, which was basically a brothel-type bar.

He nodded while I spoke, occasionally jotting things down in the notebook. Once again, his cigarette had turned to ash and it fell onto his beige trousers. He swiped at it, smudging it in.

'Where exactly is Maria's?' he asked.

I gave him the address and he wrote this down too.

Then I showed him the bracelet that I had been clutching in my hand the entire time.

'Some friends of Nisha's found this by the Green Line,' I said, 'not too far from Maria's. See how the clasp is broken?'

'May I?' he said, and opened his palm.

I placed the bracelet upon it. He looked at it closely, examining its every line, running his finger over Aliki's name on its underside.

'Who is Aliki?'

'My daughter. This bracelet was a present to Nisha from us for her birthday a few years ago.'

He gave me the bracelet and sat there, pensive. There was silence between us for a while. Ricky Martin's 'Livin' La Vida Loca' drifted in with the sounds of cutlery and conversation and laughter. Tony looked around the dining area through the glass of his office booth, like a captain at the bridge of a ship.

'Could there be a connection,' I said, 'between these three women?'

In response, he tore a piece of paper out of the notebook and wrote down the names of the women, including the date of their disappearance. 'I am assuming that you are in contact with some of Nisha's acquaintances?'

'Yes, of course,' I said.

He handed me the piece of paper. 'Please go back and ask them about these two other women. Had Nisha mentioned them? Are they known within her circle of friends? Once you start asking questions, I'm sure more questions will emerge. But you never know, there could be some answers in there, too.'

I stared for a while at the names of the women: *Rosamie Cotabu 12th October 2018* and *Reyna Gatan 23rd October 2018*.

What had happened to these women? How had they disappeared without a trace? And now Nisha would be added to this list: *Nisha Jayakody 31st October 2018.*

Tony asked for my details: my full name, Nisha's full name, my mobile number, my landline and my address. He took it all down in his notebook.

'I'm going to go back to the police,' he said. 'I'll write them emails, I'll visit, I'll camp out on their front step, if I have to. If a Cypriot woman had gone missing, they would have searched the Earth to find her. Why are they not bothering with these women? Because they are foreign. They are not Cypriot, they are not citizens. They just don't count.'

As I drove away from the sea, I could still hear the music in my ears, smell the food on my clothes. The road was almost empty on this Sunday afternoon. I was both reassured and troubled by my meeting with Tony. Most of the way home, the names and the dates flashed through my mind. Had Nisha ever mentioned these women? I really didn't think so. Perhaps their consecutive disappearances were mere coincidence. But something – something dark and sinking and sinister – told me this wasn't the case.

It was just before 6 p.m. when I arrived home. In front of her house, Mrs Hadjikyriacou had her black skirt hitched up to her knees, teaching Aliki a dance move, kicking about in her new red and cat Converse. Aliki was taking the lesson very seriously. Ruba had opened a foldable wooden table in the front yard and was bringing out bowls of steaming food.

214

When Mrs Hadjikyriacou saw me, she beamed. 'We've had the most fantastic time,' she said. 'I'm getting rather tired though.' She let her skirt drop down to her ankles and insisted that I join them for dinner.

We all sat together around the table. Aliki must have been starving because she was already holding her knife and fork, eager to start eating. She eyed the food in the bowl – a Nepalese dish of fine noodles and vegetables that instantly reminded me of the smells at the Blue Tiger. There was a jug of bright, freshly made lemonade, bowls of creamy white goats' yoghurt and warm bread.

'I was going to ask you how it went, but you look famished, so let's eat first.'

Ruba lit the outdoor heater and brought out some colourful crochet throws for Aliki and me to wrap around our shoulders; they were of the softest wool and smelled of jasmine. 'I made those after the war,' Mrs Hadjikyriacou said, 'when I first came to live here. Each is a flower that used to grow in my garden back home.' And as we ate, she listed the flowers in alphabetical order.

Aliki liked this game because she challenged Mrs Hadjikyriacou with ever more obscure flower species.

'How about the cyclamen Cyprium?'

'No, they only grow in the mountains.'

'How about the Cyprus bee orchid? They are very pretty. Our teacher likes flowers. He teaches us all about them.'

'No. They usually grow in grasslands and open pine wood-lands.'

'How about the tulipa Cypria? My teacher, Mr Thomas,

215

told us they are so hard to find, and they are the colour of deep red blood. Did you have any of those in your garden?'

'No, but I'm pretty sure that my Auntie Lucia had some of those in her garden. She had three thumbs. Talking about three thumbs . . . have you heard of the monster that lives in the underwater caves near Cape Greco?'

Aliki shook her head, eyes round.

'Some people say it has several heads and numerous limbs. But everyone who talks about the creature speaks of its friend-liness. It is said to appear from the deep sea, attracted by fish caught in a net. Some people think it is a giant sea snake or a large runaway crocodile, but I have seen it with my own eyes and I can tell you that it looks like a prehistoric Plesiosaur. It was many years ago, when I was exactly your age, Aliki, that I went with my parents and my seven siblings on a summer trip to the sparkling waters of the east coast . . .'

I listened to the story and devoured the food on my plate. Ruba ate with us and was vigilant should we need anything – occasionally refilling our glasses with lemonade, or passing around the bread and yoghurt. Her eyes darted about the table; from time to time she smiled at me or Aliki and gave a slight nod, but she never spoke.

There was a light on above my flat. Yiannis was sitting on the balcony looking out across the street. I knew that I would need to speak with him, tell him about the Blue Tiger and share the information that Tony had given me. I prayed that he would know something.

The man with the army boots and the windbreaker is sitting on a rock. He drinks some hot tea from a flask and stares without blinking at the still water of the lake. Beside him is a black suitcase, lying on its side. After a moment, he straightens his posture, focuses his eyes, looks around and places a hand on the case.

Five or more beetles are crawling over the hare's fur. Some feed on fly eggs, larvae and maggots; others devour its flesh. They like the dark, the time when they feel most free. With their flat bodies, they crawl into the empty socket of its eye, feeling their way around with long antennae. A black whip snake glides past, raises its head and continues to the edge of the crater. It trickles like a shining stream down to the lake, but it does not enter.

There is no breeze tonight and the sky is full of stars. A half-moon gleams, dropping its bone-white light upon the pecan trees and fruit trees, down upon the distant river where dragonflies swarm, down upon the sunflowers and the dirt path, leading to the homes in the village, where most people are asleep. A TV flickers in one of the bedrooms; a night light glows in another. In the guest house, a cockroach, enticed to the room by the sugared almonds, feeds on the paper of an old book of fairy tales sitting on a wooden shelf. The widow is snoring. She has left the washing out on the line. A cat, with the stripes of a tiger, watches from behind a rosemary bush, planning to catch a lone dragonfly that has found itself far from the fresh water of the river – a scarlet dragonfly with ghostly, red-veined wings.

When the breeze picks up again, the man with the army boots and the windbreaker and the suitcase is no longer there.

18

Yiannis

THERE WERE FLYERS OF NISHA all over the neighbourhood. On every corner, there she was. Even from my balcony I could see her, glued to the pole of a street lamp outside Yiakoumi's antique shop, and on my walk, hanging from the canopy at Theo's, stuck to the wooden pillars and walls of the restaurant. Passers-by glanced at them but mainly took no notice. Only the other maids paused, contemplating Nisha's picture, with something in their eyes like fear – or perhaps it was recognition, a fearful look in the mirror.

The birds from the hunt in Akrotiri had filled the fridges in the spare room. I needed to clean them, but I couldn't find the discipline to sit down and focus.

Felling uneasy, I grabbed my coat and headed downstairs.

Crossing the street, I pulled off one of the flyers from a lamp-post and headed to Lakyavitos station.

I was kept waiting for forty-five minutes before I could see the chief constable, Vasilis Kyprianou.

'I understand you're here to report a missing person,' he said, opening a notebook and clicking a silver pen.

I nodded and placed the flyer on the desk.

He glanced down at it briefly, then up at me, 'I see. Can I get you a coffee?'

'No, thanks.'

He picked up the phone and asked for one coffee and some biscuits. I proceeded to tell him about Nisha and how she had disappeared without her passport.

'I know that her employer came to report her missing but had no success,' I concluded.

He put his pen down now and with a gesture that seemed to suggest that he wasn't fussed, he closed the file. 'And who are you to her?' he asked, tapping the flyer roughly with a finger.

I hesitated.

'Her lover?' There was a slight smirk on his face.

'Well, I wouldn't put it like that.'

He smiled now. 'I don't blame you, a lot of them are extremely beautiful. I wonder sometimes, though, if they really are as beautiful as they seem or if it's because they look different, exotic, if you know what I mean?'

I didn't reply. I could feel my neck and face heating up.

'So. How would you put it then?' he asked.

'I care about Nisha very much. She has been working hard for nine years to send money to her family . . .'

His smile broadened and he started waving his hand, as if he couldn't be bothered to hear the rest. 'These people don't care about their families. They have no real roots. They would throw their families away at the drop of a hat! That's why they are able to come here, or travel even further to countries in Europe, or to the Arabic Emirates and God only knows where else. You wouldn't see a Cypriot lady making that sort of decision now, would you? Leaving her children behind? That would be unheard of, no matter the circumstances. But then again, their lives are so shitty back home. They are peasants. No prospects. They come over here and we give them more than they could have ever imagined – good accommodation, good food, higher wages. But they have no gratitude – some steal, some sell their bodies, others take off. You'd think they'd appreciate being here more. Don't make the mistake of thinking they are like us. They are made of different stuff, mark my words.'

'Whatever you say, she is missing, and I would like you to launch an investigation.'

'Look, I'm not here to be chasing after these women. They come here. They don't find what they are looking for. They run away to avoid the debts they owe to their agents. Don't you think we could put taxpayers' money to better use than launching an investigation which will inevitably be a complete waste of time and resources?'

This guy was an arsehole. His skull an impenetrable wall.

221

I focused on the blue veins that ran down from his receding hairline, the steep bridge of his nose, his yellow teeth. I clenched my fist beneath the table to trap the anger.

A woman came in with a coffee and a plate of biscuits, which she placed in front of him. He took a sip and sighed with contentment. I got up to leave, leaning over to take the flyer from his desk, but instead deciding to leave it. Let him throw it away.

At home I cleaned the birds. Mechanically, systematically. I needed to get the job done. I defeathered the blackcaps, song thrushes and chiffchaffs. These birds would be pickled, roasted, fried, eaten whole in secret. The tiny blackcap sat beside me, chirping now and then, struggling to flutter up onto the table in order to eat some berries. It succeeded, then clumsily wafted back down again to give itself a bath in the bowl I'd set out for it. It was getting stronger, its wing clearly mending, but it needed more time. I'd purposely put its food on the table and the bird bath on the floor so that it would exercise its wings, test its strength.

When I first starting poaching, I did some reading on avian intelligence, hoping to confirm the bird-brain theory, so that I would feel better about what I was doing. Instead, I learned that certain bird species were so smart that they were considered 'feathered apes'. For decades, scientists believed that birds weren't capable of higher thinking because they lacked a cerebral cortex; however, now they knew that a different part of the brain – the pallium – evolved to fill its place.

In my heart, this revelation was not surprising. I had known since I was a child – and had held that dead golden bird – that they had an inner life. Throughout my boyhood, I had known birds solve problems with cognition beyond instinct, their minds flexible and sharp. I even had a crow-friend I called Batman, whom I'd watch make tools out of twigs and wood. Sometimes I would offer Batman some metal wire and create sort of a problem – a puzzle as such – and sit beneath a tree and watch it work out a solution.

Seraphim killed Batman during one of his visits. He shot the bird with a pellet gun. His dad had given him the gun to practise aim control so that he could go out hunting with the men. He was using figs as targets. He was pretty good: I remember him scrunching up his left eye, holding the gun steady on his right shoulder. Aim. Fire. Aim. Fire. He became more proficient by the second. Then, while we were having our lunch one afternoon, Batman flew down from the sky through the pines. Seraphim swiftly put the gun to his shoulder, aimed, and fired. The bird didn't die straight away, and Seraphim held it by its legs upside down, the bird squirming in his grip, and took his trophy down the mountain to show his father.

As I made my way through the bin-bag – an indistinguishable mass of bodies, feathers and beaks tangled together – my eyes fell upon an owlet. I reached down for it. It was smaller than my palm, but its body carried heft, its feathers impossibly soft and fine. I wondered if it had flown into the

223

net while following his mother on a night hunt. Its oversized opaque black eyes in its pale, heart-shaped face looked up at me without seeing.

I thought of Nisha's story of the owl, of losing Kiyoma, and I almost dropped it on the floor. How did I not notice this bird in Akrotiri when we were sorting the birds? Did Seraphim see it and let it pass into the bag on purpose? I can imagine he would have bitten into its neck indiscriminately. To him, a bird was a bird was a bird. To me, I worked like a machine. A hunt was a job was money.

Not knowing what to do, I covered the owlet gently with my other hand, making a cocoon. I thought of Nisha's first story of loss and how she had felt and heard for the first time the stillness and silence of death. I considered the other birds. The ones I had trapped, killed and defeathered. The ones that were soaking now in the basin and the bath, and all the other species that I had discarded in a bin-liner because they would not sell. This is where the baby owl would end up. I could not bring myself to throw it in there. So I sat. I sat there on the stool with the owlet nestling between my palms and I did not move for what must have been more than an hour.

Music drifted in through the open doors in the other room. It was the woman again, at Theo's. Her voice pure gold. After a while I heard Aliki laughing out front; she must be home from school. I heard Mrs Hadjikyriacou's voice. It sounded like they were playing a game.

I thought about how simple everything used to seem. How I used to sit out on the balcony, after these sounds of the neighbourhood had ceased, when most had gone to bed, and waited for Nisha. Those nights after the miscarriage, she came to me with eyes carrying pain. But she still came. Because that's what we do. When there is love, there is a safe place for sadness.

Nisha told me told me another story of loss the second night after her miscarriage. She lay down on the bed and placed her hands over her stomach in the corpselike manner she had done before. She inhaled deeply and her chest trembled. She wanted to cry, I was sure, but she held it in.

'What's your favourite colour?' she asked.

'I don't know, I've never thought about it.'

'But what if you were given a choice, the last colour you saw before you died, what would it be?'

'I'm still not sure. It's hard to choose.'

'You have to choose one!'

'Maybe this is a game Aliki would appreciate.'

'Yes, she loves these games. But choose.'

She tilted her head in my direction, staring at me with wide eyes, as if she'd asked me the most important question in the world.

'Amber,' I said.

She nodded to herself.

'I don't know what colour Mahesh would have chosen,' she said. I held my breath at the mention of her husband – she very rarely mentioned him. 'I never got to ask him that question.'

Then, in a soft, faraway voice, she told me the second story of loss.

Nisha's parents had worked in the paddy fields. They rented a plot from a rich landowner, ploughed the earth, grew rice and sold it at the market. They lived in a simple house, not quite a mud hut, but with makeshift walls of asbestos sheets. There was a well in the back garden that brought forth cool and fresh water from the dark veins of the earth, even in the heat of the summer. They had a jackfruit tree as well as papaya, mango and passion fruit. Trellises of jasmine flowers separated their garden from the neighbour's. Nisha's father grew yams and mace in the yard. He was a tall man with lighter skin – it was well known that his ancestors had joined the Dutch East India Company fleeing Catholicism in the seventeenth century, and that was why her family carried the surname Van de Berg, which meant *from the mountains*. Her mother's colouring was rich and dark, like Nisha and Kiyoma, but Nisha had her father's amber eyes. The kids at school called her 'mango-eyes'.

Their house was at the end of a long road that divided the paddy fields from the sea, overlooking a coconut plantation on one side and the Indian Ocean on the other. From her bedroom window, Nisha could see the fishermen take the boats out in the night. She'd wake up early to watch them cast the nets in the water just before dawn and then pull them in at around nine o'clock, before it got too hot. On Saturdays, she would go with her father to buy fresh fish.

She liked the silver scales, but she didn't like the sea. It wasn't a friendly sea, rough and unforgiving, and most people in Sri Lanka had never learned how to swim because of it.

Rice-growing was a family affair. Husband and wife worked together, the children expected to follow in their footsteps. However, when Nisha had reached her teenage years, an increasing number of people were leaving the farms to work in factories – garments, ceramics, gems and jewellery. With Kiyoma gone, Nisha's father encouraged her to find a job where she could be independent and not owe rent money to the rich landowners. The country was changing. Since the 1960s, the Sri Lankan government had imposed much control over trade, with heavy tariffs for imports, even banning some imports entirely. But in 1977, a new government came into power, which introduced trade expansion under new policies. Nisha's father would sit with her in the garden and explain all this; he would bring her books and articles to read – he wanted her to understand, he wanted her to understand life, the economy and people, and how these were intertwined, so that she could make productive and logical decisions.

In 1995, when she was sixteen years old, Nisha left Galle for the alluvial gem fields in Elahera. Along the banks of the Kalu Ganga river the land was luscious and green, but the foliage had been stripped away, exposing the muddy, red earth. Men climbed down deep mine shafts in Rathnapura, hoisting gravel into baskets to the surface.

In a large reservoir next to the mine, workers washed the gravel in wicker baskets, swishing them in the water a few handfuls at a time. This was Nisha's job, and it was hard work. She spent most of the day in the sun bent over the reservoir, or wading in the cloudy water, until she would see a crystal sparkle in the light amongst the dirt: blue, yellow and pink sapphires; rubies; topaz; chrysoberyls. Nisha loved finding the blue sapphires: they were her favourite. They reminded her of the colour of the early morning sea from her bedroom window, with the silver fish that twitched in the nets.

Mahesh worked in the mines. He noticed Nisha immediately. He thought her eyes were like yellow sapphires. This is what he said during a lunch break when they sat beneath the canopy of trees drinking hot tea, looking out at the arid land where the mine shafts were, where the workers cleaned the gravel chest-deep in brown water. She laughed at him and told him that his comment was cheesy, but that made him like her even more.

They became frequent lunch companions, and Mahesh told her about the journey down the shaft and along the dark tunnels of the earth, the unbearable heat, the humidity, and the fear he had of being buried alive. He was a small, gentle man with a smile that was bigger than his face. He would sweat in the mines and nearly hyperventilate, but he gritted his teeth and kept going. Nisha admired his strength, his character and determination. She told him this and he'd said that he would remember her words, that they would give him courage. Every morning, from then on, when she saw him descend into the mines, she prayed for him.

He would descend fifteen or so metres beneath Rathnapura, looking for topaz and sapphires. He would push a metal rod

228

into the porous mine walls and listen to the sound it made, try to feel the vibrations of the earth along the rod. He could normally tell when he hit alluvial gravel or sapphire, but sometimes he would inspect the rod after pulling it out as harder gem material would scratch the metal. He was good at his job, fast and agile; he hoisted more sacks full of good, gem-filled gravel than any other worker there.

They were married in Galle some years later and bought a house in Rathnapura, which was bigger than the house she had lived in with her parents.

She loved him with all her heart. He was kind. He never raised his voice, like the neighbour who shouted at his wife day and night. He cleaned his own shoes and always put his dirty clothes in the laundry basket. He had a high-pitched laugh that made Nisha laugh. No matter how tired or wary or fed up he became, she could always see the child in his eyes. That was what she liked about him. It is possible to love someone without really liking them, but she liked Mahesh a lot.

Every night he'd have sore, swollen hands. After dinner Nisha would rub them with cream. 'You don't have to do that again,' he would say, with his huge smile. 'You are tired too. How about I rub your feet?'

But Nisha wouldn't have it. 'What, with those crusty things?' She'd point to his hands and pull a face. 'Besides, I can rub my own feet. Now lie back and think of the open sky.' He liked the open sky. It was the opposite of the mines.

He didn't like coffee, he drank sweet tea. Every Sunday they went down to the market to eat *kottu* with spicy curry sauce, a flat crispy fried bread made with *godamba roti*. Some evenings Mahesh would make a delicious green jackfruit curry with pandan leaves and coconut milk. He would climb the tree himself to get fresh coconuts. He was sexy when he chopped vegetables because his thick fringe would flop down over his eyes. Nisha would call him a shaggy dog. He would laugh and lick her face from chin to brow.

When she found out she was pregnant, Mahesh ran around the neighbourhood calling out, 'I'm going to be a father!' Then he came home sweating, beaming from ear to ear, pacing the kitchen, making plans.

One day, months later, after she had just given birth to Kumari, Nisha was in the kitchen breastfeeding the baby. Hearing a noise, she looked up and saw someone through the window, running and tripping as she went. It was one of her neighbours, a woman named Shehara, running through the fields, shouting something that at first Nisha could not understand. Then her voice flowed in through the open doors: 'It has caved in! It has caved in! It has caved in!'

She shouted this over and over again, until the words lost all meaning. *It has caved. In it has caved. It has caved in it has caved in it has caved in it has.*

Nisha understood immediately what had happened. The very thing her husband had always feared. It was why Nisha had prayed every night from that very first day when they spoke in the shade of the trees. Mahesh was stuck down there in the deep, dank well with no way out. She knew him so well that she could almost hear the beat of his heart, feel the blood pumping in his veins. She could hear the dripping

230

water, see the dripping walls, the shimmering crystals in the light of his head torch. She could smell it – the earth. The earth that produced such beautiful gems, the earth that held such brilliant colours, had now swallowed him up.

Nisha stopped her story there. She could not go on. She sat up and began coughing, as if she was the one trapped in the mine, struggling for breath.

I got up and brought her a glass of cold water. She took a few sips and handed it back to me.

'I can't tell any more,' she said, eventually. 'My tears are going into my throat and choking me.'

It was so hot that night. We were on the bed with the fan blowing on us and the patio doors wide open. Once again, Nisha lay on her back, placing her hands on her stomach. All the lost futures drifted through Nisha into me. I felt sorrow for the lost child. I had a feeling of crying internally; I recognised it from when I was a boy, when my father had returned with blood in his eyes trapped in the visions and sounds of the war, never seeing me again. He made me a desk with fresh oak from the woods. He placed the desk away from the window so that I couldn't look out. He became obsessed with my education. I was no longer allowed to roam around and look at the birds and wildlife. I could no longer go with them to the market. He wanted me to study. He checked in on me. If he saw me standing by the window, he closed the blinds.

It was this thought: that loss cannot be reversed, that I

could not bring back my father's lost mind, or the child that – this lack of control, this helplessness – made my hand tremble over Nisha's.

'I wish it could have been safe inside me,' she said.

'You know it was not your fault,' I said.

'I *do* know.'

She looked up at the night sky, through the window. The moon was not visible, only stars. I placed my palm over her hands and we stayed like that for a long time.

I thought about the dying man in the gem-filled darkness of the mine. How long would it have taken him to die? Did he have time to sit in the dark and think about his life, his wife, his baby daughter up above, about all the things he loved and those that he hated, about his triumphs and regrets? What would he have felt, meeting the inescapability of death before it had arrived? What kind of hunger did he feel? What thirst? What pains plagued his body? What memories his mind? Or was he so panicked that his death came faster?

'But I didn't know what his favourite colour was,' I heard her say.

Still cradling the owlet in my palms, I went to the balcony and saw that Petra and Aliki were having dinner with Ruba and Ms Hadjikyriacou in her front yard. This was a good time for me to go to the garden. I took a spade and buried the owlet in the soft soil beneath the orange tree. I buried it deep so that cats and wild animals could not get to it. Then I sat on the balcony holding the little bird, who had nestled deep into its feathers, and I listened to the laughter and endless chatter down below.

At exactly 5 a.m. the iPad rang again. I answered it. Kumari stared back at me, confused. Once again, she was in her school uniform, purple rucksack on her shoulders. This time her hair was down, straight as needles.

'Hello, Mr Yiannis,' she said.

'Hello, Kumari.'

'Can I speak to Amma?'

I paused for only a second: I didn't want her to pick up on my anxiety.

'I'm sorry, Kumari, your mum is at work again.'

She thought for a moment, clearly sceptical. Her eyes were round and severe. 'But it is very early in the morning there. Why she is working now?'

'She had extra duties to do.'

'With the chickens?'

'Erm, yes. With the chickens.'

She nodded, thoughtfully.

'She told me to tell you that she loves you so much, more than anything in the whole world, and to be really good at school.'

'OK, Mr Yiannis. You be good at work too.'

Once again, she smiled and she was gone.

19

Petra

THE NEXT DAY, AS I drove home from work, I decided to speak to Yiannis again. As I parked, I noticed the flyer of Nisha just outside the house was no longer on the lamp-post where I had put it. But her smiling face stared at me still further along the street.

Going through the garden and up the stairs, I knocked for Yiannis. It was the first time I had been in the flat since I had rented it to him. He kept it neat and tidy and so sparsely furnished that it looked as though he was only staying for a couple of days. He kept the patio doors in the living room wide open so that the winter light and wind flooded in. He pulled the doors closed when he saw me shudder, and offered me a hot drink, which I accepted.

In the kitchen he brewed coffee in a stainless-steel pot on

the stove. On the windowsill were two plants: a small cactus and a jasmine flower, whose summer scent reminded me of the old man on the bus to Troodos.

'*I spy with my little eye, something beginning with N.*'

'*Hm, that's a hard one.*'

I could almost hear them now: Aliki's laugh, Nisha's mock concentration, as she searched out of the window.

'I went to the police,' Yiannis said.

'Oh?'

'I couldn't sit around and do nothing.'

'What did they say?'

'Basically nothing.'

He watched the coffee brew on a low flame, making sure that it didn't boil and spoil the *kaimaki* – the marbley film of creamy froth on its surface.

'Look,' I said, 'I know about your affair with Nisha.'

'Affair? Why, who am I cheating on?'

'What would you call it then?'

'I love her. We have a relationship.'

He said this matter-of-factly, as he poured the coffee into cups and placed them on a heavy oak table, which looked more like a desk than something one might find in a kitchen. One chair was made of the same wood by the same hand, and opposite was a black plastic chair that had nothing to do with the table. I sat down on that one.

Yiannis took a sip of coffee, glancing at me momentarily over the rim of the cup.

At this point I heard a chirp and saw a tiny bird beneath

the table by his feet, one of those songbirds that sweep in from the west in the winter. I used to hear them over the sea, when I went out with my father in his fishing boat.

Yiannis reached down so the bird could hop onto his hand. He brought the bird up onto the table and it settled beside the coffee cup.

'That's an odd choice of pet,' I said.

'It's not a pet. Its wing was damaged. I'm taking care of it until it's ready to fly again.' He was silent for a moment, looking at the bird. Then he said, 'Do you have any news about Nisha – is that why you're here?'

I took the note that Tony had given me, and Nisha's bracelet, out of my pocket and placed them on the table.

'What are these?' he said, going very still.

'Two other women are missing.' I said, trying to keep my voice steady. 'These are their names and the dates when they disappeared.'

Yiannis stared at me without looking down at the paper.

'And this is Nisha's bracelet, as I'm sure you recognise. It was a gift from Aliki, and Nisha never took it off. Another maid found it on the street near Maria's.'

I could see the fear in his eyes. His hard silence reminded me of Muyia's wooden sculptures, frozen in time.

I told Yiannis about going to the Blue Tiger, how I had met Tony and what he had told me about the other two maids. While I was talking, he sat with both hands on the table, a deep frown between his brows. It was only when I finished talking that he moved, bringing his hand up to his face, pressing his temples with his thumb and finger, creasing his face in the way that he had when he'd downed the *zivania* at my apartment.

I expected that he would speak but he said nothing at all. We sat there in silence for a long time, Yiannis with his fingers pressed against his temples, me with my hands in my lap. The kitchen window was open a crack and a cold breeze drifted through the jasmine flowers, riffling their smell.

'Aliki, this is too difficult.'

'Keep going!'

'Nylon? And before you ask, the woman who is reading the novel – to your right – is wearing nylon tights.'

'That's very good. But no.'

'Necklace.'

'No.'

'Neck!'

'No.'

'Nun?'

'Nisha, where do you see a nun?'

'We passed a church and a nun was outside in the garden.'

'You see everything.'

'You should be more observant.'

'OK, do you give up?'

'Let me try one last time . . . nostril!'

'The answer is Nisha.'

'Me? That's cheating! I can't see me!'

'Why? I see you!'

'I would never have guessed that! I could have gone all week and I would never have guessed that.'

'Isn't it funny that you saw everything but yourself?'

237

'Something is really wrong,' Yiannis said, eventually.

'I know.'

'Something is really wrong,' he repeated, this time more to himself, as he scratched a knot in the wood of the table with his nail. His foot shook intermittently underneath his chair, which made the table tremble and the coffee cups rattle in their saucers. He seemed to be thinking, thinking, thinking. I imagined his mind spinning and I tried to keep mine still.

'At first I thought I might have scared her away,' he said.

'Why?'

'The night before she went missing, I asked her to marry me.'

'You wanted to marry her?'

The table stopped trembling. He exhaled deeply and brought his hand up to his face again, this time rubbing his thumb and forefinger towards each other across his eyes, as if he was scooping up tears before they fell.

'I found a ring on her dressing table. So that was from you.'

He nodded and glanced up at me, as if he was now worried about my reaction.

I wondered what conversations they may have had: the discussions about Nisha losing her job, just like other maids who had become embroiled in relationships. They were meant to be working and even when they were resting, we owned them. This was the unspoken truth.

Had his proposal scared her away? Was this a possibility? It would have been simpler and much less frightening to cling to this thought, but the piece of paper in front of us fluttered slightly in the breeze as if it was trying to take flight.

'Please,' I said. 'Have a look at these names. Do you recognise them?'

He picked up the piece of paper and read it. 'No. She's never mentioned them to me.'

'You're sure?'

He nodded. 'I would have remembered.'

'Mrs Hadjikyriacou told me she saw Nisha the night she went missing, at ten thirty, heading north up towards the buffer zone.'

'That's the street that leads to Maria's,' he said, nodding.

'Yes.'

He thought for a while. 'Spyros – the postman – told me he saw her rushing along the street. Apparently she told him that she was going to Maria's to meet Seraphim.'

I frowned. 'Seraphim, your colleague?'

'Yes.'

'I bumped into him at Maria's on Friday night. I stopped in to leave a flyer and talk to the manager. What connection does Seraphim have with Nisha?'

'Nothing, as far as I know. She'd met him and his wife a few times, that's all.'

'Have you spoken to him?'

'He denied seeing her or arranging to meet her.'

'Do you believe him?'

He didn't reply.

'Something's not right there,' I said.

Yiannis went into the living room and returned with a handful of red berries, which he placed on the table. The bird ate them one by one. I watched Yiannis as he watched the bird eat. There was a softness to this man; he seemed to have a gentle and troubled soul.

'What about Kumari?' I said. 'Won't she be trying to contact her mother? The girl must be beside herself with worry now, if she hasn't heard from her.'

'Nisha used to speak to Kumari at my place.'

I nodded, not knowing what to say, feeling ashamed that I had not known this.

'I've spoken to Kumari,' he continued. 'I'm trying not to worry her too much until we know more.'

I nodded again, concerned.

'Leave it with me,' he said. 'Kumari knows me. I'll deal with it.'

'Thank you,' I said.

'At least we can agree that she was heading in the direction of Maria's.'

'Yes. That is one thing, at least.' But it felt like nothing. 'Can't we check her bank account,' I said, 'to see if money has been taken from it?'

'It's not possible to check her account without the police.'

He offered me another coffee, but I declined. I had left Aliki alone and I needed to make dinner; it would be getting dark soon.

'Listen,' I said, as I headed to the kitchen door, 'this guy – Tony – he's going to call me to arrange a meeting with the employer and the sister of the other missing women. Would you come with me?'

'Of course,' he said, immediately. 'Thank you, Petra.'

'Thank you, too,' I said.

As I walked back down the stairs, my feet were heavy and I felt tears begin to well in my throat. I wasn't ready to face Aliki yet – I didn't want her to know I had been crying – so I made my way over to the abandoned rowing boat and got in. Clutching my sweater around me, I sat on the rough wooden plank and thought about the day that Nisha had first arrived from Sri Lanka.

It was spring, a week after Stephanos had died; I was thirty-two weeks pregnant. I had prayed that he would live to meet our baby. Before his illness, I'd envisioned our future like a storybook: we would have a beautiful garden full of fruit and flowers; Stephanos was going to build a small BBQ out of brick, on the far right by the cactus; we would have two children. We'd made these plans before I even got pregnant. If someone had told me then that soon my only hope would be that my husband would live long enough to see his only child just once, I would never have believed them. We didn't understand how bad things would get: neither of us had any experience with cancer. We had assumed that things would be tough for a while, and then return to normal. Treatment. Remission. Like so many others.

Then, one day, I had had to carry my husband to the car. With the help of a neighbour, we lifted him into the seat and we drove in silence to the hospital. My husband's eyes were yellow and his hands black, and we carried him, twelve months pregnant with bile, over the threshold to no man's land.

That Christmas Eve, when he could not lift his arms or his eyelids or his lips to smile, I kissed him. I fed him and brushed his hair and filled the creases around his eyes with cream, then I folded the white sheet beneath his chin and tucked it in around his bones and waited for him to say, 'I'm here.'

He lay in his faeces with a catheter and a keepsake from the church, and drank soup through a straw. He had no voice and no hope and no more days left.

After he was gone, a blur of people came. My mother was still alive in those days and she and my father would turn up together, at any time of the day, with shopping bags and oven-dishes of warm moussaka – which they knew was my favourite. They tried so hard to keep me from sinking. Later, after my mother's fatal stroke, my father bought a boat and moved to Greece, finding his solace on the sea where he always belonged.

Friends and neighbours visited. They would ring the door-bell, come and go like ghosts. I had hot food and hot cups of tea. They tried to keep the house tidy. They made sure I ate and bathed and slept. They bought gifts for the baby: yellow gifts – candy yellow, sunshine yellow. Life-before-death yellow. Stephanos and I had chosen the room facing the orange tree for the nursery, so that's where I stored the gifts in a pile, like a castle, on top of a changing table.

I drifted through it all, but I was not there. My mind was stuck in the life we had planned; it could not fathom this new reality. All the evidence was that Stephanos was still there. His clothes and military gear were in the wardrobe. His aftershave and cufflinks on the dressing table. His razor by the sink in the bathroom. The canister of his shaving foam still had froth on its tip. His hair was still in the comb. His shoes in the wardrobe. Our bed still held his smell.

Nisha arrived soon after. She was dropped off by the agent's representative. She had one small suitcase and copper eyes. She wore a black dress, the material too fine for the cold weather. She stood by the door behind the agency woman, looking around, then her eyes settled on me. The woman – Koula or Voula – wore a grey suit and had a blonde bob and was talking, but I wasn't really listening. I remember signing the contract on the dining table, while Nisha stood watching by the door.

'You've got a good one,' the woman said. 'She speaks English. My girl is from Nepal and doesn't know a word. It's a nightmare, I'll tell you.'

Thankfully, that was the end of the conversation.

When the woman left, I showed my girl to her room. She put her suitcase down by the bed and asked me if she could open the blinds. For the first time in a long time, the sun came in.

Dust floated about in the light. I hadn't been in this room for ages. My girl walked around touching the bedcovers and dressing table and armchair with the tips of her fingers.

'Madam,' she said, 'thank you for this beautiful room. You are very kind. Some of my friends said that I might have a dark room and sleeping on the floor.'

'I don't think that's true,' I said. 'We look after our maids here.'

She nodded.

'When is the baby coming?' she asked.

'In a few weeks.'

'I have a little girl in Sri Lanka. Her name is Kumari. She is two years of age.'

I didn't know what to say. I had no energy and no desire to hear about her life, or anybody else's, for that matter. There were no questions inside me.

Her eyes flitted to my stomach and then she glanced again around the room.

'You can have a rest,' I said, 'after your long journey. Settle in, unpack, have a good sleep and start work tomorrow.'

'Thank you, madam.'

'Then you'll be working from 6 a.m. to 7 p.m. Monday to Saturday, with a two-hour break in the afternoon. You'll have Sundays off. When you're not working in the evening, I expect you to rest in your room so that you are fresh for work the next day.'

She nodded and said nothing.

'You have very unusual eyes,' I said.

'Thank you, madam. At school my friends called me "mango-eyes".' She smiled now, and her face was radiant. I left the room and closed the door behind me.

From then on, Nisha slowly brought the house back to life. She made me fresh eggs with toast and tea every morning. She cleaned until the marble floors sparkled, the kitchen spotless. On the mantelpiece, the photo of Stephanos stood polished in its silver frame.

Mostly I stayed out of her way. The baby was due soon, and I was working as much as I could, putting in extra hours at the shop. I came home at night exhausted and falling into bed, barely eating the dinners Nisha would prepare.

But, one evening, I looked up at Nisha and smiled at her. 'Thank you,' I said. 'You've done a fantastic job.'

She nodded and smiled. 'I'm glad you're happy, madam,' she replied. Then, after a moment's hesitation, she went on: 'But there is something I need your help with.'

I followed her to the nursery. She had folded all the yellow clothes and put them away, in the drawers and cupboards. She had washed and ironed the bed sheets and throws, and made up the cot.

'It's very nice, Nisha.'

'But it is not beautiful yet,' she said.

On the changing table were ornaments and toys, gifts I barely remembered.

'I wonder, could you help me to decide where these will go?'

She picked up a snow globe and shook it – white glitter swirled around a cat with four suckling kittens at her teats. 'Where shall I place this?'

'Anywhere you like.'

'I think it's the job of the mother to decide.'

'Fine,' I said. 'On the dressing table.'

She went over to the dressing table and placed to the left of the mirror. 'Here?' she asked.

'That'll do.'

'Or how about in the middle?' She pushed the snow globe over a few inches and turned to look at me. I said nothing.

Then she picked up a string garland for the wall. White fluffy clouds and wooden stars. 'And this, madam? Over the crib, or on this wall on the other side?'

'Either will be fine.'

She contemplated for a moment and held them up over the crib and finally decided to place them on the wall adjacent to the patio doors. I watched her as she did it. Concentrating, making sure they all lined up neatly. Then there were fairy lights of moons and stars, a bedside lamp of a cottage where the windows lit up, rainbow building blocks, a family of teddy bears, cactus ornaments, a yellow pillow with the word Dream embroidered on it, and some tiny animals made of felt – a bird, a hedgehog and two bears. She placed each item with purpose and care and soon the room had been transformed. The bedside lamp glowed in the darkening evening light, a beautiful, welcoming little house.

Then she took me to my room. The bed was neatly made, the mirrored wardrobes had been cleaned and the room smelled of polish.

'I will leave all your husband's things until you tell me.'

I was grateful for this.

But, eventually, I let her clean out my husband's belongings. I felt a throb of shame that I could not bring myself to do the task, but by then I had become so used to letting Nisha do everything for me – and for the baby, when she eventually arrived – that it took almost nothing to turn to the window and sip my coffee, Aliki asleep in her bassinet, while Nisha removed every trace of my marriage from the room.

I suddenly noticed that Aliki was standing in the garden looking at me. She was holding Monkey.

'Does that cat belong to us now?' I asked, pretending to be cross.

'Ask him,' she said. At that, she released Monkey, who took the opportunity to spread out on the ground and set about licking himself. Then Aliki stepped into the boat with me.

'I'm hungry,' she said. 'Are you going to make supper?'

'Yes. Yes, my baby, I will make it in a moment. I'm sorry it's gotten so late.'

'That's OK. But I am hungry.'

'I know,' I said. 'But first, would you tell me about the Sea Above the Sky? I'm feeling sad. I'm missing Nisha and I think I would like to hear a story.'

She looked at me for a moment, then said, 'OK, then. Close your eyes.'

I did as she said.

'You mustn't peep. I can tell if you are peeping!'

I scrunched up my eyes, to prove that I wouldn't cheat.

'Most boats go forwards and backwards, but this one goes upwards,' she said. 'Into the sky. We have to go through the layers of sky and then we get to the sea.'

'Isn't the sea on the ground?' I asked.

'No. And don't interrupt. Just be patient,' Aliki said.

I smiled at the scolding. *Just be patient.* Those words reminded me of Stephanos. I was always more eager than him to get on with things, to make plans, to get married, to get pregnant. *Chill out, Petra. Just be patient.* It's not because he didn't love me, I had no doubt about that, but he was a man who wanted to take everything a step at a time, slowly, as if we had all the time in the world. It was also how we made love, so unrushed, so slow, and it made me go crazy for him.

'We're there,' Aliki said. 'But don't open your eyes.'

I nodded and kept my eyes closed.

'Up here it's eight hours ahead,' she said, 'so the sun is coming up. But *just* coming up, so it's still kind of dark. The sea is shiny, all silver and gold. The sea is as wide as the sky, it never ends, so you can sail above any country in the whole world. When you look down through the water, you can see the earth, all the trees and rivers and houses. And the people.'

'Are there people up here, too?' I asked.

'Sometimes, but not today. There are plenty of birds, though. They are birds that have died and now they are here and they make promises to each other. Some of them used to be human and they came here to find each other again. But not all – some of them were birds before.'

I opened my eyes now and looked at my daughter. Her hair was wild about her shoulders, and shining a deep glossy brown. She was wearing her pyjamas and her wrists and ankles seemed to be bursting from them. How had she grown, this child of mine? I could see the past in her eyes, Stephanos looking out at me, just for a second, before the memory of him vanished and then there was only Aliki. Aliki. Aliki in her own right. With her beautiful almost-translucent skin and silver veins on her lids and flushed cheeks and soft ridge in her brow and cheek bones like half-moons. She took my breath away.

The cat jumped on my lap and rubbed its head against my arm, my shoulder and my face, its soft purr close to my ear.

'Can we have dinner now, Mum?' she asked.

Mum.

'Yes,' I said.

'Mum?'

'Yes?'

'I miss Nisha.'

'Yes,' I said. 'So do I.'

'Is she coming back?' Aliki asked.

'I don't think so, but I don't know for sure.'

'Are you trying to find her?

'I am.'

Aliki was quiet for a while and then in a very serious voice she said, 'She was worried about the birds.'

'The birds?' I said.

'The ones that get trapped on the lime sticks by their feathers and legs. She was going to tell the man to stop stealing all the birds from the sky.'

'What man?'

'He's called Seraphim.'

I tried not to react. I chose my words carefully. 'Did she go to speak to him?' I said, as gently as I could.

'Yes. When we came back from the mountains. When she tucked me into bed, she told me that she was going out to talk to the bad man about the birds and that I should be a good girl and stay in bed. You know, because sometimes I need to wee and I knock on her door because it's too scary at night for me to go to the toilet all on my own.'

I didn't know that, but I nodded.

'I think we should go back now,' she said. 'The waves are getting bigger. We can come again another night.'

I nodded.

'Would you like to come up here again?' she said.

Once more I nodded, but I found that I couldn't speak.

The man with the army boots is walking out of the water, wet to his ribcage. He is completely dressed in black, with a windbreaker that has an orange trim around the lapel. Guided by the light of the moon, he bends down to pick up his phone, which he has left on the yellow rock by the side of the lake, and makes his way up the crater until he comes across the decomposing hare. He flashes the light of his phone over the corpse. A beetle climbs out of the empty eye socket.

The man walks away from the lake, picking up a black rucksack that he's left beneath a wild thyme bush; he catches the smell as he bends, and he pauses for a moment and inhales the scent with closed and distant eyes. Perhaps he is trying to replace the smell of death, which is clinging to his nostrils. With the rucksack over his shoulder, he walks a few yards to his car. He does not turn on the headlights as he drives away.

20

Yiannis

EARLY IN THE MORNING, THERE was a knock at the door. I jumped out of bed thinking it was Nisha, but Petra was standing there, looking pale as the moon.

'Can I come in?' she said.

'Sure.'

She was wearing pyjama bottoms and a white T-shirt. She had dark circles under her eyes. 'I haven't slept,' she said.

I led her into the kitchen and put the coffee on the stove. She looked up at the wall clock.

'My god, I didn't realise it was that early.'

She seemed disoriented in the chair, trembling hands in her lap, shoulders sagging. She reminded me of a moth. Usually she was so put-together. This wasn't a woman who cuddled or cried. She did not fall apart. Her name, Petra, means 'stone'. I'd never really liked her, to be honest. She was the wall that stood between Nisha and me. Her, and the whole damn system.

The little bird hopped around on the windowsill, bobbing its head, looking at the world outside.

'It wants to fly,' she mumbled.

'Yes. But it's not quite ready yet. It won't survive if I release it now.' I placed the coffee in front of her and she took a few large gulps. 'Watch it,' I said, 'it's scorching,' but she didn't seem to hear.

'I have some more information,' she said.

I sat down opposite her. My heart beat fast but I tried to keep calm.

'I was talking to Aliki last night. She said that on the night that Nisha went missing, she had put Aliki to bed and told her that she was going out to meet a man about birds.'

I straightened, heat creeping up my neck. 'Who?'

'Seraphim. According to Aliki, he was stealing birds out of the sky and Nisha wanted to make him stop.'

I felt sick.

'The thing is,' she continued, 'I've been up all night thinking, trying to work things out, but I'm missing all the pieces. If there is something you're not telling me, Yiannis, I think now is the time to do it.'

She said my name with bitterness, as if she knew I was guilty of something. And I was. I could tell she knew by the way she had drawn her shoulders back now, challenging me. This was the Petra I knew.

'*Is* there something I should know?' she said.

254

I instinctively looked over to the spare room.

'Look, I'm not messing about.'

'Neither am I,' I said.

'What is this thing with Seraphim and the birds? I know you know something.'

I got up and asked her to follow me to the spare room. I unlocked the door and we went in. She looked around at the fridges, the lime sticks and the hunting gear.

'Right.' She opened the fridge closest to her, looked inside, turning her face away immediately, closing it. 'So this is what you do.' It wasn't a question.

'I got involved when I was made redundant. I got in and couldn't get out.'

'Nisha knew?'

'Eventually, yes.'

'She was trying to get you to stop?'

'Yes.' I felt a wave of guilt surge through me. So big that warm liquid came up to my throat, and I remembered again Nisha's flesh and blood in the toilet.

'And Seraphim?'

'He's above me. The middle man.'

'How do they stop you from getting out?'

'Usually arson. They come at night. That's the first warning.'

'And the second?'

I didn't reply.

She nodded now and looked around the room, thinking.

'So, Nisha went to talk to Seraphim. She wanted to help to free you. Could he have hurt her?'

'I don't think so.'

'You don't sound too sure.'

I stood up and opened all the windows; my neck and face were on fire.

'She went to speak to him, then she vanished. She went to speak to him, then she *vanished*. Do you understand that?'

'Of course I do.'

'We can't go to the police.'

'No.'

'You need to find out what happened, Yiannis.'

'Yes,' I said. 'I will.'

I called Seraphim and arranged to meet him that night. He told me he would be at Maria's from 10 p.m.

'Join me anytime you want,' he said. 'I'll be there. I'm always there.'

In the meantime, I couldn't sit down, I couldn't eat, I couldn't think about anything else. I was supposed to be putting the birds in their containers and sorting them for delivery, but I spent the whole day sitting on the bed where Nisha and I used to talk and make love, staring out of the window at the street below and trying to piece the story together: I asked her to marry me. She left holding the ring. She went to speak to Seraphim. She wanted to free me. She was not seen again.

That night, I walked passed the flyers of Nisha posted around the neighbourhood. Nobody had called Petra. I watched people walk by and Nisha's smiling face looking out at them. They did not see her.

I found Seraphim sitting at a small round table near the

bar. There was a young woman sitting with him, petite with large, brown eyes – like that of a child – hair as black as coal, leaning into him, smelling his neck.

'Off you go,' he said to her, when I arrived. She obeyed. I watched her as she walked over to another table where two old men sat smoking. One of them removed some food from his tooth with his finger. The other stubbed out his cigarette. Whose fag-yellow breath would she be inhaling tonight? I hated these men. I was not one of them, I was sure of that. Had Nisha become involved in sex work? Had she got herself trapped? Maybe she was desperate to make extra money, desperate to get out of here, to get back to Kumari. There was desperation everywhere in this place: it dripped from the windows in condensation, it made the tables wet.

Seraphim clicked his fingers. A sound so sharp that I turned to face him. A waitress glided towards us with an empty silver tray.

'Two whiskies, my dolly,' he said.

'No, I don't want to drink.'

He ignored me.

'I was with her last night,' he said, flicking his eyes towards the woman sitting with the old men. 'She's lovely.'

I looked away. His face was making me feel sick.

'You've been jittery lately,' he said. 'I hope you're well.'

He didn't hope I was well. He hoped I wasn't bailing out. I'd heard him say the exact same thing to Louis before they'd burnt down his car – with his son in it.

The waitress returned with two glasses of whisky. She placed them on the table, one for me, one for Seraphim.

'Go on,' he said, 'you look like you need it.'

I downed the whole glass without flinching, just to get the damn thing out of the way. 'Seraphim,' I said, 'I miss Nisha, and I need to know what happened to her. Two people have confirmed that she was coming to meet you here the night she went missing. Please. Tell me what happened that night.'

I didn't know how else to put it. I could hear the desperation in my voice, see my pathetic self in his eyes.

He glared at me. He smiled. Deep lines around his mouth.

'This is the problem with being *in love*,' he said. 'It always creates a mess, and I like to keep things tidy, if you know what I mean?'

'So she came to see you?' I persisted.

He glanced around, over his shoulder. 'I'll tell you what,' he said. 'I don't like talking about these things in public. How about we go to mine, have a drink there?'

He downed his whisky and stood up before I replied. He left some notes on the bar, winked at the barmaid and I followed him outside and along the street to his car.

We got into his Jaguar, doors opening like wings. The interior, soft leather. He had a top-of-the-range sound system and the engine purred like a tiger. I turned my face towards the window as he goosed the gas pedal and we flew into the night.

I'd never been inside Seraphim's house before. It was a gated, white monstrosity with pillars and blue-tinted windows that looked like the sky. It was on a hill and looked down on the Famagusta Gate. It seemed to jut out of the earth at a strange angle; it reminded me of a huge cruise liner on a choppy sea.

When we stepped into the living room, a maid was standing on a chair in the middle of the room. She looked like she was in her fifties, a short woman with enormous breasts that she seemed to be carrying like an extra weight. A few lamps were on in the room and she was cleaning the chandelier – a huge crystal eyesore. When she saw us, she climbed down and turned on the main light. The crystals shimmered, the light sending thousands of orbs around the room.

'I have finished, sir,' she said, looking at Seraphim.

'Good girl. Did you do all the other things on the list?'

She nodded.

'You didn't leave anything out like last time?'

'No, sir.'

'OK, go and get us some nuts and a couple of whiskies. Put them in the back room.' He turned to me and said, 'You should always keep your lights clean.'

The maid gathered her cleaning supplies and shuffled out of the room.

'We have a dinner party tomorrow – my niece is christening her first child and the whole family is coming here. My wife is probably in bed. Let's go to the garage, we can talk privately in there,' Seraphim said.

We walked through a hallway of white marble – it was everywhere: the floors, the walls. Vivid paintings lined the walls, so extraordinary they were almost alive. Images of Troodos, orchards, streams, farms. One in particular grabbed

259

my attention: an old man with a white goatee, large hands and black trousers, a deep crease in his brow, carrying what looked like a bag of wool across a field.

'Is that—?'

'Yes,' Seraphim said behind me.

'Why?'

'These are my memories.'

I looked at the man's face more closely, remembering my grandfather. I could almost smell the funk of sheep coming off him. Then I noticed the background, the landscape stretching out behind him, green and luscious with vegetation, but down in the valley a fire, raging, and threatening to grow and expand up the hills. There had never been a fire like this as far as I could recall.

'Why is there a fire?' I asked.

'It's the war,' he said, matter-of-factly. 'And other things.'

'What other things?'

'The things that threaten all that is natural and beautiful and right with the world.'

It was then that I noticed for the first time a sadness in his expression. It reminded me of Seraphim as a boy, before the rifles, before the black crow. Something came back to me, a boy with sad eyes standing on the trunk of a fallen tree, pretending it was a mountain, saying, 'Look down there, Yiannis!'

The past echoed along the corridor. Seraphim placed a hand on my shoulder. 'Now take a look at this one,' he said.

The next painting was simply of an apple tree full of ripe

fruit, a blue sky behind it. Bright greens, yellows and blues contrasted with shadows of deep red and purple.

'That's the tree outside my house, back in the day, isn't it?'

'Yes.'

'These are phenomenal.' I could feel myself being sucked back, drawn to a time almost forgotten. I found myself surrounded by my past.

'You painted these?'

'Of course,' he said.

Then I remembered Seraphim's father. A prominent heart surgeon and hunter. Always suited and booted, even when he had a gun in his hand. He had hard eyes, that man, and a quiet but harsh tone that left Seraphim and me trembling.

Before I could say anything more, Seraphim continued on down the hallway. At the end of the long corridor was a wooden door that he unlocked with a silver key. The door opened up into a large garage, which looked more like a showroom. Three beautiful cars gleamed like water beneath halogen lights.

'Extraordinary,' I said, in spite of myself. I hadn't come here to see his cars. I wanted to talk about Nisha. He was distracting me, I could tell. He had a habit of doing this, throwing you off course.

'This one is a Lamborghini Miura. A mid-engine supercar.' He waved his hand at the nearest car, and beamed. I decided to humour Seraphim in all this, to get him in a good frame of mind.

'Metallic green,' I said, 'with tan leather seats. Very stylish.'

'Now take a look at this one,' he said.

'Wow. The Porsche 911.'

'Magic! Special order Lava Orange.'

I looked inside at the black leather interior with orange stitching and seat belts.

'This beauty has a 7-speed PDK transmission.'

'And a switchable sports exhaust system?'

'Of course.'

'Impressive,' I said.

We walked around to the silver Mercedes SL 300 Gullwing. It was beautiful. He put his hand into his pocket and pressed a fob, the lights flashed and he opened the doors on both sides, asking me to step back as if it were about to explode.

'Now, look at it,' he said. 'Didn't I tell you? Doesn't it look like it's about to fly?'

'Higher than an eagle. This is a car dreams are made of.'

He smiled in the way he had when he was a boy, after he killed Batman.

'Now the ice will be melting.'

'The ice?'

'Our whiskies. We almost forgot them.' He closed the doors of the car and clicked the fob in his pocket to lock it.

'I want to talk about Nisha.'

'Sure,' he paused, waiting. When I stayed silent, he said, 'Go ahead.'

'She came to see you the night she vanished?'

'She didn't arrive.'

His evasiveness was making my blood boil. He was playing with me. 'But she'd arranged to meet you?'

'Yes.' His eyes remained fixed on mine.

'Why didn't you tell me this, when I asked you this three days ago?'

'She's got guts, your girl, I'll tell you that. She called me, said she'd got my number from you. Said she needed to speak to me about you – she wanted me to let you go. I told her, of course, that that wasn't possible and reminded her kindly to mind her own business. That this was not the kind of thing she should be getting involved with, that she'd get herself into trouble. She insisted – she doesn't give up, your girl, I'll tell you that. She said she had something to offer me that I wouldn't be able to refuse.'

'What?'

'I have no idea. She never showed. She was meant to meet me at Maria's late that night. I waited. She never showed. I didn't mention it because your loyalty to us is solid, is it not? I didn't want to open up a pointless conversation, you know what I mean? I expect your girl will turn up in no time.' Before I could say anything, he waved his hand and smiled like nothing fazed him. 'Now, which is your favourite car?' he asked.

'Excuse me?'

'Which of these three cars do you most admire?'

'I don't have a preference' I said.

'Choose one, will you?'

'The Gullwing.'

'It's yours.'

I remained silent.

263

'Stunned, huh? Never thought you'd be in possession of such a beautiful specimen? Now look, if you exceed your target before the end of the season, it's yours.'

'I don't want your car,' I said.

'Consider it yours already. You've never let me down.'

'Seraphim,' I said, fixing my eyes on his, 'I'm telling you now that I don't want your car. Or any other reward, for that matter.'

'I see,' he said, nodding, and I saw a slight twitch beneath his right eye.

I glanced at my watch.

'I've got to go,' I said.

'There's whisky and snacks,' he said, but I told him that I had to get going. I needed to get out of there.

When I got back to the neighbourhood, it was just past midnight. I was about to go upstairs to my apartment, but something stopped me. I looked about the street almost as if I could see Nisha's footsteps, as if she'd left prints in the sand for me to follow, or crumbs for a little bird. I started walking down the street. This is the way she would have gone, heading toward Maria's.

Silver moths flew below the street lamps. Theo was just closing up for the night. He lifted his arm to greet me; I nodded. I watched the road ahead, imagined her walking. What had she been wearing? Would she have held a handbag? Hair up or down? Why hadn't I asked Spyros? I painted a picture of her for myself. Nisha in jeans and an orange jumper, the one with the sunflower on the front. She was wearing her new black trainers, the ones Petra had bought her. Hair in a ponytail. She was concerned, serious, on a mission to sort my life out. I saw her walking ahead of me, turning right onto the street where I had seen Spyros; the street lined with lemon trees where corrugated metal sheets spilt the island in two. There weeds grow. There is a dead apple tree. There is a row of mostly abandoned shops and workshops, shutters always drawn, doors bolted, some don't have doors or front walls – they were once cloth and carpet stores; some sold copper, and now they are empty.

Then Muyia's studio, dark, no one in there, his sculptures covered in white cloth. It had been a while since I'd spoken to Muyia. Could he have been there that night?

And there, at the end of the street, Christos lived in his old shack – might he have seen her? Could he have been outside? Would she have waved or stopped? The windows were dark now. I knocked. Nothing. I knocked again. Then footsteps, shuffling around. 'Who is it?'

'Yiannis!'

He didn't hear. 'I said who is it?' The door opened and he stood there in boxer shorts, pointing a hunting rifle at me. When he saw my face, he lowered it. 'What the fuck are you doing? Fuck you!' The few hairs he had stuck up on his tanned head.

'I'm sorry, Christos. I know it's late, very late.'

He narrowed his eyes at me. 'Come in,' he said.

The living room and kitchen were one room. There were

doilies everywhere – on the coffee table, the mantlepiece, the back of the sofa. People in black and white photos stared out at me from all directions. We'd spoken many times in the front yard, but I'd never been inside.

'Take a seat.' He pointed at an armchair next to the unlit fireplace. It was cold in there, but he didn't seem to notice.

'I'm sorry I woke you.'

'I'd just gone to bed. No big deal. Can I offer you a drink and a sweet?'

'Just some water,' I said. I was parched after the whisky.

'When did you take up smoking?' he asked, filling up a glass from the tap. 'You fucking reek.'

'I was at Maria's.'

'Oh, yeah?' He raised his eyebrows, placing the glass on a doily on the coffee table.

I gulped it down.

'Still poaching?'

I nodded. Christos was a hunter, not a poacher. He followed the rules of the hunting seasons, was respectful of regulations, and made a measly living.

'I need to ask you a question,' I said.

'Go ahead. Figuring it's as important as fuck for you to knock after midnight.'

'Can you think back to three Sundays ago. Were you home?'

'Well, let me see.' He rested his glass of water on his huge hairy gut. 'Last Sunday I was in Larnaca, I know that. The Sunday before I was cleaning the car.' He leaned forward, placed the glass on the table and picked up his phone. He scrolled through. 'So the one before that would have been the thirtieth?'

'Yes.'

'I was home that day.'

'Are you sure?'

'Yes. I have here: *Loula visiting with lunatic kids.* Yes. My sister came to visit with her crazy grandkids. I made us all lunch. She left around eight o'clock that evening.'

'After that?'

'I sat outside with Pavlo from down the road. I remember it well because it was the night he'd got the all clear. He had cancer, poor chap. We played backgammon for a couple of hours.'

'Did you see Nisha that night?'

'Who?' Christos asked.

'Oh, um, Petra's girl. Her name is Nisha.'

'Well, let me see . . .' He glanced up at the ceiling. 'I'm pretty sure I saw Spyros with that stupid dog of his, because he stopped to ask Pavlo about his results. It was a quiet night, not much going on. Then there was the maid. Yes, it was Petra's girl, I think. She was rushing past here like she'd missed an appointment.'

'Before or after Spyros?'

'Actually, just before. By a couple of minutes. Pavlo commented, I remember – he called out, "Come here, my little girl! You're a stunner! I'll do you when my dick works again." He'd had too much to drink. Way too much.' He laughed, his belly shaking under his T-shirt.

I paused for a moment and tried to empty my head of

267

those words, but they'd already gotten under my skin and I could feel my palms sweating.

'Did she say anything?'

'Nothing.'

'Do you remember what she was wearing?'

'I seem to recall black . . . Yes, a black dress. When she left, Pavlo said he wanted to get under it. Unzip it like the night, see the light underneath – those were his exact drunken words.' I flinched. Christos laughed even more now, rubbing his stomach, a throaty phlegmy laugh.

'Was her hair up or down?'

'Down. Ahhh, that thick, long hair. Who could not notice that? Imagine rubbing your face in it. I bet it smells like apples.'

I felt the anger again. I got up, apologised for getting him out of bed and quickly took my leave.

On my way home, I retraced Nisha's footsteps again. I could see her more clearly now. Black dress, hair down, the way it would have shone under the streetlights, light waves. I could see her rushing, turning the corner . . . Pavlo calling out, *Come here, my little girl! You're a stunner! I'll do you when my dick works again.* Then laughter. There must have been laughter. And Nisha's eyes, narrowing, lips tight, head up, thinking she wanted to belt him. That's how I imagine her. And let's take Seraphim's word for it and assume she didn't make it to Maria's. Then what? What happened to her between Christos's and Maria's? Could she have climbed over the fence? Gone into the buffer zone? But why? There was no reason for her to do this.

I could see her fingers now, dangling by her side. Calf

muscles, lean and strong as she walked. I could smell her, the faint whiff of gardens and spices and bleach.

Then she might have seen Spyros, greeted him, bent down to pet the poodle. Probably laughed at whatever silly outfit Spyros had put the dog in that night. Maybe he'd hummed the theme from *Raiders of the Lost Ark*, maybe she'd hummed it back. Perhaps she'd had it in her head as she turned the corner.

I could hear her heart beating. A clear and cold night with a full moon. Why was she rushing? Seraphim wasn't the type to have left if she was late. Unless there was another reason.

When I got home, I put all the birds into their rightful containers for the last time. I worked like a madman. I would never do it again. I should have stopped the moment I had promised Nisha and faced the consequences. She had been trying to help me, she had been trying to free me and then she was gone. If I had stopped like she'd asked me to, Nisha would have still been here. I was sure of that. My body felt heavy; I felt like there were weights on my wrists and ankles.

It took me a few hours to complete the job, working through the night. The entire time my mind retraced Nisha's steps, over and over again. I saw her in her black dress. Every time, at the end of Christos's street, she vanished. I couldn't place her after that. I couldn't imagine what had happened. It was like the ground had swallowed her up, and I remembered again Nisha's retelling of her husband's death: *The earth has swallowed him up the earth swallowed him up he has been swallowed whole by the earth.*

As soon as the tablet rang I jumped up to answer it. The sight of Kumari in her uniform, hair tied up in a ponytail like her mother, purple rucksack on her shoulders, sent a sharp pain through my head.

'Is Amma looking after the chickens again?'

'That's right.'

She looked up at the sky. I could see that she was outside this time. She took a sip from a drink with a straw.

'Are the chickens sick?'

'Yes. They seem to be.'

'Mr Yiannis, you are lying!'

'No, I'm not.'

'Yes. I know when a person is lying.'

'How?'

'Because they say silly things that they don't realise are silly things.'

'What did I say that was silly?'

'You said Amma was looking after the chickens.'

'That's because you asked me if she was.'

'But my question was a lie. Because I knew you had a lie in your sleeve. It is five o'clock in the morning where you are. I know that Amma wouldn't tend to the chickens in the middle of the night!'

I couldn't help laughing. 'Your English is very good.'

'I know. Amma teaches me on the iPad and I learn at

270

school too. And I have an auntie who is married to an Englishman up in the cold mountains and they teach me too.'

'Well,' I said, 'that's excellent.'

'Today I have my favourite subject at school.'

'What's that, then?'

'History.'

'Lovely. What do you like about it?'

'I like it because I see how people were silly in the past.'

'Like my lie with the chickens?'

'Yes.' She smiled that cheeky smile again. Then her face became serious. 'So, where is my amma?'

'I don't know, Kumari.' I couldn't lie to this girl anymore. 'I'm not sure. Usually she speaks to you on my iPad from my home, but she hasn't come to see me for a while.'

'That's unusual.' Though her voice was light, her eyes were suddenly heavy and dark.

'Why is that then?'

'Well, because you are Mr Yiannis and my amma said she loves Mr Yiannis very much because he is such a good and kind man. Why would she not come to see you if she loves you very much?'

I couldn't answer her question. In spite of her confusion and anxiety her eyes sparkled once more.

'I will call again tomorrow and I hope that she is there. You be good at work now, Mr Yiannis,' she said, and then she was gone.

21

Petra

'STILL NO SIGN OF NISHA?'

Keti was leaning on the counter, staring at me.

I filled Keti in about Nisha's relationship with Yiannis, about our discovery that Nisha had been going to visit Seraphim, and how Yiannis was going to confront him.

'Gosh,' she said. 'That's a lot to take in. So, she was on her way to meet this man, Seraphim, about poaching birds and she disappears into thin air?'

'Exactly.'

'I don't like it.'

Her words made me sink into a nearby chair.

'And Yiannis – can you trust him?'

'I think so.'

'You look exhausted,' she said.

272

'I couldn't sleep last night.'

She examined the bracelet so closely, as if she was determined to find an answer within it. Then she sighed, seemingly at a loss. She placed the bracelet in my palm and squeezed my hand. 'Go home,' she said, 'get some rest. If you burn out it won't be helpful for anyone.'

My head was pounding with a dull ache, my eyes bleary. I needed to sleep. Aliki was still at school for a few hours, Mrs Hadjikyriacou had dropped her off in the morning. I could get in a good nap before I had to go and collect her.

But after I parked the car, my feet wouldn't carry me to my front door. Instead, I found myself walking in the direction of Muyia's workshop.

'Hello?' I called, but no one answered. As I'd hoped, Muyia wasn't there. People in Cyprus used to leave all their doors open in the past, and it was as if Muyia was stuck in those bygone days. But that was good, as it wasn't him I was here to see: it was Nisha. I quickly headed over to the sculptures next to the worktop. I pulled the white sheet off and there she was, the mother and child. I put my hand on her hand and leaned my head on the worktop. Nisha had sacrificed so much to come here and I had never allowed myself to know that. Now she was gone.

I imagined the wood being hollow, and her trapped inside. I thought that if I found the seam in the wood that I could lift it and open it up like a Russian doll, and find her there.

'Petra,' a voice said, sharply.

I opened my eyes to cold light, a breeze and a person standing above me.

'Petra. What are you doing here?'

I straightened up. Muyia was staring at me, perplexed.

'How long have you been here?'

I stood up and backed away from him. His eyes were fixed on me.

'Not long,' I said. I glanced at the statue and he followed my gaze. 'Is that Nisha?' I managed to say.

'Yes. And the little child is her daughter, Kumari.'

'Why?'

His brow creased and I saw something moving at his side: he was scratching his arm.

'Nisha visits me a couple of times a week. You know, on her way to the grocery store – that sort of thing. She brings me fruit from your garden, whatever's in season. Until recently she brought me oranges. Still a bit bitter, but they were fine.'

I stared at him.

'She says I'm a lonely man who needs a woman in his life.' He laughed. 'And besides, she likes to tell me stories.'

'Stories?'

'You know, about Kumari and her life back in Sri Lanka. Also about her sister and the owl.'

The owl. I had no idea what he meant about her sister and the owl.

'I make sculptures of people and animals that leave an impression on me. Nisha has told me so many stories about

274

her life, she has brought me so many oranges and grapes and prickly pears, tomatoes . . . and, let me see . . . oh, eggs and sometimes wild greens. She says I'm too skinny, that I look like a lizard, that I need to keep up my strength if I'm going to capture the beauty and sadness of the world. So, I wanted to do something for her.' He paused. 'But what are you doing here?'

'When was the last time you saw Nisha?' I said.

'Oh, I thought you were keeping her busy. Tell her I miss her stories and her oranges, will you? And don't work her too hard – she'll do everything to please you, it's the kind of person she is.' He smiled and the cold morning light lit up the deep creases of his face.

'I haven't seen her for almost three weeks,' I said.

'How come? Gone away?'

'I don't know.'

His smile vanished.

'She went out three Sundays ago and never came back.'

'And you haven't heard from her?'

'No, I haven't.'

'Well, that's unusual.'

He sat down on the stool and remained quiet, pulling at his beard. He seemed anxious, agitated even.

'I thought she was busy,' he said. 'I didn't realise. So there's a chance I might never see her again?'

He looked up at me, waiting for an answer that I couldn't give. There was something childlike about him, as if this question had been living inside him forever, and it had finally emerged from his soul.

'She's such a good person,' he said. 'Bad things always happen to good people.'

'We don't know that anything bad has happened.'

'Sorry, don't mind me.' He stood up, as if waking from a sort of stupor. 'I tend to think the worst – always have. I am sure she is just fine. At the end of the day there will be a reasonable explanation.'

His words followed me like a shadow as I walked home. I kept my eyes on the road so that I wouldn't have to look at Nisha's flyers.

When I got home, the house was empty and hollow. I collapsed onto my bed. I imagined I was inside a seashell. The past echoed in its chamber, a far-away sea, long ago, my father's voice clear and warm above blue waves: *Look at that, Petra, look at that jellyfish, look how luminous it is, look how beautiful! No, don't reach out to touch it, baby. It will hurt you. Sometimes the most beautiful things can hurt us.*

And Stephanos, his laughter. That's what I could hear – Stephanos laughing about a cake I had baked that was as flat as a Frisbee. We spread jam on it, we ate, we made love. Then Nisha, crying in her room night after night when she first arrived. Me, stopping outside her bedroom door and listening. 'Can you hear that baby crying?' Nisha had said one night, leaning out of the window. 'I can hear a baby crying, as if it is crying for me.'

And Aliki.

Mum.

The word had disappeared. She had swallowed it up inside her. She knew, didn't she? She knew that I was far away, from the day she was born. I heard it now, that single beautiful word; I heard it inside the hollow shell over the sounds of the sea and my father's voice and Stephano's laughter and Nisha's tears.

I saw it like a jellyfish floating away in the water, and I wanted to reach out and touch it.

Mum.

And that's when I understood Nisha's tears. That's when I finally knew about her pain.

Mum.

I woke up to Aliki patting me on the cheek.

'Mum, Mum, Mum, are you awake? What are you doing home?'

'Oh, stop now, shush, girl. Do not wake your mother.' Mrs Hadjikyriacou appeared in the doorway, motioning for Aliki to come out of the room.

'It's OK,' I said. 'I'm awake.'

I thanked Mrs Hadjikyriacou, letting her get back to Ruba, and suggested to Aliki that we cook together.

'How about we make moussaka?'

Aliki's eyes lit up and she nodded. This was her favourite Greek dish too, and she had always loved helping Nisha fry the aubergines and make the béchamel sauce.

I was in bed and just about to drift off, when my phone rang. I looked at the clock and my heart dropped. It was eleven o'clock. No one called with good news this late.

'Is that Petra?' a male voice said on the other end.

'Speaking.'

A short silence followed before he said, 'Petra, this is Tony from the Blue Tiger.'

I sat up in bed. 'Yes, Tony, hello.'

'I'm wondering if you might be able to come and see me. I have some information, but this is not a matter I can discuss over the phone. I would prefer to see you face to face.'

I ran a hand through my hair, the better to wake myself up. 'I'll come tomorrow,' I said. 'I might bring someone with me this time, if that's OK with you?'

'As long as you're certain this person is trustworthy.'

'He is. Don't worry about that.'

The following morning, I took Aliki to school, and once again called Keti and asked her to cancel my appointments for the day. Back at home, I went straight up the iron staircase and knocked. It took a while for Yiannis to come to the door. He was unshaven and dishevelled. His stubble had a hint of silver.

'Did I wake you up?'

'No,' he said. 'Come in.'

In the kitchen, morning light fell through the shutters onto the table, and the bird was hopping amongst the rays. In the middle of this large table was a bowl of water and a handful of seeds.

This time Yiannis put the coffee on the stove without asking, and I sat on the plastic chair. The bird fluttered from the table to the kitchen worktop, close to Yiannis. He put his hand out to protect the bird from the flame and left it there as a barrier.

'The bird's even better today,' I said.

'Yes.'

'You'll set it free soon?'

'Of course.' He stirred the coffee gently. Then he opened a jar of *karydaki glyko* and placed two fresh, whole walnuts, husk, shell and nut, leached and soaked in honey syrup on small plates with tiny silver forks. I hadn't had one of these for years, and even the smell reminded me of this very flat, many years ago, when my aunt lived here. I suddenly remembered the lime-green curtains that had hung from the wall, embroidered with peacocks and lime trees. What had happened to them?

'So, you have more news?' Yiannis said, placing the coffee in front of me and sitting down.

'I received a call from Tony – the guy I told you about.'

He nodded.

'Late last night, he called to say he has some information that is troubling.' I swallowed hard, trying to hide my panic from Yiannis; I thought I would start to cry.

Yiannis sat up, a deep crease forming in his brow.

'He wouldn't tell me over the phone. I'm going to see him this afternoon. I thought you would want to come with me.'

'Of course,' he said, gently, but I noticed that his fists were clenched and his knuckles were white. He caught my eye. 'I'm scared,' he said.

'What of?'

But he didn't reply. We ate the *karydaki glyko* and drank our coffee in complete silence, while the bird hopped about in the rays of light between us.

'There's something else,' I said.

'Yes?'

'Kumari, Nisha's daughter. I've been thinking about her. Have you spoken to her again?'

Here he sighed deeply. 'I have,' he said. 'But I just don't know what to tell her.'

A taxi drives into the village. It stops outside the widow's house.

There you go, the driver says, glancing with a yawn out of the window.

The woman in the car double-checks the address on her phone.

It's coming up to midnight and the widow has been waiting up for them. She comes out onto the patio and raises her thumb. Yes, she says, welcome. This is the right place.

The taxi driver opens the boot and carries two medium-sized cases, one in each hand, up to the front door of the widow's home.

Round the back, she says. That's a good lad.

The widow leads the couple through the courtyard to the guesthouse and shows them around. The man picks up a sugared almond from the pillow and sucks it and says it reminds him of something, though he can't for the life of him remember what.

Tomorrow we will visit the Byzantine Museum and the Museum of Barbarism, the woman says.

They are both equally illuminating, the widow says, before she leaves them alone.

I like the word Barbarism, the woman says to the man. It strips violence of ideologies – leaves it bare, don't you think?

The other houses in the village are dark by now and so is the road leading out of the village, once the taxi has rumbled away.

Down by the lake, flesh has been removed from the head of the hare, from its abdomen and its hind legs. There are three mice feeding upon it now: one scuttles across the body as if it is running over a small hill.

The sky is dark. Clouds have gathered, thick and heavy, as a storm is brewing.

22

Yiannis

'YIANNIS, MATE. I WANT YOU to go on another hunt this weekend. We've had a number of huge orders come through. Christmas parties coming up and all that malarkey. It's gonna be busy again, like it was last year, remember?' Seraphim said, over the phone.

I was in the bedroom with the windows closed, shutters down, keeping out the winter and the light, agitating about what news this Tony guy might have about Nisha.

What exactly was Seraphim asking me to remember? How I did everything without questioning it? How I had killed inside me the boy I used to be? How I had lied to Nisha?

I remained silent.

'So,' he continued, 'this time, let's go to the west coast of Larnaca. You had a great catch there last month. I'll come with you this time, we'll be even more productive.'

283

I remained silent.

'We'll go this Friday,' he continued. 'I'll pick you up as usual, at 3 a.m., so be outside waiting, with all the gear.'

I remained silent.

'I gather you've lost your tongue.'

'I'm just looking at my diary. I still need to do all the deliveries from the last hunt.'

I saw myself in my childhood room, sitting at the oak desk, my father hovering over me. By then, I no longer called him 'father': he was *He*. My father had died in the war. I didn't know this new man, whose eyes were unfocused. He ranted. He wanted me to study, to get out of the village, to make something of myself. Was that so unreasonable?

Well, I did. Look at me. Didn't he tell me to chase money at any cost? When he died, he no longer remembered my name. But he walked the same, in the care home, along that green corridor, up and down, hovering over green lino, not knowing who he was or who I was. I guess we can die many deaths.

Seraphim cleared his throat. He'd allowed me the silence, but it had gone on too long.

'That's fine,' I said, 'I'll see you on Friday.'

I lay in the dark thinking about Nisha, the way she had held on to me in the night, grieving for the lost baby. There are many ways to lose a person, that was something Nisha had taught me. It was then she told me the third story of loss.

After her husband died in the gem mines of Rathnapura,

Nisha decided to move back to Galle to stay with her mother, in the house between the sea and the paddy fields, where she had lived as a child. By that time, her father had passed away and her mother had retired and was able look after Kumari while Nisha worked.

She found a job as a street vendor in Galle Face Green – an urban park in the jumbly city by the beach – making *kottu*. Sometimes there were rallies there and parties, and, back in the old days, horse races that she had attended with her father. Along the green now was a sizzling rainbow of street food. Every day she made the *kottu*, adding *roti*, meat, vegetables, egg and a spicy sauce called *salna*, prepared on a hot plate and chopped and mixed with silver blades.

The man who owned the stall was fat and dark. For the first few weeks, he watched over her, especially during the final step of preparing the dish, where she mashed and chopped all the ingredients together with the blunt metal blades. He wanted to make sure she got the process 'just right'. Once he was satisfied – 'This is the fucking best *kottu* in Galle. I grew up on this stuff and know what's good' – he more or less left her to it, and went off to manage his other stalls. He paid her hardly anything, but it was the only job she had been able to find: she'd walked up and down the streets practically begging for work. All day long and late into the evening, she was bathed in aromatic spices, and her sweat and her tears dripped into the food, for she did not, for a single day, stop crying and longing for her husband.

There was a carousel a few stalls down, whose music never ended, and opposite an old woman sold colourful saris. Next to her, a middle-aged man had a cart selling nuclear-orange *isso vadai* – spicy lentil cakes with prawns – and next to him a young woman who made luminous desserts with shredded coconut wrapped in betel leaf.

The park was ringed with food vendor carts lit by small puddles of electric lights at night. There were colours and smells and sounds everywhere, and Nisha was exhausted. Her mother's pension was measly, so Nisha was keeping them all afloat. When her husband had been alive, they had worked together to pay the bills, and although it had been tough, at least she had been in it with someone else, with both their wages helping them get by. They had also managed to put a bit aside for Kumari's education. It was Mahesh's wish that his daughter would be educated, and be the first in the family to attend university.

Once Nisha left for work, Kumari would cry. In fact, she cried until she turned blue. Her grandmother could do nothing to console her.

'Your daughter is a crazy genius,' Nisha's mother would say to her. 'She knows too much. I can't distract her like I could with you. She's bloody minded. Where did she get this from?'

'You, Amma!' Nisha would say, remembering her mother's obsession with her little sister's heart all those years ago. Remembering the pendant that Kiyoma had thrown into the river to free herself.

Kumari was always awake when Nisha came home from work. There was nothing Nisha's mother could do to get her to sleep. She tried everything. She sang to her, she walked her along the beachfront. Nothing – Kumari looked at the waves and laughed. Nisha's mother changed the songs to prayers, chanting beneath the hush of the trees in the garden. At one point she thought of organising a *thovil*: 'Nisha, I'm at my wits' end. This child of yours is possessed.' She was joking, of course; Kumari still smiled through it all.

Whenever Nisha came home, whether it was 9 p.m. or 11 p.m. or 1 a.m., Kumari would begin to cry. It seemed to Nisha, on reflection, that these were tears of immense relief. She would pick up her daughter, sit on the bed, and make a little nest by crossing her legs. Kumari would cluck and mutter, while Nisha put her baby to her breast. Kumari would suck vigorously, resting her left hand under Nisha's breasts, her right hand holding Nisha's fingers. When Kumari had finished, Nisha would take off her sweat-drenched clothes and lie on her back on the rug with her baby on her chest. She liked lying on the floor, feeling the firm ground beneath her: it made her feel safer, held by the Earth. And then, finally, Kumari would sigh and drift into a soft sleep.

At these times Nisha was happy. This was when her tears stopped, when she had her baby in her arms. On warm nights she'd lie like that in the garden for more than an hour and think about the world from the womb to the stars. She thought about time and space and existence and how some-where between birth and the heavens we all exist, and that somewhere out there was her husband's energy-force either waiting or being reborn.

No matter how much Nisha worked, however, her income was never enough. They had already started eating into the education fund, which left her feeling mortified. Within just a few months, there was nothing left. The three of them were surviving pay-check to pay-check.

One day, the young woman across the street who made coconut sweets with betel leaf, didn't turn up. She was replaced by an older woman with dappled skin who always wore the same purple sari. For so many months, Nisha had watched Isuri as she delicately wrapped the sweets – dark eyes down, flicking up occasionally to take in the passing crowd. Nisha and Isuri would exchange *kottu* for sweets, pleasantries for smiles, and eventually grievances for hugs. Isuri wasn't yet married and was looking for a suitable match and was progressively getting fed up with her life; she could never earn enough to support her ailing father and two much younger sisters.

Nisha and Isuri had become close, and Isuri's sudden departure had had a profound effect on Nisha. Isuri had been talking about leaving Sri Lanka, hoping to go to Europe and work as a maid. 'So many women are doing it!' she told Nisha one morning, with sparkling eyes. 'I could earn double what I'm earning here in one month! I could send money home and still have enough for myself. I'll be given nice accommodation and food. And imagine having all that freedom too! Imagine being able to go out, to be free, and not have to answer to anyone. I will be my own woman.' She had been so excited, and Nisha would never forget how Isuri looked that morning with so much hope in her heart.

At home in the evenings, with Kumari sleeping peacefully on her naked chest, drenched in drying tears, she felt her body begin to ache and her mind spin. How could she ensure that Kumari had a good life? How could she fulfil her husband's wish and send their daughter to university one day? Staying in Galle was a dead end. She had three mouths to feed and she had to do it all alone. The flour was running out in the cupboard, as was the rice. Her mother had started to ration the portions. Kumari was wearing hand-me-downs from the neighbours – this wouldn't have been a problem in itself, had Nisha been able to put money aside for Kumari's education and make sure that she was well fed, but no matter how careful she was, no matter how much overtime she worked or tips she earned, she still could not afford to buy all the food they needed for the week, let alone put money aside for the future.

Nisha felt her baby's tiny fingers, soft and warm as she slept; she gently squeezed her chubby thighs and placed her little feet in the palms of her hands and held them. Kumari sighed but did not move and did not wake. Nisha inhaled her sweet breath. Then she exhaled her decision. 'Yes,' she said out loud. *Yes. I must sacrifice these beautiful moments for Kumari's future.* And then she kissed Kumari's hands a hundred times while she slept and resolved to give her everything she could, every chance in life.

It took more than a year before her plans came into fruition, but eventually Nisha had found an agent, had filled out all the relevant paperwork and when all that was done, which took a few months in itself, she waited patiently for a suitable placement.

There had been a few opportunities that fell through –

289

one with a large family in Singapore, another with an old man in a village in Saudi Arabia, another with a young couple in a town in Cyprus. Then came Petra: a pregnant business woman who wanted help keeping the house and looking after her baby once it arrived. Nisha felt that this was perfect for her – not that she really had a choice. She would have to take what was offered or else she would have to wait longer. The island of Cyprus seemed small and homely, and she had been told that there were many women from Sri Lanka who had already made their way there, and that everyone spoke English, and that the weather was good.

The agent's fee was astronomical to Nisha, the equivalent of 10,000 euros. Of course, she couldn't afford to pay it upfront, so she would pay the debt in instalments, commencing with her first pay-check. She calculated that this would still leave her enough money to send home, and to also put aside for Kumari's education.

Meanwhile, Kumari would no longer settle on Nisha's chest when she returned from work. She would writhe and mutter and claw at her skin, then cry inconsolably, as if it was herself she had hurt. Nisha was convinced that Kumari understood on some instinctive level that her mother's heart and mind were somewhere else. Nisha couldn't bear it. She knew that Kumari knew. Kumari grew each day and became a force to be reckoned with. The muttering turned to actual words. 'No!' she would say to her grandmother when she didn't want to sleep, and 'No!' she would say to her mother when Nisha wanted a hug and a kiss on her return from work. By the time she was two and could string sentences

290

together, there was no arguing with her. 'No, Amma! You go back to work now!'

'But you were waiting for me all this time, and now you don't want me?'

'No. Not waiting. Kumari playing with Ziya. Ziya hungry.' Ziya was Kumari's favourite doll that her grandmother had made with old rags.

Kumari watched Nisha as she packed.

'Big bag, Amma?'

'I'm putting my clothes in, ba-baa.'

'Why?'

'Amma is going away.'

'Kumari going?'

'No.'

'Ziya going?'

'No, ba-baa.'

Nisha arrived in Cyprus late one Sunday night, with a small suitcase, wearing a black linen dress that a neighbour in Galle had made for her. She was picked up at the airport by the agent's representative, and taken to an old dark house in an old dark city where a forlorn pregnant woman greeted her with a broken smile and distant eyes.

Isuri had been right about one thing – she was given a lovely bedroom with antique furniture that backed onto a garden full of plants, chickens, a cactus, a fig tree and an orange tree. There was a small fishing boat in this garden, which reminded her of the fishermen in Sri Lanka – those she had seen from her bedroom window – and Nisha knew she had come to the right place.

That night, she was awakened by the sound of crying. She got out of bed and held her ear to the closed door. It was a child, very young, probably around Kumari's age. It was as clear and present as the darkness. She walked along the corridor, following the sound, and it led her out into the garden through the communal door. There the sound was louder. She thought that it might be a neighbour's child, but it seemed to have no direction. It was coming from every-where, or so it seemed to her. She sat in the unused boat in the garden and tried to understand where the crying was coming from. It came from the earth and the trees and the sky. She sat there until she fell asleep and woke at dawn to the sound of a cockerel crowing in the distance. The crying had stopped.

She only had an hour before she needed to begin work, so she decided to start straight away. She cleaned and scrubbed every surface until it shone, until the memory of the night's disturbance began to fade.

Petra was happy with Nisha's work. It was the only thing she seemed happy about. She appeared to live in a constant state of despair and she carried her stomach like an object, as if she was carrying the earth.

The following night, when she was tucked up in bed after a long day, Nisha again heard the crying. Once again, she got out of bed and followed the sound out into the garden, through the glass doors in her bedroom. It was a clear night, frosty and cold. Stars in a dome above her. The air was still, no wind, and she listened, alert as a cat, in order to locate the source of the sound. But once more it came from everywhere: from the leaves on the trees, from the branches and bark, even from the roots – it seemed to run like rivers beneath the earth, like the deep song of the trees. Equally, it came from up above, from the fabric of the sky, from the waves and particles that make up our existence; it was carried on the wings of bats and owls, and higher still, much higher, it came from the stars.

At this point in her story, Nisha paused. She stopped talking and looked at me right in the eyes, then she ran her hands along my arms as if to clarify my existence, to ground herself in the present.

'Did you find out where it was coming from?' I had asked.

But instead of replying she drew her body close to mine, so that there was no space between us; she moulded herself onto my body, she tucked her head into my neck and for the first time since the miscarriage, she had begun to cry.

23

Petra

'SO, WHEN DID IT ALL begin?' I said. 'You and Nisha? If you don't mind me asking . . . ?'

Yiannis and I had set off for Limassol. I had the radio on low. It was raining hard, so we drove with the heat on, windows up. We were passing an orchard of orange trees and then a farm. I opened the window a crack and breathed in the cold air; the smell of earth and manure rushed in.

'Two years ago,' Yiannis said.

'When you first moved in?'

'Yes. Well, that was when we started talking. It took some time after that, to get to know each other.'

I thought he might say more but he was staring into the distance, at a village on a hillside.

'How did you keep it a secret for so long?'

'She would come and see me a few nights a week. She'd

speak to Kumari at 5 a.m., always on Sundays and Tuesdays, sometimes other nights too, and then leave mine just before 6 a.m. so that she could get back to her room before you woke up.'

I kept my eyes on the road but I could see in my peripheral vision that he was looking at me now, perhaps waiting for my reaction.

'I see,' I said. 'I wish Nisha had told me.'

He didn't respond to this. I mean, what could he say? I would never have accepted it then. I was too greedy, I needed Nisha for myself – and for Aliki.

I never would have considered her right to her own life.

I was embarrassed and ashamed, because I had been so self-absorbed all these years, and I hadn't noticed. I wondered – would I have been different if Stephanos had still been alive? Would he have kept me in check? My world had become so narrow it hardly even included our daughter. I had missed so much of Aliki's life, and it was right in front of me. What had she been showing me that I couldn't see? What had she been saying all these years that I couldn't hear?

And then there were the birds. Yiannis bringing thousands of songbirds back to his apartment, selling them on the black market, being involved in what I knew to be a highly criminal organisation. Ahead, the sea was agitated by the rain. We were nearly there.

Tony was sitting in his glass booth. The atmosphere at the Blue Tiger was different today, perhaps because it was a weekday. There was a Cypriot man behind the counter making sandwiches. A few customers were dotted about at various tables and there was no music blasting from the back hall, no one walking around with trays of food and drink. It was as if the other Blue Tiger had been something I had seen in a dream. But then I spotted Devna, coming out of the kitchen area towards us. This time she had on bright red lipstick. She was wearing a different pair of dark blue jeans with a pink and white checked shirt that revealed a soft cleavage.

'Madam,' she said. 'And sir.' She nodded at Yiannis. 'Very nice to see you here again, madam. Mr Tony will be ready in only five minutes. I will bring you both a drink?'

Yiannis shook his head. He looked yellow. 'I'm fine, thank you.'

I asked for a black coffee with no sugar.

Devna went off to fetch the drink while Yiannis and I stood there awkwardly, until Tony lifted his arm and waved us in.

Yiannis shook his hand and introduced himself, simply with his first name. He looked like he was there to close a business deal, with his crisp white shirt and grey twill trousers. He was even more handsome now next to Tony, whose white hair was wild and uncombed, while large sweat marks drenched the material under his armpits. A cigarette smoked on its own in the ashtray.

He shook my hand too and we all sat down. Tony eyed Yiannis and picked up his cigarette, taking a long drag of the stub, a long stem of ash falling to the floor by his feet.

He stamped on it as if it might cause a fire and said, 'So, Yiannis, right? What brings you here today?'

'Nisha and I are close friends.'

Tony raised his eyebrows. At that moment Devna came in with a tray of coffee and biscuits. She had made one for Yiannis too, and he took it out of courtesy. Tony turned the fan on and the smoky air circulated in the booth.

'Is that a new pair of jeans, Devna?' he said, and Devna smiled at him with bright red lips. She placed the plate of biscuits on some paperwork on the desk, winked at me and left.

'They never learn, these girls,' he said to us now. 'Her employer is a middle-aged widower who treats her like a princess. He's bought her a car, he buys her new clothes every week, he's now given her a credit card with unlimited funds. So, tell me, why do you think that is?' He smiled, revealing yellow teeth, but his eyes were attentive and sharp and he fixed his gaze on Yiannis, who shifted in his seat and took a sip of coffee. 'Anyway, I trust that you are both here because you care about Nisha. I have some rather troubling news.'

Yiannis placed his coffee on the desk and sat upright. I saw that he was gripping his knees with his hands.

'Since you came to see me, Petra, two more people visited me. One was a Romanian maid, who works on the outskirts of Nicosia. She came here to tell me about a childhood friend of hers, Cristina Maier, also Romanian, who has disappeared with her daughter, Daria, who is five years old. The young girl lived here with her mother. As a Romanian citizen

297

she was able to do so. It turns out that mother and child went missing two months ago. The friend has tried everything to raise the alarm, but her employers and police are not interested. The second is again a woman from Romania, Ana-Maria Lupei with her daughter, Andreea. They were reported missing last Wednesday, exactly a week ago, this time from another town near Nicosia, and again she had her young daughter with her. Her employer, an old veteran, came here with his son to speak to me just yesterday. Apparently, she had popped out one evening to meet a friend. She took her daughter with her – and they didn't return. The old man was beside himself with worry. He is very fond of them both. He went to the police and found the encounter futile.' Tony shrugged. 'In both cases, the women disappeared without warning; in both cases, friend and employer insist that it was out of character, that they left without belongings or passports, and in both cases the police were not interested in pursuing an investigation. The only difference here, however – and what is even more disturbing – is that these two women have disappeared not on their own, but with their daughters.'

Tony was silent now, letting his words sink in. He held his cigarette with his elbow on the table, looking from me to Yiannis and back again.

Yiannis inhaled deeply and his breath came out in fragments. I did not turn to look at him. I couldn't. Any hope I might have had drained out of me: the disappearances wove together now in a complicated web. It had become so much bigger; something dark and wrong clawing at the edges of the booth.

Tony threw his cigarette butt in the ashtray and lit another. The flick of the lighter was loud, the flame cracked into existence, the smoke travelled around us.

Yiannis suddenly stood up, brought his hand up to his face, brought his palm down over his eyes and mouth.

'Are you OK, Yiannis?' I said.

'I'm sorry,' he said. 'I just don't understand.'

'Clearly,' Tony said, 'they must be connected. It's too much of a coincidence. There has to be one person or a group of people behind this. It's transpired that one of the women was going out on a date. I have no information about the person she was intending to meet –I'm working on that – but she let one of her friends know before leaving home. This confirms, more so, that the police are wrong. These women did not just decide to run away to the occupied territory in the north. I'm going to go back to the station tomorrow with all the facts I have here before me.' He placed his hand on the notebook. 'And I'm not going to leave until they agree to take this seriously.'

Yiannis was still standing, his head bowed as if he was praying. Without saying anything, he sat down again and placed his hands on his knees, as before, except this time the anguish was evident on his face.

'Do I have your permission to share the information that you've given me about Nisha?' Tony now asked.

'Of course,' I said.

'Do you have anything that you could add?'

There was a pause. Then Yiannis spoke, his voice gaining strength as he did so: 'We now know,' he said, 'that Nisha was heading out to meet a colleague of mine. His name is Seraphim Ioannou. He and I are involved in an illegal network involving poaching. Songbirds, specifically. Nisha had found out and had arranged to meet him. Apparently, she never turned up for the appointment.'

Tony's eyes turned to slits. He opened the notebook and asked Yiannis to repeat the name. 'Do you have proof that she was going to meet him?'

'Yes, Seraphim has confirmed it to me.'

Tony nodded and scribbled down a few more notes. Then he closed the pad, leaned back in his chair, looking now for the first time through the glass at his restaurant that had begun to fill up, considerably.

We drove back in complete silence. The sun vanished into the sea as the afternoon turned late. Aliki would be home from school by now. Mrs Hadjikyriacou was collecting her and probably keeping her company with her stories, while Ruba made them something warm and fragrant for supper.

Yiannis stared at the rain ahead beating down on the windscreen and only spoke when I turned into Nicosia.

'Do you mind if I turn the heating off?' he said

'No, of course not.'

I flicked my eyes towards him and noticed that his neck and face were red. I wanted to ask him what he was thinking but no words escaped my lips.

It has been raining so much that the lake has overflowed. The tunnel of the mineshaft has started filling with water.

The rain has washed away the ants and the maggots from the hare, and the mice have run for shelter. Along its hind legs there are tufts of rain-drenched fur, but mostly the skin has been stripped away. The rain falls onto its open wounds, it falls into the open space where its eye once was, into the open space where its heart once was. A part of the ribcage is visible, like a new moon.

The rain continues to fall into the red water of the lake, it pounds down upon the yellow stone, it slides down the rusty skeleton of the gallows frame and into its deep mineshaft. There, on the surface of that dark water, is the white shimmer of material – drenched linen – wrapped around something unknown. Only a tiny bit is visible, like a small, white mountain rising out of darkness, like the tip of a glowing iceberg.

In the guest house, the man and the woman lie side by side on the double bed: she is on her side, facing the window where the rain streams down; he is reading the news on his phone. Its light illuminates his face. He is young still.

The woman reaches for the brochure on the bedside table and flicks through it.

Let's go to the red lake tomorrow, she says.

The red lake? he asks, distracted.

Yes, I told you about it. There was a copper mine there once. There is a red lake there now, as red as Mars, and people say it is very strange and beautiful and otherworldly. We can see the gallows frame too. What do you say?

Yes, the man says. Sounds wonderful.

24

Yiannis

SERAPHIM PICKED ME UP IN the early hours of Friday morning, while it was still pitch-black out. The streets glistened from the past few days of rain. I had all the gear ready and was waiting for him out front, as usual.

Without a hello: 'Did you complete the deliveries?'

'Yes,' I said, getting into the passenger seat and clicking in my belt, after I had put all the stuff in the back of the van.

'When?'

'Last one yesterday afternoon.'

'Good.'

The road ahead was dark, lit only by the moon. There was a fine layer of frost in the fields, luminous in the night. It reminded me of the unusually cold late October morning, not so long ago, when I had seen the mouflon in the woods, when I had rushed home to tell Nisha.

Eventually we turned onto a dirt track and the road became darker, shadowed by trees. It was so dark I felt like we might be heading off a cliff and into the sea, but the sea was miles away. The van kept rumbling on until we came to an abrupt stop in a clearing beneath a huge oak tree.

Seraphim got out without saying a word and opened the doors at the back of the van. I followed him and he handed me the shoulder bags holding the lime sticks, calling devices, three covered-up cages with sleeping birds, one large mist net, and finally a rifle.

'A rifle?' I said.

'It's hunting season. I thought we could hunt some game. We're allowed on Wednesdays and Fridays in November.'

I took the rifle from him and he turned to me and smiled with his over-stretched grin. Since when did Seraphim care about hunting regulations? I knew that November was a good time to hunt hare, chukar partridge, black francolin, wood-pigeon and woodcocks, but there is a limit on the quotas that hunters are allowed to take – something like two hare and two partridges per hunter per hunting day. But I felt like a hypocrite thinking about the quotas when on the ground by my feet lay the rolled mist net – non-selective and indiscriminate of quotas.

We carried the gear into the woods. As we unrolled the mist net and secured it on poles between two junipers, I remembered walking with my grandfather through the forest, and how he had explained that in ancient times the

304

island was almost completely covered with impenetrable forests.

'Imagine what it would have been like back then!' he'd said. 'For wildlife to be undisturbed by human hands that take so much more than what they need.'

'Where are you?' Seraphim called out, sharply.

'Right here.'

He shook his head, pushing the pole deeper into the earth. 'You're miles away. Focus, man. Imagine you have fourteen pairs of eyes. Be alert.'

I nodded and he signalled for me to lift the covers from the cages. I did so. The birds remained true to the darkness and kept their songs to themselves for the time being.

'Oksana is pregnant,' he said.

I forced myself to sound happy. 'Wow, that's great news! Congratulations, my friend.'

'We had the first scan the other day. You should have heard the heartbeat. You know, it's the most amazing thing in the world, that this little human is growing inside her. I'm going to be a father.'

His eyes shone, but his smile held a hint of fear or apprehension and I saw in this the boy I once knew.

'You'll be great,' I said.

'I've started to do up the nursery. I'm painting murals on the walls.'

'What are they of?' I asked.

'Oh, kids' stuff. You know, a waterfall, mountains, hot-air balloons, that sort of thing.'

'Sounds nice.'

We proceeded to place the lime sticks on the bushes and trees in the dark. We didn't use torches in case the area was being patrolled. We worked in silence, listening carefully for any unusual sounds or movement.

So, Seraphim was going to be a father. Seraphim. It made my intestines turn. A flash of blood in the toilet bowl. Nisha with her hands crossed over her stomach. I watched Seraphim's movements in the darkness – they were fluid and discreet, like a shadow. I wanted to ask him again about that Sunday. Had Nisha really not turned up? Did he have something to do with her disappearance? He couldn't. I mean, he couldn't. Seraphim was an arsehole, the lowest of the low when it came to certain things, but he couldn't possibly be involved in something as sinister as a missing person, or even five missing women and two children, if they were connected. I could see the fuzzy outline of his mouth and eyes. He seemed to be smiling. He was pleased with himself.

Seraphim, of all people, was going to be a dad. The prick.

When we finished setting up, we lit a small fire and waited for dawn, for the birds to descend into the trees. The calling devices sang in the dark in preparation and the mechanical but beautiful song reached us as if in a dream. The caged birds wouldn't sing until the sun rose. We toasted olives and haloumi on skewers over the fire. Seraphim had his rifle close to him.

'What are you hoping to kill?' I said.

'Maybe some hare, that sort of thing, after we've collected the birds. Wait for the wildlife to wake up.'

I nodded and removed a warm olive from the skewer with

my teeth. A black olive, bitter and grainy. There was not much conversation between us. Seraphim was alert all the time, his head darting about whenever he heard a sound. I kept my eye on the rifle. It bothered me, the way Seraphim fingered the trigger, the way he kept it so close.

It was the moment when the light of dawn cracked through the darkness and the birds in their cages and all the free birds began to sing, that I heard the crunch of leaves. Of course, Seraphim heard it to, and he was up immediately, gazing into the dawn light. I thought that was it, finally we would be caught, and more than anything I just felt relief.

But what appeared seconds later in the clearing beneath the trees was not a man in ranger's uniform, but the mouflon ovis.

I stood up too and it peered at me as it had that day, with weary, amber eyes. Once again, it stood straight and strong and its fur and horns shone gold.

'Look at that,' Seraphim whispered. 'Extraordinary!'

He gently crouched down, levelling the rifle, without averting his eyes from the animal.

The mouflon, following his movement with its eyes, took a step back so that it was now directly in a pool of light in the rising sun. And, just then, birds came in their thousands, cutting across the sky.

'Seraphim,' I said, urgently. 'Don't shoot!'

'Don't be stupid! This is a prize!' His raspy whisper was full of excitement.

He nestled the gun more securely on his shoulder, preparing himself, watching the creature.

'It's protected,' I said.

He chuckled, a low soft sound, but it came from deep in his chest. The animal took another step back, now into the shadows beneath the trees, and it seemed to be looking straight past Seraphim, at me.

I moved closer and grabbed Seraphim's elbow. He pushed me with so much force that I stumbled sideways.

'What the hell are you doing, man?' His voice back to normal. The animal shuffled back further into a darkened, shrouded space, but its fur and horns caught the light.

I straightened up and quickly positioned myself between him and the animal, while Seraphim repositioned his gun.

He held the rifle steady on his shoulder, left eye squinting hard, right eye aiming through the muzzle. 'Come on now,' he said. 'Get out of my way.'

Seraphim tried angling to the left and to the right, to get the mouflon from a different angle.

And then I saw his finger begin to tighten on the trigger.

In the next second, without thinking, I rushed into his line of fire, and before I could think another thought, he fired.

There was a searing pain in my arm, as if it had been scorched with fire.

Even through my pain, I heard the animal behind me fall. I heard its collapse, meeting the earth among the fallen leaves. Although I had my back to it, I could see its rapid decline in my mind's eye – and I still see it, time and again.

Seraphim lowered his gun. 'Fuck,' he said.

I had grabbed my arm and could feel warm blood leaking

through a huge tear in my jacket. The bullet had sliced through my skin on route to the mouflon behind me.

I turned to look. It was lying on its side, a hole in its chest, a gradually expanding pool of blood on the ground beside it. Its eyes were open. It was still alive. I crouched down beside it and placed my bloody hand on its back, stroking its fur. 'It's all right,' I whispered. A stupid thing to say.

It glanced at me sideways, its amber eyes now pools of liquid gold. I stroked its head. It was all that I could do. Its breathing was shallow and strained. Finally, it took its last breath and its eyes lost their focus.

Crouching down on the ground beside the dead animal I began to cry in a way that I had not cried since I was a boy. I cried for loving Nisha, for missing her, for being afraid for her. I cried for this beautiful creature whose life had been cut short so senselessly. I cried for the way it had looked at me as it lay dying, and I cried for the needless deaths of so many animals.

Seraphim moved behind me, and, remembering that he was there, I turned. He had lowered his gun now and was holding it loosely at his side.

I got up. I'm not sure what expression I wore on my face, but whatever it was, he took a step back, in spite of the fact that it was he who was holding a weapon.

'Are you all right?' He seemed shaken and smaller.

'Tell me what you did with Nisha.'

He stared at me without speaking. I took another step forward; he took another back and tightened his grip on the gun.

'Where is she?'

'I don't know.'

'Seraphim!'

'I'm telling you the truth! She never came to see me. I promise you on my mother's grave.' He crossed himself and held my gaze. 'I'm sorry. I apologise, you're bleeding. Let's get you to the hospital.'

Maybe it was my face, my eyes, or maybe something had happened to him when he heard me cry, because his eyes were wide and alarmed, and now in front of me stood an uncertain man, apologetic and confused to his rotten core.

I saw that his hand was shaking and he dropped the gun as he held his hands up. 'I promise you,' he said again. 'If you still don't believe me, let me show you something.'

He glanced at me tentatively, waiting for me to respond and I nodded. He reached into his back pocket and retrieved his phone, then he scrolled through it and held it out for me to take from his hand.

He'd opened up to a series of messages between him and Nisha.

31/10   22.16
Dear Mr seraphim I am running a little late because it was difficult for me 2 leave but I will be at Marias bar in half an hour.

31/10   22.19
Ok. Please don't be too late as I need to leave earlier this evening.

31/10   22.21

Dear Mr seraphim I will try my best to get there as
soon as possible Thank you for meeting it is very
important.

31/10   23.15

I am still waiting. Are you on your way?

31/10   23.43

Hello Nisha?

01/11   00.01

I'm afraid I will have to leave now.

Then he took back the phone and scrolled through again.
This time he wanted me to look at a series of text messages
between him and his wife.

31/10   22.10

Please come home early tonight? Been a long day.
Need a hug.

31/10   22.18

I will. Don't worry. Love you

31/10   22.22

I won't be too long. Waiting for someone, have a
meeting, shouldn't take long. Hug is coming! Love you

'What does this prove? Someone else could have been involved,' I said.

Seraphim blew out a puff of frustrated air. 'What do you think happened? What are you imagining? You can go through my entire phone. Go ahead! I've got nothing to hide from you.'

Still holding the phone, I turned back to the mouflon. It lay there peacefully, unmoving, its right horn digging into the earth at an odd angle. Its eyes were still open, one looking straight up through the leaves of the trees at the morning sky, which was still half-dark. I stared down at it through watery eyes.

I sat down beside it again. I put my hand on its chest, and, as the sun rose further, the morning seemed to draw the gold from the mouflon's body and eyes.

Then I saw it. I saw the gold evaporate and merge with the air and rise into the sky. I saw the gold rise from its body like light, like one might imagine a soul leaving a body. The gold became part of the sunrise before me. The fur on its underbelly was pure white now, its body and face a soft chestnut-grey. Its beautiful curved horns were an off-white that reminded me of stone.

My hand shook on its chest. My breath shook with more tears, a fierce sadness that was tearing itself upwards from deep inside me.

Seraphim remained silent behind me.

'Did you see that?' I asked.

'See what?'

'The gold, the way it left its body; the way it dissipated into the sky.'

He didn't respond immediately, and after a few deep breaths he said, 'You haven't been right since Nisha left.'

'She hasn't left. You're an asshole, you know.'

I faced him again and I remembered everything that Nisha had wanted from me, the things she had said, the way she had cried over the photograph she had seen of me as a boy. *You were just so beautiful and so sweet.* Had those been her words?

'Seraphim, I'm out,' I said. 'From now on, you leave me alone. You don't have to pay me for this hunt or the last one, for that matter. I want nothing more to do with any of this. You can burn everything I own for all I care, but if anyone gets hurt, I swear I will kill you.'

The caged birds were still singing their hearts out.

The sun rose higher still. Time seemed to be moving faster. How long did we stand there staring at each other?

'What will you do for money?' was all he said.

I didn't bother replying.

The iPad rang at 5 a.m. I was wide awake. My arm had been stitched and bandaged and I had said nothing to the doctors about what had happened.

When I answered the phone, both Kumari and Nisha's mother stared back at me.

'What happened to your arm, Mr Yiannis?'

'I fell over, Kumari. Don't worry, it's nothing.'

She squinted her eyes at me. She wasn't convinced.

The old woman began to speak to me in Sinhalese. Her face was as smooth as a stone, her large eyes fixed on me.

Her fingers opened and closed as she spoke. 'You tell me!' she said finally, in English. Then she nudged Kumari.

'My grandmother is very worried,' Kumari said. 'She want to know where my amma is. She says that never has she not called her beloved daughter and beloved mother. She is asking what have you done with her?'

I realised my hands were shaking as I held the tablet.

I was silent for a while and they both waited. The old lady with the smooth face had her hand on Kumari's shoulder. She gripped it tightly.

The young girl glared at me from beneath a newly cut fringe.

'Kumari.' I took a deep breath. 'Kumari, I'm sorry. Please tell your grandmother that I don't know where your mother is. She went out one night, nearly three weeks ago, and she hasn't come back.'

The girl paused for a moment and opened her mouth to say something to me, but then changed her mind and turned to her grandmother to translate.

The old woman was besides herself. She began to cry and speak so fast that the young girl waved her hands before her grandmother's eyes to stop her, to make her see her perhaps. The old woman continued to speak, breathless now, and Kumari, above her grandmother's voice, began to translate: 'She is asking where is she? Why would she leave? Why would she not come back? Did something happen?'

'I don't know, Kumari,' I said. 'But we are doing everything we can to find her. You must know and understand this. Everything.' My voice broke on the last word.

'She wants more information, Mr Yiannis. She says that what you have told us is not enough. She needs to know more.'

'All I know and all I can tell you is that four other women, all of them foreign maids, and their two children, have also gone missing.'

Kumari translated for her grandmother, and the old woman began to speak faster. There were questions I could tell, so many questions, but the young girl turned to face me now with a solemnity and sudden seriousness that reminded me of her mother.

'Mr Yiannis,' she said, softly, 'why didn't you tell me this? You knew for a long time, yes?'

'Yes,' I said.

'Why did you not tell me?'

'I was afraid.'

'What were you afraid of, Mr Yiannis?'

'I was afraid to break your heart.'

As soon as I said this the screen went black and she was gone.

I sat there staring at the tablet, wondering how Nisha had managed to have an entire relationship with her daughter through this tiny screen. I wanted to break through the glass, reach Kumari, pull her into a hug and tell her not to worry. I wanted to reassure this young girl who reminded me so much of her mother, but I couldn't. Not only was there so much distance between us, but also because I really didn't know what to say to comfort her.

Two vultures are gliding and sailing beneath the clouds, wings held in V-shapes. Far below, the empty eye socket of the hare stares up at their two-toned underwings of black and silver.

What a beautiful morning it is. As blue as a sapphire, with wandering winter clouds. Years ago, vultures flocked like herds of sheep or goats in this area; now these two are a rare sight. They swerve down towards the hare, the shadows of their wings lengthening across the lake as they descend. They will clean up the dead. They land on the yellow rocks of the crater, their tiny red unfeathered heads perched upon their spindly necks. Together they inspect the hare.

They begin to feast on the flesh that's been left, soft and liquified by the rain. The lake is brilliant beneath the midday sun.

In the mineshaft, white linen has unravelled in ribbons

and the overflowing rainwater moves gently over the blue and purple flesh of a breast.

At the guest house, the man and the woman tie up the laces of their hiking boots.

It's going to be a nice day, she says, as sunshine beams into the room through the slits of the shutters.

I've been reading up on the old mines, he says. I'll tell you on the way.

He speaks about the ancient history of copper and bronze as they walk past the barley and wheat fields. As they walk past the sunflowers, he tells her everything he's read about the old mines and how the men died of silicosis, and eventually they are on the arid plane where the earth stretches lonely to the horizon. The sun is strong and she holds her hand over her eyes like a sailor setting out to sea.

Seeing the couple, the vultures abandon the corpse of the hare and flap lazily away.

25

Petra

THE PHONE RANG WHILE I was collecting grape leaves from the vine in the garden. I wanted to cook something nice for Aliki. We had spent a quiet Saturday playing board games, pretending to read, but really worrying about Nisha.

I was planning to make stuffed vine leaves for a picnic on Sunday, wrapping them in foil so that we could eat them with our fingers beneath the Famagusta Gate.

Tony's voice at the end of the phone changed everything: 'Petra, I would tell you to come but this can't wait. A body has been found in the mineshaft by the red lake of Mitsero.'

I started shaking. I managed to hang up the call, then quickly gathered up Aliki and walked her over to Mrs Hadjikyriacou. The moment she saw my face, Mrs Hadjikyriacou took her in without asking any questions.

When I turned to leave, Aliki called out, 'What it is? Where are you going? Is it about Nisha?'

I couldn't find the words to answer her, but I met her eyes and nodded, then rushed off.

Taking the stairs two at a time, I ran up to Yiannis's apartment, pounding on the door.

He opened the door with red eyes, and I saw that his arm was in a sling. It looked like he had spent the night crying.

'What happened?' I said.

'It's nothing at all to worry about.'

He looked horrified when I told him about the call from Tony. He grabbed his keys and slipped on his trainers without saying a word.

It takes twenty minutes to get Mitsero from where I live. The whole time I thought about that water, with the rusted structures of abandoned mines guarding it like ghosts.

We drove to the end of a paved road that passes by the village of Agrokipia. I left the car on the side of a cracked pavement as we had to walk from there along the dirt path, to get to the lake.

A small crowd had gathered, eager to see.

These things don't happen here!

This kind of thing – never.

I wonder who they found?

I tried to block out the voices of the crowd.

The area surrounding the lake and gallows frame had been roped off. Helicopters circled above. We were on the slant of a jagged hill of yellow rock that dropped down to the water. I could feel Yiannis standing beside me, but I didn't dare to look at his face. If I saw fear there, it would have broken me; I was just barely keeping it together myself. But I could hear him breathing, I could hear his breath shake.

The body was bound in white cloth.

Tourists, they were hiking.

The mineshaft filled up with water after the rain.

Yes, that's what I heard too!

And it brought the body up.

Yes. The body came up.

I could see Nisha as if she were standing in front of me: in flip-flops and shorts; a soft sprinkling of dark hairs on her thighs; the plait that reached the base of her spine; beads on her wrist – bracelets that her daughter had made and sent in a tattered envelope. My thoughts expanded: Nisha pulling off yellow rubber gloves, spreading orange marmalade on toast for me, stirring coffee on the stove with a long spoon, questioning me with eyes that were always curious, always sombre, dark with the past.

Far away, across the land, church bells rang. They rang again and again, but I could still hear the voices of the crowd.

The body is decomposed.

They will have to do DNA tests.

I didn't dare to say the thing that was on my mind, but I knew that Yiannis was thinking it too, because when I finally turned to look at him, he was pale and shaking.

The next moment, he had left my side. I saw him slip through the crowd, heading towards the gallows frame. I lost him for a while, then I heard a commotion. I pushed my way closer to the front and saw Yiannis having an argument with a police officer: he had managed to get over or under the rope into the investigation zone. The officer was holding his arms out, creating a barrier; another was approaching from the right. This second officer placed a hand on Yiannis's shoulder and gestured for him to calm down.

'Hey!' I shouted. 'Leave him alone! It's OK. He's knows her. It's OK, he knows her.'

It wasn't until they all turned to look at me – the police, the people in the crowd – that I understood what I had said.

We left the lake without knowing. The police told us to go home, they would have to do tests, something about DNA, testing the bones – I could barely distinguish the words.

We were driving now, and I looked over at Yiannis. He looked like the shell of a man. His eyes were sunken, his lips pressed in. He was a shrivelled bird, something featherless and old.

I was just about to take the turn off for Nicosia, when he spoke, his voice dry and hoarse, as if he hadn't used it for centuries.

'Petra,' he said.

'Yes?'

'Will you go somewhere with me?'

'Where?'

'I can't go back yet.'

'But where?'

'To the woods.'

'Why?'

'I have to check something. Will you come? Will you drive me there?'

'Of course,' I said.

Following Yiannis's directions, I drove us to the west coast of Larnaca, near the village of Zygi. I was hit by the smell of wild thyme and rosemary. In the distance I could see the beautiful oranges and yellows of the citrus plantations. He directed me to a sheltered spot by the side of the road and I parked the car. He got out and headed down a narrow path through the trees, motioning me to follow him. We were walking into a dense and dark forest of eucalyptus and acacia trees. We walked for a few minutes, picking our way among the brambles, until we came to a clearing.

There, swarming with flies, was a mouflon ovis. I took a step closer, but Yiannis grabbed my arm with his good hand.

'No,' he said. 'Not this.'

I followed him further into the woods and began to hear a cacophony of birdsong. I'd never heard anything like it, so many songs overlapping. There were thousands of them, above our heads, surrounding us, thousands and thousands of birds writhing in nets that stretched the length of the glade.

'What is this?' I asked, in horror.

'The mist nets,' he said, in a hollow voice. 'Yesterday we were hunting—'

I shot him a sharp look.

'Yes,' he said, turning down his eyes. 'We were hunting.

Seraphim and me. We left so quickly after my arm was injured. I didn't know if Seraphim had come back. It looks like he didn't.'

I looked up again. It was a cacophony. The song of thousands of birds trapped in one place. I wanted to throw up. Thousands of birds stuck in the net, trying to fly away.

'Will you help me?' Yiannis asked, 'to release the birds?'

With one hand, he began to yank at the net until each side dropped gently to the earth. He knelt down and tended to each bird, one at a time. He was struggling, working with only one arm, so I went to help him.

'My god,' I said. 'My god.' Some were dead, but those still living, I cradled in my palms, stroking the birds' feathers with my fingers, placing them on the ground, waiting to see if they would move. Some hopped away, others flew up into the leaves of the trees or into the sky. One by one. One by one. Yiannis worked beside me, though clumsily and mostly ineffectually. I saw his frustration in his failed attempts, but I knew better than to tell him to step aside.

We worked for nearly an hour, releasing the birds together. There were so many that were migrating birds, and residents of the island too. Amongst the blackcaps were grey herons and blue rock thrushes, and beautiful tiny wallcreepers with their crimson flight feathers.

By now, I was crying, my sobs mingling with the birdsong.

'There are crossbills and coal tits, jays and tree creepers,' Yiannis said, as if he was seeing them properly for the first time. 'And black kites,' he continued, 'and steppe buzzards and honey buzzards. And look . . . hundreds of finches.'

'Isn't it sad that they are still singing?' I said.

'They would have sung until they died,' Yiannis replied.

'Just listen to their music,' I said. 'Oh, look at that!'

In the middle of the mist net, tangled up with pulsating wings, was a kestrel.

'It's still alive,' I said. Its wing was stuck in the net, but I tugged at the filaments with my fingers, tore at it with my nails, careful not to scare the kestrel, not to hurt it more.

'It would have died slowly,' Yiannis said.

I held the kestrel on my lap, while working on disentangling it from the net. It lay still, looking up at me with its large, beady eyes. Above us and around us flew the birds that had been rescued. On the ground beside us lay the birds that had died.

Finally, I released the kestrel from the net and Yiannis and I both stopped to watch as the kestrel opened its spotted wings and launched into the sky. I said: 'Nisha was always smiling, you know, in spite of everything. She brought up my daughter and cleaned my home and always smiled with all of her heart. Did you see that?'

'Nisha once told me,' replied Yiannis, tracing the kestrel's path in the sky with his eyes, 'that she wanted to protect Aliki from her pain. She carried much of it – pain. I don't know if you knew that. But she wanted Aliki to see her as happy, so that the child could feel that the world was full of joy. Nisha said, "Children search our eyes to discover the world. When they see happiness or joy or love there, then they know that these things exist.'"

I knew instantly that this was the gift Nisha had given to my daughter – that Aliki had learnt to understand the world through Nisha's eyes.

Two nights later, I was tucking Aliki into bed. 'Do you remember you told me about the birds stolen from the sky?' I asked her, as I pulled the sheets up to her chin, then folded them back and patted around her arms, pulling the fabric tight as she liked it.

She nodded.

'I rescued them. Yiannis and I, we went to rescue them. We released them from the nets so they would be able to fly again.'

'So now they can carry on with their journey?'

'Yes.'

She nodded again, her eyes wide and watery in the light of the bedside lamp.

'Did some of the birds die?'

I paused. 'They did,'

'Nisha will be sad.'

On Thursday, Tony rang and asked if he could come visit that evening. He didn't sound OK.

'Is there something wrong?' I said. I had become accus-tomed to the tone of his voice, but today he sounded apprehensive, tentative. He called nearly every day to check in, give any updates, to see if Yiannis or I had any news.

'It's best if we talk when I see you,' he said.

I went up to tell Yiannis that Tony would be visiting at 7 p.m., but I did not elaborate on the nature of our conversation.

I took Aliki over to Mrs Hadjikyriacou's.

'Someone is coming to tell you something about Nisha, aren't they?' Aliki said, as we knocked on Mrs Hadjikyriacou's door.

'I think so,' I said.

'Hm,' was her response. A small sound, like a mouse.

Yiannis arrived first, just before 7 p.m. He was holding his tablet in his hand in case Kumari called: he was worried about her. His hair had grown, he was unshaven, there were dark circles under his eyes and he looked as though he'd been wearing the same clothes for days. His arm was still in a sling and I didn't bother to ask him again about it. He sat down on the sofa close to the fire. Neither of us mentioned the after-noon of the songbirds, and neither of us mentioned Nisha.

'How is Aliki?' he said.

'She's fine, thank you. She's with Mrs Hadjikyriacou.'

He nodded.

'Can I get you a drink?'

'Just water.'

I went off to the kitchen and heard the tablet ring.

'Why aren't you at school?' Yiannis said.

'I couldn't go in, Mr Yiannis . . . feel too worried. I make up stories of what has happened to Amma. Maybe she is trapped underground like my baba was. Amma told me the story about Baba. Will you tell me true things from now on, Mr Yiannis, because then my brain make up other things?'

'Of course,' he said.

'My grandmother want to know any more information. She is in the other room on the bed. She has been crying.'

'OK, Kumari,' he said. 'Listen to me carefully and remember that I'm here any time if you or your grandmother need to speak to me.' Yiannis hesitated as I returned with a jug and three glasses on a tray, placing it on the coffee table. 'A woman has been found in a lake here on the island,' he said.

I stood behind him out of the glow of the screen. Kumari remained silent at first, then with a shake in her voice, she said, 'Is the lady in the lake alive?'

'No.'

'Could the lady in the lake be my amma?'

'I don't know. I don't think so. I'm sure it's not.'

Once again there was no response for a while.

'You think it might be Amma. I know you do,' she said. 'Because if you thought it was definitely not Amma you wouldn't tell me this information. You are telling me to . . . prepare me. Isn't that right Mr Yiannis?'

'Yes, Kumari.'

Then she was gone.

Yiannis sat without moving, staring at his own reflection in the dark screen. I took a step forward and placed my hand on his shoulder.

The doorbell rang.

I left Yiannis sitting there and went to let Tony in. It was strange to see him out of the booth. He was much taller and wider than I realised and he walked slowly and heavily, like a bear.

He sat in the armchair opposite Yiannis and I poured him a glass of water.

'Can I get you anything else?' I asked. 'A coffee or tea? It's quite a long journey from Limassol.'

'No, thank you, Petra,' he said. 'And thank you for your kind hospitality.'

I smiled faintly and sat down. We both stared at him and he hesitated before speaking.

'I wanted to come and tell you before it comes out in the news.'

'They've identified the body?' said Yiannis. He was perched at the edge of the sofa and I noticed a tremor in his hands as they rested on his knees.

'Yes, they have.'

'It's Nisha?'

'No,' Tony said, and I heard Yiannis exhale. 'Allow me to finish,' said Tony. 'The woman has been identified as Rosamie Cotabu. Petra, you might recognise the name. She was one of the women I told you about during your first visit.'

I nodded and glanced quickly at Yiannis, who was looking more agitated than ever, rhythmically rubbing his right temple.

'Rosamie Cotabu,' Tony repeated slowly. 'Would you mind if I light a cigarette?'

'Not at all,' I said, and got up to bring him a saucer that he could use as an ashtray. By the time I returned from the kitchen he had lit the cigarette and the smoke was swirling amongst the light of the fire. I could see that Tony's hand was shaking too as he held the cigarette up to his lips, taking three long, hard drags so that the ash drooped from it. He moved his hand carefully to the saucer and allowed the ash to drop in there.

'I have a friend in the police force,' he said, glancing at me. 'He's junior in rank so he had no power to launch an investigation, but he's been useful in getting information.'

I nodded and sat down.

'Rosamie Cotabu,' he said, 'I told you about her didn't I? The one who worked for a man who was physically abusing her.'

'Yes,' I said. 'I remember.'

'She went to the police for help, but they told her to leave Cyprus if she wasn't happy. Nobody helped her.' He paused and with heavy eyes took another drag of smoke before stubbing out the cigarette. 'I knew Rosamie wouldn't run away. I knew something was wrong. Why didn't I do more?' He lifted his arm and dropped it down onto the arm of the chair like a dead weight. He took another cigarette out of the box and held it between his fingers but did not light it. 'Oh,' he said smiling now, 'What a joyful girl she was! She had so many friends. She said I saved her life.' At this point Tony began to cry, like a sudden storm; tears broke out of him and he apologised again and again through stifled sobs.

'I'm sorry, Petra. I did not come here to be a burden on you,' he said, composing himself, lighting the cigarette, taking in the smoke as if it would save his life.

'Don't worry, Tony,' I said. Yiannis was so quiet, I almost

330

forgot that he was there but when I turned to him, he was alert and present and trembling inside. I could see it. He reminded me of the way wheat stalks shake in the breeze in the open fields.

'The police went through her phone, which they recovered in the nearby field.' Tony continued. 'They discovered that she had communicated via text with a man whom she had met on a dating site. She had gone out that particular night, the night she went missing, to meet him for the first time. He was the last person she texted. The police discovered that his dating profile had a fake name but they managed to trace the details back to a thirty-five-year-old Greek Cypriot soldier serving at the national guard. They have taken him in for questioning. The autopsy showed that she had injuries on her body and marks around her neck.' He shook his head. 'I'll tell you, this doesn't look good.'

'No,' Yiannis said, and his voice came out hoarse and unfamiliar, as if he hadn't spoken to a soul in many years. 'But I know for a fact that Nisha wouldn't have gone on a date with anyone. I know that for sure. She loved me.'

Tony nodded sympathetically. 'It will become clearer in time,' he said, 'but for now we must wait.'

After the men left, I felt frightened and cold. A strong wind rattled the windows and bent the olive tree out front. I went into Aliki's room. She was fast asleep. I crawled into bed with her and curled up around her, smelling her hair, giving her soft kisses while she slept.

26

Yiannis

THE MURDER OF ROSAMIE COTABU had been announced on the news. People were restless. The Vietnamese maids with their rice hats kept their eyes fixed on passers-by. Downstairs, at Mrs Hadjikyriacou's, Ruba stood out front holding a broom, looking frightened.

This time I called Kumari. Once again, she was alone.

'Good morning, Mr Yiannis, do you have any more information? My grandmother is making me breakfast and she is crying all the time. She is wiping all her tears on her sleeve and cardigan.'

'Have you been crying, Kumari?'

'No. I don't cry until I know all the facts. Are there new facts now?'

'They know who the woman in the lake is and it is not your mother.'

Kumari let out a huge sigh as if she had been holding her breath and her words came out shaken and broken: 'Thank you. Oh, my! Mr Yiannis. It is not my amma.'

She left her tablet on the table with me staring up at the ceiling, and I could hear her saying things to her grand-mother, who once again seemed to be asking many questions through her tears.

Kumari picked up the tablet again.

'What is the lady's name that they found inside the lake?'

'Her name is Rosamie Cotabu.'

'Was she one of the missing ladies that you told me about?'

'Yes, she was.'

'One of the five missing ladies.'

'Yes.'

'Was she a maid like my amma is?'

'Yes.'

Kumari was silent now. I could hear the old lady in the other room, still talking.

'You think they will find Amma like they did this other lady, don't you Mr Yiannis?'

'No,' I said, 'I don't think that.'

'But she was also a missing lady, like Amma. Isn't that right, Mr. Yiannis?'

It turned out that Rosamie Cotabu was Christian and church bells rang for her departure to the next world. Meanwhile, anger was brewing. The maids were not just scared, they were livid. Rosamie Cotabu had, after all, been reported missing and the police had ignored her employer's pleas and concerns. Then she had been found in a mineshaft, wrapped up in white cloth.

The women walked by on the street below, always in pairs now, keeping their heads close together in muffled conversation, but their eyes were always roving, on the lookout for the next threat. It felt like the hours and days after a massive earthquake, where people walk around expecting it to happen again at any moment, where the walls and the ground beneath one's feet no longer seem solid and there is no certainty of safety anywhere.

A man was in custody but his name had not been released to the public and Tony had no idea of it either.

During that week, at some point one evening, Seraphim knocked on my door. This was the first time he'd ever come to my place and the first time he had arrived unannounced.

I opened the door for him and without saying anything I stepped aside to let him in.

'How is your arm?' he asked, glancing at the bandage. I'd released it now from its sling.

'Better.'

'I heard about the woman found at the Mitsero mines,' he said.

I nodded and offered him a seat.

'Have you heard from Nisha?'

'No,' I said.

He looked out of the balcony doors but said nothing.

Then he unzipped a rucksack that he'd placed by his feet and took out a wad of money. From the look of it, it was much more than what he owed me for the previous hunt.

'That looks around 10,000 euro,' I said.

'You're spot on.' He put it on the coffee table between us. 'It's yours,' he said.

'A bribe?'

'Why would I need to bribe you?'

'To keep my mouth shut.'

The little bird hopped up onto the table now and inspected the wad of notes that lay upon it. Seraphim frowned and glanced at me straight on.

'You have a pet bird now?'

'It's not a pet,' I said. I had no energy to say more.

'The money is to help you get by, until you figure out what you're going to do.'

I just stared at him blankly.

'We go a long way back, don't we?' he said.

I nodded, apprehensive, wondering what dirty plan he had up his sleeve this time.

'I remember when I used to come visit your farm with my dad, do you remember?'

I just shrugged, but he went on.

'I loved being there, getting out of the city. I saw the kind of life you had and I was jealous. I was always so jealous of you and all that freedom you had. The only time I got to be out in the open was when I had a rifle in my hand.'

His eyes had drifted away for a while and they flicked back to me now.

335

'The other day, when I saw how you reacted to the death of the mouflon, it . . . it reminded me of . . .'

I waited, but the sentence was never finished.

'I'll tell the bosses that you've been badly injured in an accident and won't be able to work anymore.'

'Thank you,' I said.

'I'll reassure them that we won't need to keep you quiet.'

I nodded.

'You know, I wasn't always such a pig. Don't you remember?'

What I remembered was Seraphim running down that mountain holding the crow he'd killed by its feet.

He must have seen the doubt on my face as he said, 'Come on, Yiannis! Don't you remember? It was as soon as they placed that gun in my hands, that's when I changed. Before that we played in the woods. You showed me all those creatures that crawled amongst the leaves. You showed me how to catch a snake and release it. We played dominos in the olive orchard. We made an igloo out of twigs and explored the North Pole! We fought sharks in the Pacific Ocean!'

He was right, of course. I remembered all of it. Those memories were exactly what had stopped me from despising him completely. I had a sudden image of him now, standing on the fallen trunk of a tree, encouraging me across a treacherous river of grass.

'We made a catapult to knock the ripe apples off the trees,' he said, 'so that we could eat and survive in the Amazon.'

'Yes,' I said.

'You do know.'

I nodded, slowly.

'Take the money,' he said. 'Please.'

'OK.'

I didn't thank him and I didn't offer him a drink.

'I have a new apprentice,' he said, as he made his way to the door. 'Young lad, very sharp. Exactly what I need. But, you know, Oskana wants me to stop all this stuff. She doesn't understand there's a huge price to pay. We are expecting a child. I cannot take risks.'

His eyes were so sad, so full of anguish.

'How *is* Oksana?' I said.

'Very well. I finally finished painting the nursery and revealed it to her, grand opening, that sort of thing. She was beside herself.'

'I'm so glad,' I said, and for a brief moment I genuinely was.

'If I'd really hurt you, I would never have been able to live with myself,' he said.

'I know.'

Then he was gone.

I glanced down at the money and I knew what I wanted to do with it. I would send it to Kumari, along with everything else I had saved.

As for me, I would start again. I'd get a job at a restaurant somewhere, maybe even at Theo's if he needed any waiters. I would do this and start over again, and when Nisha returned, she would see that I had let go of my old life, that I had understood.

There was not going to be another earthquake. One was enough. But I could hear my grandfather's voice in my head:

'The truth is in the earth, in the song of the birds, in the rhythms and whispers of the animals. If you want to see and hear it – only if you want to – it is there.'

It had been nearly a week from his last visit when we heard from Tony again. Petra knocked on my door one evening to say that he had called and he was coming late that evening. She asked if I could come down at ten o'clock, after Aliki was asleep.

I arrived early and Petra offered me a seat by the fire. I took the same spot on the sofa I had occupied before, and placed my hands on my knees. Petra kept glancing over at me, as if I were a stranger, and I smiled to myself. My hair and beard had grown even more and I was sure I looked something like a bear. A friendly one, I hoped.

'I've stopped the poaching. I should have listened to Nisha from the start,' I told her, and waited for her reaction.

'Yes, you should have,' she said and then seemed to regret her words, the heat of them. They were true, however. Fair and true. I lowered my eyes to the ground.

'I'm sorry,' said Petra. 'I'm sure Nisha will be very relieved and happy when she returns.'

I glanced at her sharply and was about to speak, but the doorbell interrupted us.

A moment later, Petra ushered in Tony. He remained standing for a moment, taking us in, before taking a seat.

'Can I get you anything?' Petra offered.

'No, nothing,' he replied, bluntly.

'So,' he said, 'I will come straight out and say this. The man they have in custody, the soldier, he has confessed to the murder of Rosamie Cotabu.'

'Why?' I blurted out. I wasn't quite sure what I was asking. Perhaps I needed quickly to see a motive for this murder so that no one could, even for a second, be able to link it to Nisha's disappearance.

'Because he is a mad man!' Tony's eyes were alight with fury. He looked as though he was about to stand up, grab something and dash it at the wall, but instead he collapsed back into the armchair, and for a moment he seemed deflated, defeated even. Then he took a deep breath, leaned forward, clutching his hands tightly together over his thighs. 'This monster is apparently devastated by what he has done, as if all he had done is steal something. He has decided to help the police. He said it's the least he can do.' Tony's voice was harsh, it shook with anger, he spat out the last sentence with venom.

He glanced at Petra, then he looked over at me and held my gaze. 'He has subsequently confessed to the murder of four more women and two of their children. The women were all foreign maids. He met two of these women on dating sites – those two he knew their names, though the police won't release the other, not yet, not until they have recovered the bodies. The rest he captured as they were walking; for them, he said he never asked their names. He is a lunatic. He needed to kill. He killed foreign maids because it was easier, he knew that nobody would search for them, he thought he would be able to get away with it. What does that tell you, huh? Tell me, what does that tell you about the shitty world we live in?'

Neither Petra nor I seemed to be able to speak.

'He threw two of the bodies into the mineshaft,' Tony said. 'The other two women and the children are in suitcases in the red lake. He put them in suitcases, he threw them away, as if they were not human.'

Tony stopped talking. He pressed his temples hard with his fingers, scrunching up his eyes. I could feel a burning sensation in my chest, fire burning. I couldn't move. Petra quietly began to recite names, ticking them off on her fingers:

'Rosamie Cotabu,

Reyna Gatan,

Cristina Maier and

her daughter, Daria,

Ana-Maria Lupei and

her daughter, Andreea.

And Nisha Jayakody.'

Petra stared at her hand, all five fingers stretched wide. She looked over at me, as if still trying to comprehend, put together the pieces of everything she had just heard.

'The search is beginning tonight,' Tony said. 'Soon, everything will be certain.'

27

Petra

WHEN I WOKE UP, I thought I had blood on my hands. I felt it, sticky and warm. When I opened the blinds, however, and held my hands up before my eyes, they were clean and white in the morning sun.

I remembered the blood of the birds. The way it had felt and smelled, the way it had stuck in my nails.

It was a cold winter Saturday and the house was silent. The dust had gathered. I sat down by an unlit fire.

'Mum, Nisha isn't coming back, is she?' Aliki was standing in the doorway, looking at me with sombre eyes.

'You're awake, baby. I was hoping you would sleep longer.'

'She's gone,' my daughter said, simply.

'I think so,' I said. 'I think she might be gone.'

'She made my heart be full of stars, now it's just dark inside me.'

I reached out and Aliki came to me. I pulled her into my lap, her gangly legs barely contained on my knees, the fug of sleep still clinging to her sweatpants and T-shirt. I stroked her hair, pulling it back from her face, and she closed her eyes.

And then we both heard it. Shouts. Cries. A murmur that was growing, beginning to swell. Aliki sprang off my lap and ran to the door. I followed her. We both stood in the doorway, watching people pass by.

First, we saw the two Filipino maids who always walked with the young girl between them, the pretty little girl with pigtails, holding each of their hands. But this time they were without the child, and heading down the street with a solemn determination. Then we saw Nilmini stepping out of Yiakoumi's shop, untying her apron and leaving it by the front door as she headed in the same direction.

When I looked back at Aliki she was crying. I put my arms around her and she cried into my chest; I felt the weight of her on me and I embraced her, tighter. Then she held herself upright and watched the maids pass by. There were so many now, all heading in the same direction. I held Aliki's hand tight. Her tears fell down her cheeks and dropped onto the cobbled street. I imagined a stream, flowing, a stream of tears flowing in the direction that the maids were heading.

The two maids at Theo's abandoned their tasks and followed the crowd. Finally, Ruba from Mrs Hadjikyriacou's house next door stepped out, closing the door behind her.

I stopped her. 'Where are they going? What is happening?'

'Come and see,' she said.

342

Aliki shoved her feet into the nearest Converse and we followed the maids.

Women that I'd never seen before in the neighbourhood were joining in. They watched from windows and came out as the women passed, without a second thought joining the rest. Most were immigrant workers and there were children, too, some Aliki's age, some even younger, who held the hands of their nannies as they followed the crowd. We walked along the backstreets from the Famagusta Gate until we reached the Cyprus Museum, then we took the main road all the way down to the Presidential Palace. There, a crowd of thousands, dressed mostly in black, spread out across the street below the palace holding lighted candles with their heads bowed in prayer. Others held banners reading 'Misogyny and Racism Must Stop' or 'End discrimination towards women and foreigners' and 'We sacrifice our lives'. I saw Soneeya and Binsa in the crowd, standing close together with candles in their hands, directing their shouts at the white palace. In her hand, Binsa held a banner that simply said: 'Where are they?'

We stayed out for hours and the sun began to set as the afternoon turned late. Someone handed Aliki a candle and she held it high above her head, joining the shouts and demands. She was still crying, but kept the candle aloft. As the darkness gathered the candles glowed, beacons everywhere. There were so many women, so many faces, so many voices raised in chorus and hope.

This was the story of Nisha Jayakody, as I understood it:

Nisha was a mother of two children, who lived in
    different worlds.
Nisha's child in Sri Lanka has straight hair, so soft it
    feels like the down of an owl.
Nisha's other child is my child.
Nisha had lost her first love.
Nisha knew how to love.
Nisha filled my daughter's heart with stars.
I owe Nisha more than I could ever repay her.

That night, when I came in to kiss Aliki goodnight, she was
sitting up in bed, looking out of the window. I followed her
gaze to Monkey, who was outside and pawing at the window-
panes, trying to get in.

'Look, Mum, it is our cat!' Aliki said. She began to laugh
and then, quite suddenly, she exhaled and gave in to a mighty
exhaustion and began to cry. She scrunched her face and her
tears flowed out. They flowed like they would never stop this
time and amongst her sobs she said, 'I'm so tired,' and, 'I miss
Nisha so much.' I sat down beside her and held her in my
arms. I held her in a way that I never had, like I should have
all those years gone, like Nisha had always wanted me to. I
felt my daughter crying on me, I felt her tears soaking into
the skin of my neck, into my veins, right through to my heart.

I rubbed her back and rocked her. 'Tell me what's in your
heart,' I said.

'I want Nisha, Mum,' she said into my neck, with shaky breath and tears. 'I want Nisha to come back. I want to sit in our boat. I want her to tell me stories and get me ready for school and . . . and . . .'

'And?'

'And do the stupid times tables with me and . . . and . . . and . . .'

'And?'

'And I wake up at night and I'm so scared because Nisha is not there. Sometimes I wake up and knock on her door and wait for her to open it, but she never opens it. She never opens it anymore.'

My chest burned and my eyes burned until I too was crying, crying and rocking Aliki.

'I want Nisha to come back so much.'

'I know baby, so do I.'

Slowly she ceased crying. Now and then she whimpered and then her breathing slowed. We remained there in silence. I stroked her hair and watched the cat jump down, glancing at us one last time before it skulked off into the dark.

28

Yiannis

IT WAS DAWN WHEN I finally slept, haunted by images of the red lake and memories of Nisha. When I finally woke up, late in the afternoon, there was a cacophony in the street below. I went out onto the balcony as hundreds of protestors filled every inch of the road, and flowed along it like a river. People marched with banners, passing the trees where Nisha's flyers hung, away from the border and into the city, to find the root of the problem and stand before it, defiant and strong.

Here we are, they were saying. *We do not simply appear from nowhere in a taxi with a suitcase and disappear once more to nowhere.*

We are human.

We love.

We hate.

We have pasts.

We have futures.
We are citizens of countries, in our own right.
We have voices.
We have families.
Here we are.

The little bird was on the table beside me and it fluttered up to the nearest tree and watched the crowd below with black eyes. Then it flicked its head back to me. Something came over me. I felt such a sadness. Such a painful despair.

'Go,' I said to it, though I wanted to hold onto the bird and all that it meant, forever. 'Go. Go fly. Go.'

In that moment, as if it understood, it opened its wings and took off into the sky.

Watching the bird leave, knowing it would probably never come back, suddenly woke me up. I dressed myself with purpose and went out onto the street. I caught a glimpse of Mrs Hadjikyriacou at her front door, watching with those observant but cloudy eyes.

I allowed myself to be taken by the current. I could hardly see for tears. I allowed myself to be taken until eventually we reached the presidential palace and I sat down on a bench, unable to stand any more. I had no strength in my legs.

I sat there and watched the women, their faces lit up by the candles they held in their hands. There was pain in those faces, and real fear, and, in the light, an anger that allowed them to stand straight and say *Here we are.*

There was a reporter beside me, and a cameraman. They were interviewing one of the women. She was probably in her twenties, with a round milky face and a French plait that

347

hung over her right shoulder. She stood there looking straight into the camera and because she was so close, I heard her voice above the crowd: 'I am one of lucky ones,' she said. 'I have a great employer, a good woman, she treats me well. My sister, she was sexually abused by her sir. She went to the police and they did nothing to help so she left her job. Now she has just three more months to find work or she will have to return to Nepal. We need to send money to my parents, they are very sick. But when I think about the women in the lake, and the children . . .' She paused and took a deep breath.

'Where does it end?' A taller, darker woman standing beside her said. 'Are we the "lucky ones" because we have not been *killed?*'

A strong wind blew and some of the candles went out. I saw Ruba amongst the crowd, and the two maids from Theo's without their rice hats, their hair long and dark. Ruba relit her candle from the flame of a woman standing beside her. She then passed her flame to a child. The sun set further into the earth.

Where was Nisha to tell her story? What would I do without her? What would Kumari do without her mother? And Aliki?

I could barely breathe. I felt like I was in the middle of a burning world. But in this moment, I imagined that it burned with gold.

It was certain. Nisha had vanished and turned to gold.

She turned to gold in the setting of this winter sun. Now, for a brief moment, I caught a glimpse of her, and I think I heard her, in the burning faces and voices of the women that surrounded me.

This is where Nisha exists.

Here.

And, in the moment, she kissed me, high up in the mountains, when she had been partly with me and partly in the world from which she had come.

The red lake at Mitsero reflects a sunset, captures it, holds it, even when the sun has died. Red lake, toxic lake, copper lake. Mothers and fathers tell their children stories about it, tales of deep passages underground, where men crawled like animals and died in darkness.

Never go near the red lake at Mitsero!

The sunset holds the expectation of the hush and darkness of the night, that time when we close our eyes and meet our true selves. The lake is at the verge of this darkness, always.

It holds all the sunsets from the beginning of time.

A helicopter hovers above like a dragonfly. Four orange rescue crafts glide on the water. Divers enter. There are three, secured to the boats with bright yellow ropes.

They will not get lost down there; they have their colleagues at the ready to pull them out.

They slide in, and once again the lake is still.

In the village, the widow stands in her front garden holding a lit candle. To protect the flame from the breeze she cradles it in her palm.

The barley fields and wheat fields are gold beneath the setting sun. The woods are alight. A hare runs out of a bush and tentatively approaches the crater, keeping its distance.

After a while, a diver emerges from the water. He signals to the people in the boat and they throw down some ropes with hooks at the end. He goes down again and when he comes back up, he raises a thumb and the people in the boat pull until a suitcase is dragged to the surface.

29

Petra

ALIKI WANTED ME TO HELP her get ready. At first, she took her time choosing what she would wear, then she stood still while I pulled the jumper over her head – Nisha's orange jumper with the sunflower. I put her feet into her jeans, pulling them up. She stared out of the glass doors at the boat in the garden, at the orange tree, at the chickens that roamed out of their pen. Then I took the bracelet out of my pocket.

'Look at this,' I said.

She turned to me now, caught my eye for a second and there I saw a depth of sadness as vast as the sea.

'That was a present from me.' She smiled, sadly.

'Yes. You know she never took it off. She wore it every single day.'

I secured the bracelet onto her wrist and she twisted her

353

hand around so that the bracelet glimmered in the late afternoon sun that streaked through the glass doors.

We went outside to sit in the boat and wait for the others. First, Mrs Hadjikyriacou came with Ruba, then Soneeya and Binsa, then Nilmini, followed by Muyia, who arrived as the sun was setting.

Apart from brief greetings, nobody spoke. We all knew why we were there – to say goodbye to Nisha. I wondered where Yiannis was. His kitchen window was shut and dark. I helped Aliki pass the candles around and when I looked again, he was standing at the foot of the stairs with his hands empty at his sides. Face pale, lids heavy, shirt buttoned up to his neck.

He stood there and watched us light the candles, hold them in front of us to light the darkness on our faces. A hush enveloped us all; the boat was empty and I imagined Nisha sitting in it.

'Nisha is going away,' Aliki said suddenly, and for a moment all eyes rose from the ground and rested on her face. 'She is drifting away on the soft waves of the faraway Sea Above the Sky.'

I put my hand on Aliki's shoulder and I felt her body shake. It wasn't a cold night, but she trembled as if an icy wind was blowing.

Then the wind did pick up and we moved back into the protection of the house, Aliki leading everyone into the warmth.

'Give me a second,' I said to her.

I walked over to the stairs where Yiannis was still standing. 'Are you coming in?'

354

He nodded. 'I've booked a flight to Sri Lanka. I'm leaving tomorrow.'

I caught his eye, inhaling deeply, not knowing what to say.

'I'm going to see Kumari,' he said.

I squeezed his hand and he began to cry. With his chin down and his eyes scrunched up, and his chest shaking, he cried, and I held onto his hand as Nisha drifted away on the Sea Above the Sky.

Later, I sat in the garden with Aliki and Nilmini. She opened her friend's journal and began to read. We sat there for hours, listening to Nisha's words. Tomorrow I would be giving Yiannis the journal to take to Kumari – its rightful owner.

Nisha's true story began to unfold. I heard the story of Kiyoma's death and the owl. I heard about how she travelled to Rathnapura, how she met her husband and the day he died in the mines. I heard about how she'd worked day and night at the market in Galle, how she had made the difficult decision to leave, and how she had felt that first year away from home, unable to hold her beautiful daughter, Kumari.

There was so much more I wished I could know. These letters were merely a handful of stars in the entire universe of her heart. But it was too late. If only I could have understood before it was too late.

Dear Kumari,

When I held you as a baby, close to my skin, and looked down into your eyes, I saw everything I loved and everything I feared. Within them, I saw the sunset over the Sri Pada (there's a story about this! Keep reading and you'll find out!). I saw rivers and waterfalls at dusk (this too!). I saw my own mother's eyes, and myself, walking beside her through the rice plantations at the end of the day. I saw peppers laid out in rows to dry in the sun, and steaming meals with lemon-grass and cardamoms and cinnamon. I saw my sister's eyes, all those years ago, when she would laugh with so much glee (you remind me of her, Kumari). I saw the dress I wore on my wedding day and your father's smile and his arms around me as we danced.

I also saw your future. This made me afraid.

In the house where I now live there is a garden and in that garden there is a small wooden boat. The boat is from far away, because there is no sea nearby. We are in the city, a very old city, with four old gates that are so big they look like they were made for giants.

I look after a baby girl called Aliki, who is two years younger than you.

Kumari, the garden is such a special place. A place that reminds me of who I am. It has an orange tree (like the ones back home, except sweeter), a cactus with prickly pears, lots of flowers, and a chicken pen. I wish you were here to see it. I've drawn pictures for you in this journal! You would love the chickens. They are so funny. One of the hens always manages to get out of the pen. She comes into the

356

living room when we forget to close the door. She sits under the coffee table and watches TV with us. I make sure my boss doesn't see her so that she doesn't throw her out. Sometimes the hen comes up to bed with me, crawls under the duvet as if it's a paper bag, and talks to herself. She has feathers that grow over her eyes so she can't see much, but she doesn't seem to mind.

By the time you are old enough to read this you will probably know all this stuff already, but I need to write it down so that I can feel close to you when I'm alone.

When I first arrived here, I could hear you crying. You might find it hard to believe, but it was you that I heard, I know that now. I thought it was a young child in another house, but then I realised that the sound was coming from the earth, the trees and the sky, that you were sending it to me as a gift. Kumari, somehow, you found a way to send me your tears. So, I sat in the little boat in the garden and sent you stories and love through the night sky.

You didn't get to know your father. I am sure you would have loved him as much as I did. I will tell you about him — although I'm sure your acci will tell you plenty as you grow up.

Your acci won't mention this because she doesn't like to talk about it, but life can change in a second. From sunlight to sudden rain, just like the weather during the monsoon when the rain comes down like the sea. But one thing your father always said was that rain doesn't last for ever, and when the sun shines again everything will gleam. He was an optimist.

357

Your father should have been an actor. He did impressions of people and animals, flicked his hand when he spoke, had a twinkle in his eye. In real life, he worked in the gem mines, that's where we met! He went down into the dark while I cleaned the gravel in the reservoir to find the gems.

I have so much to tell you. But be patient. Reality and truth need time to unravel.

Acknowledgements

I have so many people to thank for helping me to understand more deeply the sensitive issues I was researching in order to create this novel.

Thank you, firstly and especially, to Menaka Nishanthe Ramanayaka for all the work you did over the years, for all your strength, for becoming a friend, for making me lovely Sri Lankan tea, for sharing your feelings and memories with me, for listening to me and for being such a beautiful and caring person. It is because of you that I wanted to write this novel in the first place.

Thank you so much to Marissa Begonia for being such an inspiration with your insight and determination and for inviting me to visit the Voice of Domestic Workers in Holborn. You are extraordinary and the work you have done, what you have achieved, is honestly phenomenal. I'd like to thank all the women at the centre who welcomed me with so much love, for sharing your delicious food with me and allowing me to hear your stories. I'd also like to thank Loucas Koutroukides in Limassol, Cyprus, for all the wonderful humanitarian work you have done to help domestic workers on the island, for speaking with me for so many hours and for introducing me to so many wonderful people. Thank you too for all the interesting, informative and courageous articles you wrote and shared with me, for being brave enough to seek the truth and speak the truth when so many others turned a blind eye or remined silent. Thank you also to all the women at the Blue Elephant, who spoke to me, who trusted me with their stories, who shared their emotions and fears with me – thank you, I learnt so much.

Thank you to George Konstantinou at NGO Protection of the Natural Heritage and Biodiversity of Cyprus; thank you so much for answering all of my questions, for all your help and advice, and for the wonderful photographs you took and sent to me. I wish I could have attended one of your wildlife tours if we hadn't been in lockdown, but speaking to you nonetheless was so informative. Thank you also for the wonderful and important work you are doing to protect the forests and the animals on the island.

Thank you Eva Spanou for helping me to progress with my research. Thank you so much Nicolas and Sotiroulla Simou for sharing information with me about poaching.

Thank you to Peter Louizou and Tassos Louizou, for talking to me for so long last Christmas about hunting, for sharing all your knowledge with me about the poaching of songbirds and the very specific technique of making limesticks. Thank you to my lovely brother, Mario Lefteri, for giving me so much advice and information about Cyprus and about poaching locations, for being one of the first to read my novel, as you always are, and for all your help and suggestions. Thank you to Angela Stella Monaghan for your help and for introducing me to your parents. Equally, thank you to Panayiotis and Andriana Michael for spending so long talking to me about poaching and for all the useful information you shared with me.

Thank you to Nishan Weeratunge and Sajeewa Dissanayake for all the information you gave me about Sri Lanka, Sri Lankan food and culture and Sri Lankan history. It was immensely helpful and so great that I made new and wonderful friends from it. Thank you to Maryvonne and Antony for inspiring me with all of your stories and for introducing me to Nishan.

Thank you to my beautiful friend, Anna Petsas, who I should have thanked last time, for encouraging me to volunteer, to take thoughtful risks, and for sending me the article about domestic workers in the first place and alerting me to what was happening. You are so inspirational; I have often found myself taking huge steps in my life after just talking to you!

I would like to thank my friend Paul Lewis for all the inspirational writing chats. I would also like to thank Conway Road Writing Group – it means the world to me to be part of this group. Thank you all for being such great, supportive and talented and lovely people!

Thank you to Mehr at Salt and Sage Books for your thoughtful and insightful authenticity read; it was a real privilege to receive your helpful feedback on the manuscript.

Thank you to my agent, Marianne Gunn O'Connor – you are my guiding star. Thank you for your love, care, support, encouragement, vision, for being such a beautiful, inspirational person, for caring so much about the world and for also being a friend. I would never have been able to do this without you.

Thank you to my foreign rights agent at MGOC, Vicki Satlow, for being so amazing, and for everything you have done for me over the years.

Thank you so so much to my publishers at Manilla Press. Thank you Kate Parkin for your constant and unwavering support and for everything you have done, for being so caring, insightful and passionate. Margaret Stead – you have been absolutely amazing – all those conversations we had over the phone during lockdown, your insight, your suggestions, your imagination and creativity, and absolutely everything you have done to help make this novel happen.

Thank you to Perminder Mann for all of your support. Thank you Clare Kelly, Felice McKeown and Katie Lumsden – you are all so great to work with; thank you for all the hard work you have put into bringing this novel out.

Thank you to all my friends and family for your love and support over the years. Thank you to my brother, Kyri, and his wife for always encouraging me and being there for me. Thank you to Maria and Antony for being the best friends anyone can ask for. Thank you to Stellios Arseniyadis for listening to all my ideas during the editing process, and for being so helpful and supportive. Thank you to Claire and Sam Afhim for your friendship and support. Thank you to Louis Evangelou for your advice, for being so helpful, caring and endlessly patient. Thank you to the whole Evangelou family – Katerina, Tina and Chris – for all your support and help and lovely food and love, always.

362

Thank you especially to my dad and Yiota for always being there for me, encouraging me never to give up and for all your love and help. Thank you to my mum, though you are no longer with us – thank you for the love you gave me, the belief you had in me and for how funny and creative you were. I have those things with me, every step I take.

Every time I write a novel, I learn so much, and I'd really like to thank everybody who helped me to know, to under-stand, and to see things in a new way.

Dear Reader,

Around ten years ago, I became friends with a domestic worker in Cyprus who worked for a close family member. Menaka was from Sri Lanka and had not seen her two daughters for eight years. She used to speak to them on her tablet; she was a mother to them through a screen. She introduced me to her daughters, she showed me her house and the streets of her hometown through the iPad. On screen, she showed me the trees, the flowers, the sky, the food – she wanted me to know what home meant to her, what it smelled like and tasted like and how it felt. We went on virtual walks together through the town with her daughters and mother-in-law. Sometimes, like any parent, she would need to tell her daughters off, or remind them to do their homework; often she told them she loved them – always through a screen. She told me the story of how she was widowed when her husband, the love of her life, died in a farming accident. Subsequently, she had to make the difficult decision to work abroad as a domestic worker, in order to provide for her children. Since then, she has not been able to be present for her daughters as they grow up. She sends them clothes and money, but she cannot be there with them, as they grow into young adults. I could see the strength, resilience and immense love that Menaka had within her, but I also came to see the immense suffering of her sacrifice. In the meantime, I could see how the other women, in all the households along that street, went about their duties, often unseen and misunderstood. 'Ah,' one of the neighbours said to me once, 'these women don't care about their families, they drift around the world.'

While I was on tour for *The Beekeeper of Aleppo*, I was often asked: 'How can we get people to understand that refugees are not like migrants, that they have come because they do not have a choice?' This question saddened me. Migrants are often forced to leave their homes for less obvious reasons than war – but they still leave because they feel that they have no choice.

Songbirds was influenced both by this question and by a recent tragedy in Cyprus, in which five migrant women domestic workers and two of their children disappeared. When the women were reported missing, the authorities did not investigate their disappearance or search for them, because they were foreign – it was assumed that they had simply moved on. Later, however, it was discovered that the women and children had been murdered. In reality, almost two years had passed before a couple of tourists discovered the first victim in an abandoned mine shaft after a heavy rainfall. This was a woman who had been reported missing and whose disappearance had been completely dismissed.

I followed the events as they unfolded. With a broken heart, I read newspapers and watched the Cypriot news, spoke to friends. But I was not surprised at all that nobody had searched for these women and their children. I was not surprised that an investigation had not been launched, that the police had dismissed them as runaways. I felt anger, such anger, because over the years I had witnessed the reality of what had led to such gross negligence.

Most of my family live in Cyprus. I was born in the UK because my parents came as refugees after the war in 1974.

Most of the middle-class families in Cyprus – just as they do all over the world – hire domestic workers. In Cyprus, you do not have to be rich to have a domestic worker, just reasonably comfortable. So, the presence of these women, who run the households, look after children, walk the dogs, clean the restaurants/shops or whatever other businesses or properties their employers might own, is commonplace. Migrant domestic workers are a part of the fabric of Cypriot life.

This story is not an attempt to represent the voices of migrant workers or to speak for them, it is an exploration of the ideologies, prejudices, circumstances and underlying belief systems that can lead to very sad and often catastrophic events. It is an exploration of the way in which a flawed system can trap people. It is also a story about all forms of entrapment – the way we can all trap ourselves into certain ways of seeing and being.

And so, the idea of *Songbirds* began to grow.

I decided to visit Cyprus, to speak to as many women as I could, so that I could understand things more deeply. I went to visit a man who is the head of a human rights organisation aimed at caring for domestic workers; he also owned a café where the men and women would meet on Sundays. It was he who family members and employers had turned to when the police would not investigate the disappearances of these women and children. At one point, he admitted, he was the only person in Cyprus looking for what he believed to be a murderer – he turned out to be right.

I became very moved by the stories I heard. He arranged

for me to speak to many of the domestic workers who came into his café on Sundays. The stories I heard opened my eyes to the difficulties and suffering that migrant domestic workers experience. When I returned to the UK, I contacted Justice for Domestic Workers, and helped to edit some stories written by the women who visit the centre. I wanted to learn more about the problems and hardships that domestic workers face around the world, because I felt that the failure of the authorities in this particular situation was not an isolated incident, it was a result of our deeply flawed society and civilisation.

It became clear to me that although some of the women were leaving their countries in order to be able to earn more and support family members, others were searching for their freedom. Many of these women ended up finding themselves more trapped than they had been before, with no way of returning home.

I had learnt so much just by listening and opening my eyes; I understood so much more than I had before. This is why I wanted to write a story from the perspective of the people who had to learn about Nisha themselves – her employer and her lover. I struggled to write the ending. I found it so hard because I knew that Nisha had to die. She had to die because the women in reality had lost their lives, so cruelly snatched away. Although my novel isn't based on the true story, it is inspired by the essence of it, by the way in which ideologies exist like powerful undercurrents. We hear Nisha's story through the mouths of others; we have to piece together her existence through the memories of others

– this is what I often saw and felt on the streets of Cyprus. But when we listen and look carefully, we see that each person has as much beauty and depth and hope and fear and history and aspiration and courage as we do ourselves. The reader must discover this. Until the end, when Nisha finally speaks. I hope there is an echo after the last page – her voice continuing out into the silence of the ending.

Songbirds is a story about migration and crossing borders: it is about searching for freedom, for a better life, only to find oneself trapped. It is a story about the way in which systemic racism exists often unquestioned, relying upon prejudice and nationalistic ideals to survive. It is a story about learning to see each and every human being in the same way as we see ourselves.

Christy Lefteri

Reading Group Questions

1. How does *Songbirds* explore the theme of motherhood?

2. What does this novel tell us about the lives of female migrant workers?

3. How do racism and classism operate within the world of the novel?

4. Both Petra and Yiannis are complex characters. Did you like them? How did that change as you read the book?

5. What did you make of Seraphim as a character?

6. What role do animals play in this novel? What do you think the songbirds and the mouflon ovis represent?

7. What do you think Nisha really felt for Yiannis?

8. What role do you see Aliki playing in the novel – is she key to helping Petra come to realise she has to find out what has happened to Nisha?

9. Why do you think Petra struggles to connect with her daughter?

10. We never hear Nisha's voice until the end, but we see her through the other characters' eyes. What did you make of Nisha, and how did your image of her develop across the novel?

11. At the end of the book, Yiannis is going to find Kumari and her grandmother, and give them Nisha's journal and the money he has made. Do you see hope for their future, despite the fact that they have lost Nisha?

12. If you've read the author's letter, how did it affect your understanding of the novel?

Menaka

By Christy Lefteri, exclusive to this edition

I first met Menaka about a decade ago in Cyprus. It was the summer of the London riots, just a few years after my mum died and the year that I separated from my ex-husband. I remember arriving from the airport late at night, so I didn't meet Menaka until the morning, when she was up and already making breakfast.

'Madam,' she said, 'tea or coffee?'

Madam? I almost glanced behind me, but she was looking right at me.

There she stood, this woman I didn't know, greeting me in the morning with dark smiling eyes, asking me if I wanted tea or coffee. But this was no hotel, I was staying with a family member in Ayia Napa, Famagusta. They were working through the summer, so during the day I more or less had the house to myself.

'No. Thank you so much,' I said, 'I can make it, please don't worry.'

'No, madam!' she insisted. 'It is my job.'

So she made me oolong tea from the Galle district in Sri Lanka that she'd bought from the local shop to help her feel at home. The grocers along the seafront stocked all sorts of spices, teas and condiments from south and south-east Asia, because most households now hired a foreign domestic worker. Shelves were stacked with things that had never before been readily available in Cyprus: curry and pandan leaves, saffron, lemongrass, nutmeg, mace and tins and tins of coconut milk.

She made the tea with warm milk. She boiled an egg; she buttered toast. She brought it all to the table as if I were the Queen, and then she went about her duties.

I ate it with a lump in my throat. This was lovely in many ways – fresh eggs from the garden, milky sweet tea. The sun was shining and the sky was endlessly blue. I could put my feet up and enjoy this. But it didn't feel right.

The next morning, I got up early and made her breakfast. She had a go at me. We both laughed.

'I'm sorry,' I said, 'but I can't sit back while you serve me.'

'But that is what I'm going to do,' she replied, decisively.

'Fine. Well then, I will do the same for you.'

'If you must,' she said and laughed again.

The following morning I cut up some watermelon with salty slices of halloumi. I made us both some sweet oolong tea and laid the table. She ate with me, shaking her head. *What is this going to achieve?* she seemed to be saying with a disapproving and yet humorous look in her eyes. She knew so much more than I did.

In my naivety, I stuck to this routine with vehemence, disregarding Menaka's protests – as if I was going to change the world by making her breakfast. She knew, of course she did, that this would make no difference whatsoever in the bigger scheme of things. My gesture would amount to no more than a drop in the ocean.

Far beyond, the sea twinkled. I watched it through the window. I had so many questions. Where exactly had she come from? Why had she come here?

Her face became familiar to me, so familiar as the days passed that she became like an old best friend and I could not remember not knowing her. Back home in London, my flat was empty now and the streets were burning. Silenced voices had finally erupted with rage. I savoured the calm of the Mediterranean breeze, of the unchanging sky. I got so used to the tone of Menaka's voice, the slap of her flip-flops on the stairs, her warmth, her sly humour, and those conversations she had in Sinhalese on the phone at night on the porch swing in the garden, facing the darkness and the sea.

During the day she scrubbed and cleaned. She wore shorts and a T-shirt and kept her hair in a bun. Once, after a bath, she sat out on the porch to brush it and only then did I see how long it was. She scrubbed and cleaned and every surface sparkled. She did the laundry and hung the clothes out on the line to dry. I could hear her vacuuming. When it was silent, I would go upstairs and find her ironing. Often, she would go out into the orchard in the garden and pick the fallen leaves, then she would bring in fruit straight from the trees.

She peeled and sliced figs and gave them to me on a plate, as a parent would for a child, and yet she called me 'madam'. I was only two years younger than her. She seemed to hold so much wisdom and knowledge behind her eyes, it was as if she had lived a hundred lives. There was something in the way she carried herself, in the look in her eyes, in the tone of her voice.

'Where is your husband, madam?' she asked me once as we ate the breakfast that I had prepared.

'We've separated,' I said.

She nodded.

'Would you like to meet someone else one day? It's a shame to be alone.'

'I think so. I think that would be nice. Some day.'

'You're still young. You'll meet someone else, I'm sure of that.'

'What about you?' I asked.

'My husband died . . . in a farming accident, when my girls were little.'

'I'm so sorry,' I said, not knowing what else to say.

'He was such a good man. I loved him very much.'

We remained silent for a while. The cats that she fed everyday were waiting for her by the open door and a breeze swept in.

'So you have daughters?' I said.

'Yes.' She smiled. 'Two daughters. One is eight and the other ten. Their dad died seven years ago and then I had to come here. They are living with my mother-in-law.'

'How often do you get to see them?'

'I don't see them. I haven't seen them since I left. We speak on the phone.' And she smiled.

A few years back I'd been invited to my then husband's cousin's house for a summer barbeque. All of the guests brought their maids with them. We were in the garden. The maids sat at a separate table to eat with the children, probably to watch over them – I think they were on duty. The women sat at another table, sipping wine.

'Mine speaks very good English!' I heard one of them say.

'Oh, mine is useless,' replied another.

'How about yours?' asked another.

'Oh, her English is fantastic. But the Sri Lankans are usually very good.'

It struck me that none of these women had referred to their domestic workers by their names and they spoke about them like they owned them. I remained silent. Perhaps this was a mistake. This was clearly commonplace. It was unquestioned; these were everyday conversations and I happened to overhear one. It was not so long ago that Cyprus was occupied by the British, just as Sri Lanka once had been. Surely, people should know either from memory or stories passed down what it means to be subjugated.

But no. The women sipped their wine. They laughed. These facts had clearly been forgotten, or buried in the depths of the nearby sea. The maids tended to the children; their lives, their inner worlds, I assumed, remained unknown.

And just a few years later here I was now alone, on a summer break, with nothing much to do but think about the breakdown of my marriage and get to know Menaka's rhythms, and as the long hot days passed, in the silence and stillness of this simmering summer, I got to know about her life.

We talked during breakfast, we talked while we collected leaves from the garden, we talked as we played with the cats. One of them, a tabby named Simba, followed her everywhere, bit at her ankles, jumped onto her lap whenever she sat down for a moment, arching its back, purring. Years later, when she left this house, the cat prowled the garden and the porch, endlessly searching for her.

'Please, Menaka,' I said one day as we chatted in the kitchen while she prepared dinner, 'can you stop calling me "madam"?'

'Of course, madam,' she said and smiled.

'Menaka, I mean it.'

'But why?'

'I don't like it. It's weird.'

'OK,' she said, 'I'll try to remember.'

Menaka showed me pictures of her daughters. She had hopes that they would both go to university when they grew up.

I visited year after year, and every time I went back it was yet another year that she had not seen her daughters, that she had not returned home.

'There has to be some way!' I said.

'The expense of the journey is not worth it. I need to send that money to them.'

I learnt that she was paid less than the minimum wage, far less, as were all the domestic workers, on account of the fact that they were given food and accommodation. I learnt that she was not allowed to go out at night, that she could not date, and that she, like all the others, basically did everything. And that was no overstatement. They cleaned the house, the gardens, cared for children if there were any, did the shopping, served dinner, cooked, walked the dogs, accompanied their employers on outings and holidays. There seemed to be no beginning or end to their duties.

When I visited again, she was talking to her girls on a tablet. She introduced me to them. She told me so much about her home, the town where they lived and what life had been like for her.

One day, I woke up to find her in the kitchen, crying.

'What's the matter?' I said.

'Sometimes I get so lonely, and when you're not here, there's no one to say good morning to.'

We prepared breakfast together. She made the tea and buttered the toast. I cut up some watermelon with halloumi.

When I returned the following year, she had gone. She'd moved on to work with a family who had two young children.